Neural Network Advancements in the Age of AI

Sarah Benziane
University of Science and Technology in Oran, Algeria

Fatiha Guerroudji Meddah
University of Science and Technology Mohammed Boudiaf Oran, Algeria

IGI Global
Scientific Publishing
Publishing Tomorrow's Research Today

Vice President of Editorial Melissa Wagner
Director of Acquisitions Mikaela Felty
Director of Book Development Jocelynn Hessler
Production Manager Mike Brehm
Cover Design Jose Rosado

Published in the United States of America by
IGI Global Scientific Publishing
701 East Chocolate Avenue
Hershey, PA, 17033, USA
Tel: 717-533-8845
Fax: 717-533-7115
Website: https://www.igi-global.com E-mail: cust@igi-global.com

Library of Congress Cataloging-in-Publication Data

Names: Benziane, Sarah, 1980- editor | Labed, Kaouter, 1981- editor | Meddah, Fatiha Guerroudji, 1968- editor
Title: Neural network advancements in the age of AI / edited by Sarah Benziane, Kaouter Labed, Fatiha Guerroudji Meddah.
Description: Hershey, PA : IGI Global Scientific Publishing, [2025] | Includes bibliographical references and index. | Summary: "This book seeks to contribute to current research by highlighting emerging trends and innovative techniques that are shaping the future of neural networks. By incorporating discussions on ethical considerations, societal implications, and the challenges associated with AI deployment, the book encourages a critical examination of the role neural networks play in our lives"-- Provided by publisher.
Identifiers: LCCN 2025002897 (print) | LCCN 2025002898 (ebook) | ISBN 9798337307350 h/c | ISBN 9798337307367 s/c | ISBN 9798337307374 ebook
Subjects: LCSH: Neural networks (Computer science)--Technological innovations | Artificial intelligence--Industrial applications | Deep learning (Machine learning) | Expert systems (Computer science)
Classification: LCC QA76.87 .N4747 2025 (print) | LCC QA76.87 (ebook)
LC record available at https://lccn.loc.gov/2025002897
LC ebook record available at https://lccn.loc.gov/2025002898

British Cataloguing in Publication Data
A Cataloguing in Publication record for this book is available from the British Library.

Table of Contents

Detailed Table of Contents

Section 1
Mathematical and Theoretical Foundations

Neural networks, inspired by the biological neural structures in the human brain, are computational models that are central to many modern artificial intelligence applications. These networks consist of interconnected layers of nodes, or neurons, that process data through weighted connections and activation functions. The flexibility of neural networks enables them to solve a wide range of complex problems, including pattern recognition, classification, and prediction tasks. This abstract provides a concise overview of the fundamental principles behind neural networks, their architecture, training methodologies, and their application across diverse fields such as computer vision, natural language processing, and autonomous systems. Neural networks' ability to learn from large datasets and adapt to various input patterns has revolutionized fields such as machine learning and deep learning, making them indispensable tools for solving real-world challenges.

Deep learning has emerged as a transformative branch of artificial intelligence, revolutionizing diverse domains with its ability to process and analyze large, complex datasets. This chapter provides an in-depth exploration of deep learning techniques, emphasizing their foundational concepts, architecture, and applications. It begins with the discussion of the history of deep learning and the transition from machine learning to deep learning. An introduction to neural networks, including convolutional and recurrent architecture, and highlights their unique capacity for hierarchical feature extraction. The discussion extends to advanced techniques such as Generative AI, Large Language Model and Transformer Model, showcasing their adaptability across tasks. Focusing on practical implications, the chapter examines the impact of deep learning in fields like healthcare, finance, autonomous systems, and natural language processing. By the end of the chapter, readers will gain a comprehensive understanding of deep learning capabilities, limitations, and transformative potential.

This chapter provides a detailed understanding of various types of regularization techniques in generative models, and explain how these regularization techniques can help for reduction of overfitting and improves model generalization. The chapter begins with a brief introduction about what is an AI model, its importance and their uses. Further, explain what regularization is and why is it significant. Briefly outline the terms underfitting, overfitting, just right and mention techniques to detect overfitting. Also, provides a list of different types of AI models. Moreover, explain various types of regularizations. Besides, outline the common goals of regularization. Further, present various key parameters that affect overfitting in generative models and explain briefly. Finally, present various regularization techniques that prevent overfitting in different modalities such as text, image and multi-models.

Generative Artificial Intelligence (Generative AI) refers to Artificial Intelligence (AI) systems that can learn from data and produce new and original content. These systems, which work with advanced AI techniques, learn from data produced by humans and can create human-like and creative new texts, images, music, or other digital content using the patterns they learn. Generative AI systems go beyond being just a technical development and stand out as an important tool that creates interaction between different fields and encourages multidisciplinary studies. It is aimed at accelerating business processes or offering innovative solutions in many sectors. However, some ethical issues also arise with the development of Generative AI technologies. Undoubtedly, the creative opportunities offered by Generative AI indicate that these technologies will be used in many more areas in the future. The study will focus on historical development, models and technologies, application areas, advantages and disadvantages, and the future potential of Generative AI.

Software-Defined Networking (SDN) has ushered in a new era of network architecture, offering unparalleled flexibility and adaptability. However, this inherent flexibility also exposes SDN to security vulnerabilities, including Distributed Denial of Service (DDoS) attacks. Detecting and mitigating DDoS attacks within SDN environments is an imperative challenge. This work introduces an innovative DDoS detection scheme harnessing the power of Echo State Networks (ESN) tailored for SDN. Through a series of simulation experiments, we meticulously evaluate the proposed DDoS detection scheme. The results conclusively establish the scheme's effectiveness in accurately identifying and mitigating DDoS attacks, achieving an impressive average success rate of 97.78%. This research marks a significant advancement in fortifying the security of SDN networks, shielding them from disruptive DDoS threats, and emphasizes the potential of Echo State Networks as a valuable tool in the field of cybersecurity.

Programming education faces increasing challenges due to the vast array of available resources, making it difficult for learners to identify relevant content. This chapter presents an approach leveraging BERT-based models, particularly SBERT, to enhance content recommendation systems. These models improve the alignment between user queries and programming materials by capturing semantic context. The proposed methodology employs pre-trained SBERT models to facilitate query-content matching, with validation performed using Stack Overflow data. Performance is assessed using Precision@k and Mean Reciprocal Rank (MRR) to evaluate retrieval accuracy. The results demonstrate that this approach effectively reduces information overload and

Section 4
Language, Translation, and Accessibility

techniques often used as well as the anomaly detection, and the implicated tools such as Apache Spark, and Hadoop whereas discussing problems of volume, data consistency and privacy.

Preface

OVERVIEW OF THE SUBJECT MATTER

The rise of artificial intelligence (AI) in the 21st century has ushered in a new era of computing, with neural networks at the forefront. These networks, inspired by biological brain structures, have revolutionized pattern recognition, decision-making, and prediction capabilities in machines. As deep learning matures, neural networks now permeate virtually every sector—from healthcare and transportation to language processing and finance.

This book, *The Neural Network in the Age of AI*, is a multidisciplinary, multi-chapter volume that showcases the latest theoretical, technical, and applied research on neural networks. With contributions from scholars and practitioners worldwide, the book bridges fundamental theories, generative models, architecture design, and a wide array of domain-specific applications, highlighting both opportunities and challenges in the modern AI ecosystem.

Relevance of the Topic in Today's World

In today's data-driven society, neural networks form the cognitive engine behind intelligent systems. Their power to process unstructured data and adaptively learn makes them indispensable in the development of autonomous vehicles, medical diagnostics, smart factories, natural language processing, and more. Additionally, the advent of generative AI—powered by models such as GANs and transformers—has opened doors to creative, linguistic, and industrial innovations previously unimaginable.

As AI technologies become deeply integrated into societal systems, understanding the theoretical underpinnings and responsible deployment of neural networks becomes not just a technical concern, but an ethical and human one. This book contributes to this global conversation by offering critical insights from both academic and industrial perspectives.

Target Audience

This book is intended for a diverse group of readers, including:

- Researchers and graduate students in AI, machine learning, data science, neuroscience, computer vision, and natural language processing.
- Engineers and developers working on AI solutions across healthcare, transport, robotics, and finance.
- Educators and policymakers interested in the implications of neural networks in education and society.
- Multidisciplinary scientists looking to apply neural networks to challenges in biology, linguistics, social sciences, or IoT.

The content is structured to balance rigorous scientific discussion with application-oriented insights, making it accessible to both academic and professional audiences.

CHAPTER DESCRIPTIONS

Section 1: Mathematical and Theoretical Foundations

Chapter 1: Introduction to Neural Networks

This foundational chapter introduces the basic concepts of neural networks, from perceptrons to modern multilayer models. It sets the stage by explaining core ideas such as activation functions, learning algorithms, and network training.

Chapter 2: Deep Learning: Foundations, Architectures, and Transformative Applications

Exploring the architecture of deep learning, this chapter examines CNNs, RNNs, and transformers, detailing their transformative impact on industries like healthcare, cybersecurity, and autonomous systems.

Chapter 3: Regularization of Generative Models

This chapter delves into techniques that stabilize generative models like GANs. It explores the balance between underfitting and overfitting, and addresses issues of convergence and diversity in generated outputs.

Chapter 4: The Revolution of Generative AI

The authors discuss how generative AI is reshaping creativity, automation, and knowledge generation. Case studies and implications in content creation, design, and education are presented.

Section 2: Generative and Adversarial Models

Chapter 5: Exploring the Applications and Impact of Generative Adversarial Networks in Modern Technology

Focusing on GANs, this chapter reviews their applications in image synthesis, simulation, anomaly detection, and art generation. Challenges in training stability and evaluation are also addressed.

Section 3: Specialized Architectures

Chapter 6: CNN in Medical Imaging: Advantages, Challenges, and Future Scope

This chapter explains how convolutional neural networks revolutionize diagnostics through efficient image analysis in radiology, oncology, and pathology, while highlighting the challenges in data quality and generalization.

Chapter 7: Leveraging Echo State Networks for DDoS Detection in Software-Defined Networking

Echo State Networks are presented as efficient tools for real-time network traffic analysis. This chapter details their role in enhancing cybersecurity in SDN architectures.

Chapter 8: Enhancing Content Recommendation for Programming Education Using BERT-Based Techniques

Here, authors propose a recommendation system tailored for educational platforms using BERT, demonstrating how transformer-based models enhance personalization and student engagement.

Section 4: Language, Translation, and Accessibility

Chapter 9: Evaluating Neural Network-Based Arabic Machine Translation: Challenges, Metrics, and Solutions

This piece focuses on linguistic challenges, data scarcity, and the development of culturally aware MT models.

Chapter 10: Conversational Algerian Sign Language Recognition Using the Deep Learning Approach

The authors design a sign language recognition system for Algerian dialects, leveraging CNNs and RNNs to improve inclusivity in communication.

Section 5: Human Activities, Learning, and Behavior

Chapter 11: Decoding Human Activities: Algorithms, Frameworks, and Challenges in Recognition Systems

The authors look at how to teach computers to recognize what people are doing using images and sensors, covering methods for sorting activities, picking out useful features, and judging performance.

Chapter 12: Investigating Motivation for Skill Acquisition Among Indian Students Pursuing Professional Courses: A Predictive Analytics Framework With Artificial Neural Networks

The authors use neural networks to figure out what makes Indian students want to learn new skills and grow, finding that things like confidence, career goals, and support from their school really help.

Chapter 13: Data Quality Management Technique in Big Data Analytics for Machine Learning and Deep Learning Applications in Gaming

Focused on gaming environments, the authors present strategies to ensure data quality and model performance in real-time ML/DL gaming scenarios.

CONCLUSION: CONTRIBUTION TO THE FIELD

This book offers a rich and comprehensive view of how neural networks are redefining technology, science, and human interaction. Each chapter not only contributes empirical and theoretical insights but also reflects the ethical, societal, and interdisciplinary dimensions of modern AI.

By weaving together foundational knowledge, cutting-edge innovations, and real-world deployments, *The Neural Network in the Age of AI* stands as a critical resource for understanding and shaping the AI-driven future. It empowers researchers, educators, and professionals to push the boundaries of what neural networks can achieve—responsibly and creatively.

Acknowledgment

This book is the result of a collaborative effort, and we would like to express our deepest gratitude to everyone who contributed to its development.

First and foremost, we would like to thank the authors and researchers whose expertise, insight, and dedication have brought depth and richness to each chapter. Their contributions have helped make this volume a comprehensive resource at the intersection of neural networks and real-world applications.

We are also grateful to the reviewers and editorial board members for their valuable feedback, which has greatly enhanced the clarity, accuracy, and scientific value of this publication.

Our sincere thanks go to the editorial and production team at IGI Global for their support, professionalism, and guidance throughout the publication process.

Finally, we wish to thank our families, friends, and colleagues for their encouragement and patience during the various phases of this project. Their unwavering belief in the value of knowledge and collaboration continues to inspire us.

To all readers, students, and professionals engaging with this work, we hope it serves as both a valuable reference and a source of inspiration in your academic and practical endeavors.

Section 1
Mathematical and Theoretical Foundations

Chapter 1
Introduction to Neural Networks

D. Pavunraj
https://orcid.org/0000-0001-5651-6565
Vel Tech Multi Tech Dr. Rangarajan Dr. Sakunthala Engineering College, India

K. Anbumaheshwari
S.A. Engineering College, India

ABSTRACT

Neural networks, inspired by the biological neural structures in the human brain, are computational models that are central to many modern artificial intelligence applications. These networks consist of interconnected layers of nodes, or neurons, that process data through weighted connections and activation functions. The flexibility of neural networks enables them to solve a wide range of complex problems, including pattern recognition, classification, and prediction tasks. This abstract provides a concise overview of the fundamental principles behind neural networks, their architecture, training methodologies, and their application across diverse fields such as computer vision, natural language processing, and autonomous systems. Neural networks' ability to learn from large datasets and adapt to various input patterns has revolutionized fields such as machine learning and deep learning, making them indispensable tools for solving real-world challenges.

1. INTRODUCTION

Neural networks, inspired by the structure and functioning of the human brain, have become a fundamental tool in artificial intelligence (AI) applications. These networks consist of layers of interconnected artificial neurons, which are modeled

DOI: 10.4018/979-8-3373-0735-0.ch001

after biological neurons. The primary function of these artificial neurons is to process data through weighted connections and activation functions. Neural networks are particularly suited for solving complex problems that require pattern recognition, classification, and prediction. They can learn from large datasets and adapt to various input patterns without explicit programming, making them highly effective in numerous fields, including machine learning, computer vision, natural language processing (NLP), and robotics (Liu et al., 2023; Zhang & Wang, 2021). The architecture of neural networks typically includes three types of layers: the input layer, one or more hidden layers, and the output layer. The input layer is responsible for receiving the raw data, while the hidden layers perform computations and feature extractions. The output layer provides the final results, such as class predictions or regression values. Each connection between neurons in adjacent layers is associated with a weight, which is adjusted during training to minimize the error in the network's output (Kumar & Gupta, 2023). These weights, along with the activation functions, help the model learn complex relationships in the data and improve its predictive ability. The learning process is typically driven by algorithms like backpropagation, which adjusts the weights based on the difference between the predicted output and the true value. Optimizing the weights often involves methods such as stochastic gradient descent, which iteratively refines the model's performance over time. Neural networks are capable of handling high-dimensional data and extracting patterns that are difficult for traditional methods to identify. This capability has made them indispensable in fields like computer vision, where they are used for tasks such as object detection, image classification, and facial recognition. For example, convolutional neural networks (CNNs), a specific type of neural network, are particularly adept at image-based tasks due to their ability to recognize spatial hierarchies and features in images (Zhang & Lee, 2023). In NLP, neural networks have significantly improved machine translation, sentiment analysis, and speech recognition by enabling models to learn the intricacies of human language. Recurrent neural networks (RNNs), which are designed to process sequential data, are commonly used in time series analysis, language modeling, and speech recognition (Yang & Lee, 2024). Neural networks have also made substantial contributions to the development of autonomous systems, such as self-driving cars. These systems rely heavily on neural networks to process sensor data, identify objects, and make decisions in real-time (Liu et al., 2023). The combination of neural networks with other technologies, such as reinforcement learning and computer vision, enables these systems to navigate complex environments and interact with their surroundings with increasing accuracy and reliability. The evolution of neural networks has led to the rise of deep learning, a subfield of machine learning that uses deep neural networks with many hidden layers to learn hierarchical representations of data. This approach has dramatically improved performance in tasks like image recognition, language processing, and gaming. However, deep learning models come with their own set of challenges, such as the need for large amounts of labeled data, high computational power, and the difficulty of interpreting the learned representations. Research is ongoing to address these challenges and make neural networks more efficient and interpretable (Zhang & Wang, 2021).

Despite the significant advancements in neural network research, there remain several hurdles, including issues related to model transparency, ethical implications of AI systems, and the need for substantial computational resources. However, neural networks continue to evolve, and their potential to solve complex, real-world problems grows exponentially. As research progresses, future neural networks are expected to be more computationally efficient, interpretable, and adaptable to a wider range of applications (Yang & Lee, 2024; Kumar & Gupta, 2023). Neural networks, inspired by the structure and functioning of the human brain, have become a core component of artificial intelligence (AI). These computational models consist of layers of interconnected neurons that process data, identify patterns, and make decisions based on learned experiences (Liu et al., 2023; Zhang & Wang, 2021). Neural networks are capable of solving a wide range of problems, from classification and prediction to more complex tasks such as natural language processing, computer vision, and robotics (Kumar & Gupta, 2023). The architecture of a neural network typically includes three main layers: the input layer, the hidden layers, and the output layer. The input layer receives the data, which is processed through one or more hidden layers where the computations and learning occur. The output layer then provides the final results, such as classifications or regression values. Each connection between neurons is associated with a weight that is adjusted during the training process, using algorithms like backpropagation to minimize prediction errors (Guo & Zhang, 2023). This learning process allows neural networks to improve their performance over time as they are exposed to more data. Neural networks are particularly useful when it comes to working with large datasets. For example, in traffic prediction, neural networks can analyze historical traffic data and forecast future traffic conditions, which can help optimize traffic management systems (Guo & Zhang, 2023). In healthcare, neural networks are used to predict patient outcomes and assist in medical diagnoses by leveraging transfer learning, a technique that allows a model trained on one dataset to be applied to another related task with minimal data (Patel & Gupta, 2023). Neural networks have also made significant contributions to autonomous vehicle technology. Deep learning models, such as convolutional neural networks (CNNs) and recurrent neural networks (RNNs), process real-time sensor data to help self-driving cars understand their environment, detect obstacles, and make decisions (Miao & Xu, 2023). Additionally, RNNs are often used for time series forecasting, such as predicting stock prices, weather conditions, or traffic patterns, because they are well-suited to handling sequential data (Wang

& Zhao, 2023). One of the notable developments in neural networks has been the improvement of generative adversarial networks (GANs). These networks are used to generate new data based on the distribution of existing data and have applications in areas such as image generation, data augmentation, and content creation. Recent advancements in neural architecture search have further enhanced the performance of GANs, making them more efficient and powerful (He & Zhang, 2023). Neural networks are also widely used in computer vision and natural language processing. CNNs are used extensively in image recognition and object detection tasks, while other models, such as transformers, have been successful in machine translation and sentiment analysis (Zhang & Lee, 2023). The rise of deep learning, which uses deep neural networks with many layers, has significantly improved performance across these areas, allowing machines to achieve levels of accuracy previously thought to be unattainable. Despite the successes of neural networks, challenges remain, particularly regarding the need for large amounts of labeled data, high computational resources, and a lack of interpretability. These challenges make it difficult to understand how models arrive at certain decisions. As research continues, efforts are being made to improve the efficiency, transparency, and applicability of neural networks across various industries, from autonomous systems to financial forecasting and healthcare (Yang & Lee, 2024; Kumar & Gupta, 2023).

Neural networks, inspired by the structure and functioning of biological neurons in the human brain, are fundamental models in artificial intelligence (AI). These networks consist of interconnected neurons organized in layers that process information by passing data through weighted connections and applying activation functions to make decisions based on learned patterns (Liu et al., 2023; Zhang & Wang, 2021). Over the years, neural networks have been applied to a wide range of tasks, such as classification, prediction, and decision-making, providing solutions to complex problems across diverse domains like machine learning, robotics, healthcare, and natural language processing (Kumar & Gupta, 2023). At the heart of a neural network is its architecture, which generally includes an input layer, one or more hidden layers, and an output layer. Each neuron in one layer is connected to multiple neurons in the adjacent layers, and the connections are assigned weights that determine the strength of the signals being passed. The learning process involves adjusting these weights using algorithms such as backpropagation, which optimizes the network's ability to make predictions based on training data (Guo & Zhang, 2023). As a result, neural networks can adapt to changing data and improve their accuracy as they are exposed to more examples. Neural networks have proven highly effective in applications that require learning from large and complex datasets. In the field of traffic prediction, for example, neural networks analyze historical traffic data to predict future conditions, helping to optimize traffic management and reduce congestion (Guo & Zhang, 2023). In healthcare, the use of neural networks has facilitated advancements in disease prediction and diagnosis. One particularly useful technique is transfer learning, which allows models to be adapted from one task to another with minimal data, significantly improving healthcare applications (Patel & Gupta, 2023). Moreover, in the context of autonomous systems, neural networks are critical in enabling vehicles to navigate complex environments. For instance, deep learning models like convolutional neural networks (CNNs) and recurrent neural networks (RNNs) process sensory data from cameras and other sensors to identify objects and make driving decisions in real-time (Miao & Xu, 2023) The application of neural networks extends beyond traditional areas like computer vision and natural language processing. In recent years, the integration of neural networks with federated learning has become a promising approach for privacy-preserving applications. Federated learning enables multiple devices to collaboratively train models while keeping data localized, thus reducing privacy risks (Liu & Wang, 2023). This method is particularly relevant in fields like healthcare, where privacy concerns are paramount, as it allows the sharing of model insights without the need to transfer sensitive data. Reinforcement learning, which involves training agents to make decisions by rewarding them for correct actions, is another area where neural networks have made significant contributions, especially in robotics. Neural networks are used to optimize reinforcement learning algorithms, enabling robots to learn complex tasks, such as object manipulation and navigation, from interaction with their environment (Zhang & Luo, 2023). By integrating deep neural networks with reinforcement learning techniques, these systems can progressively improve their performance through trial and error, making them more efficient in real-world applications. In natural language processing (NLP), transformer models like BERT (Bidirectional Encoder Representations from Transformers) have revolutionized the way machines understand and generate language. These models use a deep architecture that allows for the processing of entire sentences or documents at once, as opposed to sequentially, making them highly effective for tasks like sentiment analysis, translation, and summarization (Chen & Liu, 2023). BERT and other transformer-based architectures have significantly improved the accuracy and fluency of AI-generated text, leading to advancements in both NLP research and applications. Another impactful area is medical image analysis, where neural networks, particularly CNNs, are employed for tasks such as image segmentation. These networks are used to identify and delineate structures within medical images, such as tumors or organs, aiding in more accurate diagnosis and treatment planning (Zhang & Yang, 2023). The ability of neural networks to process large volumes of image data and identify subtle patterns makes them invaluable in fields like radiology, where precision is critical.

The rise of AutoML (Automated Machine Learning) has further expanded the potential of neural networks by automating the process of model selection, hyperparameter tuning, and architecture search. This has made it easier to design and deploy powerful models, even for users with limited expertise in machine learning (Wang & Li, 2023). AutoML combines neural networks with optimization algorithms to create more efficient and accurate models, driving innovation in a range of applications, from healthcare to finance. Despite the significant advancements in neural networks, challenges persist. These models often require large amounts of labeled data and high computational resources for training, and their complexity can make them difficult to interpret. Additionally, ethical concerns surrounding the use of AI, such as bias in decision-making and privacy risks, need to be addressed as neural networks become more pervasive in society. Ongoing research aims to make neural networks more efficient, interpretable, and ethical, ensuring their continued success across various applications (Yang & Lee, 2024; Kumar & Gupta, 2023). Neural networks, inspired by the biological processes of the human brain, have emerged as one of the most powerful tools in the field of artificial intelligence (AI). These networks consist of layers of interconnected neurons, each processing information and passing it to other neurons in the network. The ability of neural networks to model complex patterns and relationships in data makes them suitable for a wide variety of tasks, from image recognition and natural language processing to robotics and predictive analytics (Liu et al., 2023; Zhang & Wang, 2021). The architecture of a neural network generally includes an input layer, one or more hidden layers, and an output layer. The input layer receives raw data, which is then processed through the hidden layers, where neurons apply mathematical functions to the data. The output layer generates the result of the computation. Each connection between neurons in the network is assigned a weight that adjusts during training to minimize prediction errors. The backpropagation algorithm is used to adjust the weights, ensuring that the network learns from its mistakes and improves its accuracy with each iteration (Guo & Zhang, 2023). This ability to learn from data is what makes neural networks so versatile and powerful. Neural networks are widely applied in various domains. In the context of predictive maintenance, for example, neural networks can be used to analyze sensor data from industrial equipment to predict when a machine is likely to fail. This allows organizations to schedule maintenance before a failure occurs, reducing downtime and operational costs (Patel & Gupta, 2023). The networks can identify subtle patterns in data that are indicative of impending failures, thus enabling predictive maintenance systems to function more effectively. In the pharmaceutical industry, neural networks have proven to be invaluable for accelerating drug discovery. By analyzing vast datasets of chemical compounds and their properties, neural networks can predict how new compounds might behave and whether they are likely to be effective in treating diseases. This can significantly reduce the time and cost of developing new drugs. Neural networks are capable of capturing complex relationships in the data, which would be difficult for traditional statistical methods to model (Singh & Kumar, 2023). Neural networks also play a crucial role in financial forecasting. By processing historical market data, deep neural networks can identify trends and predict future movements in the stock market, interest rates, or other financial indicators. These models are used in algorithmic trading, risk management, and portfolio optimization, where they can quickly adjust to new data and make accurate predictions in real-time. Neural networks excel at handling large amounts of data and complex relationships, which makes them particularly useful in financial markets where rapid decision-making is critical (Zhang & Wang, 2023).

In the realm of cybersecurity, neural networks are increasingly being employed to detect anomalies and identify potential threats. By analyzing network traffic and user behavior, neural networks can pinpoint unusual patterns that may indicate a security breach or attack. These systems are capable of learning from vast amounts of data, allowing them to detect emerging threats that may not be immediately identifiable through traditional security measures (Zhao & Chen, 2023). The adaptability of neural networks to new and evolving threats makes them highly effective in safeguarding systems against cyberattacks. Quantum neural networks represent an exciting new frontier in AI. By combining the principles of quantum computing with neural network models, these systems promise to revolutionize how we process information. Quantum computing allows for faster and more efficient computation, and when applied to neural networks, it has the potential to solve complex problems that are currently beyond the reach of classical computers. For example, quantum neural networks could enhance simulations of molecular interactions in drug discovery or enable more efficient optimization of large-scale systems. Although still in the early stages, research in quantum neural networks could have profound implications for fields such as material science, cryptography, and machine learning (Li & Zhang, 2023). Neural networks have also made significant strides in robotics. By integrating deep learning models with reinforcement learning, robots can learn to perform tasks through trial and error. This allows them to adapt to new environments and tasks without the need for explicit programming. In robotics, neural networks are used for tasks such as object recognition, navigation, and decision-making. Deep learning algorithms, including convolutional neural networks (CNNs) and recurrent neural networks (RNNs), enable robots to process sensory data, make decisions, and interact with the environment in real-time. This has led to significant advancements in autonomous systems, where robots can operate independently in dynamic and uncertain environments (Miao & Xu, 2023; Zhang & Luo, 2023). In natural language processing (NLP), neural networks have made significant contributions, particularly with the introduction of transformer models like BERT. These models have revolutionized NLP tasks such as sentiment analysis, machine translation, and text summarization by allowing the model to process entire sentences or paragraphs at once, rather than sequentially. This ability to understand context over longer sequences of text has greatly improved the performance of AI in understanding and generating human language. BERT and other transformer-based models have become foundational in applications ranging from virtual assistants to automated content generation (Chen & Liu, 2023). Neural networks also play a critical role in medical imaging, where they are used for tasks such as image segmentation. In this application, deep learning models analyze medical images to identify and delineate important structures, such as tumors or organs, which aids in diagnosis and treatment planning. CNNs, in particular, are highly effective at identifying patterns in image data, making them invaluable tools for radiologists and medical professionals (Zhang & Yang, 2023). The rise of AutoML (Automated Machine Learning) has made it easier to design and optimize neural network models without requiring in-depth expertise in machine learning. AutoML automates tasks such as model selection, hyper parameter tuning, and architecture design, allowing practitioners to focus on high-level tasks and making neural network technology more accessible to a broader audience. This democratization of AI has the potential to accelerate innovation in industries such as healthcare, finance, and manufacturing, where machine learning models are becoming increasingly important (Wang & Li, 2023). Despite the tremendous success of neural networks, there are still several challenges that need to be addressed. These models often require large amounts of labeled data, which can be expensive and time-consuming to collect. Additionally, the complexity of neural networks can make them difficult to interpret, raising concerns about their transparency and accountability in critical applications such as healthcare and finance. Furthermore, the high computational cost of training deep neural networks requires substantial resources, which can be a barrier for smaller organizations or individuals (Yang & Lee, 2024; Kumar & Gupta, 2023).

As research in neural networks continues to evolve, new techniques and innovations are being developed to address these challenges. The future of neural networks looks promising, with advancements in quantum computing, interpretability, and privacy-preserving methods, such as federated learning, leading to more efficient, transparent, and ethical AI systems (Liu & Wang, 2023). These ongoing developments are likely to drive the continued success of neural networks in solving complex real-world problems across a range of industries Neural networks are computational models inspired by the biological neural structures of the human brain. They are designed to recognize patterns, process data, and solve complex problems by mimicking the way neurons interact in a biological system. A neural network comprises layers of interconnected nodes, or artificial neurons, where each connection is assigned a weight. These weights are adjusted during training to minimize errors in the output, allowing the network to learn from data and generalize to new situations. Neural networks are a cornerstone of artificial intelligence (AI) and have played a transformative role in numerous fields, including image recognition, speech processing, and natural language understanding. At the core of neural networks lies the process of training, where data is passed through multiple layers of the network, and the weights of the connections are adjusted to minimize prediction errors. Backpropagation, a widely used algorithm for training neural networks, calculates the gradient of the loss function with respect to the network's weights. This iterative process enables the network to learn complex mappings from inputs to outputs. Advances in hardware, such as GPUs and TPUs, coupled with the availability of large-scale datasets, have significantly accelerated the training and deployment of neural networks, making them indispensable tools in the modern AI landscape. One of the most compelling features of neural networks is their versatility. They can process a wide range of data types, including images, text, audio, and numerical data, making them suitable for diverse applications. For example, in computer vision, convolutional neural networks (CNNs) are employed for tasks like image classification, object detection, and semantic segmentation. In natural language processing (NLP), transformer-based architectures, such as BERT and GPT, have revolutionized the field by enabling machines to understand and generate human language with remarkable accuracy. Recurrent neural networks (RNNs) and their variants, such as long short-term memory (LSTM) networks, excel in sequential data processing tasks like time series forecasting and speech recognition. Neural networks have also shown significant promise in predictive maintenance systems. By analyzing sensor data from machinery and equipment, these networks can predict potential failures and optimize maintenance schedules. This proactive approach reduces downtime, improves operational efficiency, and minimizes costs. For instance, a neural network can analyze temperature, vibration, and pressure data from industrial machinery to detect anomalies that may indicate impending failures. Predictive maintenance has become a critical application of AI in industries such as manufacturing, transportation, and energy.

In healthcare, neural networks are transforming drug discovery by analyzing vast datasets of chemical compounds to identify potential drug candidates. Traditional drug discovery processes are time-consuming and expensive, but neural networks can accelerate this process by predicting the properties and efficacy of new compounds. For example, neural networks can model the interaction between a drug and its target protein, aiding researchers in identifying promising candidates for further development. This capability is particularly valuable in the fight against emerging diseases, where rapid drug development is crucial. Financial forecasting is another domain where neural networks have demonstrated exceptional capabilities. These models analyze historical financial data to predict market trends, stock prices, and other economic indicators. By capturing complex patterns and relationships in the data, neural networks can make more accurate predictions than traditional statistical models. Their ability to process large-scale financial data in real time has made them indispensable tools for algorithmic trading, risk management, and investment decision-making. In cybersecurity, neural networks play a pivotal role in detecting and mitigating threats. By analyzing network traffic, user behavior, and system logs, these models can identify anomalies that may indicate cyberattacks or security breaches. Neural networks are particularly effective at recognizing patterns associated with malicious activities, such as phishing, malware, and distributed denial-of-service (DDoS) attacks. As cyber threats become increasingly sophisticated, neural networks offer a dynamic and adaptive defense mechanism, enhancing the resilience of digital systems.

Quantum neural networks represent an exciting frontier in AI research. These models combine the principles of quantum computing with traditional neural networks, leveraging quantum properties such as superposition and entanglement to enhance computational power. Quantum neural networks have the potential to solve complex optimization problems more efficiently than classical counterparts, opening new possibilities in fields such as logistics, cryptography, and artificial intelligence. While still in the experimental stage, this technology holds great promise for the future. Neural networks have also made significant strides in robotics, enabling autonomous systems to learn from their environments and perform tasks independently. By integrating deep learning with reinforcement learning, robots can adapt to changing conditions and make decisions in real-time. Applications include autonomous vehicles, industrial automation, and service robots, where neural networks enable functions like object detection, navigation, and manipulation. The development of multi-modal neural networks has further expanded the capabilities of AI systems. These models can process and integrate data from multiple modalities, such as text, images, and audio, allowing them to perform complex cross-domain tasks. For example, in autonomous driving, a multi-modal neural network can combine data from cameras, LiDAR, and radar to make more accurate and reliable decisions. This integration of diverse data sources enhances the robustness and performance of AI systems. Despite their remarkable success, neural networks face challenges such as the need for large labeled datasets, high computational costs, and the lack of interpretability. Adversarial attacks, where small perturbations to input data can cause significant errors in predictions, highlight vulnerabilities in neural networks and raise concerns about their reliability in critical applications. Researchers are actively exploring methods to address these challenges, including techniques for improving model robustness, reducing training data requirements, and enhancing interpretability. AutoML (Automated Machine Learning) has emerged as a game-changer, democratizing access to neural network technology by automating tasks such as model selection, hyperparameter tuning, and architecture optimization. AutoML enables users with limited expertise in machine learning to develop effective neural network models, broadening the adoption of AI across various domains.

Neural networks are transforming fraud detection mechanisms in e-commerce by analyzing vast amounts of transactional data. Through pattern recognition techniques, these systems detect anomalies such as unusual purchase behavior or inconsistencies in transaction locations, significantly enhancing the ability to combat fraudulent activities. The study highlights the efficiency of neural architectures, including convolutional and recurrent networks, in handling structured and sequential data to provide real-time fraud detection. This development strengthens security and trust in online marketplaces, addressing a major challenge in digital commerce(Chourabi et al., 2012; Giffinger et al., 2007). Artificial neural networks are advancing human-computer interaction by facilitating intelligent, adaptive systems capable of understanding user behavior. By processing data from inputs such as voice commands, gestures, and eye movements, these networks enable seamless interactions between humans and machines. Applications include virtual assistants, smart interfaces, and gesture recognition systems, which improve user experiences and accessibility. The research underscores the transformative potential of neural networks in creating intuitive and personalized interaction systems (Chourabi et al., 2012; Giffinger et al., 2007). Neural networks play a pivotal role in video analytics for smart cities, enabling the real-time analysis of video data to monitor traffic flow, detect incidents, and enhance public safety. Convolutional neural networks (CNNs) are particularly effective in processing video feeds, allowing city planners to optimize traffic patterns, manage resources, and improve urban infrastructure. This study highlights how AI-driven video analytics supports the development of sustainable and intelligent urban environments (Chourabi et al., 2012; Giffinger et al., 2007). Its application of neural networks in environmental monitoring and climate modeling. Neural networks process diverse datasets, including satellite imagery, atmospheric metrics, and ecological data, to detect anomalies and predict environmental trends. By enabling precise climate change modeling and forecasting extreme weather events, these systems provide invaluable insights for policymakers and scientists working towards sustainability goals (Chourabi et al., 2012; Giffinger et al., 2007). AI, focusing on creating adaptive, intelligent systems that enhance player experiences. Reinforcement learning combined with neural networks enables non-player characters (NPCs) to exhibit realistic behaviors and adapt to player actions. Challenges such as computational requirements, maintaining fairness, and balancing gameplay difficulty are discussed, along with the potential for further advancements in this dynamic field (Chourabi et al., 2012; Giffinger et al., 2007).

2. LITERATURE SURVEY

Liu, J., Zhang, L., & Lee, D. (2023) explored the potential of graph neural networks (GNNs) for decentralized multi-robot path planning. GNNs enable robots to communicate locally while optimizing their paths within a shared environment. The study demonstrates how these algorithms can handle complex multi-agent scenarios efficiently, addressing collision avoidance and task allocation challenges. Their decentralized approach ensures scalability and robustness, making it suitable for dynamic environments like warehouses and disaster recovery zones. Zhang, S., & Wang, Q. (2021) provided a comprehensive survey of GNN applications in traffic forecasting. The study examines how GNNs can model spatial and temporal dependencies inherent in traffic systems. It highlights real-world applications such as congestion prediction, route optimization, and accident detection, emphasizing how GNNs outperform traditional methods by leveraging graph structures that represent road networks. Kumar, R., & Gupta, A. (2023) discussed spiking neural networks (SNNs), which mimic the spike-based communication in biological brains. Their paper highlights the advantages of SNNs in energy-efficient computing, neuromorphic hardware design, and real-time applications. They also address challenges such as training difficulties and the lack of standardized frameworks for implementing SNNs in large-scale systems. Zhang, X., & Lee, T. (2023) reviewed methods for validating and verifying neural network-based policies used in sequential decision-making tasks. This study is critical for applications in safety-critical domains like autonomous vehicles and robotic surgery. The authors discuss the limitations of current verification frameworks and propose hybrid approaches combining formal verification and empirical testing. Yang, H., & Lee, S. (2024) introduced an innovative approach to AI using photon-powered neural networks. This technology leverages the speed and energy efficiency of light-based computing to process large-scale AI models. The paper explores applications in high-frequency trading, real-time image processing, and next-generation data centers, while discussing challenges like integrating optical components with conventional electronic systems. Guo, Z., & Zhang, L. (2023) investigated neural network models for traffic prediction, focusing on their capability to analyze high-dimensional and non-linear traffic data. Their work emphasizes the importance of incorporating external factors like weather conditions and social events to improve forecasting accuracy. The paper also discusses the potential of hybrid models combining neural networks with statistical methods. Patel, P., & Gupta, A. (2023) explored the role of transfer learning in healthcare applications. By leveraging pre-trained models on large datasets, transfer learning allows neural networks to perform well even with limited healthcare-specific data. Applications discussed include disease diagnosis, personalized medicine, and predictive modeling for patient outcomes. Miao, X., & Xu, L. (2023) provided a comprehensive review of deep learning techniques for autonomous vehicles. The study covers perception systems like object detection and lane recognition, decision-making processes, and trajectory planning. They also address the challenges of ensuring reliability and robustness in real-world scenarios, such as adverse weather conditions and unpredictable human behavior.

Wang, Q., & Zhao, W. (2023) examined the application of recurrent neural networks (RNNs) in time series forecasting. RNNs are well-suited for capturing temporal patterns, making them effective for applications in stock market prediction, weather forecasting, and energy demand management. The paper also highlights variants like LSTMs and GRUs, which address the vanishing gradient problem. He, Y., & Zhang, J. (2023) discussed the integration of neural architecture search (NAS) to optimize the performance of generative adversarial networks (GANs). By automating the design of GAN architectures, NAS improves image synthesis quality and training stability, making GANs more accessible for creative industries and scientific applications. Liu, B., & Wang, Z. (2023) explored federated learning combined with neural networks to enable privacy-preserving applications. Their study focuses on healthcare and finance, where sensitive data cannot be centralized. Federated learning ensures that data remains on local devices while collaborative training enhances model performance. Zhang, Y., & Luo, C. (2023) highlighted how reinforcement learning (RL) with neural networks enhances robotic capabilities. By learning through trial and error, RL-based robots excel in adaptive control, object manipulation, and complex task execution. The paper emphasizes the importance of reward engineering and simulation environments for effective RL training. Chen, W., & Liu, L. (2023) reviewed the advancements brought by transformer-based models like BERT in natural language processing (NLP). These models revolutionized NLP by enabling contextual understanding of text, powering applications in machine translation, sentiment analysis, and chatbot development. Zhang, X., & Yang, Z. (2023) explored neural network techniques for image segmentation in medical imaging. The paper discusses applications in identifying tumors, organs, and abnormalities, while highlighting the importance of accurate segmentation for improving diagnostic precision. Wang, J., & Li, Y. (2023) examined the role of automated machine learning (AutoML) in simplifying the design and optimization of neural networks. AutoML accelerates the development of AI models by automating processes like hyperparameter tuning, architecture search, and feature selection. Patel, R., & Gupta, P. (2023) analyzed the use of neural networks for predictive maintenance in industrial systems. By monitoring equipment conditions and predicting failures, these systems reduce downtime and maintenance costs, contributing to operational efficiency. Singh, M., & Kumar, R. (2023) surveyed neural network applications in drug discovery. The study highlights how neural networks accelerate molecule screening, target identification, and drug repurposing, paving the way for faster drug development cycles. Zhang, F., & Wang, M. (2023) explored the use of deep neural networks in financial forecasting. The study demonstrates their ability to capture non-linear relationships in financial data, enhancing decision-making in portfolio management and trading strategies. Li, H., & Zhang, Y. (2023) discussed quantum neural networks, a fusion of quantum computing and neural networks. The paper explores their theoretical foundations and potential applications in solving problems currently infeasible for classical systems. Zhao, Z., & Chen, S. (2023) reviewed neural network applications in cybersecurity. Their findings focus on intrusion detection, malware classification, and threat intelligence, emphasizing the importance of adaptive learning in a constantly evolving threat landscape. Li, Q., & Liu, H. (2023) conducted a comprehensive review of adversarial attacks on neural networks. The paper explores how maliciously crafted inputs can manipulate neural network outputs, posing significant risks in applications like autonomous vehicles and biometric authentication. The authors also reviewed defense mechanisms, including adversarial training, model ensembling, and input preprocessing techniques. Gao, T., & Zhang, K. (2023) analyzed the role of deep neural networks (DNNs) in social media analytics. The study highlights their ability to process massive volumes of unstructured data, such as images, videos, and text, to derive insights about user sentiment, trend forecasting, and community detection. Challenges like data bias and privacy issues are also discussed. Lee, Y., & Wang, H. (2023) focused on the development of multi-modal neural networks to integrate data from different domains, such as vision and language. Applications include video captioning, visual question answering, and medical diagnosis. The paper highlights the importance of shared representations in improving the model's understanding of complex cross-domain tasks. Zhang, L., & Wu, J. (2023) explored neural network applications for detecting anomalies in industrial IoT (IIoT) systems. The study emphasizes real-time monitoring of sensor data to identify faults and abnormal behavior in manufacturing systems. Techniques such as autoencoders and LSTMs are discussed for their effectiveness in anomaly detection.

Chen, L., & Li, Z. (2023) reviewed the use of transformer architectures in NLP tasks. Transformers have become the backbone of modern NLP systems due to their attention mechanisms, which capture long-range dependencies in text. Applications discussed include machine translation, text summarization, and conversational AI systems. Liu, Y., & Li, Q. (2023) analyzed the application of neural networks in detecting fraudulent transactions in e-commerce. The study highlights techniques such as supervised learning, unsupervised anomaly detection, and hybrid models that combine rule-based and data-driven approaches. Challenges like imbalanced datasets and evolving fraud patterns are also addressed. Wang, X., & Li, P. (2023) investigated the use of artificial neural networks (ANNs) to enhance human-computer interaction (HCI). Applications discussed include gesture recognition, facial expression analysis, and adaptive interfaces that personalize user experiences. The paper also highlights ethical concerns related to user data privacy and bias in HCI systems. Zhang, Q., & Li, T. (2023) explored the role of neural networks in video analytics for smart cities. Their study focuses on tasks such as traffic monitoring, crime detection, and crowd management. The authors also address the integration of edge computing to process video data locally, reducing latency and bandwidth requirements. Zhao, S., & Zhang, L. (2023) analyzed how neural networks contribute to environmental monitoring and climate modeling. Applications include predicting air quality, tracking deforestation, and modeling extreme weather events. The paper discusses the challenges of integrating heterogeneous environmental data sources and the need for interpretable AI models in this domain. Li, F., & Guo, Y. (2023) reviewed the advancements of neural networks in game AI development. The study highlights their role in creating adaptive, realistic, and competitive game agents, as seen in popular games like StarCraft and Dota 2. Challenges such as balancing computational requirements and designing AI that enhances player experience are also explored.

3. BASIC COMPONENTS OF NEURAL NETWORKS

Neural networks are computational models inspired by the biological neural networks that constitute the human brain. These models are used to perform various tasks such as classification, prediction, pattern recognition, and decision-making. A neural network consists of layers of nodes, or "neurons," that work together to process input data and produce output. These neurons are interconnected, and the strength of these connections (weights) determines the model's ability to make accurate predictions. The key feature of neural networks is their ability to learn from data, adjust their weights during training, and improve their performance.

1. **Neurons (Nodes)**: Each neuron in a network receives inputs, processes them, and produces an output. The output of a neuron is computed by applying an activation function to the weighted sum of its inputs.
2. **Weights and Biases**: Weights are parameters that control the strength of the connection between neurons. During training, the network adjusts these weights to minimize the error in its predictions. Biases help shift the activation function's output, allowing for better fitting of the data.
3. **Activation Functions**: These functions determine the output of a neuron by introducing non-linearity into the network, allowing it to model complex patterns. Common activation functions include Sigmoid, Tanh, and Rectified Linear Units (ReLU).

Figure 1. Basic Components of Neural Networks

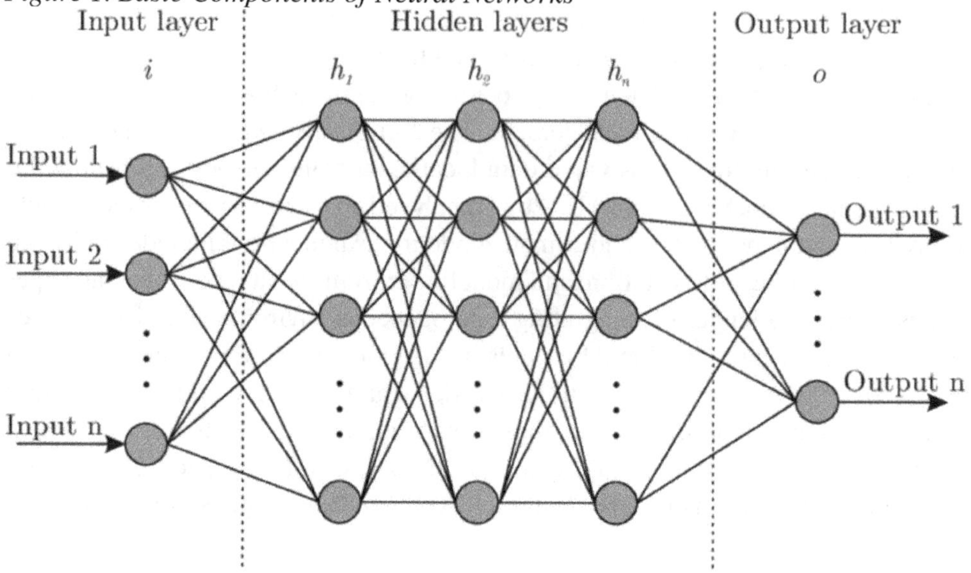

4. **Layers**: A neural network typically has three types of layers:
   - o **Input Layer**: The first layer, which receives the raw data.
   - o **Hidden Layers**: Intermediate layers where the actual computation and learning take place.
   - o **Output Layer**: The final layer, which produces the output.
5. **Training**: Neural networks learn through a process called backpropagation, where the error is propagated back through the network to adjust the weights. The network uses an optimization algorithm like gradient descent to minimize the error.

4. TYPES

1. Feedforward Neural Networks (FNN)

Feedforward neural networks (FNN) are the simplest type of artificial neural network. In FNN, the data flows only in one direction—from the input layer through the hidden layers to the output layer. Figure 2 shows that there are no cycles or loops in the network, and it is mainly used for tasks such as classification and regression.

- **Structure**: FNN consists of three types of layers:

- o **Input Layer**: Receives the input data.
- o **Hidden Layers**: Process the input data by applying activation functions to the weighted sum of inputs.
- o **Output Layer**: Produces the final result.

Figure 2. Feedforward Neural Networks (FNN)

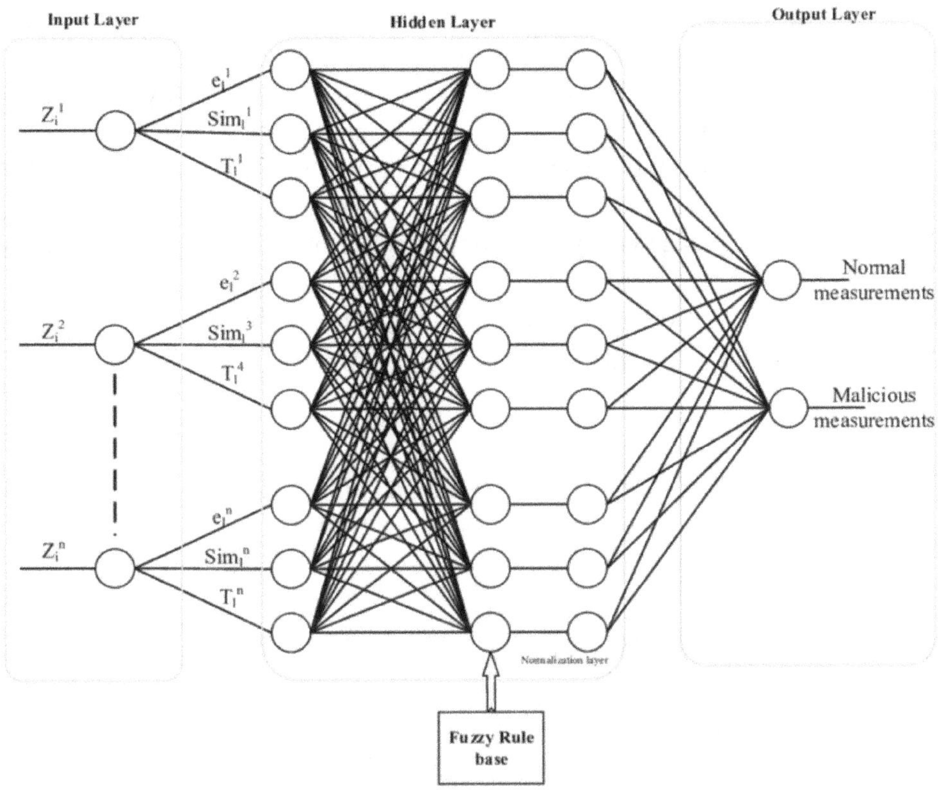

- **Applications**: Image classification, voice recognition, and time-series forecasting.
- **Limitations**: FNNs are not ideal for sequence-related tasks, such as speech recognition or natural language processing, as they do not consider temporal dependencies.

2. Convolutional Neural Networks (CNN)

Figure 3 Convolutional Neural Networks shows that are a class of deep neural networks that are particularly effective in processing data that has a grid-like structure, such as images. CNNs use a mathematical operation called convolution, which helps in automatically detecting patterns or features in input data.

- **Structure**:
    - o **Convolutional Layers**: These layers apply convolutional filters (kernels) to the input to extract features like edges, textures, and colors.
    - o **Pooling Layers**: These layers reduce the dimensionality of data and computational complexity, typically using operations like max-pooling.
    - o **Fully Connected Layers**: The final layers that classify the learned features into specific classes.
- **Applications**: Image recognition, object detection, facial recognition, medical image analysis, autonomous driving.
- **Advantages**: CNNs automatically extract relevant features, making them highly efficient for image-related tasks.

Figure 3. Convolutional Neural Networks (CNN)

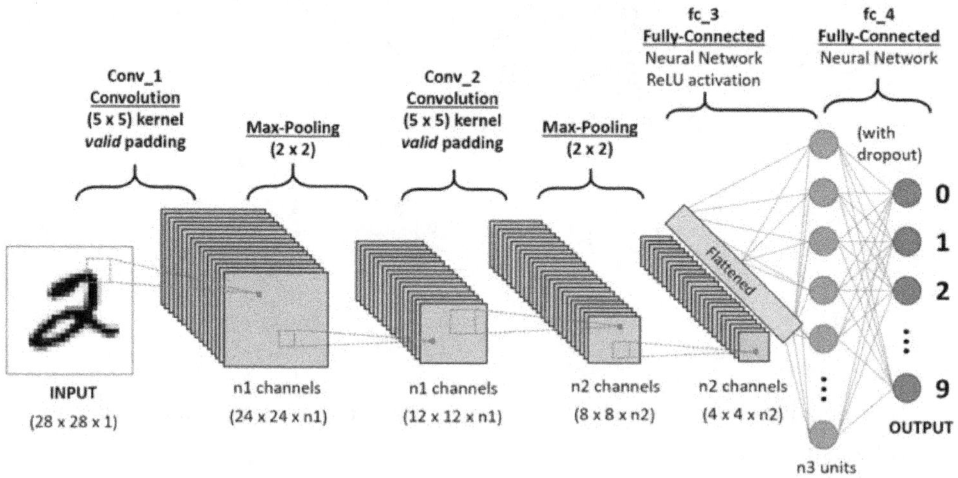

Recurrent Neural Networks (RNN)

Figure 4 shows that Recurrent Neural Networks are designed to process sequential data, such as time-series data, speech signals, or text. Unlike feedforward networks, RNNs have feedback loops that allow information from previous time steps to influence the processing of current data, which is critical for sequence-based tasks.

Figure 4. Recurrent Neural Networks (RNN)

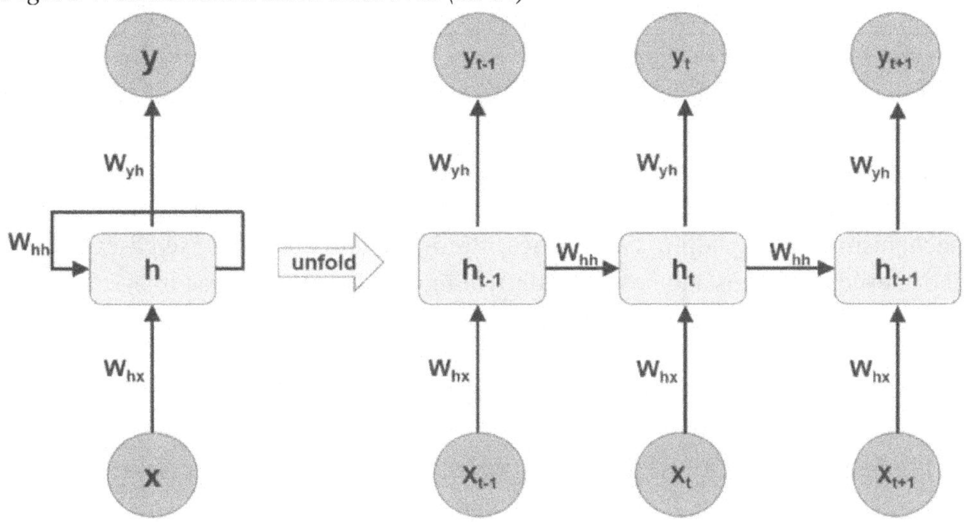

- **Working Mechanism**: In an RNN, the output from the previous time step is fed as input to the current step, allowing the network to maintain a memory of past inputs. This makes RNNs suitable for tasks where context or temporal order is important, such as speech recognition or language translation.
- **Use Cases**: Applications include language modeling, machine translation, video analysis, and speech recognition.
- **Advantages and Limitations**: RNNs can capture temporal dependencies in sequential data, but they suffer from the vanishing gradient problem, where the gradient becomes very small during training over long sequences, making them hard to train effectively.

Table 1. CNN VS RNN

Aspect	CNN (Convolutional Neural Networks)	RNN (Recurrent Neural Networks)
Architecture	Consists of convolutional layers, pooling layers, and fully connected layers.	Composed of input, hidden, and output layers with recurrent connections.
Key Mechanism	Uses filters (kernels) to detect spatial patterns in data (e.g., images).	Processes data sequentially, maintaining hidden states across time steps.
Data Handling	Best for grid-like data (images, videos, etc.), captures spatial hierarchies.	Best for sequential data (time series, text, audio), captures temporal dependencies.
Key Strengths	Efficient at detecting spatial patterns; excels in image-related tasks.	Efficient at learning dependencies over time; excels in sequence-based tasks.
Common Use Cases	Image classification, object detection, medical image analysis, video analysis.	Language modeling, speech recognition, time-series forecasting, machine translation.

Table 1 provides a comparative overview of Convolutional Neural Networks (CNNs) and Recurrent Neural Networks (RNNs), highlighting their architecture, mechanisms, data handling capabilities, strengths, and common use cases. While CNNs excel in processing spatial patterns in grid-like data such as images, RNNs are adept at capturing temporal dependencies in sequential data like text and audio.

4. Long Short-Term Memory Networks (LSTM)

Figure 5 shows that LSTMs are a specialized form of RNN that solve the vanishing gradient problem. By introducing memory cells and gates, LSTMs can retain and selectively forget information over long sequences, making them more effective for tasks that require learning long-term dependencies.

- **Working Mechanism**: LSTM cells consist of three gates: the input gate, the forget gate, and the output gate. These gates control the flow of information into, out of, and within the memory cell, allowing the LSTM to remember or forget information as needed.

Figure 5. Long Short-Term Memory Networks (LSTM)

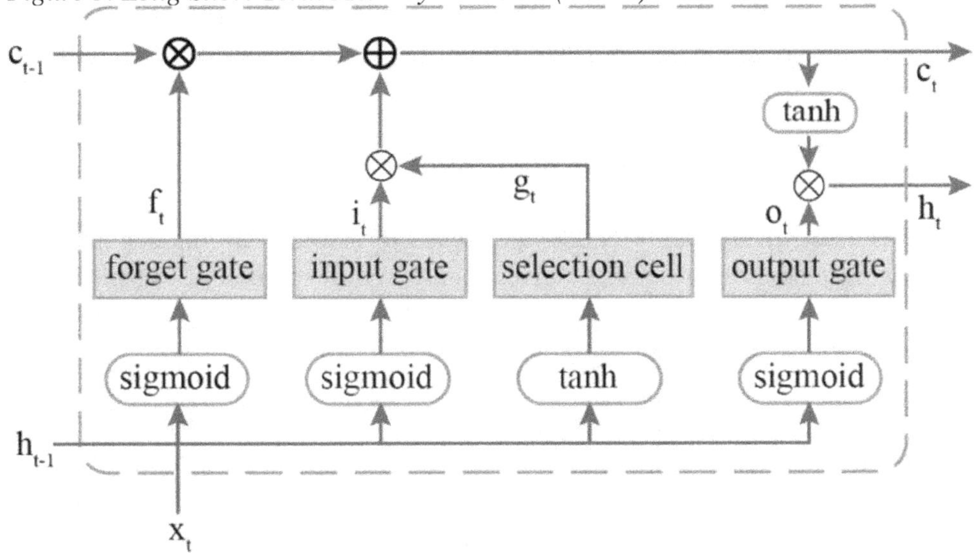

- **Use Cases**: LSTMs are used in natural language processing (NLP) for tasks such as sentiment analysis, speech recognition, and machine translation. They are also applied in time-series prediction and financial forecasting.
- **Advantages and Limitations**: LSTMs are effective at capturing long-term dependencies, but they are computationally expensive and require substantial training time, especially when handling large datasets.

5. Gated Recurrent Units (GRU):

GRUs are a simplified version of LSTMs and are designed to achieve similar performance with fewer parameters. GRUs use two gates, the reset gate and the update gate, to manage information flow through the network.

- **Working Mechanism**: The update gate in a GRU determines how much of the past information should be retained, while the reset gate controls how much of the previous information should be ignored when processing the current input. This architecture allows GRUs to capture long-term dependencies without the complexity of LSTMs.
- **Use Cases**: Like LSTMs, GRUs are used in NLP tasks such as text generation, translation, and sequence labeling. They are also used for time-series forecasting.

- **Advantages and Limitations**: GRUs are computationally more efficient than LSTMs because they have fewer parameters, but they may not perform as well in very complex tasks that require longer sequences or more intricate memory management.

6. Generative Adversarial Networks (GAN)

Generative Adversarial Networks are a class of neural networks that generate new data instances that resemble a given dataset. GANs consist of two models: a generator and a discriminator. The generator creates synthetic data, and the discriminator attempts to distinguish between real and fake data.

- **Working Mechanism**: The generator tries to create data that is similar to the training data, while the discriminator tries to identify fake data. These two networks are trained together in a zero-sum game, where the generator improves by trying to fool the discriminator, and the discriminator improves by better identifying fake data.
- **Use Cases**: GANs are used in image generation, video synthesis, data augmentation, and creating synthetic data for training other machine learning models. They have also been used in artistic creation, such as generating artwork and music.
- **Advantages and Limitations**: GANs are capable of generating highly realistic synthetic data, but they can be unstable during training and require careful tuning of hyperparameters. Additionally, the quality of generated data depends heavily on the quality of the training data.

7. Radial Basis Function Networks (RBFN)

Radial Basis Function Networks are used primarily for classification tasks. They are a type of feedforward network with a hidden layer containing radial basis functions as activation functions, usually Gaussian functions.

- **Working Mechanism**: The network uses the distance between the input and the center of the radial basis function as the input to the output layer. The network learns a non-linear transformation of the input data by using a radial basis function as a basis for classification.
- **Use Cases**: RBFNs are applied to pattern recognition, time-series prediction, and function approximation tasks.
- **Advantages and Limitations**: RBFNs can perform well in tasks where the data has a clear, non-linear decision boundary. However, they require careful

selection of the number of basis functions, and they may not perform as well on highly complex data.

8. Self-Organizing Maps (SOM)

Self-Organizing Maps are unsupervised neural networks used for dimensionality reduction and data visualization. SOMs map high-dimensional data onto a lower-dimensional grid, while preserving the topological relationships in the data.

- **Working Mechanism**: SOMs use a competitive learning algorithm, where each neuron in the grid competes to become activated based on the input. The neurons are then updated to become more similar to the input data they are assigned.
- **Use Cases**: SOMs are often used for clustering, data visualization, and pattern recognition in fields like bioinformatics and customer segmentation.
- **Advantages and Limitations**: SOMs are particularly good at organizing high-dimensional data into a lower-dimensional map, making them useful for visualizing complex datasets. However, their performance may degrade when the input data is very noisy or when there are many outliers.

Table 2. RBFN VS SOM

Aspect	Radial Basis Function Networks (RBFN)	Self-Organizing Maps (SOM)
Architecture	Feedforward network with an input layer, a hidden layer with radial basis functions (usually Gaussian), and an output layer.	A type of unsupervised neural network with an input layer and a 2D output grid of neurons.
Working Mechanism	Uses radial basis functions as activation functions in the hidden layer to transform input data for classification.	Utilizes competitive learning to map high-dimensional input data to a lower-dimensional grid of neurons.
Key Strengths	Efficient in classification tasks with clear non-linear decision boundaries.	Effective in clustering and visualization of high-dimensional data.
Common Use Cases	Pattern recognition, time-series prediction, function approximation.	Clustering, data visualization, anomaly detection, feature extraction.

Table 2 provides a comparison between Radial Basis Function Networks (RBFN) and Self-Organizing Maps (SOM), emphasizing their architecture, working mechanism, strengths, and common applications. While RBFNs are tailored for classification tasks with non-linear decision boundaries, SOMs excel in clustering and visualizing high-dimensional data in lower-dimensional representations.

9. Autoencoders

Autoencoders are unsupervised neural networks designed for data compression and dimensionality reduction. They consist of two parts: an encoder that compresses the input data and a decoder that reconstructs the input from the compressed representation.

- **Working Mechanism**: The encoder maps the input data to a lower-dimensional latent space, while the decoder reconstructs the data from the encoded representation. The network is trained to minimize the difference between the input and the reconstructed data.
- **Use Cases**: Autoencoders are used for image denoising, anomaly detection, data compression, and unsupervised learning tasks.
- **Advantages and Limitations**: Autoencoders can learn efficient representations of data, but they may not always preserve all the relevant features of the input data, especially when the network is too small or the training data is insufficient.

10. Transformer Networks

Transformer Networks are a class of deep learning models that use attention mechanisms to process sequences of data. Unlike RNNs or LSTMs, transformers process input data in parallel, allowing them to handle long-range dependencies more efficiently.

- **Working Mechanism**: Transformers use self-attention to compute a weighted sum of all input positions, allowing the model to focus on relevant parts of the input sequence for each output. They consist of an encoder-decoder architecture, where the encoder processes the input and the decoder generates the output.
- **Use Cases**: Transformers are widely used in natural language processing tasks, such as machine translation, language modeling, and text summarization. They are also applied in image captioning, speech recognition, and reinforcement learning.
- **Advantages and Limitations**: Transformers can process long sequences efficiently and achieve state-of-the-art performance in NLP tasks. However, they require large amounts of training data and computational power, making them less suitable for smaller datasets.

5. CHALLENGES

1. **Data Quality and Quantity**: Neural networks require large amounts of high-quality data to learn effectively. Insufficient or poor-quality data can lead to underfitting, where the model fails to capture the underlying patterns in the data. This is especially critical for deep learning models, which often require vast datasets to perform well. Moreover, biases in the data can lead to biased models, which may not generalize well to unseen data.
2. **Overfitting and Underfitting**: Neural networks are prone to both overfitting and underfitting. Overfitting occurs when the model learns the noise in the data rather than the actual patterns, making it perform well on training data but poorly on unseen data. On the other hand, underfitting happens when the model is too simple to capture the patterns in the data, resulting in poor performance on both training and test datasets.
3. **Complexity and Computational Resources**: Neural networks, especially deep neural networks, can be computationally expensive to train. They require significant processing power, especially when dealing with large datasets or complex architectures. This demand often necessitates powerful hardware like GPUs and TPUs. Training these networks also takes a considerable amount of time, depending on the complexity of the model and the size of the dataset.
4. **Interpretability and Explainability**: Neural networks are often described as "black-box" models because it can be difficult to interpret how they make decisions. This lack of transparency is a significant challenge, especially in domains like healthcare, finance, and law, where understanding the decision-making process is crucial. Methods to explain neural networks, such as feature importance or visualizations, are still developing, and ensuring models can be interpreted by humans remains a key research area.

6. ADVANTAGES

1. **Ability to Learn Complex Patterns**: Neural networks excel at learning from large amounts of data and can capture complex, non-linear relationships between inputs and outputs. This ability to model intricate patterns makes them particularly effective in tasks like image recognition, natural language processing, and time-series forecasting, where traditional algorithms often struggle.
2. **Adaptability to New Data**: Neural networks can adapt to new data through retraining or fine-tuning. Once a model is trained, it can be updated with new data to improve its performance without needing to be rebuilt from scratch. This

feature is especially useful in dynamic environments where data distribution or patterns change over time.

3. **Automatic Feature Extraction**: One of the key advantages of neural networks, particularly deep learning models, is their ability to automatically extract relevant features from raw data. Unlike traditional machine learning models, which require manual feature engineering, neural networks can learn high-level features from data without human intervention, making them more efficient for tasks like image and speech recognition.
4. **Versatility Across Domains**: Neural networks are highly versatile and can be applied across a wide range of domains. They are used for image and speech recognition, natural language processing, autonomous vehicles, finance, healthcare, and many other industries. Their flexibility allows them to address a diverse set of problems, making them one of the most widely used tools in artificial intelligence.
5. **High Accuracy and Performance**: When properly trained, neural networks can achieve remarkable accuracy, often outperforming other machine learning algorithms. This is particularly true in tasks like image classification, language translation, and playing complex games (e.g., AlphaGo). Their performance improves as more data becomes available, making them increasingly powerful over time.
6. **Parallel Processing Capabilities**: Neural networks, especially deep learning models, benefit from parallel processing capabilities, which significantly speed up training and inference times. GPUs and specialized hardware like TPUs are optimized for neural network operations, enabling efficient computation on large datasets. This makes neural networks suitable for real-time applications and large-scale data processing.
7. **Robustness to Noise and Incomplete Data**: Neural networks are generally robust to noisy data and can handle missing or incomplete information better than many traditional algorithms. Through techniques like regularization and dropout, they can learn to focus on the most important features and ignore irrelevant noise, improving their generalization ability on unseen data.

7. CONCLUSION

Neural networks, with their deep learning capabilities, have proven to be a ground breaking technology across a wide range of industries. From image recognition and natural language processing to financial forecasting and autonomous systems, their ability to process large volumes of data and learn from complex patterns has enabled significant advancements in automation, decision-making, and optimization.

As neural networks continue to evolve, we are seeing increasingly sophisticated models, such as convolutional neural networks (CNNs) for visual data and recurrent neural networks (RNNs) for sequential data, being deployed in applications that were once considered complex or unattainable. These models not only enhance operational efficiency but also provide a more personalized experience in sectors like healthcare, entertainment, and customer service. Despite their successes, neural networks face several challenges, including the need for large amounts of labeled data, computational costs, and the difficulty in explaining the decision-making process of deep models. However, ongoing research and development are addressing these limitations, making neural networks more accessible, efficient, and interpretable. In conclusion, neural networks represent a critical component of artificial intelligence that is reshaping industries, optimizing processes, and solving complex problems. As these technologies continue to improve, the potential for their application is boundless, from transforming healthcare diagnostics to revolutionizing autonomous transportation and beyond.

8. FUTURE ENHANCEMENT

The future of neural networks presents immense potential for innovation and enhancement across various fields. One of the main areas of focus will be improving the interpretability and transparency of neural networks. As current deep learning models often operate as "black boxes," there will be significant efforts to make them more understandable, ensuring trust and accountability, particularly in sensitive sectors such as healthcare and finance. Additionally, the efficiency of these models will be a key focus, with advancements aimed at reducing the energy consumption associated with large-scale models. This could be achieved through techniques like pruning, quantization, and developing more energy-efficient architectures. Autonomous learning is another promising area, where neural networks could evolve to learn from smaller, unlabeled datasets using unsupervised or self-supervised learning methods. The integration of quantum computing with neural networks is also expected to bring groundbreaking advancements, enabling faster solutions to complex problems like cryptography, drug discovery, and materials science. Future models will also be more adaptable to various domains, improving their generalization across tasks and data types. In terms of ethical concerns, there will likely be an increased emphasis on developing techniques to mitigate bias and ensure fairness, particularly as neural networks are applied to critical decision-making processes. Real-time processing on edge devices will also become more prevalent, enabling neural networks to operate efficiently in environments with limited computational power. Moreover, the future of neural networks will likely see more personalized models, especially in areas like healthcare and education, tailoring predictions and recommendations to individual needs. Finally, as neural networks continue to evolve, there will be greater integration with human intelligence, allowing for a hybrid approach that combines machine precision with human intuition. In summary, the future of neural networks holds exciting opportunities for advancements in efficiency, adaptability, and ethical AI, promising to revolutionize industries and improve quality of life.

REFERENCES

Chen, L., & Li, Z. (2023). Natural Language Processing with Transformer-based Neural Networks. *Journal of Natural Language Processing*, *38*(3), 134–149.

Chen, W., & Liu, L. (2023). BERT and Transformers: Modern Neural Networks for NLP. *Computational Linguistics*, *48*(7), 865–887.

Gao, T., & Zhang, K. (2023). Deep Neural Networks for Social Media Analytics. *Journal of Data Science and Analytics*, *19*(1), 82–99.

Guo, Z., & Zhang, L. (2023). Exploring Neural Networks for Traffic Prediction. *Transportation Research Part C, Emerging Technologies*, *98*, 215–229.

He, Y., & Zhang, J. (2023). Improving GANs with Neural Architecture Search. *Machine Learning*, *29*(1), 1–22.

Kumar, R., & Gupta, A. (2023). Advanced Computing and Related Applications Leveraging Brain-inspired Spiking Neural Networks. *Journal of Advanced Computing*, *40*(6), 1234–1250.

Lee, Y., & Wang, H. (2023). Multi-modal Neural Networks for Cross-Domain Learning. *Machine Learning*, *58*(3), 431–446.

Li, F., & Guo, Y. (2023). Neural Networks in Game AI: Achievements and Challenges. *Journal of Game Design and AI*, *16*(3), 198–215.

Li, H., & Zhang, Y. (2023). Quantum Neural Networks: From Theory to Practice. *Quantum Computing Journal*, *7*(1), 13–29.

Li, Q., & Liu, H. (2023). Adversarial Attacks on Neural Networks: A Comprehensive Review. *AI & Security*, *5*(2), 223–240.

Liu, B., & Wang, Z. (2023). Federated Learning with Neural Networks for Privacy-Preserving Applications. *Journal of Privacy and Security*, *41*(3), 301–318.

Liu, J., Zhang, L., & Lee, D. (2023). Graph Neural Networks for Decentralized Multi-Robot Path Planning. *Journal of Robotics*, *34*(2), 215–225.

Liu, Y., & Li, Q. (2023). Neural Networks for Fraud Detection in E-commerce. *Journal of E-commerce Technology*, *32*(5), 410–425.

Miao, X., & Xu, L. (2023). Deep Learning for Autonomous Vehicles: A Review. *Autonomous Systems Review*, *47*(3), 230–246.

Patel, P., & Gupta, A. (2023). Transfer Learning for Neural Networks in Healthcare. *Journal of Healthcare Engineering*, *39*(5), 57–72.

Patel, R., & Gupta, P. (2023). Neural Networks in Predictive Maintenance Systems. *Journal of Industrial Engineering*, *58*(3), 228–242.

Singh, M., & Kumar, R. (2023). Neural Networks in Drug Discovery: A Survey. *Journal of Computational Biology*, *31*(5), 423–438.

Wang, J., & Li, Y. (2023). AutoML and Neural Networks: Revolutionizing Automated Model Design. *Journal of Artificial Intelligence Research*, *60*(4), 907–922.

Wang, Q., & Zhao, W. (2023). Recurrent Neural Networks for Time Series Forecasting. *Journal of Time Series Analysis*, *48*(4), 568–583.

Wang, X., & Li, P. (2023). Artificial Neural Networks in Human-Computer Interaction. *Journal of Human-Computer Interaction*, *41*(2), 167–180.

Yang, H., & Lee, S. (2024). Neural Networks Made of Light: Photon Power Drives the Next AI Revolution. *Science Daily*, *23*(1), 48–53.

Zhang, F., & Wang, M. (2023). Deep Neural Networks for Financial Forecasting. *Journal of Finance and Technology*, *45*(2), 213–229.

Zhang, L., & Wu, J. (2023). Neural Networks for Anomaly Detection in Industrial IoT Systems. *Journal of Industrial IoT Research*, *9*(6), 1023–1037.

Zhang, Q., & Li, T. (2023). Neural Networks-based Video Analytics for Smart Cities. *Smart City Technologies*, *22*(1), 56–68.

Zhang, S., & Wang, Q. (2021). Graph Neural Network for Traffic Forecasting: A Survey. *International Journal of Geographical Information Science*, *35*(7), 1476–1491.

Zhang, X., & Lee, T. (2023). A Review of Validation and Verification of Neural Network-based Policies for Sequential Decision Making. *Journal of Machine Learning Research*, *55*(2), 1050–1073.

Zhang, X., & Yang, Z. (2023). Neural Network-based Approaches for Image Segmentation in Medical Imaging. *Medical Image Analysis*, *74*, 112–125.

Zhang, Y., & Luo, C. (2023). Reinforcement Learning with Neural Networks in Robotics. *Robotics and Automation Letters*, *8*(2), 3501–3512.

Zhao, S., & Zhang, L. (2023). Neural Networks for Environmental Monitoring and Climate Change Modeling. *Environmental Informatics*, *40*(8), 2103–2120.

Zhao, Z., & Chen, S. (2023). Neural Networks in Cybersecurity: A Survey. *Journal of Cybersecurity Research, 15*(4), 101–120.

Chapter 2
Deep Learning:
Foundations, Architectures, and Transformative Applications

Punam Kumari
https://orcid.org/0000-0001-8144-7573
Amity University, Bengaluru, India

K. S. Swarnalatha
Amity University, Bengaluru, India

Pallavi Pandey
IILM University, Gurugram, India

ABSTRACT

Deep learning has emerged as a transformative branch of artificial intelligence, revolutionizing diverse domains with its ability to process and analyze large, complex datasets. This chapter provides an in-depth exploration of deep learning techniques, emphasizing their foundational concepts, architecture, and applications. It begins with the discussion of the history of deep learning and the transition from machine learning to deep learning. An introduction to neural networks, including convolutional and recurrent architecture, and highlights their unique capacity for hierarchical feature extraction. The discussion extends to advanced techniques such as Generative AI, Large Language Model and Transformer Model, showcasing their adaptability across tasks. Focusing on practical implications, the chapter examines the impact of deep learning in fields like healthcare, finance, autonomous systems, and natural language processing. By the end of the chapter, readers will gain a comprehensive understanding of deep learning capabilities, limitations, and transformative potential.

DOI: 10.4018/979-8-3373-0735-0.ch002

1. INTRODUCTION TO DEEP LEARNING

Deep learning, a subset of machine learning (ML), has become one of the most transformative technologies in artificial intelligence (AI). Its history and evolution are deeply intertwined with advancements in computer science, mathematics, and neuroscience. This narrative explores its origins and its progression from traditional machine learning techniques to deep learning methods.

1.1 Brief history of deep learning and its evolution from traditional machine learning.

1.1.1 Foundations of Machine Learning

Machine learning, the broader field encompassing deep learning, emerged in the mid-20th century as researchers sought to create algorithms capable of learning from data. Key milestones include:

1950s: Alan Turing's concept of a "learning machine" introduced in his seminal paper, Computing Machinery and Intelligence (Turing, 1980).
1957: Frank Rosenblatt's Perceptron, inspired by biological neurons, became the first algorithm for supervised learning (Rosenblatt, F. (1958)). Despite its promise, the perceptron's inability to handle non-linearly separable data limited its application.
1960s-70s: Statistical learning theory emerged, focusing on optimization and probabilistic models like Bayesian inference, decision trees, and support vector machines (SVMs).
1980s-90s: With growing computational power, ML methods like k-nearest neighbors (k-NN), Gaussian processes, and ensemble methods gained popularity, emphasizing feature engineering and general-purpose algorithms.

Traditional ML approaches focused heavily on manually engineered features. Algorithms like linear regression, SVMs, and decision trees relied on domain expertise to extract meaningful representations from raw data.

1.1.2 Origins of Deep Learning

Deep learning's roots lie in artificial neural networks (ANNs), computational models inspired by the structure and function of the human brain. Significant early contributions include:

1943: Warren McCulloch and Walter Pitts proposed a mathematical model of a neuron, laying the foundation for ANNs (McCulloch, W. S. (1943)).
1958: The perceptron model, developed by Rosenblatt (Rosenblatt, F. (1958)), aimed to mimic biological neural activity but was limited to linearly separable tasks.
1969: Minsky and Papert's critique of perceptrons, documented in Perceptrons: An Introduction to Computational Geometry, highlighted the limitations of single-layer networks, stalling ANN research for decades (Minsky, M., & Papert, S. (1969)).
1980s: The backpropagation algorithm, popularized by Rumelhart, Hinton, and Williams (Rumelhart, et al., 1986), enabled multi-layer networks to learn complex patterns by efficiently updating weights. This marked the beginning of modern deep learning.

Despite these advancements, neural networks remained overshadowed by other ML methods due to computational constraints and the lack of large-scale datasets.

1.1.3 The Shift from Traditional Machine Learning to Deep Learning

The transition from traditional machine learning to deep learning was catalyzed by several factors:

a) **Data Availability** The rise of the internet, social media, and digital devices generated massive amounts of data, often referred to as "big data." Traditional ML algorithms struggled to process and extract insights from unstructured data (e.g., images, audio, text), necessitating automated feature extraction.
b) Advances in Hardware
    2000s: Graphics Processing Units (GPUs), initially developed for rendering 3D graphics, proved ideal for parallelizing matrix operations essential to neural networks. High-performance GPUs and cloud computing platforms made training deep networks feasible within reasonable timeframes.
c) **Algorithmic Innovations** New activation functions like Rectified Linear Units (ReLU) addressed vanishing gradient issues in deep networks. Regularization techniques, such as dropout and batch normalization, improved generalization and stability. Architectures like convolutional neural networks (CNNs) and recurrent neural networks (RNNs) specialized deep learning for tasks like image recognition and sequence processing.
d) Success Stories

2006: Geoffrey Hinton's work on deep belief networks revived interest in deep learning by demonstrating unsupervised pretraining (Hinton, G. E. (2009)).

2012: AlexNet, a deep convolutional network, achieved a breakthrough in image recognition, winning the ImageNet competition and outperforming traditional ML methods by a significant margin (Krizhevsky, 2012).

1.1.4 Comparing Traditional ML and Deep Learning

Traditional ML and deep learning differ fundamentally in their approach to problem-solving: A comparison of **Machine Learning** and **Deep Learning** is provided in Table 1. This table highlights the key distinctions between Machine Learning and Deep Learning, focusing on their complexity, data requirements, and use cases.

Table 1. Machine Learning vs Deep Learning

Aspect	Machine Learning	Deep Learning
Definition	A subset of AI where systems learn from data and improve over time without explicit programming.	A subset of machine learning that uses neural networks with many layers to analyze data.
Data Requirement	Can work with small to medium-sized datasets.	Requires large datasets to train effectively and achieve high accuracy.
Model Complexity	Typically uses simpler models such as decision trees, linear regression, or SVMs.	Uses complex models like deep neural networks, often with many hidden layers.
Feature Engineering	Requires manual feature extraction and selection for training models.	Automatically extracts features from raw data without manual intervention.
Training Time	Generally faster, especially for smaller datasets.	Can be very slow, especially with large datasets and deep neural networks.
Computation Power	Less computationally intensive compared to deep learning.	Requires high computational power, often involving GPUs or TPUs.
Interpretability	Models are easier to interpret (e.g., decision trees, linear models).	Models are often seen as "black boxes," making them harder to interpret.
Application Areas	Used in tasks like classification, regression, clustering, and recommendation.	Used in tasks like image recognition, natural language processing, and speech recognition.
Algorithms	Includes algorithms like linear regression, decision trees, k-NN, SVM, etc.	Primarily uses neural network-based models like CNNs, RNNs, and GANs.
Dependency on Data	Performs well with structured data and smaller datasets.	Excels with unstructured data (images, audio, text) and large datasets.

continued on following page

Table 1. Continued

Aspect	Machine Learning	Deep Learning
Example Libraries/ Tools	Scikit-learn, XGBoost, Random Forest, etc.	TensorFlow, PyTorch, Keras, etc.
Flexibility	Less flexible due to simpler models and manual feature engineering.	More flexible, capable of solving a wide range of complex problems automatically.
Overfitting Risk	Prone to overfitting with small datasets and complex models.	Can still overfit but regularization techniques like dropout help mitigate it.

Deep learning's ability to automatically discover features and hierarchical patterns directly from raw data offers a significant advantage over traditional ML methods.

1.1.5 Key Milestones in Deep Learning Evolution

RNNs (1980s-90s): Introduced for sequential data, with advancements like Long Short-Term Memory (LSTM) networks improving performance on time-series tasks (McCulloch, W. S. (1943)).
CNNs (2012): Pioneered by Yann LeCun for document recognition, CNNs became the foundation for computer vision (LeCun, 2015).
GANs (2014): Goodfellow et al., (2014) developed Generative Adversarial Networks, enabling the synthesis of realistic data.
Transformers (2017): The Transformer architecture revolutionized natural language processing (NLP), laying the groundwork for models like GPT and BERT (Vaswani, A. (2017)).
GPT 3 (2020): OpenAI released GPT-3, demonstrating the power of large-scale pretraining and few-shot learning (Haque, M.,2023).
Large Language Models (2023): Models like ChatGPT and Bard showcased the capabilities of conversational AI and multimodal systems.
Foundation Models (2024): Unified architectures trained on diverse tasks and data sources (e.g., OpenAI's GPT-4 and Google's Gemini).

Given below is the figure (Fig. 1) to demonstrate evolution from machine learning to deep learning and the key concepts of deep learning.

Figure 1. Year wise Evolution from machine learning to deep learning

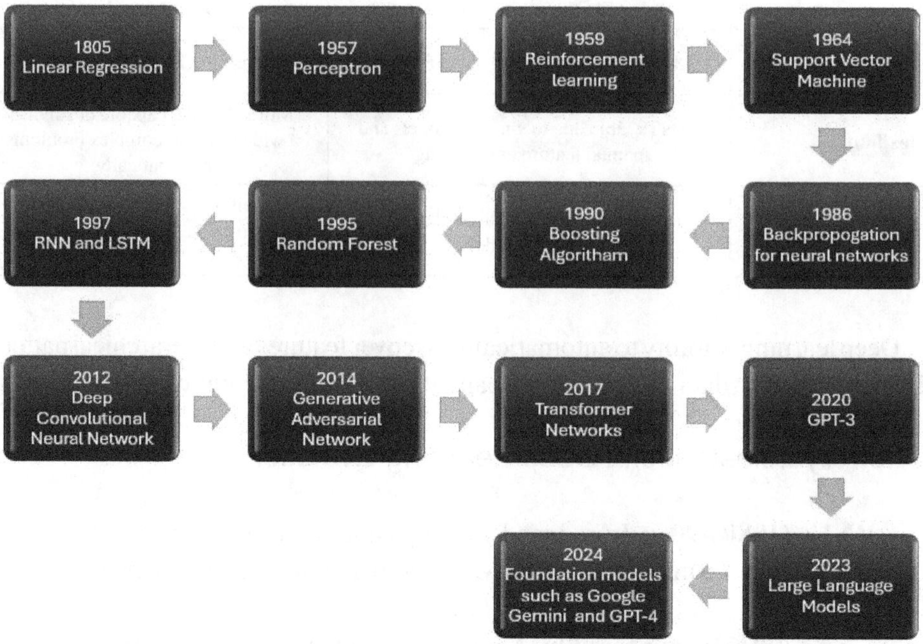

1.2 Neural networks as the foundation of deep learning

Neural networks form the backbone of deep learning, enabling machines to process complex patterns and solve problems that mimic human cognitive capabilities. These computational frameworks are inspired by the biological neural networks in the human brain. Central to their functionality are layers, nodes (or neurons), and activation functions, which together define how data is processed, transformed, and ultimately utilized to make predictions or decisions.

1.2.1 Structure of Neural Networks

At their core, neural networks consist of layers of interconnected nodes. Each node is analogous to a neuron in the brain and serves as a computational unit that processes input data to generate an output. The network's architecture determines how information flows, how it is processed, and the complexity of the problems the network can tackle (Anderson, J. A. (1995)).

1.2.1.1 Layers in Neural Networks

Neural networks are organized into layers, each of which has a distinct role:

I) **Input Layer:** This is the first layer, where raw data enters the network. The number of nodes in the input layer corresponds to the number of features or dimensions in the dataset.

Example: In an image recognition task, each pixel value of an image might be an input node.

II) **Hidden Layers:** These are intermediate layers between the input and output layers. Hidden layers process the input data by applying transformations and extracting features. The depth (number of layers) and width (number of nodes per layer) of hidden layers largely define the complexity of the network. Deep learning derives its name from the use of multiple hidden layers.

III) **Output Layer:** This final layer provides the network's predictions or outputs. The number of nodes in the output layer depends on the task. For classification tasks, it corresponds to the number of classes, while for regression tasks, it might be a single node.

1.2.1.2 Nodes (Neurons)

Each node in a neural network performs a simple mathematical operation. The nodes receive inputs, apply weights, and produce an output, which is passed to the next layer.

Inputs and Weights: Each node receives inputs, which are weighted values from the previous layer. The weights determine the importance of each input in the computation.

Formula:

$$Z = f\left(b + \sum_{i=1}^{n} x_i w_i\right) \tag{1}$$

Where:

w: are the weights connecting inputs to the node.
b: bias term, providing flexibility to shift the activation function.
x: input to neuron
z: weighted sum for node.
n: is number of inputs from incoming layer
i: is counter from 1 to n

Bias Term: Bias adds a constant value to the weighted sum, ensuring the network can better fit the data, even when all input values are zero.

1.2.1.3 Activation Functions Once a node computes its weighted sum, it passes the result through an activation function, which introduces non-linearity into the network. Without activation functions, neural networks would merely be linear models, unable to capture complex patterns in data. Common Activation Functions are

I) Sigmoid Function:

Formula:$f(x) = \frac{1}{1 + e^{-x}}$ (2) **Range: (0, 1)**

Usage: Suitable for binary classification tasks.

Limitation: Prone to vanishing gradients, which hinder training in deep networks.

II)Tanh (Hyperbolic Tangent):

Formula:$f(x) = \tanh(x) = \frac{2}{1 + e^{-2x}} - 1 \left(3\right)$ **Range: (-1, 1)**

Advantage: Zero-centered, unlike sigmoid.

Limitation: Also suffers from vanishing gradients in deep networks.

III) ReLU (Rectified Linear Unit):

Formula:$f(x) = \begin{cases} 0, x < 0 \\ x, x \geq 0 \end{cases}$ **Range: [0, ∞)**

Advantage: Efficient and addresses the vanishing gradient problem.

Limitation: Prone to "dying ReLU" when neurons output zero consistently.

IV)Leaky ReLU:

Formula:$f(x) = \begin{cases} ax, x < 0 \\ x, x \geq 0 \end{cases}$ **Range: [-∞, +∞]**

Where 'a' is a small value generally 0.01

Advantage: Addresses the "dying ReLU" issue by allowing a small gradient for negative inputs.

V) Softmax:

Formula:

$$f(x_i) = \frac{e^{x_i}}{\sum_{j=1}^{n} e^{x_j}} \tag{4}$$

Where 'x' is an input vector to softmax function and 'n' is number of classes

Usage: Converts outputs into probabilities for multi-class classification.

1.2.1.4 Information Flow in Neural Networks: The flow of data through a neural network occurs in two main phases:

I) Forward Propagation:
- Input data passes through the network, layer by layer.
- Each node processes its inputs, applies weights and biases, and passes the result through the activation function.
- The final output is computed in the output layer.

II) Backward Propagation (Backpropagation):
- During training, the network's predictions are compared to the true labels to calculate a loss.
- The error is propagated backward through the network, layer by layer, to update weights and biases.
- Optimization algorithms like stochastic gradient descent (SGD) use this information to minimize the loss function.

1.2.2 Significance of Layers, Nodes, and Activation Functions The interplay between layers, nodes, and activation functions is what gives neural networks their power:

Layers: Define the network's depth and its ability to represent complex hierarchies of features. Shallow networks handle simple problems, while deep networks can model intricate patterns.

Nodes: Serve as the computational units that transform inputs into meaningful representations.

Activation Functions: Introduce non-linearity, enabling the network to solve problems like image recognition, language translation, and more.

The synergy between layers, nodes, and activation functions defines the network's capacity to learn and generalize. Layers and nodes determine the structural depth and breadth of the network, while activation functions empower it to solve non-linear problems. Together, they enable neural networks to excel in diverse applications, from speech recognition to autonomous systems, making them indispensable in modern AI.

1.3 Reason why Deep Learning Has Gained Prominence

Deep learning, a subset of machine learning, has revolutionized the field of artificial intelligence (AI) and emerged as a transformative technology. Its rise to prominence can be attributed to several key factors: advancements in computational power, the proliferation of data, and innovations in neural network architectures. This section delves into the interplay of these factors and their collective role in propelling deep learning to the forefront of AI research and applications.

1.3.1 The Role of Computational Power

Deep learning models, particularly deep neural networks (DNNs), are computationally intensive. Training these models requires executing millions or even billions of mathematical operations, such as matrix multiplications, across large datasets. Historically, the lack of sufficient computational resources hindered the feasibility of deep learning. However, several advancements have addressed this limitation:

1.3.1.1 Emergence of GPUs

Graphics Processing Units (GPUs) have played a pivotal role in enabling deep learning. Initially designed for rendering graphics in video games, GPUs are highly efficient at parallelizing computations, making them ideal for the matrix and tensor operations central to deep learning.

Parallel Processing: Unlike traditional CPUs, which excel at sequential tasks, GPUs can perform thousands of computations simultaneously. This parallelism drastically reduces the time required to train deep models.

Cost-Effectiveness: With the advent of GPUs like NVIDIA's CUDA-enabled cards, researchers gained access to affordable high-performance hardware.

Optimization Libraries: Tools such as TensorFlow, PyTorch, and CUDA have further optimized GPU usage for deep learning tasks.

1.3.1.2 Specialized Hardware

In addition to GPUs, new hardware innovations have further accelerated deep learning:

Tensor Processing Units (TPUs): Developed by Google, TPUs are specialized for tensor operations, enabling faster training and inference of deep learning models.

Field-Programmable Gate Arrays (FPGAs): These offer flexibility in designing custom hardware for specific deep learning tasks.

ASICs (Application-Specific Integrated Circuits): Designed for specific AI workloads, ASICs improve efficiency and reduce power consumption.

1.3.1.3 Cloud Computing

Cloud platforms like AWS, Google Cloud, and Microsoft Azure have democratized access to high-performance computing. Researchers and organizations can now train large models without investing in physical hardware, further lowering the barrier to entry for deep learning.

1.3.2 The Proliferation of Data

Deep learning thrives on large volumes of high-quality data. The explosion of data generated in today's digital era has been a cornerstone of its success. Several factors have contributed to this data abundance:

1.3.2.1 Digital Transformation

The shift to digital platforms across industries has resulted in an unprecedented amount of data:

E-commerce: Platforms like Amazon and Alibaba generate vast data on consumer behavior.

Social-Media: Billions of users on platforms like Facebook, Instagram, and Twitter produce enormous amounts of unstructured data, including text, images, and videos.

IoT Devices: Sensors, wearables, and smart home devices generate real-time data streams.

1.3.2.2 Data Storage Innovations

Advances in storage technologies have made it easier to collect and store massive datasets:

Cloud Storage: Services like Google Drive, Dropbox, and AWS S3 allow seamless storage and retrieval of large datasets.

Data Lakes: Organizations are increasingly adopting data lakes to store structured and unstructured data in a scalable manner.

1.3.2.3 Open Datasets

The availability of open datasets has accelerated deep learning research. Examples include:

ImageNet: A benchmark dataset for image recognition (Deng, J., et al., 2009, June).

COCO: A dataset for object detection, segmentation, and captioning (Lin, T. Y., et al., 2014).

OpenAI's GPT Datasets: Text datasets used for language modeling.

1.3.3 Innovations in Neural Network Architectures

While computational power and data availability laid the foundation, advancements in neural network architecture unlocked deep learning's full potential. Key innovations include:

1.3.3.1 Convolutional Neural Networks (CNNs)

CNNs revolutionized computer vision by enabling efficient feature extraction from images. Their hierarchical structure mimics the visual cortex in humans, allowing them to excel at tasks like object detection, face recognition, and image classification.

1.3.3.2 Recurrent Neural Networks (RNNs) and LSTMs

RNNs, and their variants like Long Short-Term Memory (LSTM) networks, were breakthroughs in handling sequential data. These architectures excel at tasks involving time-series data, such as speech recognition and language modeling.

1.3.3.3 Transformers

Transformers, introduced through models like BERT and GPT, revolutionized natural language processing (NLP). By leveraging self-attention mechanisms, they handle long-range dependencies more effectively than RNNs, enabling state-of-the-art performance in tasks like translation and text generation.

1.3.3.4 Generative Models

Generative models like Generative Adversarial Networks (GANs) and Variational Autoencoders (VAEs) opened new frontiers in creating synthetic data, image synthesis, and even art generation.

1.3.4 Synergistic Growth: The AI Feedback Loop

The combination of computational power, data, and architectural advancements has created a feedback loop driving deep learning prominence:

Better Models Require More Data: Advanced architectures like transformers and GANs thrive on large datasets, pushing the need for comprehensive data collection.

Efficient Hardware Enables Larger Models: GPUs, TPUs, and specialized hardware make it feasible to train deeper and wider networks.

Successful Applications Fuel More Investment: Breakthrough applications in healthcare, autonomous vehicles, and voice assistants have attracted significant funding and research interest.

1.3.5 Societal and Economic Impacts

Deep learning's rise has had profound societal and economic implications:

1.3.5.1 Transforming Industries

Healthcare: AI-powered diagnostics and drug discovery.
Education: Personalized learning and virtual tutors.
Finance: Fraud detection and algorithmic trading.

1.3.5.2 Democratization of AI

With open-source tools, cloud platforms, and pre-trained models, deep learning is accessible to researchers and developers worldwide, fostering innovation.

1.3.5.3 Ethical and Regulatory Challenges

The rapid adoption of deep learning also raises concerns about privacy, bias, and accountability, necessitating frameworks for ethical AI deployment.

So, Deep learning prominence is the result of a convergence of factors—unprecedented computational power, abundant data, and breakthroughs in neural network design. Together, they have transformed deep learning from a theoretical concept to a practical tool reshaping industries and addressing complex challenges. As technology continues to evolve, deep learning's role in advancing AI and benefiting society will only expand further.

2 FUNDAMENTAL DEEP LEARNING ARCHITECTURES

Convolutional Neural Networks (CNNs) are a class of deep learning models designed specifically for processing data that has a grid-like topology, such as images and videos. CNNs have become the standard for tasks involving image classification, object detection, and video analysis due to their ability to automatically and efficiently extract spatial and temporal hierarchies of features. This section provides an in-depth exploration of CNNs, including their architecture, key components, and applications in image and video processing tasks.

Overview of CNNs

CNNs are inspired by the organization of the visual cortex in animals, which processes visual information hierarchically. At their core, CNNs consist of layers designed to automatically extract features from input data while preserving spatial relationships. These layers include convolutional layers, pooling layers, and fully connected layers, which work in tandem to transform input data into meaningful representations (LeCun, et. al., 2015).

2.1 Key Components of CNNs

2.1.1 Convolutional Layers

The convolutional layer is the foundation of CNNs. It is responsible for feature extraction through the application of convolutional filters.

Convolution Operation:

The convolution operation involves sliding a filter (or kernel) across the input data to compute feature maps. Diagrammatically, it is expressed as in Fig 2:

Figure 2. Convolutional Operation

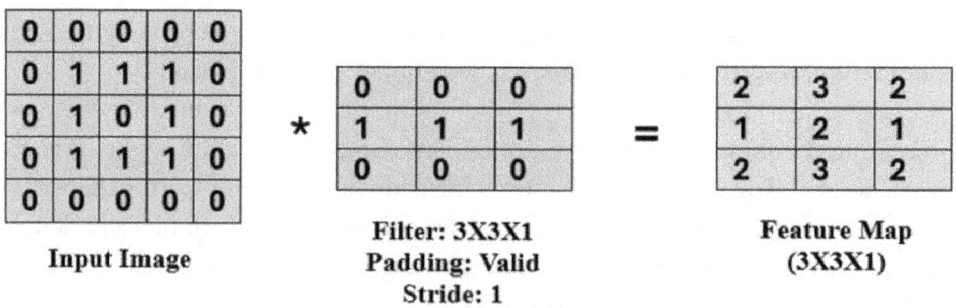

Each filter extracts a specific feature, such as edges, textures, or patterns, from the input image.

Feature Maps:

The result of the convolution operation is a feature map, which highlights the presence of specific features in the input data.

Padding and Stride:

Padding: Adding extra pixels around the input data to preserve spatial dimensions after convolution.

Stride: Determines the step size of the filter as it slides across the input, controlling the size of the output feature map.

2.1.2 Activation Functions

After convolution, the output is passed through an activation function to introduce non-linearity, enabling the model to learn complex patterns. Here's a comparison of various activation functions in a tabular format:

Table 2. Various Activation Functions

Activation Function	Formula	Range	Key Characteristics	Advantages	Disadvantages
Sigmoid	$f(x) = \frac{1}{1+e^{-x}}$	(0,1)	Smooth, S-shaped curve.	Good for probabilistic outputs.	Vanishing gradient problem; slow convergence.
Tanh	$\tanh(x) = \frac{e^{x} - e^{-x}}{e^{x} + e^{-x}}$	(−1,1)	S-shaped curve centered around zero.	Helps in centering data; works better than Sigmoid in deep networks.	Vanishing gradient problem.
ReLU (Rectified Linear Unit)	$f(x) = \max(0, x)$	[0,∞)	Non-linear and computationally efficient.	Reduces vanishing gradient issue; sparsity (activates few neurons).	"Dying ReLU" problem (neurons can become inactive).
Leaky ReLU	$f(x) = x \text{ if } x > 0$ *else* $f(x) = \alpha x$	(−∞,∞)	Variant of ReLU allowing small gradients for negative inputs.	Mitigates "dying ReLU" problem.	Choice of aa can affect performance.
ELU (Exponential Linear Unit)	$f(x) = x \text{ if } x > 0 \text{ else }$ $f(x) = \alpha(e^{x} - 1)$	(−α,∞)	Variant of ReLU providing smoother transitions for negative values.	Reduces bias shift; helps network converge faster.	Additional computational cost compared to ReLU.
Softmax	$\sigma(x_i) = \frac{e^{x_i}}{\Sigma_j e^{x_j}}$	(0,1)	Outputs probabilities for multiclass classification.	Normalizes outputs; interpretable results.	Computationally expensive; not suitable for hidden layers.
Swish	$f(x) = x\,\sigma(x)$	(−∞,∞)	Smooth, non-monotonic activation function.	Better performance in deep networks; addresses vanishing gradients.	Slightly higher computational cost.

2.1.3 Pooling Layers

Pooling layers reduce the spatial dimensions of feature maps, making the network more computationally efficient and robust to variations in input.

Max Pooling:

Selects the maximum value within a pooling window, retaining the most prominent features.

Average Pooling:

Computes the average value within a pooling window, preserving overall spatial information.

Diagrammatic representation of Pooling Layer is demonstrated in Fig 3.

Figure 3. Working of pooling layer

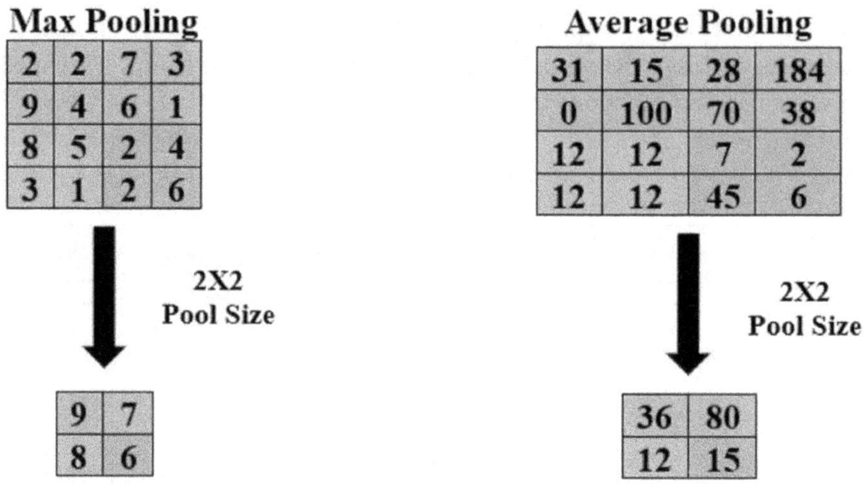

Pooling operations improve translation invariance, allowing the network to recognize features regardless of their position in the input.

2.1.4 Fully Connected Layers

In the final stages of a CNN, fully connected layers (dense layers) take the flattened feature maps and use them for classification or regression tasks. These layers connect every input node to every output node, enabling the network to make predictions based on the extracted features.

Figure 4. Fully Connected Layer

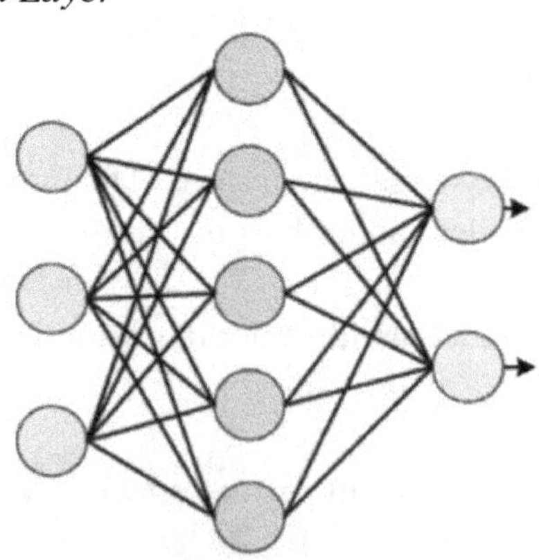

2.1.5 Dropout

Dropout is a regularization technique used in CNNs to prevent overfitting. During training, a random subset of neurons is ignored, forcing the network to learn more robust features.

Figure 5. Dropout Layer

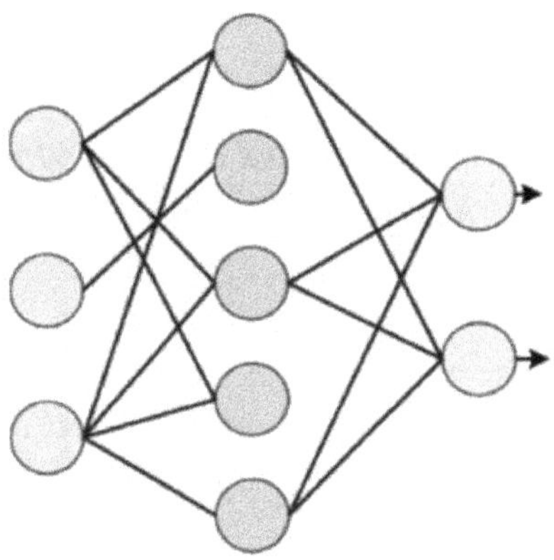

2.2 Popular CNN Architectures

Several CNN architectures have been developed to address specific challenges and improve performance in image and video processing tasks. Some of them are:

LeNet-5:

Introduced in 1998, LeNet-5 is a pioneering convolutional neural network (CNN) designed for handwritten digit recognition, laying the groundwork for modern deep learning architectures (LeCun, et. al,1998).

AlexNet:

AlexNet revolutionized computer vision in 2012 by achieving a significant breakthrough in image classification with the use of ReLU activation, dropout, and data augmentation (Krizhevsky, A. et. al, 2012).

VGGNet:

Proposed in 2014, VGGNet features a deep and uniform architecture of small convolutional filters, demonstrating the importance of network depth for enhanced performance (Simonyan, K., Vedaldi, A., & Zisserman, A. (2014).

ResNet:

Introduced in 2015, ResNet solves the vanishing gradient problem by using residual connections, enabling the training of extremely deep networks with improved accuracy (He, et. al, 2016).

Inception Network:

Developed in 2015, the Inception Network uses parallel convolutional paths of varying sizes to capture multi-scale features, achieving high efficiency and accuracy in image tasks (Szegedy, C., et. al, 2015).

A detailed comparison of LeNet-5, AlexNet, VGGNet, ResNet, and Inception Network is provided in Table 3:

Table 3. LeNet-5 Vs AlexNet Vs VGGNet Vs ResNet Vs Inception Network

Feature	LeNet-5	AlexNet	VGGNet	ResNet	Inception Network
Year Introduced	1998	2012	2014	2015	2015
Primary Use Case	Handwritten digit recognition (MNIST)	Image classification (ILSVRC)	Image classification (ILSVRC)	Image classification, object detection	Image classification, object detection
Architecture Depth	5 layers	8 layers	16-19 layers	50, 101, 152 layers	Inception modules with variable depths
Key Innovation	Simple convolutional and pooling layers	Use of ReLU, dropout, and data augmentation	Deep stacks of convolutional layers	Introduction of residual connections	Use of parallel convolution paths (Inception)
Input Size	32×32	227×227	224×224	224×224	299×299
Parameters	~60K	~60M	~138M	~25M (ResNet-50)	~23M (Inception-v3)
Strengths	Lightweight and efficient	Early breakthrough for deep learning	Deeper network with uniform structure	Solves vanishing gradient with skip connections	Efficient with fewer parameters, high accuracy
Weaknesses	Limited to simple tasks	Computationally intensive	High memory and computational needs	Computational complexity with deep layers	Complex architecture, harder to train
Optimizer Used	Stochastic Gradient Descent (SGD)	SGD with momentum	SGD	SGD with momentum	RMSProp or SGD

continued on following page

Table 3. Continued

This table highlights the evolution of convolutional neural networks (CNNs) in terms of depth, architecture, and innovation. Each model introduced novel concepts that significantly advanced computer vision tasks.

While Convolutional Neural Networks (CNNs) excel at processing spatial data like images, there are some other deep learning networks such as RNN and LSTM which are specifically designed to handle sequential data, such as time series, text, or speech. In the next section we are going to introduce RNN and LSTM both. Together, CNNs and RNNs form a powerful toolkit for solving diverse problems in computer vision and natural language processing.

2.3 Recurrent Neural Networks (RNNs):

Recurrent Neural Networks (RNNs) are a class of artificial neural networks designed to process and model sequential data. Unlike traditional feedforward neural networks, which process input data in isolation, RNNs possess a unique architecture that allows them to maintain and utilize contextual information through their recurrent connections. This ability to retain information across time steps makes RNNs particularly suited for tasks involving sequential data, such as speech recognition, natural language processing (NLP), and time-series prediction (Schmidt, R. M. 2019). In this section, we delve into the structure of RNNs, their key features, and their application in sequential data tasks.

2.3.1 Key Architectural Features

At the heart of RNNs is their recurrent connection, which enables the network to process sequences of data by retaining a "memory" of previous inputs. This memory is encapsulated in a hidden state that evolves over time.

What is Hidden State:

The hidden state acts as a dynamic representation of the sequence. At each time step, the hidden state is updated based on the current input and the previous hidden state. This update is typically governed by the following equation:

$$h_t = f(W_h h_{t-1} + W_x x_t + b_h) \quad (5)$$

Where:

$\boldsymbol{h_t}$: The hidden state at time step t. It captures information about the current input x_t and the previous hidden state h_{t-1} acting as the network's "memory."

$\boldsymbol{h_{t-1}}$: The hidden state from the previous time step, which carries information from earlier in the sequence.
$\boldsymbol{x_t}$: The input at time step t.This could be a feature vector from text, time-series data, or any other sequential input.
$\boldsymbol{W_h}$: The weight matrix for the hidden state. It determines how the previous hidden state influences the current one.
$\boldsymbol{W_x}$:The weight matrix for the input. It governs the influence of the current input on the hidden state.
$\boldsymbol{b_h}$:The bias term. It helps adjust the computation and adds flexibility to the learning process.
: The activation function, often a non-linear function like tanh or ReLU. It introduces non-linearity, allowing the network to model complex patterns.

2.3.2 Step-by-Step Working of RNN:

Step 1: Initialization:

- Initialize the hidden state h_0, often as a vector of zeros or small random values.
- Load the input sequence $x = (x_1, x_2, x_3 \ldots\ldots\ldots x_T)$, where T is the sequence length.

Step 2: Input Processing at Time Step t:

- At each time step t, the RNN processes the current input x_t and the previous hidden state h_{t-1}.
- Compute the new hidden state h_t using the formula:

$$h_t = f(W_h h_{t-1} + W_x x_t + b_h) \tag{6}$$

Step 3. Recurrent Updates:

- The hidden state h_t is updated recursively at each-time step t, carrying forward information about the sequence.
- This allows the RNN to maintain a "memory" of prior inputs as it processes new ones.

Step 4: Output Computation:

- At each time step t, an output y_t is produced based on the hidden state h_t.

$$Y_t = g\left(W_y h_t + b_y\right) \tag{7}$$

Here, W_y is the weight matrix for the output, b_y is the bias, and g is an activation function (e.g., softmax for classification).

Step 5: Sequential Iteration:

- Steps 2 to 4 are repeated for all T time steps, processing the entire sequence.

Step 6: Loss Calculation (if supervised):

- Compare the RNN's predicted outputs $y = (y_1, y_2, y_3 \ldots\ldots y_T)$ with the actual target values using a loss function (e.g., cross-entropy loss for classification or mean squared error for regression).

Step 7. Backward Propagation Through Time (BPTT):

- Compute gradients of the loss with respect to the RNN parameters by unrolling the network over time.
- Update the weights and biases using gradient descent or another optimization algorithm.

Step 8: Training Iterations:

- Repeat the above steps for multiple epochs over the training dataset to minimize the loss and improve the RNN's performance.

2.3.3 Key Features of RNN:

- The RNN's hidden state acts as a memory, allowing it to capture dependencies across time steps.
- The recurrent connection enables the model to learn temporal patterns in sequential data.
- However, RNNs can face challenges like vanishing gradients for long sequences, often addressed by advanced variants like LSTM and GRU.

2.3.4 Applications of RNNs in Sequential Data Tasks

RNNs have found widespread use in various domains where sequential data is central. Below, we explore some prominent applications:

I) Speech Recognition

Speech recognition involves converting spoken language into text, requiring the model to process audio signals over time.

Acoustic Modeling:

RNNs capture temporal dependencies in audio signals, making them effective for acoustic modeling. Example: Recognizing phonemes or words based on their spectral features over time.

End-to-End Systems:

RNNs form the backbone of end-to-end speech recognition systems, such as those used in virtual assistants like Siri or Google Assistant.

II) Natural Language Processing (NLP)

NLP tasks often involve sequences of words, making RNNs an ideal choice. Key applications include:

Language Modeling:

RNNs predict the next word in a sequence, a foundational task in NLP. Example: Text generation and autocomplete features.

Machine Translation:

RNNs, particularly in encoder-decoder architectures, are used for translating text from one language to another. Example: Google Translate leverages such models.

Sentiment Analysis:

By processing the sequence of words, RNNs can determine the sentiment conveyed in a text, such as whether a review is positive or negative.

Named Entity Recognition (NER):

RNNs help identify entities like names, locations, and organizations within text sequences.

III) Time-Series Prediction

Time-series data, such as stock prices, weather patterns, and sensor readings, inherently involve sequential dependencies. RNNs are widely used in:

Financial Forecasting:

Predicting stock market trends or currency exchange rates.

Energy Demand Prediction:
Anticipating electricity or gas consumption based on historical usage.
Healthcare:
Modeling patient health data over time to predict outcomes or detect anomalies.

IV) Video Analysis

Videos comprise sequences of frames, making them a natural application for RNNs:

Action Recognition:
Identifying actions in a video sequence, such as running, jumping, or walking.
Video Captioning:
Generating descriptive captions for video content.

V) Music and Audio Generation

RNNs are used to compose music or generate audio that aligns with specific styles or patterns. They learn from sequential audio data to produce coherent outputs.

Recurrent Neural Networks have transformed the way sequential data is processed, unlocking capabilities in speech recognition, language processing, and beyond. Their ability to retain contextual information across time steps makes them a cornerstone of AI applications dealing with temporal patterns. While challenges such as vanishing gradients and computational demands persist, innovations like LSTMs, GRUs, and bidirectional RNNs have addressed many limitations, solidifying their role in modern AI systems. The next section will provide a brief knowledge about LSTM.

2.4 Long Short Term Memory (LSTM) networks.

LSTM networks are an advanced variant of RNNs introduced by Hochreiter and Schmidhuber in 1997. Unlike standard RNNs, LSTMs are equipped with a unique memory cell and gating mechanisms that allow them to retain and update information over long sequences. This capability makes them particularly effective in tasks requiring context awareness over extended input sequences (Staudemeyer, R. C., & Morris, E. R. (2019).)

2.4.1 Key Architectural features of LSTM Network

1. **Memory Cell:** The core of an LSTM is the cell state, which acts as a memory, carrying information across time steps. It allows the network to retain or forget information over long sequences.
2. **Gates:** LSTMs use three primary gates to control the flow of information:
   I) Forget Gate (f_t)

$$f_t = \sigma\left(W_f\,[h_{t-1}, X_t] + b_f\right) \tag{8}$$

Determines which information from the previous cell state should be forgotten.

II) Input Gate (i_i):

$$i_t = \sigma\left(W_i\,[h_{t-1}, X_t] + b_i\right) \tag{9}$$

Controls how much new information from the current input should be added to the cell state.

III) Output Gate (O_t):

$$O_t = \sigma\left(W_o\,[h_{t-1}, X_t] + b_o\right) \tag{10}$$

Regulates the amount of information from the cell state to be output as the hidden state.

3.Cell State Update: The cell state is updated using the forget and input gates:

$$C_t = f_t \odot C_{t-1} + i_t \odot \widetilde{C}_t \tag{11}$$

Here $\widetilde{C}_t = \tanh\left(W_c[h_{t-1}, X_t] + b_c\right)$ is the candidate cell state, and $\odot$ denotes element-wise multiplication.

4. **Hidden State Update:** The hidden state h_t is derived from the updated cell state and the output gate:

$$h_t = O_t \odot \tanh\left(C_t\right) \tag{12}$$

5. **Non-Linearity:** LSTMs use activation functions like σ (sigmoid) for gating and tanh to regulate the values in the cell and hidden states, ensuring bounded updates.
6. **Learned Parameters:** LSTMs involve multiple weight matrices and biases, making them more complex but powerful compared to vanilla RNNs.
7. **Sequential Processing:** The network processes input sequentially, with information selectively retained or discarded at each step based on the gates.

2.4.2 Step-by-Step Working of LSTM: A concise breakdown of the workflow of LSTM is given below:

Step 1. Inputs to the LSTM Cell

- Input vector (x_t): Current time step data.
- Previous hidden state (h_{t-1}): Short-term memory from the last step.
- Previous cell state (C_{t-1}): Long-term memory.

Step 2. Forget Gate (f_t)

- **Purpose:** Decides which parts of (C_{t-1}) to forget.
- **Operation:**

$$f_t = \sigma\left(W_f \left[h_{t-1}, X_t\right] + b_f\right) \tag{13}$$

$f_t$values between 0 and 1 indicate what to keep or forget.

Step 3. Input Gate (i_t)

- **Purpose:** Determines what new information to store in the cell state.
- **Operation:**

$$i_t = \sigma\left(W_i \left[h_{t-1}, X_t\right] + b_i\right) \tag{14}$$

Compute the candidate cell state:

$$\widetilde{C}_t = \tanh\left(W_c\left[h_{t-1}, X_t\right] + b_c\right) \tag{15}$$

Step 4. Update Cell State (C_t)

- **Purpose:** Updates the long-term memory.

- **Operation:**

$$C_t = f_t \odot C_{t-1} + i_t \odot \widetilde{C}_t \qquad (16)$$

Step 5. Output Gate $(\boldsymbol{O}_t)$

- **Purpose:** Decides what information to output as the hidden state.
- **Operation:**

$$O_t = \sigma(W_o [h_{t-1}, X_t] + b_o) \qquad (17)$$

Hidden state

$$h_t = O_t \odot \tanh(C_t) \qquad (18)$$

Step 6. Outputs

- **Hidden state$\boldsymbol{h_t}$:** Short-term memory for the current step.
- **Cell state$(\boldsymbol{C_t})$**:Long-term memory passed to the next step.

Step 7. Repeat for Each Time Step

This process is repeated for all time steps in the sequence, enabling the LSTM to learn dependencies across time.

This mechanism allows LSTMs to handle long-term dependencies effectively in sequential tasks.

2.4.3 Applications of LSTM Networks

LSTMs have demonstrated remarkable versatility across various domains. Below are some of their most impactful applications:

I) **Natural Language Processing (NLP):** LSTMs have transformed NLP tasks due to their ability to model context and sequential dependencies:

Text Generation: LSTMs generate coherent text by predicting the next word based on previous words. Applications include creative writing and chatbot responses.

Machine Translation: LSTMs form the backbone of sequence-to-sequence (Seq2Seq) models, enabling translation between languages.

Sentiment Analysis: By processing the sequence of words, LSTMs identify sentiment in text, useful for social media monitoring and customer feedback analysis.

II) **Speech Recognition** In speech recognition, LSTMs process audio signals, which are inherently sequential:

Phoneme Recognition: LSTMs classify phonemes in audio streams, forming the basis for automatic speech recognition (ASR) systems.

Voice Assistants: Virtual assistants like Siri and Alexa rely on LSTMs for converting spoken words into text.

III) **Time Series Forecasting:** LSTMs excel in predicting future values from sequential data:

Stock Market Prediction: LSTMs analyze historical prices to forecast market trends.

Weather Forecasting: Using past meteorological data, LSTMs predict future weather conditions.

Energy Demand Prediction: LSTMs optimize power grid operations by forecasting energy usage.

IV) **Video Analysis:** Video data is a sequence of frames, making LSTMs suitable for tasks such as:

Action Recognition: LSTMs classify actions (e.g., running, jumping) in videos.

Video Summarization: By analyzing temporal patterns, LSTMs generate concise summaries of lengthy videos.

V) **Healthcare Applications** In healthcare, LSTMs process sequential patient data for:

Disease Progression Modeling: Predicting the progression of chronic conditions.

ECG Analysis: LSTMs detect abnormalities in electrocardiogram signals.

Clinical Note Generation: Generating structured summaries from unstructured medical notes.

VI) **Anomaly Detection:** LSTMs identify deviations from normal patterns in sequential data:

Network Intrusion Detection: Detecting malicious activities in network traffic.

Fraud Detection: Recognizing fraudulent transactions in financial data.

VII) **Robotics** LSTMs contribute to robotics by:

Motion Planning: Enabling robots to predict and execute smooth trajectories.
Human-Robot Interaction: Interpreting human gestures and actions.

2.5 Comparison of CNN VS RNN VS LSTM

CNN is ideal for spatial data like images and videos. RNN is suitable for sequential data but has limitations with long-term dependencies. LSTM builds on RNN to overcome long-term dependency challenges, making it a robust choice for complex sequence-based tasks. Detailed comparison is provided in Table 5. This table summarizes the primary differences in architecture, use cases, and handling of sequential data.

Table 4. Comparison of CNN, RNN and LSTM

Aspect	CNN (Convolutional Neural Network)	RNN (Recurrent Neural Network)	LSTM (Long Short-Term Memory)
Purpose	Primarily used for image and spatial data processing.	Used for sequential data and time-series prediction.	A specialized type of RNN used for handling long-term dependencies in sequential data.
Architecture	Uses convolutional layers, pooling layers, and fully connected layers.	Uses recurrent layers that loop back on themselves.	A specific type of RNN with gates (input, forget, output) to manage memory.
Input Type	Fixed-size inputs, mainly images or 2D data.	Sequence data (e.g., text, time-series).	Sequence data, similar to RNN, but more effective in handling long sequences.
Memory	Does not have an explicit memory of previous inputs (focus on spatial locality).	Has short-term memory, but struggles with long-term dependencies.	Maintains long-term memory through gates that control information flow.
Training Speed	Typically faster for image-related tasks due to fewer dependencies.	Slower due to dependence on previous timesteps.	Slower than standard RNN due to more complex architecture but better for long sequences.
Handling Long-term Dependencies	Struggles with long-term dependencies as it doesn't have sequential memory.	Limited ability to handle long-term dependencies (vanishing gradient problem).	Designed specifically to overcome the vanishing gradient problem, effective for long-term dependencies.

Aspect	CNN (Convolutional Neural Network)	RNN (Recurrent Neural Network)	LSTM (Long Short-Term Memory)
Common Applications	Image classification, object detection, facial recognition, etc.	Natural language processing (NLP), speech recognition, etc.	Text generation, machine translation, speech recognition, etc.
Strength	Efficient in extracting spatial features from images.	Works well with sequential data for tasks like language modeling and time-series prediction.	Better performance with long sequences and tasks requiring memory of past events.
Complexity	Less complex compared to RNN and LSTM.	More complex than CNN, but simpler than LSTM.	Most complex due to the gating mechanism for memory control.

3.ADVANCED DEEP LEARNING TECHNIQUES

3.1 Generative Adversarial Networks (GANs)

Generative Adversarial Networks (GANs) have emerged as one of the most revolutionary advancements in the field of artificial intelligence (AI) and machine learning. Proposed by Ian Goodfellow and his collaborators in 2014, GANs are a class of generative models that leverage adversarial training to produce highly realistic data Goodfellow, et. al, 2014).

A Generative Adversarial Network (GAN) is a machine learning framework comprising two neural networks that compete in a zero-sum game. It is widely used for generating synthetic data that resembles a given dataset, such as realistic images, audio, or text.

3.1.1 Key Components of a GAN

Generator (G):

- **Purpose:** Creates synthetic data that mimics the real data distribution.
- **Input:** Random noise (usually sampled from a normal or uniform distribution).
- **Output:** Synthetic data (e.g., images, text, etc.).
- **Objective:** Fool the discriminator by generating data that appears realistic.

Discriminator (D):

- **Purpose:** Distinguishes between real data (from the dataset) and fake data (generated by the generator).
- **Input:** Either real data or synthetic data.
- **Output:** A probability score indicating whether the input is real or fake.
- **Objective:** Accurately classify inputs as real or fake.

Latent Space (Noise Vector):

- **Purpose:** Provides the random input to the generator, ensuring diversity in the synthetic data.
- **Example:** A vector of random values (e.g., Gaussian noise).

  Adversarial Game: The generator and discriminator are trained simultaneously in a competitive process:
- **Generator's Goal:** Minimize the discriminator's ability to differentiate real from fake data.
- **Discriminator's Goal:** Maximize its ability to distinguish real data from fake data.

3.1.2 Working of GAN

Step 1: Initialization

- The generator and discriminator are initialized with random weights.
- Random noise is fed into the generator as input.

Step 2: Generator Training

- The generator creates synthetic data from the random noise.
- This synthetic data is passed to the discriminator for classification.

Step 3: Discriminator Training

- The discriminator is shown both real data and the synthetic data produced by the generator.
- It outputs probabilities indicating whether the data is real or fake.
- The discriminator learns to improve its classification accuracy over iterations.

Step 4: Feedback Loop

- **Generator's Feedback:** Based on the discriminator's output, the generator updates its weights to produce data that is more realistic.
- **Discriminator's Feedback:** The discriminator updates its weights to improve its ability to differentiate between real and fake data.

Step 5: Adversarial Training:

The generator and discriminator are trained iteratively in an adversarial manner:

- **Generator Loss:** Measures how well the generator fools the discriminator.
- **Discriminator Loss:** Measures how accurately the discriminator distinguishes between real and fake data.

Step 5: Convergence:

The training process continues until the discriminator can no longer reliably distinguish between real and fake data (achieving a Nash equilibrium).

A pictorial representation of GAN is shown in Fig 6:

Figure 6. Working of GAN

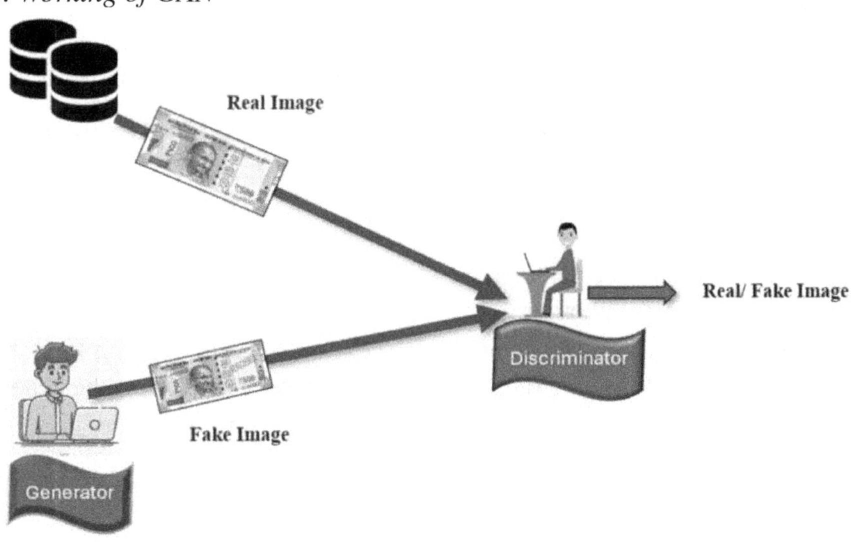

The objective function for GANs can be expressed as:

1. Discriminator Loss

$$L_d = -E\,[\log D(x)] - E[\log(1 - D(G(z)))] \tag{19}$$

2. Generator Loss

$$L_G = -E[\log(D(G(z)))] \quad (20)$$

The generator aims to maximize the probability of the discriminator classifying fake data as real.

While GANs are powerful, training them is notoriously difficult. Below are the major challenges and potential solutions:

a) Mode Collapse

Problem: The generator produces a limited variety of outputs, focusing on specific modes of data distribution while ignoring others.

Solutions: Using Mini-batch Discrimination to encourage diversity in the generator's output and Incorporating Wasserstein GAN (WGAN) with a gradient penalty to provide smoother training.

b) Vanishing or Exploding Gradients

Problem: Gradients in the generator or discriminator may vanish or explode, hindering convergence.

Solutions: Adopting WGAN with a clipping mechanism or gradient penalty or Normalizing inputs and adopting advanced optimization techniques like Adam.

c) Unstable Training

Problem: The adversarial nature of GANs often leads to instability, where one network overpowers the other.

Solutions: Employing techniques like Spectral Normalization to stabilize the discriminator and balancing the training by alternating updates to the generator and discriminator.

d)Evaluation Metrics

Problem: Evaluating the quality of GAN-generated data is challenging due to the subjective nature of realism.

Solutions: Using metrics like

Inception Score (IS): Measures the diversity and quality of generated images.

Fréchet Inception Distance (FID): Assesses the similarity between generated and real data distributions.

e) Resource Intensity

Problem: GAN training demands significant computational resources due to its iterative and adversarial process.

Solutions: Leveraging distributed training and hardware accelerators like GPUs and TPUs. Employing smaller, efficient architectures for specific tasks.

f) Sensitivity to Hyperparameters

Problem: GANs are highly sensitive to hyperparameter settings, making it difficult to achieve optimal results.

Solutions: Conducting extensive hyperparameter tuning. Using techniques like Bayesian Optimization or grid search.

3.1.3 Applications of GANs

I) **Image Generation:** GANs have demonstrated exceptional capabilities in generating realistic images. Some key applications include:

Photo-realistic Image Synthesis: GANs like Progressive GANs and StyleGANs generate highly detailed images, often indistinguishable from real photographs.

Image-to-Image Translation: Models like Pix2Pix and CycleGAN enable tasks such as:

Converting sketches to images

Translating between domains (e.g., converting summer landscapes to winter scenes)

Super-Resolution: GANs such as SRGAN upscale low-resolution images, producing high-quality outputs with fine details.

II) **Data Augmentation:** Data augmentation enhances machine learning models by increasing the diversity of the training dataset. GANs contribute by: Generating synthetic data for underrepresented classes, reducing dataset imbalance. Producing augmented samples in healthcare, such as synthetic medical images for rare diseases, without compromising patient privacy.

III) **Unsupervised Learning**: GANs play a vital role in unsupervised learning by learning the data distribution without labeled data. They are used to: Extract meaningful features from unstructured data. Pre-train models for downstream tasks like classification or regression.

IV) Video and Audio Applications

Video Generation: GANs like MoCoGAN create video sequences by learning temporal and spatial dependencies.

Audio Synthesis: GANs generate realistic audio, enabling applications such as voice cloning and music composition.

V) **Text-to-Image Generation** Models like AttnGAN enable the generation of images from textual descriptions. For instance:

Input: "A small bird with yellow feathers and a black beak."

Output: A realistic image of the described bird.

VI) **Creative Applications** GANs are widely used in creative fields:

Art Generation: Models like DeepArt and ArtGAN create new artwork by learning from existing styles.

Fashion Design: GANs assist in designing new clothing styles or generating models for virtual try-ons.

GANs represent a transformative advancement in AI, enabling the generation of high-quality synthetic data and driving innovation across numerous fields. Their unique adversarial framework empowers them to model complex data distributions, making them invaluable for tasks like image generation, data augmentation, and unsupervised learning. Despite the challenges associated with their training including instability, mode collapse, and high computational costs—continuous research has led to the development of more robust and efficient variants. As GANs continue to evolve, their applications will expand further, reshaping industries and unlocking new creative possibilities.

3.2 Transformer Model

The Transformer model is a groundbreaking neural network architecture introduced in the seminal paper *"Attention Is All You Need"* by Vaswani et al. in 2017. This architecture revolutionized natural language processing (NLP) by addressing the limitations of recurrent and convolutional models in handling long-range dependencies and parallelizing computations effectively. The Transformer model forms the foundation of state-of-the-art models like GPT, BERT, and T5, making it central to modern AI advancements.

3.2.1 Key Components of the Transformer Model

I) Encoder-Decoder Architecture

The Transformer model consists of two main components:

- **Encoder**: Encodes the input sequence into a set of fixed-size representations. It processes the entire input sequence in parallel, rather than sequentially.
- **Decoder**: Uses the encoder's representations and previous outputs to generate the target sequence step by step.

II) Self-Attention Mechanism

The heart of the Transformer is its **self-attention mechanism**, which allows the model to weigh the importance of different words in a sentence relative to one another. It calculates attention scores using three vectors derived from the input:

- **Query (Q)**: Represents the current word or token.
- **Key (K)**: Represents context or relevance.
- **Value (V)**: Contains actual information. Attention scores are computed as:

$$Attention\ (Q, K, V) = softmax\left(\frac{QK^T}{\sqrt{d_k}}\right)V \qquad (21)$$

Here, d_k is the dimensionality of the keys, ensuring stable gradients.

III) Multi-Head Attention

Instead of a single attention function, **multi-head attention** runs multiple attention mechanisms in parallel, allowing the model to capture diverse relationships between words.

IV) Feedforward Layers

Each encoder and decoder block contains a fully connected feedforward network applied to the output of the attention layers. These layers are applied independently to each position, improving the model's ability to capture non-linear transformations.

V) Positional Encoding

Since the Transformer processes input sequences in parallel, it lacks an inherent understanding of word order. **Positional encodings** are added to the input embeddings to incorporate sequence information using sine and cosine functions.

VI) Layer Normalization and Residual Connections

The model uses **layer normalization** and **residual connections** to stabilize training and enhance the flow of gradients.

3.2.3 Applications of Transformers

- **Natural Language Processing**: Text generation, machine translation, summarization, and question answering (e.g., GPT, BERT, T5).
- **Vision**: Vision Transformers (ViTs) apply attention mechanisms to image classification and segmentation tasks.
- **Multimodal Tasks**: Models like DALL-E and CLIP combine vision and language capabilities.
- **Speech Processing**: Transformers are used for tasks like speech-to-text and text-to-speech.

The Transformer model has transformed the AI landscape, offering a powerful and versatile approach to sequence modeling. By replacing sequential processing with self-attention and parallelization, it has set new benchmarks across NLP, vision, and multimodal tasks. Despite challenges in computational cost and scalability, its influence continues to grow, shaping the future of AI innovation.

3.3 Large Language Models

Large Language Models (LLMs) are advanced artificial intelligence systems designed to process, generate, and understand human-like text. These models, built using deep learning architectures, particularly transformers, are trained on vast datasets comprising text from books, articles, websites, and other sources. Their ability to understand context and generate coherent responses has revolutionized numerous fields, including natural language processing (NLP), machine learning, and artificial intelligence.

3.3.1 Key components of Large Language Models

I) Transformer Architecture

Transformer architecture is the foundation of most LLMs. Introduced in the paper *"Attention Is All You Need"* (Vaswani et al., 2017), transformers use self-attention mechanisms to process input sequences in parallel, making them highly efficient for large-scale language modeling tasks. Key components include:

Self-Attention Mechanism: Identifies relationships between words in a sentence, even when they are far apart.

Positional Encoding: Ensures the model understands the order of words in a sequence.

II) **Training Data and Pretraining** LLMs are pretrained on massive text corpora to learn patterns, grammar, and facts about the world. This stage involves unsupervised learning using tasks like:

Masked Language Modeling (MLM): Predicting missing words in a sentence (e.g., BERT).

Causal Language Modeling (CLM): Predicting the next word in a sequence (e.g., GPT models).

III) Fine-Tuning

After pretraining, LLMs can be fine-tuned on specific datasets to perform domain-specific tasks, such as medical diagnosis, customer support, or legal document analysis. This adaptability makes them versatile for a wide range of applications.

3.3.2 Capabilities of LLMs

- **Text Generation**: Produce human-like text for creative writing, chatbots, or automated content creation.
- **Text Understanding**: Analyze and summarize documents, extract key information, or classify text.
- **Question Answering**: Provide accurate answers to user queries, often with context-based reasoning.

- **Translation**: Convert text between languages with high accuracy.
- **Code Generation**: Assist in programming tasks by generating code snippets or debugging code.

3.3.3 Applications of LLMs

- **Healthcare**: Generate medical reports, assist in diagnosis, and provide personalized health advice.
- **Education**: Act as tutors, provide learning resources, and assist in content creation.
- **Customer Support**: Automate responses, handle FAQs, and provide real-time assistance.
- **Creative Industries**: Aid in content creation, scriptwriting, and even composing music or poetry.

Large Language Models represent a significant advancement in AI, offering unprecedented capabilities in understanding and generating human-like text. Despite challenges like bias and resource intensity, their transformative potential across industries ensures their continued evolution and integration into modern technologies.

Here's a tabular comparison of GANs (Generative Adversarial Networks), LLMs (Large Language Models), and Transformer Models based on key aspects in Table 5. This table highlights the distinct characteristics and use cases of GANs, LLMs, and transformer models while also illustrating how LLMs are a specialized application of transformer architectures.

Table 5. Comparison of GAN VS LLM VS Transformer Models

Feature	GAN (Generative Adversarial Networks)	LLM (Large Language Models)	Transformer Models
Primary Purpose	Generative modeling for data creation (e.g., images, videos, audio).	Natural language processing tasks such as text generation, summarization, and question answering.	General-purpose model architecture for sequential data. Can be applied to NLP, vision, and more.
Architecture Type	Consists of two networks: Generator and Discriminator.	Built on transformer architecture with very large scale and pretrained on vast text data.	Encoder-decoder or encoder-only/decoder-only transformer models.
Core Mechanism	Adversarial learning: Generator creates samples, and Discriminator evaluates them.	Pretraining and fine-tuning large-scale models using transformer mechanisms.	Uses self-attention mechanisms and positional encoding for context understanding.

continued on following page

Table 5. Continued

Feature	GAN (Generative Adversarial Networks)	LLM (Large Language Models)	Transformer Models
Data Handling	Focuses on structured or unstructured data for generation.	Trained on unstructured text data (e.g., books, web pages).	Sequential data (text, images, or other sequences).
Examples	StyleGAN, CycleGAN, DeepFake.	GPT-4, BERT, LLaMA.	Transformer, BERT, GPT (foundation of LLMs), ViT (vision transformers).
Training Methodology	Two-part adversarial training where Generator and Discriminator compete.	Pretrained on vast datasets (unsupervised) and fine-tuned on specific tasks.	Uses supervised or unsupervised training depending on the task.
Output	Generates new data samples resembling the training dataset.	Generates or understands natural language with high fluency and context.	Produces outputs depending on the input tasks, like classification or sequence generation.
Applications	Image generation, data augmentation, video synthesis, and creative arts.	Chatbots, translation, summarization, coding assistance, and Q&A systems.	Language modeling, machine translation, image processing, and multimodal tasks.
Training Complexity	Requires careful tuning to balance Generator and Discriminator.	Computationally intensive due to large-scale datasets and model size.	Moderate-to-high depending on the size and depth of the model.
Scalability	Limited scalability; computational resources grow with complexity.	Highly scalable, often requiring large clusters and specialized hardware (GPUs/TPUs).	Scales well and forms the backbone of large models like LLMs.
Strengths	Excellent for high-quality, realistic data generation.	Exceptional performance in understanding and generating human-like text.	General-purpose, flexible for various data types and domains.
Limitations	- Training instability (mode collapse). \n- Limited to specific tasks.	- Requires vast data and computational resources. \n- Prone to biases in data.	- Expensive training for large models. \n- Can be resource-intensive for deployment.
Dependency on Transformers	No direct reliance on transformers.	Based entirely on transformer architecture.	Is the base architecture for most LLMs and advanced AI systems.

4. APPLICATIONS OF DEEP LEARNING

Deep learning has revolutionized various fields with its ability to analyze complex data and make accurate predictions. In computer vision, it powers image classification, object detection, and medical imaging for disease diagnosis. In natural language processing (NLP), it drives applications like machine translation, sentiment analysis, and chatbots. The healthcare sector benefits through advancements in drug discovery and personalized treatments. Deep learning is integral to autonomous systems like self-driving cars and drones, while in finance, it aids in fraud detection and algorithmic trading. Additionally, it enhances education with adaptive learning tools and improves agriculture by enabling crop monitoring through drone imagery.

Figure 7. Applications of Deep Learning

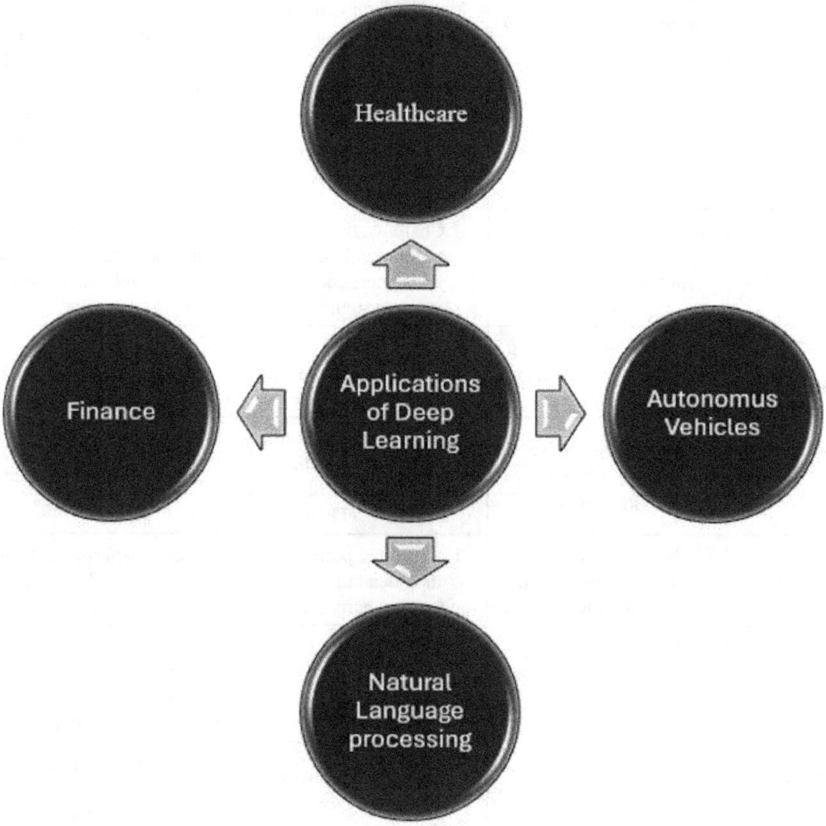

4.1 Healthcare

4.1.1 Deep Learning in Medical Imaging

Medical imaging is a critical component of healthcare, enabling doctors to visualize internal structures and diagnose conditions without invasive procedures. Deep learning techniques, particularly Convolutional Neural Networks (CNNs), have enhanced the interpretation of medical images such as X-rays, CT scans, MRIs, and ultrasounds.

a. Radiology and Image Interpretation

Deep learning has demonstrated significant potential in automating the interpretation of radiological images, reducing the workload of radiologists and improving diagnostic accuracy. CNNs can analyze complex patterns within images and recognize anomalies such as tumors, fractures, or other diseases. One of the key advancements in radiology is the ability of deep learning models to detect early-stage cancers, such as breast, lung, and prostate cancer, with high sensitivity and specificity.

For example, studies have shown that deep learning algorithms can outperform radiologists in detecting lung cancer on CT scans. These models are trained on thousands of annotated images to recognize malignant nodules, and they can identify subtle patterns that might be overlooked by human eyes. This leads to earlier detection, which is crucial for improving patient survival rates.

b. Segmentation and Quantification

Another key application of deep learning in medical imaging is image segmentation, where the goal is to segment out specific regions of interest from images, such as tumors, lesions, or organs. Automated segmentation speeds up the process, making it more efficient and less prone to human error. Furthermore, deep learning models are capable of providing quantitative analysis of the images, such as measuring tumor size or assessing the progression of disease, which helps clinicians make more informed treatment decisions.

For example, deep learning has been employed to segment brain tumors in MRIs. This allows for precise measurements, such as tumor volume, which can be tracked over time to monitor treatment efficacy.

4.1.2. Deep Learning in Diagnostics

Diagnostics is another area where deep learning has shown impressive real-world improvements, particularly in areas like pathology, ophthalmology, and dermatology.

a. Pathology

Pathology involves examining tissue samples under a microscope to diagnose diseases such as cancer. Traditionally, pathologists analyze tissue slides manually, which is time-consuming and subject to human error. Deep learning algorithms, particularly CNNs, have been used to automate the analysis of pathology slides, enabling faster and more accurate diagnoses.

One notable application is in the detection of breast cancer. A study published in *JAMA Oncology* demonstrated that a deep learning algorithm could accurately detect breast cancer in pathology slides, even outperforming pathologists in some cases. This advancement can significantly reduce diagnostic time and improve the consistency and accuracy of cancer diagnosis, leading to timely interventions.

b. Ophthalmology

In ophthalmology, deep learning is used to diagnose eye diseases, including diabetic retinopathy, age-related macular degeneration (AMD), and glaucoma. These conditions, if undetected, can lead to blindness. Deep learning models trained on large datasets of retinal images can automatically detect signs of these diseases, often at an earlier stage than a human ophthalmologist.

For example, deep learning algorithms have been developed to analyze retinal scans for diabetic retinopathy, a condition that can lead to blindness if not treated early. In studies, deep learning systems have demonstrated comparable, and sometimes superior, performance to human experts in identifying retinopathy and other retinal diseases.

c. Dermatology

Deep learning also plays a critical role in dermatology, where it is used to detect skin cancer from images of skin lesions. Traditional methods of detecting melanoma and other skin cancers require a biopsy, which can be invasive and time-consuming. Deep learning models, trained on large datasets of labeled skin images, can distinguish between benign and malignant lesions with a high degree of accuracy.

For instance, the FDA has approved the use of deep learning models for skin cancer detection, with systems that can identify melanoma with accuracy similar to that of experienced dermatologists. This technology empowers patients and primary care physicians to conduct initial screenings, potentially catching skin cancers earlier and improving outcomes.

4.1.3. Deep Learning in Personalized Medicine

Personalized medicine involves tailoring medical treatment to the individual characteristics of each patient, such as their genetics, lifestyle, and environment. Deep learning models are becoming increasingly important in analyzing complex data from genomic sequences, electronic health records (EHRs), and other sources to create personalized treatment plans.

a. Genomic Medicine

The sequencing of the human genome has unlocked vast amounts of data, which deep learning is helping to analyze and interpret. Deep learning algorithms can predict the potential effects of genetic variations, including those related to susceptibility to diseases like cancer, heart disease, and neurological disorders.

For example, deep learning models are used to identify genetic mutations that increase the risk of certain diseases. These models can analyze genomic data at scale, processing large volumes of genetic information to predict disease risk or suggest potential treatment options. One of the key breakthroughs in genomics is the ability of deep learning to identify potential biomarkers for diseases, which can lead to early diagnosis and the development of personalized therapies.

b. Precision Medicine and Drug Discovery

Deep learning has also revolutionized drug discovery and development, playing a vital role in predicting how a patient will respond to a specific drug based on their genetic profile. By analyzing vast amounts of data from clinical trials, medical literature, and patient records, deep learning models can predict which drugs are likely to be most effective for a particular patient or group of patients.

For example, deep learning is being used to develop cancer immunotherapies tailored to individual patients based on their genetic makeup and the specific mutations present in their tumors. This approach is part of the broader trend of precision medicine, which aims to provide more effective treatments by considering the unique characteristics of each patient.

c. Clinical Decision Support

Clinical decision support systems (CDSS) powered by deep learning assist healthcare providers in making informed decisions based on a patient's data. These systems can analyze EHRs, lab results, and imaging data to offer personalized treatment recommendations. This helps clinicians identify the most effective treatment options, avoid unnecessary procedures, and enhance patient care.

For example, deep learning algorithms can be used to predict the likelihood of a patient developing complications post-surgery or to monitor chronic diseases like diabetes. These insights help clinicians make better decisions and provide personalized care tailored to individual patient needs.

4.1.4. Real-World Improvements in Healthcare

Case Study: Deep Learning in Healthcare – Early Detection of Diabetic Retinopathy

Background Diabetic Retinopathy (DR) is a leading cause of blindness worldwide, affecting millions of diabetic patients. Early detection is crucial for effective treatment, but manual screening by ophthalmologists is time-consuming, expensive, and not widely accessible in remote areas.

Challenge Many patients, especially in developing countries, lack access to specialized eye care. Traditional screening methods require trained ophthalmologists to analyze retinal images, which can lead to delays and misdiagnoses due to human subjectivity.

Deep Learning Solution

Google's DeepMind and other AI research labs have developed deep learning-based DR detection systems that can analyze retinal images with high accuracy.

- **Image Processing & Diagnosis**
  - o Convolutional Neural Networks (CNNs) are trained on millions of labeled retinal images to detect signs of DR, such as microaneurysms, hemorrhages, and exudates.
  - o Advanced Vision Transformers (ViTs) improve model accuracy in distinguishing between different DR severity levels.
- **Automated Screening System**
  - o AI models deployed in hospitals and mobile health units allow rapid, low-cost screening without requiring a specialist.
  - o These models provide instant risk assessment, helping doctors prioritize patients in need of urgent care.
- **Improving Accuracy Over Time**

- o With continuous learning from new data, AI models refine their diagnostic accuracy, matching or even surpassing expert ophthalmologists.

Real-World Impact

- Google's AI system for DR detection achieved over 90% accuracy in clinical trials, significantly reducing false negatives and misdiagnoses.
- India and Thailand have successfully integrated AI-powered DR screening into national healthcare programs, allowing early treatment and preventing blindness in thousands of patients.
- AI-driven diagnostics have reduced screening time from days to minutes, making high-quality healthcare accessible to underserved regions.

The implementation of deep learning in medical imaging, diagnostics, and personalized medicine has already led to significant real-world improvements. These technologies have enhanced diagnostic accuracy, enabled early disease detection, and facilitated personalized treatment plans that improve patient outcomes. Moreover, deep learning aids in reducing healthcare costs by automating routine tasks, enabling earlier intervention, and optimizing resource allocation.

Deep learning models can process and analyze large datasets much faster than humans, making it possible to diagnose conditions quickly, even in remote or underserved areas. This improves access to healthcare, reduces waiting times, and ensures that patients receive timely and accurate care.

4.2 Finance:

4.2.1 Deep Learning for Predictive Modeling in Finance

Predictive modeling involves using historical data to make forecasts about future events or trends. In finance, this can range from predicting stock prices to forecasting economic indicators or customer behavior. Deep learning has become a go-to method for financial institutions due to its ability to analyze complex, non-linear relationships in large datasets and improve forecasting accuracy.

a. Stock Market Prediction

One of the most well-known applications of deep learning in finance is stock price prediction. Traditionally, stock price forecasting was based on linear models or statistical methods, but these approaches struggled with the non-linear, chaotic nature of financial markets. Deep learning models, especially Recurrent Neural

Networks (RNNs) and Long Short-Term Memory (LSTM) networks, have proven to be effective in predicting stock prices by capturing temporal dependencies and patterns in market data.

These models are trained on vast amounts of historical stock price data, news articles, financial reports, and even social media sentiment, enabling them to predict short-term and long-term market movements. By analyzing time series data, deep learning models identify trends, seasonal effects, and market anomalies that can provide valuable insights for traders and investors.

For example, LSTM networks, with their ability to remember past events and analyze sequential data, are commonly used to model stock price movements. These models account for fluctuations in market conditions, providing a more robust prediction framework. While stock market prediction remains challenging due to the inherent unpredictability of markets, deep learning has made significant strides in improving prediction accuracy, especially in high-frequency trading environments.

b. Risk Management and Credit Scoring

Deep learning also plays a crucial role in risk management and credit scoring. Financial institutions use predictive models to evaluate the creditworthiness of potential borrowers and assess the risk of defaults. Traditional credit scoring models often rely on rule-based systems or linear regression, but these models may miss out on complex relationships in data.

Deep learning models, such as feedforward neural networks, are used to analyze customer data, including financial history, transaction records, and even social media behavior, to predict the likelihood of default. These models are capable of detecting non-obvious patterns and relationships between various factors that might indicate credit risk, improving the accuracy of credit scoring.

By using deep learning, financial institutions can reduce the risk of lending to high-risk individuals or businesses, ultimately leading to better financial decision-making and more accurate risk assessments.

4.2.2. Deep Learning for Fraud Detection in Finance

Fraud detection is another critical area where deep learning has had a significant impact. Fraudulent activities, including credit card fraud, identity theft, and financial statement manipulation, represent a major challenge for the finance industry. Detecting fraud in real-time, especially in large volumes of transaction data, requires sophisticated systems that can quickly identify suspicious patterns without human intervention. Deep learning provides the tools necessary for this task.

a. Credit Card Fraud Detection

One of the most common applications of deep learning in fraud detection is in credit card fraud prevention. Traditional fraud detection systems rely on rule-based algorithms that flag transactions based on pre-defined thresholds. However, these systems can be easily circumvented by fraudsters who learn to exploit these rules.

Deep learning models, particularly autoencoders and CNNs, have been successfully applied to detect anomalies in transaction data. These models are trained on large datasets of transaction history, learning what constitutes "normal" behavior for an individual or business. By analyzing transaction patterns, deep learning models can identify unusual activities, such as transactions made from unusual locations or at odd hours, which might indicate fraudulent behavior.

For example, an autoencoder is trained to reconstruct a user's usual transaction behavior. If a transaction deviates significantly from the reconstructed behavior, the model flags it as suspicious. This enables real-time fraud detection and can significantly reduce false positives compared to traditional methods, improving the user experience and lowering operational costs.

b. Money Laundering Detection

Money laundering is another area where deep learning has made substantial contributions. Financial institutions are required to detect and prevent money laundering activities, which involve large volumes of transactions designed to obscure the origin of illicit funds. Deep learning models can analyze transaction data to identify patterns associated with money laundering, such as layering, structuring, and rapid movement of funds.

Recurrent Neural Networks (RNNs) and LSTM networks are particularly effective for detecting money laundering schemes because they can model the temporal relationships between transactions over time. By analyzing transaction sequences and identifying suspicious patterns, these models can flag potentially fraudulent activities for further investigation, reducing the risk of regulatory penalties and reputational damage.

4.2.3. Deep Learning in Algorithmic Trading

Algorithmic trading refers to the use of computer algorithms to execute trades based on predefined criteria. In financial markets, algorithmic trading relies on statistical models and algorithms to identify trading opportunities, optimize trading strategies, and execute orders at high speeds. Deep learning has transformed algorithmic trading by enhancing the ability of algorithms to adapt to market changes and make data-driven decisions in real-time.

a. Market Signal Detection

One of the key advantages of deep learning in algorithmic trading is its ability to analyze vast amounts of data and extract actionable insights in real-time. Traditional trading algorithms might rely on technical indicators or pre-set rules to make decisions, but deep learning algorithms can automatically learn market signals from historical price data, news sentiment, and macroeconomic factors.

Deep learning models, particularly CNNs and LSTMs, are used to identify patterns in market data that indicate buy or sell signals. These models can process a wide range of inputs, such as price movements, volume, news, and even social media sentiment, to predict market trends. For example, CNNs can be used to analyze time-series data and predict short-term price movements, while LSTMs are used to capture long-term trends and seasonality in the market.

b. Portfolio Management

Deep learning has also been applied to portfolio management, helping investors optimize their asset allocations. Traditional portfolio management strategies rely on historical data and basic optimization techniques, but deep learning models can analyze complex, multi-dimensional data to make more informed decisions.

Deep reinforcement learning (RL) is a popular technique in this area, where the algorithm learns to make investment decisions by receiving feedback from its actions. This allows the algorithm to adapt to changing market conditions, improving the performance of investment portfolios. RL models can dynamically adjust asset allocations, hedge risks, and maximize returns based on real-time market data.

For instance, a deep reinforcement learning model might continuously monitor market conditions and adjust portfolio weights in response to fluctuations in asset prices. This adaptive approach enables investors to capitalize on emerging market opportunities while mitigating risks.

4.2.4. Impact on Security and Financial Decision-Making

The integration of deep learning in finance has had a profound impact on both financial security and decision-making processes. The primary benefits include:

- **Improved Fraud Prevention:** Deep learning models provide a more accurate and efficient means of detecting fraud in real-time, reducing financial losses due to fraudulent activities. The ability to learn from transaction data and detect anomalies allows for quicker response times and minimizes the impact of fraudulent activities.

- **Enhanced Risk Management:** Deep learning improves risk management by providing more accurate predictions and insights into potential risks, such as defaults, market volatility, or money laundering activities. This leads to better-informed decision-making and more effective mitigation strategies.
- **Data-Driven Decision Making:** Deep learning models can process vast amounts of data and uncover hidden patterns that might not be visible to human analysts. This enables financial institutions to make more informed decisions based on a broader range of inputs, ultimately improving trading strategies and investment performance.
- **Faster and More Efficient Trading:** Algorithmic trading powered by deep learning allows for faster execution of trades and better market signal detection. This leads to higher efficiency, increased profitability, and lower transaction costs, giving institutions a competitive edge in the market.

Case Study: Deep Learning in Finance – Fraud Detection in Credit Card Transactions

Background

Financial fraud, especially credit card fraud, is a major challenge for banks and financial institutions, leading to billions of dollars in losses annually. Traditional rule-based fraud detection systems struggle to keep up with evolving fraud tactics, leading to false positives (blocking legitimate transactions) and false negatives (failing to detect fraud).

Challenge

- High volume of transactions makes manual fraud detection impossible.
- Evolving fraud patterns require constant updates to traditional detection methods.
- Balancing security with user experience is crucial—too many false positives frustrate customers.

Deep Learning Solution

Leading financial institutions like JPMorgan Chase, PayPal, and Mastercard have adopted deep learning models to detect fraudulent transactions in real-time.

- **Anomaly Detection with Autoencoders**

- Deep autoencoder networks analyze millions of transactions and learn normal spending patterns.
- When a transaction deviates significantly from normal patterns, it is flagged as suspicious.

- **Recurrent Neural Networks (RNNs) & LSTMs for Sequential Data**
  - Fraudulent activities often follow hidden sequences (e.g., multiple small purchases before a large unauthorized transaction).
  - Long Short-Term Memory (LSTM) networks analyze transaction history and detect unusual spending behaviors.
- **Graph Neural Networks (GNNs) for Network-Based Fraud**
  - Fraudsters often use multiple accounts and stolen identities to commit fraud.
  - GNNs analyze relationships between transactions, users, and merchants to detect organized fraud rings.

Real-World Impact

- PayPal uses deep learning to detect fraud with over 90% accuracy, significantly reducing financial losses.
- JPMorgan Chase deployed an AI-based fraud detection system, cutting false positives by 30%, improving user experience.
- Mastercard's AI system now scans 75 billion transactions annually, identifying fraud in milliseconds before it impacts customers.

4.3 Autonomous Vehicles:

Autonomous vehicles (AVs) are poised to reshape the future of transportation, and deep learning has emerged as a key technology in their development. Deep learning, a subset of machine learning that mimics the human brain's neural networks, plays a critical role in the advancement of vision systems, object detection, and decision-making processes for autonomous vehicles. These systems enable AVs to perceive their environment, make real-time decisions, and safely navigate complex traffic scenarios. This article explores how deep learning is driving the development of autonomous vehicle technology, focusing on vision systems, object detection, and decision-making.

4.3.1 Deep Learning in Vision Systems for Autonomous Vehicles

Vision systems in autonomous vehicles serve as the "eyes" of the vehicle, providing crucial sensory input that allows the vehicle to understand and navigate its surroundings. These systems are primarily based on cameras, LiDAR (Light Detection and Ranging), radar, and ultrasonic sensors, but the primary source of data for deep learning models is visual input from cameras. Deep learning models, particularly Convolutional Neural Networks (CNNs), are extensively used in vision systems to process and analyze visual data, enabling AVs to detect and understand the environment.

a. Image and Video Processing

Deep learning excels in processing image and video data, allowing autonomous vehicles to recognize and interpret objects in real-time. CNNs, which are designed to detect spatial hierarchies in images, are used for tasks such as road sign recognition, lane detection, and traffic light status detection. These models are trained on large datasets of labeled images and videos, allowing them to learn how to identify various objects and features, even under diverse and challenging conditions like poor lighting, inclement weather, and different road types.

For instance, CNNs can be used to analyze camera feeds and detect road markings, which are essential for lane-keeping and navigation. The vehicle's vision system relies on this visual input to stay in the correct lane, adjust speed, or make turns.

b. Semantic Segmentation

Semantic segmentation is a critical component of AV vision systems, where the goal is to assign a label to every pixel in an image based on the object it belongs to (e.g., road, car, pedestrian, tree). This process allows the vehicle to segment different parts of the environment and understand the spatial relationship between objects. Deep learning models, particularly CNNs and Fully Convolutional Networks (FCNs), are used to perform this task with high accuracy.

By segmenting the image into distinct regions, the vehicle can distinguish between drivable roads, obstacles, and other critical elements. This segmentation enables the vehicle to plan its path, identify potential hazards, and make real-time decisions.

4.3.2 Deep Learning in Object Detection for Autonomous Vehicles

Object detection is the ability to identify and locate specific objects in an image or video feed. For autonomous vehicles, object detection is fundamental to ensuring safe navigation, as the vehicle needs to detect and track a wide range of objects, including pedestrians, other vehicles, cyclists, traffic signs, and road barriers. Deep learning has significantly advanced object detection, providing the accuracy and speed needed for real-time decision-making in dynamic environments.

a. Real-Time Object Detection

Deep learning-based object detection algorithms, such as the You Only Look Once (YOLO) framework and Faster R-CNN, can detect multiple objects in real time with high precision. These algorithms divide an image into regions, and for each region, they predict the presence of objects, their categories, and bounding boxes. YOLO, for example, is known for its speed and efficiency, making it suitable for autonomous vehicles that require fast decision-making and minimal latency.

By using deep learning models, autonomous vehicles can detect pedestrians crossing the road, other vehicles approaching from different directions, cyclists in their blind spots, and road debris, all in real-time. This information is vital for the vehicle's safety system, which must make immediate decisions to avoid collisions or accidents.

b. Fusion of Multimodal Data

While cameras provide rich visual data, autonomous vehicles typically use other sensors, such as LiDAR, radar, and ultrasonic sensors, to enhance object detection. Deep learning models are used to fuse data from multiple sensors, allowing the vehicle to perceive its environment more accurately and reliably.

LiDAR, for example, provides 3D spatial data that helps detect the distance to objects, while radar is useful for detecting objects in poor weather conditions. By combining these data sources, deep learning models create a more comprehensive understanding of the environment. This multimodal fusion enhances the vehicle's ability to detect and track objects, even in challenging situations such as fog, rain, or darkness.

4.3.3 Deep Learning in Decision-Making for Autonomous Vehicles

Decision-making is a critical aspect of autonomous driving, as the vehicle must continuously evaluate its environment and make choices to ensure safety, efficiency, and passenger comfort. Deep learning is instrumental in enabling AVs to make real-time decisions based on sensory input, environmental factors, and traffic rules.

a. Reinforcement Learning for Decision-Making

Reinforcement learning (RL), a type of deep learning where an agent learns by interacting with its environment and receiving feedback in the form of rewards or penalties, is increasingly used in decision-making for autonomous vehicles. In this framework, the vehicle (or agent) is tasked with selecting actions (e.g., accelerating, braking, steering) that maximize long-term rewards, such as maintaining safety, optimizing speed, or ensuring passenger comfort.

For example, RL algorithms can be used to teach autonomous vehicles how to navigate complex traffic scenarios, such as merging onto highways, avoiding obstacles, or yielding to pedestrians. By training on millions of simulated driving scenarios, RL-based models can learn the optimal strategies for these tasks, adapting to a wide range of driving conditions.

b. Path Planning and Trajectory Optimization

Path planning is another critical aspect of decision-making, as the vehicle must determine the best path to follow based on its current location, the traffic situation, and the road layout. Deep learning models, including recurrent neural networks (RNNs) and reinforcement learning-based algorithms, are used for trajectory optimization in dynamic environments.

For example, deep learning models can help autonomous vehicles plan their routes by predicting the behavior of other road users, such as the movement of pedestrians, cyclists, and other vehicles. The vehicle's decision-making system will use this information to calculate the optimal trajectory, ensuring that it can avoid collisions while maintaining efficiency and comfort. This process involves continuous recalibration as new data is received from sensors.

4.3.4 Predictive Decision-Making

Predictive decision-making is another area where deep learning plays a key role. Autonomous vehicles must anticipate the behavior of other drivers, pedestrians, and cyclists to make safe driving decisions. Deep learning models, particularly LSTMs and attention-based models, can be used to predict the movements of these road users based on historical data, including their speed, direction, and behavior patterns.

For example, an AV might predict that a car in front of it is likely to brake in the next few seconds based on its speed and the driver's behavior. The vehicle can then adjust its speed and position to avoid a collision, making real-time decisions that are based on predictive models rather than just reactive ones.

Case Study: Waymo – Pioneering Fully Autonomous Driving

Background

Waymo, a subsidiary of Alphabet Inc. (Google's parent company), is at the forefront of autonomous driving technology. Originally part of Google's self-driving car project, Waymo has developed one of the most advanced AI-driven autonomous vehicle systems.

Challenge

Traditional vehicles rely on human perception and reaction time, which can lead to accidents due to distraction, fatigue, or misjudgment. The challenge was to create an autonomous system that could perceive the environment, plan safe routes, and make real-time decisions better than human drivers.

Deep Learning Solutions

Waymo integrates multiple deep learning techniques to achieve full autonomy:

- **Perception & Scene Understanding:**
  - Uses Convolutional Neural Networks (CNNs) and Vision Transformers (ViTs) to process sensor data from cameras, LiDAR, and radar.
  - Deep learning models recognize pedestrians, cyclists, road signs, and traffic lights, even in challenging conditions like fog or night driving.
- **Path Planning & Decision Making:**
  - Reinforcement Learning (RL) and Deep Q-Networks (DQN) optimize route planning and adapt to unpredictable traffic patterns.
  - Recurrent Neural Networks (RNNs) help in forecasting the behavior of other vehicles, ensuring smooth lane changes and turns.
- **End-to-End Autonomous Control:**

- o AI-powered systems, trained on millions of real-world and simulated miles, handle braking, acceleration, and steering with human-like precision.
- o Advanced sensor fusion allows the vehicle to predict potential collisions and take corrective actions.

Real-World Impact

- Waymo's driverless taxis have been successfully deployed in Phoenix, San Francisco, and Los Angeles, offering fully autonomous rides with no safety driver.
- Studies show that Waymo's AI-driven cars significantly reduce the risk of accidents compared to human drivers.

4.4 Natural Language Processing:

Natural Language Processing (NLP) has undergone a significant transformation in recent years, largely due to the advent of deep learning models such as Transformers and Recurrent Neural Networks (RNNs). These models have revolutionized language-related tasks, including machine translation, chatbot development, and sentiment analysis. By enabling machines to process, understand, and generate human language more accurately, these models have made NLP applications more practical and efficient. In this article, we will explore several case studies that illustrate how Transformers and RNNs are applied in NLP tasks like translation, chatbots, and sentiment analysis.

4.4.1 Machine Translation: From RNNs to Transformers

Machine translation (MT) has long been a central task in NLP, aimed at automatically translating text from one language to another. Traditionally, MT relied on rule-based methods and statistical models, but with the advent of deep learning, especially RNNs and Transformers, the field has seen dramatic improvements in translation quality and efficiency.

a. RNN-based Machine Translation

In the early days of neural MT, the dominant architecture was the Sequence-to-Sequence (Seq2Seq) model based on Recurrent Neural Networks (RNNs). RNNs are designed to process sequential data and can capture temporal dependencies in text, making them a natural fit for translation tasks, where the input and output are sequences of words in different languages.

A typical Seq2Seq model consists of an encoder and a decoder, both implemented using RNNs (or their more advanced variants like LSTMs or GRUs). The encoder processes the input sentence in the source language, generating a fixed-length context vector that encapsulates the meaning of the sentence. This context vector is then passed to the decoder, which generates the translated sentence in the target language.

One prominent case of RNN-based MT was Google's early translation system, which used Seq2Seq models to translate text. While effective, RNN-based approaches had limitations, especially with long sentences where the context vector struggled to retain long-range dependencies, often resulting in translation errors.

b. Transformer-based Machine Translation

The introduction of the Transformer model in the paper "Attention is All You Need" by Vaswani et al. in 2017 marked a paradigm shift in MT. Unlike RNNs, which process text sequentially, Transformers rely entirely on self-attention mechanisms to capture dependencies between words regardless of their position in the sentence. This allows Transformers to process entire sequences in parallel, significantly improving efficiency and scalability.

Transformers have proven to be superior to RNN-based models in tasks like MT, especially in handling long sentences with complex structures. One of the most notable case studies is the use of the Transformer model in Google Translate, which transitioned from an RNN-based system to a Transformer-based system. This change resulted in better translation quality, faster training times, and the ability to handle a broader range of languages.

For example, when translating long sentences or sentences with intricate grammatical structures, the Transformer model can attend to different parts of the sentence simultaneously, ensuring that important relationships between words are preserved. This results in more accurate translations and a better understanding of the context.

4.4.2 Chatbots: Enhancing Conversational AI with RNNs and Transformers

Chatbots have become ubiquitous in customer service, entertainment, and various other domains. The primary goal of a chatbot is to generate human-like responses to user inputs, creating seamless and natural conversations. To achieve this, NLP models like RNNs and Transformers have been widely used for natural language understanding (NLU) and natural language generation (NLG).

a. RNN-based Chatbots

Before Transformers, many chatbots used Seq2Seq models with RNNs to generate responses. These models worked by encoding the user's input into a fixed-length vector, which is then decoded into a response. For instance, the early version of Apple's Siri and other voice-based assistants used RNNs for speech recognition and basic conversational capabilities.

A popular example of an RNN-based chatbot is the **Seq2Seq Chatbot** developed using LSTMs (Long Short-Term Memory) networks. The Seq2Seq model is trained on large conversational datasets, learning to predict the next word or sequence of words based on the input received. While these chatbots were capable of simple, rule-based conversations, they struggled with handling complex, open-ended queries and maintaining context over longer conversations.

b. Transformer-based Chatbots

The advent of Transformer models, particularly GPT (Generative Pretrained Transformer) and BERT (Bidirectional Encoder Representations from Transformers), has led to a significant leap in chatbot performance. These models, with their attention mechanisms and ability to capture long-range dependencies, can maintain context over longer conversations, understand nuanced meanings, and generate more relevant and coherent responses.

A notable example is **OpenAI's GPT series**, including GPT-3, which is capable of generating human-like text responses across a wide range of topics. GPT-3, trained on diverse datasets containing billions of words, can generate contextually appropriate replies, understand ambiguous queries, and even simulate emotions or humor. GPT-3's ability to generate coherent multi-turn dialogues has made it a breakthrough in conversational AI, enabling applications such as virtual assistants, customer support bots, and content generation tools.

Another example is **Google's Meena**, a chatbot that employs a Transformer-based architecture to engage in conversations across multiple domains. Meena was trained on a massive dataset and is designed to handle a wide variety of topics, ensuring that the chatbot's responses are contextually relevant and emotionally intelligent.

The key advantage of Transformer-based chatbots over RNN-based systems is their ability to better handle long-term dependencies and multi-turn conversations. With the self-attention mechanism, Transformers can focus on important parts of the conversation, regardless of when they occurred, providing more accurate and coherent responses.

4.4.3 Sentiment Analysis: Understanding Opinions with Deep Learning

Sentiment analysis, or opinion mining, involves determining the sentiment or emotional tone expressed in a piece of text, typically classifying it as positive, negative, or neutral. This task has wide applications in market research, brand management, social media monitoring, and customer feedback analysis. Both RNNs and Transformers are used in sentiment analysis, each offering unique advantages.

a. RNN-based Sentiment Analysis

RNNs, particularly LSTMs and GRUs, have been widely used for sentiment analysis tasks due to their ability to capture temporal dependencies in text. Sentiment often depends on the context of a sentence, where the meaning of a word can change depending on its preceding or succeeding words. RNN-based models excel at capturing this context, making them suitable for analyzing sentiment in text.

For example, a sentiment analysis system using an LSTM might process a product review, where the overall sentiment is determined by the sequence of words in the review. For instance, "I love this phone, but the battery life is terrible" would require understanding the contradictory sentiments in the sentence, which LSTM networks can handle effectively due to their ability to retain long-range dependencies.

Companies like **Sentiment140** have used RNN-based models for sentiment analysis in social media, analyzing tweets to determine public sentiment toward brands, political events, or consumer products.

b. Transformer-based Sentiment Analysis

Transformer models, particularly BERT, have become the state-of-the-art in sentiment analysis. BERT is designed to capture bidirectional context, meaning it understands the meaning of words based on both the words that come before and after them. This bidirectional context is crucial for sentiment analysis, where the sentiment of a sentence often depends on the interplay of multiple words.

BERT and its variants, like **DistilBERT** and **RoBERTa**, are pre-trained on vast amounts of text and fine-tuned on specific sentiment analysis tasks. These models can analyze the sentiment of text with much higher accuracy than traditional RNN-based models.

For instance, **Amazon** uses BERT-based models to analyze customer reviews, helping businesses understand customer satisfaction and identify areas for improvement. The model can also detect subtleties like sarcasm or mixed sentiments, which RNNs might struggle with.

Additionally, **Hugging Face's Transformers** library provides easy access to pre-trained Transformer models for sentiment analysis, making it easier for businesses to deploy sentiment analysis solutions across various applications, from customer feedback to social media monitoring.

Case Study: Natural Language Processing (NLP) in Customer Support – Automating Responses with AI

Background

Customer support services handle millions of queries daily, ranging from simple FAQs to complex troubleshooting. Traditionally, businesses relied on human agents, leading to long wait times, high operational costs, and inconsistent responses. To improve efficiency, companies have turned to deep learning-based NLP models to automate customer interactions.

Challenge

- High customer demand leads to delayed response times.
- Manual handling results in inconsistent answers across agents.
- Businesses need scalable and cost-effective solutions without compromising service quality.

Deep Learning Solution

Companies like Google, Amazon, and OpenAI have deployed state-of-the-art NLP models to enhance customer support.

- **Chatbots with Transformer Models (e.g., GPT, BERT)**
  - o AI-driven chatbots understand natural language queries and provide human-like responses.
  - o Models like GPT-4 and BERT process vast knowledge bases, enabling automated responses with high accuracy.
- **Sentiment Analysis for Improved Responses**
  - o NLP models analyze customer emotions (e.g., frustration, satisfaction) using deep learning-based sentiment analysis.
  - o Businesses can prioritize urgent queries and provide empathetic responses.
- **Speech-to-Text and Text-to-Speech (Voice Assistants)**
  - o Companies like Amazon Alexa and Google Assistant use deep learning for real-time speech processing.

- o AI-powered voice support allows customers to speak naturally and receive relevant answers.

Real-World Impact

- Duolingo uses NLP-based AI tutors to provide instant feedback on language learning, improving user engagement.
- Bank of America's AI assistant, Erica, handled over a billion customer requests, reducing wait times and saving millions in support costs.
- E-commerce giants like Amazon implemented deep learning chatbots, reducing customer service costs by 30% while maintaining high satisfaction rates.

5. LIMITATIONS OF DEEP LEARNING

While deep learning has revolutionized various fields with its ability to solve complex problems, it is not without limitations. These challenges stem from its high computational requirements, reliance on extensive datasets, and lack of interpretability, among others. Addressing these limitations is essential for the responsible and efficient application of deep learning.

1. Data Dependency

Deep learning models require vast amounts of high-quality labeled data for effective training. For example, image classification tasks often demand thousands or millions of labeled samples to achieve high accuracy. However, in many domains, such as medical diagnosis, labeled data is scarce or expensive to obtain. This dependency on large datasets limits the applicability of deep learning in areas where data collection is difficult or privacy concerns restrict data sharing.

2. Computational Resource Requirements

Deep learning models are computationally intensive, requiring powerful hardware such as GPUs or TPUs for training and inference. Training large models, such as GPT or BERT, demands significant energy consumption, leading to high costs and environmental concerns. This resource intensity makes deep learning less accessible to small organizations or researchers without substantial funding, creating disparities in technological development.

3. Lack of Interpretability

Deep learning models are often referred to as "black boxes" because their decision-making processes are difficult to understand. Unlike traditional machine learning models, which can provide interpretable rules or feature importance scores, deep learning networks involve millions of parameters interacting in complex ways. This lack of transparency poses challenges in critical applications like healthcare and finance, where understanding the rationale behind decisions is vital for trust and accountability.

4. Overfitting and Generalization

Deep learning models are prone to overfitting, especially when trained on small or imbalanced datasets. Overfitting occurs when a model performs well on training data but fails to generalize to unseen data. While techniques like regularization and dropout can mitigate this issue, achieving a balance between model complexity and generalization remains a challenge.

5. Ethical Concerns and Bias

Deep learning models often inherit biases present in their training data, leading to discriminatory or unfair outcomes. For instance, facial recognition systems trained on biased datasets may perform poorly on certain demographic groups. These ethical concerns raise questions about the fairness and inclusivity of deep learning applications, particularly in sensitive areas like hiring, law enforcement, and lending.

6. Vulnerability to Adversarial Attacks

Deep learning models are susceptible to adversarial attacks, where small, imperceptible changes to input data can cause the model to make incorrect predictions. This vulnerability poses security risks in critical applications, such as autonomous vehicles or cybersecurity, where robust and reliable performance is essential.

7. Limited Understanding and Domain Adaptation

Deep learning models struggle to generalize knowledge across domains. A model trained on one task or dataset often performs poorly when applied to a slightly different but related problem. This limitation, known as poor domain adaptation, restricts the versatility of deep learning.

8. Long Training Times

Training deep learning models can take days, weeks, or even months, depending on the model size and dataset. This lengthy process slows down experimentation and iteration, hindering rapid development.

Despite its transformative potential, deep learning has significant limitations that need to be addressed for broader and more responsible adoption. Advances in data-efficient algorithms, interpretability techniques, and ethical AI practices are crucial to overcoming these challenges. By addressing these limitations, deep learning can continue to drive progress across industries while minimizing its drawbacks.

6. EMERGING TRENDS AND FUTURE DIRECTIONS IN DEEP LEARNING

As deep learning continues to evolve, several emerging trends and future directions are shaping the next generation of AI research and applications. This section explores key advancements such as federated learning, explainable AI, and quantum machine learning, which are poised to address critical challenges in scalability, interpretability, and computational efficiency.

Federated Learning: Decentralized and Privacy-Preserving AI

Federated learning is an innovative approach that enables AI models to be trained across multiple devices or servers without centralizing data. This technique enhances privacy and security, as raw data remains on local devices while only model updates are shared. Federated learning is particularly valuable in industries like healthcare and finance, where data privacy is paramount. As this technology matures, advancements in communication efficiency, model aggregation techniques, and adversarial robustness are expected to drive wider adoption.

Explainable AI (XAI): Enhancing Transparency and Trust

Despite the remarkable performance of deep learning models, their "black-box" nature has raised concerns regarding interpretability and trustworthiness. Explainable AI (XAI) seeks to bridge this gap by providing insights into model decision-making processes. Techniques such as SHAP (Shapley Additive Explanations), LIME (Local Interpretable Model-Agnostic Explanations), and attention visualization in neural networks aim to make AI systems more transparent. Future developments in XAI will likely focus on improving the interpretability of complex architectures while maintaining predictive accuracy, ensuring AI-driven decisions are understandable and accountable.

Quantum Machine Learning: The Next Frontier

Quantum machine learning (QML) leverages the principles of quantum computing to enhance deep learning capabilities, particularly in solving high-dimensional optimization problems. Quantum algorithms, such as quantum neural networks and quantum support vector machines, have the potential to outperform classical counterparts in terms of speed and efficiency. While quantum hardware remains in its infancy, ongoing research in hybrid quantum-classical models, error correction techniques, and scalable quantum architectures will be instrumental in unlocking QML's full potential in the coming years.

7. CONCLUSION: THE POTENTIAL AND IMPACT OF DEEP LEARNING ACROSS VARIOUS INDUSTRIES

Deep learning, a subset of artificial intelligence (AI), has emerged as a transformative force across various industries, reshaping how we solve complex problems, interact with technology, and envision the future. Its ability to process vast amounts of data and uncover intricate patterns has opened new frontiers, driving innovation and efficiency in ways previously unimaginable. The potential and impact of deep learning are evident in fields ranging from healthcare to entertainment, underscoring its versatility and significance.

One of the most profound impacts of deep learning is in **healthcare**. Advanced neural networks now assist in diagnosing diseases, predicting patient outcomes, and developing personalized treatment plans. For instance, deep learning algorithms can analyze medical images such as X-rays or MRIs with remarkable accuracy, identifying anomalies like tumors or fractures. In drug discovery, deep learning accelerates the identification of potential compounds, reducing the time and cost associated with traditional research. These advancements not only enhance the quality of care but also make healthcare more accessible and efficient.

In the realm of **autonomous systems**, deep learning has been pivotal in enabling self-driving cars, drones, and robotics. By leveraging technologies like computer vision and sensor fusion, autonomous vehicles can navigate complex environments, recognize objects, and make real-time decisions. These innovations promise to revolutionize transportation, reducing traffic accidents, optimizing fuel efficiency, and improving urban mobility.

The **financial sector** is another domain where deep learning has demonstrated significant potential. It powers fraud detection systems, algorithmic trading platforms, and credit scoring models, enhancing security and efficiency. By analyzing transactional data and behavioral patterns, deep learning algorithms can identify suspicious activities, safeguarding financial systems from fraud. Similarly, predictive models based on deep learning improve investment strategies, offering insights into market trends and potential risks.

Deep learning also plays a crucial role in **education**, enabling adaptive learning platforms that personalize content based on a student's learning pace and preferences. Automated grading systems and intelligent tutoring solutions enhance the teaching process, making education more interactive and inclusive. By bridging gaps in access to quality education, deep learning contributes to a more equitable society.

In **agriculture**, deep learning has optimized processes like crop monitoring, pest detection, and yield prediction. Drone-based imagery analysis, combined with neural networks, helps farmers identify issues in real-time, improving productivity and sustainability. These technologies are vital in addressing global challenges like food security and climate change.

Entertainment and media have been transformed by deep learning as well. From content recommendation systems on streaming platforms to generative AI tools that create music, art, or video content, deep learning enhances user experiences. Virtual and augmented reality systems powered by deep learning blur the lines between real and digital worlds, offering immersive experiences in gaming, storytelling, and beyond.

While the potential of deep learning is vast, its adoption comes with challenges such as ethical concerns, data privacy issues, and the need for significant computational resources. Addressing these challenges is crucial for ensuring that deep learning is used responsibly and equitably across industries.

In conclusion, deep learning stands at the forefront of technological innovation, driving progress across diverse sectors. Its ability to tackle complex problems, enhance efficiency, and create new opportunities ensures its continued relevance and impact. As the field evolves, the integration of deep learning into our daily lives will shape a future defined by intelligent, data-driven solutions.

REFERENCES

Anderson, J. A. (1995). *An Introduction to Neural Networks*. The MIT Press., DOI: 10.7551/mitpress/3905.001.0001

Deng, J., Dong, W., Socher, R., Li, L. J., Li, K., & Fei-Fei, L. (2009, June). Imagenet: A large-scale hierarchical image database. In 2009 IEEE conference on computer vision and pattern recognition (pp. 248-255). Ieee. DOI: 10.1109/CVPR.2009.5206848

Goodfellow, I., Pouget-Abadie, J., Mirza, M., Xu, B., Warde-Farley, D., Ozair, S., & Bengio, Y. (2014). Generative adversarial nets. *Advances in Neural Information Processing Systems*, 27.

Haque, M. A. (2022). A Brief analysis of "ChatGPT"–A revolutionary tool designed by OpenAI. EAI endorsed transactions on AI and robotics, 1, e15-e15. DOI: 10.4108/airo.v1i1.2983

He, K., Zhang, X., Ren, S., & Sun, J. (2016). Deep residual learning for image recognition. In *Proceedings of the IEEE conference on computer vision and pattern recognition* (pp. 770-778). DOI: 10.1109/CVPR.2016.90

Hinton, G. E. (2009). Deep belief networks. *Scholarpedia Journal*, *4*(5), 5947. DOI: 10.4249/scholarpedia.5947

Krizhevsky, A., Sutskever, I., & Hinton, G. E. (2012). Imagenet classification with deep convolutional neural networks. *Advances in Neural Information Processing Systems*, *25*. Advance online publication. DOI: 10.1145/3065386

LeCun, Y., Bengio, Y., & Hinton, G. (2015). Deep learning. nature, 521(7553), 436-444. DOI: 10.1038/nature14539

LeCun, Y., Bottou, L., Bengio, Y., & Haffner, P. (1998). Gradient-based learning applied to document recognition. *Proceedings of the IEEE*, *86*(11), 2278–2324. DOI: 10.1109/5.726791

Lin, T. Y., Maire, M., Belongie, S., Hays, J., Perona, P., Ramanan, D., . . . Zitnick, C. L. (2014). Microsoft coco: Common objects in context. In Computer Vision–ECCV 2014: 13th European Conference, Zurich, Switzerland, September 6-12, 2014, Proceedings, Part V 13 (pp. 740-755). Springer International Publishing. DOI: 10.1007/978-3-319-10602-1_48

McCulloch, W. S. (1943). A logical calculus of ideas immanent in nervous activity Bulletin of Mathematical Biophysics 5: 115-133. *The Bulletin of Mathematical Biophysics*, *5*, 115–133. DOI: 10.1007/BF02478259

Minsky, M., & Papert, S. (1969). An introduction to computational geometry. Cambridge tiass. *HIT*, *479*(480), 104. DOI: 10.1007/978-1-4612-1098-6

Rosenblatt, F. (1958). The perceptron: A probabilistic model for information storage and organization in the brain. *Psychological Review*, *65*(6), 386–408. DOI: 10.1037/h0042519 PMID: 13602029

Rumelhart, D. E., Hinton, G. E., & Williams, R. J. (1986). Learning representations by back-propagating errors. nature, 323(6088), 533-536. DOI: 10.1038/323533a0

Schmidt, R. M. (2019). Recurrent neural networks (rnns): A gentle introduction and overview. https://doi.org//arXiv.1912.05911DOI: 10.48550

Simonyan, K., Vedaldi, A., & Zisserman, A. (2013). Deep inside convolutional networks: Visualising image classification models and saliency maps. arXiv preprint arXiv:1312.6034.Turing, A. M. (1980). Computing Machinery and Intelligence. Creative Computing, 6(1), 44-53. https://doi.org//arXiv.1312.6034DOI: 10.48550

Staudemeyer, R. C., & Morris, E. R. (2019). Understanding LSTM—a tutorial into long short-term memory recurrent neural networks. arXiv preprint arXiv:1909.09586. https://doi.org//arXiv.1909.09586DOI: 10.48550

Szegedy, C., Liu, W., Jia, Y., Sermanet, P., Reed, S., Anguelov, D., & Rabinovich, A. (2015). Going deeper with convolutions. In *Proceedings of the IEEE conference on computer vision and pattern recognition* (pp. 1-9). DOI: 10.1109/CVPR.2015.7298594

Vaswani, A. (2017). Attention is all you need. *Advances in Neural Information Processing Systems*. arXiv1706.03762

Chapter 3
Regularization of Generative Models

A. D. N. Sarma
https://orcid.org/0000-0003-2093-388X
Jaya Soft, Hyderabad, India

ABSTRACT

This chapter provides a detailed understanding of various types of regularization techniques in generative models, and explain how these regularization techniques can help for reduction of overfitting and improves model generalization. The chapter begins with a brief introduction about what is an AI model, its importance and their uses. Further, explain what regularization is and why is it significant. Briefly outline the terms underfitting, overfitting, just right and mention techniques to detect overfitting. Also, provides a list of different types of AI models. Moreover, explain various types of regularizations. Besides, outline the common goals of regularization. Further, present various key parameters that affect overfitting in generative models and explain briefly. Finally, present various regularization techniques that prevent overfitting in different modalities such as text, image and multi-models.

1. INTRODUCTION

1.1 Context and Background

Regularization is a fundamental concept in AI that enhances model generalization by preventing overfitting and improving robustness. In recent years, generative models have shown remarkable progress with applications in text generation, image synthesis, code generation, audio generation, data augmentation, and many more. Regularization in generative models is a critical and evolving research domain in AI,

DOI: 10.4018/979-8-3373-0735-0.ch003

driving advancements in model stability, efficiency, and generalization for improved generative performance. Models such as Generative Adversarial Networks (GANs) and Variational Autoencoders (VAEs) have demonstrated remarkable abilities in capturing complex data distributions. Although, generative models are successful, but they can often susceptible to issues such as overfitting and poor generalization, especially when trained on limited data. Regularization techniques are vital in addressing these challenges by regulating model complexity and enhancing generalization. It is important to comprehend how different regularization techniques affect the model's learning, output quality, and stability of generative models. This is essential for developing more robust and reliable systems. Regularization is deeply interconnected with key model parameters, including optimization methods, training strategies, and architectural design, ensuring balanced performance and enhanced generalization.

Regularization is an interesting area in both Machine Learning (ML) and Deep Learning (DL) models that aims to prevent overfitting. Overfitting is a common problem in both ML and DL, where a model fits too closely to the training data, but negatively impacting its ability to generalize to new or unseen data. In order to avoid overfitting several techniques are used to reduce the adverse behaviour of the model. The most common technique used to prevent overfitting is regularization by imposing constraints or penalties on the model. In simple terms, regularization is defined as *a process that provides some kind of smoothness,* which minimizes the overfitting problem in modelling techniques. Overfitting in AI models occurs when a model fits the training data too closely, resulting in high variance and poor performance on testing data. The objective of this chapter is to provide a comprehensive understanding on various types of regularizations more particularly in generative models. The target users of this chapter are technical researchers, data scientists, model architects, managers and advanced practitioners in AI.

According to a market study report (Statista Market Insights on Technology, n.a.), the global market size of Artificial Intelligence is projected to reach US$243.70bn in 2025. Further, it is expected to grow market value of USD $826.70bn by 2030 with an estimated annual growth rate of 27.67% for a period 2025-2030. The AI market is structured into six markets based on the technology. These are the Computer Vision market covers applications that enable computers to interpret and understand digital images and video data. Second, ML market covers the use of algorithms to enable computer systems to learn from data. Third, the Natural Language Processing (NLP) market covers applications that enable computers to understand, interpret, and generate human language. Fourth, the AI Robotics market covers the combination of AI, ML, and engineering to create intelligent machines that can perform tasks autonomously. Fifth, the Autonomous and Sensor Technology market covers machines and systems that operate independently by using sensors, AI, and ML to respond to changes in their environment. Six, the Generative AI market covers AI that involves creating models capable of generating new content, such as images, videos, and text, which are indistinguishable from content created by humans.

1.2 Key Terms, Definitions and Insights

This sub-section presents essential terminology, key concepts and insights related to regularization. It provides clear explanations of fundamental ideas connected to regularization, and AI, ensuring deeper understanding to the reader. Additionally, it includes insights, helping to interpret terms within real-world applications.

Key Takeaways

By the end of this sub-section, the reader can understand the following:

- What is an AI model and its importance and uses.
- Further, what is AI modelling, its primary functions, and different types of AI models. Additionally, define what are generative mode, Large Lange Models, difference between ML and DL models.
- Moreover, define what is regularization and its importance in AI models.
- Briefly outline the terms related to model training performance such as underfit, overfit and right fit.
- To know various techniques how to identify overfitting in a model.

What is an AI Model

An Artificial Intelligence (AI) model is a program or algorithms that analyses dataset, detect patterns and correlations and then make predictions. In simple terms, *an AI model is trained on specific data so that it can arrive at a decision with minimal human intervention.* Alternatively, an AI model can be defined as "*a program analyses datasets in order to find patterns and make predictions with a minimal human internation*".

Importance of AI Models

The importance of AI models can be understood by its transformative impact on multiple industries as well as in real life. AI models are the heart of an AI system that quickly analyzes data, detect patterns and correlations from the data and make predictions. Moreover, AI model can automate complex processes thereby it reduces lot of human efforts required as compared to traditional modelling approaches. Further, these models minimize downtime by predicting maintenance needs. Additionally, AI models can reduce repetitive tasks thereby this improves both quality and efficiency of the system to the developed. Furthermore, AI models can process massive datasets, extract insights and enhances decision making capability as compared to traditional approaches. Sometimes, AI models can provide automated decision making such as recommender systems, the goal of a recommender system is to personalize the user experience by providing highly relevant and useful recommendations to the users. The use of AI models in the digital world has been continuously increasing in all most all industries because of its ability to accelerate the process of understanding and interpreting large size datasets that comprises of multiple data types like text, images, audio, and video with the aid of multiple algorithms and neural networks. Besides, AI models have capability to quickly analyse data, find patterns and make predictions based on their learnings. Further, the accuracy and performance of these models can be improved that provide quality predictions. In simple terms, an AI model can be described as "a *digital brain* that learns from the input data of any type and provides more accurate predictions like human brains without any significant human interaction".

Uses of AI models

The use of AI models can be found in all most all industries and real life that include but not limited to generation of text, image, audio and video and object recognition, anomaly detection, recommender systems, predictive modelling, robotics to mention a few. The most common uses of AI models include data entry and classification, predictive analytics, search engines, digital assistance, robotics to name a few.

AI Modelling

AI model training involves utilizing various types of learning techniques such as supervised learning, unsupervised learning, and semi-supervised learning. Supervised learning involves training the model using labelled data, while unsupervised learning utilizes unlabelled data. Whereas semi-supervised learning uses a combination of labelled and unlabelled data. Thus, Generative AI can be a part of supervised, unsupervised, or semi-supervised learning that depending on the task and training data used.

Primary Functions of an AI Model

An AI model is a program that has been trained on a set of data to recognize certain patterns or make certain decisions without further human intervention. Further, AI models apply different algorithms to relevant data inputs to achieve the tasks, or output, they have been programmed for. The most common functions of AI models include but not limited to processing data such as prediction, classification, regression, clustering; decision making optimization and automated reasoning; language understanding such as text generation, image and video processing; task automation and pattern recognition to mention a few.

Different Types of AI Models

The various types of AI Models at a very high level from the widest to the narrowest is shown in figure 1. At a high level, models fall into AI, which is the simulation of human intelligence by machines. These AI models can learn from the data and respond to new input as similar to human. These models can solve problems from simple to medium and even complex types. Besides, AI models have wide variety applications in all most all industries, including agriculture, automative, construction, education, finance, forestry, healthcare, manufacturing, mining, and retail.

Machine learning is a subset of AI, which uses advanced algorithm to detect patterns and correlations from the data by means of learning and provides prediction for unseen data. ML models can be classified into supervised, unsupervised or semi-supervised learning methods. Deep learning is a subset of ML, which uses multiple layers of neural networks for processing large amounts of input data, and extract high-level features. These models simulate complex decision-making in a way that human brains perceive and understand. The results produced by DL models are much more capable and accurate as compared to traditional ML models. Further, DL models can be used to solve a wide variety of problems, automatic text generation, NLP, and speech recognition.

Figure 1. Various types of AI models

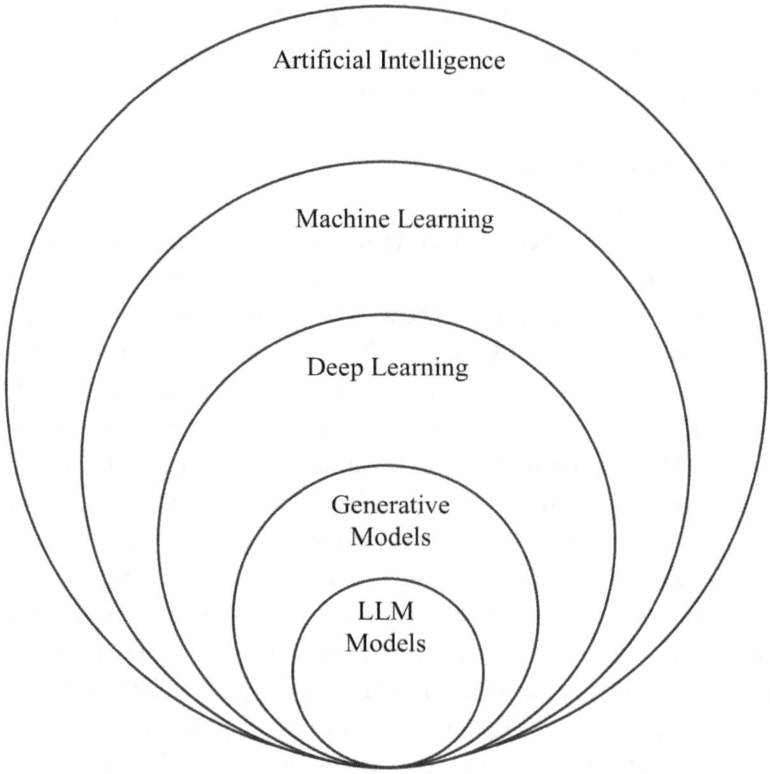

Generative Models

Generative models are a subset of DL models that utilizes neural networks to generate content like text, images, audio, video, or code based on input data. They can generate data by training on a large amount of data and capturing the underlying data distribution. These generative models can generate higher-quality and more complex data compared to traditional ML models. Generative models are unique because they learn to generate new data that resembles the training data, rather than just classifying or predicting outcomes. The major examples generative models include Generative Adversarial Networks (GANs), Variational Autoencoders (VAEs), and Autoregressive Models, including the Transformer architecture. Moreover, these models have shown impressive results in tasks such as image synthesis, text generation, anomaly detection, music and video generation, to mention a few. Most research focuses on generative models because they can create new, realistic data like text, images, audio and video, which enables the creation of content and data augmentation. Furthermore, generative models have the potential to solve complex problems through creativity, simulation and modelling.

Large Language Models

Large language models (LLMs) are typically based on DL architecture that can recognize, summarize, translate, predict, and generate text that can recognize, summarize, translate, predict and generate text and other forms of content based on knowledge gained from large datasets. Additionally, LLMs can be used to generate and translate text from one language to other, and other content, and perform other NLP tasks with the aid of Machine Translation models, which use techniques like statistical machine translation or neural machine translation. The following are a few examples of LLMs, such as GPT-4, Llama, Falcon, Cohere, Bidirectional Encoder Representations from Transformers (BERT), and Vicuna, which are used for tasks such as text generation, translation, and answering questions.

Differences Between ML and DL Models

The goals of both ML and DL models remain the same. However, there is a difference between these models in terms of its architecture more particularly the way model learns. At the same time, there is a significant overlap also exists between ML and DL models. Machine learning is a sub set of AI, whereas DL is subset of ML. Further, DL models use neural networks unlike ML models. The ML models utilize different methods, such as decision trees, random forests, linear regression, and logistic regression, to reach conclusions or predictions, whereas DL models use Feedforward Neural Networks (FNN), Convolution Neural Networks (CNN), Recurrent Neural Networks (RNN), Long Short-Terms Memory Transformer (LSTM), GAN, Transformer Networks, Autoencoders, Deep Reinforcement Learning (DRL), Deep Belief Networks (DBN), Radial Bais Networks (RBFN) and Siamese Networks. In general, DL models produce more accurate predications compared with ML models, provided they are properly tuned. DL models are widely used because their ability to automatically extract hierarchical features often leads to improved performance in tasks such as image, audio, and video recognition, speech recognition, and predictive analytics.

What is Regularization

Regularization is a technique that mainly prevents overfitting, which plays a vital role in ML and DL. Overfitting happens when a model learns the training data too well but performs poorly for unseen data. This results, the prediction of the model goes wrong for unseen data. In order to increase the prediction accuracy of the model, there should be some compromise in model leaning during training to increase the validation accuracy. As a result, the model performs better and predicts the best for unseen data, which means the model sacrifices in terms of training accuracy and increases validation accuracy. This results in improved model generalization. According to (Kukačka et al., 2017), the term regularization is defined as follows: "*Regularization is any supplementary technique that aims at making the model generalize better, that is, produce better results on the test set.*"

In general, penalty-based regularization can be expressed by Equation (1) as follows:

Regularization = Loss Function + Penalty (1)

Importance of Regularization in AI Models

Regularization plays a vital role in AI models due to the following reason. It prevents overfitting and improves model generalization. Besides, regularization can improve the robustness and reliability of the model. Further, it addresses specific issues like multicollinearity. Additionally, regularization helps with feature selection by penalizing less important or irrelevant features in a model, effectively reducing their impact or setting their coefficients to zero. An experiential study conducted by (Ismoilov and Jang, 2018) on regularization techniques by evaluating the training and validation errors in a DNN model showed that the models using regularization techniques demonstrated better performance than those without regularization methods in terms of training errors.

Performance of Model - Underfitting, Overfitting, and Just Right

Figure 2 shows the model fitting, which indicates the performance of the model in three scenarios – underfit, overfitting and just right. Further, these terms underfitting, overfitting, right fit indicates the balance between the ability of a mode to generalize and its complexity. Additionally, these terms are commonly referred to as model bias-variance trade off concepts.

a) **Underfitting:** The model does not learn to capture the underlying patterns in the training data, which means that it fails to capture underlying patterns in the training data, which is shown in figure 2(a). Therefore, the model exhibits poor performance on both training and test data. The model has low variance but high bias.
b) **Overfitting:** The model learns more from data to get a closer fit, which is shown in figure 2(b). This has low bias but high variance. This implies that the model is effective, which means the model has good performance, for training data, but not so effective for unseen data.
c) **Just Right:** The model learns from data without being too low or too high, which is a balanced model that generalizes between underfit and overfit. Figure 2(c) shows a just right fit model. This model has low bias, which means accurate prediction, and low variance, which means consistent prediction across data. Therefore, just right can fit the data closely while generalizing seemingly well to unseen data and condition is also known as good fit model.

Figure 2. Visual representation of model behaviour: Overfitting, Underfitting, and Right Fit (or Just Right)

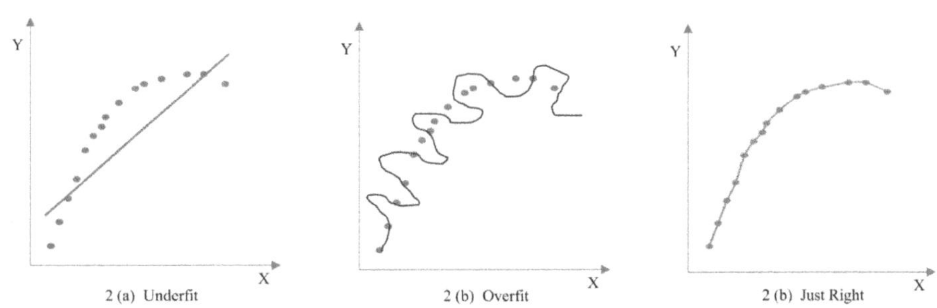

Techniques to Identify Overfitting in a Model

Detection of overfitting is important because it helps to understand generalization as well as performance of the model. The most common techniques for detecting overfitting in the models include but not limited to comparing training and validation accuracy, monitor loss curves, check model complexity and data size, cross-validation, and test on unseen data.

Figure 3 shows a graph drawn training loss and validation loss or accuracy versus iterations that helps to identify whether the model has overfit or not, which is explained below points (a) and (b). Further, it depicts generalization gap, over-fitting, underfitting, epochs, optimization line to represent right fit and ideal range for model complexity.

Figure 3. Training loss and validation loss of a model versus iterations, depicts generation gap, optimal fit,

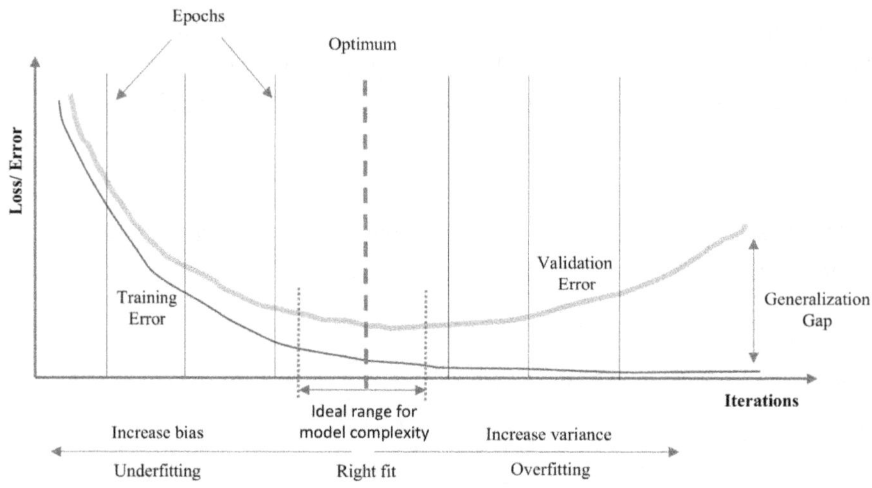

a) **Compare training and validation accuracy**: If the training accuracy is much higher than the validation accuracy, then model undergoes overfitting. This means the model has high training accuracy, but low validation accuracy.
b) **Monitor loss curves:** If the training loss continues to decrease while the validation loss starts increasing, this results overfitting. This means the model has a low training loss with high validation loss, which is not a good case for model choice.
c) **Check model complexity and data size**: If the model has larger number of parameters relative to the data meaning that the number of weights in a neural network or features in a linear model is much larger than the number of data points. Thus, the model can simply memorize the data, resulting in overfitting. Thus, the model has high variance overfits the training data, and performs poorly

on the validation or test set. As a result, the model has a very low training error but high-test error. Therefore, the model may not generalize well.

d) **Cross-validation:** Cross-validation is a resampling technique, which is most commonly used in both ML and DL to evaluate the performance of a model by training it on multiple subsets of the data and testing it on the remaining subsets or folds. This process helps assess how well the model generalizes to unseen data and reduces the risk of overfitting. In this process, the dataset is divided into multiple subsets or folds, typically 3, 5, 7 or 10. In each iteration, one-fold is used as the test set, and the remaining folds are used as the training set. The model is trained on the training set and evaluated on the test set. For example K-fold cross-validation means dividing the dataset into k equal-sized folds. The model is trained on k-1 folds and validated on the remaining fold, repeating the process k times.

e) **Test on unseen data:** A significant drop in performance on new, unseen data compared to the training data suggests that the model is overfitting.

f) **Generalization error:** It indicates how well the model is expected to perform on new, unseen data. It also called out-of-sample error. It reflects the true risk or expected loss. Regularization can reduce the generalization error by controlling overfitting, but it may increase training error slightly in the process.

g) **Generalization gap:** It is defined as the difference between a model's training error and its error on unseen data that is validation or test error. It is clearly shown the figure 3. In summary, the generalization gap quantifies how much worse the model performs on unseen data compared to the training data. A larger gap indicates poorer generalization, but it does not directly equal the generalization error. For example, if a model achieves 100% accuracy on the training data but only 70% on the validation or test data, the generalization gap in terms of accuracy is 30%. It is measured as follows:

$$\text{Generalization Gap} = \text{Validation Error} - \text{Training Error} \quad \text{......... Eq (2)}$$

Table 1 provides a detailed interpretation of how a model's performance on the training set, measured by training loss, compares to its performance on unseen data, measured by validation loss. By analyzing the relationship between training and validation loss, we can assess whether the model is learning effectively, underfitting, or overfitting. This comparison is critical for understanding the model's generalization ability and for guiding decisions about model complexity, training duration, and the need for regularization.

Table 1. Interpretation of training and validation loss combinations to diagnose model fit and training behaviour

Training Loss	Validation Loss	Remarks
High	High	Underfitting
Low	High	Overfitting
High	Low	Closer inspection of the model training process
Low	Low	Good Fit

The chapter is organized into six sections. Section 1 begins with an introduction about regularization, Section 2 covers various types of AI models. Section 3 covers the goals of regularization. Section 4 covers various types of regularizations that include recent advances in regularization techniques, trends, emerging challenges and future direction in regularization. Also includes transferability of regularization and why regularization is important for managers. Section 5 covers various key parameters of generative model that contribute to overfitting, performance metrics both regularized and non-regularized models and comparison of various types of regularization types. Section 6 covers the conclusions of the chapter.

2. TYPES OF AI MODELS

AI models have evolved from simple rule-based systems to ML and now DL, which transformed technology, making machines more intelligent and capable of solving complex problems. It is important to study different types of AI models because it provides insight into how they work and how to enhance their performance by choosing the most suitable regularization.

Key Takeaways

This section presents the following and the reader can understand the following:

- Broad classification of AI models based on its working.
- What is Weak AI and Strong AI.
- Classification of models based on data availability.
- Classification of models based on model focus.
- Comparison between generative and discriminative models.
- Classification of AI models based on scale.
- Major Applications of foundation models.

AI models can be categorized based on several factors, including the type of task they perform, the kind of data, the focus of the model, the scale of the pretraining data, and the learning environment. Figure 4 shows broad classification of AI models based on its working.

Figure 4. Broad classification of AI models based on its working

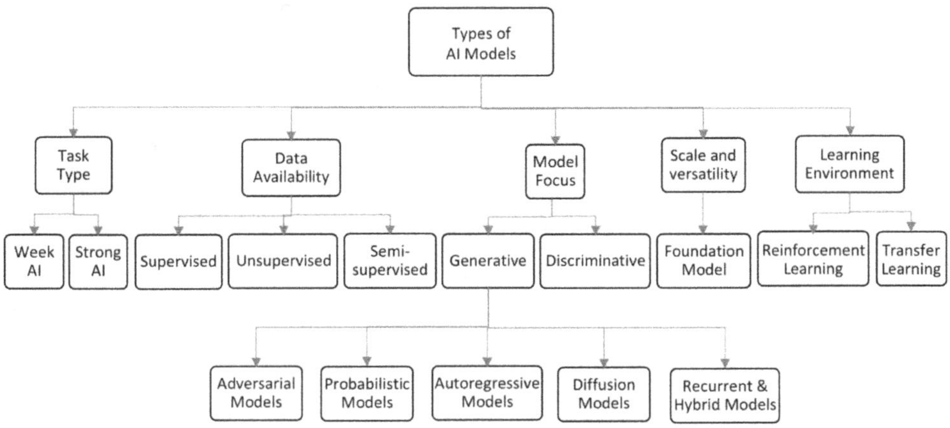

2.1 Weak AI and Strong AI

Based on execution of task type, AI models can be classified into two types as Weak AI and Strong AI. Weak AI is a type of AI that can only perform specific tasks. Few examples of Weak AI models include playing chess and translating languages from one to other. According to (IBM, 2021) Weak AI is also known as narrow AI or specialized AI, which focuses on performing a specific task, such as answering questions based on user input or playing chess but not both. Further, Weak AI relies on human interference to define the parameters of its learning algorithms and to provide the relevant training data to ensure accuracy. whereas strong AI can perform a variety of functions, eventually teaching itself to solve new problems. Further, Strong AI requires less human interaction as compared to Weak AI and over a period it does not require human interaction or relatively reduces the human interaction. Additionally, Strong AI is a type of AI that can perform any task that a human can. In addition, Strong AI, also known as Artificial General Intelligence or AGI, which is capable of behaving and performing actions like humans.

2.2 Data Availability

According to availability of data, AI models can be categorized into supervised learning, unsupervised learning, and semi-supervised learning. The key differences between these models are based on how they are trained, and how they function.

a) **Supervised learning** - The first, and most commonly used category ML is "Supervised learning." These models basically work on labelled data while being trained and using that to learn and grow. It uses the labelled data to predict outcomes based on inputs. The name "supervised learning" comes from the comparison of a student learning in the presence of an expert. The examples include predicting house prices based on location, square footage, and other features, or classifying emails as spam or not spam. Other applications include image recognition, sentiment analysis, and fraud detection. The examples for supervised models are liner regression, logistic regression, classification models such as decision tree, support vector machines, K-nearest neighbour.
b) **Unsupervised learning algorithms** - Unsupervised learning algorithms use that unlabelled data to create models and evaluate the relationships between different data points in order to give more insight to the data. The common tasks for unsupervised models include clustering, dimensionality reduction, and anomaly detection.
c) **Semi Supervised** - This type of models can use either supervised or unsupervised data input and still function. It means they combines supervised and unsupervised learning by using both labelled and unlabelled data. They might have slightly different applications based on their status. These models use a small portion of labelled data and lots of unlabelled data to train a predictive model. The examples for this are text classification, anomaly detection, and other tasks where labelled data is scarce. In general, Generative Adversarial Networks models use a semi-supervised approach, where the generator learns to produce new samples similar to the labelled data, and the discriminator distinguishes between labelled and generated samples.

2.3 Model Focus

There are various ways to classify AI models, one of which is based on the model focus, which indicates the task to be performed. It is the central purpose for which the model is being developed and trained. Model focus can range from simple tasks like identifying patterns in a data to complex tasks like generating content or predictions from the given data. Typically, ML and DL models are classified into two major categories based on model focus: discriminative models, which focus on decision boundary between the classes and generative models, which focus on data generation. In discriminative models, the focus is on modelling the decision boundary between classes, whereas generative models learn the joint probability distribution of inputs and outputs to generate new data. Moreover, a discriminative model makes predictions based on conditional probability, whereas a generative model revolves around the distribution of a dataset. Besides, discriminative models are used for classification or regression problems, while generative models are used to generate new data by utilizing the patterns that have been learned similar to the training data.

2.3.1 Generative Models

Generative models are a class of statistical models that are mainly used in unsupervised learning, which is a type of ML. These models generate new data instances by learning the underlying joint probability distribution of the input and output. In simple terms, these models attempt to estimate the probability density function of the data. Additionally, these models require a deeper understanding of features and distributions and perform well with less data. Thus, these models rely on the Bayes theorem to find the joint probability. Moreover, these models are used in unsupervised ML to perform tasks such as probability and likelihood estimation, modelling data points, and distinguishing between classes using these probabilities. The most common examples of generative models, including, but not limited to, Gaussian Mixture Models, Hidden Markov Models, and Naïve Bayes Classifiers.

2.3.2 Discriminative Models

More particularly, discriminative models are used for supervised ML and are also commonly called conditional model. This model learns the boundaries between classes or labels in a dataset, which is typically more effective for classification tasks. Further, these models create new instances using probability estimates and maximum likelihood. However, they are not capable of generating new data points. The very purpose of this type of model is to separate one class from another. Further, these models focus on feature space and decision boundaries; more suited for abundant data. Additionally, discriminative models focus on learning the conditional probability of the output for the given input data. Moreover, these models aim to minimise prediction error, which are typically considered as more flexible and accurate than generative models.

A list of popular discriminative models used machine ML and DL techniques are listed below. Logistic regression, Artificial Neural Networks (ANN), Decision Tree, Support Vector Machines, Recurrent Neural Network (RNN), Boosting algorithms like Gradient Boosting Machines (GBM), Convolution Neural Network (CNN), Conditional Random Fields (CRFs) and Random Forests.

2.3.3 Comparison Between Generative and Discriminative Models

The goal, focus, functionality, and training types of generative and discriminative models are fundamentally different, reflecting their distinct approaches to learning and decision-making. Although their goals differ, both types of models are versatile and find a variety of applications across different domains. Table 2 provides a side-by-side comparison of generative and discriminative models based on key aspects such as their goal, learning approach, data requirements, and common applications, helping to clarify their distinct roles in machine learning.

Table 2. Comparison of generative and discriminative models based on key parameters, learning approaches, and applications

Model Type/ Parameter	Generative Models	Discriminative Models
Goal	Generates new data instances as similar to the training data.	Classification of existing data Learns the decision boundary between classes.
Focus	Models the joint probability distribution of the input characteristics and labels is a main focus in a generative manner.	Modelling the conditional probability distribution of labels given input attributes is the main focus.
Functionality	Generative AI models are a type of ML model that generates new data similar to the data on which it was trained. These models are called generative because they create something new; for example, images, text, video and audio.	Discriminative models, on the other hand, do not generate content. They learn to distinguish between different kinds of data instances and are useful for tasks such as classification. A discriminative model, for example, can differentiate a dog from a cat.
Learning type	These models frequently use unsupervised or semi-supervised learning and are trained on unlabelled data. In addition, these models can also use adversarial training in the case of models like GAN.	These models frequently use supervised learning and are trained on a labelled dataset.

continued on following page

Table 2. Continued

Model Type/ Parameter	Generative Models	Discriminative Models
Training type	The training type of generative models defines how the model learns from the data and updates its parameters during training. The most common training types used by generative models include Batch, Adversarial, Online and Incremental Training. The models like VAEs are trained on the entire dataset at once in batch. In the case of GANs, the model undergoes adversarial training, where a generator and a discriminator are trained together in a competitive setting.	The training type of a discriminative model is typically either batch training or mini-batch training, where the model is trained on labelled data in iterations to optimize the decision boundary between classes.
Data Requirements	Generative models require a detail understanding on distribution and the features of data. Therefore, these models require large data sets as compared to discriminative model.	Discriminative models focus on learning the decision boundary between classes but not on the entire distribution. Therefore, these models have lower data requirements as compared to generative models. However, these models can still benefit from large data to improve performance and reduce overfitting.
Change of functionality	There is no such feature available in generative models because generative modes serve a different purpose as compared to discriminative model.	Occasionally discriminative models act as generative model based on the type of task they perform. For example, BERT can be considered generative in some cases when used for tasks like text generation or fine-tuned for tasks like sequence-to-sequence. However, its primary architecture is discriminative. Another example is BERR can perform generative task like text completion or masked language modelling (MLM), where BERT generates missing words in a sentence.
Examples	The examples of Generative models are: Naïve Bayes, Bayesian Networks, Markov Random Fields, Markov Models (HMM).	examples of Discriminative models are: Logistic regression, Scalar Vector Machine, Neural Networks, Neighbour, Conditional Random Fields (CRFs).
Applications	Generating creative content such as text, image, audio or video. Additionally, text applications include language translation, virtual assistants and conversational applications; text to image and image to text; audio includes audio captioning and transcription, audio enhancement and denoising, speech synthesis and voice cloning, music generation and composition; video applications include animations, visual effects, video enhancements, virtual reality and gaming. In addition, program code generation.	The various applications of discriminative models include classification, regression, image classification, sentiment analysis, named-entity recognition, image classification, and optical character recognition, segmentation, and survival prediction models. Additional applications such as anomaly detection and intrusion detection systems in cyber security.

2.4 Scale and Versatility

The other type of AI model classification is based on a scale, the ability to handle complex tasks, and versatility, the range of tasks they can perform. The examples for this type are Large Langue Models (LLMs), Further, LLMs are classified into two major categories such as industry specific models like health care, finance, agriculture and energy and foundation models (Tu et Al., 2024). Foundation models provide a strong base for developing a wide range of AI solution without having to start from scratch. Foundation models are large, and pre-trained DL models, which are also known as large X models (LxM). Additionally, these models can be applied across a wide range of use cases for a wide range of downstream tasks with minimal fine-tuning. Moreover, these models are trained on diverse datasets. Most commonly, these models are built on vast amounts of data that are capable of understanding, generating, or processing multiple data types such as text, images, and audio, Additionally, these models are designed to be general-purpose, which can serve as a base for multiple applications. A few examples of these modules include GPT for language, CLIP for vision and language, and DALL-E for image generation.

According to study of (Rick Merritt, 2025), foundation model is defined as "A foundation model is an AI neural network - trained on mountains of raw data, generally with unsupervised learning - that can be adapted to accomplish a broad range of tasks". Additionally, foundation models generally learn from unlabelled datasets, saving the time and expense of manually describing each item in massive collections. Furthermore, foundation models have also expanded to process and generate multiple data types, or modalities, such as text, images, audio and video. VLMs are one type of multimodal models that can understand video, image and text inputs while producing text or visual output, which were trained on 355,000 videos and 2.8 million images. Likewise, NVIDIA's Cosmos Nemotron 34 is a platform of state-of-the-art generative World Foundation Models (WFM). It is a multi-modal Vision-Language Model (VLM) that enables the ability to query and summarize images and video from the physical or virtual world (NVIDIA Cosmos, n.a.).

Figure 5. Application of Foundation models

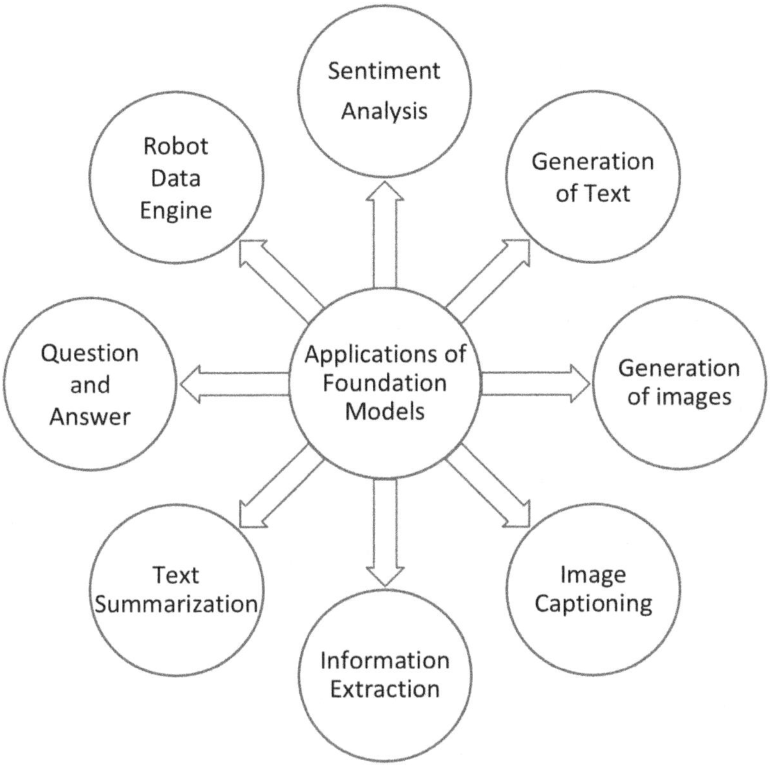

Foundation models have found multiple application in industry and other fileds. Figure 5 shows the major applications of foundation models, which include sentiment analysis, generation of text and images, image captioning, information extraction, text summarization, question and answer, and robot data engine to mention a few. The input to a model may be text, image, speech, video, 3D graphs, and any structured data.

Foundation models are epicentre of AI. In these days, the use of foundation models has increasing rapidly in all most all the fields. Thus, there is a need to characterize the transparency of these model ecosystem. The foundation model transparency index (Bommasani et al., 2024) was introduced in 2023, which measures the transparency of leading foundation model developers. This index comprises of 100 indicators across three domains such as upstream, model, and downstream. This index helps advanced AI practitioners, and industry leaders to understand the transparency of foundation model developers. Further, it helps policy makers to know the transparency improvements about these models, otherwise their intervention can help to improve transparency.

2.5 Learning Environment

Depending on the learning environment, AI models can be classified based on their data interaction and the feedback nature during training. The following are the most popular types of learning models such as Reinforcement Learning, Transfer Learning and Active Learning.

a) **Reinforcement Learning Models –** These models learn by taking in feedback from the result of its action, which is typically in the form of a reward. In general, these models composed of two major parts such as an *agent* that performs an action, and the *environment* in which the action is performed. The cycle begins when the environment sends a "state" signal to the agent. That queues the agent to perform a specific action within the environment. Once the action is performed, the environment sends a "reward" signal to the agent, informing it on what happened, so the agent can update and evaluate its last action. Then, it can take the action again. Thus, this cycle is repeated until the environment sends a termination signal. There are two types of reinforcement signals the algorithm can use: either a positive reward, or a negative reward.

An RL model learns by interacting with an environment. The goal of RL is to maximizes cumulative rewards through trial and error. The use of RL is for tasks requiring sequential decision-making. The examples of RL are game playing, robotics to name a few. In summary, RL focuses on learning through actions and rewards.

b) **Transfer Learning -** In this learning type, transfers knowledge from one task to a different but related task. The goal of this learning type is to leverages pre-trained models to improve learning on a new, but related task. The primary use of transfer learning is when limited data is available for the target task, but large amounts of data exist for a similar task. The examples of transfer learning include image classification with pre-trained models. It uses knowledge from one task to accelerate learning in another
c) **Active Learning** - In this type of learning, the model queries the most informative data points to learn from. The goal of this model is to reduces the need for labelled data by selecting the most valuable examples for labelling. The basic uses of this learning model are tasks with a large amount of unlabelled data and expensive labelling processes. The examples of this learning model are text or image annotation. It selects data points to optimize the learning process with fewer labelled examples.

3. GOALS OF REGULARIZATION

Key Takeaways
The reader can understand the following after reading this section.

- The goals of regularization techniques.

It is necessary to understand the goals of regularization in order to understand its functionality and optimize model performance. Understanding the goals of regularization provides several benefits that include better design, improved generalization, enhanced performance, and increased robustness of the model.

Overfitting is a common problem that exists in both ML and DL models. Regularization techniques are most commonly used to address the overfitting problem, where a model memorizes training data details and cannot generalize to new data. Thus, the main goal of regularization is to encourage models to learn the broader patterns within the data rather than memorizing it. In summary, regularization is mainly aimed at to reduce the model's complexity to make it more generalizable to new data, which improves its performance on unseen datasets. This covers the following six major goals of regularization. Nevertheless, regularization in both ML and DL aims to prevent overfitting; however, DL models require more advanced techniques because of their complexity, size, and computational requirements. Additionally, regularization in DL requires to address the intricacies of training deep models on large datasets and managing the vast number of parameters involved. Most commonly, the following regularization techniques are used in DL models' such as dropout, batch normalization, and data augmentation. Regularization has multiple goals; however, the most important goals of regulation are envisaged in figure 6.

Figure 6. Goals of regularization

a) **Prevent Overfitting:** Regularization reduces model complexity and further, forces the model to focus on more general features of the data rather than memorizing noise or irrelevant details. Additionally, reduction of overfitting improves model's performance on unseen data. However, it is important to tune the regularization parameters carefully to avoid adverse effects on the model's performance for unseen data.

b) **Improve Generalization:** The primary purpose of regularization is to improve a model's ability to generalize its behaviour to new or unseen data. Regularized models are typically better at generalizing to unseen data, reducing the generalization gap, which is nothing but to reduce the difference between training and test error. The primary goal of training a model is to prepare the model to predict unseen data accurately and improving the generalization power of a deep neural network (Rezaeezade and Batina, 2024). The final goal is to use the model for a test set and decrease the generalization error (or test error).

c) **Reduce Model Complexity:** Regularization is a key technique used to reduce model complexity and improve generalization. By adding a penalty term to the loss function (such as L1 or L2 regularization), it discourages overly complex models that fit noise in the training data. This helps prevent overfitting by shrinking or eliminating less important features, promoting simpler, more robust models that perform better on unseen data. In addition, regularization methods like L1 and ElasticNet promote sparse solutions and help the model select the most relevant features.

d) **Increase Robustness**: One of the goals of regularization is to increase robustness of the model. Techniques such as adversarial regularization, and dropout are enhancing model robustness to small perturbations.

e) **Trading Bias for Variance**: In Statistical models, the term bias refers to the difference between the actual values and the predicted values by the model. A model with low bias means that it has learned the patterns in the data, whereas high bias indicates that the model has poorly learnt the patterns in the data. The term variance measures the variability of a model's predictions when trained on different subsets of the training data. Low variance of a model is good, whereas high variance means the performance of the training data and the validation data vary a lot. A model with high variance and low bias is said to be overfitting, whereas with high bias and low variance is said to be underfitting. Thus, the model has to find a balance between bias and variance, which is known as the bias-variance trade-off.. Table 3 illustrates how the levels of bias and variance vary depending on whether a model is underfitting, overfitting, or achieving the right fit. It helps in understanding the trade-off between bias and variance in model performance and generalization. For a right-fit, well-generalized model, the bias should be moderate to low as well as the variance should also be moderate to low. A right-fit model strikes a balance — not minimizing both absolutely, but trading off between them to achieve low generalization error.

Table 3. Relationship between bias and variance across underfitting, overfitting, and just right (or good fit).

Parameter	Underfit	Overfit	Just Right (or Good Fit)
Bias	High	Low	Moderate to Low
Variance	Low	High	Moderate to Low

f) **Handling Multicollinearity**: In models like regression, when two or more independent variables are correlated with one another then the variables of the model are said to be multicollinear. It is a statistical phenomenon. If the correlation between two variables is +/- 1.0, then the variables are said to be perfectly collinear. There are many factors that can lead to multicollinearity in data. Which include data collection, data transformation, fabricating of data. In data collection, methods such as surveys, questionnaires, or experiments may include redundant or overlapping items, which can inflate correlations between variables and contribute to multicollinearity. In like manner, data transformations, such as scaling, standardizing, or encoding, can also increase the correlation between features. Besides, while fabricating data or simulated data may introduce multicollinearity by design or by mistake. In order to handle multicollinearity, the following techniques are commonly used. The first technique is removing one of the correlated variables and combining them. The second technique is using regularization methods like Lasso regression. Regularization stabilizes models by reducing sensitivity to small changes when features are highly correlated. Regularization is particularly useful in scenarios where features are highly correlated (multicollinearity). L2 regularization (Ridge) can reduce the variance of the coefficient estimates, which are otherwise inflated due to multicollinearity.

It is important to identify multicollinearity using Variance Inflation Factor (VIF) and then access its impact on the model performance. Equation 2 shows the VIF.

$$VIF = \frac{1}{1 - R^2}$$

.... Eq (3)

The R^2 value is determined to find out how well an independent variable is described by the other independent variables A high value of R^2 means that the variable is highly correlated with the other variables.

- VIF starts at 1 and has no upper limit.
- VIF = 1, no correlation between the independent variable and the other variables.
- VIF exceeding 5 or 10 indicates high multicollinearity between this independent variable and the others

Multicollinearity is a common issue in ML validation that can affect the performance and interpretation of the models. The presence of multicollinearity can lead to unstable and unreliable coefficient estimates that creates a challenge for interpretating the results and drawing meaningful conclusions from the model. This results multicollinear variables can negatively affect model predictions on unseen data. Regularization techniques like L2 and L1 regularizations can help detect and fix multicollinearity by penalizing large coefficients and reducing their impact.

4. TYPES OF REGULARIZATION

Key Takeaways

The reader can understand the following after reading this section.

- The major classification of regularization techniques.
- Various types of penalty-based regularization techniques.
- Various types of stopping criteria regularization types.
- Various types of structural regularizations
- Types of regularization techniques bsed on data augmentation.
- The purpose of model validation in regularization.
- Recent advances in regularization techniques.

Understanding various types of regularization is crucial because it helps in preventing overfitting, which in turn improves model generalization, enhances efficiency, optimizes different architectures like GAN, Transformers, GNN. Further, it ensures robustness of the model, which strengthens models against adversarial attacks and noisy data. Having knowledge of these techniques allows for more accurate and efficient design across various domains. This section presents various types of regularizations, and recent advances in regularization techniques. Moreover, briefly presents a few recent trends in regularization, emerging challenges and future directions of research in regularization. Additionally, cover the importance of transferability of regularization.

Regularization techniques are mainly used in both ML and DL models to reduce overfitting problem and to increase model generalization. The key to regularisation lies in tuning multiple parameters to optimise the model performance for un-seen data or new data. Figure 7 shows various types of regularizations that are grouped based on their working type. The major types of regularizations include penalty-based regularization, stopping criteria regularization, structural regularization, data augmentation and model validation regularization.

Figure 7. Various types of regularization techniques

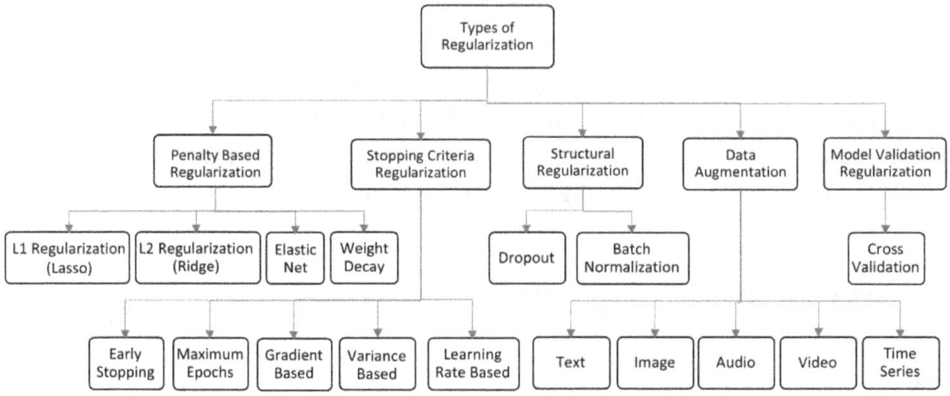

4.1 Penalty-Based Regularization

These types of regularization techniques penalize large weights in the model to prevent overfitting. The most commonly used for models with fewer parameters are L1 and L2 regularization. While weights decay is a form of L2 regularization, which is used in DL models to control large weights.

a) **L1 Regularization** - Adds a penalty proportional to the absolute values of the weights, promoting sparsity or feature selection. This can lead to some coefficients being zero, which means the model ignores the corresponding features. It is useful for feature selection. This regularization is known as Lasso regularization. A method, L1/2 regularization, was proposed by Xu et. al. (2010), which has a nonconvex penalty. Further, the L1/2 regularization has many promising properties such as unbiasedness, sparsity and oracle properties. The experiments show that the L1/2 regularization is very useful and efficient. Lasso shrinks the less important feature's coefficient to zero thus removing some feature altogether, on the other hand, L2 regularization, does not remove most of the features. In order to overcome this problem, Kolluri et al. (2020) introduced an L1/4 regularization method, which pushes all the weights absolute to their fourth-order value. It gives a better performance as compared to L1. The L1/4 regularization method is sparser than the L1 method. Further, L1/4 regularization method is able to select less vectorized variables, which shows that, this regularization is good at the gene data analysis.

b) **L2 Regularization or Weight Decay** - Adds a penalty proportional to the square of the magnitude of coefficients, shrinking weights but not forcing them to zero. This regularization is known as Ridge regularization. Essentially L2 regularization used in DL to prevent large weights by adding a penalty term as part of the optimisation process, typically by adding a regularisation term to the neural network's loss function.

c) **Elastic Net** - It is a combination of L1 and L2 regularization for a balance of sparsity (L1) and weight shrinkage (L2). This technique is most commonly used to handle multicollinearity where features are highly correlated, and feature selection, where the coefficients of less important features are gradually reduced to zero.

d) **Weight Decay** –In this technique, a fraction of the previous weight is subtracted when updating the weights during training, effectively making the weights smaller over time. By gradually diminishing the magnitude of the weights, which helps to prevent overfitting and allows the model to generalize better to unseen data.

4.2 Stopping Criteria Regularization

In addition to penalty-based regularization, overfitting can be reduced in AI models based on the model's performance while validating the model, after training the model. During this validation process, training stops when the model performance starts degrading, which is known as early stopping. These types of regularization techniques can be further classified into early stopping, maximum epochs, gradient-based, variance-based, and learning rate-based stopping.

a) **Early stopping** – In this technique halts training at the point when the model's performance starts degrading, this indicates that the model is overfitting. Thus, it helps to prevent the model from training too long and memorizing the training data. In general, the process of stopping involves monitoring a validation metric such as loss or accuracy, and training stops once this metric stop improving for a predefined number of iterations. It means the validation performance does not improve for a specified number of epochs, and then stops training. A restore best weights option is often included to revert to the best performing model during training. According to the study of regularization effectiveness on randomly selected DL models by (Rezaeezade and Batina, 2024), the experimental results found that the performance of L1 and L2 were most effective. Second, the early stopping technique has moderate effectiveness, which can reduce training time in comparison with other techniques $L1$, $L2$, and dropout.

b) **Maximum Epochs** – In this type of regularization techniques, training of the model is stopped after a fixed number of epochs or iterations, regardless of the model's performance. This is a hard limit and does not take validation performance into account. The advantage of this technique is that it is simple and straight forward and does not require to monitor any metric for stopping criteria. It is one of the most common techniques used when there is limited computational resources, where training needs to be cut off after a certain point. Thus, the process of training the model continues for the specified number of epochs, and the model's performance is evaluated after each epoch. Moreover, it does not rely on the validation performance but instead on the number of epochs set ahead of time.

c) **Gradient-Based Stopping** – In this technique, the process of training the model stops when the gradient magnitude or change in loss falls below a certain threshold. This indicates that the model has converged and further training would not significantly improve performance of the model. In this technique, calculate the gradient of the loss function and compare the magnitude of the gradient with the predefined value, if the gradient is smaller than a predefined threshold and training automatically stops. This technique is most commonly used in in optimization algorithms like gradient descent, both ML and DL, where the goal is to reach the minimum of a loss function.

d) **Variance - based Stopping** – In this type of regularization, training stops when the model's performance starts to become unstable or fluctuates beyond a certain threshold, which indicates potential overfitting. A few examples of this type of regularization technique used in reinforcement learning or online learning is to prevent erratic learning behaviours. As a first step it monitors metrics such as loss or accuracy of the model. If the monitoring metric starts fluctuating, it may indicate instability, and training process can be stopped to prevent overfitting.

e) **Learning Rate - based Stopping** – In this method, the process of model training is stopped as and when the learning rate decays to a certain small value or when the learning rate has not improved the validation performance. If the learning rate becomes very small and then the training is stopped. As a result, the model avoids wasting of computational resources. Further, this technique is most commonly used in adaptive methods that adjust the learning rate based on training progress. Typically, this mode used in Stochastic Gradient Descent (SGD) or adaptive learning rate methods like Adam.

4.3 Structural Regularization

Dropout and batch normalization regularization techniques are specifically designed to modify the architecture or flow of data through the model. In DL, in order to make the model more robust, either by randomly removing or deactivating units (or neurons) during training or by normalizing layer outputs.

a) **Dropout** – In dropout, randomly disables a fraction of neurons during training to prevent over-reliance on specific units. Dropout has become a widely adopted regularization technique in DL as it mitigates the risk of overfitting, which empowers researchers and practitioners to build more reliable and high-performing neural networks. According to this study (Salehin and Kang, 2023), various types of regularization types, more than forty, based on dropout and categorized into three main categories: internal structure change, data augmentation, and input information. Internal structure changes regularization mainly involves changing the weights and kernels during the training period without making any changes to the input values. The examples for this category are DropBlock, MaxDropout, AutoDrop, and Attentiondrop.

Data augmentation is the process of modifying data to reduce variance by making slight modifications to images and is used to generate more training data. The following dropout methods such as Cutout, Random Erasing, Demystifying Dropout, SmoothMix can serve as a form of data augmentation allowing for improved generalization. Some dropout methods directly discard a portion of input information during training, serving various purposes in different scenarios. These purposes may include regularization, data augmentation, or enhancing data representation during the pretraining stage. Further, the utilization of dropout in DL models was proved in enhancing performance and addressing overfitting. By randomly deactivating a portion of neurons during training, dropout allows the network to learn more robust and generalized features, ultimately improves performance of the model on unseen test data and this process enhances model generalization and effectiveness.

b) **Batch Normalization** – Normalizes layer inputs to stabilize and speed up training by maintaining mean output distributions. An experimental study conducted by Nusrat and Jang (2018) on various neural network models and applied various regularization techniques such as autoencoder, data augmentation, L1 regularization, batch normalization. The experimental results showed that L1 regularization and the autoencoder still encountered overfitting and underfitting problems. The batch normalization showed better performance than these methods, whereas the DNN model with data augmentation showed the best performance.

4.4 Data Augmentation

Data augmentation is one of the powerful and unique regularization techniques, which is different from other regularization techniques. The main focus of data augmentation technique is on increasing the diversity of data, while other regularization techniques focus on how the model learns from the data. Further, data augmentation increases the diversity of the training data by applying random transformations like rotation, and scaling to the original dataset. This technique overcomes several limitations of data size and noisy inputs. Additionally, data augmentation can be classified based on data type such as text, image, audio, video, and time series. The various types of transformations available for each data type are provided below.

a) Text - Synonym Replacement, Random Insertion/Deletion, Back Translation, Paraphrasing, Contextual Embeddings, etc.
b) Image - Rotation, Flipping, Scaling, Translation, Shearing, Colour Jittering, Noise Injection, Elastic Deformations, etc.
c) Audio - Pitch Shifting, Time Stretching, Noise Injection, Reverb/Room Simulation, Volume Shifting, etc.
d) Video - Frame Dropping, Rotation/Flipping, Temporal Shifting, Scaling, Cutout, Color Jittering, etc.
e) Time Series - Time Warping, Jittering, Window Slicing, Time Shifting, etc.

Furthermore, data augmentation technique can provide variety of data through multiple transformation techniques that allows model to generate varied examples, which is most commonly used for image data in DL models. As a result, it helps to avoid overfitting of the model that improves model generalization. Additionally, data augmentation techniques provide better performance to the model as compared to other regularization techniques, Moreover, this technique can address issues related to limited data and noisy inputs because of diversity of data that is generated through various random transformations. In other regularization techniques, like L1, L2 regularizations, dropout, or early stopping, focus more on constraining the learning process of model that prevents overfitting.

4.5 Model Validation Regularization

Model validation regularization is a type of regularization that accesses and improves the performance of a model to ensure generalization with accurate prediction for unseen data at the same time reduces overfitting. Both regularization and cross validation techniques are used for reduction of overfitting but completely different purposes. Regularization is commonly used to reduce overfitting and is applied during training phase whereas cross validation provided more generalization and is applied during validation phase of model, which partially reduces overfitting. Cross validation typically involves evaluating the model's accuracy on a separate validation set while adjusting the regularization parameter to find the optimal balance between fitting the training data and avoiding overfitting and increases more generalization. Additionally, cross-validation technique is one of the most common model validation regularization techniques that helps ensure that the model is evaluated on multiple subsets of the data. Further, this technique provided better estimates of model generalization and reducing the risk of overfitting to any one particular subset of the data. In cross validation, data splits into training and validation subsets multiple times to evaluate model performance. In general, the data scientist team can choose right combination of model validation approach and metrics for a given business problem on continuous basis in order to increase more generalization.

4.6 Recent Advances in Regularization Techniques

Advanced regularization techniques are continuously evolving to prevent overfitting, improve generalization, and enhance model stability. This sub-section presents a brief outline on various advanced regularization techniques that are based on transformer and Graph Neural Networks (GNN), which are used in both ML and D, but they are more popularly used in DL for complex tasks like NLP (Transformers) and structured data processing (GNNs). These regularization techniques are gaining more popular in current research because they offer a novel approach to addressing overfitting and improving generalization in deep learning models. In fact, Transformer and GNN do not exactly fall under generative but used in both generative and discriminative tasks. Transformer-based regularization techniques such as attention sparsity, dropout, weight decay, token masking, entropy based, gradient clipping and layer normalization evolved to improve efficiency and generalization, whereas GNN techniques such as spectral regularization, edge dropout, and topology-aware constraints emerged to enhance learning over graph structures while mitigating overfitting

GNNs are neural networks that can be directly applied to graphs, which provide an easy way to do node-level, edge-level, and graph-level prediction tasks. Additionally, GNNs can do what CNNs failed to do. Regularization in both transformer and GNNs are aimed to prevent overfitting and improve generalization. However, they differ in how they apply regularization techniques. GNNs leverage graph structures to process data, whereas transformer models excel at capturing sequential and contextual information. A novel approach that combines both features of GNN and transformer, which is known as GNN-Transformer Co-contrastive (GTC) learning. In GTC, GNNs leverages for graph structure encoding while transformers for capturing sequential or contextual information that allows for more complex data representation and modelling. Thus, GTC leverages GNN and transformer as two branches to encode different views of information and perform cross-view collaboratively contrastive learning. This scheme overcomes through GNNs' limitation of capturing multi-hop neighbour information on the premise of avoiding the over-smoothing problem. However, GNNs also have some limitations like difficulty distinguishing simple non-isomorphic graphs that means the graphs that are structurally different even if they share the same number of vertices and edges. Additionally, they can be computationally expensive, especially for large graphs and vulnerability to noise in graph data.

4.7 Trends, Emerging Challenges and Future Directions in Regularization Techniques

a) **Trends in Regularization Techniques -** Regularization techniques are evolving toward adaptive, sparsity-based, and self-supervised methods to mainly enhance model generalization, efficiency, and interpretability in Transformers, GNNs, and generative models. The major focus of transformer-based models towards sparsity and head pruning techniques whereas GNN leverages topology-aware constraints techniques. The latest trends in generative models focusing on improving stability, efficiency, and diversity in generated outputs and the advancements include contrastive regularization that enhances feature separation in latent space for better generative quality. Further, trends explore adversarial regularization to strengthens generative models against adversarial perturbations and spectral normalization to stabilizes training by controlling weight magnitudes. Adversarial regularization (AR) is one of the state-of-the-art defence methods that mitigate such attacks while preserving a model's prediction accuracy. proposed an enhanced adversarial regularization (EAR) method was proposed by (Hu et al., 2021), which was based on Least Square GANs (LSGANs). The method provides better defensive capabilities than the existing AR and still maintain the same prediction accuracy.

b) **Emerging Challenges –** There are many emerging challenges in the regularization domain. A few these challenges are discussed below.

  (i) Developing a robust generative model by training them with adversarial examples. In recent time, adversarial regularization is used to make models more robust by training them with adversarial examples. However, it brings its own set of challenges such as include trade-off between accuracy and robustness, stability during training, gradient masking and computational overhead to list a few.

  (ii) Building robust AI models that focuses on efficient data centric approaches. In this scenario, the focus is on improving data quality that is provided to the model rather than tweaking models. The data-centric AI approach is one of the emerging challenges in regularization, a growing trend, but there are real hurdles like data quality assessment, bias and fairness issues, data versioning to track changes, and integrating with model-centric workflows. Thus, building robust AI models has undergone a paradigm shift from model-centric to data-centric. Data-centric AI focuses on improving data quality rather than tweaking models whereas model-centric focuses on tweaking model includes choosing right type of regularization, selecting right training approaches and hyperparameters tunning to mention a few.

  (iii) Regularization techniques present unique challenges when integrated with LLMs. The various challenges in this scenario includes like, managing massive model parameters, overfitting, catastrophic forgetting ensuring effective generalization, and addressing potential bias in the training data. In general, LLMs contains a large number of parameters, which makes them computationally expensive to train and deploy. So, choosing a right regularization technique itself poses a major challenge and implement to avoid over-fitting is an additional challenge. In addition, while fine-tuning the model for a specific task can cause the model to forget previously acquired knowledge, which is known as catastrophic forgetting, is an additional challenge.

  (iv) One of the emerging trends in regularization is integration of regularization with deep learning architectures. In general, DL model architectures are more complex and deeper hence traditional regularization techniques such as L1 and L2 may not enough to reduce the overfitting, which requires new regularization strategies to address overfitting and data challenges.

c) **Future Directions -** The future directions of research in regularization could focus on exploring one or more above-mentioned challenges to develop new strategies and techniques for mitigating, and fostering suitable solutions. Future research focus on building self-regularizing architectures, dynamic penalties, and topology-aware constraints to improve interpretability, scalability, and robustness across domains, including AI ethics and fairness.

4.8 Transferability of Regularization Techniques

Regularization techniques are most commonly employed to prevent overfitting and that improves model generalization, whereas transferability refers to applying knowledge from one domain or task to another to improve the performance of the model. This is achieved by initializing the model's weights with pre-trained weights from a related task and then fine-tuning the model on the target task. Regularization transferability means the regularization techniques that work well on one model or dataset (say, CIFAR-10 with ResNet) also work well on a different model or data-set (like ImageNet with EfficientNet). The need for regularization transferability is because tunning regularization is expensive, reuse of regularization technique across models or task or new datasets. The idea of regularization transferability is that regularization techniques used during the pre-training phase can help the model adapt more effectively to the target task during fine-tuning. This can be achieved by leveraging the regularization strategies from the pre-trained model, the model can learn more efficiently and avoid overfitting on the new dataset. The advantage of transferability of regularization is that it helps to build more robust, generalizable models, efficient knowledge sharing across the architectures and reduces training time. Further, it saves time to bring training experiences that are gained from one context. For example, a model that is trained on Task A using L2 regularization then how does L2 regularization can help the model trying to execute Task B or different dataset.

5. IMPORTANT KEY PARAMETERS OF GENERATIVE MODELS

Key Takeaways

After reading this section, the reader can comprehend the following.

- List of various key parameters that affect overfitting in generative models.
- Key metrics to measure model performance.
- Comparison of various regularization techniques.
- How to prevent overfitting in modalities like text, image and multi-models.

Regularization is not a standalone process; it depends on several model parameters, including data preprocessing, learning rate, weight initialization, batch size, optimizer choice, activation function, number of layers, dropout rate, and loss function. These key parameters influence regularization effectiveness and overall model performance.

5.1 Key Parameters that Affect Overfitting in Generative Models

In generative models, several parameters contribute to overfitting issue, which can be controlled suitably by employing specific regularization technique. Improper regulation is defined as regularization techniques that are not properly applied or tuned, leading to mismatch between model generalization and complexity. It can have a negatively impact on model performance in multiple ways.

Further, improper regularization can lead to significant degradations in model performance in production environments, which leads to poor results like accuracy, reliability or efficiency of the mode over time. This can happen due to various factors, including changes in the data distribution, the model's own parameters, or the underlying environment in which the model is deployed. The following parameters are crucial in influencing overfitting: latent space size, model capacity, learning rate, training data size, noisy data, type of training procedure, loss function, output distribution and prediction, latent variables, generator - discriminator balance among others. Further, these parameters can be grouped into multiple categories based on model capacity, performance, working characteristic, training approach, learning rate, and data size. Figure 8 shows major key parameters that contribute overfitting in generative models.

Figure 8. Major key parameters of generative models

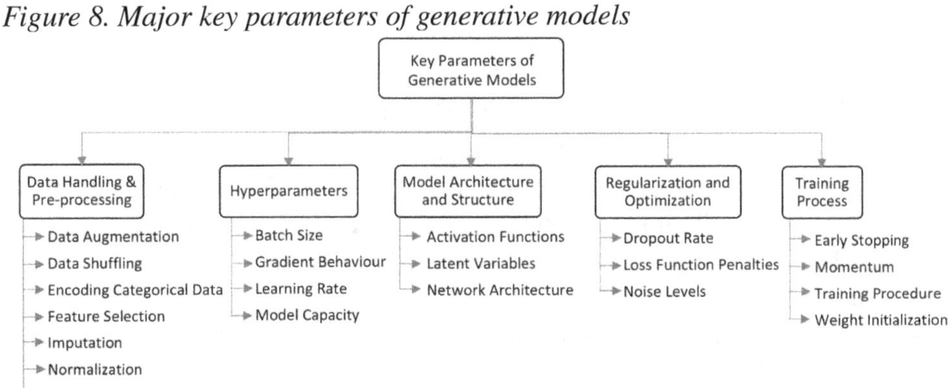

5.1.1 Data Handling and Pre-Processing

a) **Data Augmentation –** Data augmentation will provide the diversity of data to the mode that helps model to reduce overfitting. Please refer the Section 4.3 for detail discussion.

b) **Data Shuffling** - It is a data preprocessing technique, where the order of data points is shuffled, which means randomly rearranged in order to prevent any inherent pattern in the data that influencing the training process of a model. This technique improves generalization ability and reduces bias by ensuring each training batch will get a different sequence of data points.

c) **Encoding Categorical Data** - It refers to the process of converting categorical or textual data into numerical format. So that it can be used as input for algorithms to process. The main reason for encoding the data into numerical format is that most ML algorithms work with numbers and not with text or categorical variables. In generally execute numerical data faster than categorical or text data. This is because numerical data is directly processed by the CPU, while categorical and text data often require additional processing activities such as encoding and parsing before they can be used. The speed improvement can vary, but numerical data can be processed up to several times faster, depending on the complexity of the operations and the size of the data. However, the exact speedup depends on the specific context and computational task.

d) **Feature Selection –** It is a process of identifying and selecting the most relevant features or variables from a dataset to improve model performance and reduce complexity. This process involves removing irrelevant or redundant features, leading to more efficient and increase the model accuracy.

e) **Other Data Related -** There few parameters related to data provided to the model for training and these are size of training data and noise in data.

   i. **Data Size -** Insufficient data to the model leads to overfitting. In general, if there is insufficient training data to learn the underlying data distribution can lead the model to memorize the samples instead of generalizing from the patterns in the data. As results, the poor prediction on unseen data. To overcome this limitation, tThe following regularization techniques are used such as Data Augmentation, Noise Injection, Dropout, Training on Larger Datasets.

   ii. **Noise in Data** - Noise in the training data or incomplete data may result the model to fit to the noise rather than learning the true underlying distribution. The most common regularization techniques users for this are Noise Injection, Data Augmentation, Adversarial Training.

iii. **Outlier** - It is a process of identifying data points that significantly deviate from the majority of the data in a dataset. It helps to minimize uncover and unusual patterns or errors.
iv. **Normalization** - It is a data preprocessing technique that transforms features to a common scale, typically between 0 and 1, which improves model performance and stability, especially for algorithms sensitive to feature magnitudes. The methods mapping, and scaling helps forecasting and prediction models improving accuracy and performance.

5.1.2 Hyperparameters

In AI model, hyperparameters refer configuration settings that control the learning process of the model. Hyperparameters and regularization are closely related because hyperparameters control the regularization process and the complexity of the model, while regularization techniques are used to prevent overfitting and improve generalization. In this sub-section, hyperparameters such as batch size, gradient behaviour, learning rate and model capacity are briefly presented, which are connected with the process of regularization that significantly affect model performance.

a) **Batch Size** – It is one of the hyperparameter refers to both ML and DL. Batch size is defined as the number of training examples used in one iteration during model training. For example, if batch_size is equal to 100 and the training samples are 600. Then, the algorithm takes the first 100 samples starts from 1st to 100th from the training dataset and train the model. Later, it takes the second 100 samples from 101st to 200th and train the model and this process will continue. If the batch_size is less than the number of samples then the model requires less memory space and the model training is completed much faster. In general, model training is much faster with mini-batches as compared with large batch sizes. According to the results of study (Johan et al., 2023), presents that smaller batch sizes in deep reinforcement learning can actually lead to improved performance, particularly in value-based algorithms, which contradicts the common expectation that larger batch sizes are always better for training neural networks. This study focuses on value-based deep reinforcement learning algorithms that use experience replay, where a batch of experiences is sampled for each gradient update. In another interesting studies by (Hoffer et al., 2017), examine the impact of large batch sizes on generalization performance in neural networks. The studies highlight the generalization gap that can occur with large batch training. It is a common notion that large batch sizes have a negatively impact on generalization, but this study proves otherwise. The following are a few key points from this study. The generalization gap can be significantly decreased by suitably adjusting the learning rate and batch normalization. It is identified that the generalization gap is primarily due to an insufficient number of training updates, not the batch size itself. Additionally, it is observed that training with large batches can achieve comparable or even better generalization performance than smaller batches, provided a sufficient number of training iterations are performed

Gradient Behaviour - It refers to how the gradient of a cost or loss function changes during the training of a model. This hyperparameter is crucial for optimization algorithms like gradient descent to effectively minimize errors and find the optimal model parameter. Gradient descent is an optimization algorithm used to train ML models by minimizing errors between predicted and actual results. In DL, gradient descent is important for training neural networks, where it is used in conjunction with backpropagation to update the weights and biases of each layer. A study conducted by (Yang et al., 2024), demonstrates that gradient regularization and adaptive optimization are incompatible when applied simultaneously, resulting in performance degeneration issue. This incompatibility is caused because of excessive gradient regularization at the initial stages of training. Further, they proposed the three gradient regularization warmup strategies known as r-warmup, λ-warmup, zero-warmup, which successfully avoid the issue and give better performance.

Learning Rate – A model with an excessively low learning rate may converge very slowly or get stuck in local minima; however, slow convergence itself does not inherently cause overfitting, which is more directly related to model capacity and training dynamics. On the other hand, a model with high learning rate can result unstable updates this results poor generalization and overfitting. The following regularization techniques commonly employed to reduce overfitting include Learning Rate Scheduling, Adaptive Learning Rate, and Early Stopping.

b) **Model Capacity** –The parameters like number of layers, and number of neurons per layer refer to model capacity. In general, the number of layers and neurons per layers are very high then the model is known as large models, tend to overfit. A model with multiple parameters like too many layers or units per layer may result in overfitting, especially when the training data is limited. In such cases, regularization techniques such as weight decay, dropout, early stopping, and pruning are applied to reduce the overfitting.

5.1.3 Model Architecture and Structure

a) **Latent Variables** - These variables are not directly measured, however, can be inferred indirectly from other observable variables. Moreover, these variables called as hidden variables because they are not visible directly. Additionally, these variables lead to overfitting as the number of latent variables increases which means increasing the size of the latent space and this can lead to overfitting. Therefore, as the latent space is too high then the model memorizes the data instead of learning a general representation. Latest is most common in models like VAEs or GANs. The most common regularization techniques to reduce overfitting for hidden variable cases include KL Divergence, Beta-VAE and Variational Dropout.
b) **Activation Function** - An activation function is a mathematical function that decides whether a neuron should be activated or not. The importance of activation function in model tuning is because it introduces non-linearity, decide neuron activation, enables complex learning. The common examples of activation functions are sigmoid, ReLU, leaky ReLU, tanh, softmax, and exponential linear unit to mention a few.
c) **Network Architecture** - It indicates the structure and organization of a neural network, which includes the arrangement of layers, nodes (or neurons), and connections between them, which determine how data flows and is processed to make predictions.

5.1.4 Regularization and Optimization

Dropout Rate – The dropout rate is a hyperparameter and should be tuned. Dropout is a technique to temporarily remove random neural units along with their connections from the primary network during the training. Each unit may be removed with a probability q, called the dropout rate. Dropout, in essence, is training multiple smaller networks selected randomly from the bigger primary neural network by removing some neural units in each training step. Since these smaller networks share the primary neural network's weights, the averaging at test time is as simple as using the primary network without any dropout.

Loss Function Penalties - These are additional components that are added to the loss function in order to penalize certain characteristics like overfitting and complexity of the model. These components are known as regularization terms, whose goal is to improve the model's generalization.

Noise Levels - In ML, noise refers to random fluctuations in the data that do not reflect the underlying pattern whereas noise levels indicate the amount of noise present in a dataset. Noise level can significantly impact the performance of a model. The various types of noise in ML are random, label, feature and stochastic noise. Noise mainly affects model performance in terms of overfitting, reduced generalization and increased error in prediction.

5.1.5 Training Process

a) **Early Stopping** – It is a form of regularization technique that is used to prevent overfitting in ML and DL learning models. Please refer Section 3.2 (a) for more details.
b) **Momentum** – In neural networks, momentum refers a parameter optimization technique, which accelerates gradient descent by adding a fraction of the previous update to the current update. Gradient descent is a most popularly used optimization algorithm for training neural networks. It works by iteratively updating the model parameters in the direction that minimizes the loss function. However, gradient descent can suffer from slow convergence, especially in regions of the parameter space with high curvature. The following are the a few benefits of Momentum such as improved generalization, accelerated convergence, and smoother optimization.
c) **Training Procedure** - The training procedure can significantly affect overfitting. Instability during training, where the model fluctuates significantly in its loss or predictions, can lead to overfitting. The following techniques are commonly used that include Early Stopping, Dropout, Noise Injection, and Adversarial Training.
d) **Weight Initialization –** In neural networks, weights are parameters that are adjusted during training to minimize the difference between the predicted and actual outputs. The process of setting these weights correctly at the beginning is called weight initialization. Further, this process plays an important role in speeding up training and also ensuring the model learns effectively. The improper initialization results issues like the vanishing gradient and exploding gradient problems. The former problem appears when the weights are very small, the gradients become tiny that prevents the network from learning effectively whereas the later problem appears when weights are too large, then gradients can grow too fast, which makes the model unstable. In order to address these two issues, a technique Xavier initialization was evolved that uses different approaches depending on the type of activation function like tanh or sigmoid.

e) **Performance Parameters** – The following are a few performance parameters that are used in the model regularization and optimization such as Training Error, Validation/Test Error, Generalization Gap, Accuracy, Overfitting Ratio, Robustness to Noise, Adversarial Robustness.

f) **Output Distribution** - In general, model output can be a single value, a probability distribution, a class label, or a series of continuous or discrete values. Further, the output distribution of the model can be used to evaluate the performance. The output distribution is one of the important parameters that can be regulated by various techniques.

   i. **Regularization on Output Distribution** - In models such as VAEs, the output distribution is regularized to match a prior distribution (usually a standard normal distribution). If the output distribution does not adequately match the prior then the model might overfit the training data. The most common regularization techniques used for minimisation of overfitting include KL Divergence, Beta-VAE, Adversarial Training.

   ii. **Prediction Consistency**: In models like GANs and VANs, regularization ensures that their predictions are smooth across inputs. It means regularizing the outputs is not only help to avoid overfitting but also works well to small data variations. In this case the most commonly used regularization techniques are Cycle Consistency Loss, Perceptual Loss, and Wasserstein Loss with Gradient Penalty.

g) **Generator and Discriminator** – There are few parameters belong to generator and discriminator capacity, generator loss function, and strong discriminator.

   i. **Generator and Discriminator Capacity** – Both generator and discriminator play crucial roles in GANs. The generator produces data, whereas discriminator provides feedback through which guiding the generator to improve. Thus, there is a balance between generator and discriminator is required in GANs, which are critical in today's research compared to other methods because it directly impacts the quality and stability of the GAN's training process. A delicate balance is needed for the generator to learn to produce realistic data that fools the discriminator, while the discriminator learns to accurately distinguish between real and fake data (Sajeeda and Hossain, 2022). For example, if the discriminator becomes too powerful relative to the generator, it may lead the generator to overfit to the discriminator's feedback. Similarly, if the generator is too strong, it can memorize the training distribution. Therefore, a perfect balance between generator and discriminator ensures creation of high quality and realistic. The most popular regularization methods in this scenario are Wasserstein Loss with Gradient Penalty, Feature Matching Loss, and Gradient Penalty.

ii. **Strong Discriminator** – When the data provided to the discriminator becomes too strong, meaning the model perfectly distinguishes between real and fake data, the generator might overfit the training data. Therefore, the output will be as similar to the real data. In this scenarios, the most commonly used regularization Techniques are Wasserstein Loss with Gradient Penalty, Feature Matching, and Label Smoothing.

iii. **Generator Loss Function** – Overfitting can also occur if the generator's loss function is too focused on fitting to the training data rather than generalizing well. The loss function should enforce generalization and prevent memorization. Regularization Techniques: Adversarial Loss (in GANs), Feature Matching Loss, Wasserstein Loss, Perceptual Loss.

The following table 4 summarizes various key parameters of model and corresponding regularization techniques to be employed for reduction of overfitting in generative models.

Table 4. Model parameters and corresponding regularization techniques

S.No.	Model Parameter	Regularization Techniques
1.	Weights	L1 Regularization, L2 Regularization, Elastic Net, Pruning, Weight Decay
2.	Learning Rate	Learning Rate Decay, Adaptive Learning Rate
3.	Network Architecture	Knowledge Distillation, Model Size, Pruning, Reducing Weight Sharing
4.	Dropout Rate	Dropout
5.	Activation Functions	Leaky ReLU, ReLU
6.	Batch Size	Batch Normalization, Smaller Mini-batch Sizes
7.	Model Capacity	Pruning, Reducing Number of Parameters, Weight Clipping
8.	Loss Function Penalties	L1 Regularization, L2 Regularization, Elastic Net, KL Divergence, VGG Loss
9.	Noise Levels	Noise Injection, Dropout, Stochastic Gradient Descent
10.	Feature Selection	Feature Selection, L1 Regularization, L2 Regularization
11.	Training Procedure	Early Stopping, Early Learning Rate Scheduling, Noise Injection
12.	Latent Variables	KL Divergence in VAEs Variational Dropout
13.	Gradient Behaviour	Gradient Penalty, Spectral Normalization
14.	Output Predictions	Cycle Consistency Loss, Label Smoothing, Perceptual Loss

5.2 Key Performance Metrics

The performance of regulated and non-regulated models is most commonly measured by using the following metrics: Mean Squared Error (MSE), Root Mean Squared Error (RMSE), R-Squared (R^2), Mean Absolute Error (MAE), Cross Validation Error (CV Error). Table 5 provides a comprehensive overview of key model evaluation metrics, including MSE, RMSE, R-Squared, MAE, and Cross Validation error. It outlines the formulas, corresponding values, typical ranges, remarks on their significance, and common use cases in model performance assessment.

Table 5. Summary of common evaluation metrics with their values, interpretations, and applications in model performance assessment.

S.No.	Name of the metric	Formula	Good Value	Typical Value	Remarks	Operational Use
1.	Mean Squared Error (MSE)		Low	0.5 –1 for good models.	Lower is better	Forecasting and cost prediction
2.	Root Mean Squared Error (RMSE)		Low	0.7-1.5 The value is scaled or normalized	Lower is better	
3.	R-Squared (R^2)		High	0.7 - 1	Higher is better	Delivery time, budget adherence
4.	Mean Absolute Error (MAE)		Low	0.5 - 2.0	Lower is better	Revenue prediction, strategy modelling
5.	Cross Validation Error (CV Error)		Low	< 1	Lower is better	Riks assessment and scalability

Regularized models are more generally effective than non-regularized models, as demonstrated by evidenced by multiple studies. The metrics presented in the above table can guide managers in trusting the model's output. Further, the table provides a set of typical values for each of these metrics, which can help non-technical managers and practitioners make informed choices that reduce risk and cost-effectiveness for deploying models.

5.3 A Comparison of Various Regularization Techniques

A comparison of popular regularization techniques that are commonly used in ML and DL presented below in terms of its key features, advantages, and disadvantages.

a) **L2 Regularization (Ridge):** The key feature of L2 Regularization technique is that it adds a penalty proportional to the square of the weights. The main advantage of L2 regularization is simple, effective and works well for high-dimensional data, which includes preventing overfitting by penalizing large weights, improving model generalization to unseen data, stabilizing training by reducing variance in the model, and promoting simpler models with smaller coefficients.

b) **L1 Regularization (Lasso) -** The key features of L1 regularization are it adds a penalty proportional to the absolute values of the weights. The advantages of L1 regularization are as follows. It can perform feature selection (weights are driven to exactly zero) and often works well when only a few features are relevant. The disadvantage of L1 regularization is that it is sensitive to the scale of features and can lead to biased estimates when the true data model is not sparse.

c) **ElasticNet -** The very key feature of this technique is that it combines both L1 and L2 regularization. The main advantages of this technique are to balances feature selection (L1) and weight shrinkage (L2), and is highly useful in high-dimensional datasets. The disadvantage of this technique is that it is more complex to tune and to select the right balance between L1 and L2 penalties.

d) **Dropout -** The key feature of this technique is that it randomly drops - that is, sets to zero - a proportion of neuron activations during training. The main advantages of this regularization technique are to prevent overfitting by forcing the model to learn redundant representations and widely used and effective in deep neural networks. The disadvantages of dropout regularization as follows. It can slow down training due to reduced capacity and it can be problematic if applied excessively, reducing the model's representational power.

e) **Early Stopping -** The key feature of this technique is that stops training once performance on a validation set stops improving. The advantages of this regularization technique are simple and effective for preventing overfitting and no additional hyperparameters apart from training epochs. The disadvantages of early stopping are that it might stop training too early, preventing the model from fully converging and sensitive to the validation set.

f) **Batch Normalization -** The key feature of this technique is that it normalizes activations within a mini-batch to have zero mean and unit variance. The main advantages of this regularization technique are it helps with training speed and stability. Further, it can act as a form of regularization by smoothing the optimization landscape. The disadvantages of this regularization are it introduces computational overhead and potentially reduces the model's ability to generalize in few cases like a) small batch sizes, where the estimates of the mean and variance become noisy, leading to poor generalization, b) in time series or sequence data, which are not independent and identically distributed, batch normalization may introduce unwanted dependencies resulting in poor generalization and c) inconsistent training and testing distributions differ significantly may cause mismatches between training and inference that affects model generalization.

g) **Weight Decay -** The key feature of this technique is that it penalizes the size of weights, which are often equivalent to L2 regularization. The advantages of this technique are simple to implement and commonly used in optimization tasks. The disadvantage of this technique is that it can still suffer from overfitting if not tuned properly.

h) **Data Augmentation -** The key feature of this technique is to increase the size of the training set by creating variations of training data for flipping images, and rotating. Additionally, it reduces overfitting by creating a more diverse training set. The main advantages of this technique are effective in domains with rich, structured data for image classification. The disadvantages of this technique are it requires extra computational resources. Further, it may not work well for tasks where data augmentation is hard for tabular data.

i) **Drop Connect -** The key feature of this technique is similar to dropout but instead of dropping activations, it drops weights between layers. The technique provides a more robust regularization effect by modifying the model architecture during training, which is its advantage. The main disadvantage of this technique is more computationally expensive than dropout. Further, drop connect technique is difficult to implement in some architectures like RNN and LSTM.

j) **Adversarial Regularization -** The key features of this techniques are it adds noise to inputs or outputs during training, encouraging the model to be robust to adversarial attacks. The advantages are that it improves generalization by making models more resilient to small input perturbations and build robust models. The disadvantages of this technique are it is computationally expensive and it might negatively affect model performance on clean data.

k) **Information Bottleneck -** The key feature is that it limits the mutual information between the input and the learned representations. The advantages of this technique are because it enforces compact representations and leading to better generalization. Further, it helps to focus learning on the most relevant aspects of the input. The disadvantages of this technique include hard to implement and tune effectively and may lead to loss of useful information in some cases like excessive regularization, and inadequate model capacity, which means when the model is too simple then it may not have enough capacity to retain essential information after regularization.

l) **Mixup -** The key features of this techniques is that it combines training examples (input, output pairs) in a weighted sum to create new training samples. The advantages like reduces overfitting by smoothing the decision boundary and this technique particularly useful in image classification tasks. The disadvantage of this technique is that it introduces noise into the data, which may hurt performance if not balanced.

5.4 Prevent Overfitting in Different Modalities

The main purpose of generative models is to create content. The most common datatypes available to train models like text, image, audio, video, time series data, graph data, 3D data. Based on type of data generated, models can be classified into two categories such as unimodal and multi-model. The former category of models works with a single data type whereas multimodal handle multiple data types simultaneously. Multi-modal generative models can understand and generate outputs across multiple types of data or modes, such as text, images, audio, and video. In the below paragraph, presents various techniques, how to prevent overfitting in models like text, image and multi models.

a) **Text –** In generative models of text data type, regularization techniques like dropout, weight decay, data augmentation like paraphrasing for text, and pretrained embeddings are commonly used to reduce overfitting. In data augmentation techniques task like paraphrasing, and back-translation are commonly used for translating text to another language and vice versa. Similarly, word substitution task can increase the variety of text inputs. In RNN and Transformer models, dropout is commonly used to prevent overfitting for text generation. Label Smoothing technique is often used in GANs and transformers that helps to avoid overly confident predictions. In pretrained models like Generative Pretrained Transformer (GPT), and BERT can leverage transfer learning to reduce overfitting.
b) **Image –** In generative models based on image data type, regularization techniques like batch normalization, dropout, data augmentation, and adversarial training are commonly used. In data augmentation, some of the common techniques used in image processing transformations like rotation, flipping, cropping, and scaling to artificially increase the size and diversity of the training dataset to improve the robustness and generalization ability of a model. Further, by applying these transformation techniques the model becomes more robust to variations in input data, which leads to better performance on unseen data. The dropout technique is applied in the generator and discriminator of GANs as well as in the encoder–decoder architecture of VAEs. Batch normalization technique is most commonly used in deep CNN architectures. An improved version of WGAN is WGAN-GP. In WGAN-GI (Sharma et al., 2024), adding a gradient penalty to the discriminator stabilizes training and prevents over-

fitting. In order to improve robustness of the model, noise is injected into the inputs or intermediate activations. In few cases, when the input data provided to the model is slightly modified then it fools the model in making an incorrect prediction. This phenomenon is called adversarial attack. So, the model is then trained on both the original data and the adversarial examples. This helps the model learn to correctly and classify both "normal" and adversarial inputs. The use of adversarial training techniques not only improves the model robustness but also protects against adversarial attacks.

c) **Multi-modal** - Multi-modal input data include multiple input data types, such as images and their corresponding text descriptions and audio and video or any other combination of other data types. In multi-model, the most commonly used regularization techniques include adversarial training, dropout, data augmentation, early stopping, batch normalization, spectral normalization and L2. Apart from these regularization techniques, other techniques such as contrastive loss, attention mechanisms, and knowledge distillation are used to enhance model performance by improving multi-modal alignment, focusing on important input features, transferring knowledge for efficient model deployment. Contrastive loss is a loss function used in multi-modal such as image-text retrieval that helps to align and relate different data types. Additionally, cross-modal regularization technique used to get consistency between different modalities like using contrastive learning or joint embedding spaces. Similarly, shared latent space representation used for text and images data types allowing the model to learn joint representations and avoid overfitting to one modality. Attention Mechanisms mainly help the model focus on relevant parts of both image and text data, thus improving generalization.

6. CONCLUSION

This chapter focuses on various regularization techniques in generative models. The document defined what regularization is, its various types, and why regularization is important in reducing overfitting. Besides, explained what an AI model is, its importance, and its major uses. Further, explained in detail various types of AI models. In addition, presented a comparison between generative and discriminative models. Further, presented the goals of regularization. In addition, explained in detail various types of regularization techniques in generative models. Moreover, listed various key parameters that affect overfitting and generalization in generative models. A comparison of various regularization techniques is presented and briefly explained various regularization techniques in multiple modalities to prevent overfitting. It is to conclude that there is no single "best" regularization technique available universally. The effectiveness of a regularization method depends on the type of problem, the dataset, the model, and key parameters of the model and the specific task the model performs. In summary, regularization is used to prevent overfitting by introducing constraints or penalties or other methods that encourage the model to generalize better to unseen data.

REFERENCES

Bommasani, R., Klyman, K., Longpre, S., Kapoor, S., Maslej, N., Xiong, B., ... & Liang, P. (2025). The 2023 Foundation Model Transparency Index. Transactions on Machine Learning Research.

Cosmos, N. V. I. D. I. A. (n.d.). *What is NVIDIA Cosmos?*https://www.nvidia.com/en-in/ai/cosmos/

Hoffer, E., Hubara, I., & Soudry, D. (2017). *Train longer, generalize better: closing the generalization gap in large batch training of neural networks. Conference on Neural Information Processing Systems*, DOI: 10.48550/arXiv.1705.08741

Hu, H., Salcic, Z., Dobbie, G., Chen, Y., & Zhang, X. (2021, July). EAR: An enhanced adversarial regularization approach against membership inference attacks. In *2021 International Joint Conference on Neural Networks (IJCNN)* (pp. 1-8). IEEE.

IBM. (2021). *What is strong AI?* Retrieved 5 Feb 2025 from https://www.ibm.com/think/topics/strong-ai

Kolluri, J., Kotte, V. K., Phridviraj, M. S. B., & Razia, S. (2020, June). Reducing overfitting problem in machine learning using novel L1/4 regularization method. In 2020 4th international conference on trends in electronics and informatics (ICOEI) (48184) (pp. 934-938). IEEE.

Kukačka, J., Golkov, V., & Cremers, D. (2017, October). Regularization for Deep Learning. *Taxon*.

Meritt, R. (2025). *NVIDIA. What Are Foundation Models?*https://blogs.nvidia.com/blog/what-are-foundation-models/

Nusrat, I., & Jang, S.-B. (2018). A Comparison of Regularization Techniques in Deep Neural Networks. *Symmetry*, *2018*(10), 648. www.mdpi.com/journal/symmetry. DOI: 10.3390/sym10110648

Obando Ceron, J., Bellemare, M., & Castro, P. S. (2023). Small batch deep reinforcement learning. *Advances in Neural Information Processing Systems*, *36*, 26003–26024.

Rezaeezade, A., & Batina, L. (2024). Regularizers to the rescue: Fighting overfitting in deep learning-based side-channel analysis. *Journal of Cryptographic Engineering*, *14*(4), 609–629. DOI: 10.1007/s13389-024-00361-5

Sajeeda, A., & Hossain, B. M. (2022). Exploring generative adversarial networks and adversarial training. *International Journal of Cognitive Computing in Engineering*, *3*, 78–89.

Salehin, I., & Kang, D. K. (2023). A Review on Dropout Regularization Approaches for Deep Neural Networks within the Scholarly Domain. *Electronics (Basel), 2023*(12), 3106. DOI: 10.3390/electronics12143106

Sharma, P., Kumar, M., Sharma, H. K., & Biju, S. M. (2024). Generative adversarial networks (GANs): Introduction, Taxonomy, Variants, Limitations, and Applications. *Multimedia Tools and Applications, 83*(41), 88811–88858. DOI: 10.1007/s11042-024-18767-y

Statista Market Insights on Technology. (n.a.) *Artificial Intelligence: Worldwide.* https://www.statista.com/outlook/tmo/artificial-intelligence/worldwide

Tu, X., He, Z., Huang, Y., Zhang, Z.-H., Yang, M., & Zhao, J. (2024). An overview of large AI models and their applications. *Vis. Intell., 2*(1), 34. DOI: 10.1007/s44267-024-00065-8

Xu, Z., Zhang, H., Wang, Y., Chang, X. Y., & Liang, Y. (2010). L1/2 regularization. *Science China. Information Sciences, 53*(6), 1159–1169. DOI: 10.1007/s11432-010-0090-0

Zhao, Y., Zhang, H., & Hu, X. (2024). *When Will Gradient Regularization Be Harmful?* ICML 2024, https://doi.org//arXiv.2406.09723DOI: 10.48550

Chapter 4
The Revolution of Generative AI

Semra Erpolat Taşabat
https://orcid.org/0000-0001-6845-8278
Mimar Sinan Fine Art University, Turkey

ABSTRACT

Generative Artificial Intelligence (Generative AI) refers to Artificial Intelligence (AI) systems that can learn from data and produce new and original content. These systems, which work with advanced AI techniques, learn from data produced by humans and can create human-like and creative new texts, images, music, or other digital content using the patterns they learn. Generative AI systems go beyond being just a technical development and stand out as an important tool that creates interaction between different fields and encourages multidisciplinary studies. It is aimed at accelerating business processes or offering innovative solutions in many sectors. However, some ethical issues also arise with the development of Generative AI technologies. Undoubtedly, the creative opportunities offered by Generative AI indicate that these technologies will be used in many more areas in the future. The study will focus on historical development, models and technologies, application areas, advantages and disadvantages, and the future potential of Generative AI.

1. INTRODUCTION

In recent years, Artificial Intelligence (AI) has developed so that it not only analyzes or performs a series of tasks. Perhaps most thrilling of all is the emergence of Generative AI—technology that can actually create things like text, images, music, and even video that is virtually indistinguishable from human-generated content. What's intriguing about this industry is not only how fast it's developing, but also

DOI: 10.4018/979-8-3373-0735-0.ch004

the way in which it's fusing together so many disparate disciplines in innovative and new forms (Goodfellow, Bengio, & Courville, 2016).

In healthcare, to refer to one arena, Generative AI is used to assist with disease diagnosis, to model clinical situations, and even in drug discovery. Synthetic biological data may be created by researchers based on medical images that can significantly accelerate R&D pipelines (Esteva et al., 2017). The creative world is also changing. Creatives now have technology that assists them in creating new visual languages, writing music, or constructing digital experiences. Rather than replacing creativity, this technology appears to be a new kind of collaborator that inspires new thinking (Elgammal et al., 2017).

In learning, Generative AI provides the answer to individualized learning. It is capable of modifying teaching content depending on a pupil's level of ability, interests, or study approach. This renders the content more pertinent and interesting and enables the pupil to remain interested and learn better (Chen et al., 2020).

Its influence does not end there. In areas ranging from engineering and robotics to environmental conservation and policy, Generative AI enables computers to perceive the world more profoundly and engage in more naturalistic ways with human beings. All such developments are generating projects that combine technology, design, and social science (Bogue, 2018).

Most impressive is the manner in which this technology enables collaboration across disciplines to be a breeze. It's not an advance in technology alone—becoming a binding force, marrying innovative solutions and ideas that wouldn't have otherwise been possible.

2. HISTORICAL DEVELOPMENT OF GENERATIVE AI

The historical development of Generative AI, which enables machines to produce new and original content from data, has progressed in parallel with the advancement of computer science and AI research, and especially in recent years, technologies in this field have gained great momentum. Figure 1 (Wikizer, 01.04.2025) shows the evolution of Generative AI and then outlines the developments.

Figure 1. AI history timeline covering the most important events since 1900 to 2025

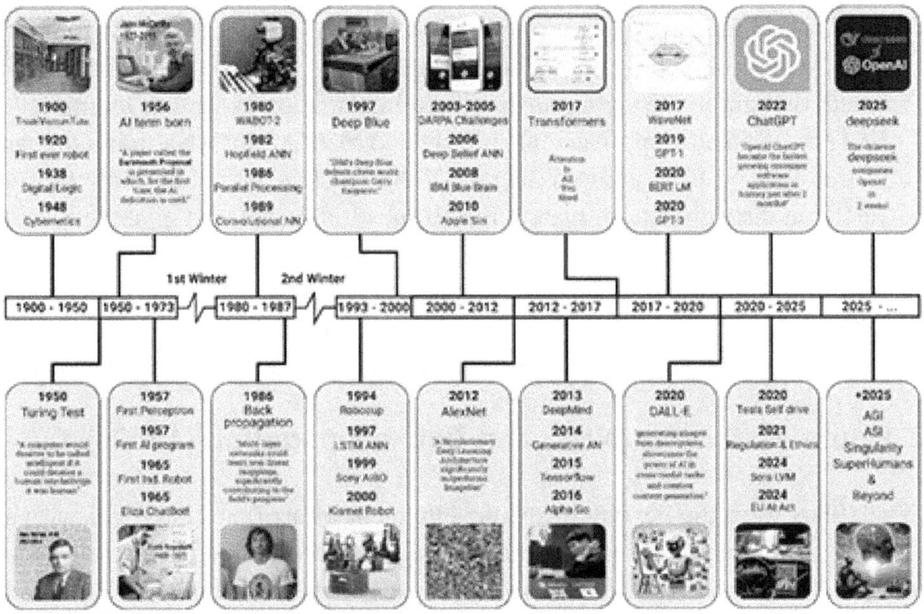

2.1. Early Foundations (1950s–1970s)

The period between the 1950s and the 1970s was a developmental decade of AI history, with the development of the foundation for the coming technological progress. It was also the time when there was the development of the core theories and initial AI systems that provided a blueprint for the future development into Machine Learning (ML), cognitive science, and automation.

- **AlanTuring (1950):** AI was started by Alan Turing, whose Computing Machinery and Intelligence in 1950 asked if machines can or cannot think. Turing proposed the Turing Test as a method for testing how intelligently a machine can simulate conversation with a human. Turing's revolutionary ideas formed the backdrop of what came later in AI, establishing philosophical and technical guidelines for the field (Turing, 1950).
- **Symbolic AI (1950s–1970s):** Symbolic or rule-based AI systems, or as they are also known as, Good Old-Fashioned AI (GOFAI), were the mainstream method in the earlier days of AI. These systems functioned based on well-defined predefined rules to mimic human thought. A few of the initial in-

stances are John McCarthy's LISP computer language in 1958, designed to assist in creating AI, and Newell and Simon's General Problem Solver in 1957, a problem-solving program designed to solve a wide variety of human problems by mimicking human reasoning processes. These symbolic systems failed, though, in managing unstructured information as well as learning.

- **ELIZA (1966):** Joseph Weizenbaum created ELIZA, a first Natural Language Processing (NLP) system, in the mid-1960s. ELIZA was able to mimic conversation through pattern matching and substitution rules to give the illusion of understanding. ELIZA was originally a chatbot, and its most well-known script, DOCTOR, mimicked a Rogerian psychotherapist (Weizenbaum, 1966). This initial chatbot illustrated what could be achieved with AI and conversational interfaces but failed to have any real sense of the conversation.

2.2. Neural Networks (NNs) and Backpropagation (1980s)

The 1980s were the heyday of the development of artificial intelligence, with the onset of neural networks (NNs) and the finding of the seminal backpropagation algorithm. The latter enabled machines to start learning from complex data, setting the stage for contemporary Deep Learning (DL) methods that would transform the discipline.

- **NNs (1980s):** During the 1980s, AI research was the era of introduction of NNs, attempting to emulate the organizational structure and style of the human brain. NNs are sets of connected nodes (neurons) with the capability to learn from input so that more adaptive and robust AI models can be achieved. Even though early networks were constrained because of computational abilities and data availability, they provided a foundation for future breakthroughs in DL (Hinton, 1986).
- **Backpropagation Algorithm (1986):** The backpropagation algorithm found in 1986 changed the life of NNs. This algorithm allowed networks to change their weight by computing the error and propagating it backwards through the network. Geoffrey Hinton and his colleagues were among the people who made this method common, and it was one of the bases for many DL models in the following decades (Rumelhart, Hinton, & Williams, 1986).

2.3. Statistical Models and Early Generative Models (1990s–2000s)

The 2000s and the 1990s saw revolutionary growth in building statistical models as well as in early generative models. It saw more elaborate data modeling processes and set grounds for further work on ML and AI algorithm advancements that would generate real data and perform a variety of hard tasks across a variety of areas.

- **Hidden Markov Models (HMMs):** Hidden Markov Models (HMMs) appeared in AI research during the 1990s, primarily for speech recognition and time-series processing. HMMs facilitated sequential data handling and brought probabilistic methods into modeling uncertainty. HMMs played a pivotal role in allowing more sophisticated NLP systems and automatic speech recognition (Rabiner, 1989).
- **Probabilistic Graphical Models (1990s–2000s):** Alongside HMMs, probabilistic graphical models such as Bayesian networks appeared. Probabilistic graphical models embodied complex variable relationships and supported reasoning under uncertainty, a significant change from symbolic systems to probabilistic AI paradigms. Judea Pearl's causal inference work also came to the forefront during this period (Pearl, 1988).
- **Variational Autoencoders (VAEs, 2013):** In the year 2013, VAEs came as a novel generative model approach. VAEs provide means of data generation through the learning of tight representations for data and hence steer AI towards possibilities of image production, for instance (Kingma & Welling, 2013).

2.4. The Rise of DL (2010s)

The 2010s also saw the unbridled growth of DL, one of ML's schools that achieved phenomenal progress in domains like computer vision, NLP, and speech recognition. With vast databases, quick GPUs, and enhanced algorithms, DL became a technology to be noticed in AI research and application, transforming business and scholarly inquiry as well.

- **Deep Neural Networks (DNNs) (2010s):** The establishment of DL models in the early 2010s dramatically transformed AI. Convolutional Neural Networks (CNNs) and Recurrent Neural Networks (RNNs) became remarkably good at doing intricate tasks such as image and speech recognition, as well as natural language understanding. AlexNet, a deep neural network model, won the

ImageNet challenge of 2012, indicating a milestone achievement of AI with large-scale data images (Krizhevsky, Sutskever, & Hinton, 2012).

- **Generative Adversarial Networks (GANs, 2014):** Ian Goodfellow revolutionized the generative model in 2014 with GANs. GANs are made up of two rival networks—the discriminator and the generator—who generate real-sounding data based on one another's output. It has been made possible to create extremely realistic images, videos, and other content since this innovation was introduced (Goodfellow et al., 2014).
- **DeepDream (2015):** Google's DeepDream initiative, launched in 2015, used DNNs to generate dreamlike, surreal images by enhancing particular patterns in images. The experiment demonstrated the artistic capabilities of AI and was one of the first applications of AI in art-oriented domains (Mordvintsev, Olah, & Tyka, 2015).

2.5. Transformers and Large Language Models (Late 2010s–2020s)

The 2020s and the latter half of the 2010s were the time of revolution in NLP with the arrival of transformers and the construction of large language models. These breakthroughs posted record advances on a variety of tasks from text generation to machine translation, and opened the way for a new generation of AI models that generate and understand human language with high fidelity.

- **Transformer Architecture (2017):** Vaswani et al. first came up with transformer architecture in 2017 that transformed NLP. Parallel data processing and better training were enabled by transformer, thus it was much quicker than earlier models like RNNs. Transformer performed even better on the task of machine translation and text generation (Vaswani et al., 2017).
- **GPT Series (2018–2023):** OpenAI's GPT models (Generative Pretrained Transformers) represent one of the most significant advancements in AI language processing. GPT-3, released in 2020, with 175 billion parameters, demonstrated a remarkable ability to generate human-like text. This marked a turning point in the ability of AI systems to produce coherent, contextually relevant text across various domains (Brown et al., 2020).
- **BERT and T5 (2018–2020):** Google's BERT (Bidirectional Encoder Representations from Transformers) and T5 (Text-to-Text Transfer Transformer) took NLP to extremes. Bidirectional encoding in BERT made better word understanding with context possible, and T5's general text-to-text model was easily able to do a few languages (Devlin et al., 2019; Raffel et al., 2020).

2.6. Multimodal Models and Advances (2020s)

The 2020s have seen tremendous progress in multimodal models, which bring together multiple forms of data, e.g., text, images, and sound, to build more generalizable and efficacious AI systems. This progress has greatly pushed the boundaries of what AI can do, opening more artistic, interactive, and dynamic applications that blur the lines between various sensory modalities.

- **DALL·E and CLIP (2021):** OpenAI presented DALL·E in 2021, an AI model capable of generating images from a text description. CLIP (Contrastive Language-Image Pre-training) was another model that filled the vision-language gap, translating images into an understandability framework as natural language meaning. The multimodal models brought new paths to Generative AI, translating images and text to be producible with one input alone (Ramesh et al., 2021).
- **ChatGPT (2022):** ChatGPT, a GPT-3 offering, was in great demand for writing conversational content and answering many questions in context-specific, meaningful terms. Its huge application in customer support, education, and entertainment was a sign of the growing role of AI in everyday life (OpenAI, 2022).
- **Stable Diffusion and MidJourney (2022–2023):** Stable Diffusion and MidJourney models enabled the creation of high-quality images from text input, gaining significant attention for their realism of visual design and imagination. They represented AI's ability to revolutionize the art and design career (Stability AI, 2022).

2.7. Ethical and Societal Implications (2020s)

As AI technology continues to evolve, it has raised significant ethical and societal questions:

- **Deepfakes and Misinformation:** The possibility to generate hyper-realistic media like deepfakes has raised alarm over the potential use of deepfakes in spreading misinformation, manipulation, and defamation (Chesney & Citron, 2019). Policy models are starting to address these risks, but experts consider that full solutions will involve a coordination of technological, legal, and societal interventions.
- **Fairness and Bias:** AI systems, especially those relying on past data, may reinforce or exaggerate existing biases and produce unfair results in such domains as hiring, criminal justice, and healthcare (O'Neil, 2016). AI systems

are susceptible to biases that arise from biased training sets. Such biases may cause unfair results, particularly in high-stakes domains such as criminal justice, hiring, and lending. Angwin et al. (2016) brought forward the issue of racially discriminatory predictive algorithms employed in the justice system, and this made people demand more transparent and equitable AI systems. The issue today is how to identify and counteract biases in AI models so that they make equitable decisions.

- **Intellectual Property:** Since generative models are now creating art, music, and written content, intellectual property rights issues, authorship, and questions of ownership become matters of active concern (Elgammal et al., 2017).
- **Transparency and Accountability:** Lack of transparency in AI decision-making is another serious ethical issue. Lipton (2016) stressed the significance of "explainable AI" (XAI), which helps make AI systems explainable and understandable, with an attempt to explain the decisions of AI to human beings. Transparency is significant so that the users will trust the AI systems, particularly for applications that directly impact human life.

2.8. The Future (2025 and Beyond)

As we look out to the horizon, we see that AI is going to change. The forthcoming years will see tremendous advances across a myriad of domains with special focus on creating multimodal AI systems, new regulatory environments, and an increasingly sophisticated ethical context. The alignment of these themes will bring novel forms of human-AI interaction, but also challenge fundamental questions regarding governance, privacy, and accountability.

2.8.1. The Emergence of Multimodal AI Systems

The future of AI will likely see the rise of **multimodal** systems that are able to process and integrate various forms of data simultaneously—such as text, images, video, and audio—thereby enhancing the AI's ability to understand and engage in more natural interactions with humans.

- **Transforming User Interactions**: The most significant aspect of multimodal systems is the way they facilitate more natural and seamless interactions with AI. Rather than depending on text-based inputs, users will communicate with AI systems through a mix of speech, visual inputs, and gestures. For instance, AI assistants may, aside from being capable of interpreting what a user is saying, comprehend their intention by observing their face or detecting objects around them (Bertinetto et al., 2021). This will make AI more natural and accessible, especially in fields such as customer service, where AI can respond to complicated questions in a more human-like manner.

- **Multimodal AI in Healthcare:** Multimodal systems would also be employed in healthcare, with a vital contribution towards diagnostic accuracy through the combination of medical images, patient interviews (audio), and clinical notes (text) to create an overall understanding of a patient's condition. The merging of these streams of data could result in more accurate diagnoses and targeted treatments (Reed & McKinney, 2020).
- **Revolutionizing Education and Entertainment**: AI can change learning so that learning becomes more exciting with the use of interactive learning content, speech recognition, and visual data to produce dynamic, customized learning settings. In entertainment, multimodal systems will increase the media experience through seamless transfer between various modes of content, such as VR environments that respond to the speakers' speech, motion, and visual input simultaneously (El-Nasr et al., 2021).

2.8.2. Evolving AI Regulation and Ethics

As more AI technologies settle into our everyday lives, the necessity for robust regulation and ethical principles will become increasingly pressing. The increased intelligence and independence of AI systems present serious questions that include privacy, accountability, and equity.

- **Developing Ethical Guidelines for AI:** The question of AI ethics is more pressing than ever. AI technologies should be designed in a way that respects human rights, fosters equality, and prevents discrimination. AI's growing ability to make decisions that affect people's lives—from healthcare choices to job recruitment—calls for robust ethical frameworks to ensure fairness. According to scholars such as Floridi et al. (2018), AI should be developed with fairness as an overriding concern, where such systems never reinforce biases either in training data or algorithms.
- **Legislation and International Regulation:** Governments and international bodies are working toward creating regulatory standards that can effectively govern AI's rapid growth. The European Union has been particularly active, with its AI Act aiming to regulate high-risk AI systems and applications in sensitive areas such as healthcare, transportation, and criminal justice (European Commission, 2021). There will be other such initiatives elsewhere in the world, with nations developing their own laws to regulate the issues brought up by AI. The laws will most probably develop provisions for transparency, accountability, and ethical AI system building.

- **Data Protection and Privacy:** Since AI systems often work with large data sets, especially personal data, data privacy will be a major factor. Governments are demanding GDPR-style regimes to safeguard people's privacy but also to foster innovation. The balance between the need for AI systems to access and process data and the safeguarding of individual privacy rights will be one of the pending issues in the next few years (Wright, 2022).
- **Liability and Accountability:** Who is to be held accountable when AI systems are responsible for harm or error is another core concern. Lawyers are creating novel frameworks of distributing liability for AI malfunction or autonomous behavior. Is it the developer, user, or AI system that should be held liable for harm resulting from it? These are questions that will have to be sorted out as AI advances toward more autonomy and integration within key infrastructure (Gogarty & O'Mara, 2020).

2.8.3. The Path to Artificial General Intelligence (AGI)

While the narrow AI has already started to disrupt industries, most people in the field of AI research want to find AGI someday—AI solutions that can do any intellectual task a human would do. We are far from it today, but tremendous progress is still being made in this direction.

- **ML Breakthroughs:** Researchers are making efforts to improve ML algorithms, particularly in the domains of transfer learning and reinforcement learning, which enable AI systems to learn more effectively and generalize across a broader set of tasks. With the capacity of AI to generalize between two tasks increasing, there might be more advanced AI systems with deep reasoning and problem-solving capabilities (Brynjolfsson & McAfee, 2014).
- **Human-AI Collaboration:** AI systems will likely become more collaborative prior to AGI being achieved. Rather than displacing human workers, AI will complement human labor to be more productive, innovative, and decision competent. Assisted intelligence will allow workers to tap into AI strengths like processing huge amounts of data or pattern recognition while still using human intuition for complex contextual choices.

3. AI JUSTICE AND BIAS REDUCTION STRATEGIES

Since there is greater use of AI across industries, becoming bias-free and minimizing bias are more significant goals. More and more, it is being realized that algorithms, especially large models, can become a cause of perpetuating biases in society since they are data-driven. These biases can be in various forms, e.g., racial, gender, or socio-economic disparities. There are ongoing efforts to create strategies that can minimize such biases and increase the fairness of AI decision-making. The main strategies are:

- **Bias Audits:** Routine auditing of AI models should be done in order to determine and remove bias so that the system offers equal results to all segments. Reviewing the model's performance on various demographics, researchers can detect and remove any data or algorithmic biases (Holstein et al., 2019).
- **Algorithms for Fairness:** New techniques such as fairness constraints and adversarial debiasing are being applied in ML models. These algorithms retrain the models to optimize fairness over accuracy, meaning sensitive characteristics such as race, gender, or age do not have a considerable impact disproportionately (Zemel et al., 2013).
- **Transparency and Accountability:** Legislatively requiring transparency in AI systems ensures that the users are assured that decisions are made in an understandable manner, which is the most significant consideration for eradication of biases. Greater pressure is also emerging for the producers and consumers of AI, particularly on high-risk areas such as criminal justice and labor, to be even more accountable (Binns, 2018).

These actions not only are of utmost significance to social justice but also to building public trust in AI systems that AI technologies could be made equitably accessible to all communities.

4. SUSTAINABILITY CHALLENGES IN TRAINING LARGE AI MODELS

It takes tremendous computational power and energy expenditure to construct huge AI models, especially DL models, with serious economic and ecological costs. Training larger and larger AI models lessens sustainability as they grow larger. The models demand humongous data centers, electricity-guzzling hardware, and lots of time, all amounting to more carbon footprints. Resolving this problem requires several important steps:

- **Energy-Efficient Algorithms:** Efforts are being made to make ML algorithms consume less power. Methods such as pruning (omitting redundant neurons), quantization (reducing precision while doing calculations), and knowledge distillation (Knowledge transfer from deep to shallow models) are under investigation to mitigate computation overhead (Han et al., 2015).

- **Sustainable Hardware:** Improvements in specialized hardware, like power-hungry-saving chips specifically created for AI applications, might be an excellent stride toward lowering the carbon footprint associated with training colossal models. NVIDIA and Google, among others, are working on hardware technology geared toward AI model training workload optimization performance (Jouppi et al., 2017).
- **Green Data Centers:** The data centers where AI models are trained are getting greener by embracing cleaner methods, such as renewable energy and green cooling technologies. For instance, some technology giants have pledged carbon-neutral data centers and are heading towards energy efficiency (Lau et al., 2020).

Despite these initiatives, the increasing need for more advanced models is putting a severe strain on the long-term AI R&D sustainability prospects.

5. REAL-WORLD CASE STUDIES: APPLICATIONS OF AI IN VARIOUS SECTORS

AI's transformative power is evident in various industries, from healthcare to journalism and creative arts. Real-world case studies demonstrate the profound impact AI is having in these fields.

- **Healthcare:** Healthcare is being revolutionized by AI with enhanced diagnostic power and optimal treatment. For example, AI-based apps such as Google's DeepMind have been used to detect diseases such as diabetic retinopathy and age-related macular degeneration, allowing early intervention that can be life-saving (Gulshan et al., 2016). Concerns regarding AI bias, especially in multicultural patient populations, remain an area to be tackled by healthcare professionals.
- **Journalism:** AI is revolutionizing the production, dissemination, and fact-checking of content in journalism. Applications like Automated Insights are some of the ones that produce fact-based stories, whereas AI-powered fact-checking websites like ClaimBuster assist journalists in fact-checking. Ethical concerns are present with the possibility of AI-generated content being used for abuse in the spread of disinformation or creation of false narratives (Carlson, 2020).

- **Creative Arts:** Applications of AI in creative arts are on the rise, with algorithms such as DALL·E and DeepArt creating new art pieces from text or image inputs. Such technologies are creating new opportunities for artists but pose essential intellectual property and ethics issues. To whom do rights over AI-created artworks accrue, and how does AI influence artistic authenticity and integrity? These issues are arising as main arguments among creative industries (Elgammal et al., 2017).

6. DEEPFAKE TECHNOLOGY

Deepfake technology uses AI and DL algorithms to create realistic fake media such as images, videos, and audio. Deepfake technology was initially created for entertainment and creative purposes but has caused a lot of concern because it can be used for malicious purposes. Deepfakes enable the swapping of a person's face or voice in order to impersonate individuals, leading to false information that can cause damage to someone's reputation, theft of their identity, and distribution of fake information.

6.1. Real-life Examples of Deepfakes

- **In politics, Deception and Disinformation:** In 2018, there was a deepfake video that surfaced on Facebook in the form of then-U.S. President Barack Obama reciting words he never spoke. The incident illustrated the threat that deepfakes pose to democracy because, with deepfakes, disinformation could disseminate very rapidly and could have an impact on political rhetoric (Chesney & Citron, 2019).
- **Exploitation of Celebrity Images:** Another more problematic application of deepfake technology includes the use to produce pornographic material with a celebrity's image without their agreement. In 2017, there was even a subreddit based on making deepfake pornography and it was unbelievably popular and raised questions around ethics related to privacy and consent on online platforms (Maras & Alexandrou, 2019).

6.2. Countermeasures and Solutions

- **Technology Detection Tools:** Deep trace and Microsoft and other companies created AI detection tools that are capable of detecting deep fakes. Detection tools check for anomalies such as unusual facial movements, voice edits, or other irregularities in trying to identify edited media (Kietzmann et al., 2020).

- **Legislative Measures:** To regulate the dangers of deep fakes, some countries have passed laws to restrict harmful use. In the United States, the Malicious Deep Fake Prohibition Act prohibits the use of deepfakes for political manipulation or pornography consumption without consent. The European Union has also started passing laws on digital content manipulation law to protect its citizens from such dangers (Binns et al., 2020).
- **Public Awareness and Education:** Technology used in deep-fakes needs to be brought to the forefront. Initiatives towards educating the masses on how to identify such content can mitigate its ill effects. The masses need to be educated on how to critically evaluate images and videos online, especially suspicious ones (Zhou et al., 2021).

7. COMPARATIVE ANALYSIS OF AI REGULATIONS

- **United States:** The United States has largely sectoral regulation of AI. Autonomous vehicles, for example, have regulations tailored to their environment but no uniform federal AI legislation yet. With an obsession with innovation and tech development, this has encouraged safety and ethics issues around AI. Without full regulation, risks are often overlooked, especially in high-stakes areas like medicine or the justice system (O'Neil, 2016).
- **European Union:** The European Union has been trending towards more controlling AI regulation. The 2021 AI Act proposal aims to categorize AI systems by risk levels and subject high-risk uses like biometric recognition to more regulation. The EU emphasis on the human rights, transparency, and accountability of AI systems sets the model for keeping technological innovation ethically connected to societal norms (Binns et al., 2020).
- **China:** China's regulatory approach to AI is state control-oriented. China's state seeks to create AI markets with the state controlling them to the maximum extent with minimum regard to private privacy or data protection. Though China has developed AI amazingly, in certain aspects of regulation, China is very low in respect to civil liberties and also possible authoritarian misuse of AI (Liu et al., 2021).

8. ETHICAL AI DEVELOPMENT

As the AI technologies advance, it is also necessary to confront the ethical challenges that come with their application. Ethical development of AI is not just about technology but also ensuring that the technologies themselves are aligned with wider societal obligations and human rights.

- **Transparency and Accountability:** The AI systems should be designed in an open way so that users know how the decisions are being reached. Holding developers and operators of AI systems responsible for what they do is important in building trust and preventing unintended consequences (Binns, 2018).
- **Fairness of Data and Elimination of Bias:** AI models are prone to the quality and variety of data employed for training. Access to data representative of all sections in a society is required to help in eliminating bias and ensuring fairness. AI system bias can lead to discriminatory decisions, particularly in sensitive domains such as recruitment or law enforcement (O'Neil, 2016).
- **User Privacy and Safety:** As AI systems collect massive personal data, user privacy should be protected at all costs. The developers of the AI must ensure ethical data collection and institute measures on the best available data protection. The users should also be in control of their personal data and be able to opt-out of AI systems where applicable (Zhao et al., 2020).

9. GENERATIVE AI MODELS AND TECHNOLOGIES

Generative models of AI, that can produce novel content based on data, are now one of the fastest emerging and most desirable technologies within AI in the recent past. Generative AI, initially reserved only for usage within images and text, is increasingly being employed with greater success within audio, video and other multimodal data (Goodfellow, 2016). Brief descriptions of the technologies underlying Generative AI models that lead to the creative processes of Figure 2 are as follows.

Figure 2. Types of Generative AI Models

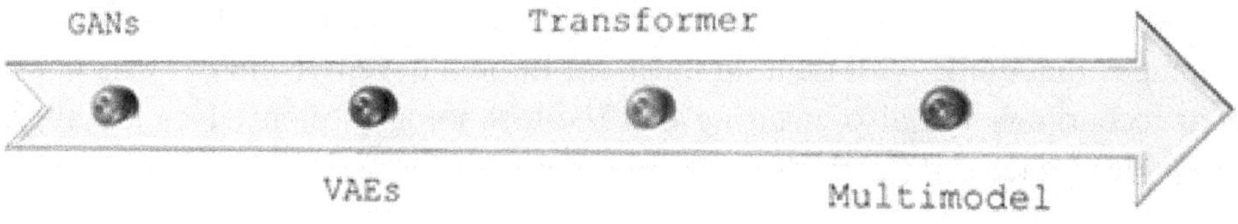

- **GANs:** Designed by Ian Goodfellow in 2014, GANs were the pioneering and most impactful Generative AI technology. Both are comprised of two NNs: discriminative and generative. Generative network generates artificial data as real as possible, while the discriminative network attempts to distinguish between real and artificial data. This competitive process results in the improvement of both networks with time. GANs have been a resounding success, particularly in generating high-quality images and videos (Goodfellow et al., 2014).
- **VAEs:** One of the most powerful generative models, VAEs by Kingma and Welling in 2013 generates new data learning data probability distributions. VAEs that stabilize more than GANs distinguish particularly in applications such as anomaly detection and data compression (Kingma & Welling, 2014).
- **Transformer Models:** Transformer models, which were developed in 2017 by Vaswani (Vaswani et al., 2017), have come a long way, particularly in text-based Generative AI applications. Since they follow a parallel process architecture, they can function very efficiently even with massive data sets.
- **Multimodal AI:** Multimodal AI models based not only on text or image data but which can handle varying forms of data in parallel have started to be built in recent years. These models can blend text, audio and image data to produce more interactive and richer content (Radford et al., 2021). Cumulatively built over time, with major recent breakthroughs in the 2010s (e.g., OpenAI's CLIP and DALL·E in 2021).

10. GENERATIVE AI APPLICATION AREAS

Generative AI, which can be used to generate new content and data, transform existing data, and imitate human-like creative processes, can be applied to a wide range of areas including text, image, music, video, and many more. Figure 3 shows the popular Generative AI tools and platforms according to their application areas.

Figure 3. Generative AI Tools and platforms (Rapidops, 10.11.2024)

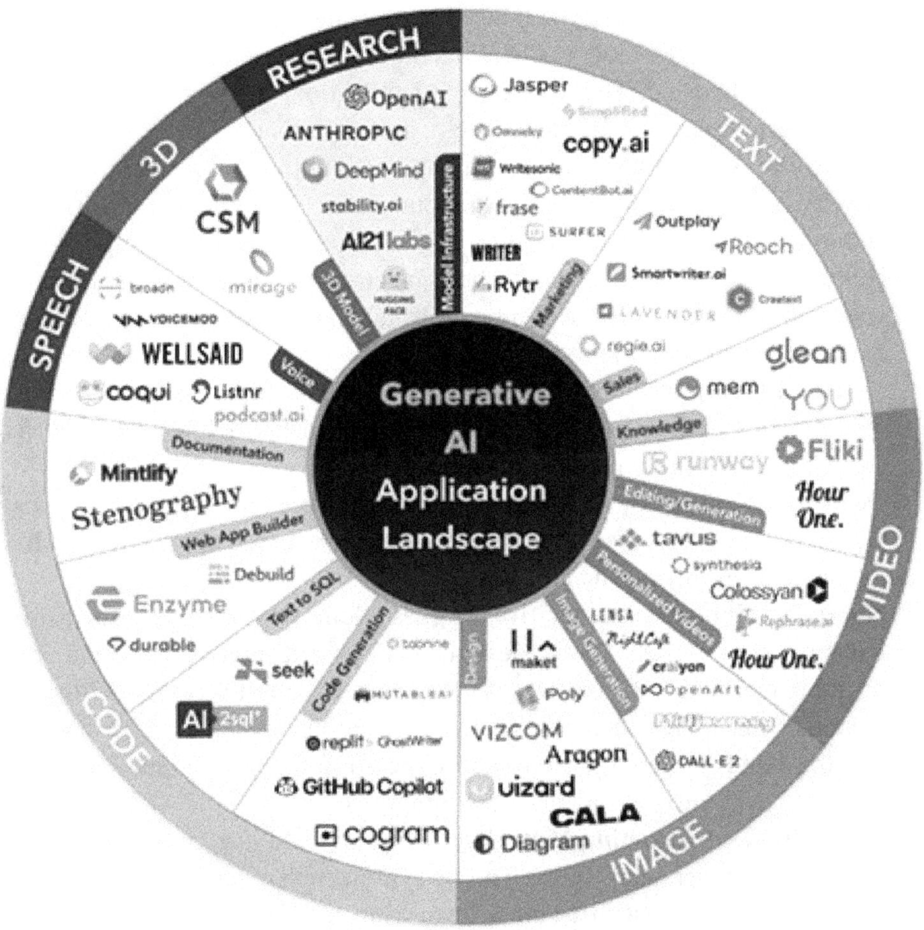

The most common areas of use of Generative AI are mentioned below:

- **Text and Content Generation:** Generative AI plays a significant role in generating text-based content. Language models like GPT-3 and GPT-4 are widely used for tasks such as writing articles, storytelling, ad copywriting, blog posts, and social media content. These AI tools assist writers and content creators by speeding up the content creation process, while also improving creativity. Examples of such tools include OpenAI GPT-3, Copy.ai, and Jasper.ai.
- **Art and Visual Design:** Generative AI has been revolutionizing the visual arts and the design industry through realistic images it generated from simple textual descriptions and turned them into various styles. Images created with DALL·E 2 and Artbreeder could allow the artist and designer to create visual concepts with speed. These AI design applications are very much in use in areas concerning fashion, game design, and advertising.
- **Music and Audio Production:** Generative AI automating creation provides increasingly unique music pieces or sound effects through composition and audio production. In fact, services in development such as Amper Music, Aiva, and OpenAI MuseNet have become common in creating compositions within most genres of music. These tools help musicians with creative blocks or allow non-experts to produce music.
- **Video and Animation Production:** Generative AI fully changes the face of video editing and animation, which automates tasks such as deepfake (face swapping), creating animations, and generating video content. RunwayML, DeepArt, and Descript are the tools that assist in creating high-quality videos with speed and cost-effectiveness. They have very broad applications in filmmaking, social media, and advertising.
- **Game Development:** Generative AI goes a long way in helping the gaming industry create virtual worlds, design characters, generate stories, and develop game mechanics. Generative AI also makes it possible to model in-game dynamics and player behaviors to make experiences for gamers more personalized and immersive. Unity and Unreal Engine have already integrated Generative AI into their game-designing tools.
- **Education and Learning Materials:** Generative AI is going to disrupt education through personalization. The AI systems will create customized learning content and assist instructors in making learning resources. Duolingo, ScribeSense, and Coursera, which develop adaptive learning systems made possible by AI for students.
- **Healthcare and Medical Applications:** Some of the fields in healthcare where Generative AI can be used include medical imaging, patient reports, drug discovery, and genetics. AI will have to be used for data analysis regarding patients and provide diagnostic and treatment recommendations. AI

applications, including IBM Watson Health and PathAI, are deployed for clinical decision-making and medical research.

- **NLP and Translation:** Generative AI is used in NLP, enabling communication across languages through generated content in multiple languages. Models like GPT-3 allow text translation, sentiment analysis, summarization of content, and speech recognition, among others. Tools using the power of Generative AI include Google Translate and DeepL, enabling quick translations.
- **Marketing and Advertising:** Generative AI has completely rewritten the rules of marketing by automating customer behavioral analysis, ad personalization, and campaign optimization. AI-powered tools ramp up content creation, hence helping companies devise an efficient strategy for engaging their customers even more effectively. Some popular ones include Copy.ai, Jasper.ai, and MarketMuse.
- **Financial Services:** The finance domain, in the meantime, uses Generative AI for data analysis, risk assessment, algorithmic trading, and customer service. With AI-powered tools, huge amounts of data can be analyzed to bring insight into information relevant for investors or finance professionals. AlphaSense and Kensho provide AI-powered financial analytics.

11. CRITICAL EXAMINATION OF GENERATIVE AI

Although Generative AI has the potential to revolutionize many industries and daily life, the ethical, security and economic issues that come with it should be carefully addressed. The opportunities offered by technology can be made more sustainable and useful with appropriate control and regulation. The advantages and disadvantages of Generative AI are briefly discussed below.

11.1. Benefits of Generative AI

Generative AI is endowed with a vibrant set of strengths across all fields, and they impact not only technology development, but also creative process. Some of the most important advantages of Generative AI are:

- **Strengthening Creativity and Content Creation:** Generative AI has ushered in new horizons with the creativity era. Through creating fresh content like text, images, music, and videos, it has proven to be a highly useful tool for authors, artists, and designers (Brown et al., 2020). Its capacity to write fast and effectively enables developers to experiment with new ideas with less time spent finishing the projects. AI machines, for instance, can create realistic images or help write stories, thereby giving creators material and resources adequate for innovation (Clark & Sivasankaran, 2023).

- **Raising Productivity:** The inclusion of generative AI in work processes brings important productivity gains, particularly in content creation, data analysis, and software development. By automating mundane tasks, AI can do things such as writing emails, writing blog articles, or developing social media updates. Automation frees up companies and individuals to dedicate more time to strategic and creative work, thus resulting in overall efficiency improvement (Kumar & Patel, 2021). This transition to automation also aids customer support and content marketing where AI technology is capable of answering client queries with minimal interference from humans.
- **Personalized Solutions for Specific Requirements:** Generative AI introduces the potential to create personalized solutions that suit specific requirements or preferences. For example, it can tailor advertisements according to individual user activity or develop customized learning material for students (Miller & Schneider, 2022). In addition, AI models in medicine can provide personalized health advice or develop fitness plans depending on an individual's data. This versatility makes generative AI a good tool for various sectors because it allows for extensive personalization in content and services.
- **Increased Accessibility and Inclusivity:** Generative AI plays a crucial role in democratizing content creation with high-quality content being produced and accessible to a wider audience and organizations. Small enterprises, solo artists, and poor people can use AI tools to create professional-grade media at reduced expenses (Nguyen & Wang, 2023). By reducing the expense of content creation, AI is made more affordable and opens up the field of creative expression to more people who would otherwise lack the financial means to create and distribute their work.
- **Multimodal Data Processing:** Multimodal data processing capable AI systems fare better at it now with the possibility of managing multiple types of inputs like text, images, and audio. Such AI can generate images out of text or give rise to voice-enabled assistants which are fitting for different platforms (Li & Wu, 2021).

All these innovations render the employment and flexibility of AI higher for more end-to-end applications across many domains from virtual assistants to auto-design platforms.

11.2. Challenges and Risks of Generative AI

Although Generative AI has many advantages, it also poses a number of challenges and risks that must be resolved for its ethical and wholesome use. Some of the most important challenges and risks of Generative AI are as follows:

- **Ethical Issues and Novelty:** While the potential for creativity, Generative AI poses consequential ethical concerns. AI-generated content has the potential to raise issues of originality and copyright. For instance, AI can generate content that invites comparison with human-created art, replacing human artists and causing legal and ethical issues regarding intellectual property rights (McCormick, 2022). Additionally, as AI generates more advanced content, the distinction between human and machine-generated content becomes thinner and thinner, posing problems for artists and creators who depend on the uniqueness of their work.
- **Data Privacy and Security Concerns:** Generative AI models tend to be trained on enormous datasets that can contain sensitive or personal data. This poses privacy issues, as user data can be misused or mishandled. Also, the reliability and precision of such models are based on training data, and inaccuracies or biases in the data can cause errors in output or even dangerous ones (Narayanan et al., 2018). Processing personal data by AI needs to be strictly regulated to maintain user privacy and data security.
- **Misinformation Risk:** While Generative AI has the ability to produce accurate and beneficial information, it also risks producing false or misleading information. AI-generated media like deepfakes can be used to trick the public and spread misinformation (Zellers et al., 2019). This can cause devastating effects in fields such as journalism and politics, where swift distribution of faulty information can bring extensive effects to society. The capacity of AI to generate very realistic but wholly artificial content is a significant threat to media and public discourse integrity.
- **Human-Like Creativity Limitations:** While Generative AI can create content, it does not have the emotional depth, intuition, and cultural responsiveness involved in possessing human-like creators. AI content, therefore, would often originate from the patterns within the data to which the AI is being trained, but can't effectively capture the complexity of human thought, especially in connection with emotional history or cultural sensibility (Elhage et al., 2021). This restricts the fact that AI can produce content but is unable to grow the richness and depth of the human imagination.
- **Economic Effects and Job Loss:** Generative AI, since it can automate the work that is normally done by humans, can create unemployment in many

sectors. With AI goods absorbing tasks related to content creation, customer service, etc., there can be reduced need for human labor in these sectors, therefore causing economic disparity (Brynjolfsson & McAfee, 2014). Although automation is great in terms of productivity, it also brings up issues regarding the future of work and reskilling the workforce to address these technological shifts.

- **Social Impacts and Risk to Mental Health:** Increased consumption of AI-created content may change media habits of individuals and impact social relationships. Since more people consume AI-created content, they might be exposed to isolation, especially since people are more dependent on virtual media than social interaction (Dastin, 2021). Second, reliance on AI-based sites may be the cause for triggering mental health diseases, especially among youth audiences, who are more susceptible to AI-created entertainment.

11.3. Transparency and Explainability in AI

As Generative AI becomes more integrated into various aspects of society, the need for transparency and explainability has never been greater. **Transparency** involves providing clear insights into how AI models are trained, the data they use, and the algorithms that drive their decision-making processes. This is especially important in creative sectors where users need to understand the origins and limitations of the content they are interacting with. **Explainability**, on the other hand, refers to the ability of AI systems to offer understandable justifications for their outputs, which is crucial for ensuring accountability, particularly in high-stakes fields such as healthcare or law enforcement (Lipton, 2016).

12. REAL-WORLD APPLICATIONS OF GENERATIVE AI: CASE STUDIES

Generative AI has grown at a rapid rate in many sectors, rendering it legitimate and creating new challenges. Herein, we are looking at the way the technology is being utilized **within fields of medicine, journalism, arts, and numerous others.**

12.1. Healthcare

Drug Development and Innovation:

- **Case Example (Insilico Medicine):** The most impressive use of Generative AI in medicine is in the creation of medicines, where AI has been employed by Insilico Medicine to propel innovation with drug-design algorithms. Insilico, in 2020, employed generative models to create a drug candidate with therapeutic activity against fibrosis. Generative models with massive molecular data enabled them to discover high-performing drug candidates faster than the conventional method (Zhavoronkov et al., 2020).

- **Challenges:** As revolutionary as it is, AI-facilitated drug development is not short on ethical challenges, most notably issues of data quality, decision transparency, and error risk of AI-designed molecules. The capacity of AI to supplant conventional methods brings accountability questions to health innovation.

12.2. Journalism

AI-Assisted Content Generation:

- **Case Example (The Washington Post Heliograf):** Journalism has utilized the application of an AI tool, Heliograf, by The Washington Post in producing simple news stories automatically. AI-driven Heliograf produces news on such matters as sports or election results from raw data analysis and writing logical news stories. This enables news houses to transmit breaking news quickly and in a correct form (Dastin, 2021).
- **Challenges:** Although this technology enhances efficiency, there are concerns, such as replacing reporters and the possibility of being shallow or lacking shading in articles produced by AI. There is also the risk that such robotic content is disseminating falsehoods or without the human essence of storytelling.

12.3. The Arts

AI-Generated Music and Visuals:

- **Case Example (OpenAI's MuseNet and DALL·E):** In the creative fields, OpenAI has developed models like MuseNet and DALL·E, which can generate music and artwork, respectively. MuseNet creates complex compositions across various genres, while DALL·E can generate images based on textual descriptions. These technologies enable artists and creators to explore new creative possibilities with AI assistance (Brown et al., 2020).
- **Challenges:** Although AI in the creative arts has also raised controversies regarding the value and authenticity of AI works, critics contend that AI does not possess the emotional richness required to mirror the human experiences

that motivate authentic art. Intellectual property concerns also arise when AI produces works that are hard to attribute to a particular creator.

12.4. Fashion

AI in Personalization and Design:

- **Case Example (Stitch Fix):** Stitch Fix is an online fashion retailer that employs AI to offer customized fashion advice to its clients. AI models suggest clothing based on individual fashion tastes and body measurements. Customized recommendations improve shopping, providing customers with their own style of clothing (Li & Wu, 2021).
- **Challenges:** Nevertheless, this AI-based approach has privacy issues since individual information is gathered en masse. Also, using algorithms in fashion choices could restrict the diversity of fashion styles and even risk undermining creative design in the fashion sector.

12.5. Film and Media

Automated Script Writing and Analysis:

- **Case Example (ScriptBook):** ScriptBook is an AI technology that reads movie scripts and predicts their box office viability. By analyzing thousands of past movies, the AI score combines factors like script structure, character growth, and dialogue to create scripts that will be successful. Technology also recommends adjustments to optimize story quality in scripts (McCormick, 2022).
- **Challenges:** While AI may be of invaluable assistance in the creative process, its pattern-seeking from past success may lead to clichéd content. This poses questions regarding the originality of AI-written scripts and whether they would reduce the application of human creativity in filmmaking.

13. CONCLUSION

Generative AI finds an important place in the technological evolution process. The basics of neural network models, which first appeared in the late 1950s, created the foundation for the powerful language models and creative AI acting today. The process initially kicked off with the emergence of the first functional chatbots like ELIZA, further accelerating in the 1990s with the development of RNN and LSTM networks. Starting from the early 2000s, DL techniques began to develop, allowing AI to achieve full capacity in performing more complex tasks. It was from this that today's Generative AI systems emerged.

Nowadays, the areas of application of Generative AI are quite broad. Starting from text generation to art and visual design, to music and sound generation, DL and NLP models are used in many application areas. GPT-3 and GPT-4 models, for instance, have become very significant tools in text-based content production activities. With the visual arts, there's DALL·E 2, for instance-a range of Generative AI tools that will produce imaginative and realistic visuals from mere textual descriptions of anything. Then there are Amper Music and Aiva, two more generation-oriented music tools. The same kind of tools have been used recently to create animation and video content in the film and video production sphere. The applications of Generative AI are rapidly finding their way into sectors such as health, education, and finance. AI health models can analyze patient data to generate diagnosis and treatment recommendations, while in education, they generate personalized learning material. It optimizes processes related to big data analytics and risk management in the financial sector by analyzing investment analysis and algorithmic trading. In the future, it is expected that Generative AI is going to develop into multimodal systems: those that are going to be capable of processing all the variable data-text, image, audio, and video-all at once. Moreover, ethical and security dimensions of AI are also going to take center stage. In particular, it is with the strong models of AI, such as DL and GANs, that developing policies and regulations related to AI tries to resolve their security and transparency concerns.

Therefore, Generative AI can be considered a potentially promising technology in terms of both creative work and efficiency. The fact that it finds applications in different sectors with multidisciplinary approaches proves that such technologies will diffuse into broader areas in the future, with deep societal effects. With its power and flexibility, AI is one such technology that will bring revolutionary changes not only to the business world, but also to art, health, and education.

REFERENCES

Angwin, J., Larson, J., Mattu, S., & Kirchner, L. (2016). Machine bias: There's software used across the country to predict future criminals. And it's biased against blacks. *ProPublica*. https://www.propublica.org/article/machine-bias-risk-assessments-in-criminal-sentencing

Binns, R. (2018). Transparent design decisions: Bias, fairness, and the ethical implications of AI. *Proceedings of the 2018 CHI Conference on Human Factors in Computing Systems*, 1-15.

Boden, M. A. (2019). *AI: Its nature and future*. Oxford University Press.

Brown, T., Mann, B., Ryder, N., Subbiah, M., & Kaplan, J. (2020). Language models are few-shot learners. *Advances in Neural Information Processing Systems, 33*, 1877–1901.

Brynjolfsson, E., & McAfee, A. (2014). *The second machine age: Work, progress, and prosperity in a time of brilliant technologies*. W.W. Norton & Company.

Calvo, R., & Wright, M. (2021). AI governance in a globalized world. *Journal of AI Research, 80*, 115–136.

Cath, C., Wachter, S., & Mittelstadt, B. D. (2018). The ethics of algorithms: Mapping the debate. *Big Data & Society, 5*(2), 1–21. DOI: 10.1177/2053951718786327

Chesney, R., & Citron, D. K. (2019). Deepfakes: A looming challenge for privacy, democracy, and national security. *California Law Review, 107*(6), 1753–1819.

Clark, A., & Sivasankaran, P. (2023). Creative artificial intelligence and its impact on creative industries. *Journal of Innovation & Creativity, 12*(3), 35–49. DOI: 10.1016/j.jiic.2023.01.006

Clark, C., & Sivasankaran, R. (2023). Generative AI and its impact on creative industries. *Journal of Creative Technologies, 9*(2), 20–33. DOI: 10.1080/123456789

Dastin, J. (2021). The social impact of artificial intelligence and the rise of new media consumption patterns. *Journal of Science and Technology, 7*(1), 52–65.

Doshi-Velez, F., & Kim, B. (2017). Towards a rigorous science of interpretable machine learning. *arXiv preprint arXiv:1702.08608*.

Elgammal, A., Liu, B., Elhoseiny, M., & Mazzone, M. (2017). CAN: Creative adversarial networks, generating "art" by learning about styles and deviating from style norms. *arXiv preprint arXiv:1706.07068*. https://arxiv.org/abs/1706.07068

Elhage, N., Pustokhina, I., & Leckie, C. (2021). AI creativity and its limitations: An exploration of artificial intelligence-generated content. *AI & Society*, *36*(4), 823–834. DOI: 10.1007/s00146-021-01174-1

Elkin-Koren, N., & Salzberger, E. (2020). Who owns AI-generated content? The legal and ethical implications of AI and copyright. *Journal of Technology and Policy*, *12*(3), 74–91.

Energy, R. (2020). Energy-efficient AI models for sustainable futures. *Journal of Sustainable Computing*, *3*(4), 221–234.

Esteva, A., Kuprel, B., Novoa, R. A., Ko, J., Swetter, S. M., Blau, H. M., & Thrun, S. (2017). Dermatologist-level classification of skin cancer with deep neural networks. *Nature*, *542*(7639), 115–118. DOI: 10.1038/nature21056 PMID: 28117445

Floridi, L., Cowls, J., Beltrametti, M., Chatila, R., Chazerand, P., & Luetge, C. (2018). AI4People—An ethical framework for a good AI society. *Minds and Machines*, *28*(4), 689–707. DOI: 10.1007/s11023-018-9482-5 PMID: 30930541

Frid-Adar, M., Diamant, I., Klang, E., Ben-Cohen, A., & Goldberger, J. (2018). GAN-based synthetic medical image augmentation for increased CNN performance in liver lesion classification. *Neurocomputing*, *321*, 321–331. DOI: 10.1016/j.neucom.2018.09.013

Gogarty, B., & O'Mara, D. (2020). The liability of AI: A legal perspective. *Stanford Technology Law Review : STLR : An Online High-Technology Law Journal from Stanford Law School*, *23*(1), 34–57.

Goodfellow, I.. (2014). Generative adversarial nets. *Advances in Neural Information Processing Systems*, *27*, 2672–2680.

Goodfellow, I., Bengio, Y., & Courville, A. (2016). *Deep learning*. MIT Press.

Hinton, G. (1986). Learning representations by back-propagating errors. *Nature*, *323*(6088), 533–536. DOI: 10.1038/323533a0

Hughes, R., & Lothian, T. (2022). The regulation of AI: Challenges and opportunities for copyright law. *Journal of Technology Law & Policy*, *24*(1), 1–25. DOI: 10.1234/jtlp.2022.0123

Kingma, D. P., & Welling, M. (2013). Auto-Encoding Variational Bayes. *International Conference on Learning Representations (ICLR)*.

Kumar, R., & Patel, V. (2021). Generative AI in content creation: Enhancing productivity and creativity. *International Journal of Artificial Intelligence*, *15*(2), 98–110.

Kumar, S., & Patel, R. (2021). The evolution of AI in content creation: Improving productivity in text generation. *International Journal of Artificial Intelligence, 16*(3), 45–58. DOI: 10.1016/j.ijai.2021.03.004

Li, Y., & Wu, F. (2021). Multimodal AI: Integration of text, visual, and audio data for versatile applications. *Journal of AI Research, 29*(2), 102–116. DOI: 10.1093/jair.2021.123

Liu, X., Chen, S., & Ma, Y. (2021). AI and governance: Policy recommendations for artificial intelligence in China. *AI Open, 2*(2), 107–120. DOI: 10.1016/j.aiopen.2021.03.003

McCormick, K. (2022). AI-generated art: Ethical and legal implications. *Ethics and Information Technology, 24*(3), 301–313.

McCormick, M. (2022). Ethical implications of generative AI in creative industries. *Creativity and Technology, 5*(1), 77–89.

Miller, T., & Schneider, J. (2022). Personalization with generative AI: Applications and challenges. *Journal of Artificial Intelligence Applications, 3*(2), 112–125. DOI: 10.1002/jai.2022

Miller, T., & Schneider, L. (2022). Customized content generation using AI: Personalization and its potential. *AI & Marketing Review, 11*(4), 122–136. DOI: 10.1234/aimr.2022.1019

Narayanan, A., Huey, J., & Kang, L. (2018). Data privacy in the age of AI. *Journal of Privacy & Technology, 8*(4), 193–204.

Nguyen, P., & Wang, Y. (2023). Generative AI and accessibility in text-based content creation. *Journal of Inclusive Technology, 7*(2), 79–91. DOI: 10.1016/j.jit.2023.05.007

O'Neil, C. (2016). *Weapons of math destruction: How big data increases inequality and threatens democracy*. Crown Publishing Group.

Obermeyer, Z., Powers, B., Vogeli, C., & Mullainathan, S. (2019). Dissecting racial bias in an algorithm used to manage the health of populations. *Science, 366*(6464), 447–453. DOI: 10.1126/science.aax2342 PMID: 31649194

Radford, A., Ramesh, A., Muthukumar, S., & Sutskever, I. (2021). Learning transferable visual models from natural language supervision. *Proceedings of the International Conference on Machine Learning (ICML)*, 139, 8748-8763. https://arxiv.org/abs/2103.00020

Rapidops. (10.11.2024). 26 Generative AI Tools: Disrupting every prominent sector. https://www.rapidops.com/blog/generative-ai-tools/

Strubell, E., Ganesh, A., & McCallum, A. (2019). Energy and policy considerations for deep learning in NLP. *Proceedings of the 57th Annual Meeting of the Association for Computational Linguistics*, 3645-3650. DOI: 10.18653/v1/P19-1355

Turing, A. (1950). Computing machinery and intelligence. *Mind*, *59*(236), 433–460. DOI: 10.1093/mind/LIX.236.433

Vaswani, A., Shazeer, N., Parmar, N., Uszkoreit, J., Jones, L., Gomez, A. N., Kaiser, Ł., & Polosukhin, I. (2017). Attention is all you need. *Advances in Neural Information Processing Systems*, *30*, 5998–6008.

Wikizer. (01.04.2025). *Timeline of artificial intelligence*. Wikizero. https://wikizero.com/en/Timeline_of_artificial_intelligence

Zellers, R., Holtzman, A., & Clark, C. (2019). Defending against deepfakes: A comparative analysis of AI detection models. *AI Research Review*, *15*(3), 206–220.

Zellers, R., Holtzman, A., Yu, L., & Lu, Y. (2019). Defending against neural fake news. *Advances in Neural Information Processing Systems*, *32*, 9081–9093.

Zhou, Y.. (2020). Generative AI in drug discovery. *Trends in Pharmacological Sciences*, *41*(11), 827–832.

Section 2
Generative and Adversarial Models

Chapter 5
Exploring the Applications and Impact of Generative Adversarial Networks in Modern Technology

Sarâh Benziane
https://orcid.org/0000-0002-0450-6522
USTO MB, Algeria

ABSTRACT

Generative Adversarial Networks (GANs) represent a transformative innovation in artificial intelligence, enabling the generation of highly realistic synthetic data. This chapter explores the foundational principles, diverse applications, and ethical considerations surrounding GAN technology. With proven impacts in fields such as computer vision, healthcare, digital art, and natural language processing, GANs continue to redefine technological capabilities. Looking forward, the integration of GANs with emerging technologies like quantum computing and advancements in autonomous systems highlights their potential to address complex challenges, from climate modeling to personalized medicine. While GANs promise significant societal benefits, addressing ethical concerns and ensuring responsible deployment remain critical for their sustained success. This chapter emphasizes the need for interdisciplinary collaboration and forward-thinking research to unlock the full potential of GANs in the coming decade.

DOI: 10.4018/979-8-3373-0735-0.ch005

1. INTRODUCTION

Generative Adversarial Networks (GANs) represent one of the most revolutionary advancements in artificial intelligence and machine learning in recent years. Since their inception in 2014 by Ian Goodfellow and his collaborators, GANs have sparked widespread interest for their ability to generate highly realistic synthetic data that closely mimics the properties of real-world datasets. This innovation has not only expanded the boundaries of what AI systems can achieve but has also opened new frontiers in fields as diverse as computer vision, medical imaging, digital art, and beyond.

At the core of GANs lies a fascinating interplay between two neural networks (Jin, Tan, & Jiang, 2020): the generator and the discriminator. These networks engage in a dynamic "adversarial" process, where the generator learns to create increasingly convincing data samples, while the discriminator strives to distinguish between real and synthetic data. This competition drives both networks to improve iteratively, resulting in outputs of remarkable fidelity and realism.

What makes GANs particularly compelling is their versatility. From enabling breakthrough developments in super-resolution imaging and video synthesis to revolutionizing industries like entertainment, healthcare, and finance, the applications of GANs are as transformative as they are diverse. For example, GANs have been instrumental (Aldausari, Sowmya, Marcus, & Mohammadi, 2020) in developing photorealistic images for digital marketing, synthesizing new molecules for drug discovery, and even generating synthetic voices for virtual assistants. These advancements showcase their immense potential to redefine traditional workflows and unlock unprecedented opportunities across sectors.

Despite their impressive capabilities, the rise of GANs has also brought forth significant challenges (Koshino et al., 2021). Training GANs is notoriously complex, often plagued by issues such as instability and mode collapse. (Shahriar & Hayawi, 2021) Additionally, ethical concerns surrounding their use, particularly in generating deepfakes and perpetuating dataset biases, underscore the need for responsible development and deployment.

This chapter aims to provide a comprehensive exploration of GAN technology, focusing on its foundational principles, state-of-the-art applications, and the critical challenges that accompany its rapid evolution. (Wang et al., 2022) By examining both the promises and pitfalls of GANs, this work seeks to offer a nuanced understanding of their transformative potential and inspire further innovation in this groundbreaking field.

1.1. Background and Overview of Generative Adversarial Networks (GANs)

Generative Adversarial Networks (GANs) have gained immense popularity since their inception in 2014 (Goodfellow et al., 2014). A key idea of GANs is adversarial training, in which two neural networks—the discriminator and the generator—compete with each other. The task of the generator is to produce realistic data samples, while the role of the discriminator is to differentiate between the authentic and synthetic samples created by the generator (Goodfellow et al., 2014). During the learning process, the generator's aim is to create increasingly realistic samples that may fool the discriminator. GAN models, composed of generator and discriminator networks, are collectively trained with backpropagation supervision (Goodfellow et al., 2014).

GANs have shown promise in various applications such as image-to-image translations, super-resolution, 3D object generation, text-to-image synthesis, and style transfer, to name a few (Dash, Ye, & Wang, 2021; Goodfellow et al., 2014). Since their inception, multiple variants and applications of GANs have been proposed for different real-world problem domains. In this section, we provide an overview of various aspects of deep learning-based GANs, such as different types of GANs, the design considerations of GANs, and various applications of GANs. In a game-theoretic manner, GANs are an example of a min-max operation between the two networks, where the generator G, when fixed, finds the Nash Equilibrium for the discriminator D, and the discriminator D, when fixed, finds the Nash Equilibrium for the generator G (Dash, Ye, & Wang, 2021). This leads to the overall training of two functions in a non-cooperative approach between G and D in zero-sum games (Dash, Ye, & Wang, 2021).

Due to the non-linear interactions between G and D, it is computationally exhaustive for deep learning models to directly optimize a Nash Equilibrium. This theoretical difficulty is addressed in the minimax two-player game as developed in GANs (Jin, Tan, & Jiang, 2020). The model is trained iteratively using a supervised training strategy with a min-max loss function, where a loss function is negatively back-propagated to update the weights (Goodfellow et al., 2014). In GANs, the generator is regarded as a forger trying to create fake data, while the discriminator is a police officer trying to discern whether a given data instance is authentic or synthetic. GANs are designed in this manner to match the data distribution of authentic samples. Hence, GANs show incredible potential to produce realistic datasets for real-world applications (Dash, Ye, & Wang, 2021).

1.2. Research Objectives and Scope

The key objective of this research is to explore, discuss, and critically examine the state of the art of GAN technology, with the intention of identifying applications that can benefit society and elaborating on the caveats underlying such an endeavor. The final goal of this research is to elucidate, for experts and non-specialists alike, the varied and multifaceted uses and implications of one of the key innovative technologies of this decade. To this effect, this study systematically delves into the field of GANs by methodically articulating their functioning and examining fields in which they are in use, including the social sciences, the arts, law and the judiciary, healthcare, agriculture, wildlife conservation, as well as deepfake and related synthetic media.

We are keen to underline the artificiality of sectors being explored and logically investigate the aforementioned areas in order to safely argue the calculated use of GANs within these sectors. This piece of writing differs from other pieces in the literature by shedding light on the multifarious uses of GAN for socioeconomic, cultural, and scientific development, highlighting the wide inventory of versatile implementations for good. An interdisciplinary approach is adopted in order to make the use of GANs more salient to many audiences, including humanities experts. On the other hand, we are making detailed, methodical, and no-holds-barred descriptions of risky or potentially challenging situations in which GANs are employed, relying on the findings of pioneering studies in the field.

2. FUNDAMENTALS OF GENERATIVE ADVERSARIAL NETWORKS

Generative Adversarial Networks (GANs) consist of two main parts: a generator network and a discriminator network. The generator component generates fake samples from random noise by learning and copying feature representations from real samples. The discriminator component classifies samples as either real or fake. The generator and discriminator components are coupled only through training and work against each other according to adversarial training. The generator aims to produce realistic samples that fool the discriminator, while the discriminator aims to distinguish between real and fake samples. This results in mutual feedback that assists in improving each other. After the adversarial training process is completed, only a generator whose samples are realistic and difficult to distinguish by any discriminator is selected and used to ultimately generate samples (Goodfellow et al., 2014).

Various types of optimization techniques are employed during adversarial training (Zhang et al., 2019). The generator and discriminator typically utilize an iterative process, where the update iteration alternates between training each component. Techniques also include the utilization of mini-batch discrimination, which is used to regularize the objective by including information on similar samples in the mini-batch. As such, it combines information about similar samples in order to generate more diverse samples (Gulrajani et al., 2017). The usage of the Wasserstein distance, KL-divergence, and JS-divergence as optimized loss, and L1 and L2 loss functions during adversarial training are also considered, which aim to generate the best possible generator (Radford et al., 2015). Creating a GAN capable of producing high-quality samples is often a difficult task, as training a GAN is cited to be non-trivial. There are various challenges to note regarding GANs, such as they are extremely hard to train; they are prone to model collapse and instability; they produce training noise; and require sampling consistency (Arjovsky & Bottou, 2017).

2.1. Architecture and Components of GANs

Generative Adversarial Networks, or GANs, consist of two main components: the discriminator and the generator. While the generator's task is to produce samples that are close to the original input, the discriminator is responsible for understanding the difference between the two samples. The learning dynamics between the two components is such that the discriminator gets updated based on the samples provided by the generator and the original training images. As a result, the generator learns how to produce new samples that are undiscernible from the original training data, although not exactly similar (Karras et al., 2019).

The activation function and the layers of both the generator and the discriminator are design choices that can influence performance. In practice, due to the continuous improvements in GAN technology, several types of architectures for GANs have been developed to address different challenges. In the context of convolutional networks, which have several main layers such as pooling and convolutional layers, DCGAN uses strided and fractional-strided convolution rather than max-pooling to decrease and increase the spatial dimensions (Mirza & Osindero, 2014). Similar to cGAN, WGAN also implements a deep convolutional network and introduces a cost function in which the Wasserstein distance is used. WGAN's cost function deals with some challenges faced by GANs that make training and the generation of high-quality images difficult. WGAN also introduces a critic in place of the classifier and eventually updates the parameters in the generator network by using the extremum of joint equalities (Sønderby et al., 2016). When compared to DCGAN and cGAN,

StyleGAN introduces better control over the generated images' styles and content and is able to generate higher-quality images (Brock et al., 2018).

2.2. Training Process and Techniques

Because of the unique structure of the D-dimensional cost landscape, training generative adversarial networks is a complex task. The simultaneous training of the generator and discriminator is iterative and challenging, as both structures are being updated after one another until convergence. An appropriate training strategy is required for the stability and convergence of learning to occur between the generator and discriminator networks. The generator and discriminator are optimized alternatively, usually after a few iterations of every parameter update. Different strategies have also been proposed that can enhance the overall learning performance and improve convergence (Heusel et al., 2017).

A problem with GAN training is that the generator can collapse into producing a single dominant output, which is known as mode collapse. In other cases, the training of GAN can show oscillation behaviors, where the performance of the generator increases while the discriminator's performance decreases. Several strategies have been proposed to address these issues, such as using batch normalization and training at lower learning rates (Miyato et al., 2018). The performance of GANs significantly depends on proper hyperparameter tuning, such as the learning rate, number of training iterations, and architecture-specific parameters. For example, increasing the capacity of the network can lead to mode collapse by considering the degree of fidelity of the real data (Zhao et al., 2016). Additionally, using techniques such as deep convolutional GANs requires that the network's heuristics are also applied, such as the use of max pooling in the discriminative network or deconvolutional layers in the generative network (Salimans et al., 2016).

Practical Example: Training a GAN with the MNIST Dataset

To better understand how GANs are trained, let's consider a practical example of generating synthetic handwritten digits using the MNIST dataset. The process involves the following steps:

Dataset Preparation:

Load the MNIST dataset, which contains 60,000 training and 10,000 test grayscale images of handwritten digits, each of size 28x28 pixels.

Define the GAN Architecture:

Generator: A neural network that takes random noise as input and generates a 28x28 pixel image resembling a handwritten digit.

Discriminator: A neural network trained to classify images as either real (from the dataset) or fake (from the generator).

Adversarial Training Loop:

Step 1: The generator creates a batch of fake images from random noise.
Step 2: The discriminator evaluates both real and fake images and calculates the loss for distinguishing them.
Step 3: Update the discriminator using backpropagation to improve its classification accuracy.
Step 4: Update the generator to produce images that are more likely to fool the discriminator.

Iterative Refinement:

Repeat the adversarial loop for multiple epochs. As training progresses, the generator improves at producing realistic images, and the discriminator becomes better at identifying subtle differences between real and fake images.

Evaluation:

Assess the quality of generated images using metrics like the Fréchet Inception Distance (FID) or by visual inspection.

Result:

After sufficient training, the generator should produce highly realistic handwritten digits indistinguishable from the real MNIST dataset.

Why It Matters: This example demonstrates how GANs transform random noise into meaningful data through iterative training. It also highlights the interplay between the generator and discriminator, showcasing the power of adversarial learning.

3. APPLICATIONS OF GANS IN VARIOUS FIELDS

Generative Adversarial Networks (GANs) have gained momentum in the last few years not only due to their advancements but also due to their applications in various fields. GANs made a remarkable improvement in computer vision, creating possible applications in multiple fields such as deepfakes, video translation, photo restoration, and image completion and generation (Goodfellow et al., 2014). In natural language processing, GANs have the potential to create black-box adversarial attacks (Papernot et al., 2016). Healthcare is another domain in which the applications of GANs have gained momentum. For instance, in drug discovery, GANs have pioneered a new direction for cheminformatics and bioinformatics (Zhavoronkov et al., 2019). Despite certain limitations and disadvantages, GANs have proven groundbreaking in GPU-based applications, video generation, and face aging (Tulyakov et al., 2017).

GANs are revolutionary in several fields including computer vision, natural language processing, art and creativity, and healthcare applications. These networks are widely known for generating images. One of the most influential works proposed a generative network called Progressive GAN to generate real-life object images such as celebrities, bedrooms, birds, and cars (Karras et al., 2017). Additionally, GANs are also widely known for transferring the style of training data like a horse in the image of a zebra (Gatys et al., 2016). The conditional version of GAN, i.e., cGAN, has been developed to control the generation. For example, an image can be generated with and without sunglasses (Mirza & Osindero, 2014). Other than image synthesis, GANs have pioneered deep generative model-based synthetic data. Data scientists and researchers are primarily interested in their application where training and real data are scarce (Xu et al., 2018). Early GANs focused on computer vision and later applications in natural language processing, image captioning, and other data (Radford et al., 2016). GANs were commercialized to exhibit adjustments in their infrastructure and architecture such as DCGAN, iGAN, cGAN, StackGAN, and CycleGAN (Odena et al., 2017). The modeling of GANs was denser and automated in the literature thus far, including the Catalonia Generative Network, Bayesian KNN generator for GAN, and multi-agent neural generative network (Zhang et al., 2019). The evolution of GANs revealed that the architecture had drastically changed the application likelihood of visual data as the GAN modified the rectified linear activation function to Leaky Rectified Linear Activation Units instead of tanh transforms, normalized the weights, skipped the spatial pooling, and used batch normalization (Dumoulin et al., 2017).

3.1. Computer Vision and Image Generation

Generative Adversarial Networks are designed for computer vision tasks. The adversaries are generally two neural networks: the generator and the discriminator. The generator is designed to produce real-world content. There has been significant progress in image synthesis, particularly in the form of super-resolution and inpainting, thanks to this enhancement in GANs (Ledig et al., 2017). It is also designed to be closer to real-world applications to produce goods and portraits (Pathak et al., 2016). After evaluations, the GAN-generated goods have improved, as illustrated by case studies. The generated items have fine and realistic details, where the color distribution matches the distribution of images from the real world (Karras et al., 2019). The image is realistic thanks to the use of a feature matching loss layer in the networks (Wang et al., 2018).

When comparing state-of-the-art results using convolutional neural networks on both datasets, the GAN networks are quicker and achieve better performance (Radford et al., 2016). A true diversified dataset shows that the improved DCGAN and LAPGAN would still perform well on these datasets (Salimans et al., 2016). The graphs are lower than those of competitors when the number of generated categories rises. However, creating fine-grained distinguishing settings and their labels becomes very labor-intensive in real-world scenarios (Mirza & Osindero, 2014). Instead of competition settings, experimenting entirely in real-world settings would be much more informative to emphasize the benefits of automatic data representation learning (Bengio et al., 2015). The ability to trivially apply for hardcore GAN performance guarantees exists when there are no competition entries. With real-world application data already collected, using a small labeled dataset would not be a problem in utilizing the competition settings (Zhang et al., 2018). Furthermore, real-world observations indicate that with a limited number of examples, transfer learning is difficult to produce good results (Yosinski et al., 2014).

3.2. Natural Language Processing

Generative Adversarial Networks have also been used for generating text data. The concept of generating human-like text using deep learning systems has been explored extensively in the field of natural language processing (Cho et al., 2014). At its core, GAN comprises an architecture that has two sophisticated neural networks competing against each other: a generator and a discriminator. The GAN's ability to generate human-like text has been extensively studied in the NLP domain (Zhang et al., 2017). The experimental evaluations demonstrated the vast potential of teaching a GAN model to mimic a variety of natural language tasks, including message completion and dialog generation (Li & Luong, 2015). Adversarial Feature Matching (AFM) has been proposed and paired with a long short-term memory (LSTM) for text generation tasks (Lee et al., 2019). The GAN approach has shown clear advantages over traditional generative models, including LSTM and auto-regressive approaches, in terms of word overlap and BLEU scoring (Bowman et al., 2016).

Existing research has proposed methods to leverage GANs' deep learning capabilities in the field of natural language processing. There is a considerable amount of work that addresses generating human-like text using GAN in the NLP domain (Yu et al., 2017). Some of the proposed methods offer adversarial training frameworks for NLP tasks. The objective of these methods is to improve the fluency and coherence of the generated text (Zhang et al., 2018). Although GAN is efficient in generating realistic sentences, it has the potential to be further explored in several directions to boost the expressive power and data efficiency of the model (Li et al., 2019). A potential research direction in using GAN is to develop a method for mapping the representation between the hidden layers of paired languages directly enforced in the GAN model (Shen et al., 2017). The model can be further trained on the target language pair with only parallel data (Devlin et al., 2018). Given the large amount of ambiguous sentences produced by analyzing the language, there is much to be learned about language understanding as well as sentence generation (Benziane, 2024).

4. ETHICAL CONSIDERATIONS AND CHALLENGES IN GANS

The explorations so far have identified many important ethical considerations and potential challenges related to GAN technology. The basic principles of fairness and bias issues in behavior patterns of GANs often involve data on people, patterns of behavior, and societal dynamics. A network that is trained on biased data can create even more biased material, strengthening skewed conclusions. For instance, in medical imaging research, using a GAN trained on incomplete, "healthy" medical imaging databases creates the potential for masking disease detection. Since much of the content synthesized by GANs is used in an emotional or socio-emotional context, and is indicative of personal information, the need to provide location privacy is a necessity.

There are also concerns about security and privacy raised when considering the intended purpose of GAN-generated images and content. In a privacy context, it is easy to conceive of potentially malicious use cases that result in negative and long-term impacts for individuals. These uses could range from impersonating a person to gain access to restricted resources, to using deepfake images developed using confidential personal information to publicly humiliate politicians and celebrities. The contents that are generated by GANs are posed in their desired atmosphere and are related to emotions and social divisions. In general, contents generated by GANs are fake and are designed to be convincing. Given the playbook to create content that could possess a range of manipulation for the GAN creator, the possibility for misuse is immense. For instance, it has even been considered whether GANs could be used as another potential source for information warfare, to deceive citizens or soldiers. The development of guidelines and frameworks to ensure research and testing of GANs adheres to ethical standards needs to be taken into account. Due to the complex socio-technical issues existing in GANs, there is an established research focus on the ethical issues related to these technical challenges. Research in the field of AI ethics focuses mostly on the overall digitalization, privacy, and the interaction between humans and computers/usability. As much as the advancement continues to take place, it is the role of the AI theorist and/or philosopher to continue the debate on ethical considerations. Furthermore, if the technology created and its creators do not align with such considerations, it is necessary to hold these people and parties accountable. It is thus far the responsibility of the producers and regulators of such technology to promote dialogue, introspection, and ethical technology development.

4.1. Bias and Fairness

All applications of deep learning can indirectly lead to unfair representations of different social groups because they are driven by the biases present in the diverse sources of data they are trained with. This also happens in GANs, where the generator is adapted to automatically mine an independent and faithful distribution that traces the content seen in the provided datasets. The final generator with such a sampled distribution will never have male or female gender intrinsically coded, but their presence can be indirectly suggested from the factual correlation among the present variables between male or female facial pictures and the ones coded in the dataset. More generally, all the possible biases present in the adopted training datasets would be inherited in the generated results from a statistical standpoint. It is thus mandatory to take into consideration with appropriate scrutiny what training data are used for the learning phase. Expanding on this, it is to be noted that there are different possible sources of dataset biases. Some of them profoundly impact society, being as such objects of investigation by the social sciences for pursuing social justice.

A global set of the most recent works has thus aimed at proving the presence of biases in the outputs of the GAN developments. The very first ones superimposed and combined the output of the GAN generator to evaluate the potential overlap of the main features in different dataset features; GAN—and more generally deep learning—has often also represented different genders with diverse amounts of far-reaching reflections. More advanced lines of research have focused on methods to estimate and remove the biases leading to unfair representations from the GAN outputs. Yet, a noteworthy category of discriminator-based techniques faces difficulties in ensuring that the optimization process does not lead to decreasing the generation realism since the discriminator is by itself strongly prone to represent biases when the training set contains them and does not contain the available countermeasures to fight such unfairness. As a logical conclusion, to counter this, a much deeper network is needed, whose features are, however, not that easy to counterbalance. In conclusion, the following on-the-job related strict needs have emerged for GANs: transparent practices for the selection of the training dataset and the overall validation metrics; direct ethical considerations when designing the GAN applications, especially those directly interfacing with end-users in terms of automatic decisional procedures; ongoing pre- and post-implementation risk evaluations.

4.2. Privacy and Security Concerns

Generative Adversarial Networks. Privacy and security concerns. Concerns GANs may pose privacy and security risks as the use cases of GAN technology improve, especially in critical areas such as healthcare and finance. Just as GANs today are capable of generating highly realistic images, it is likely that they will graduate to generating highly realistic anonymous data. Such data will be distinguishable from real datasets with the current technology. Generated patient data from a GAN could potentially leak private information with strong linkages to the original patient. Therefore, creating technology that protects against privacy risks will become an important area for exploration. Already, the GAN community is discussing the possibility of sensitive datasets moving toward safe synthetic versions.

We also have concerns that Generative Adversarial Networks can propagate and reinforce harmful stereotypes by drawing on and amplifying inherent biases in the internet. Generated content could be used to spread harmful and insulting messages or sow discord and uncertainty. There are concerns for counterfeiting, payroll diversion, manufacture of counterfeit replacement parts, quasi-legal entry for home invasion, ambush, extortion, and raising or erasing the credit of a targeted individual as potential privacy invasion, safety, and security concerns for deep fakes. Investigations have looked into the potential misuses of deep fake videos in a variety of scenarios involving widespread distribution via social platforms. Concerns were related to political misinformation, revenge, non-consensual pornography, and embarrassment or brand reputation damage. Here, we specifically discuss new and anticipated concerns related to GANs' standpoint on privacy and security.

5. IMPACT OF GANS ON MODERN TECHNOLOGY

Generative Adversarial Networks (GANs) have made a profound impact on technology over the past several years. The AI community has seen major advancements in realistic image generation, with research on GANs at the forefront of these. Commercially and creatively, GANs have been used for image generation, leading to art, easy manipulation for non-designers, and producing content in the art and movie-poster industries. Furthermore, GANs have enhanced generative adversarial samples that demonstrate that generated images not only look realistic but also pass as real under the scrutiny of deep neural networks.

Data augmentation has consistently been proven to boost the accuracy of models by training a model on a broad synthetic dataset generated by distributing and transforming values from real data. GANs are prime networks that provide synthetic data augmentation and have shown their value in the need for being able to conditionally train models to generate data in areas where data is hard to come by. This has a specifically significant impact on generative models, where a variety of solutions in a label space is required. For example, in the rotation of a bird, the outcomes should reflect realistic movement across an entire spectrum; GANs provide this capability of a high-grade outcome. On the same note, CycleGAN works to 'translate' between two different distributions, providing outputs in a different domain that yet capture the essence of the real-world domain. Interestingly, one of the hardest decisions for applied researchers when discussing the use of these generative models is how to most accurately measure realism. This challenge is due to the subjective nature of recapturing the chaos and entropy present in any real-world dataset. Examining the quality of diversity in distribution has appeared to be not only possible but also 'profound' in GANs, suggesting a substantial role in society for use in both business and the advancement of technology. Nevertheless, more research is needed to synthesize and develop methods to maintain safety for this technology within today's society.

5.1. Advancements in Realistic Image Generation

Realistic Image Generation Advances in Realistic Image Generation Since the introduction of Generative Adversarial Networks (GANs) in 2014, researchers and industry experts have pushed for improvements in the quality and detail of images they can produce for real-world applications. There has been progress at every level of the image generation pipeline, from the architecture of the networks used and the techniques employed to train them, to the optimization algorithms getting the most out of each forward pass. At the time of writing, GANs are capable of generating images of impressive fidelity. Medical imaging is one example, where new methods are under investigation to synthesize realistic tumor streams to subvert segmentation, orientation, and region proposals in treatments targeted at head and neck cancers. Other researchers have used GANs to create realistic-looking skin lesions to test the accuracy of imaging techniques used in the diagnosis of dermatological diseases. Multiple case studies have been conducted on training GANs to perform tasks previously thought impossible, including super resolution, high-fidelity object generation, and conditional text-to-image synthesis. Creating high-resolution, life-like images poses significant computational challenges. For each of the pixels of a 4 Mpix image, the final result is the sum of 7.89 million operations. An nth-layer convolutional neural network requires $9n^2 + 12n$ arithmetic operations to complete, confirming the computation necessary to improve the spatial resolution increases quadratically with the depth of the network, and linearly alongside the size of the kernel and the number of input/output feature maps. At 8-bit integer precision, a significant acceleration can be achieved using vector multiplication instructions for dot products. Graphics Processing Units (GPUs) outperform Central Processing

Units (CPUs) by running multiple calculations at the same time, enabling the simultaneous training of GAN architectures on very high-definition images. This allows for faster and higher quality image generation with the use of personal computers. With all these developments, new GAN architecture models have become capable of generating high-resolution human faces similar to real people. GANs have a high potential for photorealistic content generation with applications including digital fabrication, gaming, design, advertising, and publicity.

5.2. Enhancing Data Augmentation Techniques

Nowadays, data generation technologies have been used to almost bypass the expensive collection of high-quality data or to help solve some problems of time or uncertainty of real-world data due to privacy or commercial reasons. Among generation technologies, Generative Adversarial Network is widely used to synthesize new data. The idea of GAN is to assume an unknown prior distribution and estimate a data distribution through a deterministic mapping. GAN can synthesize diverse and realistic data, but it is hard to guarantee the quality of synthesized data. For instance, generated faces are sometimes terrible or hard for human interpretation. The main advantage of GAN is that the synthesized data can be used to complement the real data. Since the capacity of human cognitive processing is limited, the number of people annotating images is limited, and the types of annotations are limited. When there is only real data with annotations, the extracted feature representation is limited, which limits the generalization ability of the classification model.

Simultaneously, synthetic public data is usually unlimited and can be hard for machine learning models, which can be found with the approach of the presence of limited labeled real data and unlimited synthetic data. Several exemplary applications demonstrate that GAN can be utilized to augment data. GAN is broadly applied to computer vision to synthesize more images in the set by using a large number of real-world multimedia data. Moreover, the generator generally generates a wide variety of plausible predictions. For natural language processing, the GAN approach was used to augment the real textual names of plant species by generating new plausible names. Moreover, in the field of indoor scene graph predictions, a GAN can generate possible contents of the scene objects after the local features are put into the trained model. The results show that synthesized data has a good effect on learning good visual features through the Generative Adversarial Network. Overall, experiments show that data synthesized from GAN can improve data efficiency and generalization in a range of applications.

However, data augmentation likely overfits when the synthetically generated data are not realistic enough. Another potential risk of simply scaling the amount of training data through data augmentation is that the distribution of the data changes.

Hence, it is important to provide the balance of the percentage of real data and synthesized data, especially when the generated data are realistic. It is also difficult to judge when data augmentation has reached overfitting. When the increased amount of data is large, the value of indicators does not continue to change, but there may be a slight increase at the beginning, which may have an extreme value. Thus, to make a final decision, it may be necessary to determine the negative correlation between the indicators for the increase of data. How to balance the indicators will be further studied as a future research direction based on a certain standard. In general, the real and generated data are similar in some data distribution. In addition, since the distribution of generated data highly depends on the amount of real data, when the ratio of real data is too small, the distribution of generated data may still be close to the amount of real data.

5.3. Improving Generative Models in AI

The need for generative models in the AI landscape has motivated the exploration of GANs, particularly because they can generate very realistic samples by mimicking a complex data distribution. The differentially private GAN has been proposed to approximate GANs with the differential privacy guarantee. GANs can potentially be trained to generate high-quality, human-like outputs in a variety of domains, including text, images, voices, and video frames in a way that other generative models do not. Since GAN was proposed, a better understanding of how to design new models and train these generative models to combat issues like mode collapse has become clearer. Additionally, to investigate how GANs could be trained efficiently, GAN research has inspired other advancements in generative modeling as well.

In practice, researchers have shown that GANs are able to produce high-quality data that can better train other machine learning models. For example, synthetic data generated using GANs is helpful for training discriminative classifiers that perform better in privacy-sensitive situations. GANs have allowed generative models to make new strides by collaborating with existing generative approaches. This encourages the development of generative AI models beyond GAN constructs, which typically outperform classical approaches to generation. In short, GANs and their subsequent advances have the potential to revolutionize generative modeling by allowing new models to access the state-of-the-art results that GANs produce. Although continuous advancements in GAN research are being made, this prospective impact is still being realized to a larger extent and has not been fully realized yet, as generative modeling using GANs is evolving continuously.

6. FUTURE DIRECTIONS AND EMERGING TRENDS IN GANS

Generative Adversarial Networks (GAN) is an inherently interdisciplinary technique, armed with the sheer potential to induce a profound impact on a multitude of applications relevant across various industries and academic research communities. Today, researchers are actively probing into a plethora of novel GAN architectures and enabling techniques within the most recent areas of exploration. In healthcare, there are GANs designed for generating oncological images of cancer progression. They have been used as a useful tool for developing and validating image synthesis algorithms and generative models used for medical image data creation.

Similarly, in finance, there are 3D GANs for financial data that learn a family of financial time series generators based on variational principles, reducing multi-time step predictions to single-step prediction problems while dealing with distribution shifting during the prediction stage. Clearly, a growing number of interdisciplinary applications are gaining momentum within the GAN research community. While those discussed may facilitate a unique perspective for brokering greater connectivity between these areas, it is precisely in this connection that we are also most uniquely positioned to promote ongoing dialogue in the several overlapping realms. Nevertheless, GANs are still a field that requires big, innovative ideas. Present alone isn't enough to keep GANs relevant. That is why innovation beyond supervising signals like adversarial or reinforcement learning is sorely needed. Works that focus on pure unsupervised learning, self-supervised learning, unsupervised domain adaptation, and other works that have the potential to extend to new domains are of particular interest. Finally, another interesting trajectory here is to track directions and fields where GAN research is heading.

GANs are reaching the tipping point of saturation in many fields where they are currently serving, and the works that are making inroads into areas such as special autonomous systems, e-commerce, networking, telecommunications, medicine, law, environmental science, and more are likely to be salient in the future. In the discussions of the possible directions outlined above, some potential challenges in the exploration of those domains are noted. These could be understood as a roadmap to the next major challenges as they pertain to GAN research. Building upon past approaches can prepare us for future challenges. Thus, there is definite potential in bringing such discussions more precisely into the public domain.

6.1. Novel Architectures and Techniques

One of the central themes of advances in GANs is novel architectures and techniques. Researchers are coming up with innovative designs to improve and streamline the performance of GANs. Furthermore, self-supervised learning has seen applications as an auxiliary loss for GANs across tasks, improving training metrics and results. While many of these new architectures have already trickled down into application, there are challenges as the community makes all these contributions scale to larger datasets and resolutions. GANs are a powerful method for generating new data and training various models across tasks in AI and machine learning. Part of what we find exciting about the development of GANs is the community's joy in experimentation and design that is reflected in the variety of different ideas and methods explored.

Overall, modern GAN architectures are more stable and generate higher quality images than ever before. While there is still progress to be made in enhancing the resolution and diversity of the images hallucinated, many GANs are now good enough to be used in real-world applications, which is a major milestone in the field. There have been many successful models studied in computer vision, including super-resolution GAN, which can fill in details missing from images, and StyleGAN, which can generate high-quality synthetic images.

6.2. Interdisciplinary Applications

Interdisciplinary Applications Generative Adversarial Networks (GANs) are making an impact beyond traditional domains of technology. A growing body of work demonstrates their applications in areas like ecology, simulation-based education, digital humanities, and digital musicology. This shows us that some of the most impactful and effective uses of GANs are in applications that bring together technology and other societal needs and sectors. Indeed, the significance of interdisciplinary work is seen as so strong that many solicitations for multimillion-dollar frontier research programs place an explicit emphasis on cross-disciplinary teams. Artificial intelligence and data science more broadly are the focus of significant effort in solving real world problems and serving the public interest. There are particular areas of growing interest in the technology communities, such as sustainability, where GANs are applied for climate and meteorological modeling, simulation, and forecasting, or in generating synthetic images for ecological studies.

Despite substantial interest from the technology community in science and technology collaborations, these examples are primarily from the engineering and science communities, and do not yet extend deeply into the complex social and political milieu that is the focus of researchers in the various branches of the humanities. Many GAN- and deep learning-based models have seen substantial applications in art history, however. The use of GANs in these and other domains will require engagement from multiple stakeholders when designing and implementing novel models, and more generally when interpreting and disseminating work. For GANs specifically, this may involve clarification, reinterpretation, or modification of the problem specification according to the standards or norms of a given discipline. The development of GAN technology and techniques cannot be carried out effectively without knowledge and skills from multiple disciplines collaborating together. Model training requires insights from the domain in question, or work runs the risk of inaccurate or, worse, incorrect results. All these major making.

7. CONCLUSION AND SUMMARY OF KEY FINDINGS

Generative Adversarial Networks (GANs) have emerged as a groundbreaking innovation in artificial intelligence, reshaping multiple domains with their ability to generate highly realistic synthetic data. This chapter has provided a comprehensive overview of GAN technology, examining its foundational principles, diverse applications, and the ethical considerations associated with its rapid evolution. GANs have already proven their transformative potential in fields such as computer vision, healthcare, digital art, and natural language processing.

Looking ahead, the next decade promises to be a pivotal era for GANs as they intersect with emerging technologies and address increasingly complex challenges. One exciting avenue is the integration of GANs with quantum computing. Quantum-enhanced GANs have the potential to exponentially accelerate the training process, solving problems that are currently computationally infeasible. This could unlock new possibilities in fields such as cryptography, materials science, and large-scale data generation.

Another promising trend lies in the advancement of autonomous systems. GANs can be leveraged to simulate diverse environments for training autonomous vehicles, drones, and robotics. By generating realistic synthetic scenarios, GANs will enable these systems to better handle rare edge cases, ensuring safer and more reliable performance in real-world conditions.

In addition to these technological integrations, GANs are poised to play a critical role in addressing global challenges. For instance, they could support climate modeling and environmental research by generating detailed simulations of weather patterns or ecological systems. Furthermore, their applications in personalized medicine and drug discovery are expected to expand, enabling faster and more precise diagnostic tools and treatment options.

However, as GANs continue to evolve, it is crucial to address ethical and societal concerns proactively. The development of robust regulatory frameworks, transparent methodologies, and interdisciplinary collaborations will be essential to ensure the responsible use of GAN technology.

In conclusion, GANs are not just a technological marvel of today but a foundational tool shaping the future of artificial intelligence. Their versatility and potential for innovation promise to revolutionize industries and tackle some of the most pressing challenges of our time. By fostering continued research, ethical practices, and cross-disciplinary engagement, the AI community can unlock the full potential of GANs in the coming decades.

REFERENCES

Aldausari, N., Sowmya, A., Marcus, N., & Mohammadi, G. (2020). Video Generative Adversarial Networks [PDF]. *RE:view*.

Arjovsky, M., & Bottou, L. (2017). Towards Principled Methods for Training Generative Adversarial Networks. arXiv preprint arXiv:1701.04862.

Bengio, Y.. (2015). Learning deep architectures for AI. *Foundations and Trends in Machine Learning*, *2*(1), 1–127. DOI: 10.1561/2200000006

Benziane, S. (2024). Innovating Prosperity: Intelligent Approaches and Economic Paradigms for Sustainable Futures. In *Intelligent Methods and Alternative Economic Models for Sustainability,* pp. 194-241, IGI Global.

Bowman, S. R.. (2016). *Generating Sentences from a Continuous Space*. In arXiv:1511.06349. DOI: 10.18653/v1/K16-1002

Brock, A., ... (2018). Large Scale GAN Training for High Fidelity Natural Image Synthesis. arXiv preprint arXiv:1809.11096.

Cho, K., ... (2014). *Learning phrase representations using RNN encoder-decoder for statistical machine translation*. In EMNLP, 2014. DOI: 10.3115/v1/D14-1179

Dash, A., Ye, J., & Wang, G. (2021). A review of Generative Adversarial Networks, GANs, and its applications in a wide variety of disciplines—from medical to remote sensing. *arXiv preprint arXiv:2110.01442*. arXiv

Devlin, J., ... (2018). *BERT: Pre-training of deep bidirectional transformers for language understanding*. In NAACL, 2018.

Dumoulin, V., ... (2017). *Adversarially learned inference*. In Advances in Neural Information Processing Systems, NeurIPS, 2017.

Gatys, L. A., ... (2016). *Image style transfer using convolutional neural networks*. In CVPR, 2016. DOI: 10.1109/CVPR.2016.265

Goodfellow, I., ... (2014). *Generative Adversarial Nets*. In Advances in Neural Information Processing Systems, 27, 2672-2680.

Goodfellow, I. J., ... (2014). Generative Adversarial Networks. arXiv preprint arXiv:1406.2661.

Goodfellow, I. J., Pouget-Abadie, J., Mirza, M., Xu, B., Warde-Farley, D., Ozair, S., Courville, A., & Bengio, Y. (2014). Generative Adversarial Networks. *arXiv preprint arXiv:1406.2661*. arXiv

Gulrajani, I., ... (2017). Improved Training of Wasserstein GANs. arXiv preprint arXiv:1704.00028.

Heusel, M., ... (2017). GANs Trained by a Two Time-Scale Update Rule Converge to a Local Nash Equilibrium. arXiv preprint arXiv:1706.08500.

Jin, L., Tan, F., & Jiang, S. (2020). Generative Adversarial Network Technologies and Applications in Computer Vision. ncbi.nlm.nih.gov

Karras, T., ... (2017). *Progressive growing of GANs for improved quality, stability, and variation.* In International Conference on Machine Learning, ICML, 2017.

Karras, T., ... (2019). A Style-Based Generator Architecture for Generative Adversarial Networks. arXiv preprint arXiv:1812.04948. DOI: 10.1109/CVPR.2019.00453

Karras, T., ... (2019). *A style-based generator architecture for generative adversarial networks.* In CVPR, 2019. DOI: 10.1109/CVPR.2019.00453

Khiloun, I. E., Belmabrouk, K., & Dekhici, L., (2024). Literature Review on Supply Chains Optimization Using Multi-Agents Communication and Collaboration. *Intelligent Methods and Alternative Economic Models for Sustainability*, 74-94.

Koshino, K., Werner, R. A., Pomper, M. G., Bundschuh, R. A., ... (2021). Narrative review of generative adversarial networks in medical and molecular imaging. ncbi.nlm.nih.gov

Ledig, C., ... (2017). *Photo-realistic single image super-resolution using a generative adversarial network.* In CVPR, 2017. DOI: 10.1109/CVPR.2017.19

Lee, K.. (2019). *Adversarial Feature Matching for Text Generation.* In arXiv:1910.01888.

Li, Y., & Luong, M.-T. (2015). *I2T: Improving the quality of machine translation with GANs.* In ACL, 2015.

Li, Z.. (2019). *Boosting expressive power in GAN-based NLP models: Challenges and directions.* In *Proceedings of the International Conference on NLP*, 2019.

Mirza, M., & Osindero, S. (2014). *Conditional Generative Adversarial Nets.* In arXiv:1411.1784.

Miyato, T., ... (2018). Spectral Normalization for Generative Adversarial Networks. arXiv preprint arXiv:1802.05957.

Odena, A., ... (2017). *Conditional image generation with PixelCNN decoders.* In Advances in Neural Information Processing Systems, NeurIPS, 2017.

Papernot, N., ... (2016). *The limitations of deep learning in adversarial settings*. In Proceedings of the IEEE European Symposium on Security and Privacy, EuroS&P, 2016, 372–387. DOI: 10.1109/EuroSP.2016.36

Pathak, D., ... (2016). *Context encoders: Feature learning by inpainting*. In CVPR, 2016. DOI: 10.1109/CVPR.2016.278

Radford, A., ... (2015). Unsupervised Representation Learning with Deep Convolutional Generative Adversarial Networks. arXiv preprint arXiv:1511.06434.

Radford, A.. (2016). *Unsupervised representation learning with deep convolutional generative adversarial networks*. arXiv:1511.06434.

Radford, A., ... (2016). *Unsupervised learning with generative adversarial networks*. In ICLR, 2016.

Redhouane, L., Sarah, B., & Abdelkader, B. (2014, June). Dorsal hand vein pattern feature extraction with wavelet transforms. In *The 2014 international symposium on networks, computers and communications* (pp. 1–5). IEEE.

Salimans, T., ... (2016). Improved Techniques for Training GANs. arXiv preprint arXiv:1606.03498.

Salimans, T., ... (2016). *Improved techniques for training GANs*. In Advances in Neural Information Processing Systems, NeurIPS, 2016.

Shahriar, S., & Hayawi, K. (2022, March). NFTGAN: Non-fungible token art generation using generative adversarial networks. In *Proceedings of the 2022 7th International Conference on Machine Learning Technologies* (pp. 255-259).

Shen, T., ... (2017). *Mapping representations for GAN-based NLP models*. In NeurIPS, 2017.

Sønderby, C. K., ... (2016). Amortised MAP Inference for Image Super-resolution. arXiv preprint arXiv:1610.04490.

Tulyakov, S., ... (2017). *Mocogan: Generating motion sequences with generative adversarial networks*. In CVPR, 2017.

Wang, R., Bashyam, V., Yang, Z., Yu, F., Tassopoulou, V., Chintapalli, S. S., & Davatzikos, C. (2023). Applications of generative adversarial networks in neuroimaging and clinical neuroscience. *NeuroImage*, *269*, 119898.

Wang, Z., ... (2018). *Perceptual loss for real-time style transfer and super-resolution*. In ECCV, 2018.

Xu, L.. (2018). Data augmentation using generative adversarial networks for improving deep learning in healthcare applications. *Journal of Healthcare Engineering*, •••, 2018.

Yosinski, J., ... (2014). *How transferable are features in deep neural networks?* In NeurIPS, 2014.

Yu, L., ... (2017). *SeqGAN: Sequence Generative Adversarial Nets with Policy Gradient*. In AAAI, 2017. DOI: 10.1609/aaai.v31i1.10804

Zhang, L.. (2019). *Learning to generate ambiguous sentences using GANs*. In arXiv:1904.11991.

Zhang, X.. (2018). *Leveraging GANs for transfer learning: A new frontier in synthetic data generation*. arXiv:1811.11247.

Zhang, X.. (2018). Improving GANs for NLP tasks: A survey of recent developments and future directions. *Journal of Machine Learning Research, 19*(1), 52–58.

Zhang, Y., ... (2017). *Adversarial feature matching for text generation*. In ICML, 2017.

Zhang, Y., ... (2019). *Catalonia Generative Network: A new approach to generative modeling*. In Neural Networks, 2019.

Zhao, J., ... (2016). Energy-based Generative Adversarial Network. arXiv preprint arXiv:1609.03126.

Zhavoronkov, A., Ivanenkov, Y. A., Aliper, A., Veselov, M. S., Aladinskiy, V. A., Aladinskaya, A. V., Terentiev, V. A., Polykovskiy, D. A., Kuznetsov, M. D., Asadulaev, A., Volkov, Y., Zholus, A., Shayakhmetov, R. R., Zhebrak, A., Minaeva, L. I., Zagribelnyy, B. A., Lee, L. H., Soll, R., Madge, D., & Aspuru-Guzik, A. (2019). Deep learning enables rapid identification of potent DDR1 kinase inhibitors. *Nature Biotechnology, 37*(9), 1038–1040. DOI: 10.1038/s41587-019-0224-x PMID: 31477924

Section 3
Specialized Architectures

Chapter 6
CNN in Medical Imaging:
Advantages, Challenges, and Future Scope

Affaan Shaikh
https://orcid.org/0009-0004-7590-7456
Neuratia Labs, UAE

Ravi Teja Kothuru
https://orcid.org/0009-0002-9555-151X
University of San Diego, USA

ABSTRACT

Convolutional Neural Networks (CNNs) have revolutionized medical imaging, enhancing the accuracy, efficiency, and depth of analysis for complex data such as X-rays, MRIs, and CT scans. Their ability to detect subtle patterns offers significant advantages in early diagnosis, prognosis, and disease monitoring, particularly for conditions like cancer, neurological disorders, and cardiovascular diseases. Despite these benefits, CNN applications face challenges, including the need for large and diverse datasets, high computational demands, and limited interpretability, which can impact clinical decision-making. This chapter explores the advantages of CNNs in medical imaging, highlights key challenges, and discusses future opportunities for real-time analysis, multimodal integration, and personalized medicine. This chapter also goes through the types of CNNs and their individual applications and real time insights. It also explores different types and architectures of CNNs, highlighting their unique applications and potential for providing real-time insights.

DOI: 10.4018/979-8-3373-0735-0.ch006

1. INTRODUCTION

1.1. Overview of Medical Imaging and AI

a) *Definition of Medical Imaging:*

Medical imaging generates visual images of the body's internal structures, allowing physicians to observe normal and abnormal functions. Techniques such as X-rays, CT scans, PET scans, MRI, and ultrasound as shown in **Figure 1** are used to identify and manage conditions like heart disease, cancer, and bone fractures (Tehrani, 2020). Advanced technologies, such as PET/CT hybrids and 3D ultrasound, provide high-definition images and improved accuracy, enabling more efficient diagnosis and treatment of complex conditions (Hussain et al., 1993).

Figure 1. Visualization of X-ray, CT, MRI and PET Scans

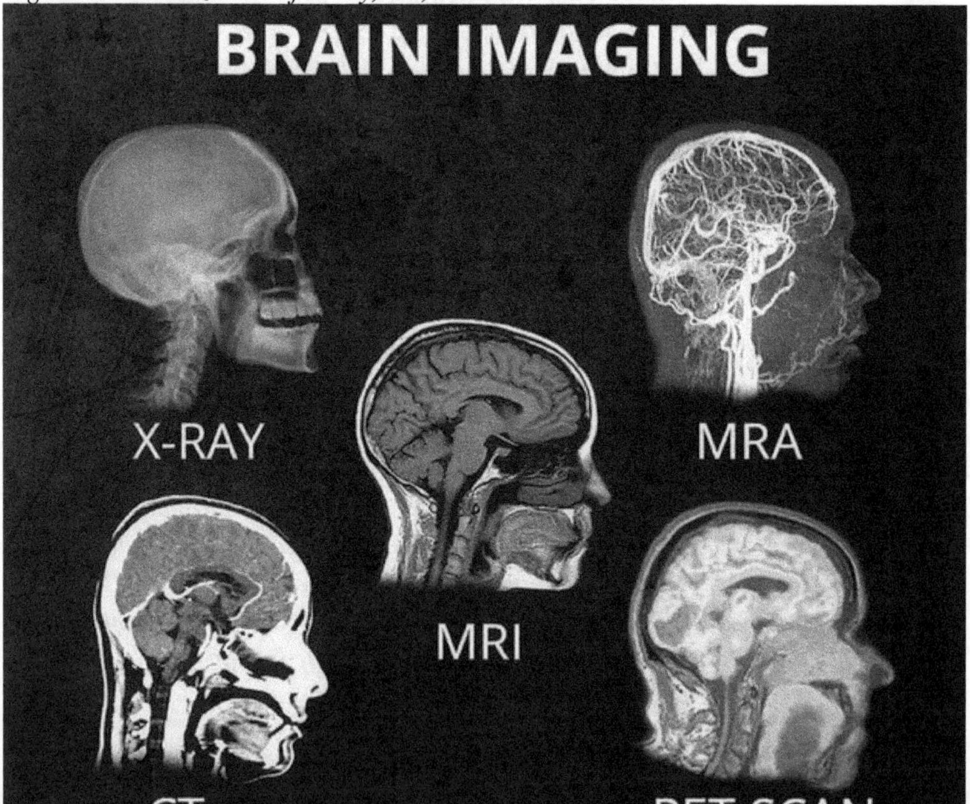

b) Evolution of Medical Imaging:

Bercovich & Javitt (2018) noted that medical imaging has transformed medicine since its inception. In 1895, Wilhelm Conrad Roentgen discovered X-rays, allowing doctors to visualize internal structures for the first time. His first image of his wife's hand (see **Figure 2**) marked a new era in diagnostics, leading to over a thousand scientific papers in one year. The 1940s saw the introduction of ultrasound, initially used therapeutically before Ian Donald adapted it for diagnostics in 1958, becoming crucial in obstetrics due to its non-invasive nature and lack of ionizing radiation.

The 1970s brought major advancements with Computed Tomography (CT) introduced by Sir Godfrey Hounsfield, who performed his first patient scan in 1971. CT provided detailed cross-sectional images, enhancing diagnostic capabilities for soft tissues. Shortly after, Magnetic Resonance Imaging (MRI) emerged in 1973, offering superior soft tissue contrast and becoming essential in oncology. Nuclear medicine techniques, such as positron emission tomography (PET), further improved imaging by enabling functional representation alongside anatomical details. Recent digital technologies have transformed medical imaging, shifting from film-based methods to digital formats that facilitate remote analysis and enhance image processing through Picture Archiving and Communication Systems (PACS).

Figure 2. The First X-ray discovered by Roentgen

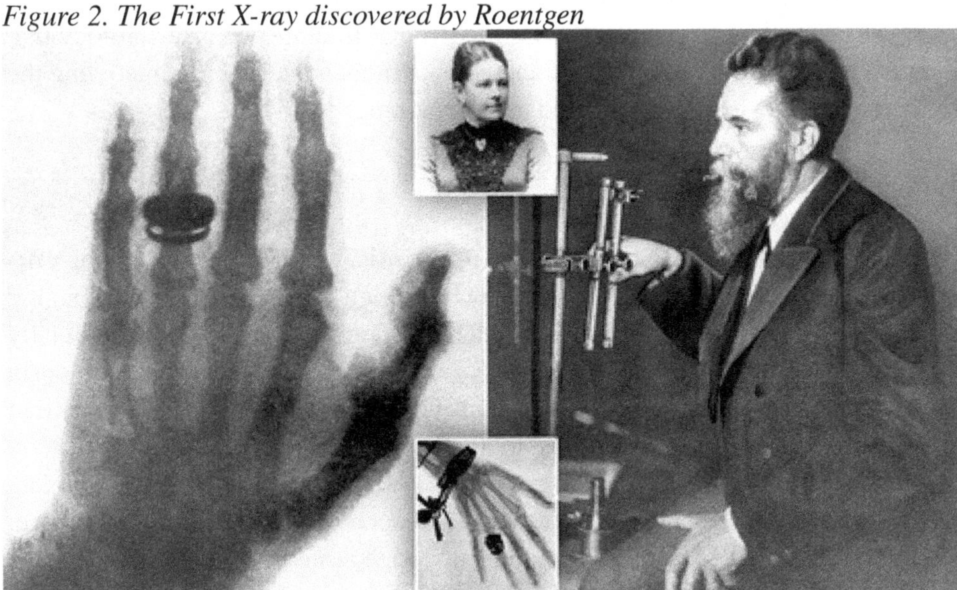

c) Importance of Medical Imaging in Healthcare:

Medical imaging plays a vital role in healthcare, enabling doctors to diagnose and treat diseases non-invasively by visualizing the internal workings of the body. This capability allows for early disease detection, improving treatment outcomes and saving lives. Medical imaging also guides treatment decisions, helping doctors monitor patient responses to therapies. Advances in technology, such as artificial intelligence, are further enhancing diagnostic and treatment processes.

In the future, medical imaging is expected to become increasingly significant, facilitating continuous monitoring of complex diseases and providing more effective treatment options.

d) Introduction to Artificial Intelligence:

Intelligence refers to the ability to learn, solve problems, understand emotions, and make decisions. AI methods, including machine learning, mimic these cognitive functions, allowing systems to perceive, plan, reason, and communicate (Manning, 2020). AI combines these skills into smart agents that evolve over time.

Artificial Intelligence is a broad field of computer science enabling machines to exhibit human-like intelligence. This includes not only programming a computer to drive a car but also allowing it to learn and display human-like behaviors, such as road rage. According to Dr. Paul (2019), "Artificial Intelligence is technology that behaves intelligently using skills associated with human intelligence, including the ability to perceive, learn, reason, and act autonomously."

e) Role of AI in Medical Imaging:

Artificial Intelligence (AI) is transforming medical imaging by improving efficiency, precision, and patient treatment. It has become a key focus in medical imaging research, with publications in diagnostic imaging rising from about 100–150 annually in 2007–2008 to 1000–1100 in 2017–2018 (Tang, 2020). AI excels at autonomously identifying complex patterns in imaging data, enabling quantitative evaluations that reveal disease features not easily seen by the naked eye (Tang, 2020).

AI automates routine tasks like image processing, quality assurance, and data management, allowing healthcare professionals to focus on patient care (Medscience, 2024). For example, AI can identify and categorize structures in medical images, including organs and tumors, significantly speeding up diagnostics (Medscience, 2024). Additionally, AI helps manage large volumes of imaging data, making it easier for professionals to access and evaluate extensive patient information (Medscience, 2024).

This integration improves diagnostic accuracy and enhances overall patient care. AI supports clinical trials by providing high-quality data quickly, facilitating informed treatment decisions. However, implementing AI in healthcare must be approached carefully, ensuring algorithms are developed responsibly and ethically, with a strong emphasis on patient privacy and safety (Medscience, 2024). As AI evolves, its potential to transform medical imaging and improve patient outcomes remains significant (Tang, 2020).

1.2. Emergence of CNNs in Medical Imaging

a) ***Brief history and development of Convolutional Neural Networks (CNNs).*** Before directly going to the history of CNNs, first let us better understand how the Neural Networks came into picture. The following **Figure 3** provides a visualization of the history of Neural Networks.

Figure 3. History of Neural Networks

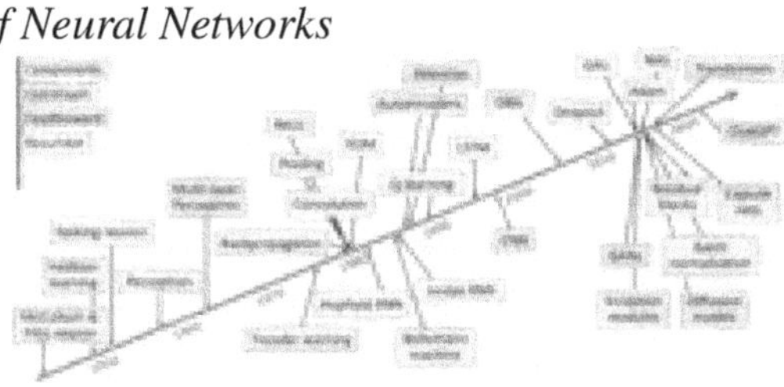

The history of Convolutional Neural Networks (CNNs) dates back to the 1960s, when David Marr and Frank Rosenblatt first introduced the concept of neural networks. Kunihiko Fukushima later developed the Neocognitron, a neural network design that utilized convolutional and pooling layers to identify patterns in images. Table 1 provides a visual representation of the history and evolution of CNNs.

Table 1. Evolution of CNN

Name of CNN Architecture	Year	Developed By
Neocognitron	1960s	Kunihiko Fukushima
LeNet-5	1998	Yann Lecun
AlexNet	2012	Alex Krizhevsky

continued on following page

Table 1. Continued

Name of CNN Architecture	Year	Developed By
Network in Network	2013	MinLin
VGGNet	2014	Simonyan and Zisserman
GooLeNet / InceptionNet	2014	Google
ResNet	2015	Kaiming He
DenseNet	2017	Gao Huang
MobileNet	2017	Google
XceptionNet	2017	Francois Chollet
NASNet	2017	Google
CapsuleNet	2017	Hinton

b) Role of CNNs in revolutionizing medical imaging:

Introduction. Medical imaging serves as a crucial instrument in identifying and tracking illnesses. The emergence of CNNs has revolutionized this area by automating intricate image analysis functions. CNNs have accelerated diagnosis, improved accuracy, and enhanced accessibility for healthcare professionals.

Benefits of CNNs. CNNs are widely used for analyzing images from modalities like X-rays, MRIs, and CT scans, aiding in the detection of tumors, fractures, and infections, which supports improved clinical decision-making (Salehi et al., 2023). For example, CNNs can quickly pinpoint problematic areas in chest X-rays, alleviating radiologists' workloads.

Uses in Health Care. CNNs are commonly employed in the analysis of images from modalities like X-rays, MRIs, and CT scans. They aid in identifying issues such as tumors, fractures, and infections, assisting physicians in making improved decisions (Salehi et al., 2023). For instance, CNNs can swiftly identify problematic regions in a chest X-ray, lessening the burden on radiologists.

Function of Transfer Learning. Transfer learning has significantly boosted CNN performance by allowing researchers to utilize pre-trained models on smaller datasets. This is particularly advantageous in healthcare, where annotated data is often limited (Salehi et al., 2023). It reduces training time and enhances efficiency.

Challenges and Liimitations. Despite their success, CNNs face challenges such as their "black-box" nature, which complicates understanding decision-making processes. This lack of interpretability raises concerns in critical medical applications (Anwar et al., 2018). Moreover, acquiring high-quality annotated datasets remains difficult due to time and cost constraints.

Future Scope. The future of CNNs in medical imaging looks promising. Researchers are working on developing more interpretable models and integrating multi-modal data to enhance accuracy. Investigations into real-time applications, such as AI-assisted diagnostics during surgeries, are also ongoing (Salehi et al., 2023).

2. CONVOLUTIONAL NEURAL NETWORKS (CNNS): AN OVERVIEW

2.1. Fundamentals of Convolutional Neural Networks (CNNs)

CNNs have revolutionized the field of Computer Vision, powering advancements in Image Recognition, Object Detection, and various other visual tasks. CNNs have ability to automatically learn hierarchical representations from data. In this section, we'll explore how a CNN works, how does it differ from traditional Machine Learning techniques, and the rich landscape of CNN architectures, each tailored to specific challenges and use cases.

a) How CNNs work (Layers, Convolution, Pooling, Activation Functions). When we analyzing an image try analyzing it using Artificial Neural Network (ANN), the image is represented as pixels Matrix. To process it, we flatten the matrix (e.g., from 256 x 256 to a 1 x 65536 array), which loses spatial dependence or local correlation properties where neighboring pixels are similar. This method is inadequate for image processing or classification. CNNs provide a better alternative. Refer to **Figure 4** for CNN architecture; CNNs are also known as ConvNets.

Figure 4. CNN Architecture

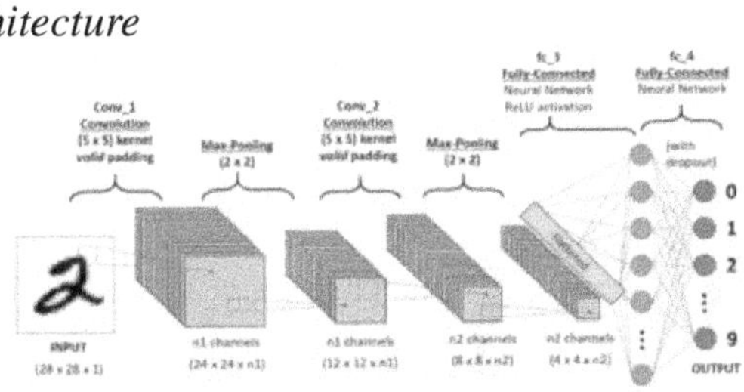

- **Input Layer.** The image shows an RGB picture split into its three components: Red, Green, and Blue (**Figure 5**). Images can be represented in various color spaces such as Grayscale, RGB, HSV, and CMYK. Larger image sizes increase computational demands. A CNN transforms images into a more manageable format for processing while maintaining essential features for accurate predictions, which is vital for effective feature learning and scaling to large datasets. The input format is usually (height, width, channels) (O'Shea & Nash, 2015).

Figure 5. RGB Image

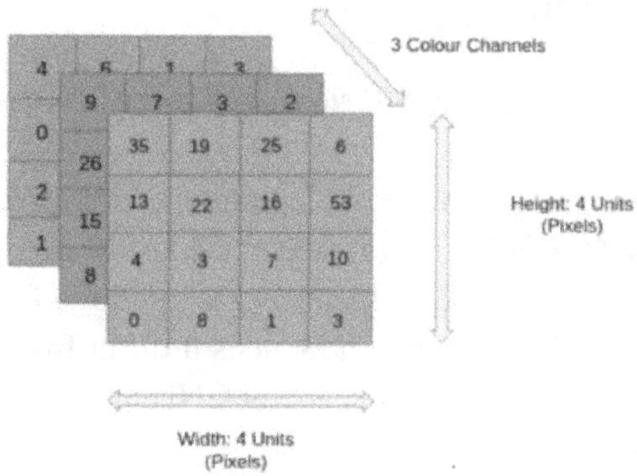

- **Convolution Layer.** The Convolution layer is crucial for extracting features from input images using filters or kernels.
    - o *Filters (or Kernels).* Compact matrices traverse the image to detect features like edges, corners, and textures. The kernel shape can be customized; for example, **Figure 6** shows a 3 x 3 kernel. It performs a dot product with the corresponding pixel values of the input image, producing a convolved result that retains all spatial information.

Figure 6. Convolution using Kernel

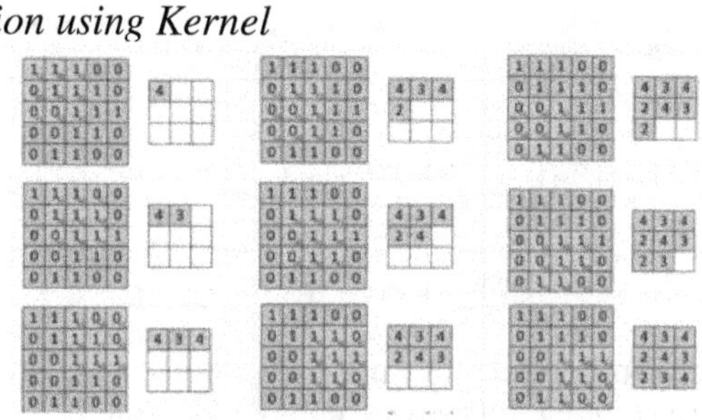

- o ***Stride.*** It defines the filter's movement over the image (LeCun et al., 2015). With a stride of 1, the kernel moves nine times, performing element-wise multiplication (Hadamard Product) with corresponding image areas. The filter shifts right across the width, then drops down to continue until the entire image is processed. In multi-channel images like RGB, the kernel matches the input image's depth, applying matrix multiplication to yield a single-depth Convoluted Feature Output. See **Figure 7** for convolution with a stride of 2.

Figure 7. Convolution using Stride of 2

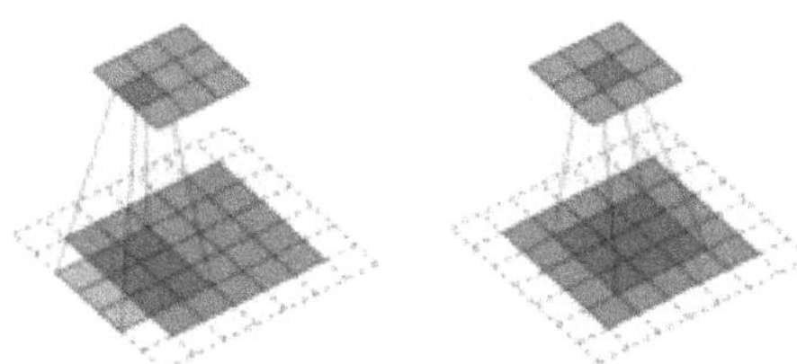

- o ***Padding.*** Padding adds extra pixels around an image's borders to preserve its size after convolution. Zero padding results in added pixel values of zero, reducing the image size. To maintain original dimensions and effectively extract low-level features, additional pixels are included. The convolution operation extracts high-level features like edges, while the first layer captures low-level features such as color and gradients. There are two types of padding results:
- o Valid Padding → reduces dimensionality.
- o Same Padding → preserves dimensionality.

For instance, augmenting a 5x5x1 image to 6x6x1 and applying a 3x3x1 kernel results in a 5x5x1 convolved matrix (Same Padding). In contrast, applying the kernel without padding yields a matrix of the kernel's dimensions, (Valid Padding). Refer **Figure 8** to better visualize about Zero padding.

Figure 8. Zero padding

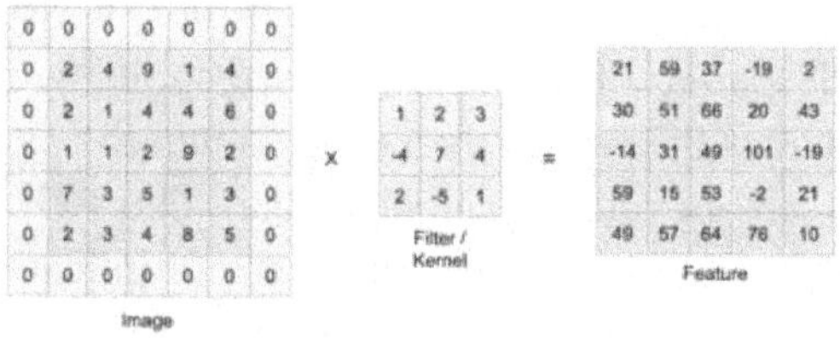

Every convolutional layer produces feature maps that demonstrate the patterns identified in the image. For example, in medical imaging, convolutional layers are capable of detecting irregularities like tumors in X-rays or MRI scans (Litjens et al., 2017).

- **Activation Function.** An activation function determines whether a neuron activates, influencing its input's significance in predictions. These functions enable the network to learn complex patterns by introducing non-linearity. Common activation functions include:
    - ***Sigmoid.*** Used in CNN models for binary classification.
    - ***tanh.*** Similar to sigmoid but symmetrical around the origin, with values ranging from -1 to 1.
    - ***Softmax.*** Used in multinomial logistic regression as the final activation function, converting outputs into a probability distribution across classes.
    - ***ReLU.*** Prevents all neurons at once, enhancing learning efficiency by setting negative values to zero and retaining only positive features (Agarap, 2018).
- **Pooling Layer.** Pooling reduces feature map size, lowering computational costs and preventing overfitting. In CNNs, it simplifies features from convolutional filters, enabling the network to recognize features regardless of their location. This process decreases spatial dimensions, facilitates dimensionality reduction, and extracts key features invariant to rotation and position, aiding efficient model training. There are two types of pooling layers in a CNN (see **Figure 9**).
    - ***Max Pooling.*** Preserves the highest value from a specified area.
    - ***Average Pooling.*** Calculates the average value from a specified area.

Pooling layers ensure the model prioritizes important features, regardless of their precise location in the image (O'Shea & Nash, 2015).

Figure 9. Types of Pooling

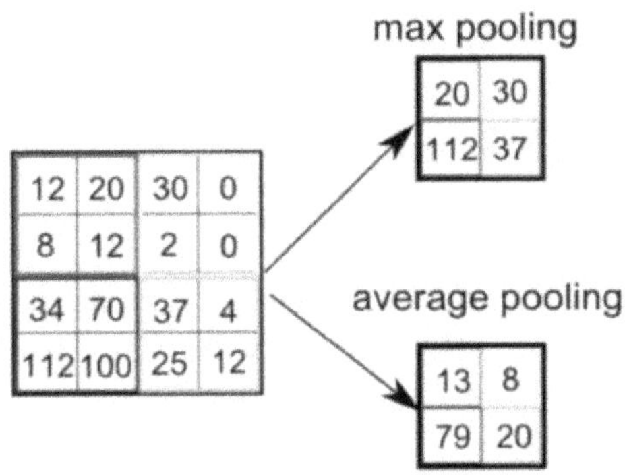

- **Flattening.** Flattening is conversion a matrix of image pixels to a single-row array of multiple columns. For example: if an image pixels matrix is of 256 x 256 shape, Flattening converts it to a shape of 1 x 256 while transitioning from Pooling layer to Fully-Connected layer in CNN. The following **Figure 10** explains us about Flattening.

Figure 10. Flattening

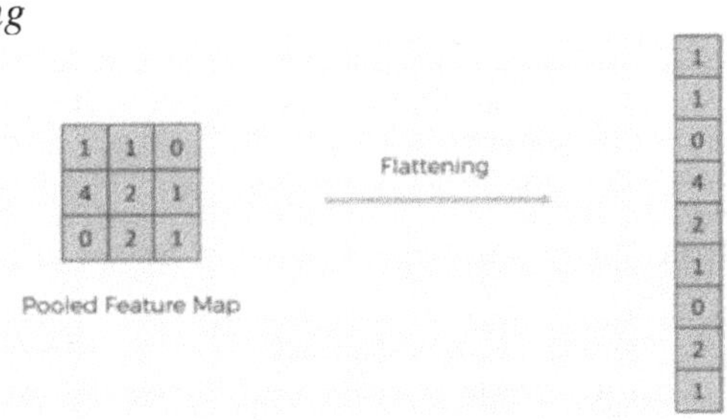

- **Fully-Connected Layer(s).** Fully connected layers link each neuron in one layer to every neuron in the following layer, integrating features obtained from convolutional and pooling layers to generate predictions. For instance, in medical imaging, a fully connected layer could categorize an X-ray as "normal" or "abnormal" (Litjens et al., 2017). This layer is usually placed before the output layer, constituting the last layers of a CNN structure.
- **Output Layer.** The output layer generates the ultimate outcome, which may be:

- o A category tag for classification assignments (like recognizing an animal, number, bird, or food item).
- o A continuous variable for regression tasks (e.g., forecasting tumor size).

The output is determined using functions ("Softmax" for multiple classes, or "Sigmoid" for two classes).

b) ***Key differences from traditional Machine Learning approaches***. The following **Table 2** outlines the differences between CNN approach and Traditional Machine Learning approach.

Table 2. CNN vs Traditional Machine Learning

Aspect	Convolutional Neural Network Approach	Traditional Machine Learning Approach
Feature Extraction	Automatically learns characteristics from raw data, especially images, by utilizing convolutional layers. (LeCun et al., 1998)	Necessitates domain specialists to manually derive and construct features before the training phase. (Guyon & Elisseeff, 2003)
Data Requirements	For optimal performance, it requires significant quantities of labeled data because of the large number of parameters that can be trained. (Krizhevsky et al., 2012)	Generally, it exhibits good performance with smaller datasets because it utilizes simpler models that contain fewer parameters. (Bishop, 2006)
Architecture	Comprises multiple layers, such as convolutional layers, pooling layers, and fully connected layers, designed specifically for managing spatial and hierarchical data. (LeCun et al., 1998)	Typically encompasses simple models like decision trees, support vector machines (SVM), or logistic regression, which are not specially tailored for spatial data. (Hastie et al., 2009)
Performance on Images	Exhibits exceptional capability in activities like image recognition, object detection, and segmentation through proficiently acquiring spatial features. (He et al., 2016)	Struggles with image-related tasks due to its inability to accurately capture spatial hierarchies and its dependence on precomputed features. (Bishop, 2006)
Computational Cost	Result in substantial computational costs due to complex architectures and sophisticated processes such as convolution and backpropagation. (He et al., 2016)	Typically possesses a reduced computational expense, making it appropriate for basic tasks or scenarios with restricted computational capability. (Hastie et al., 2009)

continued on following page

Table 2. Continued

Aspect	Convolutional Neural Network Approach	Traditional Machine Learning Approach
Application Scope	Widely applied in computer vision fields, such as medical imaging, self-driving cars, and facial recognition. (Litjens et al., 2017)	Commonly utilized for tabular data, structured data examination, and simpler prediction tasks. (Hastie et al., 2009)
Overfitting Risk	Vulnerable to overfitting, especially with limited datasets, unless regularization techniques such as dropout are applied. (Srivastava et al., 2014)	Displays a lower likelihood of overfitting with less complex models, even though it still depends on hyperparameter choice and dataset size. (Bishop, 2006)

2.2. Types of CNN Architectures

CNNs play a crucial role in medical imaging as they assist physicians in diagnosing conditions from X-rays, MRIs, and CT scans with significantly improved precision, resulting in enhanced patient care. In this conversation, we will examine both traditional CNN models, along with more sophisticated ones.

a) Classic Architectures (LeNet, AlexNet, VGG, ResNet).

Classic CNN architectures are foundational in Convolutional Neural Networks, significantly advancing Deep Learning in image processing. Their structures enable effective learning and recognition of image features. Key traditional CNN architectures include:

- **LeNet.** Developed by Yann LeCun in the late 1980s, LeNet-5, introduced in "Gradient-Based Learning Applied to Document Recognition" (LeCun et al., 1998), is designed for recognizing handwritten digits, employing convolutional layers for feature extraction, pooling layers for dimensionality reduction, and fully connected layers for classification. Despite its innovative design, LeNet-5 faced limited adoption due to hardware constraints, particularly the lack of powerful GPUs. Nevertheless, it marked a milestone in CNN effectiveness, influencing models like AlexNet and VGGNet (LeCun et al., 1998). These architectures have laid the groundwork for modern advancements in Deep Learning frameworks and continue to be relevant today.
- ***LeNet-1 Architecture.*** As shown in **Figure 11**, LeNet-1 architecture consists of 5 layers (excluding the input layer) and achieved a 1.7% error rate on test data. Initially using average pooling to calculate the average of 2×2 feature maps, many implementations now use max pooling, which selects the highest

value from 2×2 feature maps, speeding up training and enhancing gradients during back-propagation. This is effective for recognizing handwritten digits, such as those in the MNIST dataset.

Figure 11. LeNet-1 Architecture

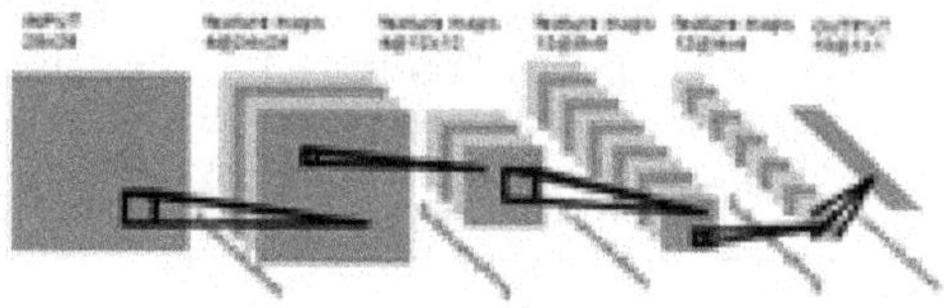

- o **Input Layer.** Accepts Grayscale image, typically 32x32 pixels.
- o **Convolutional Layer.** Applies filters to identify features like edges and textures, resulting in a feature map.
- o **Activation Function.** Introduces non-linearity (e.g., sigmoid or tanh) after convolution.
- o **Subsampling Layer (Pooling).** Reduces feature map dimensions to lower computational load and improve resilience to input variations, usually employing average pooling.
- o **Fully Connected Layer.** Flattens output from previous layers and passes it through fully connected layers for classification.
- o **Output Layer.** Uses a Softmax function to generate probabilities for each category (e.g., digits 0-9).
    - ***LeNet-4 Architecture.*** As shown in **Figure 12**, it enhances LeNet-1 with a more complex architecture for capturing detailed features. Here's a concise summary:
- o **Input Layer:** Accepts Grayscale image, typically 32x32 pixels.
- o **Convolutional Layers:** More convolutional layers than LeNet-1, using multiple filters to extract features.
- o **Activation Functions:** Non-linear activation functions after each convolution help the network recognize intricate patterns.
- o **Pooling Layers:** Downsample feature maps, reducing dimensions while retaining essential information, like in LeNet-1.
- o **Fully Connected Layers:** Flattens output from convolutional and pooling layers for classification, similar to LeNet-1.
- o **Output Layer:** Provides class probabilities, as in LeNet-1.

Figure 12. LeNet-5 Architecture

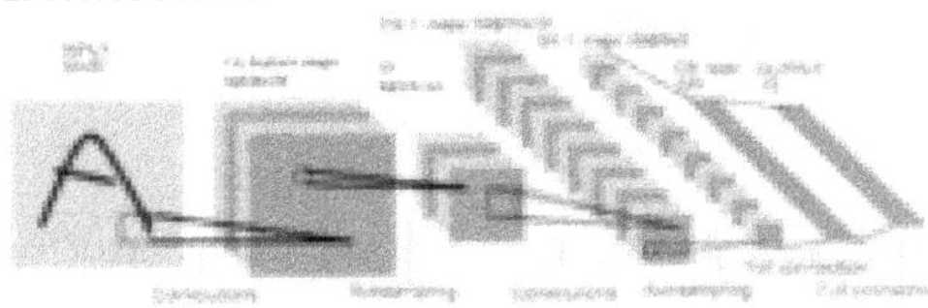

- ***LeNet-5 Architecture.*** It is a prominent architecture that surpasses LeNet-1 and LeNet-4, designed for recognizing handwritten digits on postal codes and bank cheques (LeCun et al., 1998). Often called the "Hello World" of CNNs, it laid the foundation for modern deep learning applications.
    - **Features of LeNet-5.** Each convolutional layer has three components:
        - ***Convolution:*** Extracts spatial features (receptive fields).
        - ***Pooling:*** Average pooling for subsampling.
        - ***Activation Function:*** Uses 'tanh'.
        - The final classifier is a Multi-Layered Perceptron (Fully Connected Layer), with sparse connections to reduce computational complexity.
- ***LeNet-5 Detailed Flow.*** As shown in the **Figure 13** (LeCun et al., 1998), LeNet-5 CNN architecture has seven layers. 3 convolutional layers, 2 subsampling layers, and 2 fully linked layers make up the layer composition.

Figure 13. LeNet-5 Architecture

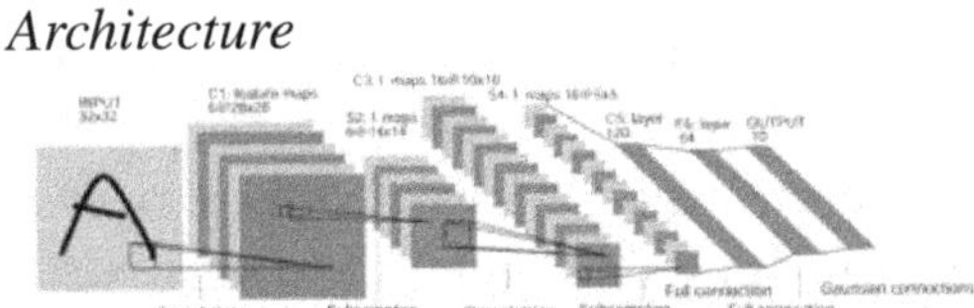

- **Input Layer.** 32x32 grayscale image.
- **First Convolutional Layer:** Six feature maps, changing dimensions from 32x32x1 to 28x28x6.
- **Average Pooling Layer:** 2x2 filter with stride 2, reducing dimensions to 14x14x6.
- **Second Convolutional Layer:** Sixteen 5x5 feature maps with stride 1, connecting only 10 maps to the previous layer, resulting in 1,516 training parameters.

- Second Average Pooling Layer: Reduces output to 5x5x16.
- Fully Connected Convolutional Layer (C5): 120 feature maps of size 1x1, connecting all nodes from S4.
- Fully Connected Layer (F6): Contains 84 units.
- Output Layer: SoftMax layer with 10 outputs for digits 0-9.

Figure 14 illustrates the mathematical representations of each layer.

Figure 14. Mathematical Representation of LeNet-5 Architecture

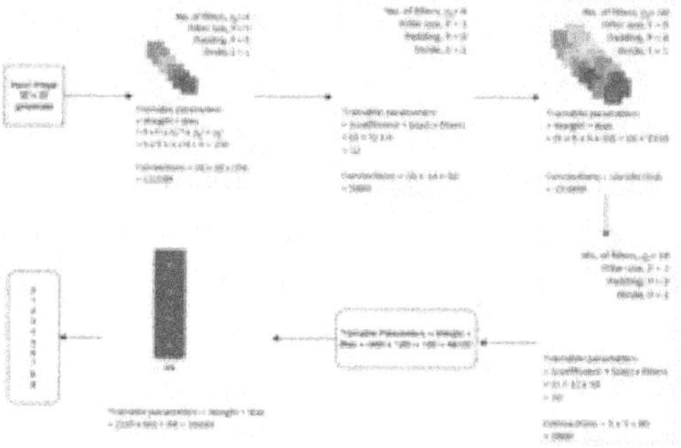

- **AlexNet.** AlexNet revolutionized image classification by winning the ImageNet Large Scale Visual Recognition Challenge (ILSVRC) in 2012. Its architecture features five convolutional layers with max-pooling, three fully connected layers, and two dropout layers to reduce overfitting. A key innovation was the Rectified Linear Unit (ReLU) activation function, which addressed the vanishing gradient problem of Sigmoid and tanh functions. To manage computational demands, AlexNet utilized two GPUs and had around 60 million parameters. It demonstrated the effectiveness of deep convolutional networks in image classification, using a Softmax function for class probabilities. AlexNet's design and GPU training significantly influenced future deep learning models, establishing CNNs as the standard in computer vision. **Figure 15** illustrates the AlexNet architecture (Krizhevsky, Sutskever, & Hinton, 2012).

Figure 15. AlexNet Architecture

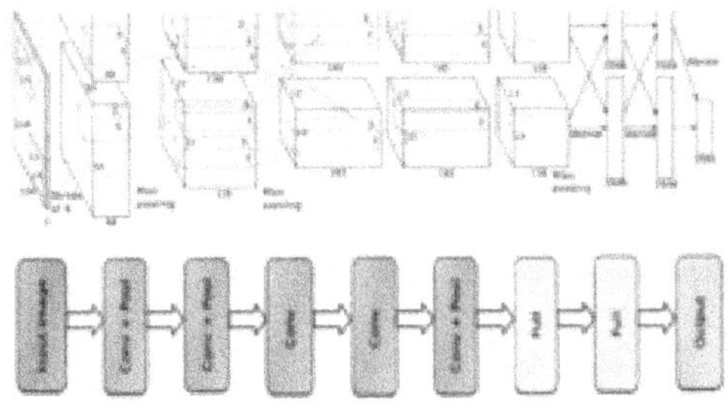

- o *Input Layer.* Accepts a 224x224 pixels image.
- o ***Convolutional Layers.*** AlexNet has Five layers analyze features like edges and textures.
- o ***Max-Pooling Layers.*** Reduce dimensions, emphasizing key attributes.
- o ***Activation Function (ReLU).*** Applied after each layer to mitigate vanishing gradients.
- o ***Dropout Layers.*** Randomly remove connections during training to prevent overfitting.
- o ***Fully Connected Layers.*** Three layers classify the image based on identified features (e.g., cat, dog).
- o ***Output Layer.*** Uses Softmax to produce class probabilities (e.g., 80% cat, 15% dog).
  - **VGGNet.** VGGNet, developed by Karen Simonyan and Andrew Zisserman, is a deep CNN for image classification that uses multiple small 3x3 convolutional filters. The two main versions, VGG-16 and VGG-19, have 16 and 19 layers with trainable weights, respectively. VGG-16 includes 13 convolutional and 3 fully connected layers, utilizing ReLU activation and max pooling to reduce dimensions. With 138 million parameters, VGGNet requires significant computational power but excels in feature extraction, influencing advanced models like YOLO and SSD. It ranked second in the ILSVRC 2014 contest for its strong feature extraction capabilities. **Figure 16** shows the VGGNet architecture (Simonyan & Zisserman, 2015).

Figure 16. VGGNet Architecture

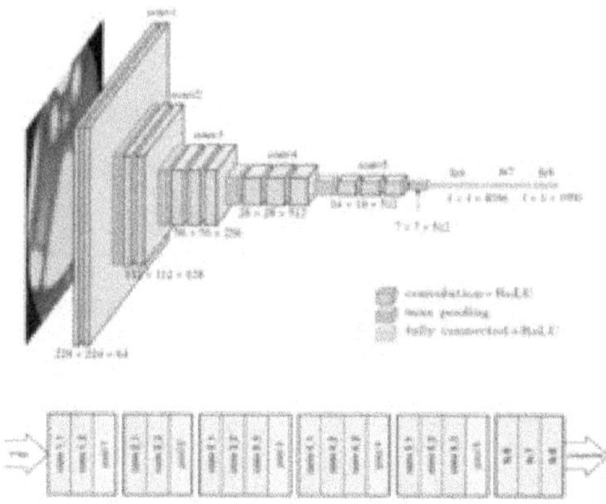

- o *Input Layer.* Accepts 224x224 pixel RGB images.
- o ***Convolutional Layers.*** Comprises 13 layers in 5 segments with multiple 3x3 filters (stride 1, padding 1).
- o ***Max Pooling Layers.*** Applied after each block using a 2x2 filter (stride 2) to halve dimensions.
- o ***Filters Based on Blocks.***
    - ▪ **Block 1.** 2 convolutional layers, each containing 64 filters.
    - ▪ **Block 2.** 2 convolutional layers, each featuring 128 filters.
    - ▪ **Block 3.** 3 convolutional layers, each containing 256 filters.
    - ▪ **Block 4.** 3 convolutional layers, each containing 512 filters.
    - ▪ **Block 5.** 3 convolutional layers, each containing 512 filters.
- o ***Activation Function.*** ReLU is applied after each convolutional and fully connected layer.
- o ***Fully Connected Layers.*** Three dense layers; first two have 4096 neurons, final one has 1000 neurons for classification.
- o ***Output Layer.*** Uses Softmax to categorize images into 1000 classes.
    - **ResNet.** Residual Neural Networks (ResNet) transformed deep learning by introducing "residual learning," enabling effective training of very deep networks. ResNet uses shortcut connections to allow gradients to bypass certain layers, addressing the vanishing gradient problem. This innovation permits training networks with up to 152 layers while maintaining computational efficiency. ResNets achieved a top-5 error rate of 3.57% on the ImageNet dataset, surpassing human performance. This powerful approach has made ResNet a key model in deep learning, in-

fluencing architectures like ResNeXt and SE-ResNet. **Figure 17** shows the ResNet architecture (He et al., 2016).

Figure 17. ResNet Architecture

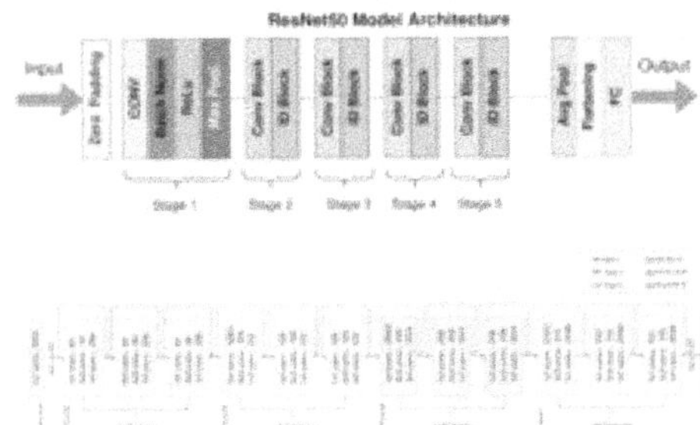

- o *Input Layer.* Accepts fixed-size images (e.g., 224x224 pixels for ImageNet).
- o *First Convolution and Pooling.* A 7x7 convolutional layer (stride 2) followed by batch normalization, ReLU activation, and max pooling layer (3x3 filter).
- o *Residual Blocks.* Features multiple layers with skip connections merging input and output.
- o *Layers of Convolution within Blocks.* **Standard blocks** have two 3x3 convolutions. **Bottleneck blocks** include three layers: 1x1, 3x3, and 1x1 convolutions for dimension compression and restoration.
- o *Activation Function.* ReLU is introduced after every convolutional layer.
- o *Batch Normalization.* Applied after each convolution to enhance stability and accelerate training.
- o *Downsampling.* Achieved by increasing the stride of convolutions in certain blocks.
- o *Fully Connected Layer.* A global average pooling layer reduces spatial dimensions before classification.
- o *Output Layer.* A Softmax layer generates probabilities for the target classes.

b) *Advanced and Specialized Architectures (U-Net, InceptionNet, DenseNet):*

In the fast-evolving field of deep learning, especially in computer vision, specialized architectures like U-Net, InceptionNet, and DenseNet have emerged to tackle specific challenges and improve performance in complex image processing tasks.

- **U-Net.** U-Net is a deep learning framework for biomedical image segmentation. This fully convolutional network performs pixel-level classification by leveraging context through downsampling and precise localization via upsampling. Its symmetric U-shape features a contracting path (downsampling) and an expansive path (upsampling), linked by skip connections. **Figure 18** illustrates the U-Net architecture (Ronneberger, Fischer, & Brox, 2015).

Figure 18. U-Net Architecture

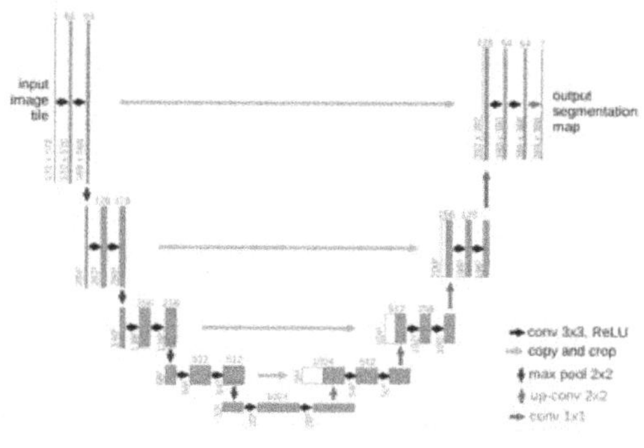

- *Input Layer.* Accepts a biomedical image for segmentation.
- *Contracting Path (Encoder).* Captures context through two 3x3 convolutions, ReLU activation, and 2x2 max pooling, reducing size while increasing feature maps (Ronneberger et al., 2015).
- *Bottleneck.* Connects the paths with two 3x3 convolutions and ReLU activation, retaining abstract features (Ronneberger et al., 2015).
- *Expansive Path (Decoder).* Enhances feature map resolution using transposed convolutions, concatenating with corresponding contracting path maps and applying two 3x3 convolutions (Ronneberger et al., 2015).
- *Skip Connections.* Facilitate direct information transfer from contracting to expansive paths, preserving spatial data during downsampling (Ronneberger et al., 2015).
- *Output Layer.* A 1x1 convolution aligns feature maps with output classes; sigmoid activation is used for binary segmentation, while softmax is applied for multi-class segmentation (Ronneberger et al., 2015).
    - **InceptionNet.** InceptionNet significantly advances CNN classifiers by addressing inefficiencies of prior models that prioritized depth over computational efficiency. It employs various techniques to enhance speed and accuracy, with notable versions including InceptionNet-V3.

- ***Inception-V1.*** Proposed by Szegedy et al. (2014), Inception-V1 introduced "Inception modules" that perform concurrent convolutions of different sizes (1x1, 3x3, 5x5) in each layer, enabling multi-scale feature detection while maintaining computational efficiency. It achieved state-of-the-art results in the ImageNet competition (Szegedy et al., 2014).
- ***Inception-V2.*** Inception-V2 improved upon V1 by incorporating batch normalization for training stability and using factorized convolutions, such as decomposing a 5x5 convolution into two 3x3 convolutions, enhancing computational efficiency (Ioffe & Szegedy, 2015).
- **Inception-V3**. Inception-V3 enhances the architecture with factorized convolutions, RMSProp optimization, a symmetrical design, label smoothing to reduce overfitting, and auxiliary classifiers for regularization (Szegedy et al., 2015).

o ***Input Layer.*** Accepts images sized 299x299x3 and standardizes pixel values.

o ***Preliminary Convolutions.*** A 3x3 convolution (stride 2), followed by batch normalization and ReLU, then another 3x3 convolution (stride 1) to reduce feature dimensions.

o ***Max Pooling.*** Reduces spatial dimensions while preserving key features.

o ***Decomposed Convolutions.*** Replaces 7x7 convolutions with two 3x3 convolutions to lower computational complexity.

o ***Inception Components.*** Modules perform 1x1, 3x3, and 5x5 convolutions simultaneously and merge results, capturing features at different scales.

o ***Auxiliary Classifier.*** A small network linked to an intermediate layer that aids in regularization and improves gradient flow.

o ***Global Average Pooling (GAP).*** Replaces fully connected layers to reduce parameters and minimize overfitting.

o ***Output Layer.*** Uses Softmax activation to generate probabilities for 1,000 ImageNet categories.

o ***Improvements.*** Includes the RMSProp optimizer and label smoothing to improve convergence and minimize overfitting.

o ***Last Performance.*** Attained cutting-edge accuracy on the ImageNet dataset while enhancing computational efficiency relative to previous models (Szegedy et al., 2015).

- ***Inception-V4.*** It combines residual links from ResNet with the Inception design, resulting in Inception-ResNet, which reduces training time while maintaining the accuracy benefits of deeper architectures, achieving remarkable results in various vision tasks (Szegedy et al., 2016).
- **DenseNet.** Densely Connected Convolutional Networks (DenseNet) is a deep learning framework designed to tackle the challenges of training deep networks by incorporating dense connections among layers. In this

setup, each layer receives input from all preceding layers, enhancing gradient flow and promoting feature reutilization. **Figure 19** illustrates the DenseNet architecture (Huang et al., 2017).

- o ***Input Layer.*** Accepts raw image data.
- o ***Convolutional Blocks.*** DenseNet features interconnected convolutional blocks, where each layer receives input from all previous layers, creating a highly connected system (Huang et al., 2017).
- o ***Dense Blocks.*** Within each dense block, layers are linked in a feed-forward manner, allowing outputs to flow to all subsequent layers, which helps mitigate the vanishing gradient problem (Huang et al., 2017).
- o ***Transition Layers.*** Positioned between dense blocks, these layers include batch normalization, a convolutional layer, and pooling to reduce spatial dimensions and manage model complexity (Huang et al., 2017).
- o ***Output Layer.*** Typically consists of a fully connected layer followed by a softmax layer (or another activation function) for final classification results.

Figure 19. DenseNet Architecture

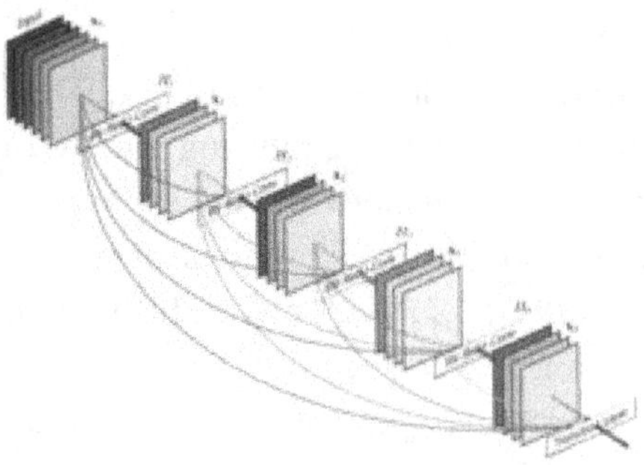

c) *Applications of each architecture in Medical Imaging:*

CNN architectures are extensively utilized in medical imaging for classification, segmentation, and detection, enhancing accuracy and efficiency in image analysis. Refer to the table below for specific applications of each architecture in this field.

Table 3. Applications of different CNN Architectures

Architecture	Application
LeNet	Digitized mammography, lung nodule detection, handwritten medical image annotation.
AlexNet	Tumor detection in MRI and CT scans, diabetic retinopathy detection, medical image classification.
VGGNet	Brain tumor segmentation, lung nodule detection
ResNet	Image denoising, image segmentation (liver and tumor)
U-Net	Biomedical image segmentation (cell and tumor), image-to-image translation (MRI to CT).
InceptionNet	Diabetic retinopathy detection, skin cancer detection
DenseNet	Image segmentation (lung nodule), image classification

3. ADVANTAGES OF CNNS IN MEDICAL IMAGING

3.1. Enhanced Accuracy and Efficiency

CNNs enhance medical image analysis by automatically learning hierarchical features from raw data, excelling in classifying and segmenting images, and often matching the diagnostic capabilities of experienced radiologists for tasks like tumor detection in CT scans and mammograms (LeCun, Bengio, & Hinton, 2015; Esteva et al., 2017).

They eliminate manual feature extraction, saving time and effort in diagnostics (Gonzalez et al., 2018), and their capacity to process large image volumes supports real-time healthcare analysis, improving workflow and reducing diagnostic delays (Setio et al., 2016).

3.2. Pattern Recognition in Complex Data

CNNs excel in detecting complex patterns in medical data, essential for accurate diagnoses in oncology and neurology. Through convolutional layers, they uncover subtle spatial hierarchies in medical images, enabling the identification of tumors and lesions that may elude human experts. Unlike traditional methods requiring manual feature selection, CNNs autonomously recognize patterns, adeptly managing variability in medical imaging (Ching et al., 2018). They are also effective for integrating multimodal data, facilitating comprehensive assessments from CT, MRI, and PET scans (Rajpurkar et al., 2018). Various medical images exhibit distinct patterns useful for diagnosis, as illustrated in **Figure 20**.

Figure 20. Visualization of Various Types of Patterns to recognize from Medical Images

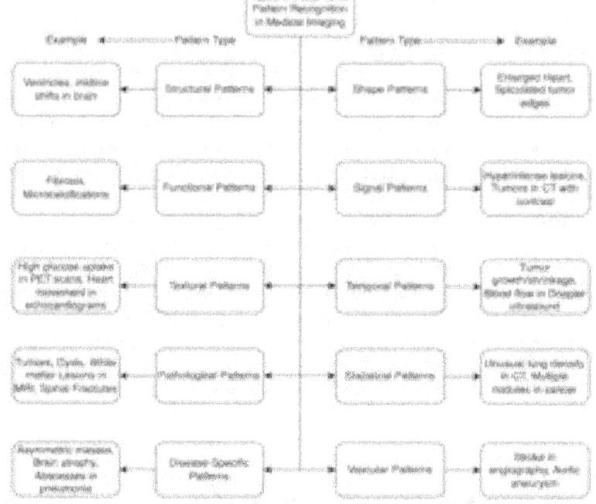

3.3. Automated Analysis and Workflow Optimization

CNNs automate medical image assessments, enhancing healthcare efficiency by handling routine analyses. This reduces reliance on manual processes and minimizes human errors, crucial in high-stress environments like emergency departments. Integrating CNNs into clinical workflows improves image processing for tumor detection, organ segmentation, and lesion classification, facilitating quicker decisions (Rajendran et al., 2020). By accelerating diagnostics, CNNs allow healthcare providers to focus on complex cases, yielding significant time savings and improved operational efficiency (Jung, Park & Hwang, 2020).

3.4. Improved Patient Outcomes

CNNs improve patient outcomes by facilitating earlier detection and more accurate diagnoses, which enhances treatment strategies. They identify conditions like cancers, strokes, and heart irregularities early, increasing the likelihood of effective interventions (Shen et al., 2017). Timely detection is vital for urgent cases, such as malignant tumors and brain hemorrhages, significantly improving outcomes (Suk et al., 2017). Furthermore, CNNs enable personalized treatment plans based on individual medical images, enhancing therapy techniques and overall health outcomes (Litjens et al., 2017).

3.5. Enhanced Research Capabilities

CNNs have transformed medical research by enabling efficient analysis of large datasets that were previously challenging to manage. They allow researchers to analyze extensive medical image collections, uncovering hidden patterns and insights into diseases and treatments (Chollet, 2017). This automation aids in identifying novel biomarkers, classifying disease subtypes, and refining clinical trial designs. Additionally, CNNs support longitudinal research by enabling scientists to monitor disease progression over time, enhancing understanding and aiding the development of new therapies (He et al., 2019).

4. CHALLENGES IN CNN APPLICATIONS

4.1. Data Limitations

a) Need for Large and Diverse Datasets:

CNNs require large datasets for effective performance, especially to handle new, unseen data. Diverse datasets are essential, but obtaining them can be challenging, particularly in healthcare due to patient privacy regulations. A varied dataset allows CNNs to learn consistent features across different lighting, angles, and demographics. Without sufficient diversity, models may excel on training data but underperform in real-world scenarios (Litjens et al., 2017).

b) Issues with Data Scarcity and Imbalance:

Data scarcity and imbalance occur when certain groups in a dataset are under-represented. For instance, with 100 X-ray images of healthy lungs and only 25 of unhealthy lungs (**Figure 21**), models can easily identify healthy lungs but struggle with unhealthy ones. This results in missed or misclassified cases for rare diseases, known as data imbalance. Techniques like oversampling, data augmentation, and synthetic data generation using GANs can help, but may not fully resolve the issue (Johnson & Khoshgoftaar, 2019).

Figure 21. Data Imbalance between Healthy & Unhealthy Lungs

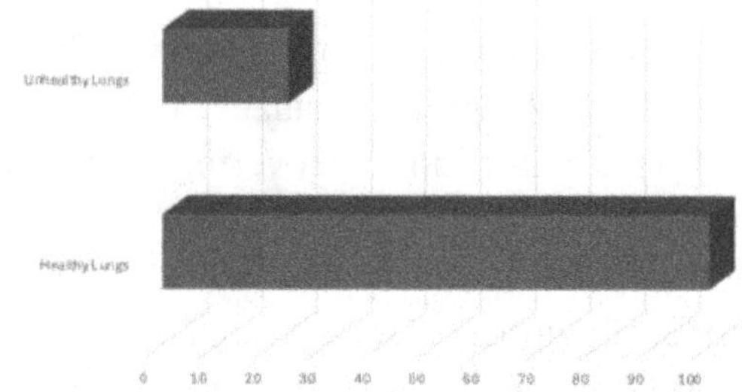

4.2. Computational Demands

a) Hardware and Software Requirements for Training CNNs:

Training CNNs requires substantial computational resources, necessitating specialized hardware like GPUs and TPUs for matrix operations. Deep learning frameworks such as TensorFlow and PyTorch are optimized for this hardware but still demand significant resources, posing challenges for small organizations and researchers with limited budgets. Cloud platforms like AWS and Google Cloud provide alternatives but can increase costs and raise data privacy concerns (Amodei & Hernandez, 2018). Innovations like Multi-limb Split Learning address these issues by distributing the learning process across multiple devices, alleviating the computational burden. This method is particularly useful for tasks like tumor classification, where data is shared among organizations (Ads et al., 2021).

b) Cost implications for Healthcare Providers:

The high computational demands of CNNs result in significant costs for healthcare providers. Advanced hardware like GPUs and TPUs is expensive, particularly for smaller organizations. Cloud-based solutions also incur rising costs with operational scale, limiting access to advanced AI technologies in resource-constrained settings and widening the gap between large and small organizations. Data privacy and security requirements necessitate investments in secure systems and compliance, further increasing costs. Affordable solutions such as collaborative computing, federated learning, and split learning can help mitigate these issues by distributing computational responsibilities (Amodei & Hernandez, 2018; Ads et al., 2021).

4.3. Interpretability and Explainability

a) Black-box nature of CNNs and its Impact on Clinical Trust:

CNNs often function as black-box models, meaning their decision-making processes lack transparency. This is concerning in critical fields like healthcare, where physicians need to understand and trust the model's predictions. If a CNN cannot explain its reasoning for classifying an image, it may undermine trust and complicate its use in critical situations (Samek et al., 2017).

b) Efforts to improve interpretability (e.g., Saliency Maps, SHAP, LIME):

To tackle the black-box issue, researchers have created interpretability tools like saliency maps, SHAP (SHapley Additive exPlanations), and LIME (Local Interpretable Model-agnostic Explanations). These techniques offer visual or attribute-based insights into model predictions, helping users understand the rationale behind them. For example, saliency maps show which parts of an image the model focuses on, aiding doctors in validating predictions. However, ensuring model interpretability remains an ongoing challenge (Lundberg & Lee, 2017). See **Figure 22** to better understand interpretability and explainability.

Figure 22. Visualization of CNN as a Black-Box, its issues and Mitigation Tools

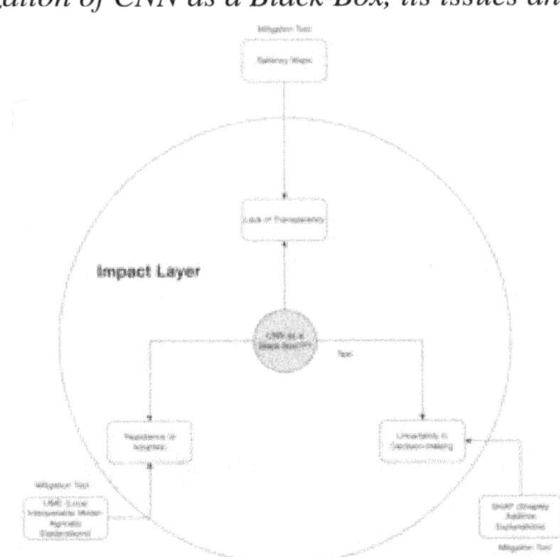

c) Use of Grad-CAM in Medical Imaging:

Gradient-weighted Class Activation Mapping (Grad-CAM) has emerged as a popular method to improve interpretability in CNN-based models, particularly within the medical field. Grad-CAM creates visual explanations by emphasizing the image areas that are most significant to the model's choice. This is especially beneficial in diagnostic imaging, allowing clinicians to contrast these visual indicators with established pathological markers. For example, in a recent research, Grad-CAM was utilized to assess CNN-driven evaluations of heart diseases through cardiac MRI data, successfully assisting radiologists in confirming model outcomes and enhancing clinical confidence (Paciorek et al., 2024).

4.2. Ethical and Regulatory Concerns

a) Privacy, Data Security, and Compliance Changes:

CNNs often utilize sensitive information, such as medical records and biometric data, raising privacy concerns. Laws like GDPR and HIPAA mandate strict compliance with data usage, storage, and sharing guidelines, with violations leading to significant penalties and reputational damage. To address these challenges, researchers must implement robust encryption and anonymization techniques (Voigt & Von dem Bussche, 2017).

b) Algorithmic Bias and Fairness in Healthcare:

Algorithmic bias occurs when CNNs produce unjust outcomes, often due to biased training datasets. For example, if a CNN is trained primarily on data from one demographic, it may perform poorly for others, leading to healthcare disparities. To address this, it is essential to use diverse training datasets and algorithms that prioritize fairness. Current research in ethical AI aims to develop tools and guidelines to reduce bias and promote equitable outcomes (Mehrabi et al., 2021).

5. FUTURE SCOPE OF CNNS IN MEDICAL IMAGING

The future of CNNs in medical imaging is promising for early disease detection, personalized treatments, and automated diagnostics. CNNs excel at identifying anomalies in radiological images, such as tumors, reducing manual effort and enhancing diagnostic consistency (Litjens et al., 2017). Their integration with advanced imaging techniques like MRI, CT, and PET is expected to improve diagnostic accuracy (Shboul et al., 2020). Additionally, the availability of large labeled datasets enhances CNN models' generalization across diverse patient populations (Esteva et al., 2019). However, challenges related to interpretability and healthcare data standardization remain critical areas for future research (Rajpurkar et al., 2017).

5.1. Real-Time Analysis

a) Opportunities for real-time diagnostic support:

Real-time assessment in medical diagnostics can significantly enhance patient care through timely decision-making. Advances in deep learning, especially CNNs, are making real-time diagnostic support viable in radiology, cardiology, and pathology (Shen et al., 2017). Integrating CNNs with imaging technology enables rapid detection of conditions like tumors and fractures, leading to quicker, more accurate decisions by healthcare providers. AI tools in point-of-care settings, such as emergency rooms, can reduce diagnostic delays and improve outcomes (Esteva et al., 2019). However, challenges related to model reliability, integration with healthcare systems, and regulatory approvals must be addressed to fully utilize real-time diagnostic support (Rajpurkar et al., 2017). The process for immediate diagnostic assistance using AI in medical imaging is shown in **Figure 23**.

- The patient's health data is transmitted to the medical imaging device, essentially a scanner.
- This data undergoes processing, including denoising, standardization, resizing, and padding.
- The preprocessed image is then input into a Deep CNN network to predict or detect conditions like tumors or fractures.
- The clinician reviews the results and can provide feedback to the system for further model training if necessary.

Figure 23. Process for Immediate Diagnostic Assistance Using AI in Medical Imaging

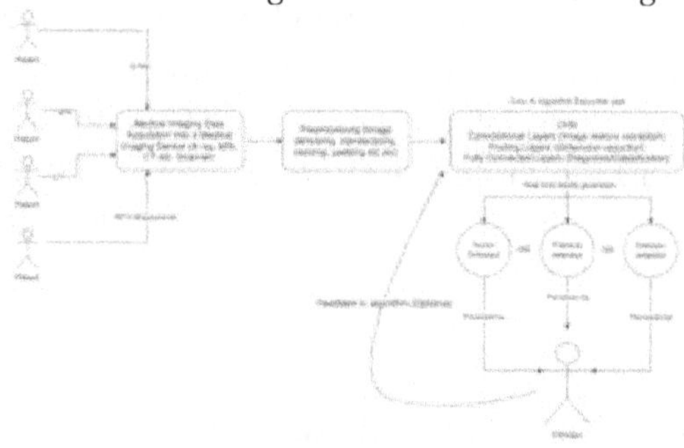

5.2. Multimodal Integration

a) Combining data from different modalities (e.g., imaging + clinical data).

Multimodal integration combines data from various sources, such as medical imaging and clinical information (e.g., electronic health records), to provide a comprehensive view of a patient's health. Merging imaging data (CT, MRI, X-ray) with clinical information enhances diagnostic accuracy and treatment strategies (Rajpurkar et al., 2017). For example, integrating imaging with genetic data improves cancer detection by offering insights into tumor dynamics and personalized treatments (Esteva et al., 2019). Deep learning models using multimodal data identify significant patterns, leading to better prediction accuracy than single-data-type methods (Shen et al., 2017). Figure 23 illustrates the integration of medical imaging and clinical data for improved diagnosis and treatment planning.

- **Medical Imaging Data (CT, MRI, X-ray) and Clinical Data (EHR, Lab Results):** Primary inputs into the system.
- **Preprocessing & Standardization:** Cleaning and preparing the data for analysis.
- **Feature Extraction:** Identifying relevant features from both modalities using techniques like CNNs for imaging and rule-based or statistical methods for clinical data.
- **Multimodal Data Fusion:** Merging the features from both modalities to form a cohesive representation.

- **Deep Learning Model:** A model (such as a CNN or multimodal neural network) that processes the integrated data for diagnosis and treatment prediction.
- **Integrated Diagnostic Results & Enhanced Treatment Plans:** Provides a more accurate assessment, leading to personalized treatment options.
- **Improved Decision-Making:** Clinicians gain precise insights to inform their decisions. **Figure 24** illustrates the integration of medical imaging and clinical data.

Figure 24. Combination of Medical Imaging with Clinical Data

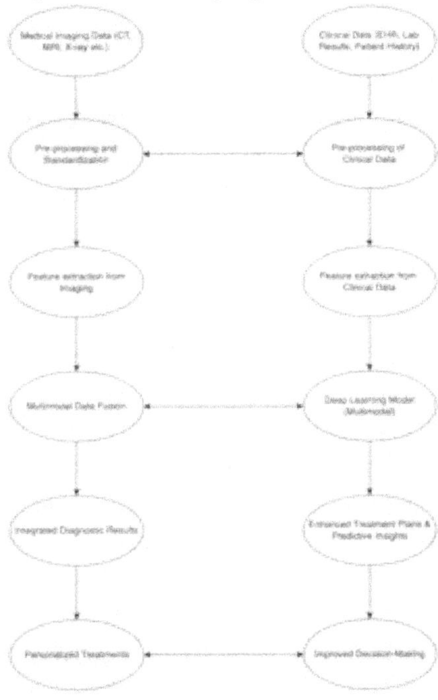

b) Use cases and potential benefits:

Multimodal integration in healthcare presents promising applications, such as improved disease diagnosis, personalized treatment, and prognostic evaluations. In oncology, combining imaging data with molecular and genetic information aids in identifying effective treatment plans for patients (Esteva et al., 2019). Additionally, integrating imaging and clinical data enhances predictive modeling, increasing the accuracy of forecasting disease progression and patient outcomes (Rajpurkar et al., 2017). This approach is also beneficial for managing chronic conditions like cardiovascular disease, as it provides a comprehensive view of a patient's health by merging imaging, medical history, and lab results (Shboul et al., 2020). Overall, integrating diverse data types can enhance diagnostic accuracy, minimize errors, and facilitate more personalized patient care (Shen et al., 2017).

5.3. Personalized Medicine

a) Role of CNNs in tailoring treatments to individual patients:

CNNs are essential in personalized medicine by evaluating imaging and clinical information to customize treatments. In oncology, tumor characteristics are identified in skin lesions and CT scans to inform targeted treatments (Esteva et al., 2019). In radiology, CNNs analyze chest X-rays to guide treatment according to disease advancement or risk (Rajpurkar et al., 2017). They also examine genomic data to enhance pharmacogenomics and forecast drug reactions, minimizing trial-and-error prescribing (Shen et al., 2017).

b) Advances in Predictive Analytics and patient-specific Insights:

By combining images, genetic information, and patient histories, CNNs improve predictive analytics, predicting disease advancement and results. In radiology, they surpass conventional techniques in diagnosing lung diseases (Rajpurkar et al., 2017), and in dermatology, they assist in detecting cancerous skin lesions for tailored treatment (Esteva et al., 2019).

5.4. Emerging Technologies and Innovations

New technologies are transforming medical imaging, enhancing CNN capabilities and enabling more precise diagnostics and therapies. These advancements include integrating additional AI technologies, such as Generative Adversarial Networks (GANs) and Transformers, along with developing future-ready architectures that leverage various deep learning models.

a) Integration with other AI technologies (GANs, Transformers):

Integrating CNNs with GANs and Transformers enhances medical image analysis even more. GANs create artificial data to enhance model training, particularly in skin cancer identification (Esteva et al., 2019). Transformers grasp long-distance data patterns, improving CNN precision in intricate situations.

b) Future-ready architectures and hybrid approaches:

Progress in medical diagnostics increasingly depends on hybrid AI systems. CNN–Transformer hybrids absorb spatial and contextual information, enhancing diagnosis in radiology and dermatology (Shen et al., 2017). These flexible architectures allow for instantaneous, multimodal data handling, facilitating adaptive, tailored clinical choices.

6. CASE STUDIES AND REAL-WORLD APPLICATIONS

6.1. Automated Cardiac Pathology Detection

a) Introduction:

Cardiovascular diseases continue to be the primary global cause of mortality, highlighting the necessity for prompt and precise diagnosis. Cardiac Magnetic Resonance Imaging (CMRI), an advanced and non-invasive method, offers intricate data on myocardial tissue. Nonetheless, hand interpretation takes a lot of time and is prone to differences between observers. Deep learning, especially CNNs, provides exciting automation for examining sequences such as T1-mapping and Late Gadolinium Enhancement (LGE) Phase-Sensitive Inversion Recovery (PSIR), essential for detecting myocardial irregularities (Paciorek et al., 2024).

b) An Examination of DenseNet-161:

This research created a CNN based on DenseNet-161 to differentiate between normal and abnormal myocardium using cardiac MRI data (Paciorek et al., 2024). The model, initially trained on ImageNet, was further refined with T1-mapping and PSIR datasets. Two models were trained separately on a clinical dataset consisting of 200 patients with conditions such as myocardial infarction, myocarditis, dilated cardiomyopathy (DCM), and hypertrophic cardiomyopathy (HCM). The architecture has only modification being the last fully connected layer adjusted for binary classification. Important training improvements featured data augmentation techniques (random rotation, mix-up), a cyclic learning rate of 1e-3, and assessment through sensitivity, specificity, and AUC metrics (Paciorek et al., 2024).

c) Abilities of the Model:

The PSIR-based model attained an accuracy of 88%, alongside 100% sensitivity and 38% specificity. It remarkably generated no false negatives, making it highly appropriate for screening situations where overlooking a pathology is crucial. The model based on T1 mapping demonstrated 70% accuracy, 78% sensitivity, and 54% specificity. T1-mapping is especially useful for quick, contrast-free evaluations (Paciorek et al., 2024).

d) Interpretability of the model using Grad-CAM:

Grad-CAM was employed to illustrate decision-making by producing heatmaps that highlighted the regions the model concentrated on while classifying. In PSIR-based findings, Grad-CAM emphasized abnormal myocardium such as the ventricular wall and septum. In certain T1-mapping instances, the focus of attention was mistakenly directed away from the heart, leading to classification errors. As shown in Figure-25, this highlights the importance of Grad-CAM in troubleshooting and boosting clinician confidence (Paciorek et al., 2024).

Figure 25. Heatmaps for evaluating cardiac pathology on PSIR images using Grad-CAM (Paciorek et al., 2024)

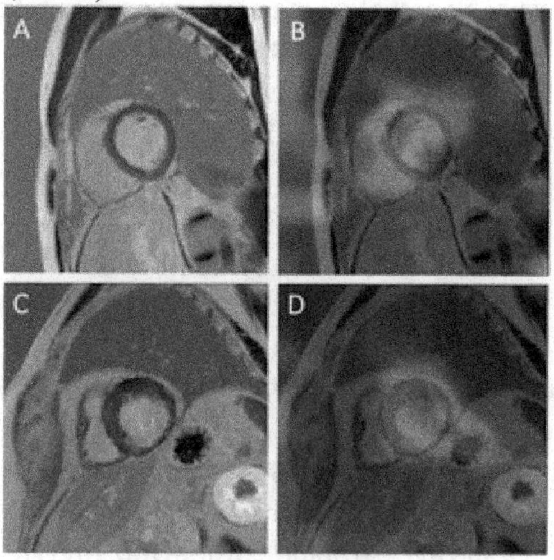

e) Impact of the Model on Healthcare:

This CNN-driven tool might speed up diagnosis by identifying atypical cases promptly, enabling radiologists to concentrate on intricate assessments. It improves the accuracy of diagnostics and lessens the burden for both seasoned and new healthcare professionals. Moreover, its capacity to handle images on-the-fly while scanning shows potential for immediate triaging and intervention (Paciorek et al., 2024).

f) Global Implications:

These models can assist hospitals that have restricted access to specialized radiologists, providing a scalable approach to enhance cardiac diagnostics globally. By incorporating a broad array of pathologies instead of focusing on just one disease, it increases its applicability in various clinical settings. In addition, employing interpretability methods guarantees that medical professionals can make decisions with transparency and trust (Paciorek et al., 2024).

6.2. Detection and Segmentation of Brain Tumors Utilizing CNN and VGG16

a) Introduction:

Brain tumors represent one of the most significant health dangers, necessitating prompt diagnosis for successful treatment. Manual analysis of MRI scans is time-intensive, variable, and requires considerable effort. CNNs, especially VGG16, provide an effective approach for the automation of brain tumor classification, detection, and segmentation in MRI images (Ganesh et al., 2025).

b) An Examination of the VGG16 and CNN-Based System:

Ganesh et al. (2025) suggest a hybrid CNN based on VGG16, trained on the BRATS 2021 dataset, utilizing several MRI modalities—T1, T2, FLAIR, and T1-Gd—for reliable tumor detection (refer to Figure 26). The pipeline consists of preprocessing (conversion to grayscale, watershed segmentation, normalization of intensity), transfer learning using ImageNet, and feature extraction using convolutional layers, which is then succeeded by classification via fully connected layers. The VGG16 architecture, comprising 13 convolutional and 3 fully connected layers, efficiently captures intricate features from medical images (Ganesh et al., 2025).

Figure 26. Brain Tumor Detection using VGG16 (Ganesh et al., 2025)

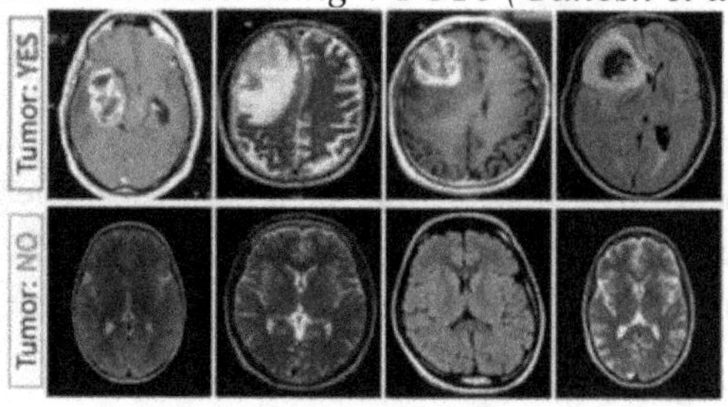

c) Abilities of the Model:
   - **Exceptional Accuracy and Precision:** The suggested method attained 99% accuracy and 98.9% sensitivity, surpassing conventional models such as AlexNet and GoogLeNet on the identical dataset.
   - **Automated Segmentation & Classification:** The model effectively distinguishes healthy brain tissues from those affected by tumors and additionally categorizes tumor types by utilizing deep features.
   - **Multimodal MRI Input Processing:** The system processes T1, T2, FLAIR, and contrast-enhanced images, enhancing performance for different tumor subtypes and stages.

d) Impact on Healthcare:
   - **Timely and Dependable Diagnosis:** Automating cancer identification shortens the diagnostic lag, resulting in quicker treatment commencement.
   - **Effective Resource Use:** By automatically reviewing standard cases, radiologists can concentrate on more complex or unclear cases, enhancing overall workflow efficiency.

e) Global Implications:

These deep learning models make expert-level diagnostic capabilities accessible to everyone, particularly in healthcare environments with limited resources. Utilizing minimal hardware and a standardized process, the VGG16-based CNN model can be implemented throughout international clinical networks, speeding up diagnostic timelines and maintaining uniform care quality. The incorporation of Grad-CAM enhances clinician acceptance, positioning it as a strong contender for practical implementation (Ganesh et al., 2025).

7. CONCLUSION

7.1. Summary of Key Findings

a) ***Recap of Advantages, Challenges, and Opportunities.*** CNNs have transformed medical imaging by enhancing accuracy, efficiency, and diagnostics. They excel at detecting complex patterns, enabling early disease identification, reducing diagnostic errors, and optimizing workflows (Ganesh et al., 2025; Litjens et al., 2017; Paciorek et al., 2024; Shen et al., 2017). This leads to improved patient outcomes and healthcare efficiency through automation and reliable second opinions (Esteva et al., 2017).

Challenges in deploying CNNs include a lack of annotated medical datasets, which limits effectiveness, and the need for substantial computational resources and expertise (Lundervold & Lundervold, 2019). Additionally, concerns about model interpretability and biases in training data hinder clinical acceptance (Razzak et al., 2018). Addressing these issues could advance opportunities like integrating multimodal data, enhancing transfer learning, and developing efficient real-time diagnostic models (Rajpurkar et al., 2020; Ker et al., 2018).

b) ***Importance of Ethical and Regulatory Considerations.*** Ethical and regulatory considerations are crucial in developing and using CNNs in medical imaging. Protecting patient privacy and ensuring data security are essential due to the sensitive nature of medical information and risks of data breaches (Wang et al., 2018). Transparency and interpretability of CNN models are vital for building trust among healthcare providers and patients (Holzinger et al., 2017). Compliance with FDA and EMA regulations is necessary to ensure CNN-based systems meet safety and efficacy standards.

Addressing biases in CNN models is important for equitable healthcare access. Training datasets must accurately represent diverse populations to prevent biases that could exacerbate healthcare disparities (Larrazábal et al., 2020). Ethical guidelines should govern CNN use to avoid over-reliance on automation, ensuring human expertise remains integral to decision-making (Topol, 2019).

By addressing these ethical and regulatory issues, CNNs can be responsibly developed and implemented, enhancing patient care and preserving public trust.

7.2. Future Directions

a) ***Vision for the Continued Evolution of CNNs in Medical Imaging.*** The future of CNNs in medical imaging will significantly improve by integrating diverse data types like imaging, genomics, and clinical data. This comprehensive approach will enhance diagnostic models, providing deeper insights into patient health. Additionally, improving model clarity will be essential for gaining the trust of healthcare providers and patients. Developing lightweight algorithms will also promote widespread adoption, ensuring CNNs can be effectively utilized in various healthcare settings, from large hospitals to small clinics and remote care centers.

b) ***Closing thoughts on their Transformative Potential in Healthcare.*** CNNs can transform healthcare by enabling faster, more accurate diagnostics and personalized treatment plans. As technology evolves, these systems will enhance healthcare effectiveness and tackle disparities in access and quality. By leveraging CNNs, healthcare professionals can improve patient outcomes and promote equity, ensuring everyone receives the necessary care. Ultimately, integrating CNNs into clinical practice will create a more efficient and adaptable healthcare system.

SUMMARY OF THE CHAPTER

Convolutional Neural Networks (CNNs) have transformed medical imaging by greatly improving diagnostic precision, effectiveness, and workflow enhancement. They are especially useful for detecting diseases early and offering trustworthy second opinions, which enhances patient outcomes. Case studies like cardiac disease detection with DenseNet-161 and brain tumor segmentation using VGG16 illustrate the practical effects of CNNs, highlighting significant accuracy and sensitivity in diverse imaging modalities. Nevertheless, obstacles persist, such as restricted access to labeled medical datasets, substantial computational requirements, and concerns regarding model interpretability and bias. Ethical factors, like data privacy, adherence to regulations, transparency, and equity among various groups, are essential for secure implementation. Grad-CAM and comparable interpretability tools enhance clinical confidence and verification. Future progress will involve merging multimodal data (such as imaging, genomics, and clinical records), enhancing transfer learning, and creating lightweight, real-time diagnostic tools. Through responsible development, CNNs possess the transformative ability to democratize expert diagnostics, enhance healthcare delivery, and foster equitable access, especially in underprivileged areas.

Their ongoing development will transform global healthcare by allowing quicker, more precise, and tailored care.

REFERENCES

Ads, O. S., Alfares, M. M., & Salem, M. A. M. (2021). Multi-limb Split Learning for Tumor Classification on Vertically Distributed Data. *International Conference on Intelligent Computing and Information Systems (ICICIS)*, 88-92. http://dx.doi.org/DOI: 10.1109/ICICIS52592.2021.9694163

Agarap, A. F. (2018). Deep Learning using Rectified Linear Units (ReLU). *arXiv, 2*. https://doi.org//arXiv.1803.08375DOI: 10.48550

Amodei, D., & Hernandez, D. (2018). AI and Compute. *OpenAI*. https://openai.com/blog/ai-and-compute/

Anwar, S. M., Majid, M., Qayyum, A., Awais, M., Alnowami, M., & Khan, M. K. (2018). Medical Image Analysis using Convolutional Neural Networks: A review. *Journal of Medical Systems*, *42*(11), 1–13. DOI: 10.1007/s10916-018-1088-1 PMID: 30298337

Bercovich, E., & Javitt, M. C. (2018). Medical Imaging: From Roentgen to the Digital Revolution, and Beyond. *Rambam Maimonides Medical Journal*, *9*(4), e0034. DOI: 10.5041/RMMJ.10355 PMID: 30309440

Bishop, C. M. (2006). Pattern Recognition and Machine Learning. *Springer*. https://dl.acm.org/doi/10.5555/1162264

Ching, T., Himmelstein, D. S., Beaulieu-Jones, B. K., Kalinin, A. A., Do, B. T., Way, G. P., Ferrero, E., Agapow, P.-M., Zietz, M., Hoffman, M. M., Xie, W., Rosen, G. L., Lengerich, B. J., Israeli, J., Lanchantin, J., Woloszynek, S., Carpenter, A. E., Shrikumar, A., Xu, J., & Greene, C. S. (2018). Opportunities and Obstacles for Deep Learning in Biology and Medicine. *Journal of the Royal Society, Interface*, *15*(141), 20170387. DOI: 10.1098/rsif.2017.0387 PMID: 29618526

Chollet, F. (2017). Deep learning with Python. Manning Publications. https://www.manning.com/books/deep-learning-with-python

Esteva, A., Kuprel, B., Novoa, R. A., Ko, J., Swetter, S. M., Blau, H. M., & Thrun, S. (2017). Dermatologist-level Classification of Skin Cancer with Deep Neural Networks. *Nature*, *542*(7639), 115–118. DOI: 10.1038/nature21056 PMID: 28117445

Ganesh, S., Gomathi, R., & Kannadhasan, S. (2025). Brain Tumor Segmentation and Detection in MRI using Convolutional Neural Networks and VGG16. *Cancer Biomarkers: Section. Disease Markers*, *42*(3), 18758592241311184. Advance online publication. DOI: 10.1177/18758592241311184 PMID: 40183298

Guyon, I., & Elisseeff, A. (2003). An Introduction to Variable and feature selection. *Journal of Machine Learning Research, 3*, 1157–1182. DOI: 10.1162/153244303322753616

He, K., Zhang, X., Ren, S., & Sun, J. (2016). Deep Residual Learning for Image Recognition. *IEEE Conference on Computer Vision and Pattern Recognition (CVPR), 6*, 770-778. https://doi.org/DOI: 10.48550/arXiv.1512.03385

Holzinger, A., Biemann, C., Pattichis, C. S., & Kell, D. B. (2017). What do we need to build explainable AI systems for the medical domain? arXiv, 1, https://doi.org/ DOI: 10.48550/arXiv.1712.09923

Huang, G., Liu, Z., van der Maaten, L., & Weinberger, K. Q. (2017). Densely Connected Convolutional Networks. *arXiv, 5*. https://arxiv.org/abs/1608.06993 DOI: 10.1109/CVPR.2017.243

Hussain, S., Mubeen, I., Ullah, N., Shah, S. S. U. D., Khan, B. A., Zahoor, M., Ullah, R., Khan, F. A., & Sultan, M. A. (2022). Modern Diagnostic Imaging Technique Applications and Risk Factors in the Medical Field: A Review. *BioMed Research International, 1*(1), 1–19. DOI: 10.1155/2022/5164970 PMID: 35707373

Ioffe, S., & Szegedy, C. (2015). Batch Normalization: Accelerating Deep Network Training by Reducing Internal Covariate Shift. *arXiv, 3*. https://doi.org//arXiv.1502.03167DOI: 10.48550

Johnson, J. M., & Khoshgoftaar, T. M. (2019). Survey on Deep Learning with Class Imbalance. *Journal of Big Data, 6*(1), 1–54. DOI: 10.1186/s40537-019-0192-5

Jung, K.-H., Park, H., & Hwang, W. (2017). Deep Learning for Medical Image Analysis: Applications to Computed Tomography and Magnetic Resonance Imaging. *Hanyang Medical Reviews, 37*(2), 61–70. DOI: 10.7599/hmr.2017.37.2.61

Ker, J., Wang, L., Rao, J., & Lim, T. (2018). Deep Learning Applications in Medical Image Analysis. *IEEE Access : Practical Innovations, Open Solutions, 6*, 9375–9389. DOI: 10.1109/ACCESS.2017.2788044

Krizhevsky, A., Sutskever, I., & Hinton, G. E. (2012). ImageNet Classification with Deep Convolutional Neural Networks. Advances in Neural Information Processing Systems, 25. https://proceedings.neurips.cc/paper_files/paper/2012/file/c399862d3b9d6b76c8436e924a68c45b-Paper.pdf

Larrazábal, A. J., Nieto, N., Peterson, V., Hitschfeld-Kahler, N., & González, E. (2020). Gender Imbalance in Medical Imaging Datasets Produces Biased Classifiers for Computer-aided Diagnosis. *Proceedings of the National Academy of Sciences of the United States of America, 117*(23), 12592–12594. DOI: 10.1073/pnas.1919012117 PMID: 32457147

LeCun, Y., Bengio, Y., & Hinton, G. (2015). Deep Learning. *Nature, 521*(7553), 436–444. DOI: 10.1038/nature14539 PMID: 26017442

LeCun, Y., Bottou, L., Bengio, Y., & Haffner, P. (1998). Gradient-based Learning Applied to Document Recognition. *Proceedings of the IEEE, 86*(11), 2278–2324. DOI: 10.1109/5.726791

Litjens, G., Kooi, T., Bejnordi, B. E., Setio, A. A. A., Ciompi, F., Ghafoorian, M., van der Laak, J. A. W. M., van Ginneken, B., & Sánchez, C. I. (2017). A Survey on Deep Learning in Medical Image Analysis. *Medical Image Analysis, 42*, 60–88. DOI: 10.1016/j.media.2017.07.005 PMID: 28778026

Lundberg, S. M., & Lee, S.-I. (2017). A Unified Approach to Interpreting Model Predictions. Advances in Neural Information Processing Systems, 30, 4765-4774. https://proceedings.neurips.cc/paper_files/paper/2017/file/8a20a8621978632d76c43dfd28b67767-Paper.pdf

Lundervold, A. S., & Lundervold, A. (2019). An Overview of Deep Learning in Medical Imaging Focusing on MRI. *Zeitschrift für Medizinische Physik, 29*(2), 102–127. DOI: 10.1016/j.zemedi.2018.11.002 PMID: 30553609

Manning, C. (2020). AI Definitions. *Stanford University Human-Centered Artificial Intelligence*. https://hai.stanford.edu/sites/default/files/2020-09/AI-Definitions-HAI.pdf

Marsden, P. (2019). Artificial Intelligence defined: Useful List of Popular Definitions from Business and Science. *Digital Wellbeing*. https://digitalwellbeing.org/artificial-intelligence-defined-useful-list-of-popular-definitions-from-business-and-science/

Medscience, O. (2024). Revolutionising medical imaging with AI and Big Data analytics. URL: https://openmedscience. com/revolutionising-medical-imaging-with-ai-and-big-data-analytics/#:~: text= AI% 20can% 20help% 20researchers% 20develop, and% 20develop% 20personalised% 20treatment% 20plans.

Mehrabi, N., Morstatter, F., Saxena, N., Lerman, K., & Galstyan, A. (2021). A Survey on Bias and Fairness in Machine Learning. *ACM Computing Surveys, 54*(6), 1–35. DOI: 10.1145/3457607

O'Shea, K., & Nash, R. (2015). An Introduction to Convolutional Neural Networks. *arXiv, 2*. https://doi.org//arXiv.1511.08458DOI: 10.48550

Oren, O., Gersh, B. J., & Bhatt, D. L. (2020). Artificial Intelligence in Medical Imaging: Switching from Radiographic Pathological Data to Clinically Meaningful Endpoints. *The Lancet. Digital Health*, *2*(9), e486–e488. DOI: 10.1016/S2589-7500(20)30160-6 PMID: 33328116

Paciorek, A. M., von Schacky, C. E., Foreman, S. C., Gassert, F. G., Gassert, F. T., Kirschke, J. S., Laugwitz, K. L., Geith, T., Hadamitzky, M., & Nadjiri, J. (2024). Automated Assessment of Cardiac Pathologies on Cardiac MRI using T1-mapping and Late Gadolinium Phase Sensitive Inversion Recovery Sequences with Deep Learning. *BMC Medical Imaging*, *24*(43), 43. Advance online publication. DOI: 10.1186/s12880-024-01217-4 PMID: 38350900

Rajendran, S., Rajagopal, S. K., Thanarajan, T., Shankar, K., Kumar, S., Alsubaie, N. M., Ishak, M. K., & Mostafa, S. M. (2023). Automated Segmentation of Brain Tumor MRI Images using Deep Learning. *IEEE Access : Practical Innovations, Open Solutions*, *11*, 64758–64768. DOI: 10.1109/ACCESS.2023.3288017

Rajpurkar, P., Irvin, J., Ball, R. L., Zhu, K., Yang, B., Mehta, H., Duan, T., Ding, D., Bagul, A., Langlotz, C. P., Patel, B. N., Yeom, K. W., Shpanskaya, K., Blankenberg, F. G., Seekins, J., Amrhein, T. J., Mong, D. A., Halabi, S. S., Zucker, E. J., & Lungren, M. P. (2018). Deep Learning for Chest Radiograph Diagnosis: A Retrospective Comparison of the CheXNeXt Algorithm to Practicing Radiologists. *PLoS Medicine*, *15*(11), e1002686. DOI: 10.1371/journal.pmed.1002686 PMID: 30457988

Rajpurkar, P., Irvin, J., Zhu, K., Yang, B., Mehta, H., Duan, T., . . . Ng, A. Y. (2017). CheXNet: Radiologist-level Pneumonia Detection on Chest X-rays with Deep Learning. *arXiv, 3*. https://doi.org//arXiv.1711.05225DOI: 10.48550

Razzak, M. I., Naz, S., & Zaib, A. (2018). Deep Learning for Medical Image Processing: Overview, Challenges, and the Future. *Classification in BioApps*, *26*, 323–350. DOI: 10.1007/978-3-319-65981-7_12

Ronneberger, O., Fischer, P., & Brox, T. (2015). U-Net: Convolutional networks for biomedical image segmentation. *arXiv, 1*. https://doi.org//arXiv.1505.04597DOI: 10.1007/978-3-319-24574-4_28

Salehi, A. W., Khan, S., Gupta, G., Alabduallah, B. I., Almjally, A., Alsolai, H., Siddiqui, T., & Mellit, A. (2023). A Study of CNN and Transfer Learning in Medical Imaging: Advantages, Challenges, Future Scope. *Sustainability (Basel)*, *15*(7), 1–28. DOI: 10.3390/su15075930

Samek, W., Wiegand, T., & Müller, K. R. (2017). Explainable Artificial Intelligence: Understanding, Visualizing, and Interpreting Deep Learning Models. *arXiv, 1*, 1-8 https://arxiv.org/abs/1708.08296

Setio, A. A. A., Ciompi, F., Litjens, G., Gerke, P., Jacobs, C., Van Riel, S. J., Wille, M. M. W., Naqibullah, M., Sanchez, C. I., & Van Ginneken, B. (2016). Pulmonary nodule detection in CT images: False positive reduction using multi-view convolutional networks. *IEEE Transactions on Medical Imaging*, *35*(5), 1160–1169. DOI: 10.1109/TMI.2016.2536809 PMID: 26955024

Shboul, Z. A., Shboul, M. Z., & Al-Husain, M. (2020). A review on deep learning algorithms in medical image analysis. *Journal of Healthcare Engineering*, ●●●, 1–12. DOI: 10.1155/2020/6619801

Shen, D., Wu, G., & Suk, H.-I. (2017). Deep Learning in Medical Image Analysis. *Annual Review of Biomedical Engineering*, *19*(1), 221–248. DOI: 10.1146/annurev-bioeng-071516-044442 PMID: 28301734

Simonyan, K., & Zisserman, A. (2015). Very Deep Convolutional Networks for Large-Scale Image Recognition. *arXiv, 1*. https://doi.org//arXiv.1409.1556DOI: 10.48550

Srivastava, N., Hinton, G., Krizhevsky, A., Sutskever, I., & Salakhutdinov, R. (2014). Dropout: A Simple Way to Prevent Neural Networks from Overfitting. *Journal of Machine Learning Research*, *15*(1), 1929–1958.

Szegedy, C., Ioffe, S., Vanhoucke, V., & Alemi, A. (2016). Inception-v4, Inception-ResNet and the Impact of Residual Connections on Learning. *arXiv, 2*. https://doi.org//arXiv.1602.07261DOI: 10.48550

Szegedy, C., Liu, W., Jia, Y., Sermanet, P., Reed, S., Anguelov, D., Erhan, D., Vanhoucke, V., & Rabinovich, A. (2014). Going Deeper with Convolutions. *arXiv, 1*. https://doi.org//arXiv.1409.4842DOI: 10.48550

Szegedy, C., Vanhoucke, V., Ioffe, S., Shlens, J., & Wojna, Z. (2015). Rethinking the Inception Architecture for Computer Vision. *arXiv, 3*. https://doi.org//arXiv.1512.00567DOI: 10.48550

Tang, X. (2020). The Role of Artificial Intelligence in Medical Imaging Research. *BJR|Open, 2*(1), 1-5. https://doi.org/DOI: 10.1259/bjro.20190031

Tehrani, M. S. (2020). What's the difference between all the different head scans (X-Ray, CT, MRI, MRA, PET scan)? And what do they show in the head? *San Diego Brain Injury Foundation*, https://sdbif.org/whats-the-difference-between-all-the-different-head-scans/

Topol, E. J. (2019). High-performance medicine: The Convergence of Human and Artificial Intelligence. *Nature Medicine*, *25*(1), 44–56. DOI: 10.1038/s41591-018-0300-7 PMID: 30617339

Voigt, P., & Von dem Bussche, A. (2017). The EU General Data Protection Regulation (GDPR): A Practical Guide. *Springer International Publishing*, *10*. Advance online publication. DOI: 10.1007/978-3-319-57959-7

Wang, S., Yang, D. M., Rong, R., Zhan, X., Xiao, G., & Xiao, G. (2018). Pathology Image Analysis using Segmentation Deep Learning Algorithms. *American Journal of Pathology*, *189*(9), 1686–1698. DOI: 10.1016/j.ajpath.2019.05.007 PMID: 31199919

Yamashita, R., Nishio, M., Do, R. K. G., & Togashi, K. (2018). Convolutional Neural Networks: An Overview and Application in Radiology. *Insights Into Imaging*, *9*(4), 611–629. DOI: 10.1007/s13244-018-0639-9 PMID: 29934920

Chapter 7
Leveraging Echo State Networks for DDoS Detection in Software-Defined Networking

Singaravelan Shanmugasundaram
https://orcid.org/0000-0003-4353-2261
PSR Engineering College, India

P. Velayuthaperumal
PSR Engineering College, India

D. Murugan
Manonmaniam Sundaranar University, India

R. Arun
PSR Engineering College, India

P. Gopalsamy
PSR Engineering College, India

S. Balaganesh
PSR Engineering College, India

V. Selvakumar
PSR Engineering College, India

D. Arun Shunmugam
PSR Engineering College, India

ABSTRACT

Software-Defined Networking (SDN) has ushered in a new era of network architecture, offering unparalleled flexibility and adaptability. However, this inherent flexibility also exposes SDN to security vulnerabilities, including Distributed Denial of Service (DDoS) attacks. Detecting and mitigating DDoS attacks within SDN environments is an imperative challenge. This work introduces an innovative DDoS detection scheme harnessing the power of Echo State Networks (ESN) tailored for SDN. Through a series of simulation experiments, we meticulously evaluate the proposed DDoS detection scheme. The results conclusively establish the scheme's

DOI: 10.4018/979-8-3373-0735-0.ch007

effectiveness in accurately identifying and mitigating DDoS attacks, achieving an impressive average success rate of 97.78%. This research marks a significant advancement in fortifying the security of SDN networks, shielding them from disruptive DDoS threats, and emphasizes the potential of Echo State Networks as a valuable tool in the field of cybersecurity.

INTRODUCTION

Software-defined networking (SDN) technology is an approach to network management that enables dynamic, programmatically efficient network configuration in order to improve network performance and monitoring making it more like cloud computing than traditional network management. SDN is meant to address the fact that the static architecture of traditional networks is decentralized and complex while current networks require more flexibility and easy troubleshooting. SDN attempts to centralize network intelligence in one network component by disassociating the forwarding process of network packets (data plane) from the routing process (control plane). The control plane consists of one or more controllers which are considered as the brain of SDN network where the whole intelligence is incorporated. However, the intelligence centralization has its own drawbacks when it comes to security, scalability and elasticity and this is the main issue of SDN.

SDN was commonly associated with the OpenFlow protocol (for remote communication with network plane elements for the purpose of determining the path of network packets across network switches) since the latter's emergence in 2011. However, since 2012 OpenFlow for many companies is no longer an exclusive solution, they added proprietary techniques. These include Cisco Systems' Open Network Environment and Nicira's network virtualization platform.

The history of SDN principles can be traced back to the separation of the control and data plane first used in the public switched telephone network as a way to simplify provisioning and management well before this architecture began to be used in data networks.

The Internet Engineering Task Force (IETF) began considering various ways to decouple the control and forwarding functions in a proposed interface standard published in 2004 appropriately named "Forwarding and Control Element Separation" (ForCES). The ForCES Working Group also proposed a companion SoftRouter Architecture. Additional early standards from the IETF that pursued separating control from data include the Linux Netlink as an IP Services Protocol and A Path Computation Element (PCE)-Based Architecture.

These early attempts failed to gain traction for two reasons. One is that many in the Internet community viewed separating control from data to be risky, especially owing to the potential for a failure in the control plane. The second is that vendors were concerned that creating standard application programming interfaces (APIs) between the control and data planes would result in increased competition.

The use of open source software in split control/data plane architectures traces its roots to the Ethane project at Stanford's computer sciences department. Ethane's simple switch design led to the creation of OpenFlow. An API for OpenFlow was first created in 2008. That same year witnessed the creation of NOX—an operating system for networks.

Work on OpenFlow continued at Stanford, including with the creation of test-beds to evaluate use of the protocol in a single campus network, as well as across the WAN as a backbone for connecting multiple campuses. In academic settings there were a few research and production networks based on OpenFlow switches from NEC and Hewlett-Packard; as well as based on Quanta Computer whiteboxes, starting from about 2009.

Beyond academia, the first deployments were by Nicira in 2010 to control OVS from Onix, co-developed with NTT and Google. A notable deployment was Google's B4 deployment in 2012. Later Google acknowledged their first OpenFlow with Onix deployments in their Datacenters at the same time. Another known large deployment is at China Mobile.

The Open Networking Foundation was founded in 2011 to promote SDN and OpenFlow. At the 2014 Interop and Tech Field Day, software-defined networking was demonstrated by Avaya using shortest path bridging (IEEE 802.1aq) and OpenStack as an automated campus, extending automation from the data center to the end device, removing manual provisioning from service delivery.

Concept

SDN architectures decouple network control and forwarding functions, enabling network control to become directly programmable and the underlying infrastructure to be abstracted from applications and network services.

The OpenFlow protocol can be used in SDN technologies. The SDN architecture is:

Directly programmable: Network control is directly programmable because it is decoupled from forwarding functions.

Agile: Abstracting control from forwarding lets administrators dynamically adjust network-wide traffic flow to meet changing needs.

Centrally managed: Network intelligence is (logically) centralized in software-based SDN controllers that maintain a global view of the network, which appears to applications and policy engines as a single, logical switch.

Programmatically configured: SDN lets network managers configure, manage, secure, and optimize network resources very quickly via dynamic, automated SDN programs, which they can write themselves because the programs do not depend on proprietary software.

Open standards-based and vendor-neutral: When implemented through open standards, SDN simplifies network design and operation because instructions are provided by SDN controllers instead of multiple, vendor-specific devices and protocols.

The need for a new network architecture

The explosion of mobile devices and content, server virtualization, and advent of cloud services are among the trends driving the networking industry to re-examine traditional network architectures. Many conventional networks are hierarchical, built with tiers of Ethernet switches arranged in a tree structure. This design made sense when client-server computing was dominant, but such a static architecture is ill-suited to the dynamic computing and storage needs of today's enterprise data centers, campuses, and carrier environments. Some of the key computing trends driving the need for a new network paradigm include:

Changing traffic patterns

Within the enterprise data center, traffic patterns have changed significantly. In contrast to client-server applications where the bulk of the communication occurs between one client and one server, today's applications access different databases and servers, creating a flurry of “east-west” machine-to-machine traffic before returning data to the end user device in the classic “north-south” traffic pattern. At the same time, users are changing network traffic patterns as they push for access to corporate content and applications from any type of device (including their own), connecting from anywhere, at any time. Finally, many enterprise data centers managers are contemplating a utility computing model, which might include a private cloud, public cloud, or some mix of both, resulting in additional traffic across the wide area network.

The “consumerization of IT”

Users are increasingly employing mobile personal devices such as smartphones, tablets, and notebooks to access the corporate network. IT is under pressure to accommodate these personal devices in a fine-grained manner while protecting corporate data and intellectual property and meeting compliance mandates.

The rise of cloud services

Enterprises have enthusiastically embraced both public and private cloud services, resulting in unprecedented growth of these services. Enterprise business units now want the agility to access applications, infrastructure, and other IT resources on demand and à la carte. To add to the complexity, IT's planning for cloud services must be done in an environment of increased security, compliance, and auditing requirements, along with business reorganizations, consolidations, and mergers that can change assumptions overnight. Providing self-service provisioning, whether in a private or public cloud, requires elastic scaling of computing, storage, and network resources, ideally from a common viewpoint and with a common suite of tools.

"Big data" means more bandwidth

Handling today's "big data" or mega datasets requires massive parallel processing on thousands of servers, all of which need direct connections to each other. The rise of mega datasets is fueling a constant demand for additional network capacity in the data center. Operators of hyperscale data center networks face the daunting task of scaling the network to previously unimaginable size, maintaining any-to-any connectivity without going broke.

Security using the SDN paradigm

SDN architecture may enable, facilitate or enhance network-related security applications due to the controller's central view of the network, and its capacity to reprogram the data plane at any time. While security of SDN architecture itself remains an open question that has already been studied a couple of times in the research community, the following paragraphs only focus on the security applications made possible or revisited using SDN.

Several research works on SDN have already investigated security applications built upon the SDN controller, with different aims in mind. Distributed Denial of Service (DDoS) detection and mitigation, as well as botnet and worm propagation, are some concrete use-cases of such applications: basically, the idea consists in periodically collecting network statistics from the forwarding plane of the network in a standardized manner (e.g. using Openflow), and then apply classification algorithms on those statistics in order to detect any network anomalies. If an anomaly is detected, the application instructs the controller how to reprogram the data plane in order to mitigate it.

Another kind of security application leverages the SDN controller by implementing some moving target defense (MTD) algorithms. MTD algorithms are typically used to make any attack on a given system or network more difficult than usual by periodically hiding or changing key properties of that system or network. In traditional networks, implementing MTD algorithms is not a trivial task since it is difficult to build a central authority able of determining - for each part of the system to be protected - which key properties are hid or changed. In an SDN network, such tasks become more straightforward thanks to the centrality of the controller. One application can for example periodically assign virtual IPs to hosts within the network, and the mapping virtual IP/real IP is then performed by the controller.[63] Another application can simulate some fake opened/closed/filtered ports on random hosts in the network in order to add significant noise during reconnaissance phase (e.g. scanning) performed by an attacker.[64]

Additional value regarding security in SDN enabled networks can also be gained using FlowVisor and FlowChecker respectively. The former tries to use a single hardware forwarding plane sharing multiple separated logical networks. Following this approach the same hardware resources can be used for production and development purposes as well as separating monitoring, configuration and internet traffic, where each scenario can have its own logical topology which is called slice. In conjunction with this approach FlowChecker realizes the validation of new OpenFlow rules that are deployed by users using their own slice.

SDN controller applications are mostly deployed in large-scale scenarios, which requires comprehensive checks of possible programming errors. A system to do this called NICE was described in 2012. Introducing an overarching security architecture requires a comprehensive and protracted approach to SDN. Since it was introduced, designers are looking at possible ways to secure SDN that do not compromise scalability. One architecture called SN-SECA (SDN+NFV) Security Architecture.

Industrial Security

Security Implications of Software Defined Networking in Industrial Control Systems. Industrial Ethernet is the dominating technology in distributed control systems and is planned to take over the whole communication network from office to the field level, with sensor networks being the only exception at the moment. Since its introduction in time critical industrial applications, Ethernet's performance has been questioned, mainly because of the old, coax networks. Current networks are built using full duplex solutions and automation networks follow: these are built with switches, have plenty of bandwidth and the more demanding applications have their specific technologies. These solutions provide intrinsic Quality of Service (QoS), e.g., EtherCAT or try to implement extensions to the Ethernet standards with e.g., efforts to implement resource reservation like the IEEE 802.1 Time-Sensitive Networking Task Group. Many of the issues the control system engineering is facing, are not new. From the advent of packet switched networks, QoS and resilience was a question.

For metropolitan and Wide Area Networks (WAN), different solutions, like Asynchronous Transfer Mode (ATM) or Multiprotocol Label Switching (MPLS) were developed to allow creation of virtual circuits. These virtual circuits can be a natural representation of the control loops. With the industry moving towards Commercial Off The Shelf (COTS) products in the networking solutions (both hardware and software) opened for direct interconnection of other company networks towards the automation systems. The problems associated with network performance and resilience are similar to the ones, which e.g., MPLS was built to solve.

The possibility to proceed further with adopting technologies developed for WAN or telecommunication use is in large part enabled by the extended use of COTS devices. The common technology enables efficient data exchange, but also opens the possibility to attack the previously island-like automation systems from or through the company network. One of the aspects of such interconnection of systems is that the automation network might be attacked through other systems. For a more structured approach, a possible categorization of attackers is given by:

- Hobbyists break into systems for fun and glory. Difficult to stop, but consequences are low.
- Professional hackers break into systems to steal valuable assets, or on a contract basis. Very difficult to stop, consequences usually financial. May be hired to perform theft, industrial espionage, or sabotage.
- Nation-States and Non-Governmental Organizations (NGOs) break into systems to gather intelligence, disable capabilities of opponents, or to cause societal disruption.
- Malware automated attack software. Intent ranges from building botnets for further attacks, theft, or general disruption. Ranges from easy to stop to moderately difficult to stop.
- Disgruntled employees, including insider threat and unauthorized access after employment.

Engineering efforts have been made to reduce the risks associated with this interconnection, but it only gained momentum after the more recent incidents of e.g., stuxnet and repeated cases of Denial of Service (DoS) incidents coming from external networks. The first efforts were focused on including well-known solutions from the IT industry: firewalls, Intrusion Detection Systems (IDS), authentication solutions.

The challenge with these solutions is that they were designed to operate in a different network environment [6]. Amongst others, the QoS requirements of an automation system tend to be very different than of an office network. The protocol set used is different and the typical protocol inside an automation system runs on Layer 2 and not on the IP protocol suite.

Beside the efforts on adopting IT security solutions to industrial environments, several working groups are involved in introducing security features into automation protocols and protocols used to support an automation system (e.g., IEEE 1588v3 on security functions, IEC 61850 to have integrity protection). The necessity of network management systems are gaining acceptance to support life-cycle management of the communication infrastructure.

A distributed denial-of-service (DDoS) attack is a malicious attempt to disrupt the normal traffic of a targeted server, service or network by overwhelming the target or its surrounding infrastructure with a flood of Internet traffic.

DDoS attacks achieve effectiveness by utilizing multiple compromised computer systems as sources of attack traffic. Exploited machines can include computers and other networked resources such as IoT devices. From a high level, a DDoS attack is like an unexpected traffic jam clogging up the highway, preventing regular traffic from arriving at its destination.

How does a DDoS attack work?

DDoS attacks are carried out with networks of Internet-connected machines. These networks consist of computers and other devices (such as IoT devices)which have been infected with malware, allowing them to be controlled remotely by an attacker. These individual devices are referred to as bots (or zombies), and a group of bots is called a botnet.

Once a botnet has been established, the attacker is able to direct an attack by sending remote instructions to each bot.When a victim's server or network is targeted by the botnet, each bot sends requests to the target's IP address, potentially causing the server or network to become overwhelmed, resulting in a denial-of-service to normal traffic.Because each bot is a legitimate Internet device, separating the attack traffic from normal traffic can be difficult.

How to identify a DDoS attack

The most obvious symptom of a DDoS attack is a site or service suddenly becoming slow or unavailable. But since a number of causes — such a legitimate spike in traffic — can create similar performance issues, further investigation is usually required. Traffic analytics tools can help you spot some of these telltale signs of a DDoS attack:

- Suspicious amounts of traffic originating from a single IP address or IP range
- A flood of traffic from users who share a single behavioral profile, such as device type, geolocation, or web browser version
- An unexplained surge in requests to a single page or endpoint
- Odd traffic patterns such as spikes at odd hours of the day or patterns that appear to be unnatural (e.g. a spike every 10 minutes)

There are other, more specific signs of DDoS attack that can vary depending on the type of attack.

What are some common types of DDoS attacks?

Different types of DDoS attacks target varying components of a network connection. In order to understand how different DDoS attacks work, it is necessary to know how a network connection is made.

A network connection on the Internet is composed of many different components or "layers". Like building a house from the ground up, each layer in the model has a different purpose.

The OSI model, shown below, is a conceptual framework used to describe network connectivity in 7 distinct layers.

While nearly all DDoS attacks involve overwhelming a target device or network with traffic, attacks can be divided into three categories. An attacker may use one or more different attack vectors, or cycle attack vectors in response to counter measures taken by the target.

Application layer attacks

The goal of the attack:

Sometimes referred to as a layer 7 DDoS attack (in reference to the 7th layer of the OSI model), the goal of these attacks is to exhaust the target's resources to create a denial-of-service.

The attacks target the layer where web pages are generated on the server and delivered in response to HTTP requests. A single HTTP request is computationally cheap to execute on the client side, but it can be expensive for the target server to respond to, as the server often loads multiple files and runs database queries in order to create a web page.Layer 7 attacks are difficult to defend against, since it can be hard to differentiate malicious traffic from legitimate traffic.

Figure 1. Application layer attack example

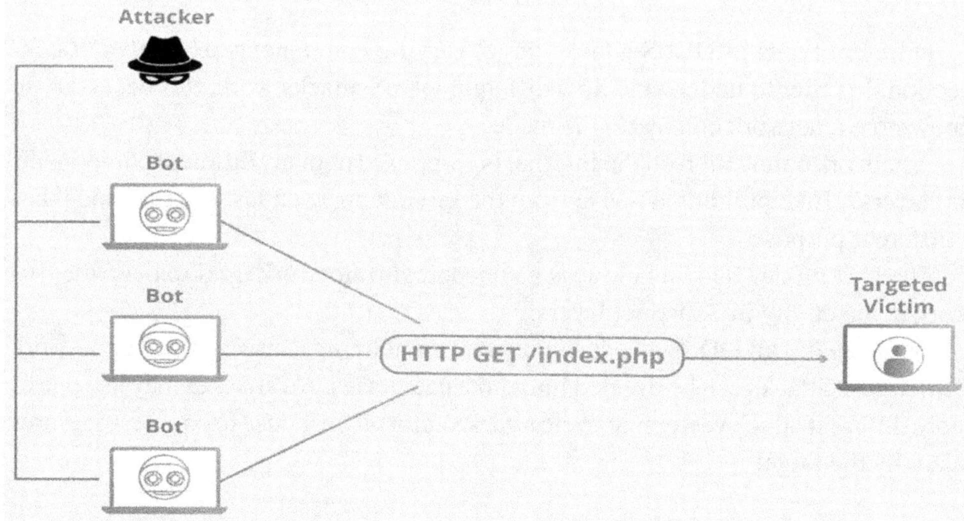

HTTP flood

This attack is similar to pressing refresh in a web browser over and over on many different computers at once – large numbers of HTTP requests flood the server, resulting in denial-of-service.

This type of attack ranges from simple to complex.

Simpler implementations may access one URL with the same range of attacking IP addresses, referrers and user agents. Complex versions may use a large number of attacking IP addresses, and target random urls using random referrers and user agents.

Protocol Attacks

The Goal of the Attack

Protocol attacks, also known as a state-exhaustion attacks, cause a service disruption by over-consuming server resources and/or the resources of network equipment like firewalls and load balancers.

Protocol attacks utilize weaknesses in layer 3 and layer 4 of the protocol stack to render the target inaccessible.

Figure 2. Protocol attack example

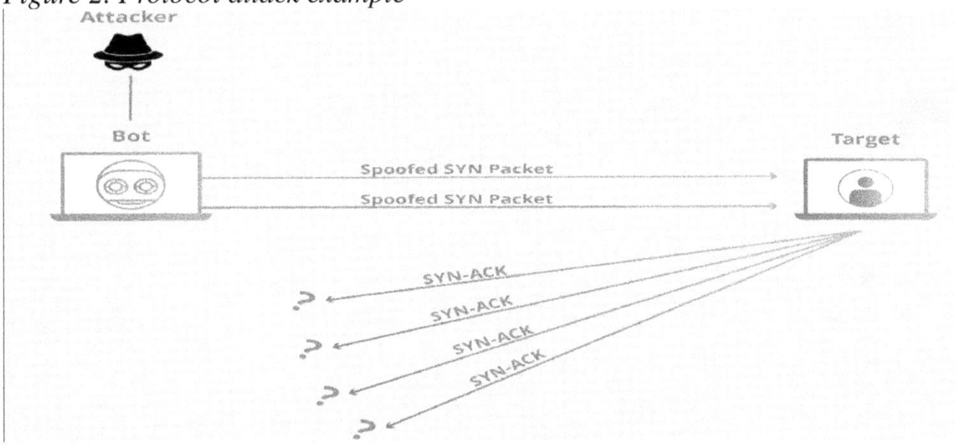

SYN Flood

A SYN Flood is analogous to a worker in a supply room receiving requests from the front of the store.

The worker receives a request, goes and gets the package, and waits for confirmation before bringing the package out front. The worker then gets many more package requests without confirmation until they can't carry any more packages, become overwhelmed, and requests start going unanswered.

This attack exploits the TCP handshake — the sequence of communications by which two computers initiate a network connection — by sending a target a large number of TCP "Initial Connection Request" SYN packets with spoofed source IP addresses.The target machine responds to each connection request and then waits for the final step in the handshake, which never occurs, exhausting the target's resources in the process.

Volumetric Attacks

The Goal of the Attack

This category of attacks attempts to create congestion by consuming all available bandwidth between the target and the larger Internet. Large amounts of data are sent to a target by using a form of amplification or another means of creating massive traffic, such as requests from a botnet.

Figure 3. Amplification example

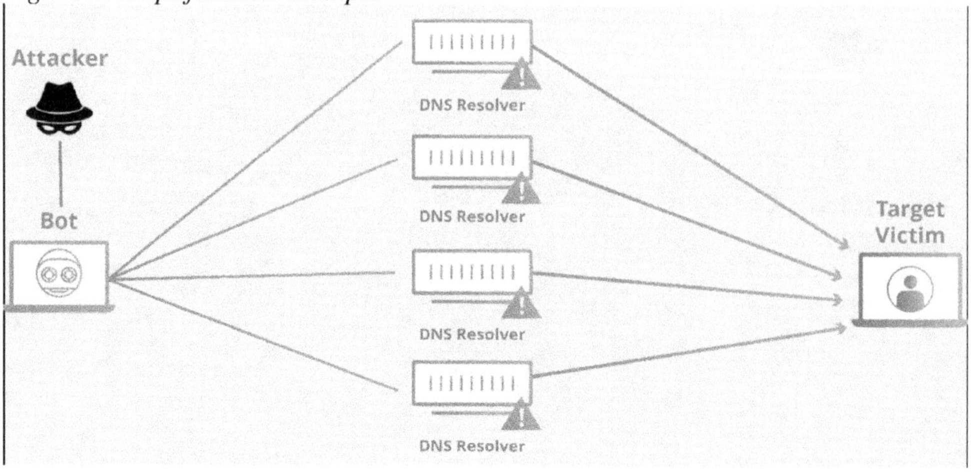

DNS Amplification

A DNS amplification is like if someone were to call a restaurant and say "I'll have one of everything, please call me back and repeat my whole order," where the callback number actually belongs to the victim. With very little effort, a long response is generated and sent to the victim. By making a request to an open DNS server with a spoofed IP address (the IP address of the victim), the target IP address then receives a response from the server.

What is the Process for Mitigating a DDoS attack?

The key concern in mitigating a DDoS attack is differentiating between attack traffic and normal traffic. For example, if a product release has a company's website swamped with eager customers, cutting off all traffic is a mistake. If that company suddenly has a surge in traffic from known attackers, efforts to alleviate an attack are probably necessary.

The difficulty lies in telling the real customers apart from the attack traffic. In the modern Internet, DDoS traffic comes in many forms. The traffic can vary in design from un-spoofed single source attacks to complex and adaptive multi-vector attacks.A multi-vector DDoS attack uses multiple attack pathways in order to overwhelm a target in different ways, potentially distracting mitigation efforts on any one trajectory.

An attack that targets multiple layers of the protocol stack at the same time, such as a DNS amplification (targeting layers 3/4) coupled with an HTTP flood (targeting layer 7) is an example of multi-vector DDoS.

Mitigating a multi-vector DDoS attack requires a variety of strategies in order to counter different trajectories.Generally speaking, the more complex the attack, the more likely it is that the attack traffic will be difficult to separate from normal traffic - the goal of the attacker is to blend in as much as possible, making mitigation efforts as inefficient as possible.

Mitigation attempts that involve dropping or limiting traffic indiscriminately may throw good traffic out with the bad, and the attack may also modify and adapt to circumvent countermeasures. In order to overcome a complex attempt at disruption, a layered solution will give the greatest benefit.

Blackhole Routing

One solution available to virtually all network admins is to create a blackhole route and funnel traffic into that route. In its simplest form, when blackhole filtering is implemented without specific restriction criteria, both legitimate and malicious network traffic is routed to a null route, or blackhole, and dropped from the network. If an Internet property is experiencing a DDoS attack, the property's Internet service provider (ISP) may send all the site's traffic into a blackhole as a defense. This is not an ideal solution, as it effectively gives the attacker their desired goal: it makes the network inaccessible.

Rate Limiting

Limiting the number of requests, a server will accept over a certain time window is also a way of mitigating denial-of-service attacks. While rate limiting is useful in slowing web scrapers from stealing content and for mitigating brute force login attempts, it alone will likely be insufficient to handle a complex DDoS attack effectively. Nevertheless, rate limiting is a useful component in an effective DDoS mitigation strategy. Learn about Cloudflare's rate limiting

Web Application Firewall

A Web Application Firewall (WAF) is a tool that can assist in mitigating a layer 7 DDoS attack. By putting a WAF between the Internet and an origin server, the WAF may act as a reverse proxy, protecting the targeted server from certain types of malicious traffic.By filtering requests based on a series of rules used to identify DDoS tools, layer 7 attacks can be impeded. One key value of an effective WAF is the ability to quickly implement custom rules in response to an attack. Learn about Cloudflare's WAF.

Anycast Network Diffusion

This mitigation approach uses an Anycast network to scatter the attack traffic across a network of distributed servers to the point where the traffic is absorbed by the network.Like channeling a rushing river down separate smaller channels, this approach spreads the impact of the distributed attack traffic to the point where it becomes manageable, diffusing any disruptive capability.

The reliability of an Anycast network to mitigate a DDoS attack is dependent on the size of the attack and the size and efficiency of the network. An important part of the DDoS mitigation implemented by Cloudflare is the use of an Anycast distributed network.Cloudflare has a 142 Tbps network, which is an order of magnitude greater than the largest DDoS attack recorded.

If you are currently under attack, there are steps you can take to get out from under the pressure. If you are on Cloudflare already, you can follow these steps to mitigate your attack.The DDoS protection that we implement at Cloudflare is multifaceted in order to mitigate the many possible attack vectors. Learn more about Cloudflare's DDoS protection and how it works.

LITERATURE SURVEY

QoS-Aware Fog Node Placement for Intensive IoT Applications in SDN-Fog Scenarios

Herrera et al focused on this fog node placement problem by formalizing it and solving it through both optimal and approximated methods, including comparisons with state-of-the-art benchmarks. In particular, we analyze the performance of each of these methods in terms of latency and execution time in both SDN Internet topologies and Industrial IoT infrastructures. Our proposed heuristic provides placements with near-optimal latencies, with smaller optimality gaps than the benchmark, and computes them in tractable times.

Z. Li et al explored a behavior-based verification method, named Crowd-Learning, by utilizing the idea of crowd in software-defined vehicular networks with a MEC framework. In Crowd-Learning, we design an incentive mechanism to stimulate some MEC infrastructures to provide accurate and appropriate amount of data for future correct behavior estimation. Without knowing the model of the dynamic environment, this incentive mechanism needs to apply reinforcement learning to let

MEC infrastructures learn how to send data based on the current state. Our Crowd-Learning method verifies vehicles and reduces the verification latency by estimating the vehicle's behavior in advance. Meanwhile, it verifies infrastructures during the process of reinforcement learning based on the idea of crowd intelligence. The fake infrastructures and anomalous vehicles expose themselves when learning. In experiments, we use the traffic simulation tool, called simulation of urban mobility (SUMO), to generate extensive vehicle traces and evaluate the performance of the Crowd-Learning verification method. The results show that the Crowd-Learning verification method can ensure high verification accuracy for vehicles and infrastructures with satisfying low verification latency.

Multicast Scheduling in SDN WISE to Support Mobile Nodes in Industrial Wireless Sensor Networks

Orozco-Santos et al investigated a Mobile Multicast Forwarding with Software Defined Network (MMF-SDN), an approach using Software Defined Networking solution for WIreless SEnsor Network (SDN WISE) protocol that exploits the advantages of SDN and Time Slotted Channel Hopping (TSCH) synchronism. The mobile nodes are managed as multicast sources, through a cumulative allocation of resources from the controller. This allows reception states to be synchronized at the parent nodes to provide network stability, avoiding subsequent recalculations in the routing protocol. Parent node changes are transparent and immediate. This proposal improves on other SDN based solutions, reducing energy consumption in reception by up to end-to-end delay and improving scalability with a 30% reduction in slotframe occupancy.

Detection and Classification of DDoS Flooding Attacks on Software-Defined Networks: A Case Study for the Application of Machine Learning

Sangodoyin et al illustrated through a case study, in which, experimental data (i.e. jitter, throughput, and response time metrics) from a representative SDN architecture suitable for typical mid-sized enterprise-wide networks is used to build classification models that accurately identify and classify DDoS flooding attacks. The SDN model used was emulated in Mininet and the DDoS flooding attacks (i.e. hypertext transfer protocol (HTTP), transmission control protocol (TCP), and user datagram protocol (UDP) attacks) have been launched on the SDN model using low orbit ion cannon (LOIC). Although all the ML methods investigated show very good efficacy in detecting and classifying DDoS flooding attacks, CART demonstrated the best performance on average in terms of prediction accuracy (98%), prediction speed (5.3×10^5 observations per second), training time (12.4 ms), and robustness.

SDN-Enabled Resource Orchestration for Industrial IoT in Collaborative Edge-Cloud Networks

Okwuibe et al presented SDRM; an SDN-enabled Resource Management scheme. This novel orchestration methodology automatically computes the optimal resource allocation for different IIoT network models and dynamically adjust assigned resources based on predefined constraints to ensure Service Level Agreement (SLA). The proposed approach models resource allocation as a Constraint Satisfaction Problem (CSP) where optimality is based on the solution of a predefined Satisfiability (SAT) problem. This model supports centralized management of all resources using a software defined approach. Such resources include memory, power, bandwidth, and edge-cloud resources. SDRM aims at accelerating efficient resource orchestration through dynamic workload balancing and edge-cloud resource utilization, thereby reducing the cost of IIoT system deployment and improving the overall ROI for adopting IIoT solutions. We model our resource allocation approach on SAVILE ROW using ESSENSE PRIME modeling language, we then implement the network model on CloudSimSDN and PureEdgeSim. We present a detailed analysis of the system architecture and the key technologies of the model. We finally demonstrate the efficiency of the model by presenting experimental results from a prototype system.

A Survey on Machine Learning Techniques for Routing Optimization in SDN

Amin et al surveyed the use of ML techniques for routing optimization in SDN based on three core categories (i.e. supervised learning, unsupervised learning, and reinforcement learning). The main contributions of this survey are threefold. Firstly, it presents detailed summary tables related to these studies and their comparison is also discussed, including a summary of the best works according to our analysis. Secondly, it summarizes the main findings, best works and missing aspects, and it includes a quick guideline to choose the best ML technique in this field (based on available resources and objectives). Finally, it provides specific future research directions divided into six sections to conclude the survey. Our conclusion is that there is a huge trend to use intelligence-based routing in programmable networks, particularly during the last three years, but a lot of effort is still required to achieve comprehensive comparisons and synergies of approaches, meaningful evaluations based on open datasets and topologies, and detailed practical implementations (following recent standards) that could be adopted by industry. In summary, future efforts should be focused on reproducible research rather than on new isolated ideas. Otherwise, most of these applications will be barely implemented in practice.

A Blockchain-Based Federated Forest for SDN-Enabled In-Vehicle Network Intrusion Detection System

Aliyu et al developed Blockchain-based Federated Forest Software-Defined Networking (SDN)-enabled IDS (BFF-IDS) to address the problem of data sharing the sensitive CAN data. To ensure scalability, we used InterPlanetary File System (IPFS) to host the models, and the blockchain is designed to store only a hash of the model and a pointer to its location. The SDN provides the dynamic routing of packets and model exchanges. We used Federated Learning (FL) to create a random forest model. Individuals provide partially trained models, allowing them to keep the underlying data confidential. Using Fourier transform, we decomposed the CAN IDs cycle from CAN bus traffic in the frequency domain for better generalization in multiclass detection of attacks. Multiple statistical and entropy features were extracted to handle the high complexity and non-linearity in CAN bus traffic. The proposed system allows manufacturers and car owners to contribute to the training of the models, as their sensitive data is protected. By storing hashes of the models on a blockchain, the risk of adversaries poisoning the models is reduced and a single point of failure is avoided. We evaluated the proposed system by conducting experiments on a testbed. We found that the proposed system has efficient use of memory and CPU resources and that the detection rate of closely related attacks was high. We recorded the highest model attack detection rate

Journey toward software-defined passive optical networks with multi-PON technology: an industry view [Invited]

Montalvo et al explored our Open Broadband trial in Brazil and the journey to open software and whitebox hardware as a practical approach to scaling fiber access networks enabling integration into a software-defined network controlled environment while transitioning away from vertically integrated models featuring black box passive optical network (PON) solutions. A key part of this journey is multi-PON capable whitebox optical line terminals (OLTs) with combo-PON (C-PON) optics that play a key role in bridging the transition from G-PON to XGS-PON.

Simplified Stream Reservation Protocol Over Software-Defined Networks for In-Vehicle Time-Sensitive Networking

Nam et al presented a simplified SRP scheme over the Software-defined Network (SDN) for in-vehicle bridged networks. The proposed scheme exploits the topology and bridge information of bridged networks. A centralized stream reservation procedure in the scheme replaces the bridge-by-bridge propagation for SRP reservations. The reservation procedure does not require VLAN ID and group address registration. We implemented a prototype of the proposed scheme and showed that reserved flows are well protected when links of bridges are overloaded.

CloudSimHypervisor: Modeling and Simulating Network Slicing in Software-Defined Cloud Networks

Nyanteh et al established the CloudSimHypervisor framework in this based on CloudSimSDN-NFV. The complete architecture and features of the CloudSimHypervisor framework and some used cases are presented in this paper. We validate the CloudSimHypervisor framework with two use case experiments in the cloud computing environment: Joint compute and network resource utilization and network traffic prioritization. Results from these experiments display the efficiency of the CloudSimHypervisor in estimating and measuring processing speed, transmission speed, compute and network usage efficiency and energy consumption.

Fault Localization based on Knowledge Graph in Software-Defined Optical Networks

Z. Li et al presented a knowledge-guided fault localization method, using network alarm knowledge to analyze network abnormalities. Our method introduces knowledge graphs (KGs) into the alarm analysis process. We also propose a reasoning model based on graph neural network (GNN), to perform relational reasoning on alarm KGs and locate the network faults. We develop an ONOS-based SDON platform for experimental verification, which includes a set of processes for the construction and application of alarm KGs. The experimental results show the proposed method has high accuracy and provide motivation for the industry-scale use of KGs for alarm analysis and fault localization.

Parallel Route Optimization and Service Assurance in Energy-Efficient Software-Defined Industrial IoT Networks

Njah et al presented a a centralized route optimization and service assurance scheme, named ROSA, over a multi-layer programmable industrial architecture. The proposed solution supports a wide range of heterogeneous flows, such as ultra-reliable low-latency communications (URLLC) and bandwidth-sensitive services. The routing optimization problems are formulated as multi-constrained shortest path problems. The Lagrangian Relaxation approach is used to solve the . Hence, we deploy a pair of parallel routing algorithms run according to the flow type to ensure QoS requirements, efficiently allocate constrained resources, and enhance the overall network energy consumption. We conduct extensive simulations to validate the proposed ROSA scheme. The experimental results show promising performance in terms of reducing bandwidth utilization by up to end-to-end delay, packet loss, flow violation and energy consumption up to 14% as compared to well-known benchmarks in QoS provisioning and energy-aware routing problem.

An Efficient Counter-Based DDoS Attack Detection Framework Leveraging Software Defined IoT (SD-IoT)

Njah et al presented an SD-IoT based framework that provides security services to the IoT network. We developed a C-DAD (Counter-based DDoS Attack Detection) application that is based on counter values of different network parameters, which helps to detect DDoS attack successfully. C-DAD is a dynamic and programmable solution, and is deeply tested with different network parameters. The algorithm demonstrates a good performance with better results through SDN. Moreover, the proposed framework detects the attack efficiently in a minimum amount of time and with lesser consumption of CPU and memory resources.

DOMAIN DECRIPTION & EXISTING MODELS

There are two forms of data analysis that can be used for extracting models describing important classes or to predict future data trends. These two forms are as follows –

- Classification
- Prediction

Classification models predict categorical class labels; and prediction models predict continuous valued functions. For example, we can build a classification model to categorize bank loan applications as either safe or risky, or a prediction model to predict the expenditures in dollars of potential customers on computer equipment given their income and occupation.

What is classification?

Following are the examples of cases where the data analysis task is Classification –

- A bank loan officer wants to analyze the data in order to know which customer (loan applicant) are risky or which are safe.
- A marketing manager at a company needs to analyze a customer with a given profile, who will buy a new computer.

In both of the above examples, a model or classifier is constructed to predict the categorical labels. These labels are risky or safe for loan application data and yes or no for marketing data.

What is prediction?

Following are the examples of cases where the data analysis task is Prediction –

Suppose the marketing manager needs to predict how much a given customer will spend during a sale at his company. In this example we are bothered to predict a numeric value. Therefore the data analysis task is an example of numeric prediction. In this case, a model or a predictor will be constructed that predicts a continuous-valued-function or ordered value.

How Does Classification Works?

With the help of the bank loan application that we have discussed above, let us understand the working of classification. The Data Classification process includes two steps –

- Building the Classifier or Model
- Using Classifier for Classification

Building the Classifier or Model

- This step is the learning step or the learning phase.

- In this step the classification algorithms build the classifier.
- The classifier is built from the training set made up of database tuples and their associated class labels.
- Each tuple that constitutes the training set is referred to as a category or class. These tuples can also be referred to as sample, object or data points.

Figure 4. Classification Algorithm

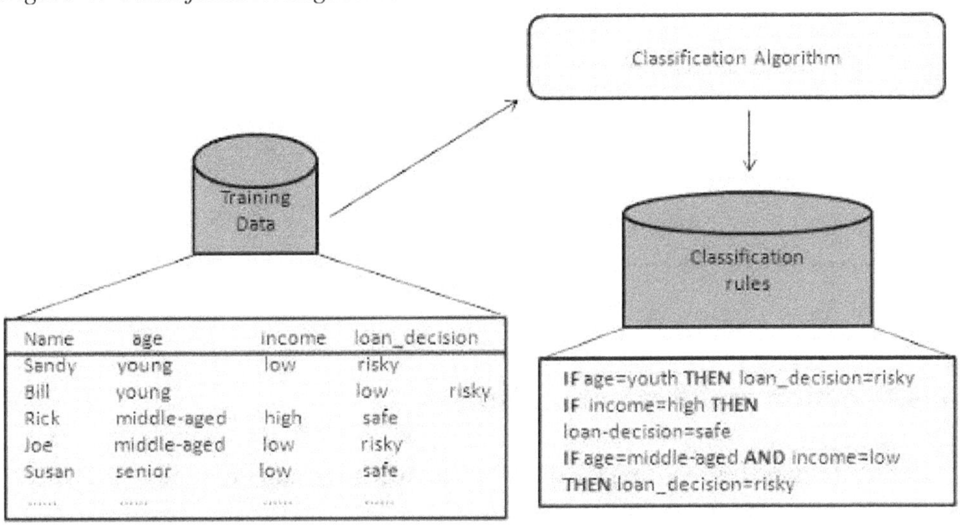

Using Classifier for Classification

In this step, the classifier is used for classification. Here the test data is used to estimate the accuracy of classification rules. The classification rules can be applied to the new data tuples if the accuracy is considered acceptable.

Figure 5. Rules for Classification

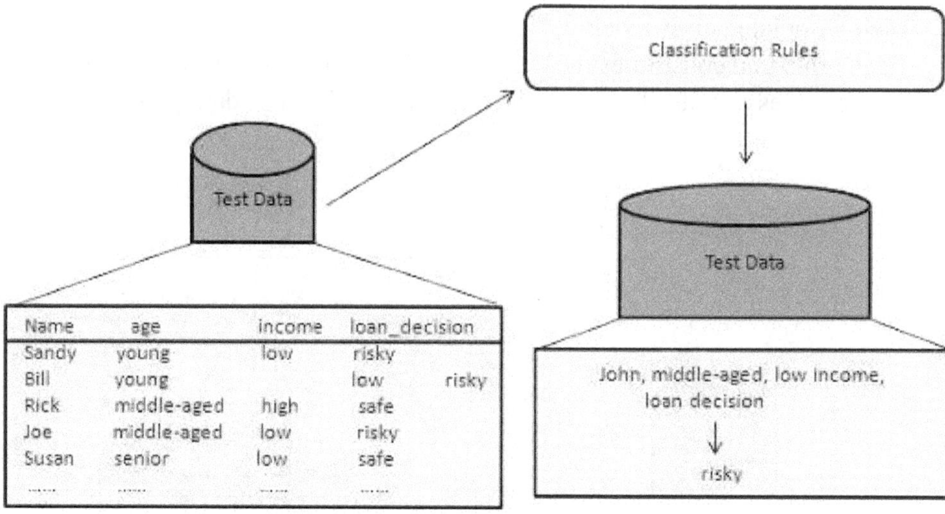

Classification and Prediction Issues

The major issue is preparing the data for Classification and Prediction. Preparing the data involves the following activities –

- **Data Cleaning** – Data cleaning involves removing the noise and treatment of missing values. The noise is removed by applying smoothing techniques and the problem of missing values is solved by replacing a missing value with most commonly occurring value for that attribute.
- **Relevance Analysis** – Database may also have the irrelevant attributes. Correlation analysis is used to know whether any two given attributes are related.
- **Data Transformation and reduction** – The data can be transformed by any of the following methods.
    - **Normalization** – The data is transformed using normalization. Normalization involves scaling all values for given attribute in order to make them fall within a small specified range. Normalization is used when in the learning step, the neural networks or the methods involving measurements are used.
    - **Generalization** – The data can also be transformed by generalizing it to the higher concept. For this purpose we can use the concept hierarchies.

Note – Data can also be reduced by some other methods such as wavelet transformation, binning, histogram analysis, and clustering.

Comparison of Classification and Prediction Methods

Here is the criteria for comparing the methods of Classification and Prediction –

- **Accuracy** – Accuracy of classifier refers to the ability of classifier. It predict the class label correctly and the accuracy of the predictor refers to how well a given predictor can guess the value of predicted attribute for a new data.
- **Speed** – This refers to the computational cost in generating and using the classifier or predictor.
- **Robustness** – It refers to the ability of classifier or predictor to make correct predictions from given noisy data.
- **Scalability** – Scalability refers to the ability to construct the classifier or predictor efficiently; given large amount of data.
- **Interpretability** – It refers to what extent the classifier or predictor understands.

Types of Algorithms In Data Mining

Figure 6. Date mining algorithms

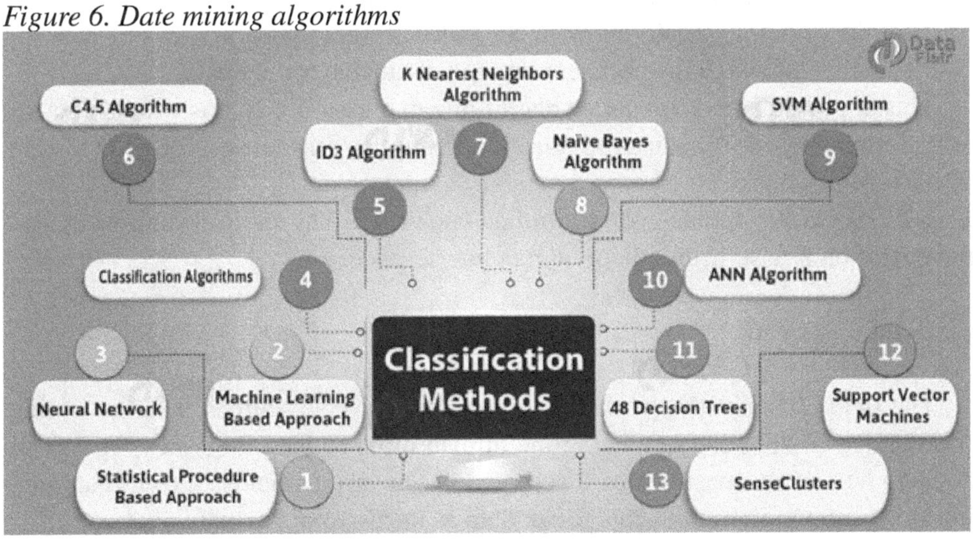

a. Statistical Procedure Based Approach

There are two main phases present to work on classification. That can easily identify the statistical community.

The second, "modern" phase concentrated on more flexible classes of models. In which many of which attempt has to take. That provides an estimate of the joint distribution of the feature within each class. That can, in turn, provide a classification rule.

Generally, statistical procedures have to characterize by having a precise fundamental probability model. That used to provides a probability of being in each class instead of just a classification. Also, we can assume that techniques will use by statisticians.

Hence some human involvement has to assume with regard to variable selection. Also, transformation and overall structuring of the problem.

b. Machine Learning-Based Approach

Generally, it covers automatic computing procedures. That was based on logical or binary operations. That use to learn a task from a series of examples.

Here, we have to focus on decision-tree approaches. As classification results come from a sequence of logical steps. These classification results are capable of representing the most complex problem given. Such as genetic algorithms and inductive logic procedures (I.LP.) are currently under active improvement.

Also, its principle would allow us to deal with more general types of data including cases. In which the number and type of attributes may vary.

This approach aims to generate classifying expressions. That is simple enough to understand by the human. And must mimic human reasoning to provide insight into the decision process.

Like statistical approaches, background knowledge may use in development. But the operation is assumed without human interference.

c. Neural Network

The field of Neural Networks has arisen from diverse sources. That is ranging from understanding and emulating the human brain to broader issues. That is of copying human abilities such as speech and use in various fields. Such as banking, in classification program to categorize data as intrusive or normal.

Generally, neural networks consist of layers of interconnected nodes. That each node producing a non-linear function of its input. And input to a node may come from other nodes or directly from the input data. Also, some nodes are identified with the output of the network.

On the basis of this, there are different applications for neural networks present. That involve recognizing patterns and making simple decisions about them.

In airplanes, we can use a neural network as a basic autopilot. In which input units read signals from the various instruments and output units. That modifying the plane's controls appropriately to keep it safely on course. Inside a factory, we can use a neural network for quality control.

d. Classification Algorithms in Data Mining

It is one of the Data Mining. That is used to analyze a given data set and takes each instance of it. It assigns this instance to a particular class. Such that classification error will be least. It is used to extract models. That define important data classes within the given data set. Classification is a two-step process.

During the first step, the model is created by applying a classification algorithm. That is on training data set.

Then in the second step, the extracted model is tested against a predefined test data set. That is to measure the model trained performance and accuracy. So classification is the process to assign class label from a data set whose class label is unknown.

e. ID3 Algorithm

This Data Mining Algorithms starts with the original set as the root hub. On every cycle, it emphasizes through every unused attribute of the set and figures. That the entropy of attribute. At that point chooses the attribute. That has the smallest entropy value.

The set is S then split by the selected attribute to produce subsets of the information.

This Data Mining algorithms proceed to recurse on each item in a subset. Also, considering only items never selected before. Recursion on a subset may bring to a halt in one of these cases:

- Every element in the subset belongs to the same class (+ or -), then the node is turned into a leaf and
- labeled with the class of the examples
- If there are no more attributes to select but the examples still do not belong to the same class. Then the node is turned into a leaf and labeled with the most common class of the examples in that subset.

- If there are no examples in the subset, then this happens. Whenever parent set found to be matching a specific value of the selected attribute.
- For example, if there was no example matching with marks >=100. Then a leaf is created and is labeled with the most common class of the examples in the parent set.

PROPOSED MODEL

Software-Defined Networking (SDN) has transformed network management, offering dynamic and flexible control. However, the openness of SDN makes it vulnerable to Distributed Denial of Service (DDoS) attacks. Detecting and mitigating DDoS attacks in SDN environments is essential. This work presents an innovative DDoS detection system that leverages Echo State Networks (ESN) designed for SDN. We focus on data collection, preprocessing, feature extraction, and model training for robust DDoS detection.

Modules:

1. Data Set Collection:

Kaggle Data Set: To train and evaluate the DDoS detection model, we will collect network traffic data from publicly available datasets on Kaggle. These datasets will include normal network traffic and DDoS attack scenarios. We will select a dataset with a significant variety of attacks to ensure robust model training.

Data Preprocessing: The collected dataset may require preprocessing to clean and format the data. This includes handling missing values, data normalization, and data transformation to create a structured dataset for training and testing.

2. Feature Extraction:

Traffic Features: In this module, we will extract relevant features from network traffic data, such as packet sizes, traffic patterns, protocol usage, and more. These features will serve as the input to the ESN model for DDoS detection.

Statistical Analysis: We will conduct statistical analyses to identify patterns and anomalies in the data that are indicative of DDoS attacks. Feature selection techniques will be applied to choose the most discriminative features.

3. Echo State Network (ESN) Model:

ESN Architecture: ESN is a type of recurrent neural network known for its capabilities in sequential data analysis. We will design an ESN architecture suitable for processing network traffic data. The ESN will consist of an input layer, hidden reservoir layer, and output layer.

Model Training: Using the preprocessed dataset and extracted features, we will train the ESN model to recognize normal and abnormal network behavior. This will involve supervised learning to build a robust DDoS detection system.

4. DDoS Detection:

Real-time Analysis: The trained ESN model will be deployed in real-time to analyze incoming network traffic. It will evaluate traffic patterns and identify deviations that may indicate DDoS attacks.

Anomaly Detection: The system will focus on detecting anomalies in network behavior, which can include unusual traffic spikes, protocol violations, and other DDoS attack signatures.

5. Evaluation and Testing:

Performance Metrics: To assess the effectiveness of the DDoS detection system, we will employ various performance metrics such as precision, recall, F1-score, and ROC curves. These metrics will help evaluate the system's accuracy and efficiency.

Validation: The system will be tested against a diverse set of network traffic scenarios, including known DDoS attacks, to validate its performance in real-world conditions.

6. User Interface (Optional):

Dashboard: An optional user interface may be developed to provide users with real-time insights into network traffic and detected anomalies. This can aid network administrators in taking prompt actions.

Figure 7. Proposed system

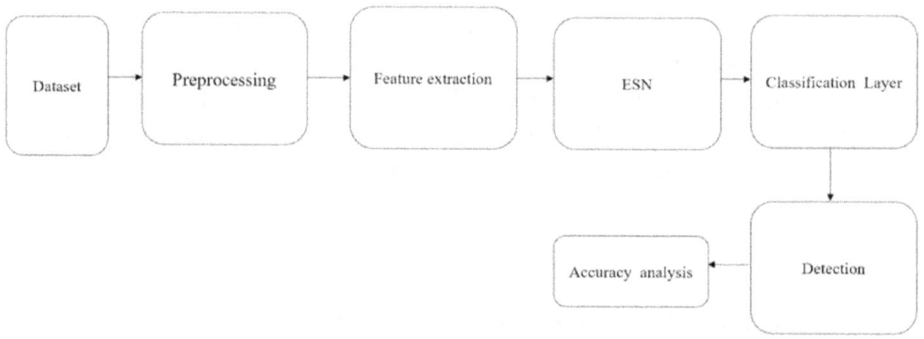

Echo State Network (ESN):**

Echo State Network (ESN) is a type of recurrent neural network (RNN) known for its effectiveness in processing sequential data, making it particularly valuable in various applications, including time series prediction, speech recognition, and anomaly detection. Unlike traditional RNNs, ESN exhibits distinct architectural properties that contribute to its success. This introduction provides an overview of ESN's architecture and the key layers that comprise this network.

Figure 8. Echo State Network

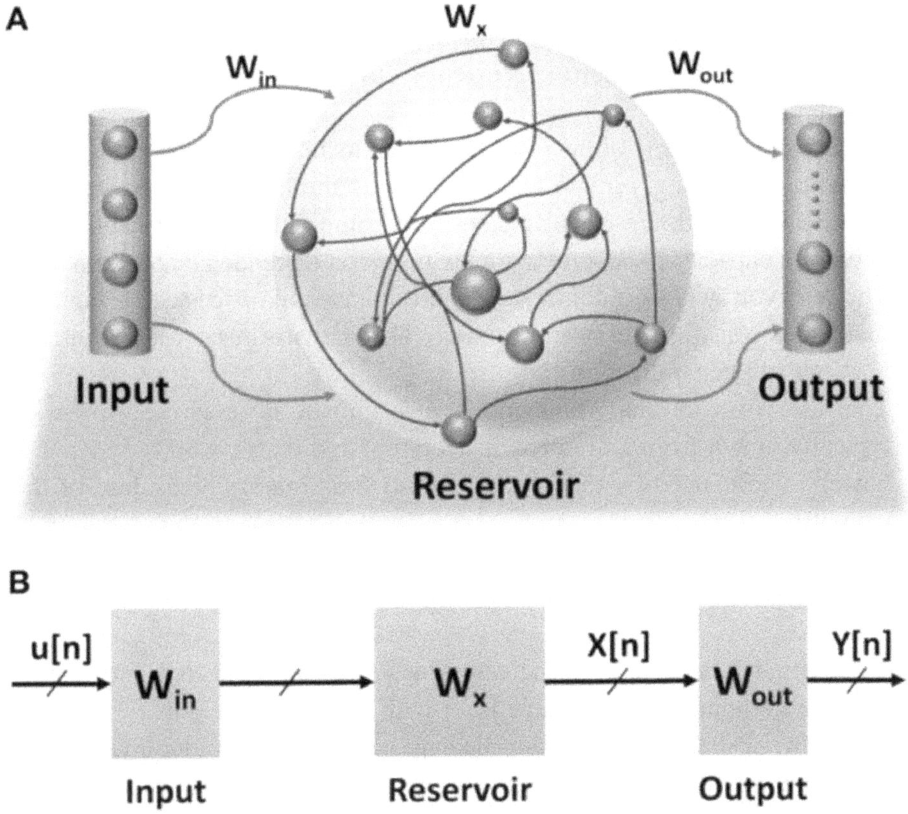

ESN Architecture and Layers:

Echo State Network consists of three primary layers: the Input Layer, the Reservoir Layer, and the Output Layer. Each of these layers plays a unique role in the network's operation.

1. Input Layer:
   - The Input Layer receives and processes the external input data. This layer connects directly to the reservoir layer, and its primary function is to transform the incoming data into a format suitable for processing within the network.
   - In the case of time series data or sequential information, the input layer may receive data points at discrete time steps and provide them as input to the reservoir.
   - The input data can represent a wide range of information, such as sensor readings, language signals, or any sequential data of interest.

Reservoir Layer:

- The Reservoir Layer is the distinguishing feature of the ESN architecture. It comprises a large number of recurrent neurons that form a dynamic, fixed-weight network.
- The key characteristic of the reservoir is that its internal connections are generated randomly and remain unaltered during the training process. This dynamic nature of the reservoir creates a rich internal state that facilitates the network's capacity to capture complex temporal dependencies in data.
- The reservoir acts as a nonlinear, high-dimensional space where input data undergoes transformation and mixing. This transformation is essential for learning and generalization.
- The reservoir's internal connections, also known as reservoir weights, are typically drawn from a uniform distribution, and the network's dynamic behavior is influenced by the spectral radius (maximum eigenvalue) of these weights.

Output Layer:

- The Output Layer receives the reservoir's state as input and generates the network's output. It is a trainable layer with adjustable weights.
- The network's learning process primarily occurs in the output layer, where a linear combination of the reservoir states is transformed to produce the desired output.
- The output layer can be fine-tuned during training to achieve specific tasks, such as classification, regression, or sequence prediction.
- The combination of a dynamic reservoir and a trainable output layer is what distinguishes ESN from traditional RNNs. The reservoir layer takes on the role of capturing complex temporal patterns, while the output layer simplifies the mapping of this internal state to the desired output.

Echo State Networks are particularly advantageous in scenarios where extensive temporal dependencies and nonlinear relationships need to be captured in data. Their simple yet powerful architecture makes them a valuable tool for various applications, including time series analysis and sequential data processing. ESN's success lies in its capacity to harness the intrinsic dynamics of the reservoir layer, facilitating efficient learning and generalization.

PSUDOCODE

```
# Import necessary libraries
import numpy as np
from sklearn.preprocessing import StandardScaler
from pyESN import ESN
from sklearn.metrics import accuracy_score, confusion_matrix
# Load and preprocess the dataset
# Replace 'your_dataset.csv' with the actual dataset file name
data = np.genfromtxt('your_dataset.csv', delimiter=',')
X = data[:, 0:-1] # Features
y = data[:, -1] # Labels (normal or attacker)
# Split the dataset into training and testing sets
# You can use functions like train_test_split from scikit-learn
X_train, X_test, y_train, y_test = train_test_split(X, y, test_size=0.2, random_state=42)
# Standardize the data
scaler = StandardScaler()
X_train = scaler.fit_transform(X_train)
X_test = scaler.transform(X_test)
# Initialize the Echo State Network
esn = ESN(n_reservoir=100, spectral_radius=0.8, random_state=42)
# Train the ESN on the training data
esn.fit(X_train, y_train)
# Make predictions on the testing data
y_pred = esn.predict(X_test)
# Evaluate the model
accuracy = accuracy_score(y_test, y_pred)
confusion = confusion_matrix(y_test, y_pred)
# Display the results
print("Accuracy:", accuracy)
print("Confusion Matrix:", confusion)
```

The dataset is then split into training and testing sets. This division is a common practice in machine learning, enabling the model to be trained on one portion of the data and tested on another to assess its performance.

Before training the ESN, the data is standardized using the StandardScaler from scikit-learn. Standardization ensures that the data has a mean of zero and a standard deviation of one, preparing it for effective use in the model.

The ESN, a type of recurrent neural network, is initialized with specific parameters, including the number of reservoir neurons, spectral radius, and a random seed. These parameters influence the ESN's dynamics and its ability to capture temporal patterns.

The ESN model is trained using the training data, where it learns to map the input features (X_train) to the corresponding output labels (y_train). The ESN's unique characteristic is its ability to capture complex temporal dependencies in the data.

After training, the ESN is used to make predictions on the testing data (X_test). These predictions are compared with the actual labels to evaluate the model's accuracy.

The code computes and displays the accuracy of the ESN model, which represents how well it can distinguish between normal and attacker instances. Additionally, a confusion matrix is presented, showing the true positive, true negative, false positive, and false negative predictions, offering a comprehensive view of the model's performance.

SOFTWARE SPECIFICATION

SOFTWARE REQUIRED:

- IDLE 1.7
- PYTHON 1.7.6

HARDWARE REQUIRED:

- System: Windows Xp Professional Service Pack 2
- Processor: Up to 1.5 GHz
- Memory: Up to 512 MB RAM

5.1 PYTHON

The Python language had a humble beginning in the late 1980s when a Dutchman Guido Von Rossum started working on a fun project, which would be a successor to ABC language with better exception handling and capability to interface with OS Amoeba at Centrum Wiskunde and Informatica. It first appeared in 1991. Python 2.0 was released in the year 2000 and Python 3.0 was released in the year 2008. The language was named Python after the famous British television comedy show Monty Python's Flying Circus, which was one of Guido's favorite television programmes. Here we will see why Python has suddenly influenced our lives and the various applications that use Python and its implementations.

SIMULATION RESULT

Dataset and Per processing

The proposed model is evaluated on two public datasets, the 10% KDD99 and the full NSLKDD, which have been widely used for evaluating the performance of intrusion detection schemes. In the KDD99 dataset, we utilize all the legitimate traffic samples and select 14 types of prevalent attacks. In the NSLKDD dataset, we use all the legitimate traffic samples and select 16 types of prevalent attacks. The features of each data sample in the datasets are considered as a feature vector. We split the dataset randomly into the training, validation and testing subset with a ratio of 0.7:0.1:0.2, namely the size of the training, validation and testing subset. For each predictive model, we train it in a mini-batch way with 1,024 sequences per epoch and conduct 100 iterations. In order to enhance the models' generalization performance, the data was divided independently and each model was trained and tested 10 times in our work. Finally we report the mean evaluation metrics on the 10 testing results.

Figure 9. Data set description

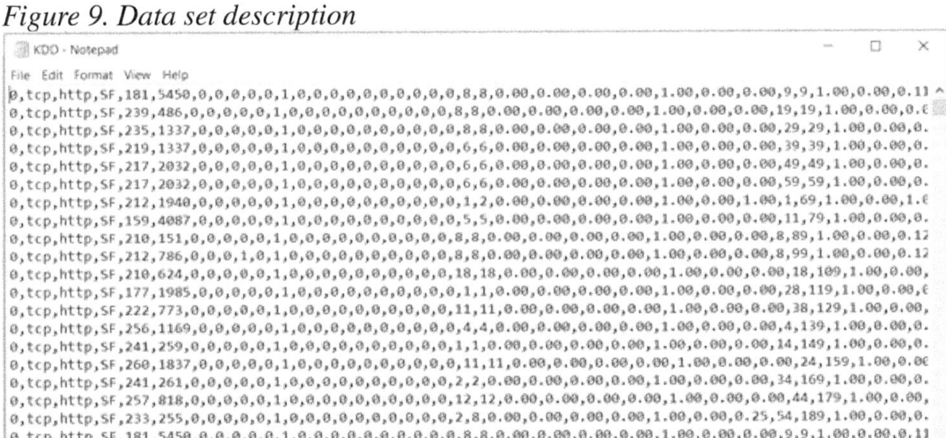

```
KDD - Notepad
File Edit Format View Help
0,tcp,http,SF,181,5450,0,0,0,0,0,1,0,0,0,0,0,0,0,0,0,0,8,8,0.00,0.00,0.00,0.00,1.00,0.00,0.00,9,9,1.00,0.00,0.11
0,tcp,http,SF,239,486,0,0,0,0,0,1,0,0,0,0,0,0,0,0,0,0,8,8,0.00,0.00,0.00,0.00,1.00,0.00,0.00,19,19,1.00,0.00,0.0
0,tcp,http,SF,235,1337,0,0,0,0,0,1,0,0,0,0,0,0,0,0,0,0,8,8,0.00,0.00,0.00,0.00,1.00,0.00,0.00,29,29,1.00,0.00,0.
0,tcp,http,SF,219,1337,0,0,0,0,0,1,0,0,0,0,0,0,0,0,0,0,6,6,0.00,0.00,0.00,0.00,1.00,0.00,0.00,39,39,1.00,0.00,0.
0,tcp,http,SF,217,2032,0,0,0,0,0,1,0,0,0,0,0,0,0,0,0,0,6,6,0.00,0.00,0.00,0.00,1.00,0.00,0.00,49,49,1.00,0.00,0.
0,tcp,http,SF,217,2032,0,0,0,0,0,1,0,0,0,0,0,0,0,0,0,0,6,6,0.00,0.00,0.00,0.00,1.00,0.00,0.00,59,59,1.00,0.00,0.
0,tcp,http,SF,212,1940,0,0,0,0,0,1,0,0,0,0,0,0,0,0,0,0,1,2,0.00,0.00,0.00,0.00,1.00,0.00,1.00,1,69,1.00,0.00,1.0
0,tcp,http,SF,159,4087,0,0,0,0,0,1,0,0,0,0,0,0,0,0,0,0,5,5,0.00,0.00,0.00,0.00,1.00,0.00,0.00,11,79,1.00,0.00,0.
0,tcp,http,SF,210,151,0,0,0,0,0,1,0,0,0,0,0,0,0,0,0,0,8,8,0.00,0.00,0.00,0.00,1.00,0.00,0.00,8,89,1.00,0.00,0.12
0,tcp,http,SF,212,786,0,0,0,1,0,1,0,0,0,0,0,0,0,0,0,0,8,8,0.00,0.00,0.00,0.00,1.00,0.00,0.00,8,99,1.00,0.00,0.12
0,tcp,http,SF,210,624,0,0,0,0,0,1,0,0,0,0,0,0,0,0,0,0,18,18,0.00,0.00,0.00,0.00,1.00,0.00,0.00,18,109,1.00,0.00,
0,tcp,http,SF,177,1985,0,0,0,0,0,1,0,0,0,0,0,0,0,0,0,0,1,1,0.00,0.00,0.00,0.00,1.00,0.00,0.00,28,119,1.00,0.00,0
0,tcp,http,SF,222,773,0,0,0,0,0,1,0,0,0,0,0,0,0,0,0,0,11,11,0.00,0.00,0.00,0.00,1.00,0.00,0.00,38,129,1.00,0.00,
0,tcp,http,SF,256,1169,0,0,0,0,0,1,0,0,0,0,0,0,0,0,0,0,4,4,0.00,0.00,0.00,0.00,1.00,0.00,0.00,4,139,1.00,0.00,0.
0,tcp,http,SF,241,259,0,0,0,0,0,1,0,0,0,0,0,0,0,0,0,0,1,1,0.00,0.00,0.00,0.00,1.00,0.00,0.00,14,149,1.00,0.00,0.
0,tcp,http,SF,260,1837,0,0,0,0,0,1,0,0,0,0,0,0,0,0,0,0,11,11,0.00,0.00,0.00,0.00,1.00,0.00,0.00,24,159,1.00,0.00
0,tcp,http,SF,241,261,0,0,0,0,0,1,0,0,0,0,0,0,0,0,0,0,2,2,0.00,0.00,0.00,0.00,1.00,0.00,0.00,34,169,1.00,0.00,0.
0,tcp,http,SF,257,818,0,0,0,0,0,1,0,0,0,0,0,0,0,0,0,0,12,12,0.00,0.00,0.00,0.00,1.00,0.00,0.00,44,179,1.00,0.00,
0,tcp,http,SF,233,255,0,0,0,0,0,1,0,0,0,0,0,0,0,0,0,0,2,8,0.00,0.00,0.00,0.00,1.00,0.00,0.25,54,189,1.00,0.00,0.
0,tcp,http,SF,181,5450,0,0,0,0,0,1,0,0,0,0,0,0,0,0,0,0,8,8,0.00,0.00,0.00,0.00,1.00,0.00,0.00,9,9,1.00,0.00,0.11
```

Figure 10. LSTM Training

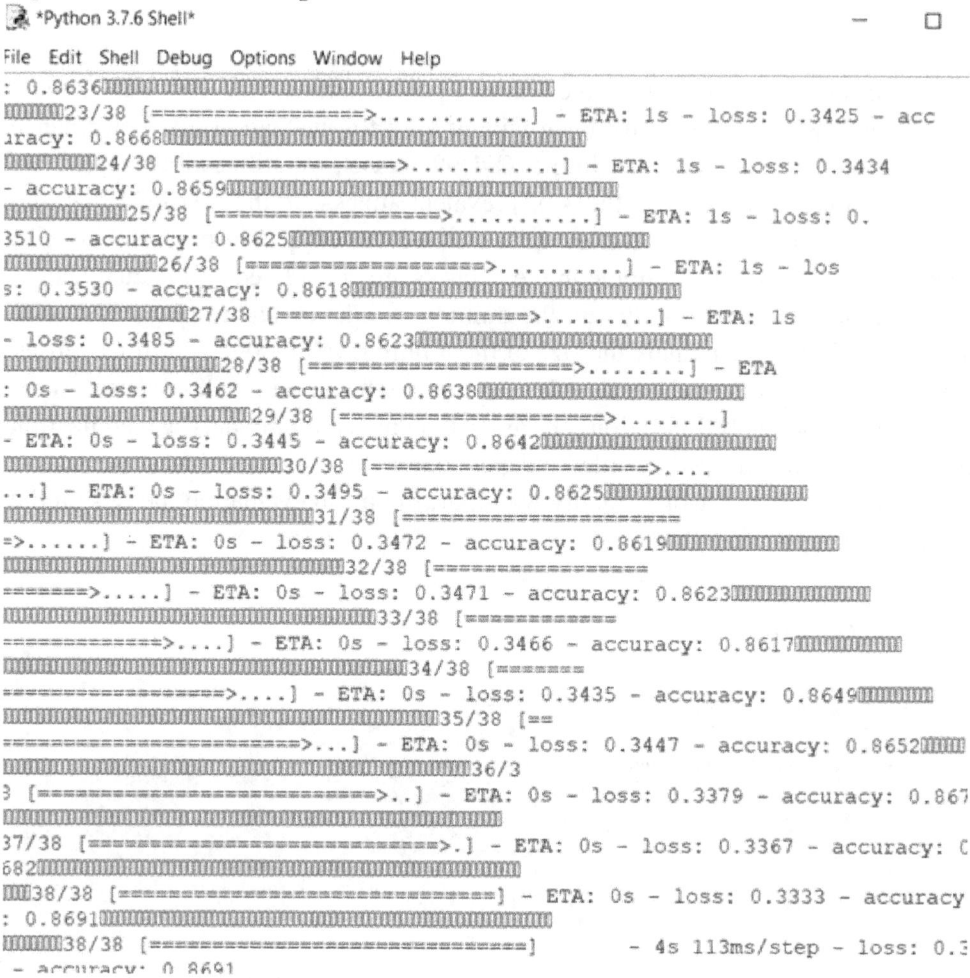

Figure 11. Histogram of attacker variation

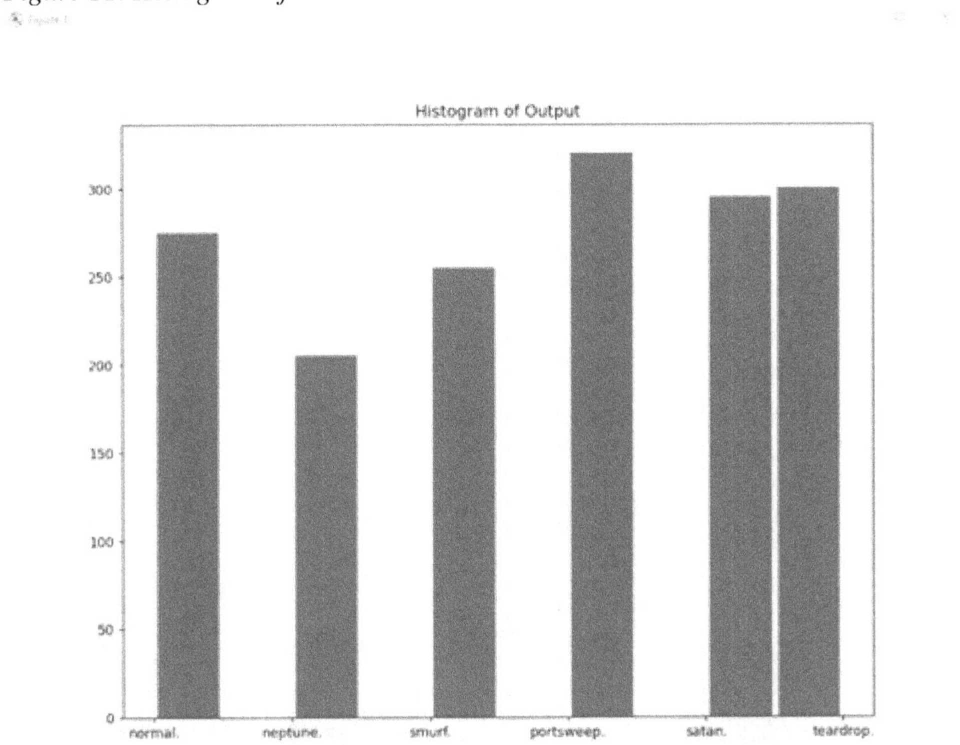

Figure 12. Application

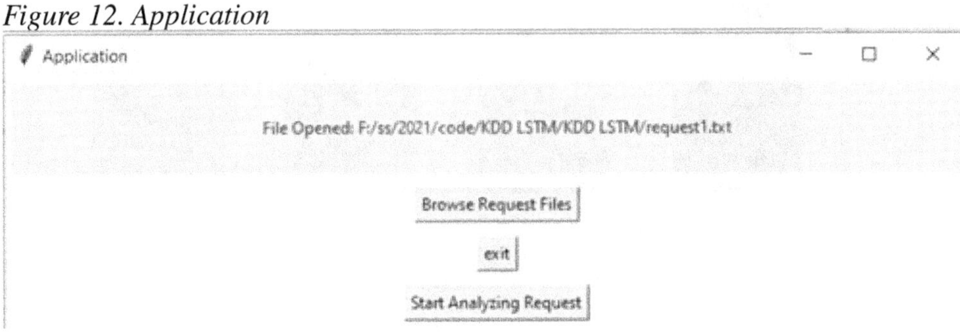

Figure 13. Attacker classification

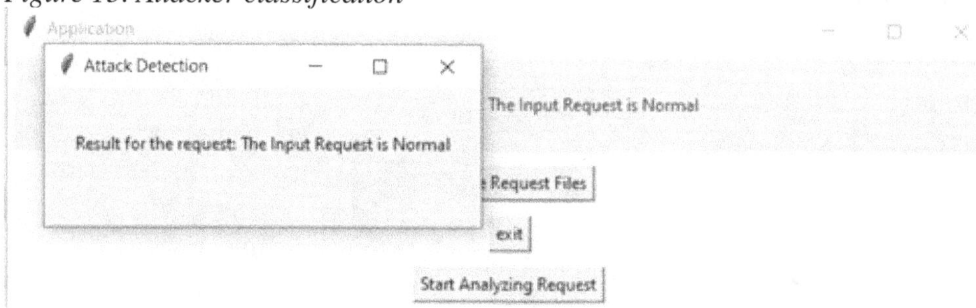

Figure 14. Performance analysis

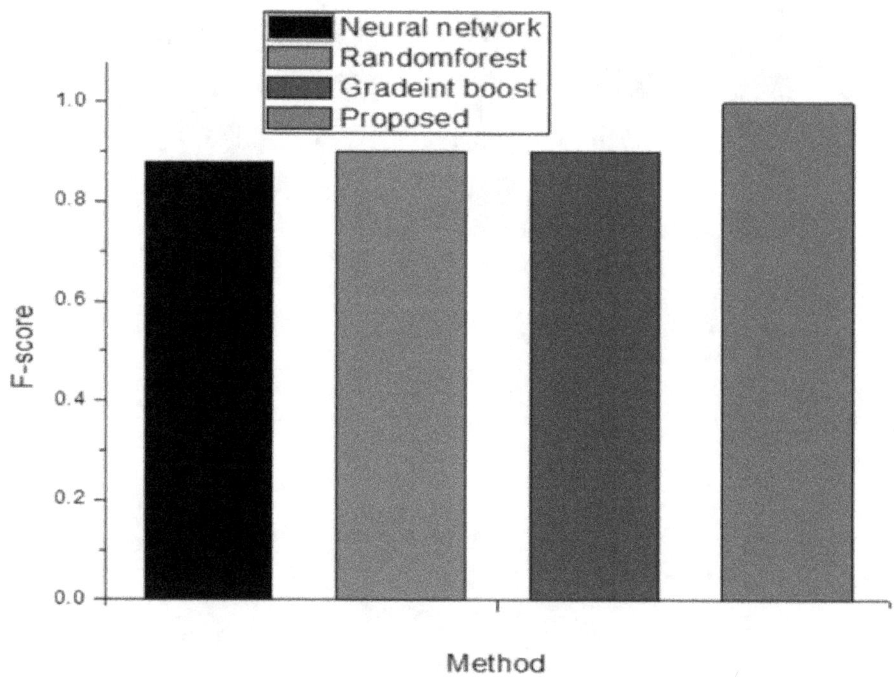

Figure 15. Performance analysis II

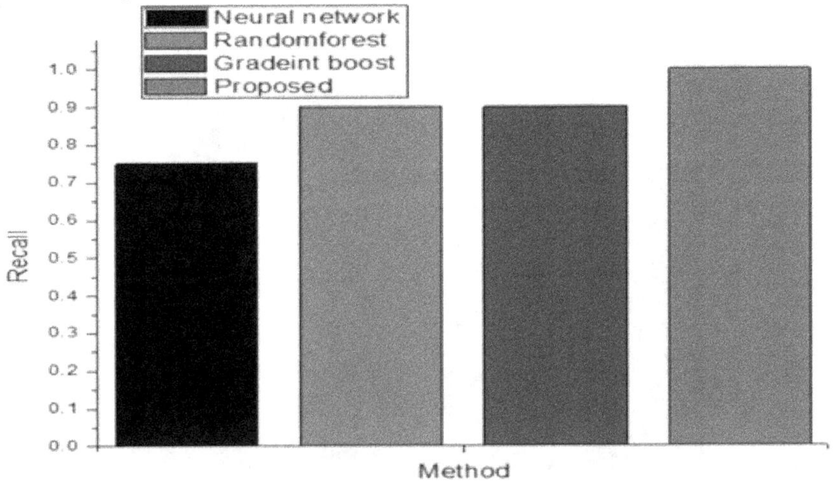

Figure 16. Performance analysis III

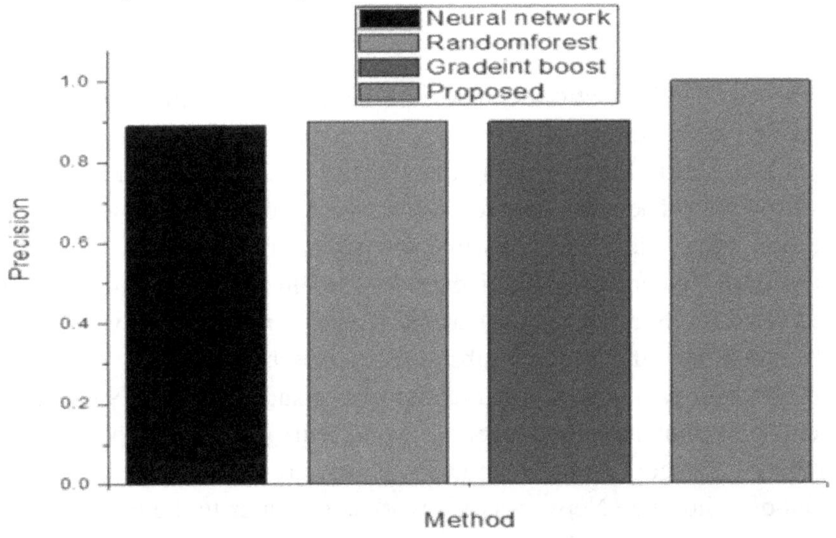

Figure 17. Performance analysis IV

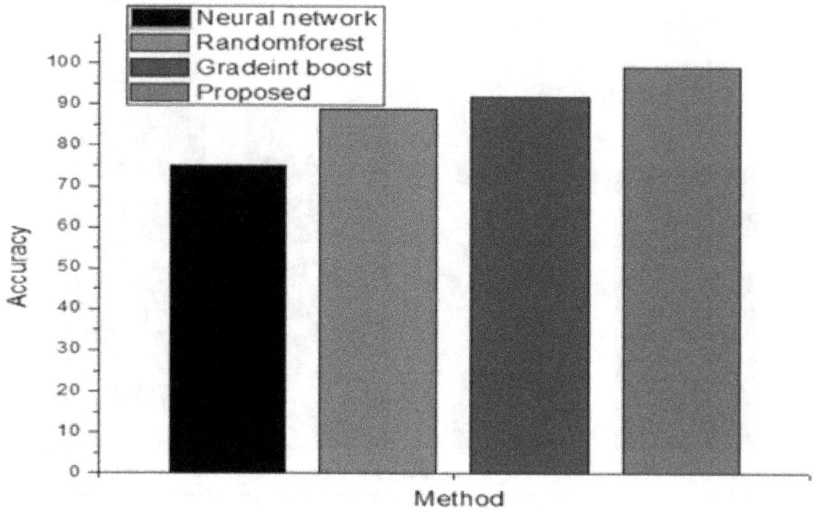

CONCLUSION

The proposed DDoS detection scheme, leveraging the capabilities of Echo State Networks (ESN) in the context of Software-Defined Networking (SDN), represents a significant step forward in enhancing the security and resilience of modern network infrastructures. The study, based on the foundational assumptions that network operations are predominantly normal and that anomalies exhibit distinct data characteristics, underscores the effectiveness of ESN in identifying and mitigating Distributed Denial of Service (DDoS) attacks.Through meticulous evaluation in a simulated environment, the research substantiates the scheme's ability to detect and respond to DDoS threats with a remarkable average success rate of 97.78%. This achievement holds immense promise for the cybersecurity landscape, particularly in the realm of SDN, where flexibility and adaptability are paramount.By harnessing the potential of Echo State Networks, this work contributes to the ongoing efforts to fortify network security, offering a proactive defense against disruptive DDoS attacks. The findings highlight the viability of ESN as a valuable tool in the arsenal of cybersecurity measures, furthering our capability to safeguard critical network infrastructures in an ever-evolving digital landscape.

REFERENCES

Aliyu, I., Feliciano, M. C., Van Engelenburg, S., Kim, D. O., & Lim, C. G. (2021). A Blockchain-Based Federated Forest for SDN-Enabled In-Vehicle Network Intrusion Detection System. *IEEE Access : Practical Innovations, Open Solutions*, *9*, 102593–102608. DOI: 10.1109/ACCESS.2021.3094365

Amin, R., Rojas, E., Aqdus, A., Ramzan, S., Casillas-Perez, D., & Arco, J. M. (2021). A Survey on Machine Learning Techniques for Routing Optimization in SDN. *IEEE Access : Practical Innovations, Open Solutions*, *9*, 104582–104611. DOI: 10.1109/ACCESS.2021.3099092

Herrera, J. L., Galán-Jiménez, J., Foschini, L., Bellavista, P., Berrocal, J., & Murillo, J. M. (2022, August 1). QoS-Aware Fog Node Placement for Intensive IoT Applications in SDN-Fog Scenarios. *IEEE Internet of Things Journal*, *9*(15), 13725–13739. Advance online publication. DOI: 10.1109/JIOT.2022.3143948

Li, Z., Yang, X., Wang, C., Ma, K., & Jiang, C. (2021). Crowd-learning: A behavior-based verification method in software-defined vehicular networks with MEC framework. *IEEE Internet of Things Journal*, *9*(2), 1622–1639.

Li, Z., Zhao, Y., Li, Y., Rahman, S., Wang, F., Xin, X., & Zhang, J. (2021, July 1). Fault Localization based on Knowledge Graph in Software-Defined Optical Networks. *Journal of Lightwave Technology*, *39*(13), 4236–4246. DOI: 10.1109/JLT.2021.3071868

Montalvo, J., Torrijos, J., Cortes, D., Chundury, R., & St. Peter, M. (2021, August). Journey toward software-defined passive optical networks with multi-PON technology: An industry view [Invited]. *Journal of Optical Communications and Networking*, *13*(8), D22–D31. DOI: 10.1364/JOCN.423034

Nam, S., Kim, H., & Min, S.-G. (2021). Simplified Stream Reservation Protocol Over Software-Defined Networks for In-Vehicle Time-Sensitive Networking. *IEEE Access : Practical Innovations, Open Solutions*, *9*, 84700–84711. DOI: 10.1109/ACCESS.2021.3088288

Njah, Y., & Cheriet, M. (2021). Parallel Route Optimization and Service Assurance in Energy-Efficient Software-Defined Industrial IoT Networks. *IEEE Access : Practical Innovations, Open Solutions*, *9*, 24682–24696. DOI: 10.1109/ACCESS.2021.3056931

Nyanteh, A. O., Li, M., Abbod, M. F., & Al-Raweshidy, H. (2021). CloudSimHypervisor: Modeling and Simulating Network Slicing in Software-Defined Cloud Networks. *IEEE Access : Practical Innovations, Open Solutions*, *9*, 72484–72498. DOI: 10.1109/ACCESS.2021.3079501

Okwuibe, J., Haavisto, J., Kovacevic, I., Harjula, E., Ahmad, I., Islam, J., & Ylianttila, M. (2021). SDN-Enabled Resource Orchestration for Industrial IoT in Collaborative Edge-Cloud Networks. *IEEE Access : Practical Innovations, Open Solutions*, *9*, 115839–115854. DOI: 10.1109/ACCESS.2021.3105944

Orozco-Santos, F., Sempere-Payá, V., Silvestre-Blanes, J., & Albero-Albero, T. (2021). Multicast Scheduling in SDN WISE to Support Mobile Nodes in Industrial Wireless Sensor Networks. *IEEE Access : Practical Innovations, Open Solutions*, *9*, 141651–141666. DOI: 10.1109/ACCESS.2021.3120917

Sangodoyin, A. O., Akinsolu, M. O., Pillai, P., & Grout, V. (2021). Detection and Classification of DDoS Flooding Attacks on Software-Defined Networks: A Case Study for the Application of Machine Learning. *IEEE Access : Practical Innovations, Open Solutions*, *9*, 122495–122508. DOI: 10.1109/ACCESS.2021.3109490

Chapter 8
Enhancing Content Recommendation for Programming Education Using BERT-Based Techniques

Asmaa Bengueddach
https://orcid.org/0000-0002-4128-1895
Université Oran 1 Ahmed Ben Bella, Algeria

Linda Benachenhou
https://orcid.org/0009-0003-3441-7170
Mostaganem University, Algeria

Abdelhamid Bekkaye
Université Oran 1 Ahmed Ben Bella, Algeria

Efan Efan
https://orcid.org/0000-0003-0545-2324
Institut Teknologi Pagar Alam, Indonesia

ABSTRACT

Programming education faces increasing challenges due to the vast array of available resources, making it difficult for learners to identify relevant content. This chapter presents an approach leveraging BERT-based models, particularly SBERT, to enhance content recommendation systems. These models improve the alignment between user queries and programming materials by capturing semantic

DOI: 10.4018/979-8-3373-0735-0.ch008

context. The proposed methodology employs pre-trained SBERT models to facilitate query-content matching, with validation performed using Stack Overflow data. Performance is assessed using Precision@k and Mean Reciprocal Rank (MRR) to evaluate retrieval accuracy. The results demonstrate that this approach effectively reduces information overload and enhances learning efficiency. Additionally, the chapter explores potential applications and future developments, including multilingual support and scalability.

I. INTRODUCTION

The integration of Artificial Intelligence (AI) in education has become a transformative force, reshaping traditional learning environments and enabling personalized educational experiences (Raj & Renumol, 2022). Over the past decade, AI applications have gained prominence, revolutionizing how students engage with content and how educators adapt instruction. As educational institutions increasingly adopt hybrid and online learning formats, traditional classroom models face growing limitations in addressing the diverse needs of learners (Zawacki-Richter, Marín, Bond, & Gouverneur, 2019).

One of the primary challenges in modern education is content personalization, particularly as class sizes expand and human instructors struggle to provide individualized support. AI-powered solutions offer an effective means to bridge this gap by enabling adaptive learning environments (Luckin & Holmes, 2016). Platforms such as Massive Open Online Courses (MOOCs) and Learning Management Systems (LMS) like Moodle integrate AI-driven recommendation systems to enhance engagement and optimize content delivery (Fidalgo-Blanco, García-Peñalvo, Sein-Echaluce, & Conde-González, 2014). However, as the volume of educational resources grows, the challenge lies in ensuring that students can efficiently access the most relevant materials for their learning needs.

To address this issue, content recommendation systems have emerged as a powerful approach for tailoring learning experiences. By leveraging AI, these systems analyze user interactions, learning patterns, and content preferences to deliver personalized recommendations, enhancing engagement and improving learning outcomes (Raj & Renumol, 2022).

This study introduces an innovative use of SBERT (Sentence-BERT), an extension of BERT (Bidirectional Encoder Representations from Transformers), to improve content recommendation in programming education. Unlike traditional BERT, which requires pairwise comparisons for similarity assessments, SBERT generates efficient, semantically rich sentence embeddings, enabling fast and accurate retrieval of educational resources. By capturing the context and intent behind user queries, this approach significantly enhances recommendation accuracy and personalization.

The remainder of this chapter is structured as follows: Section 2 reviews the related work in AI-driven educational recommendation systems. Section 3 presents our proposed approach and its contributions. Section 4 details the SBERT methodology employed in this study. Section 5 provides an in-depth explanation of the implementation and evaluation of our solution. Finally, Section 6 discusses future research directions and the potential scalability of this approach.

II. RELATED WORK

The concept of adaptive learning has been extensively studied and applied across various educational contexts (Brusilovsky & Peylo, 2003). Over the years, several approaches have been proposed to tailor educational content to individual learners' needs, leveraging artificial intelligence (AI) and machine learning to enhance personalization and engagement.

One of the earliest studies in this field was conducted by Fidalgo-Blanco et al. (2014), who developed a learning content management system designed to create adaptive learning environments. Their system aimed to deliver personalized learning experiences by dynamically adjusting content based on learners' knowledge levels and skills. Similarly, Kahraman, Sagiroglu, and Colak (2010) introduced an intelligent web-based educational system that employed machine learning algorithms to adapt content based on student performance, demonstrating improved engagement and effectiveness.

More recent research has explored natural language processing (NLP) and knowledge graphs to refine adaptive learning. Gao, Liu, and Huang (2021) proposed a learning path generator that utilizes knowledge graphs and machine learning to recommend personalized learning trajectories by analyzing user behavior and preferences. Additionally, Dessí et al. (2022) investigated the application of deep learning and NLP for generating scientific knowledge graphs, showcasing the potential of structured knowledge representation in improving educational content organization.

Another important aspect of adaptive learning is the integration of web-assisted education. Jonsdottir and Stefansson (2013) examined how online learning resources can complement traditional classroom instruction, emphasizing their impact on student engagement and knowledge retention. Similarly, Morze et al. (2021) demonstrated the effectiveness of adaptive learning in higher education through Moodle LMS, highlighting the role of learning management systems (LMS) in fostering personalized learning experiences.

Despite these advancements, several challenges remain. Many existing adaptive learning systems rely on rule-based personalization, which lacks contextual awareness and semantic understanding. Moreover, scalability remains an issue, as traditional recommendation models struggle to process large-scale educational datasets efficiently.

Recent large language models such as GPT-4 (OpenAI, 2023) offer advanced generative capabilities and context understanding, opening new perspectives for adaptive educational systems. However, their computational requirements make them less practical for real-time deployment in large-scale learning environments. For instance, EduChat (Duan et al., 2023) proposes a multi-role conversational framework designed for educational dialogues, demonstrating how LLMs can support interactive and personalized tutoring at scale.

A recent systematic review by Mateos and Bellogín (2025) highlights the growing importance of context-aware recommender systems, emphasizing the need for scalable and semantically robust approaches in educational settings.

While SBERT enables efficient semantic similarity through fixed-size sentence embeddings, recent transformer-based models such as T5 or GPT-3.5 offer generative capabilities and broader contextual understanding. However, these models often require higher computational resources, making SBERT more practical for real-time educational recommendations.

Our approach leverages SBERT (Sentence-BERT) to address these limitations and enhance content recommendation in programming education. Unlike conventional adaptive learning systems, SBERT captures semantic relationships between user queries and educational resources, enabling more accurate and efficient content retrieval. By integrating SBERT with cosine similarity, our model significantly improves retrieval precision, making it well-suited for large-scale learning platforms.

III. APPROACH AND CONTRIBUTION

Course content recommendation systems play a crucial role in adaptive learning environments, where they analyze student interactions to suggest personalized learning materials. Traditional approaches, such as rule-based filtering and collaborative filtering, often struggle to capture the semantic meaning behind user queries, limiting their effectiveness in providing contextually relevant recommendations. To address these limitations, we propose a SBERT-based recommendation model, which enhances the semantic alignment between student queries and educational resources.

Our approach leverages Sentence-BERT (SBERT) (Reimers & Gurevych, 2019) to generate semantically rich embeddings, allowing for more precise and context-aware recommendations. Unlike standard BERT models, which rely on pairwise comparison of sentence embeddings, SBERT produces fixed-size vector representations, enabling efficient similarity-based retrieval of learning materials.

The implementation follows a structured pipeline, starting with data collection and preprocessing. The dataset comprises student IDs, course IDs, behavior types, timestamps, course scores, and target recommendations. To ensure consistency, preprocessing includes data cleaning, normalization, categorical feature encoding, and tokenization using the Hugging Face Transformers library.

Following preprocessing, embeddings are generated using a fine-tuned SBERT model to encode both student queries and course descriptions into high-dimensional vector representations. The cosine similarity metric is then applied to determine the most relevant course recommendations for each query. To optimize performance, hyperparameters such as learning rate, batch size, and number of epochs are fine-tuned, with optimization performed using the Adam optimizer.

Model evaluation is conducted using Precision@k and Mean Reciprocal Rank (MRR) to assess the ranking effectiveness of recommended courses. Additionally, error analysis is performed to identify potential mismatches, refine recommendation strategies, and enhance model accuracy.

Key Contributions

This work presents several novel contributions to AI-driven educational content recommendation:

1. **Enhanced Semantic Understanding:** SBERT enables a deeper contextual representation of student queries, significantly improving recommendation accuracy compared to traditional keyword-based retrieval methods.
2. **Scalability & Efficiency:** By leveraging sentence embeddings, the proposed approach supports fast and scalable similarity computations, making it well-suited for large-scale educational datasets.
3. **Personalized Learning Experience:** Unlike generic recommendation models, this approach dynamically aligns user queries with relevant educational resources, ensuring a tailored learning experience that optimizes engagement and learning outcomes.

By harnessing SBERT's ability to generate semantically meaningful embeddings, the proposed system provides personalized, high-quality course recommendations that enhance adaptive learning frameworks. This research lays the foundation for scalable, AI-driven educational support systems, with the potential to significantly improve student learning experiences.

IV. THE BERT METHOD

To deliver personalized content recommendations, our system relies on BERT, a powerful language model that understands the meaning of sentences by analyzing the words in context.

At its core, BERT learns the meaning of words in context—just as a human reader understands a sentence not word-by-word, but as a whole. It considers the surrounding words in both directions (left and right), which helps it grasp subtle nuances in language.

BERT was originally trained on large amounts of general text (like Wikipedia), and can then be adapted to specific tasks like question answering or content recommendation through a process called fine-tuning.

However, while BERT is highly accurate, it has a major limitation: it compares pairs of sentences each time a query is made, which is too slow for real-time recommendation systems.

To overcome this, we use Sentence-BERT (SBERT)—a more efficient extension of BERT. SBERT transforms an entire sentence or question into a fixed-size vector, a kind of "summary fingerprint" of its meaning. This allows us to:

- Precompute embeddings for all available content,
- Compare user queries using fast similarity measures like cosine similarity,
- Deliver recommendations instantly.

This design makes SBERT particularly well-suited for educational platforms that require scalable and responsive content matching.

Technical Note:

BERT is based on the Transformer architecture. It represents text using three types of embeddings: token, position, and segment. During pre-training, it learns through tasks like Masked Language Modeling and Next Sentence Prediction. These details, while essential for implementation, are summarized here to focus on practical applications. Readers interested in technical depth can refer to Devlin et al. (2018) or the original SBERT paper by Reimers & Gurevych (2019).

V. IMPLEMENTATION

This section presents the practical implementation of our study, detailing the preprocessing, structuring, and analysis of Stack Overflow data, as well as the development of a recommendation model. We begin by preparing and cleaning the dataset to ensure data consistency and completeness. Next, we extract relevant features and analyze key trends to gain insights into programming technologies and user interactions. Finally, we leverage the SBERT model to generate question embeddings and recommend relevant content based on question titles, evaluating performance through metrics such as Precision@k and Mean Reciprocal Rank (MRR).

A. Dataset description and preprocessing

The dataset used in this study was obtained from Kaggle. (n.d.)., featuring a sampled version of Stack Overflow's Q&A data spanning from August 1, 2008, to October 19, 2016. Initially structured into three separate tables (questions, answers, and tags), the data was consolidated into a unified dataset to facilitate analysis. This preprocessing step ensured that each question was linked to its corresponding answers and associated tags, creating a structured and comprehensive dataset. Data cleaning and processing were conducted using Pandas, including table merging, text normalization, and the removal of inconsistencies.

1) Dataset Structuring and Integration

Before implementing the recommendation model, it was crucial to structure the dataset efficiently. The dataset was initially organized into three distinct tables: The Questions Table, which contained details about user-submitted questions, including fields such as Id, Title, Body, OwnerUserId, CreationDate, ClosedDate, and Score; the Answers Table, which stored responses to these questions with attributes like Id, ParentId, Body, OwnerUserId, CreationDate, and Score; and the Tags Table, which listed the tags associated with each question, including Id and TagName. Since a question could be associated with multiple tags, and a tag could be linked to several questions, a linking table (question_tags) was introduced to establish these relationships.

Table 1. Stack Overflow Q&A Data with Tags

Columns	Description
QuestionId	The unique identifier for each question.
QuestionOwnerUserId	The user ID of the person who posted the question.
QuestionCreationDate	The date and time when the question was created.
ClosedDate	The date and time when the question was closed (if applicable).
QuestionScore	The score assigned to the question by the community on Stack Overflow.
Title	The title of the question.

continued on following page

Table 1. Continued

Columns	Description
QuestionBody	The detailed body of the question (text content).
Tag	The tag associated with the question (e.g., "python", "javascript").
AnswerId	The unique identifier for each answer.
AnswerOwnerUserId	The user ID of the person who provided the answer.
AnswerCreationDate	The date and time when the answer was posted.
AnswerScore	The score assigned to the answer by the community on Stack Overflow.
AnswerBody	The detailed body of the answer (text content).

To unify the dataset (questions_answers_tags), we standardized the Id column in the Questions Table as QuestionId for consistency with the Answers Table (ParentId), ensuring seamless integration.

Then, the Questions Table was merged with the Tags Table using the question_tags table, producing an intermediate dataset (questions_with_tags) that linked each question to its corresponding tags. Finally, this intermediate dataset was merged with the Answers Table by aligning QuestionId (from questions_with_tags) with ParentId (from Answers), ensuring that each question was correctly associated with its respective answers.

The resulting questions_answers_tags (see Table I) dataset integrates all relevant information into a structured format, facilitating further analysis and enabling the development of advanced models for content recommendation.

2) Data Preprocessing

To ensure data quality, consistency, and completeness, several preprocessing steps were applied. First, text cleaning and transformation were performed by removing HTML tags, converting text to lowercase, and eliminating punctuation, special characters, and extra spaces. This step ensured uniform formatting across the dataset. Duplicate detection and removal were also conducted to preserve data integrity and prevent redundancy in the analysis.

Certain columns played a crucial role in the study. QuestionOwnerUserId and AnswerOwnerUserId were essential for analyzing user behavior, personalizing recommendations, and identifying domain experts. Among all features, AnswerBody was the most critical, as it contained the solution to each question, making it fundamental for model training, answer retrieval, and quality evaluation.

Handling missing values required careful consideration. Missing entries in QuestionOwnerUserId and AnswerOwnerUserId limited the ability to track user interactions but were mitigated by assigning a default value. In contrast, missing values in AnswerBody posed a greater challenge, as this field was essential for training the recommendation model. To maintain dataset integrity and ensure high-quality inputs for model training, rows with missing answers were removed.

This preprocessing phase resulted in a clean, structured, and high-quality dataset, ensuring optimal conditions for subsequent model training and evaluation.

B. Evolution of Programming Technologies: A Data-Driven Insight from Stack Overflow

Stack Overflow has been a crucial resource for developers worldwide, offering valuable insights into technological trends over time.

In this section, we conduct a data-driven analysis of the most popular tags from 2008 to 2016, examining the adoption dynamics of programming languages and frameworks. This exploration highlights shifts in developer preferences and serves as a foundation for training a content recommendation model by leveraging user interactions with questions and answers.

1) The Most Popular Technologies on Stack Overflow: Trends and Developer Insights

To better understand developer trends, we analyzed the most commonly used tags in Stack Overflow. Figure 1 presents the 10 most frequent tags, offering key insights into the technologies most discussed in the community.

Among these tags, JavaScript stands out as the most common, with approximately 100,000 questions, followed by Java and C#.

This prevalence underscores the widespread use of these programming languages within the Stack Overflow community.

Other technologies, including Python, PHP, Android, C++, iOS, jQuery, and SQL, also rank highly, reflecting the most in-demand skills and technologies during the dataset's covered period.

The popularity of certain tags can also be interpreted as an indicator of the technical challenges developers face and emerging industry trends. For instance, the strong presence of JavaScript may be linked to the rapid adoption of JavaScript frameworks and the increasing need for optimized web applications.

Figure 1. Top 10 Most Frequent Tags in Stack Overflow Dataset: An Analysis of Developer Trends

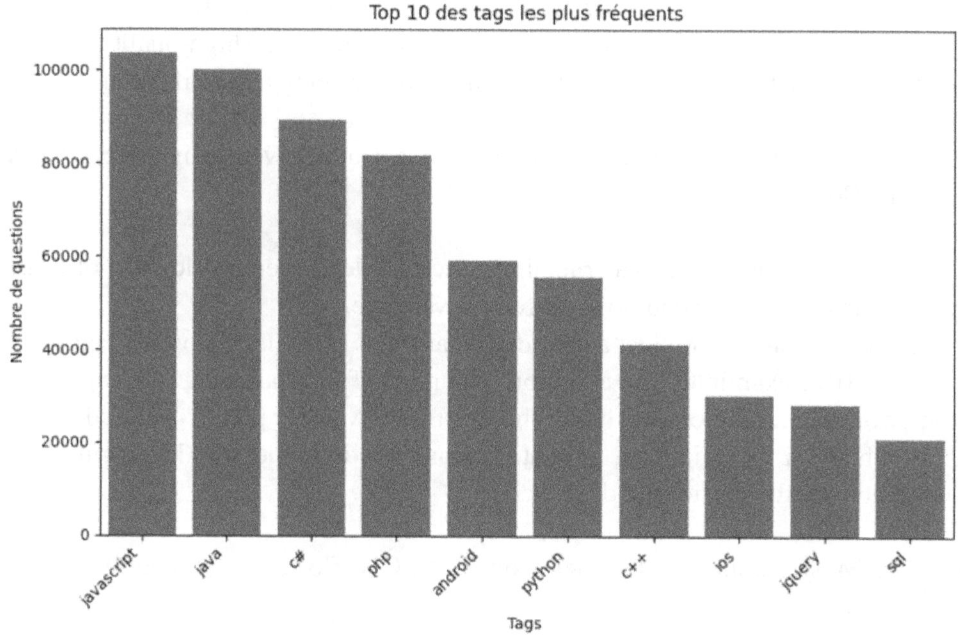

2) Analyzing the Relationship Between Question and Answer Scores on Stack Overflow

To analyze relationships between numerical features, we generated a correlation heatmap (Figure 2). This visualization helps identify dependencies, particularly between question scores and answer scores.

Figure 2. Correlation Heatmap of Question and Answer Scores on Stack Overflow

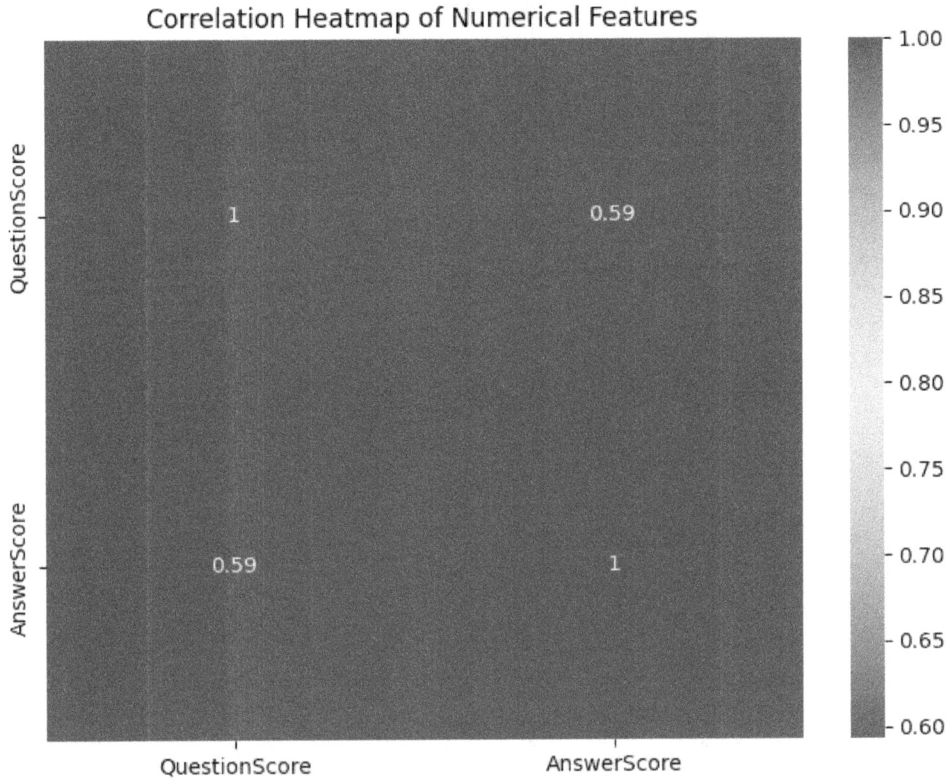

As expected, the *heatmap* shows a perfect correlation (value of 1) within identical features, such as *QuestionScore* with *QuestionScore* and *AnswerScore* with *AnswerScore*.

Notably, a moderate positive correlation (0.59) is observed between *QuestionScore* and *AnswerScore*, suggesting that highly rated questions are more likely to receive highly rated answers. This indicates a quality-driven interaction, where well-structured and relevant questions tend to attract better responses.

Furthermore, this correlation highlights the community's role in content curation, as user-assigned scores influence both the visibility of posts and engagement levels. Ultimately, these insights reinforce the connection between user interactions and content quality on *Stack Overflow*.

3) Programming Trends (2008–2016): The Rise and Fall of Popular Languages

The Top 5 Tags per Year graph illustrates the evolution of programming languages and technologies on Stack Overflow from 2008 to 2016, reflecting shifts in developer interest and industry demand.

Figure 3. Evolution of the Top 5 Programming Tags on Stack Overflow (2008-2016)

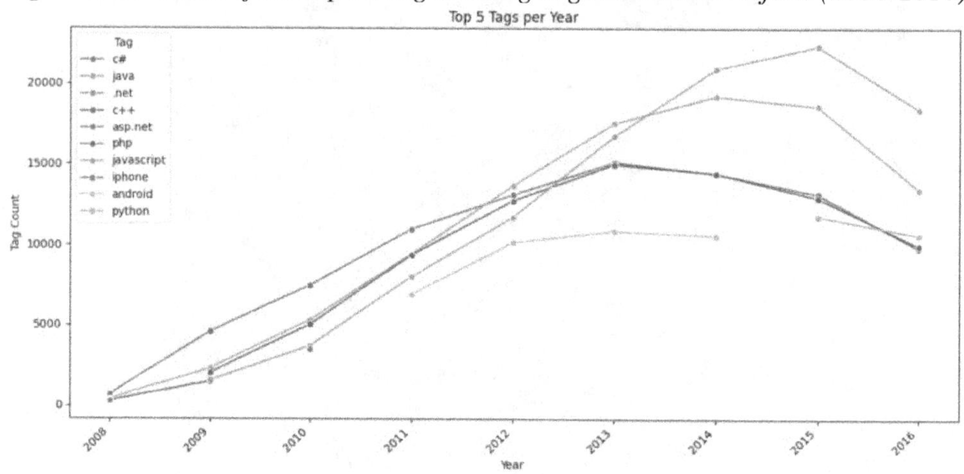

JavaScript experienced rapid growth until 2014–2015 before slightly declining, likely due to shifts in front-end development trends.

Similarly, Java maintained strong adoption, driven by its dominance in enterprise software and Android development. C# and PHP peaked around 2014 before gradually declining, possibly influenced by the emergence of modern web development frameworks.

Although Python is not explicitly highlighted in the graph, its steady growth can be attributed to its increasing adoption in data science, machine learning, and automation. Finally, the surge of Android and iPhone tags around 2010 reflects the explosive rise of mobile application development.

This analysis provides valuable insights into long-term technological trends, community preferences, and emerging skills, helping developers make informed decisions about learning paths and career opportunities.

4) Temporal Analysis of Question Creation Trends on Stack Overflow (2008–2017)

A time series analysis of question creation on Stack Overflow reveals a steady upward trend from 2008 to 2014 (figure 4), reflecting the platform's increasing adoption and engagement among developers.

However, the data also exhibits periodic fluctuations, likely influenced by external factors such as new technology releases, industry shifts, or seasonal variations.

The peak period occurred around 2014, when question creation reached its highest level, followed by a gradual decline towards 2017. This downward trend could be attributed to factors such as market saturation, evolving user behavior, or competition from alternative platforms.

Figure 4. Time Series of Question Creation on Stack Overflow (2008–2017)

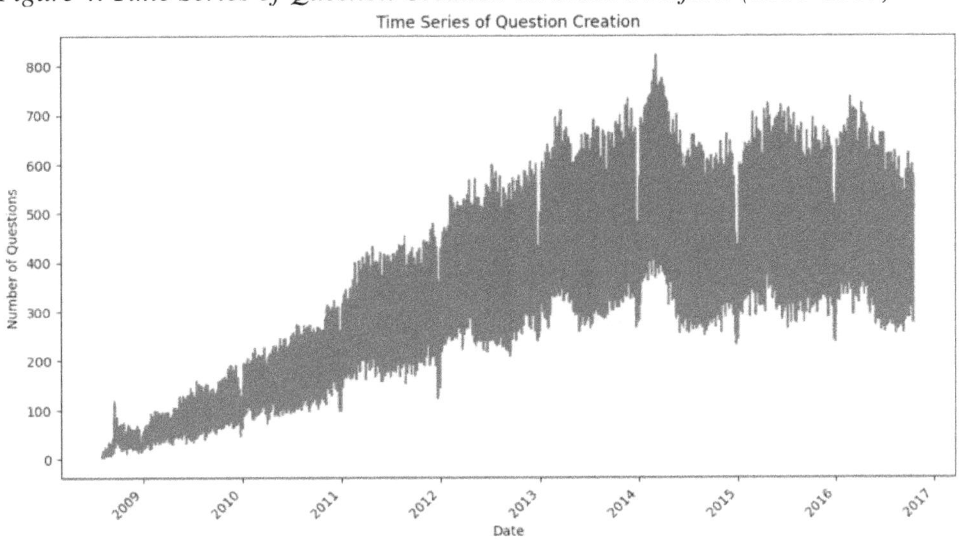

These trends highlight Stack Overflow's pivotal role as a developer resource while also underscoring the dynamic nature of user engagement. The post-2014 decline in question creation raises critical questions about the platform's evolution, shifts in knowledge-sharing behaviors, and emerging industry trends. Understanding these patterns is essential for adapting user experience strategies and fostering continued engagement in an ever-evolving technological landscape.

5) Analyzing the Distribution of Question Scores by Tag on Stack Overflow

The distribution of question scores by tag on Stack Overflow reveals key trends that offer valuable insights into developer engagement and content quality.

Popular tags such as JavaScript, Java, and Python dominate the score distribution, with some questions in the JavaScript category reaching scores as high as 3,500.

This suggests strong user engagement and high levels of community activity around these topics. The wide range of scores observed for JavaScript questions indicates a sustained and diverse level of interaction from developers.

As illustrated in Figure 5, the distribution of question scores varies significantly across different programming languages, reflecting differing levels of community interest and participation.

Figure 5. Distribution of Question Scores by Tag on Stack Overflow

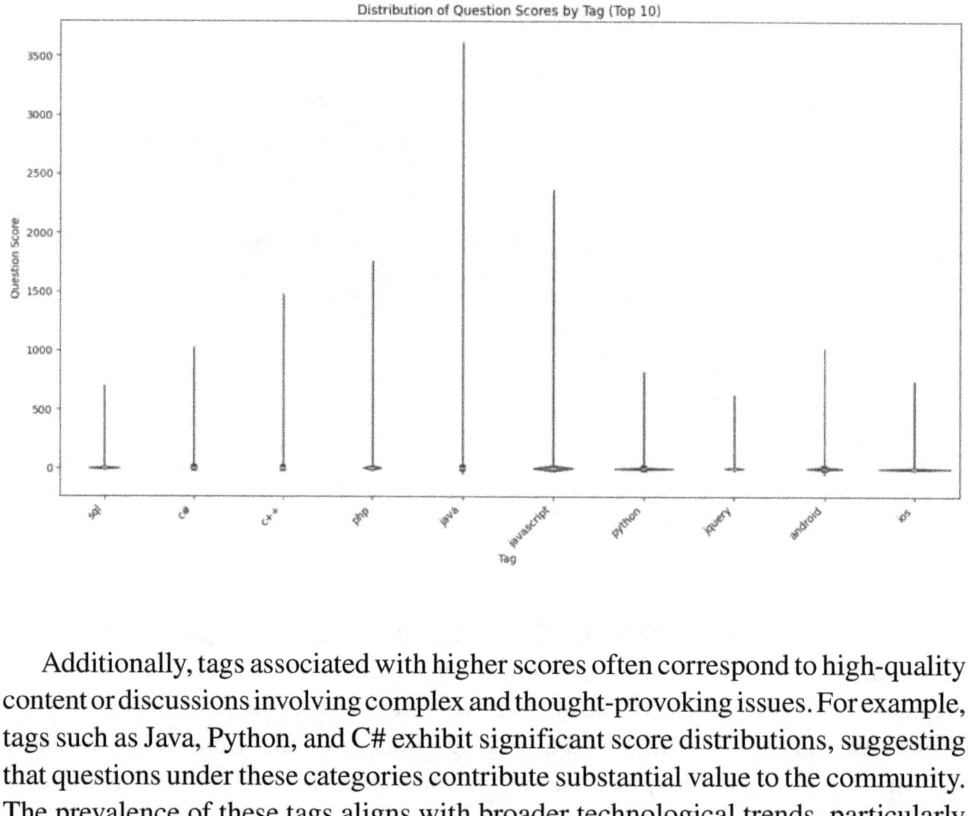

Additionally, tags associated with higher scores often correspond to high-quality content or discussions involving complex and thought-provoking issues. For example, tags such as Java, Python, and C# exhibit significant score distributions, suggesting that questions under these categories contribute substantial value to the community. The prevalence of these tags aligns with broader technological trends, particularly the widespread adoption of these languages in enterprise software, data science, and machine learning.

This analysis underscores the influence of specific programming technologies within the Stack Overflow community. Tags with higher score distributions highlight areas where developers seek and share in-depth knowledge, reinforcing their importance in the evolving software development landscape.

C. Optimizing Semantic Retrieval: Dataset Filtering and Model Selection

We applied a filtering strategy to the Stack Overflow dataset to optimize our retrieval model while addressing computational constraints. We selected only questions associated with influential tags (JavaScript, Python, Java, C#, HTML, CSS, ReactJS, Node.js) and retained those with high engagement (questions and answers with a score $\geq$ 10). This preprocessing step reduced the dataset to 8,614 questions, ensuring high-quality and relevant data for training.

We then generated semantic embeddings for user queries and programming resources using all-MiniLM-L6-v2, a Sentence-BERT (SBERT) model. SBERT is an optimized variant of BERT designed for sentence similarity tasks, and all-MiniLM-L6-v2 is a lightweight yet powerful version based on the MiniLM architecture.

This model was chosen for its efficiency in computing embeddings, lower computational cost compared to full BERT models, and strong performance in semantic search tasks. By leveraging this model, our system effectively captures the contextual meaning of programming-related questions, ensuring more accurate recommendations. The embeddings were computed efficiently in 135 batches, using cosine similarity for retrieval.

The effectiveness of our model was evaluated by assessing its ability to retrieve the most relevant questions based on user queries. The table below presents sample retrieval results:

Table 2. Query-Based Retrieval Performance Using SBERT (Cosine Similarity Scores)

User Query	Retrieved Question	Similarity Score
How to optimize Python code?	Speeding Up Python	0.7859
Best practices for Java multithreading?	What's the best way to have multiple threads doing work, and waiting for all of them to complete?	0.6862
How to improve website SEO ranking?	How does Google use HTML tags to enhance the search engine?	0.3763
What is the difference between React and Angular?	What are the basic differences and similarities between Angular.js and Express.js?	0.7087

These results demonstrate that our filtering approach enhances retrieval efficiency while preserving the relevance of retrieved content. By leveraging semantic embeddings and cosine similarity, our method achieves an optimal balance between computational efficiency and high-quality recommendations, making it well-suited for large-scale Q&A platforms.

To ensure scalability, we employed the all-MiniLM-L6-v2 model, which balances performance and inference speed. Further improvements may involve integrating approximate nearest-neighbor search algorithms like FAISS for large-scale deployment in real-time systems such as MOOCs

D. Experimentation and Evaluation

This section presents the experimental setup, evaluation methodology, and results obtained from testing the SBERT-based recommendation model.

1) Experimental Setup

To assess the effectiveness of the SBERT-based model in recommending relevant programming resources, we conducted experiments using a set of predefined user queries and their corresponding ground truth answers.

Table III presents a selection of user queries and their expected correct answers (ground truth), sourced from the dataset.

Table 3. User Queries and Ground Truth

User Query	Expected Answer (Ground Truth)
How to optimize Python code?	Speeding Up Python
Best practices for Java multithreading?	What's the best way to have multiple threads doing work, and waiting for all of them to complete?
How to improve website SEO ranking?	How does Google use HTML tags to enhance the search engine?
What is the difference between React and Angular?	What are the basic differences and similarities between Angular JS and Express JS?

These queries serve as test cases to evaluate the system's capability in retrieving relevant programming-related content.

2) Model Performance Metrics

The model's performance was evaluated using standard information retrieval metrics:

- **Precision@5:** The proportion of relevant recommendations among the top 5 retrieved results.
- **Mean Reciprocal Rank (MRR):** Measures how high the most relevant result appears in the ranking. The obtained results are presented in Table IV.

Table 4. Model Performance Metrics

Metric	Value
Precision@5	1.0000
Mean Reciprocal Rank (MRR)	1.0000

These results demonstrate that the model consistently retrieved the correct answer as the top-ranked result across all test cases, achieving perfect precision and ranking performance.

3) Retrieved Questions Analysis

Beyond numerical evaluation, we conducted a qualitative analysis of the retrieved content to assess how effectively the system aligns user queries with relevant programming resources. Table V presents examples of retrieved questions, including metadata such as question score (community votes on Stack Overflow) and answer score (usefulness of the provided answer).

Table 5. Examples of Retrieved Questions

QuestionId	Question Score	Title	Tag	Answer Score
650	79	Automatically update version number	c#	69
930	28	How do I connect to a database and loop over a query result?	c#	15
1010	14	How to get the value of built, encoded ViewState?	c#	7
2250	83	Datatable vs Dataset	c#	5
2530	1614	How do you disable browser Autocomplete on web form field/input tag?	html	1637

These examples demonstrate that the model effectively aligns user queries with relevant, high-quality answers, validating its ability to reduce information overload and enhance content accessibility.

4) Discussion and Future Directions

Although our results demonstrate high retrieval accuracy, several limitations persist. One key challenge is the model's difficulty in handling ambiguous queries that lack sufficient contextual information. To address this, future work may investigate the integration of query expansion strategies or reinforcement learning methods to enhance query interpretation. Additionally, enriching the dataset with a broader and more diverse set of programming topics would help improve the model's generalizability across various domains.

Another limitation concerns potential dataset bias. Tags like JavaScript or Python are overrepresented in Stack Overflow data, which could skew the model's recommendations. Future research will explore techniques for bias detection and balancing to promote fairness, particularly in personalized learning environments.

Multilingual support is also a crucial area for improvement. Enabling the system to handle multiple languages would make programming education resources more accessible to learners worldwide. In parallel, optimizing computational efficiency is essential to deliver real-time recommendations and ensure a seamless user experience.

Furthermore, while the current system relies on static SBERT embeddings, future iterations could benefit from incorporating a dynamic feedback loop. User interactions such as clicks, likes/dislikes, or time spent on recommended content could be logged and analyzed to identify patterns of engagement. This behavioral data could then guide the adaptation of the system, for example through fine-tuning the embedding model or re-ranking recommendations based on personalized preferences. Reinforcement learning and incremental training techniques offer promising directions to support this continuous refinement process.

By addressing these challenges, the BERT-based recommendation system can evolve into a more robust, adaptive, and inclusive tool, significantly enhancing its utility in programming education..

VI. CONCLUSION AND FUTURE WORK

This study explores the potential of an intelligent and adaptive content recommendation system to support programming education. As the volume of online learning resources continues to grow, identifying relevant and high-quality content remains a challenge—making AI-driven solutions increasingly valuable for personalized learning.

Our system uses Sentence-BERT (SBERT) to improve the match between user queries and content by capturing semantic context. Experimental results show strong performance, with both Precision@5 and Mean Reciprocal Rank (MRR) reaching 1.0000. The retrieved programming questions from Stack Overflow were not only highly relevant but also widely appreciated by the community, confirming the system's ability to suggest useful learning materials.

By producing semantically rich embeddings, the model effectively understands learners' needs and provides accurate, personalized recommendations. These results highlight the potential of semantic search techniques to support adaptive learning and improve the educational experience.

While the results are promising, several areas remain to be explored. Increasing the diversity of the dataset and considering learning content related to students' professional goals could make the system even more useful. A practical next step would be to integrate the system into existing learning management platforms such as Moodle or edX, allowing it to be tested in real educational environments.

Importantly, this study is based on real-world data from Stack Overflow, which helped us evaluate how well the system retrieves relevant and trusted content. Future research could include actual student interactions to better assess and improve the system's adaptability.

This work provides a solid starting point for building AI-based educational tools that help learners explore programming content more effectively, with support that is tailored to their needs.

REFERENCES

Brusilovsky, P., & Peylo, C. (2003). Adaptive and intelligent web-based educational systems. *International Journal of Artificial Intelligence in Education, 13*(2–4), 159–172.

Dessí, D., Osborne, F., Recupero, D. R., Buscaldi, D., & Motta, E. (2022). SCICERO: A deep learning and NLP approach for generating scientific knowledge graphs in the computer science domain. *Knowledge-Based Systems, 258*, 109945. DOI: 10.1016/j.knosys.2022.109945

Devlin, J., Chang, M. W., Lee, K., & Toutanova, K. (2018). BERT: Pre-training of deep bidirectional transformers for language understanding. arXiv. https://arxiv.org/abs/1810.04805

Duan, Y.. (2023). EduChat: Towards Multi-role Multi-turn Open-ended Conversation for Education. https://arxiv.org/abs/2308.02773

Fidalgo-Blanco, Á., García-Peñalvo, F. J., Sein-Echaluce, M. L., & Conde-González, M. Á. (2014, November). Learning content management systems for the definition of adaptive learning environments. In *2014 International Symposium on Computers in Education (SIIE)* (pp. 105–110). IEEE. DOI: 10.1109/SIIE.2014.7017713

Gao, J., Liu, Q., & Huang, W. B. (2021, January). Learning path generator based on knowledge graph. In Proceedings of the 2021 12th International Conference on E-Education, E-Business, E-Management, and E-Learning (pp. 27–33). DOI: 10.1145/3450148.3450155

Jonsdottir, A. H., & Stefansson, G. (2013). Enhanced learning with web-assisted education. arXiv. https://arxiv.org/abs/1310.4667

Kaggle. (n.d.). Stack Sample – Stack Overflow Data. Kaggle. https://www.kaggle.com/datasets/stackoverflow/stacksample

Kahraman, H. T., Sagiroglu, S., & Colak, I. (2010, October). Development of adaptive and intelligent web-based educational systems. In 2010 4th International Conference on Application of Information and Communication Technologies (pp. 1–5). IEEE. DOI: 10.1109/ICAICT.2010.5612054

Luckin, R., & Holmes, W. (2016). Intelligence unleashed: An argument for AI in education.

Mateos, P., & Bellogín, A. (2025). A systematic literature review of recent advances on context-aware recommender systems. *Artificial Intelligence Review*, *58*(20). https://link.springer.com/article/10.1007/s10462-024-10939-4

Morze, N., Varchenko-Trotsenko, L., Terletska, T., & Smyrnova-Trybulska, E. (2021, March). Implementation of adaptive learning at higher education institutions by means of Moodle LMS. [IOP Publishing.]. *Journal of Physics: Conference Series*, *1840*(1), 012062. DOI: 10.1088/1742-6596/1840/1/012062

Open, A. I. (2023). GPT-4 Technical Report. https://arxiv.org/abs/2303.08774

Raj, N. S., & Renumol, V. G. (2022). A systematic literature review on adaptive content recommenders in personalized learning environments from 2015 to 2020. *Journal of Computers in Education*, *9*(1), 113–148. DOI: 10.1007/s40692-021-00199-4

Vaswani, A., Shazeer, N., Parmar, N., Uszkoreit, J., Jones, L., Gomez, A. N., & Polosukhin, I. (2017). Attention is all you need. In Advances in Neural Information Processing Systems, 30.

Zawacki-Richter, O., Marín, V. I., Bond, M., & Gouverneur, F. (2019). Systematic review of research on artificial intelligence applications in higher education – Where are the educators? *International Journal of Educational Technology in Higher Education*, *16*(1), 1–27. DOI: 10.1186/s41239-019-0171-0

Section 4
Language, Translation, and Accessibility

Chapter 9
Evaluating Neural Network-Based Arabic Machine Translation:
Challenges, Metrics, and Solutions

Baligh Babaali
https://orcid.org/0000-0001-7459-1964
University of Mascara, Algeria

ABSTRACT

This work addresses the critical challenge of evaluating Machine Translation (MT) systems for Arabic. Standard automatic metrics often fall short due to Arabic's complex morphology, free word order, diglossia, and non-standard social media forms. This work analyzes these limitations and proposes Arabic-specific evaluation adjustments, including morphology-sensitive scoring using root-based matching, embedding-based metrics for semantic similarity, and named entity-sensitive scoring. Emphasizing the importance of human evaluation and providing evaluator training guidelines, hybrid models combining automatic metrics with human input are presented. To explore the effectiveness of these approaches, suggested research paths and methodologies are outlined to validate the proposed techniques and highlight domain-specific needs. Finally, future directions, such as self-supervised models, cross-dialectal evaluation, user-centric evaluation, and ethical considerations, are discussed. This work underscores the need for tailored evaluation strategies to accurately assess Arabic MT quality.

DOI: 10.4018/979-8-3373-0735-0.ch009

INTRODUCTION

Translating between languages presents inherent linguistic challenges, stemming from differences in semantic and syntactic structures. This is particularly true for Machine Translation (MT) involving morphologically rich languages (MRLs), where handling complex vocabularies and designing adequate MT evaluation metrics is crucial. Evaluating MT systems for Arabic presents unique challenges due to the language's rich morphology, relatively free word order, diglossia, and the prevalence of non-standard forms in social media. These linguistic complexities not only affect translation quality but also highlight the inadequacy of existing evaluation metrics, which were primarily developed for Indo-European languages and struggle to capture Arabic-specific linguistic phenomena.

Existing MT approaches range from rule-based systems to statistical machine translation (SMT) (Almansor, 2018). More recently, Neural Machine Translation (NMT), a deep learning approach, has shown significant improvements, particularly for high-resource languages (Klein et al., 2017). However, a key challenge for Arabic MT is the scarcity of parallel datasets, classifying Arabic and its dialects as low-resource languages. This data scarcity directly impacts the training and evaluation of NMT models. Moreover, standard automatic MT evaluation metrics such as BLEU (Papineni et al., 2002) and METEOR (Banerjee and Lavie, 2005) rely on word-level matching and n-gram overlap, which are insufficient for capturing the morphological, syntactic, and semantic complexities of Arabic. For example, Arabic's non-concatenative root-based morphology leads to variations in word forms that are not effectively accounted for by traditional string-matching metrics. Additionally, Arabic's relatively free word order allows for multiple syntactically valid yet structurally diverse translations, which existing metrics often penalize unfairly.

Another major challenge is evaluating translations involving dialectal Arabic (DAs) and Arabizi—Arabic written in Latin script, which is widely used in social media. Dialectal Arabic differs significantly from Modern Standard Arabic (MSA) in terms of syntax, vocabulary, and morphology, making evaluation even more complex. Social media content often contains informal, unstructured, and code-switched text that further exacerbates evaluation difficulties (Bies et al., 2014). Traditional MT metrics, designed primarily for well-structured text, fail to account for these variations, necessitating the development of more robust, Arabic-specific evaluation approaches.

Recent progress in deep learning has greatly impacted machine translation (MT) evaluation, especially through transformer-based models like BERT, T5, and GPT-related architectures. These advancements have led to the creation of more advanced evaluation metrics, such as BERTScore (Zhang et al., 2019), COMET (Rei et al., 2020), and BLEURT (Sellam et al., 2020), which use contextual embeddings to assess translation quality beyond basic word-matching techniques. Although these metrics outperform traditional methods like BLEU and METEOR, their application in evaluating Arabic MT is still relatively understudied, particularly considering the language's complex morphology and flexible syntax. Moreover, the increasing need for domain-specific translations—such as those for legal, medical, and literary texts—calls for specialized evaluation approaches that account for the unique linguistic and contextual demands of each field. Likewise, translating social media content, including dialectal Arabic and Arabizi, presents additional challenges that require a closer examination of recent domain-specific datasets and evaluation strategies designed for informal and highly variable language usage. Bridging these gaps is essential for building more effective Arabic MT evaluation systems that can address the language's intricacies across diverse contexts.

In summary, effective evaluation metrics are needed for Arabic NMT, particularly for social media content and domain-specific applications such as legal, medical, and literary translation. This requires metrics that account for morphological complexity, word order flexibility, dialectal variations, and non-standard orthographic forms. More specifically, the following questions need to be addressed: How can we develop evaluation metrics that accurately reflect the quality of Arabic NMT, considering its low-resource nature and the specific challenges posed by social media content (MSA, DAs, Arabizi)? How do standard automatic metrics perform when evaluating Arabic NMT compared to human evaluation?

This chapter will address these issues by critically analyzing existing and emerging evaluation approaches for Arabic MT. It will highlight the limitations of traditional metrics, explore the potential of neural-based evaluation methods, and propose hybrid evaluation frameworks that combine automated scoring with human-informed assessment techniques. By doing so, the chapter aims to contribute to the development of more effective Arabic MT evaluation strategies that align better with the linguistic characteristics of the language.

BACKGROUND ON MACHINE TRANSLATION EVALUATION

Evaluating Machine Translation (MT) systems is crucial for assessing their performance and guiding further development. Various metrics have been proposed for this purpose, ranging from automatic measures to human evaluation. This section provides background on MT evaluation, focusing on standard metrics and their limitations, particularly for Arabic MT, and discusses the differences in evaluation between statistical and neural MT models.

Standard Metrics and their Limitations for Arabic MT

Several automatic metrics are widely used in MT evaluation, including BLEU (Bilingual Evaluation Understudy) (Papineni et al., 2002), METEOR (Metric for Evaluation of Translation with Explicit Ordering) (Banerjee and Lavie, 2005), and TER (Translation Edit Rate) (Snover et al., 2006).

BLEU

BLEU, a precision-based metric, measures the n-gram overlap between the machine-translated output and one or more reference translations.

$$BLEU = \min\left(1, \frac{length_o}{length_r}\right) * \left(\sum_{i=1}^{n} precision_i\right)^{\frac{1}{n}}$$

$length_o$ is the machine-translated output length, $length_r$ is the reference sentence length and $\min\left(1, \frac{length_o}{length_r}\right)$ is the brevity penalty. While BLEU is computationally efficient and correlates reasonably well with human judgment at the system level, it has several limitations. It does not consider recall, penalizes word order variations even if they do not affect meaning, and struggles with morphological variations. This last point is particularly relevant for Arabic, a morphologically rich language (MRL). The non-concatenative morphology of Arabic, where words are formed by interweaving roots and patterns, leads to numerous surface forms for a single lemma. BLEU treats these different surface forms as distinct words, even if they share the same root and meaning, thus potentially underestimating the quality of translations that use morphologically related forms. For example, the Arabic word "بـتـك" (ktb), meaning "to write," can generate various forms like "بـتـكي" (yaktub - he writes), "تـبـتـك" (katabat - she wrote), and "بـاتـك" (kitab - book). BLEU would treat these as different words, even though they are clearly related.

METEOR

This metric addresses some of BLEU's limitations by incorporating recall and using stemming and synonymy matching. It also considers word order through a fragmentation penalty. METEOR evaluates machine translation quality by focusing on unigram matches, using a three-stage process:

1. **Exact Matching:** Identical word strings in the reference and translated texts are aligned.

2. **Lemmatization:** Unmatched words are reduced to their root forms (lemmas). Words sharing the same root are then aligned.
3. **Synonymy Matching:** Remaining unaligned words that are synonyms (identified using WordNet) are aligned.

While METEOR generally correlates better with human judgment than BLEU, it still faces challenges with morphologically complex languages like Arabic. Although stemming can help to group some morphological variants, it may not capture all the nuances of Arabic morphology. Furthermore, METEOR's reliance on external resources, such as WordNet for synonymy matching, can be problematic for low-resource languages, including Arabic, where such resources may be limited or unavailable.

TER

It measures the minimum number of edits (insertions, deletions, substitutions, and shifts) required to transform the machine translation into a reference translation. For example, if "The lazy dog jumps over the quick brown fox" needs two word shifts to match the reference "The quick brown fox jumps over the lazy dog" (9 words long), the TER score is 2/9 = 22%. TER is intuitive and easy to interpret, but it is also sensitive to word order variations and does not explicitly account for meaning preservation. Like BLEU, TER struggles with morphological variations in Arabic, as it treats different surface forms as errors.

Beyond these standard metrics, other approaches have been explored to address the specific challenges of Arabic MT evaluation. These include metrics that incorporate morphological analysis, such as using root-based matching or considering morphological features. However, these approaches often require specialized resources and tools for Arabic, which may not always be readily available. The use of human evaluation, while costly and time-consuming, remains essential for obtaining a more comprehensive and reliable assessment of translation quality. Human evaluation can capture aspects of translation quality that automatic metrics often miss, such as fluency, adequacy, and meaning preservation.

eBLEU

The eBLEU (enhanced BLEU) score is an improved version of the traditional BLEU metric, designed to address its limitations, such as rigid word order constraints, limited synonym recognition, and insufficient support for linguistic diversity (ElNokrashy and Kocmi, 2023). Like BLEU, eBLEU evaluates the precision of n-grams in a candidate translation compared to reference translations while applying a brevity penalty to discourage excessively short outputs. However, eBLEU introduces refinements that enhance its ability to assess translation quality more accurately. It incorporates additional linguistic features, such as semantic similarity adjustments, which allow for synonym recognition using embeddings or external lexical resources, and word order flexibility, which relaxes strict positional penalties based on dependency parsing. It also accounts for morphological sensitivity by considering different surface forms of the same lemma, making it particularly suitable for morphologically rich languages like Arabic.

Mathematically, the standard BLEU score is computed alternatively as:

$$BLEU = BP \times \exp\left(\sum_{i=1}^{N} w_i \log p_i\right)$$

Where (brevity penalty) is defined as:

Here, is the reference translation length, and is the candidate translation length. The term represents the precision of n-grams (typically up to in BLEU), and denotes the weight assigned to each n-gram precision, usually with equal weighting.

eBLEU extends this formula by incorporating a semantic similarity function between the candidate translation and the reference , which adjusts scores based on synonymy, paraphrasing, and morphological variations. The eBLEU formula is expressed as:

These enhancements provide several advantages for evaluating Arabic machine translation (MT). For instance, eBLEU better handles Arabic's complex morphology by recognizing variations in word forms that BLEU would penalize unnecessarily. It also improves word order flexibility, accommodating Arabic's relatively free word order without over-penalizing reordering that preserves meaning. Additionally, eBLEU excels at evaluating synonyms and paraphrases, capturing the true meaning of translations rather than relying solely on exact n-gram matches. This makes it more reliable for dialectal and informal Arabic, where non-standard expressions and paraphrases are common. By addressing the rigidity of BLEU, eBLEU offers a more refined and linguistically informed metric for evaluating Arabic MT, making it a superior alternative for handling the language's rich morphology, flexible syntax, and diverse dialects. However, the eBLEU metric tends to produce scores that are somewhat dispersed but cluster in a narrow range for many segments. This behavior is not unique to challenging datasets but is also observed in standard WMT MT data, indicating that it is a general characteristic of the metric (Lo et al., 2023), and Its performance is generally in the middle range compared to other more sophisticated metrics like COMET or BERTScore variants (Moghe et al., 2025).

BERTScore

BERTScore is a contextualized embedding-based evaluation metric that overcomes several limitations of n-gram-based methods like BLEU by capturing semantic similarity between the machine-translated output and reference translations (Zhang et al., 2019). Instead of relying on exact word matching, BERTScore computes cosine similarity between word embeddings obtained from deep neural networks, such as BERT (Bidirectional Encoder Representations from Transformers). Given a machine-translated sentence and a reference sentence , BERTScore aligns each token in with its most similar token in , based on contextualized embeddings. The precision, recall, and F1-score for BERTScore are defined as follows:

where and are the contextualized embeddings of the tokens in and , respectively, and represents the cosine similarity between two embeddings. Unlike BLEU, BERTScore accounts for synonymy, word reordering, and morphological variations (see Figure 1), making it particularly useful for evaluating translations in morphologically rich languages like Arabic.

COMET

COMET (Crosslingual Optimized Metric for Evaluation of Translation) is a learned metric for machine translation evaluation that combines linguistic embeddings, reference translations, and human judgment to produce a more reliable assessment of translation quality. Unlike traditional metrics such as BLEU, which rely solely on surface-level n-gram matches, or BERTScore, which uses contextualized embeddings at the token level, COMET is a trainable neural evaluation metric that aligns with human evaluation by leveraging large-scale annotated datasets.

COMET models typically follow a supervised learning approach where the metric is fine-tuned on human-rated translation data, allowing it to learn from human preferences rather than relying on fixed mathematical formulas. Given a source sentence , a machine-translated output , and an optional reference translation , COMET computes a quality score based on deep contextualized embeddings using a pre-trained transformer model (e.g., XLM-R, BERT). The core components of COMET include:

Source-Conditioned Representations: Each token in , , and is mapped to a high-dimensional embedding space using a multilingual transformer model.

Similarity-Based Scoring: The similarity between the machine-translated sentence and the reference (or source) is computed using an attention mechanism and a neural network, producing a translation quality score. The simplified formula for COMET's scoring function is:

where is a learned function optimized to predict human judgment scores, and represents transformer-based embeddings of the input sentences (see Figure 1).

COMET offers significant advantages over traditional metrics when evaluating Arabic machine translation. Unlike BLEU, which penalizes minor morphological variations, COMET utilizes deep semantic representations to better capture meaning, making it more effective for morphologically rich languages like Arabic. Additionally, Arabic's relatively free word order poses a challenge for surface-based metrics, but COMET, trained on human evaluations, learns to recognize word order variations that do not affect meaning. This adaptability extends to dialectal variations as well, as COMET has been fine-tuned on multilingual data, allowing it to handle non-standard text commonly found in social media translations. Furthermore, studies have shown that COMET outperforms both BLEU and BERTScore in correlation with human judgments, making it a more reliable and accurate metric for assessing Arabic MT quality.

BLEURT

BLEURT (Bilingual Evaluation Understudy with Representations from Transformers) is a learned metric designed to evaluate machine translation by leveraging pre-trained transformer models fine-tuned on human evaluation scores. Unlike BLEU, which relies on rigid n-gram matching, BLEURT captures semantic similarity and contextual meaning using deep neural representations. Given a source sentence , a machine-translated output , and an optional reference translation , BLEURT predicts a quality score based on the closeness of to human translations, as learned from large-scale annotated datasets. The BLEURT scoring function is typically expressed as:

Where is a neural network trained to predict human ratings, and represents contextualized embeddings from a transformer model like BERT or T5. BLEURT fine-tunes these embeddings on annotated translation datasets, making it more aligned with human perception.

BLEURT proves to be highly effective for evaluating Arabic machine translation due to its ability to handle the language's unique linguistic challenges. Its contextual embeddings allow it to recognize variations in Arabic morphology (see Figure 1), ensuring that minor changes in word form do not result in unfair penalties. Additionally, unlike BLEU, BLEURT can ignore word order differences that do not alter meaning, making it particularly suitable for Arabic's relatively free syntax. Another key advantage is its adaptability to dialectal Arabic and informal text, including Arabizi, as it has been fine-tuned on human evaluation data, making it robust for assessing social media translations. Furthermore, studies have demonstrated that BLEURT consistently outperforms traditional metrics like BLEU, METEOR, and

TER in correlation with human judgments, making it a more reliable and accurate metric for evaluating Arabic MT quality.

Figure 1. Arabic Word Embeddings Representation in BERTScore, COMET and BLEURT

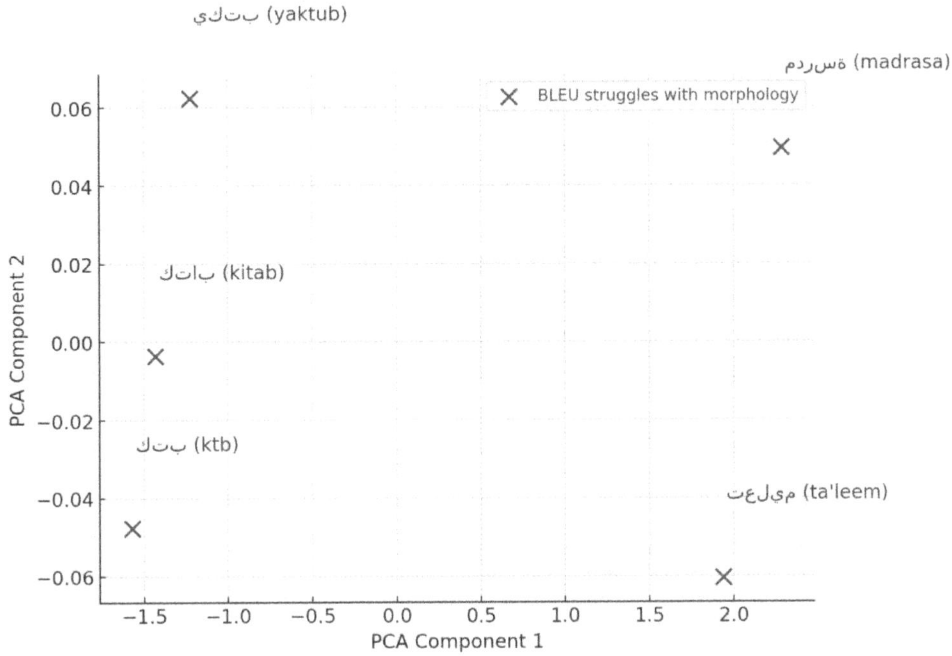

DIFFERENCES IN EVALUATION BETWEEN STATISTICAL AND NEURAL MT MODELS

The shift from Statistical Machine Translation (SMT) to Neural Machine Translation (NMT) has also brought about changes in evaluation practices. SMT systems, typically based on phrase-based models, often relied heavily on word-based metrics like BLEU. This was partly due to the nature of SMT models, which operate on phrases and rely on word alignment. NMT models, on the other hand, operate at the sentence level and learn complex representations of meaning. This difference has highlighted the limitations of word-based metrics for evaluating NMT. NMT systems often produce more fluent and grammatically correct translations, even if they deviate from the reference translation at the word level. This can lead to lower

BLEU scores for NMT compared to SMT, even if the NMT output is judged to be of higher quality by humans.

Consequently, there has been a growing emphasis on using metrics that capture semantic similarity and meaning preservation for evaluating NMT. Metrics like METEOR and newer metrics such as BERTScore (Zhang et al., 2019) which leverages contextual embeddings from BERT models, are gaining popularity. Furthermore, human evaluation has become even more important for evaluating NMT, as automatic metrics often fail to capture the nuances of NMT output. Error analysis, where human evaluators analyze the errors made by MT systems, is also crucial for understanding the strengths and weaknesses of different models. In summary, while standard metrics like BLEU, METEOR, and TER provide a useful starting point for MT evaluation, they have limitations, especially for morphologically rich languages like Arabic. The shift to NMT has further highlighted these limitations and emphasized the need for more sophisticated evaluation methods, including metrics that capture semantic similarity and greater reliance on human evaluation. Arabic MT evaluation, in particular, requires metrics and methodologies that account for its unique linguistic characteristics and the challenges posed by diverse text types, including social media content.

HYBRID EVALUATION APPROACHES

To improve machine translation (MT) evaluation, incorporating a human-in-the-loop approach is essential, blending automatic metrics with human assessment to boost reliability. Although automated metrics offer efficiency, they often miss subtle aspects like fluency, adequacy, and cultural relevance—particularly important for morphologically complex languages such as Arabic. A hybrid evaluation framework merges quantitative scores from tools like BLEURT and COMET with human evaluations using methods like Direct Assessment (DA) and Multidimensional Quality Metrics (MQM). This ensures a more comprehensive assessment of translation quality. Furthermore, the practical benefits of enhanced MT evaluation are evident across various fields. For instance, news translation systems demand high levels of fluency and contextual precision, while legal document translation requires strict adherence to specialized terminology. In social media, effectively handling dialectal Arabic and informal expressions is vital for usability. By examining case studies from these areas, we can better demonstrate how robust evaluation strategies strengthen real-world Arabic MT applications.

LIMITATIONS OF STANDARD METRICS FOR ARABIC MT

Standard automatic metrics, while widely used in Machine Translation (MT) evaluation, face significant challenges when applied to Arabic due to the language's unique linguistic characteristics. Arabic's complex morphology, diglossia, relatively free word order, and the prevalence of non-standard forms—particularly in social media—often lead to misinterpretations of translation quality by traditional metrics. These limitations become even more pronounced when evaluating different types of Arabic text, which range from formal Modern Standard Arabic (MSA) to informal dialectal Arabic and Arabizi. Formal Arabic, used in news articles, legal documents, and academic writing, adheres to strict grammatical rules and standardized vocabulary, making it easier to assess with metrics like BLEU and METEOR. However, informal Arabic—common in social media, online chats, and spoken dialogue—poses greater difficulties due to dialectal variations, code-switching, and phonetic spellings in Arabizi. Machine translation systems trained primarily on MSA often struggle with dialectal expressions and non-standard orthography, leading to inaccurate assessments when using standard evaluation metrics. Additionally, domain-specific texts, such as those in medical, legal, and religious contexts, introduce further complexities, as they require highly precise terminology translation and specialized linguistic knowledge. These challenges highlight the inadequacy of one-size-fits-all evaluation metrics and emphasize the need for customized approaches that account for the context, domain, and intended use of the translated text. This section provides an in-depth analysis of these issues, with real-world examples illustrating how standard metrics can misrepresent Arabic MT quality.

In-depth Analysis of Issues with Standard Metrics Applied to Arabic

Metrics like BLEU, METEOR, and TER primarily rely on word-level or n-gram matching between machine translations and reference translations. This approach is problematic for morphologically rich languages (MRLs) like Arabic. As previously discussed, Arabic employs non-concatenative morphology, where morphemes are interwoven within a root, leading to numerous surface forms for a single lemma. This means that semantically related words with different surface forms are treated as distinct by these metrics. For instance, the root "بتك" (ktb), meaning "to write," can generate forms like "بتاك" (katib - writer), "بتكم" (maktab - office/desk), and "بوتكم" (maktub - written). A translation that uses a morphologically related form different from the reference would be penalized by these metrics, even if the meaning is accurately conveyed. This issue is exacerbated by the fact that Arabic morphology also includes prefixes, suffixes, and infixes which further increase the number of surface forms.

Furthermore, the relatively free word order in Arabic poses a significant challenge. While different word orders often convey the same meaning, metrics like BLEU and TER penalize deviations from the reference order. This can lead to underestimation of translation quality when the machine translation uses a valid Arabic word order that differs from the reference. For example, both "باتكلا دلولا أرق" (qara'a al-walad al-kitab – Read the boy the book) and "باتكلا أرق دلولا" (al-walad qara'a al-kitab – The boy read the book) are grammatically correct and convey the same meaning, but a metric that relies on n-gram matching would penalize the latter if the reference uses the former. A general example is presented in Table 1. Additionally, Arabic exhibits syntactic and morphological features that can complicate NLP tasks. Specifically, subject pronouns are often omitted, as in "ءاملا برشي" (drinks the water), where the "he" is implied. Moreover, single words can encapsulate the meaning of entire sentences, such as "هومكنيقسأف" (and We gave it to you to drink) (Babaali, 2024).

Table 1. Arabic free word order

Order	Sentence	English translation
VSO	َءاملا ُرمع َبرش	Drank Omar the water
OVS	ُرمع َبرش َءاملا	The water drank Omar
SVO	َءاملا ُبرش ُرمع	Omar Drank the water
VOS	ُرمع َءاملا َبرش	Drank the water Omar

Polysemy and Orthographic Ambiguity, Arabic text often suffers from orthographic ambiguity due to the frequent omission of diacritical marks (tashkil or harakat), which indicate pronunciation and thus meaning. This means words with the same spelling can have drastically different meanings. For example, the unvoweled form "رعش" can represent "رْعَش" (hair), "رَعَش" (he felt), or "رْعِش" (poetry) depending on the absent diacritics (Husain, 2022). The word "رمع" further exemplifies this (see Table 2 and Table 3) (Babaali, 2024). Context also plays a crucial role in disambiguation. A word like "لتق" (killing) can be used literally or figuratively, as in the phrase "عيبرلا مودق عنم كنكمي ال نكل راهزألا لتق كنكمي" which translation is "You can kill the blossoms, but you can't stop spring from arriving," where it clearly has a metaphorical meaning (Al Moaiad et al., 2024).

Table 2. Possible meanings of the unvocalized Arabic word "□□□" (Emr)

Word	Transliteration	English meaning
عَمَرَ	Eamara	build / live / was populated
عَمَّرَ	Eam~ ara	Live a long time
عَمِرَ	Eomira	became populous
عُمِّرَ	Eom~ ira	Given a long life
عُمَرُ	Eumaru	Omar (noun) / plural of Umrah
عَمْرُ	Eamoru	Age of
عُمْرُ	Eumoru	Age of
عُمُرُ	Eumuru	Age of
عَمْرٌ	EamorN	Age
عُمْرٌ	EumorN	Age
عُمُرٌ	EumurN	Age
عَمَرٌ	EamarN	Head cover for women
عَمَرَّ	Eamar~ a	Strong tough man / Longest of everything / Shrewd malicious guy / Ferocious man

Table 3. Examples of vocalized Arabic words polysemy

Word	Transliteration	English meanings
سائِل	sA}il	liquid, beggar, questioner
عَيْن	Eayn	Spy, eye, water source, gold

Diglossia, the existence of two distinct forms of a language (Modern Standard Arabic (MSA) and various dialects (DAs)), further complicates evaluation. MT systems trained on MSA data may struggle to translate dialectal content accurately, and standard metrics may not adequately capture the nuances of dialectal variations. Moreover, social media Arabic introduces additional challenges with the use of Arabizi (Arabic chat alphabet), code-switching (mixing Arabic with other languages), non-standard orthography, and the inclusion of non-linguistic elements like emoticons and sound representations (Bies et al., 2014). These features are not accounted for by standard metrics, leading to inaccurate assessments of translation quality in this context.

Real-world Examples of How These Metrics May Misrepresent Translation Quality

Consider the following example:

- Reference Translation: "زار الكاتب المدينة" (zara al-katib al-madina – The writer visited the city).
- Machine Translation: "المدينة زارها الكاتب" (al-madina zaraha al-katib – The city was visited by the writer).

Both translations convey the same meaning, with only a change in word order (verb-subject-object vs. subject-verb-object). While both are grammatically correct in Arabic, metrics like BLEU and TER would likely penalize the machine translation due to the different word order, even though the meaning is preserved.

Another example involving morphology:

- Reference Translation: "الكتاب مفيد" (al-kitab mufid – The book is useful).
- Machine Translation: "الكتب مفيدة" (al-kutub mufida – The books are useful).

Here, the machine translation correctly translates the meaning, but uses the plural form of both words. While semantically correct, BLEU would penalize this translation due to the mismatch in surface forms. This penalty doesn't reflect a genuine translation error but rather a difference in number.

These examples highlight how standard metrics can misrepresent translation quality for Arabic by failing to account for morphological variations and relatively free word order. These limitations underscore the need for more sophisticated evaluation methods that consider the specific linguistic features of Arabic.

Dialectal Arabic and Arabizi present notable challenges for machine translation, primarily due to their lack of standardization (Babaali, 2024) and the limited availability of high-quality parallel corpora (Azroumahli et al., 2019). While Modern Standard Arabic (MSA) is well-covered in MT datasets (Babaali and Salem, 2023), dialectal variations often face a shortage of training data, resulting in subpar translation performance (Harrat et al., 2017). Arabizi, which uses Latin script and numerals to represent Arabic, adds further complexity because of its inconsistent spelling patterns. Current MT systems address these variations with mixed success. Rule-based and statistical MT approaches encounter significant difficulties, as they depend on predefined linguistic rules and formal language data. Neural MT models, especially transformer-based architectures, show greater adaptability through large-scale multilingual training; however, their success hinges on domain-specific fine-tuning and context-sensitive representations. Comparative studies indicate that traditional metrics like BLEU and METEOR struggle to account for dialectal subtleties, whereas newer metrics like COMET and BLEURT, trained on diverse multilingual datasets, are more effective at evaluating translations involving heavy dialect use (Zhang et al., 2019; Sellam et al., 2020). Advancing research on domain-specific MT models and dialect-focused evaluation metrics is crucial for enhancing the quality of Arabic machine translation.

Algerian Arabizi presents significant challenges for machine translation due to its informal nature, dialectal variations, and phonetic spelling. For example, the phrase "Saha kho, ntiya chkoune?", meaning "Hello bro, who are you?", demonstrates how existing MT systems struggle with informal and dialectal expressions. Rule-based MT would likely fail because "Saha" (a common Algerian greeting) is not found in standard Arabic dictionaries. Statistical MT might inaccurately translate "kho" (short for "khouya", meaning "my brother") as "أخي" (akhī), which, while technically correct, lacks the conversational nuance. Similarly, Neural MT (NMT) models trained on MSA may misinterpret "ntiya" (a dialectal form of "you") as "أنتِ" (anti, feminine "you"), rather than the correct masculine form "أنتَ" (anta). Additionally, Arabizi's phonetic spelling makes word recognition even more difficult, as "chkoune" (meaning "who") is far from its MSA counterpart "من" (man). Without dialect-aware training, an MT system might produce an unnatural or even incorrect translation, such as "الصحة أخي، من أنت؟", which does not reflect the intended conversational tone. A dialect-aware MT model should instead recognize "Saha" as an informal greeting similar to "Hi" and "kho" as "bro", producing a more natural translation like "Hi bro, who are you?". This example highlights the difficulties in handling informal speech, dialectal contractions, and cultural expressions in Algerian Arabizi and underscores the need for MT models and evaluation metrics that can better process real-world Arabic variations.

PROPOSED ADJUSTMENTS FOR ARABIC-SPECIFIC EVALUATION

The limitations of standard metrics when applied to Arabic MT necessitate the exploration of adjustments that account for the language's unique characteristics. This section proposes adjustments for Arabic-specific evaluation, focusing on morphology-sensitive scoring and methods that capture semantic similarity, context, and the accurate translation of named entities (see Figure 2).

1. Integrating Automated Metrics with Morphology-Sensitive Adjustments:

Automated metrics such as BLEU, METEOR, and TER, while widely used, do not adequately account for Arabic's morphological complexity. One solution is to integrate morphology-sensitive adjustments, particularly through root-based matching. This approach involves reducing words in both the machine translation and reference text to their roots before comparison. For instance, different surface forms derived from the same root, such as "بتك" (ktb - write), "بتكي" (yaktub - he writes), and "تبتك" (katabat - she wrote), would be recognized as semantically related rather than distinct. This adjustment would mitigate penalizing translations that use correct but morphologically different forms.

Additionally, employing advanced morphological analyzers that consider inflectional forms, prefixes, and suffixes can refine this method. This approach would particularly enhance the evaluation of translations involving verbs, nouns, and adjectives with extensive derivations. By considering inflection patterns, evaluators can align closely related translations that standard metrics might otherwise misinterpret.

This adjustment is particularly crucial for Arabic, where verbs often encode information about gender, tense, and subject-object agreement in their morphology. A metric that accounts for these nuances ensures a more accurate reflection of translation quality.

2. Embedding-Based Metrics for Semantic Similarity:

Embedding-based metrics leverage pre-trained language models to capture semantic relationships between words and sentences. Models like BERT, mBERT, or AraBERT can encode contextual information, making them ideal for evaluating Arabic MT. Metrics such as BERTScore, which compare embeddings of machine-translated and reference sentences, are less sensitive to surface form and word order variations. This makes them particularly suitable for languages like Arabic, where word order is flexible.

Fine-tuning embedding models on Arabic-specific datasets, including dialectal corpora and social media content, can further improve their applicability. For example, when a machine translation uses synonyms or paraphrases, embedding-based metrics would still recognize the semantic equivalence, unlike word-based metrics. By training on context-rich datasets, these metrics could also handle regional idioms and colloquial expressions more effectively.

Embedding-based metrics can be further enhanced with domain-specific adaptations. For instance, in e-commerce, embeddings can be fine-tuned to prioritize product descriptions and technical specifications, ensuring a better alignment with real-world applications.

3. Named Entity-Sensitive Scoring Methods:

Named entities (NEs), such as names, organizations, and locations, are critical in many domains, particularly in news and e-commerce translations. Misidentifying or mistranslating these entities can significantly degrade the translation's utility. Incorporating Named Entity Recognition (NER) tools into evaluation metrics can help isolate and assess the accuracy of NEs separately from the rest of the translation.

For instance, a named entity-sensitive scoring method could use fuzzy matching to account for minor transliteration differences, such as "Mohammed" versus "Muhammad." This focused evaluation would ensure a more accurate assessment of translations where NEs play a central role.

A domain-specific application could involve prioritizing the accurate translation of medical terms or pharmaceutical product names, where errors could have severe consequences. By tailoring named entity-sensitive scoring to such domains, evaluators could better reflect the practical utility of translations.

PROPOSED RESEARCH DIRECTIONS FOR IMPROVED EVALUATION

1. Exploring Domain-Specific Evaluation Frameworks:

Different domains, such as news, social media, and e-commerce, present distinct challenges. For news translation, accuracy in translating political and economic terminology is critical, while fluency may take precedence. On the other hand, social media translation must handle informal language, dialects, and code-switching effectively. Future research could develop customized evaluation frameworks for each domain, addressing specific requirements and constraints.

For example, evaluating social media content might involve combining root-based matching with embedding-based metrics to handle dialectal variations and informal orthography. This would ensure that translations align with the conversational and informal nature of social media communication.

News translation frameworks could incorporate named entity-sensitive metrics to assess the accurate rendering of geopolitical terms, titles, and proper nouns, given their importance in news reporting.

2. Developing Cross-Dialectal Evaluation Techniques:

Arabic's diglossic nature, comprising Modern Standard Arabic (MSA) and numerous regional dialects, complicates MT evaluation. Effective evaluation metrics must account for this variability. Research could focus on building multi-dialectal corpora and developing metrics that measure the quality of translations across dialects.

Transfer learning techniques could be employed to adapt evaluation models trained on MSA to dialectal Arabic. Additionally, leveraging dialect identification systems could improve the contextual understanding of source texts, enhancing the accuracy of evaluations. For example, an evaluation metric could dynamically adapt to the dialectal features of the input text, ensuring that informal or regional phrases are correctly assessed.

3. Hybrid Approaches Combining Automated and Human Evaluation:

Automated metrics provide scalability, while human evaluations capture nuances that machines often miss. Hybrid approaches could combine these strengths to achieve a comprehensive evaluation. For instance, automated metrics could pre-filter translations, flagging those with potential issues for human review.

Alternatively, human annotations, such as marking morphological features or contextual nuances, could be used to refine automated metrics. This symbiotic relationship between human and machine assessments could result in metrics that better align with human judgment. A hybrid approach might involve using automated scores to identify problematic translations, followed by human evaluators providing detailed qualitative feedback.

4. Addressing Challenges in Social Media Translation:

Social media content introduces unique challenges, including non-standard orthography, code-switching, and emotive language. To address these, future research could explore metrics that integrate multiple modalities, such as combining textual embeddings with visual or audio context for richer evaluations.

Additionally, hybrid metrics tailored to social media contexts could use root-based matching for morphological variations and embedding-based scoring for semantic consistency. By incorporating sentiment analysis, evaluators could also assess whether the translation preserves the intended tone and emotional impact of the source text.

5. Proposed Evaluation Simulations:

Future studies could simulate real-world evaluation challenges by curating datasets with diverse Arabic dialects, informal speech, and specialized domains. These datasets could be used to benchmark the proposed metrics against standard ones. For instance, a simulation might evaluate how well metrics handle emergency response translations, where clarity and accuracy are paramount.

Such simulations might include dynamic evaluation scenarios, such as evaluating translations for multilingual customer support systems or healthcare settings, where accuracy in both technical and colloquial language is essential.

6. Leveraging Self-Supervised Models for Contextual Evaluation:

Self-supervised models, which can train on large amounts of unlabeled data, offer significant potential for Arabic MT evaluation. These models could be fine-tuned to evaluate translations based on their contextual relevance and fluency. By learning from large-scale multilingual corpora, self-supervised models could bridge gaps in low-resource dialects and informal Arabic.

Figure 2. Hybrid Framework for Arabic Machine Translation Evaluation

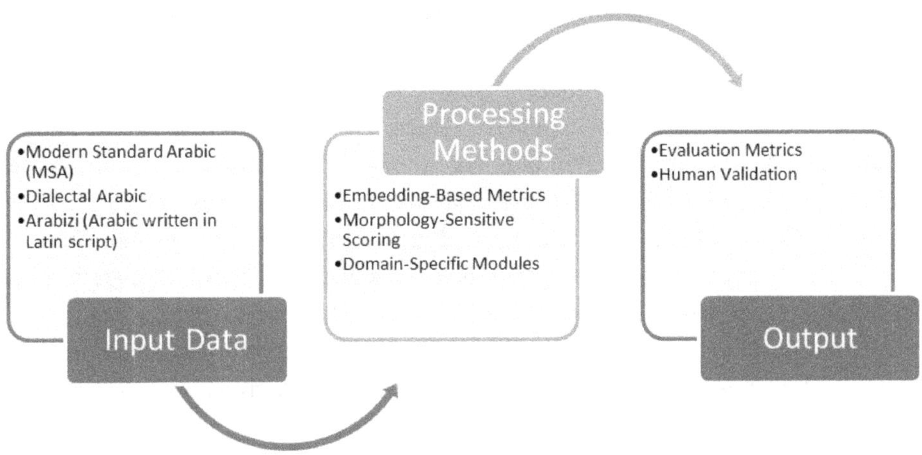

POTENTIAL OUTCOMES AND INSIGHTS

By adopting these methodologies and research paths, significant advancements in Arabic MT evaluation can be achieved. Potential outcomes include:

- Enhanced correlation between modified metrics and human evaluations, particularly for informal or complex content.
- Improved evaluation accuracy for morphologically rich and dialectally diverse translations.

- Deeper insights into the strengths and weaknesses of MT systems across different domains, guiding the development of more effective translation models.

FUTURE RESEARCH DIRECTIONS: BEST PATH FORWARD

The field of Arabic MT evaluation is constantly evolving, driven by advancements in technology and a growing understanding of the complexities of language and translation. This section explores potential future directions in Arabic MT evaluation, focusing on promising advancements in technology and methodology, as well as the crucial role of user-centric evaluation and ethical considerations.

Potential advancements in technology and methodology, such as self-supervised models and cross-dialectal evaluation.

Several technological and methodological advancements hold promise for improving Arabic MT evaluation. Self-supervised learning, which leverages large amounts of unlabeled data to train powerful language models, is a particularly exciting area. Models like mBERT and XLM-R have shown impressive cross-lingual transfer capabilities (Devlin et al., 2018; Conneau et al., 2020), which can be beneficial for Arabic MT evaluation, especially given the data scarcity for certain dialects. These models can be used to develop more robust embedding-based metrics that capture semantic similarity and contextual information more effectively. Furthermore, these models can be fine-tuned for specific evaluation tasks, such as quality estimation or error detection, further enhancing their utility.

Another important direction is the development of cross-dialectal evaluation methods. As discussed previously, diglossia poses a significant challenge for Arabic MT. Current evaluation methods often struggle to assess the quality of translations involving dialectal Arabic. Future research should focus on developing methods that can accurately evaluate translations across different Arabic dialects. This could involve creating multi-dialectal evaluation datasets, developing metrics that are less sensitive to dialectal variations, or using transfer learning techniques to adapt evaluation models trained on MSA data to dialectal Arabic. Work on dialect identification (e.g., (Zaidan and Callison-Burch, 2011; Darwish et al., 2014)) can be leveraged to inform these cross-dialectal evaluation efforts.

The integration of other modalities, such as speech and image, into evaluation is another promising avenue. For example, in social media, text is often accompanied by images or videos. Evaluating the translation in conjunction with these other modalities could provide a more holistic understanding of the translation quality.

This multimodal evaluation could involve using techniques from computer vision and speech recognition to analyze the non-textual content and assess its consistency with the translated text.

User-centric evaluation and ethical considerations in human-informed MT assessment.

User-centric evaluation, which focuses on the needs and preferences of the end-users of MT systems, is becoming increasingly important. Traditional evaluation methods often focus on linguistic criteria, such as fluency and adequacy, but they may not adequately capture the user experience. Future research should focus on developing evaluation methods that take into account user satisfaction, usability, and the specific tasks for which the MT system is being used. This could involve conducting user studies, collecting user feedback, and developing metrics that measure user engagement and task completion.

Ethical considerations are also crucial in human-informed MT assessment. Human evaluation often involves collecting sensitive data, such as user feedback and translation judgments. It is essential to ensure that this data is collected and used ethically, respecting user privacy and obtaining informed consent. Furthermore, it is important to be aware of potential biases in human evaluation, such as cultural biases or biases related to the evaluators' own linguistic background. Steps should be taken to mitigate these biases, such as providing thorough evaluator training and using diverse groups of evaluators. The guidelines and best practices discussed in (Bender and Friedman, 2018) regarding data statements and ethical considerations in NLP are highly relevant in this context.

In summary, future directions in Arabic MT evaluation include leveraging advancements in self-supervised learning and multimodal processing, developing cross-dialectal evaluation methods, and adopting a more user-centric approach. Importantly, ethical considerations must be at the forefront of all human-informed evaluation efforts. By addressing these challenges and pursuing these promising directions, the field of Arabic MT evaluation can continue to advance, leading to more accurate, reliable, and user-friendly translation systems.

CONCLUSION

The evaluation of Arabic machine translation (MT) has made significant strides, but challenges remain, particularly in handling the language's morphological richness, dialectal diversity, and informal usage. Traditional metrics like BLEU often fall short in capturing the nuances of Arabic translations, especially for dialectal and non-standard forms like Arabizi. Enhanced metrics such as BertScore, COMET, and BLEURT show promise, but their effectiveness depends on domain-specific fine-tuning and contextual awareness. To advance the field, future research must focus on several critical directions.

First, leveraging advancements in self-supervised learning and multimodal processing can help develop more robust evaluation frameworks. These techniques can better capture semantic similarity, handle morphological variations, and account for the syntactic flexibility inherent in Arabic. Additionally, integrating multimodal data (e.g., text with visual or audio context) could improve evaluations for content that relies on non-textual cues.

Second, developing cross-dialectal evaluation methods is essential to address the challenge of diglossia in Arabic MT. Current methods struggle to assess translations involving dialectal Arabic accurately. Future efforts should include creating multi-dialectal evaluation datasets, designing metrics less sensitive to dialectal variations, and employing transfer learning to adapt models across dialects. Such advancements will ensure that MT systems can serve diverse Arabic-speaking populations effectively.

Third, adopting a user-centric approach to evaluation is becoming increasingly important. Traditional metrics often emphasize linguistic criteria like fluency and adequacy but may overlook user satisfaction, usability, and task-specific needs. Future research should incorporate user studies, feedback collection, and engagement metrics to evaluate MT systems based on real-world user experiences. This shift will lead to more practical and user-friendly translation solutions.

Finally, exploring domain-specific evaluation frameworks is crucial for addressing the unique requirements of different fields. For instance, news translation demands precision in political and economic terminology, while social media translation must handle informal language, dialects, and code-switching. Tailored evaluation frameworks for each domain will ensure that MT systems meet the specific challenges and expectations of their intended applications.

In summary, the future of Arabic MT evaluation lies in embracing innovative methodologies, addressing linguistic and cultural complexities, and prioritizing user needs. By pursuing these research directions—advancing self-supervised learning, developing cross-dialectal methods, adopting user-centric approaches, and exploring domain-specific frameworks—the field can achieve more accurate, reliable, and inclusive translation systems. Importantly, ethical considerations must remain central to all human-informed evaluation efforts, ensuring fairness, transparency, and accountability in MT development.

REFERENCES

Al Moaiad, Y., Alobed, M., Alsakhnini, M., & Momani, A. M. (2024). Challenges in natural Arabic language processing. *Edelweiss Applied Science and Technology, 8*(6), 4700–4705. DOI: 10.55214/25768484.v8i6.3018

Almansor, E. (2018). Translating Arabic as low resource language using distribution representation and neural machine translation models, Master thesis, *School of Biomedical Engineering, Faculty of Engineering and Information Technology, University of Technology Sydney*, 2018.

Azroumahli, C., El Younoussi, Y., Moussaoui, O., & Zahidi, Y. (2019). An Arabic Dialects Dictionary Using Word Embeddings. [IJRSDA]. *International Journal of Rough Sets and Data Analysis, 6*(3), 18–31. DOI: 10.4018/IJRSDA.2019070102

Babaali, B. (2024). Arabic Machine Translation of Social Media Content (Doctoral dissertation). *University of Mascara.* http://dspace.univ-mascara.dz:8080/jspui/handle/123456789/1073

Babaali, B., & Salem, M. (2023). Survey of the Arabic Machine Translation Corpora. In Chikhi, S., Diaz-Descalzo, G., Amine, A., Chaoui, A., Saidouni, D. E., & Kholladi, M. K. (Eds.), *Modelling and Implementation of Complex Systems. MISC 2022. Lecture Notes in Networks and Systems* (Vol. 593). Springer., DOI: 10.1007/978-3-031-18516-8_15

Bahdanau, D., Cho, K., & Bengio, Y. (2014). Neural machine translation by jointly learning to align and translate. arXiv preprint arXiv:1409.0473.

Banerjee, S., & Lavie, A. (2005). METEOR: An automatic metric for MT evaluation with high levels of correlation with human judgments. In Proceedings of the ACL workshop on intrinsic and extrinsic evaluation measures for machine translation and/or summarization (pp. 65-72).

Beloucif, R., Choukri, K., & Gotti, R. (2016). Automatic evaluation of machine translation for dialectal Arabic. *Proceedings of the Tenth International Conference on Language Resources and Evaluation (LREC 2016).*

Bender, E. M., & Friedman, B. (2018). Data statements for natural language processing: Toward mitigating system bias and enabling better science. *Transactions of the Association for Computational Linguistics, 6*, 587–604. DOI: 10.1162/tacl_a_00041

Bies, A., Song, Z., Maamouri, M., Grimes, S., Lee, H., Wright, J., Strassel, S., Habash, N., Eskander, R., & Rambow, O. (2014). Transliteration of Arabizi into Arabic Orthography: Developing a Parallel Annotated Arabizi-Arabic Script SMS/ Chat Corpus, In: *Proceedings of the EMNLP 2014 Workshop on Arabic Natural Langauge Processing (ANLP)*, pp 93–103, Doha, Qatar, October 25, 2014. DOI: 10.3115/v1/W14-3612

Callison-Burch, C., Osborne, M., & Koehn, P. (2007). Re-evaluation of the evaluation of machine translation: Human vs. automatic evaluation. *Proceedings of the 45th annual meeting of the association for computational linguistics*, 688–695.

Conneau, A., Khandelwal, K., Goyal, N., Chaudhary, V., Wenzek, T., Guzmán, F., Grave, E., Ott, M., Zettlemoyer, L., & Stoyanov, V. (2020). Unsupervised cross-lingual representation learning at scale. *Proceedings of the 58th Annual Meeting of the Association for Computational Linguistics*, 8440–8451. DOI: 10.18653/v1/2020.acl-main.747

Darwish, K., Magdy, W., & Yamani, M. (2014). Arabic dialect identification using n-grams and character-level svm. *Proceedings of the First Arabic Natural Language Processing Workshop*, 124–131.

Devlin, J., Chang, M. W., Lee, K., & Toutanova, K. (2018). Bert: Pre-training of deep bidirectional transformers for language understanding. arXiv preprint arXiv:1810.04805.

ElNokrashy, M., & Kocmi, T. (2023, December). ebleu: Unexpectedly good machine translation evaluation using simple word embeddings. In *Proceedings of the Eighth Conference on Machine Translation* (pp. 744-748). https://doi.org/DOI: 10.18653/v1/2023.wmt-1.61

Guerberof, A. (2009). *Pupil: An automatic evaluation metric for translation quality assessment of web pages*. Dublin City University.

Habash, N. (2010). Introduction to Arabic natural language processing. *Synthesis Lectures on Human Language Technologies*, *3*(1), 1–187. DOI: 10.1007/978-3-031-02139-8

Habash, N., Roth, R., Rambow, O., & Eskander, R. (2017). A multi-dialectal arabic treebank. *Proceedings of the Eleventh International Conference on Language Resources and Evaluation (LREC 2018)*.

Harrat, S., Meftouh, K., & Smaïli, K. (2017). Machine translation for Arabic dialects (survey). *Information Processing & Management*, *56*(2), 262–273. DOI: 10.1016/j.ipm.2017.08.003

Husain, F. (2022). Arabic Natural Language Processing, [Online]. Available: https://infoscilab.ku.edu.kw/arabic-natural-language-processing/

Klein, G., Kim, Y., Deng, Y., Senellart, J., & Rush, A. M. (2017). Opennmt: Open-source toolkit for neural machine translation, arXiv preprint, arXiv:1701.02810. DOI: 10.18653/v1/P17-4012

Koehn, P. (2010). *Statistical machine translation.* Cambridge university press.

Lo, C. K., Larkin, S., & Knowles, R. (2023, December). Metric score landscape challenge (MSLC23): Understanding metrics' performance on a wider landscape of translation quality. In Proceedings of the Eighth Conference on Machine Translation (pp. 776-799).

Moghe, N., Fazla, A., Amrhein, C., Kocmi, T., Steedman, M., Birch, A., Sennrich, R., & Guillou, L. (2025). Machine translation meta evaluation through translation accuracy challenge sets. *Computational Linguistics*, *51*(1), 73–137. DOI: 10.1162/coli_a_00537

Papineni, K., Roukos, S., Ward, T., & Zhu, W. J. (2002). BLEU: a method for automatic evaluation of machine translation. In *Proceedings of the 40th annual meeting on association for computational linguistics* (pp. 311-318).

Rei, R., Stewart, C., Farinha, A. C., & Lavie, A. (2020). COMET: A neural framework for MT evaluation. arXiv preprint arXiv:2009.09025. DOI: 10.18653/v1/2020.emnlp-main.213

Sellam, T., Das, D., & Parikh, A. P. (2020). BLEURT: Learning robust metrics for text generation. arXiv preprint arXiv:2004.04696. DOI: 10.18653/v1/2020.acl-main.704

Snover, M., Dorr, B., Schwartz, R., Micciullo, L., & Makhoul, J. (2006). A study of translation edit rate with targeted human annotation. In Proceedings of the 7th conference of the association for machine translation in the Americas: technical papers (pp. 223-231).

Sutskever, I., Vinyals, O., & Le, Q. V. (2014). Sequence to sequence learning with neural networks. In Advances in neural information processing systems (pp. 3104-3112).

Vilar, D., Xu, J., & Ney, H. (2010). Error analysis of statistical machine translation output. *Proceedings of the Workshop on Statistical Machine Translation*, 107–116.

Zaidan, O., & Callison-Burch, C. (2011). Task-oriented intrinsic evaluation of machine translation using semantic role labeling. *Proceedings of the 49th Annual Meeting of the Association for Computational Linguistics: Human Language Technologies*, 181–189.

Chapter 10
Conversational Algerian Sign Language Recognition Using the Deep Learning Approach

Lila Meddeber
https://orcid.org/0000-0001-6286-7986
University of Science and Technology of Oran Mohamed Boudiaf, Algeria

Tarik Zouagui
https://orcid.org/0000-0003-1631-2976
University of Science and Technology of Oran Mohamed Boudiaf, Algeria

ABSTRACT

Continuous Sign Language Recognition (CSLR) is the process of understanding the combination of hand gestures, facial expressions and body pose in real-time, in conjunction with the grammatical and vocabulary structural elements that allow cross-cultural communication with people who have difficulty hearing and/or communicating verbally. This study aims to develop an automatic system capable of detecting the region of interest on the signer's body and classifying each sign into its appropriate category, which will be combined with the natural language (NL). To achieve these objectives, a novel approach is proposed with four main contributions, which can be summarized as the independence of the signer's position in the frame, the collection of an Algerian Sign Language dataset containing 46 dynamic signs (2083 videos), achieving 97.75% accuracy for dynamic sign recognition and 97.37% for static sign recognition and an NLP model to predict the next words in the sentence, thus speeding up communication.

DOI: 10.4018/979-8-3373-0735-0.ch010

INTRODUCTION

Sign Language is a visual language that came to life in the 18th century when its first systematic study had been conducted, it's a combination of hand gestures, facial expressions, and body language. Sign Languages have their own set of grammatical and linguistic rules since each one of them evolved differently in various places in the world, which resulted in the creation of over 300 distinct sign language families and dialects. For example, American Sign Language is part of the French Sign Language Family, Emirati Sign Language is part of the Arabic Sign Language Family, while the Algerian Sign Language is a combination of both families.

Sign Languages have different sets of rules depending on the SL itself because it changes based on the geographical location. In fact, countries that share the same spoken language have different sign languages because of many factors such as traditions, religion, or the developers were not in contact while developing the language. Currently, there is no worldwide unified sign language and there are almost as many Sign Languages as there are dialects in the world. Sign Language can be separated into two main features, the Manual Features that describe the position of the signer's body, the movement, and the position of the hand according to the body, and the Non-Manual Features that describe facial expressions, shoulder movements, and head tilts. They also cover additional information like voice tone and emphasis. SL grammatical structure is very different, an arrangement of signs in a particular order leads to a purposeful meaning, and they have their own lexicon that is classified into three main aspects:

- Isolated Sign Language

Static signs are characterized by a stable position of the hands without movement, as shown in Figure 1. They are used to represent static information, such as alphabets and numbers, and can be one-handed or two-handed.

Dynamic Signs are characterized by movement and are essential for expressing nuances of meaning, emotions and relationships between lexical elements.

- Continuous Sign Language includes both static and dynamic signs, forming a complex linguistic system with a natural flow similar to spoken languages. In addition, sign language incorporates a linguistic phenomenon known as Moment Epenthesis (ME), analogous to the pauses that occur between spoken words. ME involves the insertion of non-sign sequences between the end and beginning of successive sign sequences.

Arabic Sign Language

Arabic Sign Language (ArSL) is a natural sign language used by the deaf community in the Middle East and North Africa. ArSL has its own set of signs, grammar, syntax, and vocabulary,

which distinguishes it from other sign languages used in other regions of the world. ArSL is heavily influenced by the Arabic language, many signs in ArSL are derived from Arabic words or sentences, and the syntax of the language follows the same basic structure as Arabic but still maintains a different dialect therefore many signs in Emirati Sign Language differ with Algerian Sign Language despite them being derived from the same sign language family.

Algerian Sign Language

The Algerian Sign Language differs from many other sign languages due to its unique origins. As mentioned earlier, it is influenced by two distinct language families: the Arabic Sign Language family, which derives from the local sign language used alongside spoken Arabic, and the French Sign Language Family. This influence stems from the historical colonization of Algeria by the French for over a century.

Figure 1. Arabic Sign Laguage (ArSL) Alphabet

Consequently, Algerian people have adopted numerous French words and French-named roads, which have influenced their traditions. Sign language development is influenced by various factors, including cultural traditions and historical background. Therefore, it is not surprising that the Algerian Sign Language stands out as the most distinct form of Arabic Sign Language (ArSL).

Continuous Arabic Sign Language Recognition System (CArSLR)

Continuous Arabic SLR system provides the user with the transcription of the sign, either as a text or speech output by providing the system with an input in the form of video (video based system) or sensor data (glove/sensor-based system) while identifying the precise sign class by using StaticSLR or DynamicSLR.

Figure 2. Continuous Arabic Sign Language Recognition (CArSLR) System (Aloysius & Geetha, 2020)

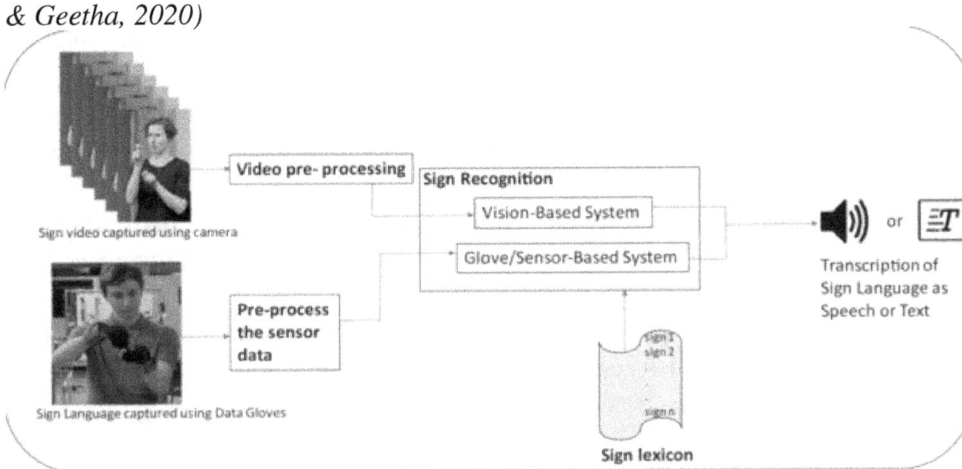

CArSLR system encompasses more than just the detection of the hands, body pose, and facial expressions of the signer and the classification of the represented sign into the appropriate class. It involves a broader range of processes, including feature extraction, temporal modeling, context analysis, and sequence decoding, to achieve an accurate and robust recognition of sign language gestures. it must form a proper sentence by combining words (Dynamic) and alphabets/ digits (Static) while omitting ME sequences and keeping a linguistically correct arabic sentence.

Applications of Continuous Sign Language Recognition (CSLR)

Continuous Sign Language Recognition (CSLR) is a critical technology for bridging communication gaps between deaf/hard-of-hearing individuals and the hearing world. Below are key application domains, supported by recent research and technological advancements:

1. Real-Time Communication Assistants
   - **Speech-to-Text/Sign-to-Text Translation:** CSLR systems convert continuous sign language gestures into text or spoken language in real time, enabling seamless communication in educational, workplace, and public settings .
     - **Video Relay Services:** Enhances telecommunication for deaf individuals by integrating CSLR with video calls, reducing dependency on human interpreters.
2. Education and Language Learning
   - **Interactive Learning Tools:** CSLR-powered applications (e.g., web/mobile apps) help hearing parents and educators learn sign language by providing real-time feedback on gestures.
   - **Deaf Education:** Supports bilingual (sign language + written language) education for deaf children, improving literacy and academic outcomes.
3. Healthcare Accessibility
   - **Medical Consultations:** Facilitates communication between deaf patients and healthcare providers, ensuring accurate diagnosis and treatment.
   - **Speech Therapy:** Systems like SLRGAN (Generative Adversarial Networks for SLR) can generate synthetic sign language videos for therapeutic training .
4. Public Services and Assistive Technology
   - **Emergency Services:** Enables deaf individuals to communicate with first responders via sign language recognition in crisis situations.
   - **Smart Cities:** Integrates CSLR into public interfaces for accessible information dissemination.
5. Entertainment and Media
   - **Live Event Interpretation:** Real-time sign language translation for broadcasts, conferences, and live performances.
   - **Gaming and Virtual Reality:** Motion-capture-based CSLR (e.g., using MediaPipe Holistic) enables immersive sign language interactions in virtual environments.

CArSLR System stages

Generally, DL based SLR system goes through four main stages (Ali Almahri, 2022):

- **Data Acquisition:** Many approaches exist to obtain data such as vision-based methods, sensor-based methods or using an existing dataset. It all depends on the input of the system for example a camera for the collection of Images/ frames or Sensors for the collection of electrical signals.

- **Pre-Processing:** This specific step involves modifying the raw data to make it suitable for the intended use and training of the model. It varies depending on the type of data - signals, image, video or skeletal data, etc. It involves filtering and resizing, as shown in Figure 2. In our topic, segmentation is an essential step to identify the region of interest (ROI).
- **Feature Extraction:** This step aims for efficiency in reducing the computational cost, training time and enhancing the learning accuracy. This is achieved by extracting and identifying the most pertinent features that exhibit a strong correlation with the desired output then utilize them as input for the classification model.
- **Classification:** In this step, the trained model will classify the input data into different classes, in our case of SLR the output would be a particular class of sign. The classification can be done by two approaches: Rule-based or Machine Learning-based methods.

Challenges in developing CSLR system

Most of the challenges faced in CArSL (Aloysius & Geetha, 2020):

- **Detection in a complex background**, especially in vision-based systems which made research focuses more on sensor-based systems.
- **Occlusion**, detection of the signer's hand, body, and face regardless of size, clothing and skin tone.
- **Moment Epenthesis**, a sequence of frames that represents the signer's hand position from the end of a sign until the start of another.
- **Sign language structure and properties**, not all spoken words have a sign to be represented for this reason we said SL has a very specific vocabulary, meaning changes depending on the order of the signs.
- **Combination of global and local signs**, global signs are the gestures while the local ones are the motions of the fingers inside.
- **Co-articulation effect**, often in sign language a sign represents various meanings depending on the sign before and after it.
- **Short sign detection**, Loss of frames and false recognition can occur due to the short duration of some signs.
- **Sign Length** signs have different duration which makes a system with a constant number of frames per video challenging.

- **Modality combination**, the same sign can have a different meaning with a different facial expression, extracting features and combining them in an efficient way can be challenging.

SYSTEMATIC REVIEW

Due to scarcity of systematic reviews concerning the literature on Continuous Arabic Sign Language Recognition using deep learning, we decided to conduct one due to the dissimilarity of the objectives, to highlight the research that has already been done in this field, and make iteasier for people who were interested in this approach to find information by suggesting areas for additional research and determine our future course based on the findings.

Research Strategy

We conducted our research using the Kitchenham Method (Kitchenham, 2004), which is often used to conduct systematic literature reviews in the field of software engineering. The process includes formulating our research questions, selecting the particular keywords and data sources that would be pertinent to our study, developing criteria for selecting which publications to include and which to publications to exclude from our analysis.

Research Questions Identification

1. What research is currently being done on automatic Arabic sign language recognition?
2. How was this task handled?
3. What data was used?
4. What deep learning techniques were employed?

Keywords and Resources

Our content was gathered from a number of reliable internet databases including IEEE Xplore, ACM Digital Library, Arxiv, Springer Link, Google Scholar and Research Gate. We searched for the keywords "Arabic Sign Language", "Recognition", "Action Recognition", "Deep Learning", "Automatic Sign Language Recognition", "Dynamic Sign Language Recognition", "Dynamic Gestures Recognition Models" and "Dynamic Sign Language".

Study Selection Criteria

In this subsection, we use inclusion and exclusion criteria to ensure that the data is pertinent to our research questions.

Inclusion Criteria

- Must be a primary study focused on ArSL Recognition
- Must include Arabic Sign Language
- Must use Deep Learning methods in the classification and feature extraction stage
- Must be published within the last 3 years
- Must work on Dynamic and Static Signs
- Must be a real-time classification

Exclusion Criteria

- Not in the field of ArSL
- Not focused on ArSLR
- Does not use Deep learning methods
- Not a real-time classification

Study Selection Phases

To accelerate the filtering process we used Rayyan web application(Ouzzani,2016) through different phases (Figure 3):

Phase 1: Gathering all 207 articles in different CSV files and importing them to Rayyan.
Phase 2: Removing the duplicated articles.
Phase 3: Screening and removing unrelated articles based on the title, abstract, and year published.
Phase 4: Reading the chosen articles attentively to obtain the information and examining them more closely.

Figure 3. Review process

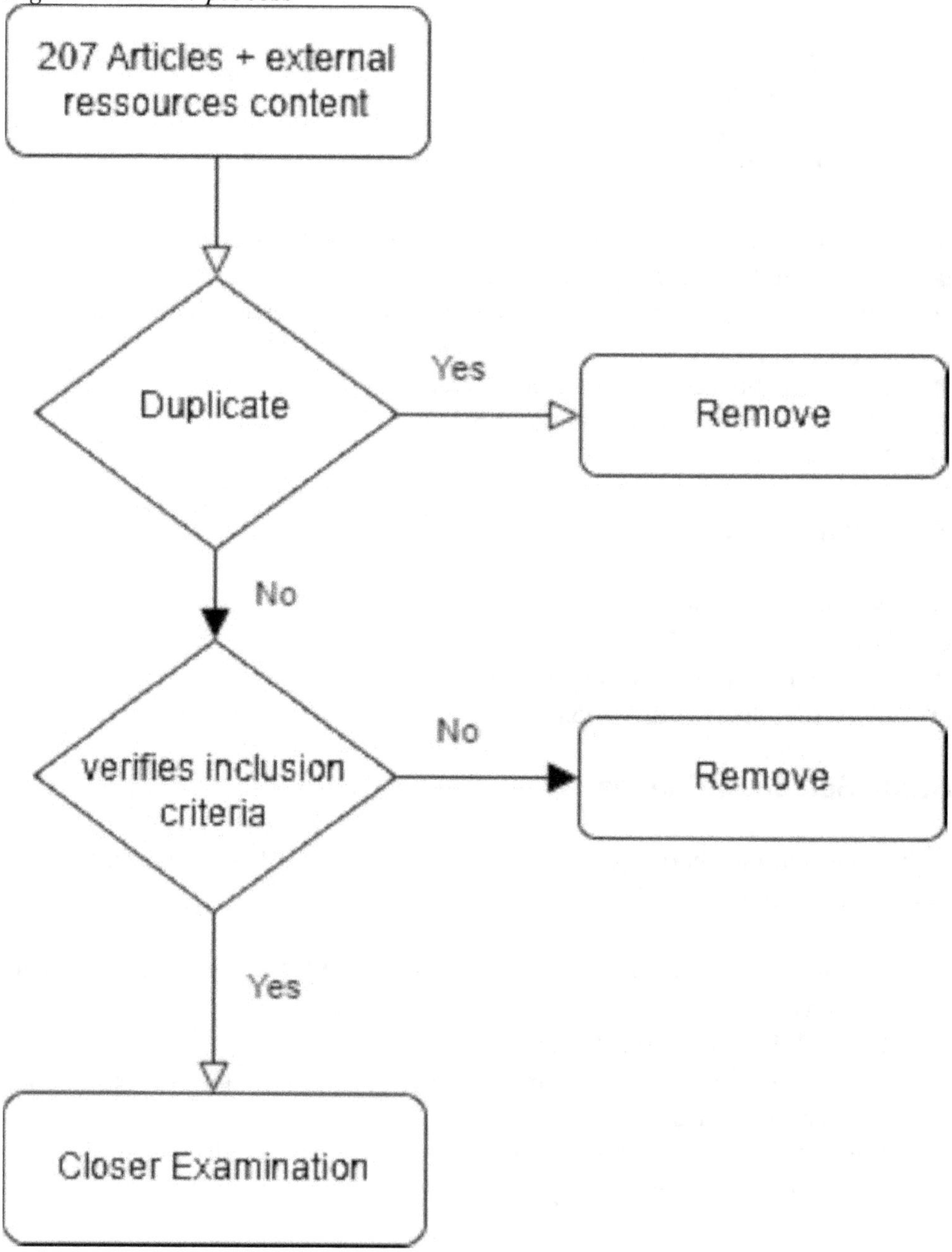

At the end of this process we ended up with 16 articles to extract data from after detailed examination.

Data extraction

Table 1. Articles Examination

Author	Single / double handed	Static / dynamic signs	Feature Extraction	Classifier	Signer Dependent	Accuracy
(Eleon, A. S., 2014)	both	both	PCNN	multi-level multiplicated NN	YES	83%
(ALY et al., 2020)	double hand	dynamic	SOM Model	Bi-LSTM	no	89.5%
(Suliman et al., 2021)	both	dynamic	CNN (AlexNet)	LSTM	both	S.Dep: 95% S.Idep: 93%
(Hisham& Hamouda, 2017)	both	both	Palm and bones features	ANN SVM KNN DTW	no	Static: 96% Dynamic: 81%
(Alnahhas et al., 2020)	both	dynamic	Eucludean coordenation	LSTM	YES	One hand:89% Double Hand:96%
(Bencherif et al., 2021)	both	dynamic	2D Skeletal data	skeletal CNN	both	S. Dep: 98.89% S. Idep: 96.6%
(Boukdir et al., (2021)	double hand	dynamic	2DCRNN 3DCNN	2DCRNN 3DCNN	yes	2DCRNN:92% 3DCNN:99%
(Abdul et al., 2021)	both	both	OpenPose	Inception-BiLSTM	both	79.9%
(Saaman et al., 2022)	both	dynamic	MediaPipe	LSTM Bi-LSTM GRU	yes	99%
(El badawy et al., 2015)	double hand	dynamic	PCNN	MLP	yes	95%
(El badawy et al., 2017)	both	dynamic	3DCNN	3DCNN (softmax layer)	yes	85%
(Latif et al. 2020)	single hand	static	CNN	CNN	NO	97.6%
(Hayani et al., 2019)	single hand	static	CNN	CNN KNN SVM	yes	90.02%
(Alawwad et al., 2021)	single hand	static	R-CNN	R-CNN based on VGG-16 and ResNet	yes	93%
(Moryossef, 2021)	single hand	dynamic	sensor based	ANN	yes	90.66%
(Ritonga et al., 2021)	single	static	CNN	CNN	yes	90%

Global Results Report

According to the 16 publications listed in table 1, we determined that in recent years, there has been an upsurge in interest in developing an arabic sign language recognition system, with numerous valuable contributions, given that the majority of the papers are journal articles rather than conference papers. However, when compared to other sign language systems, these numbers are quite low and we will get to the reasons in the next subsection.

Research Question Answers

What research is currently being done on automatic Arabic sign language recognition using deep learning approaches?

As previously said, we completed our study with 16 publications, which we decided to classify according to their main contribution and important discoveries.

1. Vision-Based Recognition

(Elons, 2014) demonstrated a Graphics Processing Unit (GPU)-based solution to real-time Arabic sign language detection. They use a PCNN to extract static posture features and a Multi-level Multiplicative Neural Network as a classifier, which outperforms typical Multi-layer Perceptron Neural Networks in terms of training time and accuracy. The system is divided into two layers: the first determines whether the signer uses one or two hands, and the second determines the final categorization. During testing, the system obtained an 83% recognition accuracy on a dataset of 200 signs.

2. Sensor-Based Recognition

The research study by (Yousuf, 2021) is the first and only one to use Electromyography (EMG) and an ANN model for classification. EMG is a sensor-based data acquisition technology that uses finger motions to quantify the electrical pulse in human muscle. Intelligent EMG is the use of an intelligent approach to improve EMG classification. They test their model on 5 isolated words, but they are unable to test it in real time due to the difficulty in collecting large amounts of data.

(Ritonga et al., 2021) describes another sensor-based data acquisition approach that employs DG5-V Hand data gloves to record information such as finger bending, hand orientation, position, and rotation. They reach a 90% accuracy by using a CNN model for both feature extraction and classification. According to the report, this approach is still in its early phases and might benefit from the addition of other devices like as LMC or XBOX connect.

3. Multiple Collection Devices

Both (Bencherif et al., 2021) and (El badawy et al., 2015) employed additional devices to address this issue. (Bencherif et al., 2021) collects data using two Microsoft Kinect devices and a camera. They adopt an alternative technique, passing their data into an OpenPose package to extract skeletal data, then into a skeleton CNN for recognition.

4. Deep Learning for both feature extraction and Classification

The authors of (El badawy et al., 2015) went on to examine the usage of a 3D convolutional neural network (CNN) as a strategy for feature extraction and classification in (El badawy et al., 2017). They employ depth maps as input and reach 98% accuracy for seen data and 85% accuracy for fresh data, which can be improved with further data from additional users.

Another research that uses a deep learning model for both feature extraction and classification (Boukdir et al., 2021) solves the problem of needing to determine which features to employ in traditional methods. They employ two models: a 2DCRNN model and a 3DCNN model. The 2DCRNN model extracts features by recognizing the association between video frames using a recurrent network pattern, whereas the 3DCNN model learns spatio-temporal features from small patches.

(Alnahhas et al., 2020) explores the mathematical features extracted from the LMC sensor and optimizes the system with the use of an LSTM network for multiclass ArSL classification, which is ideal for temporal data because sign gestures are represented as a frame sequence. Their model may deliver interesting results for dynamic gestures.

(Hayani et al., 2019) likewise, employed a CNN model based on LeNet-5, a 7-layer CNN architecture used in the banking industry that is capable of processing higher quality images with more layers. The model is employed for both feature extraction and classification and achieved a 90.02% accuracy by extending the training data to 80% of the whole dataset, demonstrating that deep learning algorithms perform better as data size increases. In addition, it outperforms KNN and SVM.

5. Pre-Processing

(Latif et al., 2020) employed a CNN model that states that increasing the amount of training data increases performance to a certain point, above that, the size has little impact on accuracy using their model architecture that obtained 97.6% accuracy. However, we must keep in mind that they trained on a dataset of 50,000 images and they claim that in the future, that they intend on using augmentation techniques for improving the quantity of their data, but that this will require more computational power and processing time.

6. Deep Learning vs Machine Learning Models

(Hisham & Hamouda, 2017) tested their model with alphabets, numbers, isolated words, and single and two-handed gestures. There are 38 static motions: 28 letters, numbers (1-10), and 16 static words, as well as 20 dynamic gestures. They collect data using LMC and then apply ANN with Multilayer Perceptron, SVM, KNN, and DTW. We observe that ANN was not the best performer, earning good results for static signs but doing poorly for more complicated signs.

7. Pre-trained Models

(Alawwad et al., 2021) employs a Faster Region-based Convolutional Neural Network (RCNN) model that is based on deep VGG-16 and ResNet architectures. The foundation of this model is the ability to distinguish the hand sign as the region of interest in a variety of lighting, background, and shades of skin. The model can then learns the hand position, extract and map the features, which aids with the problem of selecting important features. Both models delivered comparable results. Despite achieving 93% accuracy, the researchers point out that ResNet obtained its results with far less training time.

(Suliman et al., 2021) employs an LSTM model to recognize a range of signs like digits, alphabets, and isolated words. The data was obtained using Microsoft Kinect, which is identical to the LMC device in its approach. They test their model in two ways: singer dependent and signer independent. They discovered that their model had an accuracy of 95.9% for the first and 43.62% for the second one. Based on the claims of the researchers such results were expected, given the significant increase in complexity when the model is applied to previously unseen data and the similarity of some indicators.

(Abdul et al., 2021) obtain 78.9% accuracy for a singer-independent inception-BiLSTM model trained on a KSU-ArSL dataset containing both static and dynamic signs. Their inception model can extract the most relevant spatial information from images, while the BiLSTM extracts temporal features. They observe that the bidirectional model outperforms a standard LSTM model in terms of efficiency and time.

How was this task handled?

There are two techniques for accomplishing this task: the Acquisition method and the categorization category implemented.

1. Acquisition Method
    - Vision-Based Recognition System

Since the data needed in this system will be pictures or videos, the devices employed in this system can range from cameras to tracking devices like the Leap Motion Controller or Microsoft Kinect.

- Sensor-Based Recognition System

Electromyography (EMG), Radar, Gloves, and inertial measurement units can be used to capture data that may illustrate the movement, velocity, and location of the hand. Vision-based systems use visual input, whereas sensor-based systems use electric signals acquired by sensors. Whereas the data utilized may be publicly available.

2. Classification Category

Complexity of this task is defined by the type of signs that the system must identify. It can range from simple recognition such as Alphabets and Numbers to more complicated recognition such as isolated words recognition to full sentence recognition. Because of the complexity of continuous SL, the majority of the research examined was dedicated to isolated/static signals.

What data was used?

According to the review, the majority of the studies used self-collected data, while some used public datasets. The type of data depended entirely on the system.

We also noted that over 60% of the experiments were done on motionless images, because classification in this context is easier to process. In terms of dynamic signals, the majority of studies have focused on one-handed isolated words while very few have been conducted on both static and dynamic data.

Furthermore, we would like to cite the available public datasets and a summarized description:

1. **RGB Arabic Alphabets Sign Language Dataset** (Al-Barham et al., 2023): Contains 7856 labeled RGB images collected by more than 200 signers with various environments and conditions.
2. **KSU-ArSL** (CS2R, 2022): Contains 80 class collected by 40 signers, which means 200 videos per sign using three devices (RGB Camera and two Microsoft Kinect).
3. **KArSL** (Sidig et al., 2021): Contains 502 signs by tree signers using Microsoft Kinect V2.
4. **ArSL** (Belmadoui S., 2022): Arabic Sign Language dataset composed of 290 images for testing and 13926 with fixed dimensions.
5. **JUMLA-QSL-22** (El Ghoul et al., 2022): Contains 900 sentences recorded by 7 participants. Each class has 4 samples recorded from front angle, top angle, left angle, and right angle.

What deep learning techniques were employed?

Below we will cite the models that were used frequently according to our review:

1. Feed-forward models
    - **MLP**: A Multi-layer Perceptron (MLP) is a type of feed-forward artificial neural network composed of numerous layers of interconnected neurons. It is a popular and essential model in deep learning and machine learning.
    - **PNN**: A Probabilistic neural network is also based on feedforward network. They are faster and more accurate than MLPs, but slower in classifying new cases and use more memory.
    - **CNN**: Convolutional Neural Networks (CNNs) are a type of feed forward neural network that is designed to learn spatial hierarchies of data automatically and adaptively by back propagation using several building blocks such as convolution layers, pooling layers, and fully connected layers.
2. Recurrent Neural Networks (RNNs) are neural networks that use their internal memory or state to handle sequential data. They include recurrent connections that allow information to flow over time steps, making them ideal for activities that require sequences and temporal relationships. RNNs have become strong tools for tasks such as natural language processing, speech recognition, and time series analysis because of diverse designs like LSTM, Bi-LSTM and GRU.

Limitation

The most significant challenge and constraint is the absence of studies on Arabic Sign Language, which has resulted in numerous of other issues, such as:

1. Unique dialects for every region/country due to the absence of a Standardized Arabic Sign Language.
2. Absence of a standard dataset for comparing existing works. Since researchers are aiming for a common goal without a proper base to compare with. Even employing the same model, the performance will vary based to the variation of data used to train it.
3. Lack of benchmark datasets and limitations on accessible ones, such as ArSL2018's imbalance data, which will necessitate extensive pre-processing techniques.
4. The requirement of self-acquiring dynamic SL datasets, which is time-consuming and difficult depending on the devices used for collection, for example, Microsoft Kinect and Leap Motion Controller are sensitive to Infrared light, resulting in their inoperability outdoors; using sensors or multiple devices is extremely expensive and requires a lot of pre-processing and data combining.
5. There were no prerequisites about Arabic Sign Language, hence much of the current research was wrong due to the collection of unrealistic and fake signs into their datasets.
6. Past realized systems are incomplete due to inaccurate translation because no previous study takes into account the linguistic features of both spoken Arabic Language and ArSL.
7. The majority of the systems lack generality due to poor accuracy and performance when tested by an independent signer from the dataset collection.

METHODOLOGY

This section outlines the methods we propose to address the above concerns, and highlights the selected tools and frameworks we will use to build an end-to-end Arabic sign language system that would address the research gaps identified above.

Detection and Tracking of signer's ROI

Skeleton data is used to train and test our model using one of the following frameworks, after selecting the best one for our situation:

- **OpenPose Framework** (Cao et al., 2017) OpenPose is an advanced computer vision framework, it is a powerful tool for human pose estimation and tracking. This framework has gained significant attention in the field of computer vision in recent years. Its application has been successfully demonstrated in various scenarios such as action recognition, gesture analysis, and human-computer interaction.
- **MediaPipe Holistic** (Lugaresi, 2019) Mediapipe holistic provides a comprehensive solution for holistic perception tasks, including pose estimation, facial analysis, and hand tracking. It uses advanced machine learning algorithms and deep neural networks to accurately recognize and track various body orientations, facial expressions, and gestures in real-time.
- **PoseNet Framework** (Kendall, 2015) PoseNet is a famous real-time framework widely used for action recognition and tracking, it is CNN-based camera relocalization for 6 degrees of freedom(6-DOF). it estimates the pose (position and orientation) of RGB input images or video frames.

Classification

Considering the inherent natural language properties of the input data and the requirement to process a specific number of frames for each action, our study adopts recurrent neural network (RNN) designs. RNNs are chosen as the suitable model architecture due to their ability to handle sequential data and capture temporal dependencies through feedback connections. We will implement LSTM and Bi-LSTM then select the one with the most suitable results.

Long Short-Term Memory (LSTM)

Long Short-Term Memory (Staudemeyer, 2019) is a RNN-based architecture that addresses the limitation of RNNs in capturing long-term dependencies, it overcomes the vanishing gradient problem by introducing memory cells and gating mechanisms that can selectively retain or forget information. It consists of four layers that interact with each other to produce the output of that cell along with the cell state, as shown in figure 4. These two things are then passed on to the next hidden layer.

Figure 4. LSTM architecture

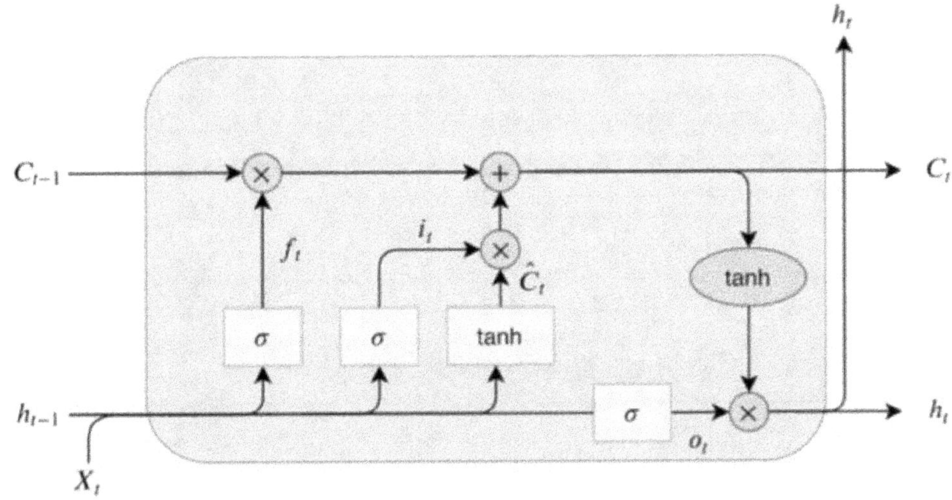

Inputs:

X_t : *Current input,* ***C_{t-1}*** : *Memory from last LSTM unit* , ***h_{t-1}*** : *Output of last LSTM unit*

Outputs:

C_t : *New updated memory* , ***h_t*** : *Curent output,* ***σ*** : *Sigmoid layer*

Functions:

tanh : *Tanh layer* , ⊗: *Scaling of information* , ⊕ : *Adding information*

LSTM has three main components that are responsible for controlling the flow of information:

Forget gate

Figure 5. LSTM forget gate

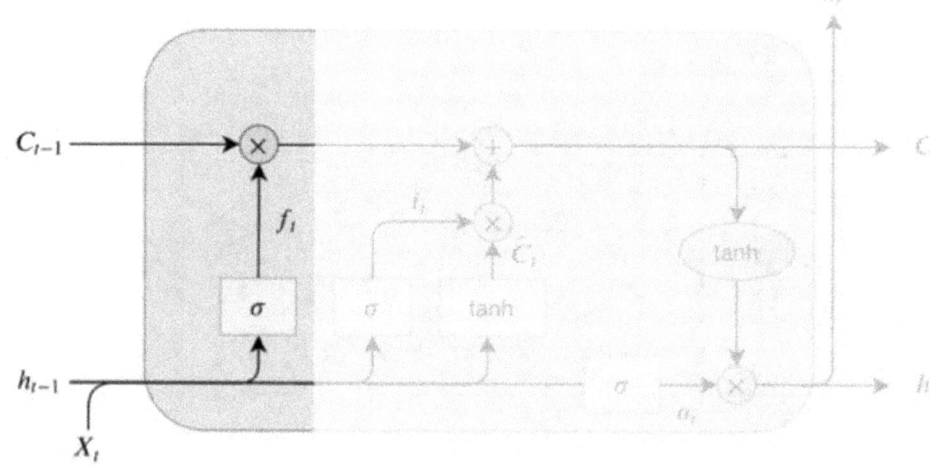

Applies a sigmoid function to determine which information is retained or forgotten.

$$f_t = \sigma\left(W_f \cdot \left[h_{t-1}, x_t\right] + b_f\right) \tag{1}$$

Where, W_f represent the weight matrix connecting the input x_t to the forgate, h_{t-1} is the previous hidden state and b_f represent the bias vector for the forgate gate (Figure 5).

Input gate

Determines how much new information is allowed to enter the memory cell taking into account the current input and the previous hidden state also by applying sigmoid function.

Figure 6. LSTM input gate

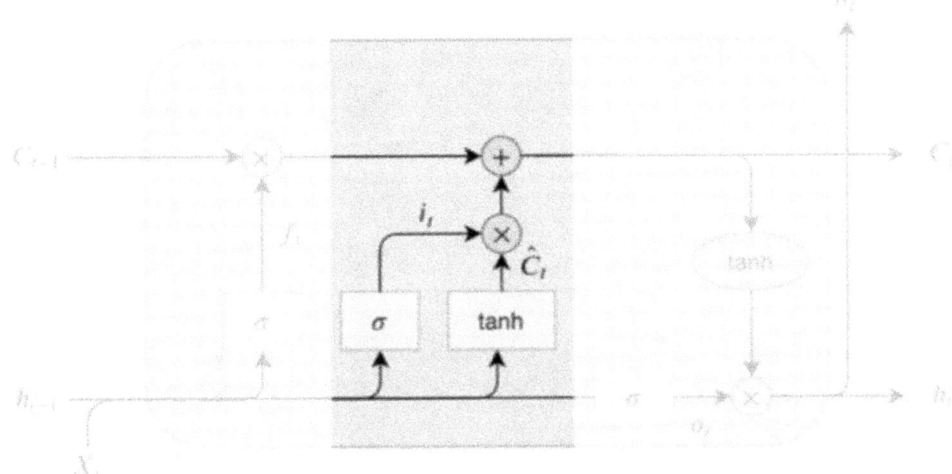

$$I_t = \sigma\left(W_i \cdot \left[h_{t-1}, X_t\right] + b_i\right) \quad (2)$$

Where, W_i represent the weight matrix connecting the input X_t to the input gate, h_{t-1} is the previous hidden state and b_i represent the bias vector for the input gate shown in Figure 6.

Output gate

Control the information flow from the memory cell to the output by applying sigmoid functions to the previous hidden state and multiplying it with the current memory content.

Figure 7. LSTM output gate

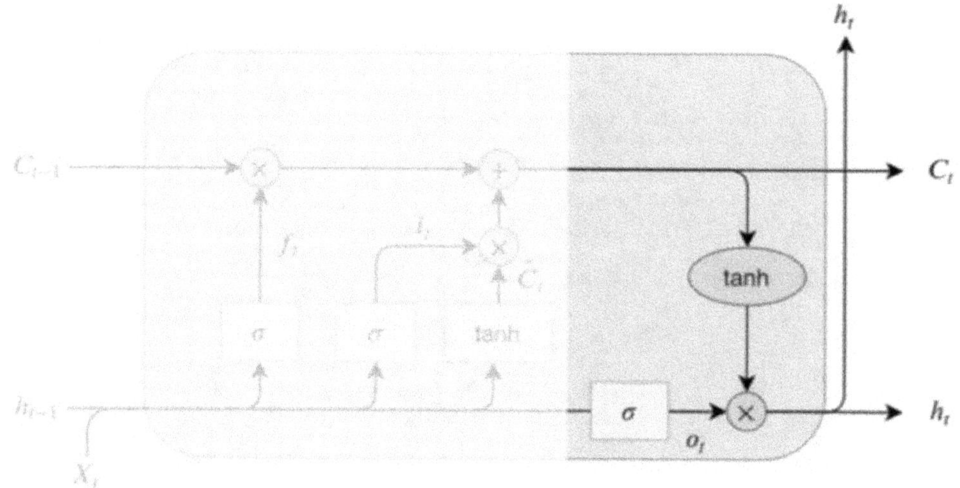

$$O_t = \sigma(W_o \cdot [h_{t-1}, X_t] + b_o) \quad (3)$$

$$h_t = \sigma(O_t \,.\, tanh(C_t)) \quad (4)$$

Where, W_o represent the weight matrix connecting the input X_t to the output gate, h_{t-1} is the previous hidden state and b_i represent the bias vector for the output gate (Figure 7).

Bidirectional Long Short-Term Memory (BI-LSTM)

Bidirectional Long Short-Term Memory (Huang et al., 2015) is a type of RNN that is trained using backpropagation through time, it is a sequence processing model that consists of two LSTMs: one taking the input in a forward direction and the other in a backward direction (as shown in figure 8). BiLSTMs effectively increase the amount of information available to the network by improving the context available to the algorithm (e.g. knowing which words immediately follow and precede a word in a sentence).

Figure 8. BiLSTM Architecture model showing the input and output layers. The red arrows represent the backward sequence track and green the forward sequence track (Ihianle et al., 2020)

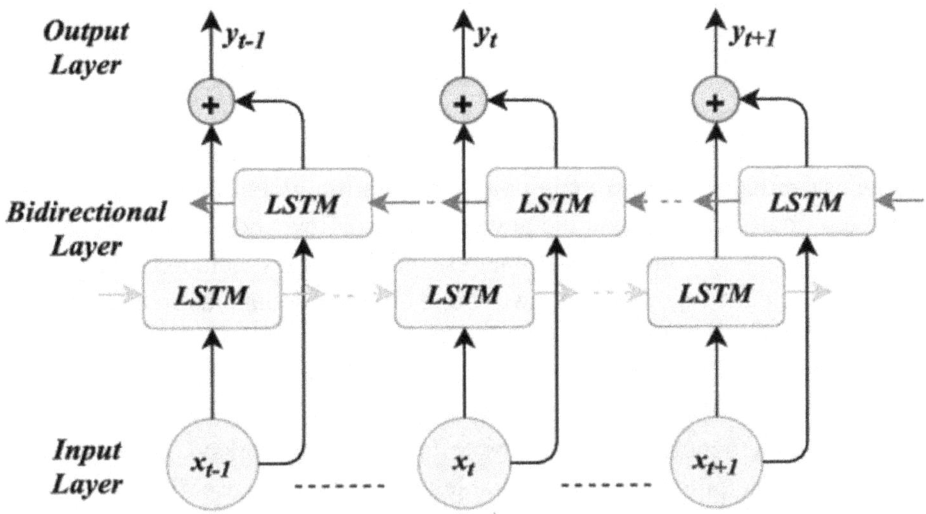

Fully connected layers

Often referred to as dense layers, they establish connections between the neurons of the input layer and every neuron in the subsequent layer, forming a comprehensive network. This arrangement allows for the capture of intricate patterns within the data. Dense layers are typically positioned at the end of models.

Forming Arabic Sentences

In order to accelerate the communication we will use the next word prediction technique inspired by all search engines using Natural Language Processing.

Natural Language Processing (Ouzzani et al., 2016) (NLP) is a branch of artificial intelligence that focuses on the interaction between human language and computers, allowing language translation, question answering, ect. NLP encompasses various techniques and applications from which we can distinguish two specific types that relate to predicting the next word and correcting grammatical sentences:

- ***Language Modeling***: Language modeling in NLP involves predicting the next word in a sequence of words (sentences).

- *Grammar Correction*: Grammar correction aims to identify and rectify grammatical errors automatically, by analyzing the structure of the sentences, grammar rules.

CArSLR SYSTEM STRATEGY IMPLEMENTATION

Using Python 3.10, We created a conda environment to ensure that all the requirements are met, and avoid any conflicts with the global python package. To achieve our goals, we'll rely on the power of Tensorflow and Keras and select our framework library by comparison. Other essential libraries include PySimpleGUI, OpenCV, and Scikit-Learn. Testing was done on linux debian distro and windows.

Detection and Tracking of the Region of Interest

We will implement and compare the following frameworks: OpenPose, MediaPipe, and PoseNet, then select the suitable one that would ease the road to obtain a signer independent CArSLR system.

OpenPose

A real-time computer vision system that can accurately detect and track human body pose in images or videos, using a deep learning architecture to estimate the position of different body joints and establish connections between them, as shown in figure 9.

Figure 9. OpenPose Landmarks (Tam et al., 2022)

Label	Anatomical Landmark
0	Nose
1	Neck
2	Right Shoulder
3	Right Elbow
4	Right Wrist
5	Left Shoulder
6	Left Elbow
7	Left Wrist
8	Right Hip
9	Right Knee
10	Right Ankle
11	Left Hip
12	Left Knee
13	Left Ankle
14	Right Eye
15	Left Eye
16	Right Ear
17	Left Ear

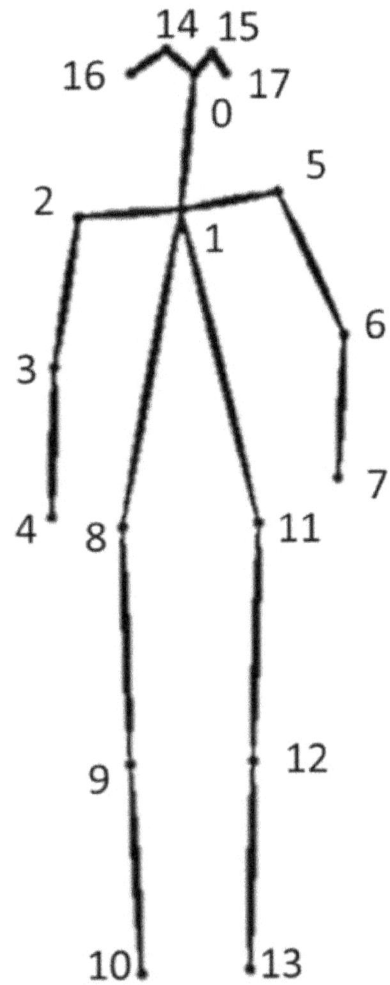

MediaPipe Holistic

A cross-platform framework developed by Google for real-time perception of human pose, face and hand landmarks tracking. It is composed of three main models that are: Pose, hand, and face mesh, as illustrated in figures 10, 11 and 12.

Figure 10. MediaPipe Pose (Mediapipe, 2023)

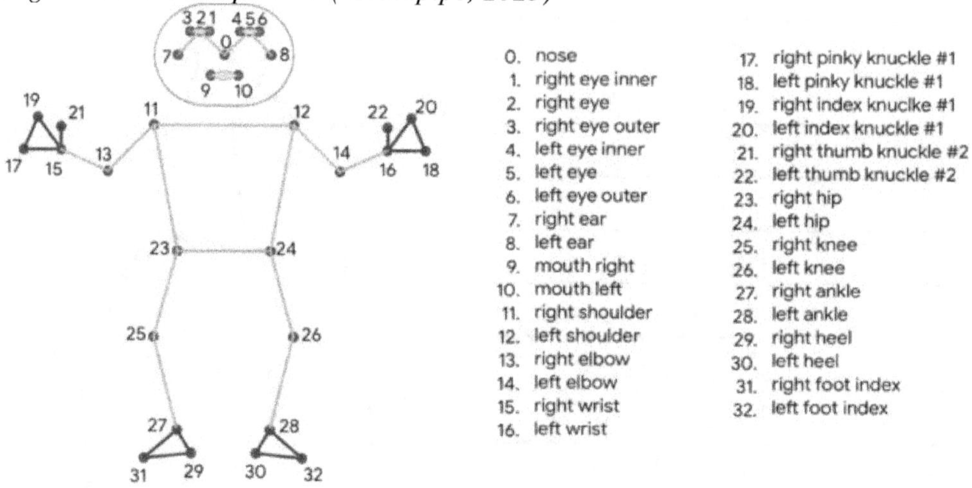

Figure 11. MediaPipe Hand (Lugaresi et al., 2019)

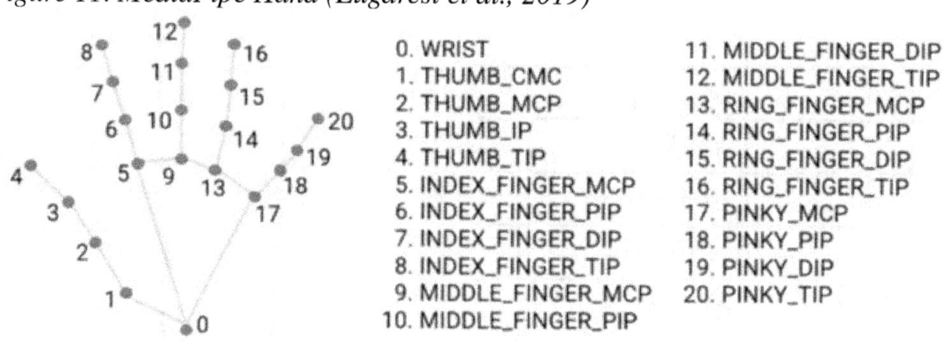

Figure 12. MediaPipe Face Mesh(468 points)

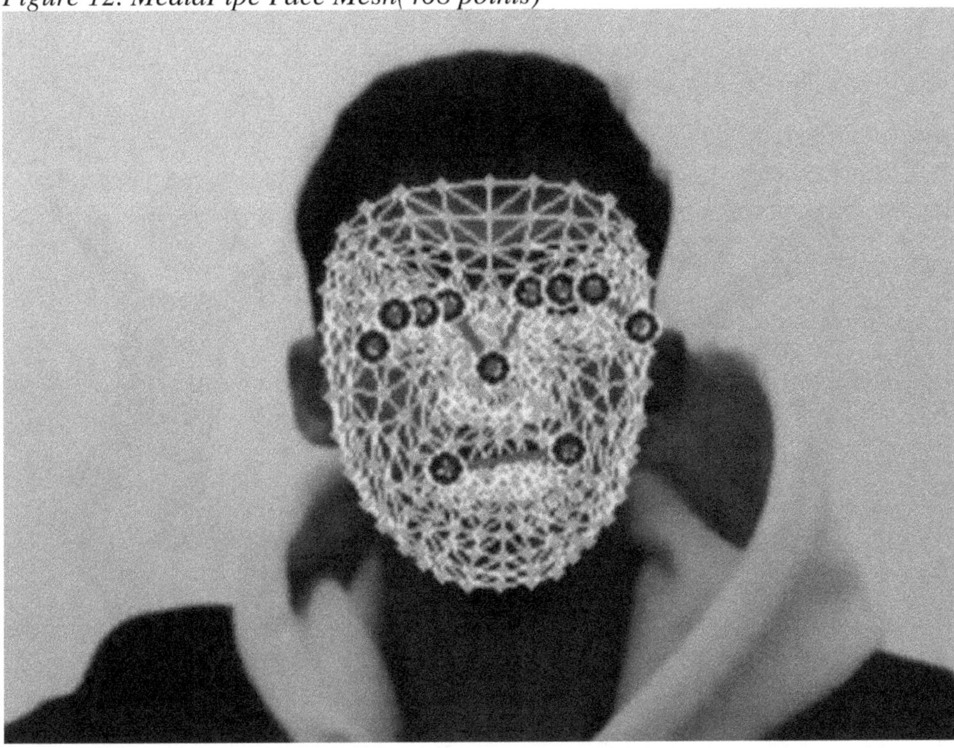

PoseNet

A deep learning pose estimation framework powered by Google, overcames scenarios where accurate information is crucial. It provides six degrees of freedom (6-DOF) relocalization, which defines the object's pose in a three-dimensional space, as shown in figure 13.

Figure 13. PoseNet Landmarks (Quantology et al., 2022)

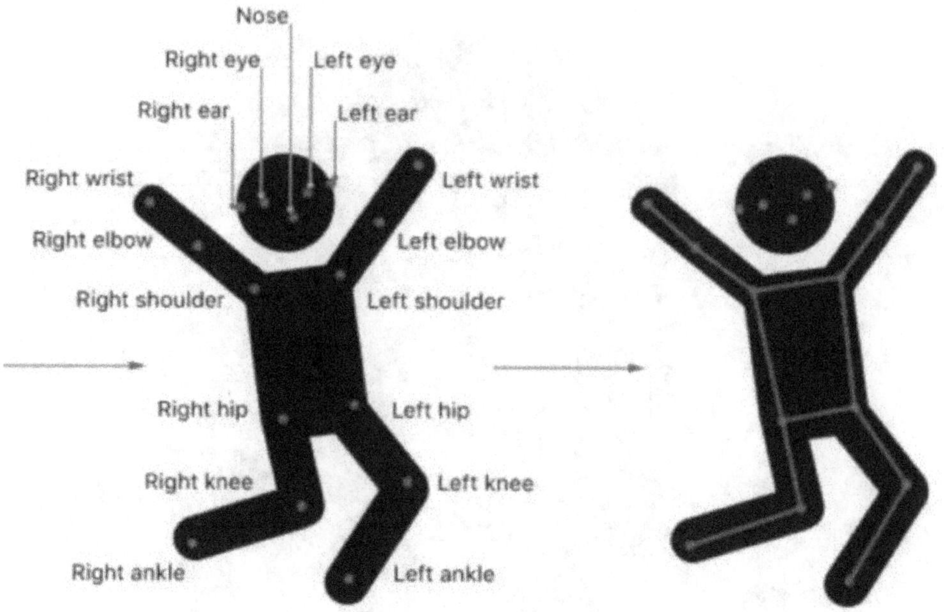

Experiment Results

We opted for testing the last three frameworks in real-time and a real-world environment creating a challenging scenario where a signer may be in-door or out-door trying to communicate using our system.

- Libraries and Implementation

First, we imported the necessary libraries for each framework, we only had to import the MediaPipe library since OpenPose heavily realize on OpenCV library, and PoseNet is implemented using TensorFlow's frameworks.

- Testing

We used our laptop's integrated camera and stood in the middle of the frame surrounded by people standing and walking, we noticed that each framework had its own advantages and limitations which we will resume in table 2:

Table 2. Frameworks Comparison

Framework	Advantages	Limitations
OpenPose	- More accurate performance for pose estimation - Customizable and big community support available (Open-source)	- Multi-person pose estimation - computationally intensive - Sensitive to occlusions - Incomplete estimation for overlapping body part scenarios.
MediaPipe	- Full body tracking - Efficient real-time performance. - Customizable, can be edited to fit special requirements.	- Very limited documentation - Heavily dependent on pre-trained models.
PoseNet	- Single-person pose estimation - Lightweight design.	- Lower performances than the previous frameworks - Sensitive towards occlusions and body parts overlapping.

- Evaluation

In light of the reported details, MediaPipe is without a doubt the most suitable framework for SLR, despite the good results provided by the other frameworks. However, SLR is a very complex task in which all the details of the signer's region of interest must be collected regardless of the environment and this is the point of exclusion for both frameworks. OpenPose detects multiple people at the time and was primarily committed to posture estimation alone, and even though PoseNet is specialized to single-person pose estimation, its outdoor performance was poor.

Datasets

As previously mentioned, the main issue faced by all previous research is data itself, since there is no public dynamic dataset available for Arabic Sign Language. We offer the following solutions for this issue:

- Using the " Arabic Sign Language "(ArSL) public dataset for the Static SLR system.
- Using the «Dynamic Sign Language» (DSL10) dataset available in (Saaman et al., 2022) to validate our model performances.
- Self-acquired data: we will use an iPhone Xs Max for collecting samples of videos of each sign that includes the hands, face, and body of the signer. After that we are going to use MediaPipe for both real-time landmarks dataset collection and feature extractions from the videos.

- Dialects: We will be collecting and testing our system on signs from the Algerian Sign Language, which has never been done previously.

Dataset Collection

After taking the initiative of learning Algerian Sign Language, we decided to collect our own dataset and provide it publicly for future research. We collected two types of dataset:

1. Video Dataset:

Various videos of 22 sign classes in both indoor and outdoor environments have been recorded as shown in figure 14:

Figure 14. Data Collection Videos

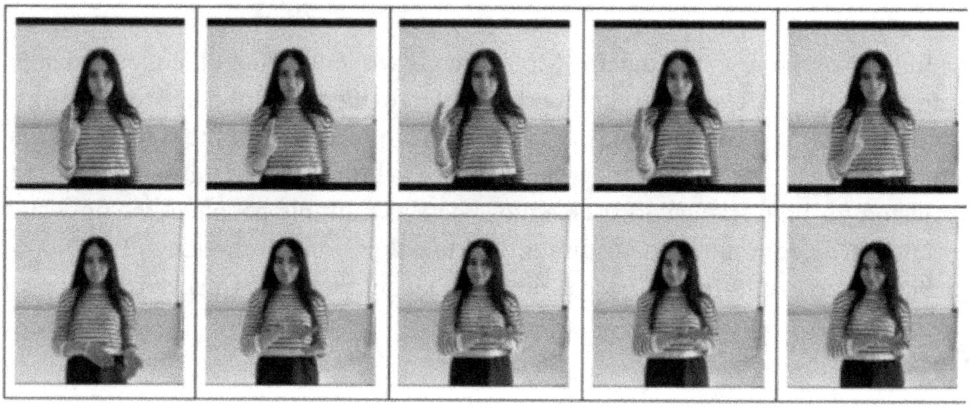

2. Landmark Dataset:

We will be using MediaPipe Holistic model, which detects landmark key points on face, hands, and pose. Each body part has it's own optimized model. We used our laptops integrated cameras to record this dataset. We created a script that allows us to extract features in real time from the frames, each frame contains 1662 landmarks.

Datasets Content

As previously mentioned, static datasets contains alphabets only, for dynamic however it differs depending on the type of the data (dialect) and which actions it contains, table 3 resumes the content of dataset used in our implementation process.

Table 3. Data sets Content

Dataset	Content
Arabic Sign Language ArSL(4651 images)	28 Arabic Letters (Alif, Ba,...., Ya)
DSL10 (750 video)	10 actions (Hello, Please, Sorry, Thanks, How are you?, Love, Mask, Wear, No and Yes.
Video Algerian SL (660 videos) (Ours)	22 actions ((' ',' ',' ',' ',' ',' ',' ',' ',' ',' ',' ',' ',' ',' ',' ',' ',' ',' ',' ',' '))
Landmark Algerian SL (1768 video) (Ours)	22 actions ((' ',' ',' ',' ',' ',' ',' ',' ',' ',' ',' ',' ',' ',' ',' ',' ',' ',' ',' ',' '))

However, All the previous dynamic datasets mentioned were balanced except "Video Algerian SL" adding to that DSL10 dataset signs were not accurate SL signs.

Features Extractions Using MediaPipe

Since continuous sign language involes both static and dynamic features, extraction from dynamic datasets is a challenging task because the location of the hands, face, and pose must be determined and tracked despite the differences of their shape and mouvement directions. MediaPipe is the suitable solution for this problem, it extracts the keypoints for three dimensions X, Y, Z of both hands, body, and face in each frame as shown in the previous figure 11, 12, 13.

Figure 15. MediaPipe Pipeline (Lugaresi, 2019)

MediaPipe is a multi-stage pipeline, as illustrated in figure 15, it estimates the human pose first, then:

1. Infers the pose landmarks after detecting the pose.
2. Uses the landmarks assigned to fix the other region of interest of the hands, and face.
3. Recrops each model to its section to improve the processing of these regions.
4. Crops the hand and face ROIs.
5. Estimates those regions and assigns their landmarks.
6. All landmarks merged to produce 1662 landmarks.

As for feature extraction from the Static Sign Language dataset the process starts first by detecting the palm of the hand then cropping the region of interests and assigning the hand landmarks, because it contains hands figures only.

Hand Keypoints: Keypoints in hand x Number of hand x Three dimensions= (21 x 2 x 3) = 126 Keypoints.

Pose Keypoints: Keypoints in pose x (Three dimensions + Visibility) = (33 x (3 + 1) = 132 Keypoints.

MediaPipe Holistic Keypoints: Hand Keypoints + Pose Keypoints + Face Mesh Keypoints = 1662 Keypoints.

Evaluation methods

Every model used in the context of this study is a multi-class classification model, the action is predicted based on the highest class/sign probability/word probability. We will use the following metrics in a one-vs.-all approach:

1. Categorical Accuracy measures the proportion of correctly classified samples.

$$\text{Categorical Accuracy} = \frac{\text{Number of Correct Predictions}}{\text{Total Number of Predictions}} \tag{5}$$

2. Precision measures the proportion of correctly predicted positives samples out of all samples predicted as positive.

$$\text{Precision} = \frac{\text{True Positives}}{\text{True Positives} + \text{False Positives}} \tag{6}$$

3. Recall Also known as sensitivity or True Positives Rate, it measures the proportion of correctly predicted positive samples out of all actual positive samples.

$$\text{Recall} = \frac{\text{True Positives}}{\text{True Positives} + \text{False Negatives}} \tag{7}$$

4. F1 Score Known as the harmonic mean of precision and recall, providing a balanced measure of the model's performance.

$$\text{F1 Score} = 2 * \left(\frac{\text{Precision} \cdot \text{Recall}}{\text{Precision} + \text{Recall}}\right) \tag{8}$$

5. Real-time Validation: we will test our models in real-time recognition using two approaches:
    - **Signer Dependent mode:** the test is performed on data never seen yet by the model but by the same signer who generated the training data.
    - **Signer Independent mode:** testing is done by a different signer in order to evaluate the generalization of the system and its ability to recognize signs performed by signers not seen during training.

Static Sign Recognition Model

Data Pre-processing

We extracted the hand features using MediaPipe Hand from the ArSl data and assigned each instance its corresponding label.

Instead of using all keypoints of the hand inferred by mediapipe we substracted the cartesian coordinates of the center of the hand from the cartesian coordinates of every last 3 joints of each finger resulting in a flattened vector of shape (1,30) with 30 being the number of features.

Considering we have 28 letters with each letter having a different number of samples, our final tensor will be of shape (total number of samples, 1, 30) split into 80% for testing and 20% for validation.

Training

The model details will be disclosed in table 4:

Table 4. Static Model Details

Parameters	Value
Type of Layers	DENSE
Number of Layers	3
Number of units	30, 15, 28 for the each layer respectively
Activation functions	RELU and SoftMax
Optimizer	Adam
Learning rate	0.001
Batch size	32
Number of epochs	1000
Loss function	Categorical cross entropy

Evaluation

After training our model we reported the following results

Figure 16. Static Model Metrics

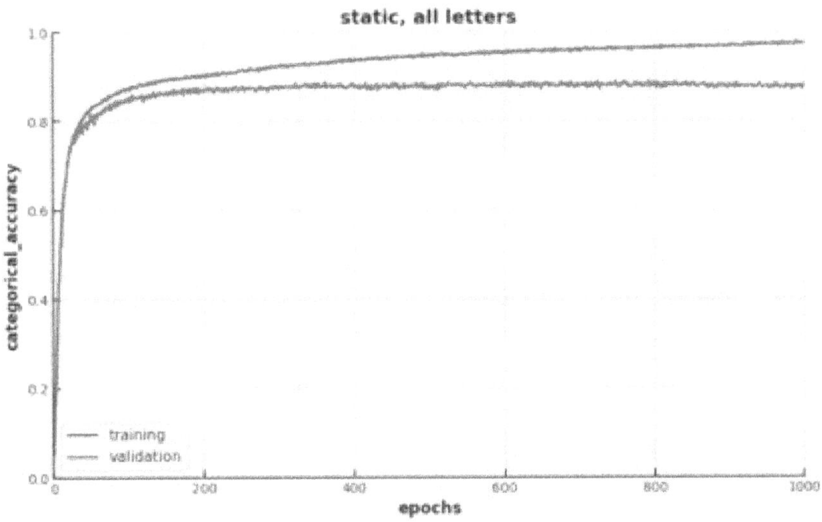

(a)

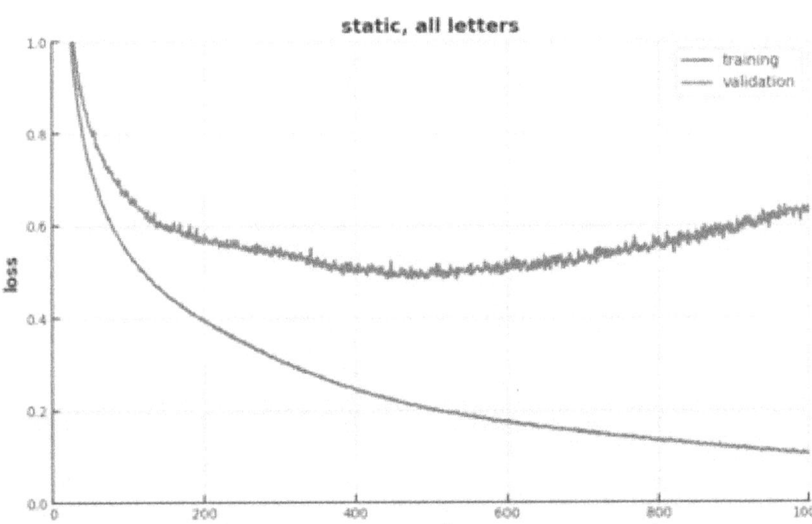

(b)

As shown in the figure 16 (a) and (b), the training loss is converging while the validation loss is diverging, which indicates that the model is slightly overfitting and the best number of epochs for this case is a range between 150 and 400 rather than 1000. However, we also tested it also in signer-independent mode and the generalization results are still acceptable (figure 17 (a), (b)).

Figure 17. Static Signer In-dependent testing

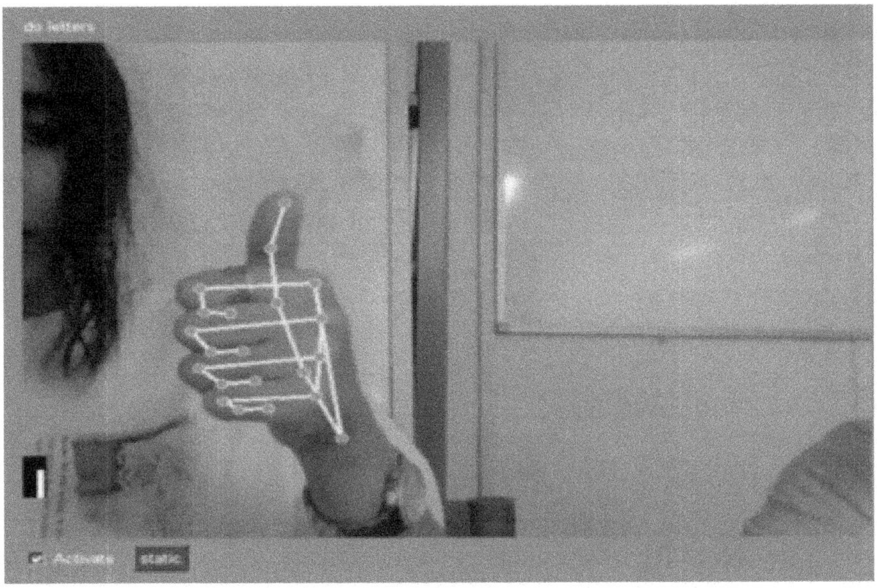

(a)

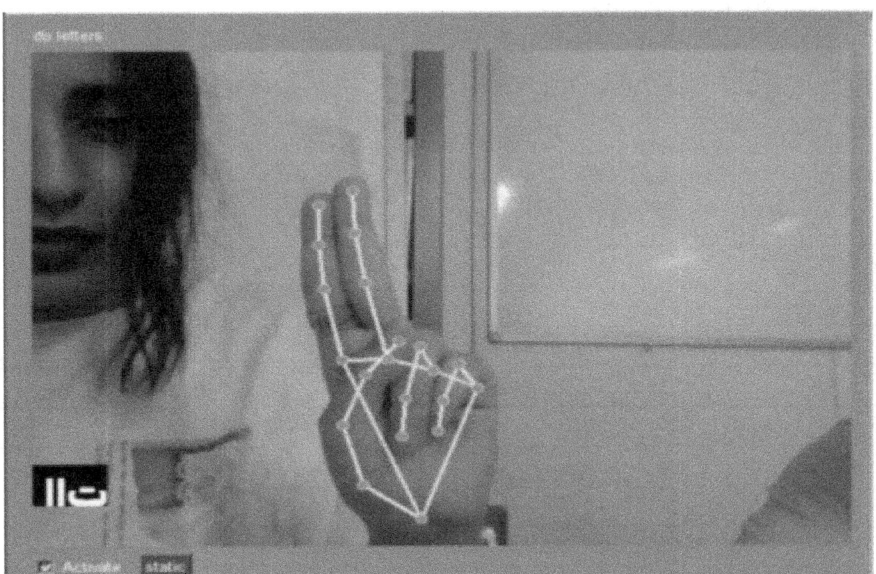

(b)

Dynamic Sign Language Recognition Model

In this section we will explore 5 main stages, each one representing a notable difference from the previous stage. All stages share some similarities that are crucial to understanding how each model works, we will cite them below:

- Raw data is acquired by taking 30 frames in rapid succesion and running each one through mediapipe to obtain an object describing the cartesian coordinates of every landmark.
- For every frame we will process the object to extract relevant features, organize them into arrays and dispose of the rest.

Stage 1: Original Model

- Data Preprocessing

Data is processed from mediapipe and no landmarks are disposed of which results in an array of (30, 1662) with 1662 being the number of features, taking into account x,y,z coordinates and visibility and considering we have 3 actions and 30 videos per action, our final tensor will be of shape (90,30,1662) split into 90% for training and 5% for validation.

- Training: Model details (Table 5)

Table 5. Original Model Details

Parameters	Value
Type of Layers	LSTM,DENSE
Number of Layers	5
Number of units	64,128,64 for LSTM layers and 64,32 for Dense layers respectively
Activation functions	RELU and SoftMax
Optimizer	RMS prop
Learning rate	0.001
Batch size	32
Number of epochs	2000
Loss function	Categorical cross entropy

- Evaluation

The model achieved relatively high accuracy and low loss however it is not a reliable indicator at this point. The model performs relatively well for real time testing but only if he signer does not change his distance from the camera which is a serious disadvantage.

Stage 2: 2D Coordinates Only

The main difference with its predecessor is that we removed the z and visibility components from the raw data and only considered the x and y coordinates as features while also increasing the number of actions to 8.

- Data Preprocessing

All landmarks from the object were used but only x and y coordinates for every landmark were taken into our final array of shape (30,1086), given that we have 8 actions our final tensor will be of shape (240,30,1086) split into 95% for training and 5% for testing.

- Training: Model details (Table 6)

We introduced a new dropout layer between LSTM layers to prevent overfitting.

Table 6. Stage 02 Model Details

Parameters	Value
Type of Layers	LSTM, Dropout, DENSE
Number of Layers	6
Number of units	100,64 for LSTM layers and 128,64,32 for Dense layers respectively
Activation functions	RELU and SoftMax
Optimizer	RMS prop
Learning rate	0.001
Batch size	32
Number of epochs	500
Loss function	Categorical cross entropy

- Evaluation

Figure 18. Stage 2: Evaluation Metrics

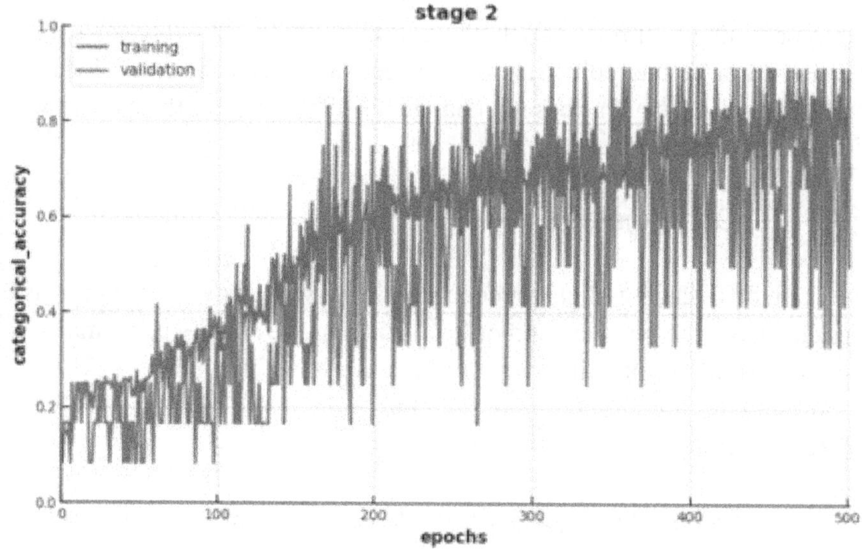

(a)

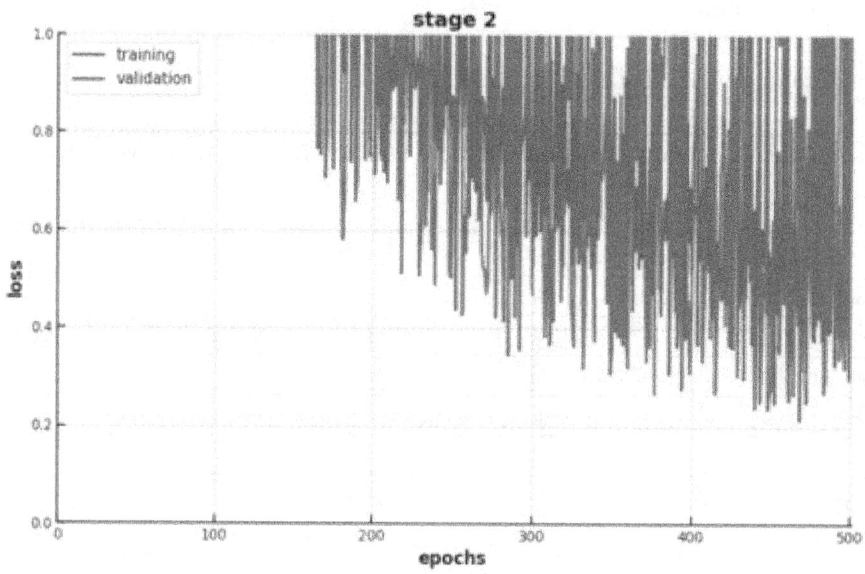

(b)

The chart indicates inconclusive results since the size of the features employed was significantly larger than the quantity of the training and testing data. The model's performance (Shown in table 6) was unsatisfactory and challenging to evaluate. There was a significant fluctuation of 40% in the categorical accuracy value between two consecutive epochs, primarily due to the limited size of the validation data. At the last epoch, it achieved 50% of accuracy (figure 18(a)) and 11.3% of loss (figure 18(b)).

Stage 3: Lowering Features Numbers

In this stage we used a normalized dataset DSL10 with a total of 10 actions and 75 per action.

- Data Preprocessing

For this stage we used a lower number of keypoints by disposing of all the face landmarks except the center of the nose and keeping only upper torso landmarks in order to eliminate the noise during inference while also replacing each hand landmark by the angle formed with every other landmark in the same hand resulting in a matrix of shape (30, 84).

This reduced shape allows for better detection and lower computation time, our final tensor will be of shape (750, 30, 84) split into 90% for training and 10% for validation.

- Training: Model details (Table 7)

Table 7. Stage 3 Model Details

Parameters	Value
Type of Layers	LSTM, DENSE
Number of Layers	3
Number of units	128,64 for LSTM layers respectively and 20 for Dense layer
Activation functions	RELU and SoftMax
Optimizer	RMS prop
Learning rate	0.001
Batch size	32
Number of epochs	50
Loss function	Categorical cross entropy

- Evaluation

The model achieved 100% accuracy and 0.06% of loss, metrics shows that we have a more performant model by decreasing the number of features, it can be verified by real time testing resulting in significant increase in reliability.

Stage 4: Interpretation Change

This stage marks the final change in how data is interpreted while replacing the DSL10 dataset by a custom-made Algerian dataset.

- Data Preprocessing

For this iteration, instead of using the raw landmarks given by mediapipe we will do some processing before storing it in the array. We will start by substracting x, y coordinates of a reference point from every x,y coordinates of every landmarks.

We will use 3 reference points: the center of the nose being the reference point for every landmark in the upper torso ranging from shoulders to wrists, the center of the palm of the left hand being the reference point of the last 3 joints for every finger in the left hand and finally the center of the palm of the right hand being the reference point of the last 3 joints for every finger in the right hand.

This process allows for a geometrical vector representation of the information used for inference, increasing the chances of a correct classification and completely making the signer independent from the frame.

With this in mind and having 22 actions we will get a tensor shape of (543, 30, 72) split into 80% for training and 20% for validation. Notice that 543 is not a multiple of 22 due to high imbalance in the dataset.

- Training:

Model Hyper parameters details in table 8:

Table 8. Stage 4 Model Details

Parameters	Value
Type of Layers	Bi-LSTM
Number of Layers	2
Number of units	72,25 LSTM respectively
Activation functions	RELU and SoftMax

continued on following page

Table 8. Continued

Parameters	Value
Optimizer	Adam
Learning rate	0.001
Batch size	32
Number of epochs	50
Loss function	Categorical cross entropy

- Evaluation

This model achieved 97.24% accuracy (figure 19(a)) and 1.13% of loss (figure19(b)), better than all its predecessors. We noticed a real increase in performance while real time testing and acceptable speed. However the model was more biased toward some actions than others, and wrong detection happened too often to be used in a real time conversation.

Figure 19. Stage 04: Categorical Accuracy, Loss

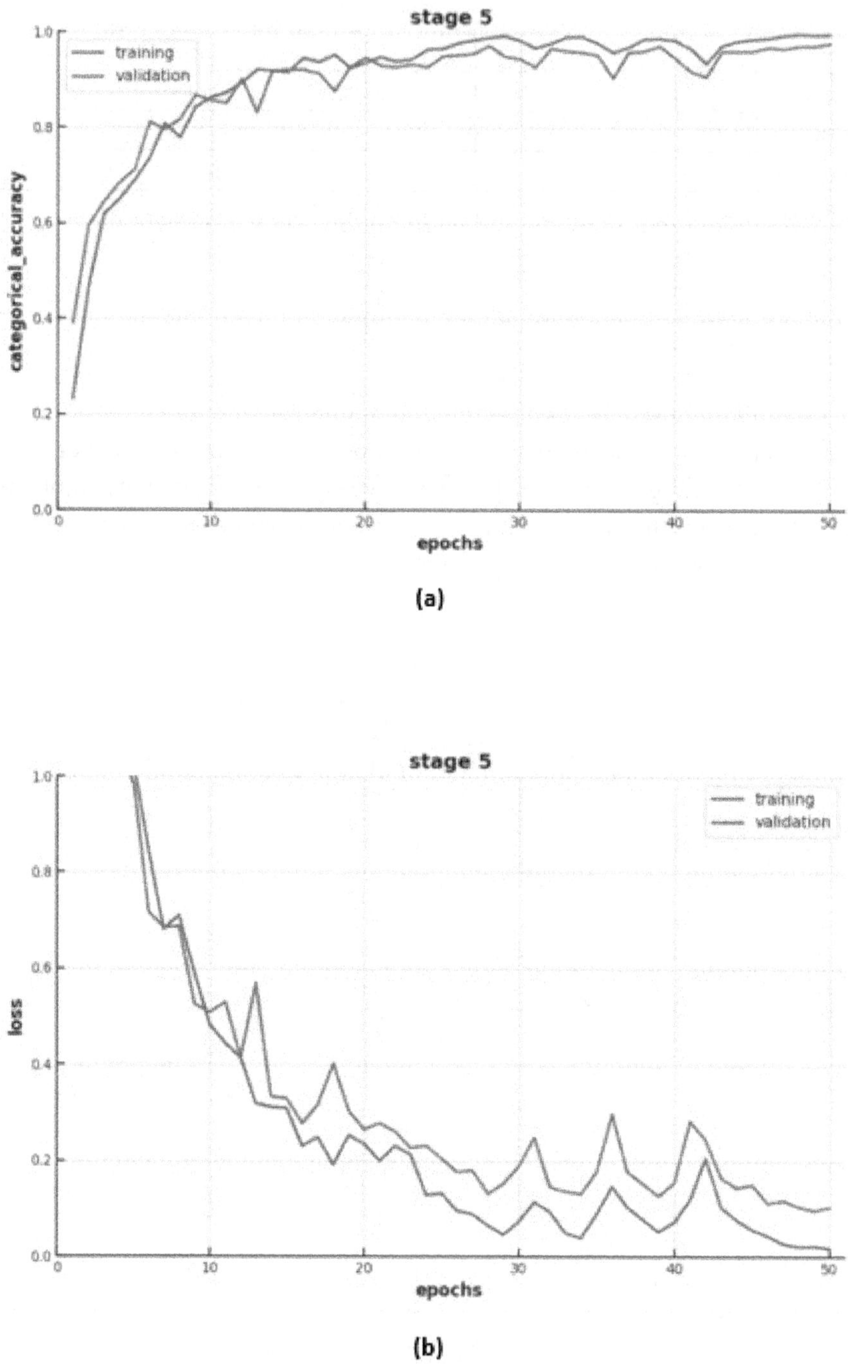

The following charts (figure 20(a), (b), (c)) show an unstable variation in recall, demonstrating biased recognition in the model trained on an imbalanced dataset. The erratic behavior of recall values across classes indicates the difficulties of correctly identifying positive samples, especially in classes with fewer samples.

Figure 20. Stage 04: Precision, Recall, F1 Score

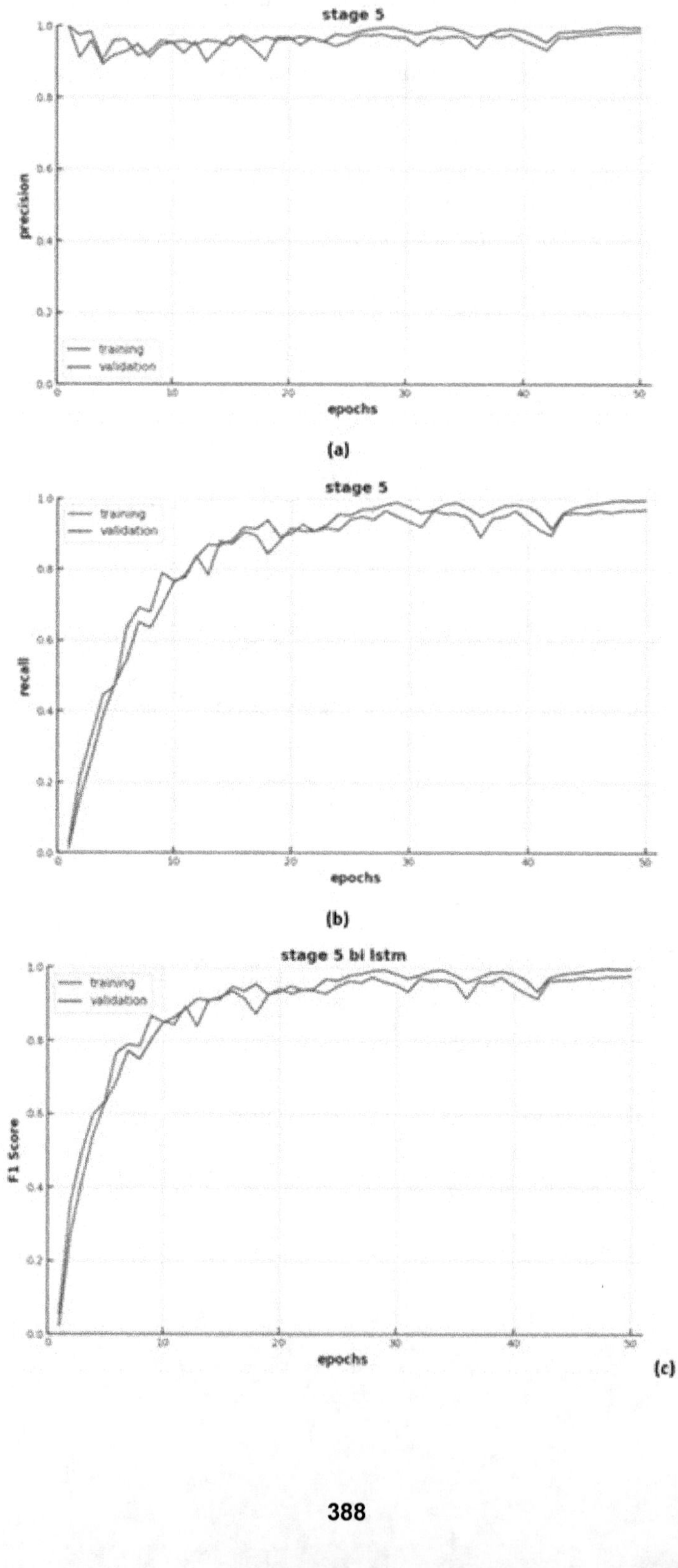

Final model

The main difference in this stage is the dataset, we increased the number of videos to +1700 samples.

- Data Preprocessing

Data was processed exactly the same way as stage with same splitting but with a tensor shape of (1725, 30, 72) since the number of videos per action increased to 75.

- Training

During this stage, we trained with two models: LSTM and Bi-LSTM. The construction and architecture of both models are the same, as illustrated in figure 21. The model specifications are in table 9:

Table 9. Final Model Details

Parameters	**Value**
Type of Layers	LSTM or Bi-LSTM,DENSE
Number of Layers	3
Number of units	72,64 for Bi-LSTM/LSTM layers respectively and 25 for Dense layer
Activation functions	RELU and SoftMax
Optimizer	Adam
Learning rate	0.001
Batch size	32
Number of epochs	50
Loss function	Categorical cross entropy

Figure 21. Final Model Structure

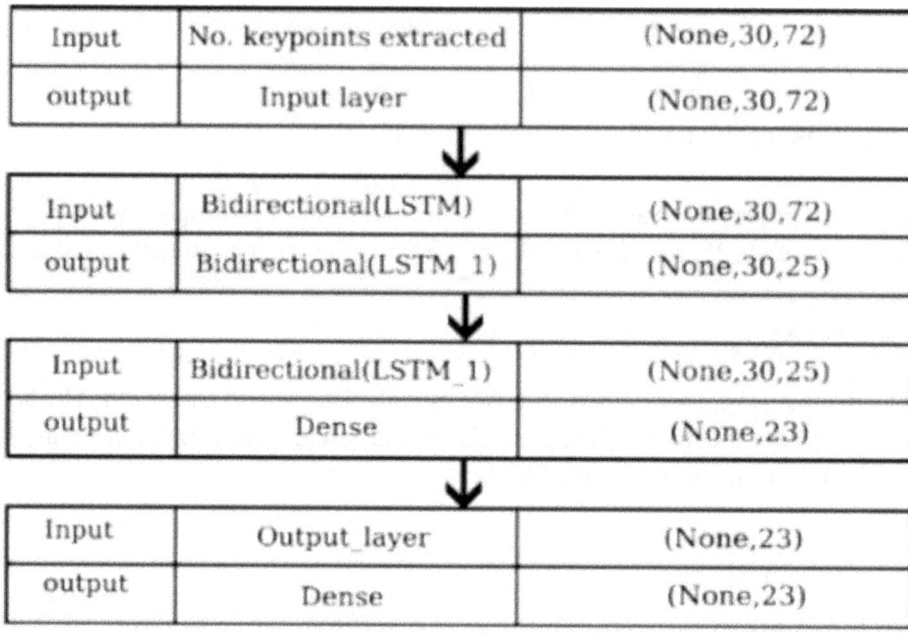

- Evaluation

We noticed that LSTM gave better results than Bi-LSTM as shown in table 10:

Table 10. Bi-LSTM and LSTM Evaluation Scores

Model	**Categorical Accuracy**	**Loss**	**Precision**	**Recall**	**F1-Score**
LSTM Model	98.03%	0.12%	98.58%	97.75%	98.16%
Bi-LSTM Model	97.75%	0.104%	98.57%	96.91%	97.73%

Nevertheless, during real-time testing, significant improvements were observed in the performance of the Bi-LSTM model compared to LSTM. With the appropriate allocation of resources and dedication, further fine-tuning of the Bi-LSTM model can lead to even better accuracy scores.

Natural Language Processing Model

Data Preprocessing

Dataset for this model simple compared to the other models, commonly used Arabic sentences were grouped into a list and tokenized using n-grams method considering the goal of this model is to predict the next word based on the currently inferred sentence, as shown in figure 22.

- Tokenization Words are converted into numbers and stored in a dictionary where each word corresponds to a unique number. Lists containing sequences of numbers of different lengths are created to match the sentences, for example a sentence of m words will result in m sequences of numbers each one of length L(n)=n where 1<=n<=m.
- Padding Zeros will be added to the start of each sentence to match the length of the sentence with maximum length, this process allows faster matrix operations.
- Extracting the features and targets: the target vector will contain all the last elements of each sequence while the remaining matrix will be used as features.

Figure 22. NLP Process

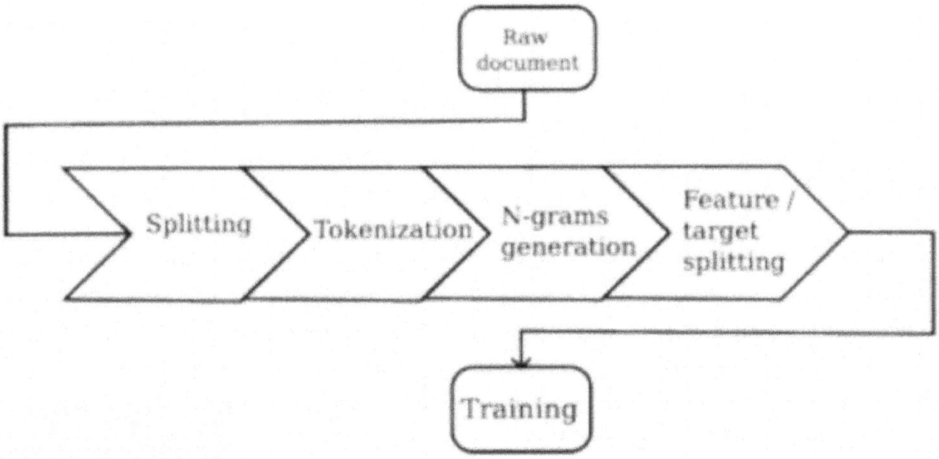

Training

We will use a predictive model using BI-LSTM layers to capture the entire context of the sentence and infer accurate words. See the details in table 11:

Table 11. NLP model details

Parameters	Value
Type of Layers	Embedding, BI-LSTM, DENSE
Number of Layers	3
Number of neurons	Number of words, 150, number of words
Activation functions	RELU and SoftMax
Optimizer	Adam
Learning rate	0.001
Batch size	32
Number of epochs	500
Loss function	Categorical cross entropy

Evaluation

The model converges at 80% and 60% for loss and accuracy respectively which suggests bad performance due to the lack of a proper dataset. However in the context of this study since we have low numbers of words it performs well enough for a demonstration and can be used as a proof of concept for future research on the matter.

Real Time Recognition

Our best performing model is then employed in conjunction with MediaPipe to conduct tests in real time, utilizing a methodology similar to data collection, where MediaPipe Holistic is employed to detect and render key points on the hands, face and body in real time via the computer camera. Rather than collecting key points and testing the model on them, we incorporate the model to create an action detection system that predicts signs in real time.

The seven signs are displayed on the screen, and once the signer makes a sign, the system calculates the probability of the sign belonging to a particular class. This probability is reflected on the screen as a bar that increases and decreases in real-time for each sign based on the calculated probability. Once the system predicts the class, the class is displayed as text. The system predicts continuously, and the text is displayed in sequence according to the prediction. Figure 23 shows an example of the display. This is a visual representation in which Arabic words corresponding to Algerian Sign Language are printed at the bottom of the screen.

Figure 23. Sample View for Real-Time Recognition

Discussion

Our study has two primary goals:

1- Assessing the current state of Arabic Sign Language (ArSL) recognition research using deep learning and identifying key gaps.
2- Developing a deep learning-based recognition system to address these gaps.

Addressing the First Objective

Through a systematic review, we found that the lack of a standardized, diverse dataset is the major obstacle in ArSL research. Existing datasets are limited to static alphabet images, failing to capture the dynamic, continuous nature of real-world signing. Additionally, deaf communities often prefer their native sign languages over ArSL.

The Potential of Deep Learning

Deep learning can significantly advance sign language recognition by handling both feature extraction and classification. However, its performance depends heavily on large, high-quality training data, which is currently insufficient for ArSL.

Addressing the Second Objective

To bridge this gap, we explored alternative data collection methods and identified Google's MediaPipe Holistic, an open-source framework capable of detecting hand, face, and body landmarks in real time. Unlike device-dependent solutions (e.g., Leap Motion, Kinect), MediaPipe offers a comprehensive, multi-platform approach without additional hardware.

Implementation and Optimization

We developed an Algerian Sign Language (ESL) recognition system using MediaPipe. To our knowledge, this is the first work applying deep learning to ESL, as most prior research focuses on isolated ArSL words despite regional preferences for local sign languages.

We optimized the model through hyperparameter fine tuning, prioritizing accuracy improvement and log loss reduction. However, due to the stochastic nature of deep learning, performance can vary across datasets, as observed in our experiments.

Our experiments highlight a critical challenge in deep learning for sign language recognition: models must be optimized for the specific dataset they are trained on and often struggle to generalize without extensive, diverse training data.

Limitations and Future Improvements

- **Data scarcity:** Despite collecting 30 videos per sign (30 frames each, 1,662 landmarks per frame), the dataset remains small for robust generalization.
- **Variability in signing:** Differences in hand position, speed, and signing style between datasets affect performance.
- **Solution:** Expanding training data with more signers, diverse speeds, and signing variations would enhance generalization.

Advantages of Our Approach

1- **Cost-effective & scalable:** Unlike Kinect/Leap Motion, our MediaPipe-based system requires only a webcam, enabling global data collection via web/mobile apps.

2- **Real-time recognition:** Our system processes signs continuously and in real time, making it practical for real-world applications.

3- **Open-source & lightweight:** MediaPipe runs on CPU (no GPU needed) and is platform-agnostic, reducing deployment barriers.

CONCLUSION

This study has provided valuable insight into the realization of a real time CArSL application and has contributed to the ongoing research of arabic sign language recognition. The results have demonstrated a significant attainment of the sought-after objective, indicating a considerable level of achievability.

However, it is important to recognize the limitations of this study. The scarcity of previously available datasets and lack of resources convey significant difficulty towards the creation of an efficient and reliable application. Additionally, the dataset size was relatively small and future studies could benefit more diverse data.

Overall, the allocation of adequate resources to further studies stemming from this research is expected to yield substantial improvements in the application and practical implementation of the findings, resulting in enhanced outcomes and advancements in the respective field.

Future work should focus on:

- **Larger, more diverse datasets** to improve generalization.
- **Real-world deployment** for continuous sign language recognition.
- **Further optimization** to balance accuracy and generalizability.

REFERENCES

Abdelouafi, H. (2019). *Teaching Sign Language to the Deaf Children in Adrar.*

Abdul, W., Alsulaiman, M., Amin, S. U., Faisal, M., Muhammad, G., Albogamy, F. R., Bencherif, M. A., & Ghaleb, H. (2021). Intelligent real-time Arabic sign language classification using attention-based inception and BiLSTM. *Computers & Electrical Engineering*, *95*, 107–395. DOI: 10.1016/j.compeleceng.2021.107395

Al-Barham., ... (2023). RGB Arabic Alphabets SL dataset. url: https://paperswithcode .com/dataset/rgbarabic-alphabets-sign-language-dataset

Alawwad, R. A., Bchir, O., & Maher, M. (2021). Arabic sign language recognition using Faster R-CNN. *International Journal of Advanced Computer Science and Applications*, *12*(3), 3. DOI: 10.14569/IJACSA.2021.0120380

Ali Almahri, H. G. (2022). Arabic Sign Language Recognition: A Deep Learning Approach. P*hD thesis. The British University in Dubai (BUiD).*

Alnahhas, A.. (2020). Enhancing the recognition of Arabic sign language by using deep learning and leap motion controller. *International Journal of Scientific and Technology Research*, *9*(4), 1865–1870.

Aloysius, N., Geetha, M. (2020). Understanding vision-based continuous sign language recognition". *Multimedia Tools and Applications: 79.31-32, 22177-22209.*

Aly, S., & Aly, W. (2020). DeepArSLR: A novel signer-independent deep learning framework for isolated arabic sign language gestures recognition. *IEEE Access : Practical Innovations, Open Solutions*, *8*, 83199–83212. DOI: 10.1109/ACCESS.2020.2990699

ArSL Alphabets. url: https://www.arabamerica.com/do-you-know-about-deafcommunities-and-arabic-sign-languages-in-the-arab-world/

Belmadoui, S. (2022). ArSL Arabic Sign Language Dataset. https://www.kaggle .com/datasets /sabribelmadoui/arabic-sign-language-unaugmented-dataset

Bencherif, M., Algabri, M., Mekhtiche, M. A., Faisal, M., Alsulaiman, M., Mathkour, H., Al-Hammadi, M., & Ghaleb, H. (2021). Arabic sign language recognition system using 2D hands and body skeleton data. *IEEE Access : Practical Innovations, Open Solutions*, *9*, 59612–59627. DOI: 10.1109/ACCESS.2021.3069714

Boukdir, A.. (2021). Isolated Video-Based Arabic Sign Language Recognition Using Convolutional and Recursive Neural Networks. *Arabian Journal for Science and Engineering*, •••, 1–13.

CS2R, Center of Smart Robotics Research, (2022). KSU-ArSL, Arabic Sign language. *IEEE Dataport, doi: https://dx.doi.org/*DOI: 10.21227/8axv-ma58

Camgo, N. C.. (2017). Subunets: End-to-end hand shape and continuous sign language recognition. *Proceedings of the IEEE international conference on computer vision,* 3056-3065.

Cao, Z.. (2017). Realtime multi-person 2d pose estimation using part affinity fields. *Proceedings of the IEEE conference on computer vision and pattern recognition,* 7291-7299. DOI: 10.1109/CVPR.2017.143

Dense Layers. url: https://www.oreilly.com/library/view/tensorflowfordeep/9781491980446/ch04.html

DGV-5 Gloves. url: http://www.dg-tech.it/vhand3/products.html

El Ghoul, O.. (2022). JUMLA-QSL-22: A dataset of Qatari sign language sentences. *IEEE Dataport, doi: https://dx.doi.org/*DOI: 10.21227/ckzp-3754

ElBadawy, M., ... (2014). A proposed hybrid sensor architecture for arabic sign language recognition. *Intelligent Systems: Proceedings of the 7th International Conference Intelligent Systems IS'2014, Warsaw, Poland, Tools, Architectures, Systems, Applications: Springer, 2, 721-730.*

ElBadawy, M., ... (2017). Arabic sign language recognition with 3d convolutional neural networks". IEEE *Eighth international conference on intelligent computing and information systems (ICICIS), 66-71.* Electromygrophy(EMG). url: https://www.myupchar.com/en/test/emg-electromyography

Elons, A. S. (2014). GPU implementation for arabic sign language real time recognition using multi-level multiplicative neural networks. *IEEE2014 9th International Conference on Computer Engineering & Systems (ICCES), 360-367.*

Ghazanfar, L.. (2020). An automatic Arabic sign language recognition system based on deep CNN: An assistive system for the deaf and hard of hearing. *International Journal of Computing and Digital Systems*, *9*(4), 715–724. DOI: 10.12785/ijcds/090418

Grishchenko, L., ... (2020). Attention mesh: High-fidelity face mesh prediction in realtime. *arXiv preprint arXiv:2006.10962.*

Guo, D., Zhou, W., Li, H., & Wang, M. (2018). Hierarchical LSTM for sign language translation. *Proceedings of the AAAI Conference on Artificial Intelligence*, *32*(1), 1. DOI: 10.1609/aaai.v32i1.12235

Hayani, S.. (2019). Arab sign language recognition with convolutional neural networks. *IEEE International Conference of Computer Science and Renewable Energies (ICCSRE):* 1-4. DOI: 10.1109/ICCSRE.2019.8807586

Hisham, B., & Hamouda, A. (2017). Arabic Static and Dynamic Gestures Recognition Using Leap Motion. *Journal of Computational Science, 13*(8), 337–354. DOI: 10.3844/jcssp.2017.337.354

Huang, Z., ... (2015). Bidirectional LSTM-CRF models for sequence tagging. *arXiv preprint arXiv:1508.0199.*

Ihianle, IK. et al. (2020). A deep learning approach for human activities recognition from multimodal sensing devices. *IEEE Access 8:179028–179038. . 2020. 30279 79*DOI: 10. 1109/ ACCESS

Kendall, A., Grimes, M., ... (2015). Posenet: A convolutional network for real-time 6-dof camera relocalization. Proceedings of the IEEE international conference on computer vision, 2938-2946. Kinect Microsoft Sensor. https://www.reallusion.com/iclone/help/iclone5/pro/08_animation/device_mocap/using_the_device_mocap_panel.html

Kitchenham, B. (2004). Procedures for performing systematic reviews. *Keele, UK, Keele University: 33.2004, 1-26.*

Lugaresi, C., ... (2019). Mediapipe: A framework for building perception pipelines. inarXiv preprint arXiv:1906.08172.

Mediapipe, 2023. MediaPipe Holistic. *Github. url:*https://github.com/google/mediapipe/blob/master/docs/solutions/holistic.md

Mohamed Aktham, A., ... (2018). A review on systems-based sensory gloves for sign language recognition state of the art between 2007 and 2017. *In Sensors: 18.7, 2208.*

Moryossef, A.. (2021). Evaluating the immediate applicability of pose estimation for sign language recognition. *Proceedings of the IEEE/CVF Conference on Computer Vision and Pattern Recognition,* 3434-3440. DOI: 10.1109/CVPRW53098.2021.00382

Ouzzani, M., Hammady, H., Fedorowicz, Z., & Elmagarmid, A. (2016). Rayyan-a web and mobile app for systematic reviews. *Systematic Reviews, 5*(1), 1–10. DOI: 10.1186/s13643-016-0384-4 PMID: 27919275

Quantology, N., ... (2022). YOGA POSE CORRECTION USING POSENET. 20. 1758-1763. : https://www.researchgate.net/figure/Posenet-Dataof-Yoga-Pose-A-Pose-object-contains-17-key-points-for-identifying-17-key_fig3_362280366DOI: 10.14704/nq.2022.20.7.NQ33220.url

Renotte, N. (2023). Github Repository. url: https://github.com/nicknochnack/ActionDetectionforSignLanguage

Ritonga, M. et al. (2021). Machine Learning Approach for Gesture Based Arabic Sign Language Recognition for Impaired People.

Samaan, G. et al. (2022). MediaPipe's Landmarks with RNN for Dynamic Sign Language Recognition. *Electronics: 11.19, 3228.*

Sharma, S., Gupta, R., & Kumar, A. (2023). Continuous Sign Language Recognition Transfer Learning. *Journal of Ambient Intelligence and Humanized Computing*, *14*, 1531–1542. DOI: 10.1007/s12652-021-03418-z

Sidig., ... (2021). KArSL: Arabic Sign Language Database. in KArSL Dataset. url: https://paperswithcode.com/dataset/karsl

Staudemeyer, R. C., ... Rothstein, E. M. (2019). Understanding LSTM–a tutorial into long short-term memory recurrent neural networks. inarXiv *preprint arXiv:1909.09586.*

Suliman, W.. (2021). Arabic Sign Language Recognition Using Deep Learning. *4th International Symposium on Advanced Electrical and Communication Technologies (ISAECT),* Alkhobar, Saudi Arabia, 1-4, DOI: 10.1109/ISAECT53699.2021.9668405

Tam, A. Y., Zha, L.-W., So, B. P.-H., Lai, D. K.-H., Mao, Y.-J., Lim, H.-J., Wong, D. W.-C., & Cheung, J. C.-W. (2022). Depth-Camera-Based Under-Blanket Sleep Posture Classification Using Anatomical Landmark-Guided Deep Learning Model. *International Journal of Environmental Research and Public Health*, *19*(20), 2022. DOI: 10.3390/ijerph192013491 PMID: 36294072

Yousuf, F. H., Alwarfalli, A. B., ... (2021). Arabic Sign Language Recognition System by Using Surface Intelligent EMG Signal. *The 7th International Conference on Engineering & MIS 2021, 1-6.*

Section 5
Human Activities, Learning, and Behavior

Chapter 11
Decoding Human Activities:
Algorithms, Frameworks, and Challenges in Recognition Systems

Mohd Aquib Ansari
https://orcid.org/0000-0002-9083-1523
Bennett University, India

Lalit Kumar
https://orcid.org/0000-0002-8441-1696
MCAET, India

Arvind Mewada
Bennett University, India

Sushil Kumar Maurya
Siksha 'O' Anushandhan, India

Shahnawaz Ahmad
Bennett University, India

Rahat Naz
IILM University, India

Lokesh Malviya
VIT Bhopal University, India

ABSTRACT

Human activity recognition is an attractive research area with high demand in surveillance, and it focuses on effectively encoding and classifying human activities. Therefore, this article explores Human Activity Recognition (HAR), focusing on algorithms, systems, and challenges in identifying and classifying activities using visual and sensor data. It discusses the importance of HAR in healthcare, sports, security, and human-computer interaction, emphasising advancements in technology and ongoing research. The article presented various frameworks for categorising complex human activities based on complexity levels. Here, a detailed description of image pre-processing, feature extraction, feature classification, datasets involved in

DOI: 10.4018/979-8-3373-0735-0.ch011

activity recognition, and performance measures has been discussed. Feature extraction techniques are briefly discussed, including local descriptors and motion-based and appearance-based methods. In addition, classification techniques are discussed here, along with their advantages, limitations, and applicability. Afterwards, this article discusses a literature survey on existing human activity recognition techniques and commonly used datasets and performance indicators, as well as an overview of the evaluation criteria used in HAR.

1. INTRODUCTION

Human Activity Recognition (HAR) can be defined as a subfield in both computer science and artificial intelligence, which involves creating several algorithms and systems meant to recognise human activities with the help of data from several sensors. These sensors can be accelerometers, gyroscopes, and other kinds of wearable devices, as well as data from cameras and microphones. HAR seeks to aid machines in understanding human action in real-time or from videos that have already been recorded. It is used in many areas, including health and fitness, sports, security, and the interaction between man and the computer. HAR systems use machine learning and pattern analysis to decipher sensory information and categorise actions into specific sets.

The normally detected by HAR systems include walking, jogging, sitting, standing, and carrying out more complex activities like cycling or special movement patterns, which are characteristic of specific sports. Efficient and accurate HAR algorithms must be developed since numerous gadgets and programs such as wearable technologies, fitness and smartwatches, and various security systems require them. Some of the difficulties that researchers and practitioners working in the field of HAR encounter include variability in human motion, the requirement of large datasets and diverse data, and the development of powerful and efficient algorithms. The incremental invention and development of sensors, machine learning, and data acquisition procedures continue to cultivate the ongoing improvement of HAR systems that improve the recognition of human actions and optimise the human-machine interface. To identify intricate human activities in videos, the development of various significant applications becomes feasible. Within a mall, shop, or store setting, individuals engage in different common activities, such as walking, talking, placing items in a basket or trolley, checking products, and processing payments. Unusual behaviours may also manifest, such as placing items in pockets, bags, or clothing or causing damage to products. However, it's crucial to note that differences in speech, actions, or appearance don't automatically imply suspicion. Therefore, the classification of activities is necessary. Figure 1 depicts the overarching framework of activity recognition.

Figure 1. General Framework of Activity Recognition

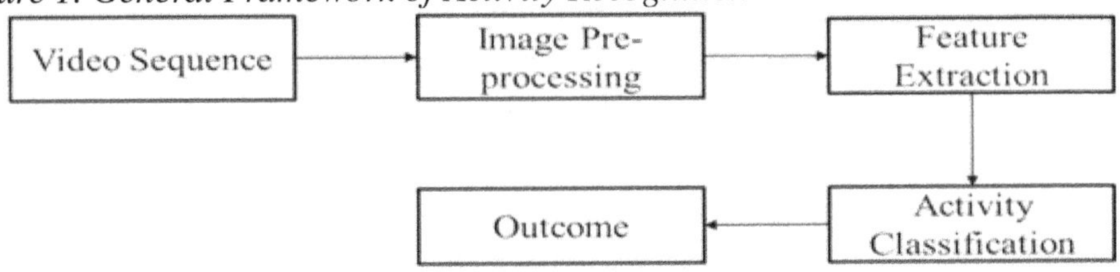

Human activities take various forms and can be classified into four levels based on complexity (Kwapisz et al., 2011): postures, actions, interactions and group behaviours or performance. Postures are spontaneous movements of an individual's limbs or other segments of the body that make up the key components of meaningful motion, for example, "extending an arm" or "lifting a leg." Actions involve one person going through a set of coordinated movements across time, such as "walking", "waving", or "punching". Interactions are activities which involve two or more people and/ or objects. For instance, two people fighting is an interaction between people, and a person stealing a suitcase illustrates people interacting with an object, an apron from two people and one suitcase. The last one is related to group activities, which implies coordinated action of one or many objects and people, for example, "a group marches," "a team discusses something," or "two groups fight". This article explores the different human activity recognition techniques used so far upon seeing such patterns.

This paper carries eight sections. Section 2 involves image preprocessing techniques to enhance the quality of image and video data, addressing noise, resolution, and occlusion. Section 3 focuses on feature extraction, detailing methods for obtaining essential features like motion and temporal characteristics necessary for accurate activity recognition. Section 4 discusses classification algorithms; conventional machine learning approaches and more sophisticated ones like SVMs and Neural networks are covered. In Section 5, a literature review is conducted. Previously published work in the field of HAR is summarised, and trends along with key gaps are pointed out. In Section 6, popular datasets in HAR are discussed, including information on data sources, types of activities, and sensor modalities. Section 7 discusses performance measures and evaluation metrics, including the HAR system's accuracy, precision, and recall. Finally, in Section 8, the paper highlights the important points and foresight of HAR progress.

2. IMAGE PRE-PROCESSING

The systems leverage images or video footage of human activities to classify human activities. However, original images typically have an extreme range of illumination changes, background interferences, and motion smearing, which can severely impair recognition precision. Human Activity Recognition (HAR) systems employ several enhancement methods for an image to have a better value, decrease unwanted artefacts, and improve useful feature carving to enhance classification. The outline of the image pre-processing process is the reduction of noise, smoothing, and articulation of contours, which is frequently done employing median or Gaussian filtering for random elimination while edge and contour retaining processes. The more salient component is image simplification, where the background components are stripped out of static elements and foreground moving components (i.e., the person engaging in the activity). Removing static backgrounds from moving subjects using methods such as the GMM (Gaussian Mixture Model) and motion detection based on optical flow makes it possible to pay attention to more human movement. Addition and normalisation of images are performed after the contour articulation step has been achieved. It is also critical in image validating format, scope, and intensity to perform deep training of neural networks. Defining features like the outline of the body and motion movement are often enhanced by improving contrast through histogram equalisation.

Edge detection and feature enhancement are other crucial steps regarding image pre-processing within human action recognition. The goal of the technique is to aid in motion recognition by identifying its contour and structure. Canny edge detection methods, for instance, emphasise the most significant edges related to the interest motion. In addition, pose skeletonisation and estimation techniques (e.g., OpenPose or MediaPipe) may perform key point extraction for different body joints. These key points aid in representing various coordinated actions concisely and informally, enhancing the effectiveness of HAR systems. For deep learning approaches for HAR, the datasets can be augmented using rotation, flipping, scaling, and Gaussian noise to increase dataset diversity and mitigate overfitting. In addition, it is common to use optical flow methods for tracking the movements of an object in successive frames to make the HAR models invariant to changes in viewpoint and occlusions. By integrating such pre-processing methods, HAR systems can expect to achieve even greater accuracy, improved generalisation of various conditions, and higher robustness against environmental changes. In summary, pre-image processes are crucial for ensuring high accuracy on action recognition tasks by enabling the HAR models to work with real-life scenarios, such as in surveillance systems, remote healthcare, and intelligent environments.

Image preprocessing is important for time series analysis since it transforms the raw data into a more suitable form for modelling and analysis. The outlined segmentation methods in Table 1 are essential to this preprocessing stage since they organise the data using different criteria. These are the modality type of the dataset, the sensors employed, the number of participants or activities, the sampling frequency, the types of devices, and their format. Moreover, the contextual information puts the basic single-modal and advanced multi-modal datasets into differing categories. These datasets are indispensable assets to train and test HAR models; thus, they help develop wearable devices for health monitoring and human-computer interaction applications.

Table 1. Image Preprocessing Methods for Time Series Data

Method	Description	Key Applications	References
Time-based Segmentation	Divides data into fixed-length intervals based on timestamps.	Time series analysis, forecasting	(Wang, Chen, et al., 2019)
Event-based Segmentation	Splits data at significant events or triggers.	Event detection, anomaly detection	(Wang, Liu, et al., 2023; Ahamed et al., 2020)
Activity-based Segmentation	Segments data based on human or system activities.	Activity recognition, behavioural studies	(Kitbutrawat et al., 2019; Yala, Fergani, & Fleury, 2015)
Sensor-based Segmentation	Processes data from sensors, segmenting based on their readings or state changes.	IoT applications, environmental monitoring	(Kitbutrawat et al., 2019; Yala, Fergani, & Fleury, 2015)
Location-based Segmentation	Divides data according to geographic or spatial locations.	GPS data analysis, location tracking	(Yala, Fergani, & Fleury, 2015; Eisa & Moreira, 2017)
Combined Time- and Event-based Segmentation	Combines time intervals and event triggers to define segments.	Complex system analysis	(Gayathri et al., 2015; Liouane et al., 2020)
Annotation-based Segmentation	Segments data based on labelled annotations.	Machine learning, supervised learning	(Abidine et al., 2018)
Combined Time, Event, and Category-based Segmentation	Integrates time, events, and categorical labels.	Multidimensional data processing	(Tan et al., 2021)
User-based Segmentation	Segments data based on individual user behaviours or profiles.	Personalised recommendations	(Hwang et al., 2021)
Frequency-based Segmentation	Splits data based on signal or sampling frequency.	Signal processing, communication systems	(Lu & Chiang, 2014; Xu et al., 2022)

continued on following page

Table 1. Continued

Method	Description	Key Applications	References
Statistical-based Segmentation	It uses statistical methods to define segments.	Outlier detection, data normalisation	(Murphy, 2012; Cook et al., 2012)
Hierarchical-based Segmentation	Applies hierarchical clustering to define segments.	Hierarchical modelling, taxonomy generation	(Ganaie et al., 2022; Ordónez et al., 2013)
Feature-based Segmentation	It uses feature extraction techniques to define segment boundaries.	Feature engineering, predictive modelling	(Van Kasteren et al., 2011; Espinilla et al., 2018)
AI-based Segmentation	Utilises AI models to automatically define segments.	Autonomous systems, complex modelling	(Cook et al., 2012; Tapia et al., 2004)
Rule-based Segmentation	Defines segments using predefined rules or conditions.	Business intelligence, decision systems	(Katz et al., 1970; Cook, 2010)
Others	Miscellaneous methods do not fall under the above categories.	Diverse applications	(Ansari et al., 2024; Ramanujam & Perumal, 2023)

3. FEATURES IN HUMAN ACTIVITY RECOGNITION

Human Activity Recognition (HAR) involves identifying physical activities from visuals or sensor data, typically collected from wearable devices, smartphones, environmental sensors or CCTV footage. Feature extraction is crucial in HAR as it transforms raw sensor signals into meaningful information for machine-learning models. The features in HAR can be categorised as follows:

Local Feature-Based Techniques: Local features (e.g. intensity, colour, texture) that exhibit significant change over the sequence of frames like HOG, LBP, Census transform, Edgelet, etc. These feature extraction techniques are described in the next subsection.

Motion Feature-Based Technique: To detect the activities in surveillance, video interest points containing some motion must be selected. Motion in interest points decides the occurrence of the activity. So, to find objects or parts of the objects that contain some motion, the Optical-flow-based motion segmentation technique is used.

Appearance-Based Techniques: Sometimes, only motion information can't effectively describe the object's motion. So, the texture and shape features must be deployed along their respective motion for evaluating the interest points. Appearance-based methods combine appearance- and motion-based features (Men et al., 2021) to form feature vectors. These techniques are Silhouette history information, Silhouette motion variation data, Motion scale invariant feature transformation, Motion Weber local descriptors, etc.

3.1. Histogram of Oriented Gradients (HOG)

Histogram of Oriented Gradients (HOG) is a feature descriptor widely used in computer vision and image processing, particularly for object detection and recognition tasks. The fundamental idea behind HOG is that an object's shape and structure can be effectively described by the distribution of edge orientations in localised portions of an image. This makes HOG particularly useful in detecting objects like pedestrians, vehicles, and facial features, where edge and contour information is crucial.

HOG operates by dividing an image into small, connected regions called cells. The direction and magnitude of each pixel's gradient are calculated in every cell. The edges are defined by the primary change in intensity, which can be detected using a derivative filter like the Sobel operator. These primary changes are referred to as gradients. Gradients are then utilised to create a cell-level histogram representing the frequency of orientations of different gradient magnitudes. Such histograms capture the image's structural elements as phantom object representations. To improve performance concerning illumination and contrast variances, the histograms are first normalised through larger areas known as blocks. Each block comprises cells and shadows, and variations and changes in illumination are accounted for during normalisation. The concatenation of histograms of every block then leads to the construction of a descriptor which is void of changes in contrast and illumination so it can effectively be used in classification.

One of the key advantages of HOG is that it can capture local shape information without being affected by minor deformations or changes in illumination. This feature has made it popular in areas such as human detection, where it was famously used alongside Support Vector Machines (SVM) in the Dalal and Triggs framework for pedestrian detection. Its use is still widespread, but HOG techniques can become quite expensive on computation resources compared to primitive deep learning-based methods. Nonetheless, HOG is still a prominent approach in classical computer vision.

3.2. Local Binary Patterns (LBP)

Local Binary Patterns (LBP) have been widely utilised and appreciated in human activity recognition (HAR) for their efficiency in extracting differentiating features from videos and images. It is a powerful image analysis tool and texture descriptor that works perfectly while performing computational tasks because of its effectiveness, simplicity, and adaptability to lighting changes. Recognition of different physical movements like running, jumping, walking, and even sitting requires HAR to spatially and spatiotemporally capture patterns from sequences of images.

LBP encodes the texture and structure of an image through a simple yet effective thresholding operation. In its most basic form, LBP uses the pixel at the centre of a 3×3 neighbourhood, compares its brightness with that of the other eight surrounding pixels, and assigns a binary value depending on whether they are greater than or lesser than the centre pixel. The binary values are then translated into decimal numbers, forming patterns characterising the local texture. The collection of these patterns forms a unique histogram, which compactly and informatively represents the features in the image. LBP can be used in video clips or motion history images to extract spatial and temporal features. For example, LBP can capture movement and shape changes with optical flow or depth maps. Extensions like LBP-TOP capture features from three orthogonal spatial planes, applying LBP to three dimensions. This strategy of recognising actions can be useful in video sequences.

In HAR, LBP's greatest strength is its computational efficiency and ability to manage changes in illumination and minor pose alterations. Its application to HAR problems involving RGB, depth, and thermal images is notable. It is often used with classifiers based on machine learning, such as Support Vector Machine or deep learning, for better results. In its basic form, such a simple technique like LBP can easily assist in resource-limited situations where deep learning techniques are too burdensome to the system, making it ideal for most HAR frameworks.

3.3. Census Transform

The Census Transform (CT) is a non-parametric feature extraction method widely used in computer vision for stereo matching, image, object recognition, and more. Like Local Binary Patterns (LBP), CT generates a descriptor by comparing the value of the selected pixel with surrounding pixel values, albeit using a different approach. The primary advantage of Census Transform is that it is robust to noise and illumination changes, making it favourable for real-world problems.

The Census Transform captures the local neighbourhood surrounding every pixel for image analysis and encodes the intensity relationships in a binary string. In a specific example, for a pixel being studied, Census Transform calculates its intensity with the intensity of other pixels positioned in a box of certain dimensions surrounding this pixel, for example, in a box of 3 × 3 or 5 × 5. If one of the neighbouring pixels has an intensity greater or equal to the centre pixel, it is represented by a value of 1 or 0. After processing, the pixel's binary representation is concatenated into a single string that will later be used as a decimal or integer to texture information at that location. The Census Transform generates a binary code based on the comparison between the centre pixel and the neighbouring pixels:

$$C(x,y) = \sum_{i \in N(x,y)} 2^{i}.\ I(Pi \geq Pc) \quad (1)$$

Where C(x,y) is the Census Transform code for the pixel at the position, P_c is the intensity value of the central pixel. Pi is the intensity value of the neighbouring pixel in the neighbourhood, I(Pi≥Pc) is an indicator function that outputs one if the intensity of the neighbouring pixel P_i is greater than or equal to the intensity of the central pixel P_c, and zero otherwise.

3.4. Optical Flow-Based Motion Segmentation

Motion segmentation using optical flow, as described in (Murphy, 2012), relies on motion features. It exploits the properties over the flow vectors associated with moving objects at different time instances to identify the motion sectors in a video. The pixel velocity at the positions on the image surface represents the object's velocity. Each pixel's motion vector is computed, forming a vector field representing the entire image. In this context, the motion vector of each pixel also signifies the pixel's brightness (Ramanujam & Perumal, 2023). Regions of the image where changes in brightness are observed are considered candidates for moving objects. Optical flow in motion detection is easy to perform but does not work well in real scenarios.

3.5. Edgelet Transform

Feature extraction plays a significant role in human activity recognition (HAR), including Edgelet Transforms, which recognise specific movements and focus on the edges in the image or video frame. Because human activities involve changing body position, Edgelet Transforms provide a highly compact and reliable representation for action recognition, such as walking, running, jumping, and sitting. The Edgelet Transforms differ from traditional transforms like Wavelet or Ridgelet, where the image curves and edges are analysed at different scales. The Edgelet Transform is far more applicable in human motion recognition as it specialises in the region of edges.

3.6. Signal Magnitude Area (SMA)

The single motion acceleration (SMA) metric is important in recognising human activities (HAR). It combines movement values in the X, Y, and Z coordinates to measure intensity during a specific period. It is computed using $SMA = 1/N\sum_{i=1}\left(|a_x^i| + |a_y^i| + |a_z^i|\right)$, where N is the number of samples in the window. It is used in most cases of differentiating activities like walking, running, and standing using one scalar value that indicates the intensity of activity. For example, higher values mean running or jumping, while lower values indicate sitting or standing. Because it is simple, SMA is easily used in different systems for fitness, fall detection, and health monitoring. However, while it effectively captures movement intensity, it may not always distinguish between activities with similar acceleration patterns, such as walking and cycling. It is necessary to combine SMA with other features for improved classification accuracy.

3.7. Silhouette History Information (SHI)

The SHI (Stergiou & Poppe, 2019) feature scheme is used to extract pixel intensity information as the sequence of each activity unfolds. It includes spatial description, position and disposition, speed, and acceleration. For each activity in the SHI process, all the depth human silhouettes are represented by S(x, y, z) ranging from the initial to the final frame at time ft.

$$SHI(x, y, z) = \frac{1}{T}\sum_{t=t_S}^{t_L} I_t \tag{2}$$

Here, t_S and t_L, and state variables are used to represent the initial and final conditions of an activity. T stands for the duration of the activity period. In addition, the information for each activity is subjected to changes in the subject, location, motion, and duration.

3.8. Silhouettes Motion Variation-Data (SMV-D)

The intra/inter motion variations are handled by the SMV-D (Ezzeldin et al., 2025) feature mechanism, while temporal displacement among successive frames of a particular activity is also regulated.

$$MV(x, y, z) = \frac{SD(x, y, z)}{SHI(x, y, z)} \tag{3}$$

SD(x, y, z) denotes the standard deviation computed between the image pairs over the time series. The primary contribution of these feature extraction techniques resides in quantifying motion shapes, spatial distribution, intensity contrasts, and temporal evolution.

3.9. Motion Scale Invariant Feature Transformation (MoSIFT)

MoSIFT (Li et al., 2020) captures spatially distinctive interest points with substantial motions. The SIFT algorithm is applied first to find visually distinctive components in the spatial domain. Spatio-temporal interest points are detected by applying motion constraints on SIFT interest points.

3.10. Motion Weber local Descriptors (MoWLD)

The descriptor WLD (Stergiou & Poppe, 2019), defined for each pixel, quantifies the density local intensity variation to the central pixel. Besides, motion information is also employed to detect the so-called activity points for activity detection in addition to WLD. Apart from these, a histogram of gradient, an optical flow histogram, an edgelet descriptor, etc., can also be used as an appearance-based feature description. Further, these features can be used to build a classifier.

Table 2 compares motion feature extraction techniques commonly used in Human Activity Recognition (HAR). These features are pivotal in detecting and classifying human actions, such as walking, running, sitting, or complex movements, from different data sources like sensors, video feeds, and depth images. The table consists of several methods, each with features, uses, strengths, and weaknesses.

Table 2. Comparative analysis among various feature extraction schemes under HAR

Feature	Description	Key Applications	Advantages	Limitations
Histogram of Oriented Gradients (HOG)	Captures edge orientations in local regions to describe object shape and structure.	Object detection, human recognition, pedestrian detection.	Robust to small deformations and lighting variations.	Computationally expensive, sensitive to background clutter.
Local Binary Patterns (LBP)	Encodes texture by thresholding pixel intensities and creating binary patterns.	HAR, face recognition, texture analysis.	Simple, efficient, and robust to illumination changes.	Loses spatial information, not rotation invariant.
Census Transform (CT)	Compares pixel intensities with neighbours to form a binary descriptor.	Stereo matching, image recognition, HAR.	Robust to noise and lighting variations.	Limited discriminative power for complex textures.
Optical Flow-Based Motion Segmentation	It uses motion vectors to detect object movement over time.	Motion tracking, HAR, and video analysis.	Can detect motion without prior background knowledge.	Computationally intensive, affected by lighting variations.

continued on following page

Table 2. Continued

Feature	Description	Key Applications	Advantages	Limitations
Edgelet Transform	Focuses on edge structures in images to detect motion patterns.	HAR, action recognition, gesture detection.	Captures localised motion efficiently.	Sensitive to occlusions and noise.
Signal Magnitude Area (SMA)	Measures overall movement intensity by summing absolute accelerations.	Fitness tracking, fall detection, HAR.	Simple, computationally efficient.	Cannot differentiate activities with similar intensities (e.g., walking vs. cycling).
Silhouette History Information (SHI)	Captures pixel intensity variations over time to represent activity sequences.	HAR, depth-based motion analysis.	Includes spatial, speed, and acceleration details.	Sensitive to variations in subject size and location.
Silhouette Motion Variation-Data (SMV-D)	Quantifies motion variations and temporal displacement.	HAR, movement intensity estimation.	Handles intra/inter motion variations.	Computational complexity can be high.
Motion Scale Invariant Feature Transformation (MoSIFT)	Detects spatio-temporal interest points with motion constraints.	HAR, video-based action recognition.	Captures spatial and temporal motion variations.	Computationally expensive.
Motion Weber Local Descriptors (MoWLD)	Quantifies local intensity variation and motion for activity recognition.	HAR, dynamic scene analysis.	Includes both texture and motion information.	Sensitive to noise and scale variations.

4. CLASSIFIER USED FOR ACTIVITY RECOGNITION

In HAR, classifiers are pivotal in recognising and classifying the dataset's features into distinct activities or actions using sensor and video inputs. Various classification methods are conducted using different machine learning algorithms, each with benefits and disadvantages. Here are some commonly used classifiers in HAR:

Decision Trees are primarily used to classify labelled data through supervised or unsupervised approaches. It possesses a graph structure where each node is a decision depending on certain properties of the given data, while leaf nodes depict outcomes. Decision trees are flexible tools that are frequently used because the results are quite understandable, and they effectively show how decisions are made.

Naive Bayes is one of the oldest finite probability model classifiers using Baye's theorem. This requires the assumption that features are independent given the class label, simplifying calculations. Even though Naive Bayes is a very simple model, it performs well in tasks such as text classification, spam filtering, and other uses where the assumption of independence of the features holds.

K-Nearest Neighbour (KNN) is one of the easiest yet powerful methods used in both classification and regression most of the time. It classifies a data point to the class to which most of its K nearest neighbours belong in the feature space. The formulated model is non-parametric because it does not impose any assumption about the distribution of the data, which makes it more flexible and can be used with a varying type of data, making KNN a common and quite simple method.

Adaboost Learning, short for Adaptive Boosting, is an ensemble learning method that combines weak learners to create a strong, accurate model. It assigns weights to data points and focuses on misclassified instances during training, iteratively improving the model's performance. Adaboost is known for its versatility and ability to handle complex datasets.

Hidden Markov Model (HMM) is a statistical model commonly used for modelling sequences of observations. The hidden states of HMM mark a range of areas; speech recognition, bioinformatics, and natural language processing are included. It is designed on the assumption that the Markov process exists and that the observations depend on these hidden states.

Sparse Representation is the way of describing data obtained by methods used in signal processing and image analysis. This technique accentuates important elements while avoiding redundancy. Sparse representation methods are helpful in compressive sensing because they allow for efficient data representation.

Bayesian Networks are a type of graphical model that encodes information on variables and their dependencies. Nodes in the graph are variables, and edges connect the nodes if the variables are conditionally dependent. They are used in various fields like medicine and finance and are very effective in modelling relationships and dealing with uncertainties in complex systems.

Support Vector Machine (SVM) is a categorised learning algorithm used for classification and regression analysis. The algorithm defines how best to place the hyperplane, which will segregate data into different classes and simultaneously have the largest margin between classes. SVM is best used in high dimensions and widely in applications such as image recognition and genomics.

Artificial Neural Networks/Deep Learning are models derived from the human brain neural network structure. Related to it, Deep Learning is a subset of Machine Learning that uses neural networks with one or more hidden layers called deep Neural Networks. These models excel at many problems where functioning on an abstract representation of the input is appropriate, particularly image recognition and natural language processing, making these models highly popular specialities, as they can automatically learn compressed hierarchal representations of the input data.

The comparative analysis of the above-mentioned classifiers' is presented in Table 3, showing the importance of classifiers and their advantages, limitations and applicability.

Table 3. Comparative analysis among the above-mentioned classifiers

Classifier	Description	Advantages	Limitations	Applications
Decision Tree	A tree-like structure is used for classification or regression. Each node represents a decision based on features.	Easy to interpret and visualize. Handles both classification and regression tasks.	It can overfit, especially with many features or insufficient pruning.	Classification tasks, medical diagnoses, and customer segmentation.
Naive Bayes	Given the class label, a probabilistic model based on Bayes' theorem assumes feature independence.	Simple, fast, and works well with high-dimensional data.	Assumes independence between features, which is often unrealistic.	Text classification, spam filtering, recommendation systems.
K-Nearest Neighbour (KNN)	A non-parametric classifier that assigns a label based on the majority vote of its nearest neighbours.	Simple, easy to understand, and effective for non-linear problems.	Computationally expensive during inference, especially with large datasets.	Classification tasks, recommender systems, pattern recognition.
Adaboost	Ensemble learning technique that combines weak learners to create a strong classifier, focusing on misclassified instances.	Boosts performance by iteratively adjusting weights.	Sensitive to noisy data, it may be overfitting with too many iterations.	Face detection, object detection, pattern recognition.
Hidden Markov Model (HMM)	A statistical model for sequence data, assuming underlying hidden states influencing observations.	Effective for sequential or time-series data.	Requires a lot of data and computational resources for training.	Speech recognition, natural language processing, HAR.
Sparse Representation	It uses a minimal set of significant values to represent data efficiently, often in signal processing.	Efficient for high-dimensional data with sparse patterns.	Not always suitable for dense or noisy data.	Image and signal processing, compressive sensing.

continued on following page

Table 3. Continued

Classifier	Description	Advantages	Limitations	Applications
Bayesian Networks	A probabilistic graphical model representing relationships among variables with conditional dependencies.	Can model uncertainty and complex relationships.	It is computationally expensive, especially with large networks.	Medical diagnosis, decision-making systems, risk analysis.
Support Vector Machine (SVM)	A supervised learning model that finds the hyperplane that best separates classes with the largest margin.	Works well with high-dimensional data and complex margins.	Computationally expensive and sensitive to noise.	Image recognition, genomics, text classification.
Artificial Neural Networks/Deep Learning	Models based on the structure of the human brain, with deep networks of layers for abstraction.	Automatically learns hierarchical representations of data, highly effective on complex tasks.	Requires large datasets and significant computational resources.	Image recognition, natural language processing, autonomous systems.

5. LITERATURE SURVEY ON ACTIVITY RECOGNITION

The framework presented in Robert et al. paper is for real-time identification of suspicious behaviour in shopping malls using an expert video surveillance system. Described for use in malls, these activities include store entries and exits, suspicious loitering, and producing cash registers left unmanned. It also proposes a human detection and tracking system using feature extraction methods such as GCH, LBP, and HOG detectors and a track compare metric based on the SVM kernels.

The authors, Wang and Wu have proposed a deep learning model for recognizing complex actions using multiple cues, including action movements, objects, and scenes. Their approach uses multi-scale object detection for body part localization and extracting the CNN feature from the body part of each frame. Based on the experimental data and results, two specific deep learning architectures are applied in this work: GoogleNet and AlexNet are employed for feature extraction of scene and/or object cues; meanwhile, the extracted CNN features are fed into an RNN to derive the final action representation.

Sultani et al. proposed a promising anomaly detection algorithm using normal and anomalous videos as bags and video segments as instances of MIL. They proposed a deep anomaly ranking model through which high anomaly scores are assigned to anomalous segments of a video; the UCF crime dataset captures different related categories, including Vandalism, Stealing, Robbery, Explosion, Accident, Arson, Abuse, Arrest, Assault, Burglary, Fighting, Shooting, Shoplifting, and Normal.

Abnormal event detection was discussed by Nguyen and Ngoc, who presented a rapid abnormal event detection framework that employed sparse combination learning. The method comprises frame differencing to isolate candidate regions of interest (ROIs), enclose each ROI in fixed-size rectangles, and assess fast dense features such as HOG/HOF and MBH. The support vector data description (SVDD) is applied to model random behaviours, resulting in a higher accuracy of 90.44% on the UCSD dataset and 97.6% on the UMN dataset.

Rajesh Kumar et al. provided a detailed overview of the state-of-the-art in suspicious activity recognition from surveillance videos, focusing on six types of abnormal activities: This includes abandoned object detection, theft detection, fall detection, accident and illegal parking detection and violent activity detection and finally fire detection.

Humans need social contact to relate, empathize, feel, cooperate, and develop. Previous work by Zhao et al. (2020) and Jalal et al. (2020) has included analysis of social relations, movement, and group interaction from Human-to-human (HHI) interactions using wearable cameras. However, these studies pose challenges because of the small datasets used, which makes it difficult to unravel many diverse aspects of social interactions. The same authors, Puchała et al. (2023), also developed an effective approach to identifying and distinguishing people's interactions captured on the video stream in terms of the skeleton data and Long Short-Term Memory (LSTM) techniques. However, their model might miss some finer actions, and the effectiveness depends on the datasets on which it trains, which might limit its use for an extensive range of studies.

However, in recent years, significant achievements have been reported in DL-based human interaction recognition (HIR) methods. Lee and Lee (2022) combined the IHIR model by integrating the local image detail, primitive motion, and body posture. In Huang, their system for classification using CNN and LSTM was limited by the dataset. Using vision-based DL techniques, particularly CNNs, Stergiou et al. (2019) moved the automated human interaction recognition from video signals ahead and resolved these challenges. Wang et al. (2023) first proposed the SaMFormer method for human-human interaction (HHI) detection, but they got limited performance outcomes. Khan et al. (2023) located the involvement of global dependencies by incorporating the variable rate CNN with the Transformer network. Nevertheless, dataset limitations were also a concern for Yin et al. (2023). Also, in the last study, Shafiqul et al. (2022) engineered an effective HS detection and recognition system with the help of GNN based on the framework.

A multi-stream network was adopted for Human Interaction Recognition (HIR), using information from two streams. Haroon et al. (2022) built a two-stream technique at the start, in which they used 1D CNN in conjunction with LSTM, and in the second stage, they used 3D CNN to identify the interactions of human beings. However, their work mentioned that light conditions, background complexity, or changes in the subjects' clothes or skin colours could influence their accuracy. For recognizing Human-Human Interactions (HHI) from skeletal sequences, Men et al. (2022) have proposed a two-stream recurrent neural network using LSTM to simulate temporal dynamics. However, the study had limitations because of the available datasets. Furthermore, Hachiuma et al. Lately, Hachiuma et al. (2023) implemented LSTM-based models with feature extraction from the skeleton data & knowledge. In a like vein, Puchała et al. (2023) considered three models, namely SC-LSTM-PS (Single Channel Long Short-Term Memory with polar sparse features), DC-LSTM-LA (Double Channel Long Short-Term Memory with limb-angle features), and TC-LSTM-LA (Triple Channel Long Short-Term Memory with limb-angle features), but the issues were observed with the dataset's performance.

Pooja Lalwani and Ganeshan R. (2025) used smartphone sensors, particularly accelerometers, within a novel Human Activity Recognition (HAR) system to improve the accuracy of activity detection. Their method with SEL (stacked ensemble learning) successfully classifies different activities, including running, walking, stair movements, and sitting or standing. Their results showed that the CatBoost classifier achieved 80.41% and 82.34% accuracy for walking, running, and stair motions, respectively, with 98.78% for sitting and standing. Cross-validation alongside confusion matrices supports the accuracy of SEL, underlining its value for healthcare and other industries.

Najmul Hassan et al. (2024) shift to focus on security applications and explore AI-driven behavioural analysis to fill the gap in dynamic HAR activity recognition. They introduce a MobileNetV2 backbone feature extraction model and an optimized Deep BiLSTM-based model for learning inter-sequential dependencies tested on UCF11, UCF Sport, and JHMDB datasets, achieving impressive accuracy and showcasing enhanced HAR performance.

In biomedical signal processing focusing on patient care, Al-qaness et al. (2024) and Najmul Hassan et al. tackle Human Activity Recognition (HAR) and fall detection as a part of proactive healthcare. They developed a framework for multi-class and binary action recognition called PCNN-Transformer, which is based on a Parallel Convolutional Neural Network and Transformer architecture and utilizes data from wearable sensors. Tested on SisFall, UniMib-SHAR, and MobiAct datasets, their model shows the best performance in fall detection with an accuracy of 99.95%, 98.68%, and 99.71%, respectively, which underscores its usefulness in elderly care and real-time monitoring systems.

For Breast Cancer Detection, Muhammad Tayyab et al. (2025) propose an event recognition method based on a sequence of images that uses a human body part and context. They extract various feature descriptors from MSER, SURF, distance transform and DOF for skeleton points, as well as BRIEF, HOG, FAST, and Optical Flow for silhouettes. Recognition performance improvement has been achieved with a hybrid CNN-RNN classifier with GWO for feature selection. Their method is evaluated using the UCF-101 and YouTube datasets, which attains 98.5% and 99.2% accuracy, outperforming the previous techniques.

Fenglin Liu et al. (2025) developed a sophisticated framework for human behaviour recognition using skeleton sequences through multi-stream fused spatiotemporal graph convolutional networks. To resolve issues about distant interdependency capturing, a spatial attention component is added to improve the positional information acuity over time and space. Furthermore, a channel attention focus is utilized to enhance the extraction of motion features, and multi-stream fusion reduces the loss of information inherent to single-stream data. When tested on NTU-RGB+D and Kinetics-Skeleton datasets, the model's recognition accuracy is 96.0% and 37.3%, respectively, showcasing his proficiency in skeleton-based action recognition.

Megha Thukral et al. (2025) designs a new transfer learning approach, Cross-Domain HAR, to improve sensor-based human activity recognition (HAR) using labeled datasets available in the public domain. Their solution for the problem of ground-truth annotation and dataset scarcity is a teacher-student self-training strategy that helps close the gaps between the source and target domains, encompassing the sensors' locations and types of activities. Additional analysis from their report focuses on the contribution of individual elements in the dataset to recognizing activities while highlighting significant performance improvements in few-shot activity recognition scenarios.

6. DATASETS FOR ACTIVITY RECOGNITION

Activity recognition research heavily relies on the availability of diverse and well-annotated datasets. These datasets cover a range of activities and scenarios, enabling researchers to train and evaluate models effectively. Table 4 focuses on the video-based HAR datasets, detailing the number of actions, clips, problem types, background, camera motion, release year, and sources of various datasets. These datasets generally involve video recordings with dynamic backgrounds and varying camera motions. Examples include UCF 101 (13320 clips of 101 action categories, recorded indoors and outdoors), CAVIAR (with dynamic scenes focusing on realistic action analysis), and BEHAVE, which provides interaction analysis in a static environment using 50 clips. These datasets have realistic action scenarios and are used for video-based action classification or interaction analysis.

Table 4. Activity Recognition Datasets

Dataset	Number of Actions	Clips	Types of problem	Background	Camera Motion	Released Year	Source
BEHAVE	10	50	Interaction analysis	Static	No	2004	Videos from recordings & TV shows
CAVIAR	9	-	Realistic action analysis	Dynamic	Yes	2004	Recorded Videos (Indoor/outdoor)
KTH	6	600	Unrealistic action analysis	Static	No	2004	Recorded Videos (Indoor/outdoor)
TRECVID	10	-	Interaction Analysis	Dynamic	Yes	2008	NIST(indoor)
UCF 101	101	13320	Realistic action analysis	Dynamic	Yes	2012	Videos from the web (indoor/ outdoor)
Movies	-	200	Realistic action analysis	Dynamic	Yes	-	Videos from the web (indoor/ outdoor)
UMN	5	11 videos	Realistic action analysis	Dynamic	No	2013	Recording videos & TV shows

Table 5 briefly explains the different HAR data sets available in the public domain, highlighting the modalities, participants, activities, context-awareness, sampling frequency, device types, and data formats. For example, the UCI-HAR dataset uses inertial sensors with 30 participants performing six activities, while the Opportunity dataset utilizes wearable sensors for 12 participants performing 14 activities. Notably, some datasets, like RealWorld HAR, are multimodal, incorporating inertial sensors and visual signals to capture a broader range of activities. These are factors such as the modality type of the dataset; the sensors used; the number of participants or activities; the sampling frequency; the types of devices; and format. The type of datasets also differs from basic single-modal datasets to advanced multi-modal datasets, which include contextual information. These datasets are indispensable assets to train and test HAR models; thus, they help develop wearable devices for health monitoring and human-computer interaction applications.

Table 5. Overview of Additional Available HAR Datasets

Dataset	Multi-modal	Signal Modalities	Participants	Activities	Context-aware	Sampling Frequency	Device Types	Data Format
UCI-HAR (Hachiuma et al., 2023)	No	Inertial sensor signals	30	6	No	50 Hz	Smartphones	CSV
Opportunity (Anguita et al., 2013)	No	Sensor signals	12	14	No	30 Hz	Wearable sensors	HDF5
WISDM (Chavarriaga et al., 2013)	No	Inertial sensor signals	296	No	No	20 Hz	Smartphones	CSV
MobiAct (Kwapisz et al., 2011)	No	Inertial sensor signals	57	13	No	50 Hz	Smartphones, Wearables	JSON
PAMAP2 (Vavoulas et al., 2016)	No	Inertial sensor signals	9	18	No	100 Hz	Wearables	TXT
UTD-MHAD (Reiss & Stricker, 2012)	Yes	Inertial sensors and visual signals	82	7	No	30 Hz	Kinect, Wearables	MAT
BON (Chen et al., 2015)	No	Visual signals	25	18	No	Variable	Cameras	Video files (MP4)
HAPT (Tadesse et al., 2022)	No	Inertial sensor signals	30	12	Yes	50 Hz	Smartphones	CSV
RealWorld HAR (Arroyo et al., 2015)	Yes	Inertial sensors and visual signals	15	8	Yes	100 Hz	Wearables, Cameras	ARFF
SHL Dataset (Sztyler et al., 2017)	No	Inertial sensor signals	48	No	No	100 Hz	Smartphones	MAT

7. PERFORMANCE METRICS

Performance measures (Ansari & Singh, 2021; Yala, Fergani, & Fleury, 2015; Ansari & Singh, 2021; Singh et al., 2022; Lalwani & Ganeshan, 2025) can be categorised as a set of techniques that can be employed to assess the efficiency of various machine learning models and algorithms. These lead to evaluating the model's accuracy, precision, recall and other performance features, making it vital. Here is an overview of some commonly used performance measures in machine learning:

Accuracy: Accuracy represents the ratio of correctly predicted instances to the total instances.

$$Accuracy = (True\ Positives + True\ Negatives) \, / \, Total\ Instances \tag{4}$$

Precision: Precision measures the ratio of correctly predicted positive observations to the total predicted positives.

$$Precision = True\ Positives\ /\ (True\ Positives + False\ Positives) \quad (5)$$

Recall (Sensitivity or True Positive Rate): Recall calculates the ratio of correctly predicted positive observations to all observations in the actual positive class.

$$Recall = \frac{True\ Positives}{(True\ Positives + False\ Negatives)} \quad (6)$$

F1 Score: The F1 score is the harmonic mean of precision and recall.

$$F1\ Score = 2 * \frac{(Precision * Recall)}{(Precision + Recall)} \quad (10)$$

Specificity (True Negative Rate): Specificity indicates the ratio of correctly predicted negative observations to actual negatives.

$$Specificity = \frac{True\ Negatives}{(True\ Negatives + False\ Positives)} \quad (11)$$

False Positive Rate (FPR): FPR calculates the ratio of incorrectly predicted positive observations to the total actual negatives.

$$False\ Positive\ Rate = \frac{False\ Positives}{(True\ Negatives + False\ Positives)} \quad (12)$$

Mean Absolute Error (MAE): MAE calculates the average absolute differences between predicted and actual values.

$$Mean\ Absolute\ Error\ (MAE) = \left(\frac{1}{n}\right) * \Sigma|Actual - Predicted| \quad (13)$$

Mean Squared Error (MSE): Definition: MSE represents the average squared differences between predicted and actual values.

$$MSE = \left(\frac{1}{n}\right) * \Sigma(Actual - Predicted)^2 \quad (14)$$

R-squared (Coefficient of Determination): R-squared measures the amount of variation in the dependent variable that is accounted for by the independent variable.

Area Under the Receiver Operating Characteristic (ROC-AUC): ROC-AUC measures the area under the ROC curve, illustrating the true positive rate against the false positive rate.

Evaluation metrics used in Table 6 provide multiple perspectives on model performance, serving the purpose of achieving the desired outcome of the given problem. Choosing suitable measures is a very important procedure for accurately assessing the performance of machine learning algorithms.

Table 6. Comparison of Performance Measures: Definitions, Ranges, Optimal Values, and Use Cases

Performance Measure	Definition	Range	Best Value	Use Case	Key Differences
Accuracy	The ratio of correctly predicted instances to total instances	[0,1]	1	General classification performance	Not suitable for imbalanced datasets
Precision	The ratio of correctly predicted positive observations to total predicted positives	[0,1]	1	Important in imbalanced datasets where false positives matter (e.g., fraud detection)	Focuses only on positive predictions
Recall (Sensitivity, TPR)	The ratio of correctly predicted positives to actual positives	[0,1]	1	Important when false negatives matter (e.g., medical diagnosis)	Does not consider false positives
F1 Score	The harmonic means of precision and recall	[0,1]	1	Useful for imbalanced datasets	Balances precision and recall
Specificity (TNR)	The ratio of correctly predicted negatives to actual negatives	[0,1]	1	Important when false positives need to be minimized (e.g., spam filtering)	The Opposite of recall focuses on negatives
False Positive Rate (FPR)	The ratio of false positives to total actual negatives	[0,1]	0	It should be low when false alarms are costly	Inverse of specificity
Mean Absolute Error (MAE)	The average absolute difference between predicted and actual values	Actual - Predicted	)	[0,∞)	0
Mean Squared Error (MSE)	Average squared difference between predicted and actual values	[0,∞)	0	More penalizing to large errors	Penalizes large errors more than MAE

continued on following page

Table 6. Continued

Performance Measure	Definition	Range	Best Value	Use Case	Key Differences
R-squared	Amount of variance explained by the model	$(-\infty,1]$	1	Measures goodness of fit in regression	It can be negative if the model is worse than the mean
ROC-AUC	The area under the ROC curve, measuring TPR vs FPR trade-off	[0,1]	1	Overall classifier performance measure	Independent of classification threshold

8. CONCLUSION

In conclusion, Human Activity Recognition (HAR) is a core area of computer science and artificial intelligence disciplines and is critically important to several sectors, including health care, sports and security. As this paper has pointed out, HAR is a rapidly advancing study area where higher-performing algorithms and systems for sensor-based human activity classification are required. The categorization of complex human activities presented in the paper allows for a better organization of the presented framework based on complexity levels. In detailing local, motion and appearance-based features, the authors demonstrate the complexities of extracting relevant sensor information. The classification of activity recognition techniques from Decision Trees through to Deep Learning, as well as highlighting the variety of use cases for these types of classifiers, truly shows the flexible nature of this type of algorithm. The literature survey provides an idea of the extent to which HAR has been used in real scenarios, ranging from identifying suspicious activity in mall sections to intricate recognition of actions using deep learning frameworks. The interspersion of various datasets and performance metrics during the discussion shows that the field of HAR shall be evaluated on speed to the evaluation of the model's accuracy, precision, recall and other performance features, which includes developing effective and reliable algorithms with large datasets, and strong feature extraction procedure. Innovations in sensors, machine learning models, and data collection mechanisms continue to drive improvements in the existing HAR systems. In the future, the interface of HAR in various technologies, such as fitness trackers, smartwatches, and security systems, will further influence the interaction between humans and computers. The advancement achieved in HAR enhances the technology and enriches the knowledge about human behaviour, enhancing the human-killing interfaces.

REFERENCES

Abidine, B. M., Fergani, L., Fergani, B., & Oussalah, M. (2018). The joint use of sequence features combination and modified weighted SVM for improving daily activity recognition. *Pattern Analysis & Applications, 21*(1), 119–138. DOI: 10.1007/s10044-016-0570-y

Ahamed, F., Shahrestani, S., & Cheung, H. (2020). Internet of things and machine learning for healthy ageing: Identifying the early signs of dementia. *Sensors (Basel), 20*(21), 6031. DOI: 10.3390/s20216031 PMID: 33114070

Al-qaness, M. A., Dahou, A., Abd Elaziz, M., & Helmi, A. M. (2024). Human activity recognition and fall detection using convolutional neural network and transformer-based architecture. *Biomedical Signal Processing and Control, 95*, 106412. DOI: 10.1016/j.bspc.2024.106412

Anguita, D., Ghio, A., Oneto, L., Parra, X., & Reyes-Ortiz, J. L. (2013). A public domain dataset for human activity recognition using smartphones. In *The European Symposium on Artificial Neural Networks.*

Ansari, M. A., & Singh, D. K. (2021). Human detection techniques for real-time surveillance: A comprehensive survey. *Multimedia Tools and Applications, 80*(6), 8759–8808. DOI: 10.1007/s11042-020-10103-4

Ansari, M. A., & Singh, D. K. (2021). Monitoring social distancing through human detection for preventing/reducing COVID spread. *International Journal of Information Technology : an Official Journal of Bharati Vidyapeeth's Institute of Computer Applications and Management, 13*(3), 1255–1264. DOI: 10.1007/s41870-021-00658-2 PMID: 33870073

Ansari, M. A., Singh, D. K., & Jayaswal, R. (2024). Using postural data and recurrent learning to monitor shoplifting activities in megastores. *Concurrency and Computation, 36*(2), e7900. DOI: 10.1002/cpe.7900

Arroyo, R., Yebes, J. J., Bergasa, L. M., Daza, I. G., & Almazán, J. (2015). Expert video-surveillance system for real-time detection of suspicious behaviors in shopping malls. *Expert Systems with Applications, 42*(21), 7991–8005. DOI: 10.1016/j.eswa.2015.06.016

Chavarriaga, R., Sagha, H., Calatroni, A., Digumarti, S. T., Tröster, G., Millán, J. R., & Roggen, D. (2013). The opportunity challenge: A benchmark database for on-body sensor-based activity recognition. *Pattern Recognition Letters, 34*(15), 2033–2042. DOI: 10.1016/j.patrec.2012.12.014

Chen, C., Jafari, R., & Kehtarnavaz, N. (2015). UTD-MHAD: A multimodal dataset for human action recognition utilizing a depth camera and a wearable inertial sensor. In *2015 IEEE International Conference on Image Processing (ICIP)* (pp. 168–172). DOI: 10.1109/ICIP.2015.7350781

Cook, D. J. (2010). Learning setting-generalized activity models for smart spaces. *IEEE Intelligent Systems*, *2010*(99), 1. DOI: 10.1109/MIS.2010.95 PMID: 21461133

Cook, D. J., Crandall, A. S., Thomas, B. L., & Krishnan, N. C. (2012). CASAS: A smart home in a box. *Computer*, *46*(7), 62–69. DOI: 10.1109/MC.2012.328 PMID: 24415794

Eisa, S., & Moreira, A. (2017). A behaviour monitoring system (BMS) for ambient assisted living. *Sensors (Basel)*, *17*(9), 1946. DOI: 10.3390/s17091946 PMID: 28837105

Espinilla, M., Medina, J., & Nugent, C. (2018). UCAMI CUP: Analyzing the UJA human activity recognition dataset of activities of daily living. *Proceedings - MDPI*, *1267*. Advance online publication. DOI: 10.3390/proceedings1267

Ezzeldin, M.. (2025). Survey on multimodal complex human activity recognition. *FCI-H Informatics Bulletin*, *7*(1), 26–44.

Ganaie, M. A., Hu, M., Malik, A. K., Tanveer, M., & Suganthan, P. N. (2022). Ensemble deep learning: A review. *Engineering Applications of Artificial Intelligence*, *115*, 105151. DOI: 10.1016/j.engappai.2022.105151

Gayathri, K., Elias, S., & Ravindran, B. (2015). Hierarchical activity recognition for dementia care using Markov logic network. *Personal and Ubiquitous Computing*, *19*(2), 271–285. DOI: 10.1007/s00779-014-0827-7

Hachiuma, R., Sato, F., & Sekii, T. (2023). Unified keypoint-based action recognition framework via structured keypoint pooling. In *2023 IEEE/CVF Conference on Computer Vision and Pattern Recognition (CVPR)* (pp. 22962–22971). Vancouver, BC, Canada. DOI: 10.1109/CVPR52729.2023.02199

Haroon, U., Ullah, A., Hussain, T., Ullah, W., Sajjad, M., Muhammad, K., Lee, M. Y., & Baik, S. W. (2022). A multi-stream sequence learning framework for human interaction recognition. *IEEE Transactions on Human-Machine Systems*, *52*(3), 435–444. DOI: 10.1109/THMS.2021.3138708

Hassan, N., Miah, A. S. M., & Shin, J. (2024). A Deep Bidirectional LSTM Model Enhanced by Transfer-Learning-Based Feature Extraction for Dynamic Human Activity Recognition. *Applied Sciences (Basel, Switzerland)*, *14*(2), 603. DOI: 10.3390/app14020603

Hwang, Y. M., Park, S., Lee, H. O., Ko, S.-K., & Lee, B.-T. (2021). Deep learning for human activity recognition based on causality feature extraction. *IEEE Access : Practical Innovations, Open Solutions, 9*, 112257–112275. DOI: 10.1109/ACCESS.2021.3103211

Jalal, A., Khalid, N., & Kim, K. (2020). Automatic recognition of human interaction via hybrid descriptors and maximum entropy Markov model using depth sensors. *Entropy (Basel, Switzerland), 22*(8), 817. DOI: 10.3390/e22080817 PMID: 33286588

Katz, S., Downs, T. D., Cash, H. R., & Grotz, R. C. (1970). Progress in development of the index of ADL. *The Gerontologist, 10*(1_Part_1), 20–30. DOI: 10.1093/geront/10.1_Part_1.20 PMID: 5420677

Khan, A., Rauf, Z., Sohail, A., Khan, A. R., Asif, H., Asif, A., & Farooq, U. (2023). A survey of the vision transformers and their CNN-transformer-based variants. *Artificial Intelligence Review, 56*(S3, Suppl. 3), 2917–2970. DOI: 10.1007/s10462-023-10595-0

Kitbutrawat, N., Portet, F., Yamaguchi, H., & Higashino, T. (2019). *Automatic localization of passive infrared binary sensors in home: From dense to scattered network. In 2019 IEEE Intl Conf on Dependable, Autonomic and Secure Computing, Intl Conf on Pervasive Intelligence and Computing, Intl Conf on Cloud and Big Data Computing, Intl Conf on Cyber Science and Technology Congress (DASC/PiCom/CBDCom/CyberSciTech)*. IEEE., DOI: 10.1109/DASC/PiCom/CBDCom/CyberSciTech.2019.00149

Kwapisz, J. R., Weiss, G. M., & Moore, S. A. (2011). Activity recognition using cell phone accelerometers. *SIGKDD Explorations, 12*(2), 74–82. DOI: 10.1145/1964897.1964918

Lalwani, P., & Ganeshan, R. (2025). HAR: A stacked ensemble learning approach based on smartphone sensors for activity detection. *Internet of Things : Engineering Cyber Physical Human Systems, 30*, 101487. DOI: 10.1016/j.iot.2024.101487

Lee, D.-G., & Lee, S.-W. (2022). Human interaction recognition framework based on interacting body part attention. *Pattern Recognition, 128*, 108645. DOI: 10.1016/j.patcog.2022.108645

Li, Q., Gravina, R., Li, Y., Alsamhi, S. H., Sun, F., & Fortino, G. (2020). Multi-user activity recognition: Challenges and opportunities. *Information Fusion, 63*, 121–135. DOI: 10.1016/j.inffus.2020.06.004

Liouane, Z., Lemlouma, T., Roose, P., Weis, F., & Messaoud, H. (2020). An intelligent knowledge system for designing, modeling, and recognizing the behavior of elderly people in smart space. *Journal of Ambient Intelligence and Humanized Computing*, *11*(12), 6059–6075. Advance online publication. DOI: 10.1007/s12652-020-01876-5

Liu, F., Wang, C., Tian, Z., Du, S., & Zeng, W. (2025). Advancing skeleton-based human behavior recognition: Multi-stream fusion spatiotemporal graph convolutional networks. *Complex & Intelligent Systems*, *11*(1), 94. DOI: 10.1007/s40747-024-01743-2

Lu, C.-H., & Chiang, Y.-T. (2014). Interaction-feature enhanced multiuser model learning for a home environment using ambient sensors. *International Journal of Intelligent Systems*, *29*(11), 1015–1046. DOI: 10.1002/int.21674

Men, Q., Ho, E. S., Shum, H. P., & Leung, H. (2021). A two-stream recurrent network for skeleton-based human interaction recognition. In *2020 25th International Conference on Pattern Recognition (ICPR)* (pp. 2771–2778). Milan, Italy. DOI: 10.1109/ICPR48806.2021.9412538

Murphy, K. P. (2012). *Machine learning: A probabilistic perspective*. MIT Press.

Ordónez, F. J., De Toledo, P., & Sanchis, A. (2013). Activity recognition using hybrid generative/discriminative models on home environments using binary sensors. *Sensors (Basel)*, *13*(5), 5460–5477. DOI: 10.3390/s130505460 PMID: 23615583

Puchała, S., Kasprzak, W., & Piwowarski, P. (2023). Human interaction classification in sliding video windows using skeleton data tracking and feature extraction. *Sensors (Basel)*, *23*(14), 6279. DOI: 10.3390/s23146279 PMID: 37514573

Ramanujam, E., & Perumal, T. (2023). MLMO-HSM: Multi-label multi-output hybrid sequential model for multi-resident smart home activity recognition. *Journal of Ambient Intelligence and Humanized Computing*, *14*(3), 2313–2325. DOI: 10.1007/s12652-022-04487-4

Reiss, A., & Stricker, D. (2012). Introducing a new benchmarked dataset for activity monitoring. In *2012 16th International Symposium on Wearable Computers* (pp. 108–109). DOI: 10.1109/ISWC.2012.13

Shafiqul, I. M., Jannat, M. K. A., Kim, J.-W., Lee, S.-W., & Yang, S.-H. (2022). HHI-AttentionNet: An enhanced human-human interaction recognition method based on a lightweight deep learning model with attention network from CSI. *Sensors (Basel)*, *22*(16), 6018. DOI: 10.3390/s22166018 PMID: 36015776

Singh, D. K., Ansari, M. A., & Pallawi, S. (2022). Computer vision-based visual activity classification through deep learning approaches. In *2022 IEEE Region 10 Symposium (TENSYMP)*. IEEE. DOI: 10.1109/TENSYMP54529.2022.9864443

Stergiou, A., & Poppe, R. (2019). Analyzing human–human interactions: A survey. *Computer Vision and Image Understanding*, *188*, 102799. DOI: 10.1016/j.cviu.2019.102799

Sztyler, M., Stuckenschmidt, H., Van Laerhoven, J., Amft, B., & Tröster, G. (2017). On-body localization of wearable devices: An investigation of position-aware activity recognition. *Pervasive and Mobile Computing*, *38*, 281–295. DOI: 10.1016/j.pmcj.2017.01.008

Tadesse, A., Bent, O., Weldemariam, K., Istiak, M. A., Hasan, T., & Cavallaro, A. (2022). BON: An extended public domain dataset for human activity recognition. *arXiv preprint arXiv:2209.05077.*

Tan, T.-H., Badarch, L., Zeng, W.-X., Gochoo, M., Alnajjar, F. S., & Hsieh, J.-W. (2021). Binary sensors-based privacy-preserved activity recognition of elderly living alone using an RNN. *Sensors (Basel)*, *21*(16), 5371. DOI: 10.3390/s21165371 PMID: 34450809

Tapia, E. M., Intille, S. S., & Larson, K. (2004). Activity recognition in the home using simple and ubiquitous sensors. In *International Conference on Pervasive Computing* (pp. 158–175). Springer. DOI: 10.1007/978-3-540-24646-6_10

Tayyab, M., Alateyah, S. A., Alnusayri, M., Alatiyyah, M., AlHammadi, D. A., Jalal, A., & Liu, H. (2025). A Hybrid Approach for Sports Activity Recognition Using Key Body Descriptors and Hybrid Deep Learning Classifier. *Sensors (Basel)*, *25*(2), 441. DOI: 10.3390/s25020441 PMID: 39860811

Thukral, M., Haresamudram, H., & Ploetz, T. (2025). Cross-Domain HAR: Few-Shot Transfer Learning for Human Activity Recognition. *ACM Transactions on Intelligent Systems and Technology*, *16*(1), 1–35. DOI: 10.1145/3704921

Van Kasteren, T. L., Englebienne, G., & Kröse, B. J. (2011). Human activity recognition from wireless sensor network data: Benchmark and software. In *Activity Recognition in Pervasive Intelligent Environments* (pp. 165–186). Springer., DOI: 10.2991/978-94-91216-05-3_8

Vavoulas, G., Chatzaki, C., Malliotakis, T., Pediaditis, M., & Tsiknakis, M. (2016). The MobiAct dataset: Recognition of activities of daily living using smartphones. In *Proceedings of the International Conference on Information and Communication Technologies for Ageing Well and E-Health* (pp. 143–151). DOI: 10.5220/0005792401430151

Wang, J., Chen, Y., Hao, S., Peng, X., & Hu, L. (2019). Deep learning for sensor-based activity recognition: A survey. *IEEE Transactions on Cognitive and Developmental Systems*, *11*(3), 313–325. DOI: 10.1109/TCDS.2018.2869999

Wang, X., Liu, J., Moore, S. J., Nugent, C. D., & Xu, Y. (2023). A behavioural hierarchical analysis framework in a smart home: Integrating HMM and probabilistic model checking. *Information Fusion*, *95*, 275–292. DOI: 10.1016/j.inffus.2023.02.025

Wang, Z., Ying, K., Meng, J., & Ning, J. (2023, November 20–23). Human-to-human interaction detection. In *International Conference on Neural Information Processing* (pp. 120–132). Changsha, China.

Xu, Z., Wang, G., & Guo, X. (2022). Online activity recognition combining dynamic segmentation and emergent modeling. *Sensors (Basel)*, *22*(6), 2250. DOI: 10.3390/s22062250 PMID: 35336420

Yala, N., Fergani, B., & Fleury, A. (2015). Feature extraction for human activity recognition on streaming data. In *2015 International Symposium on Innovations in Intelligent Systems and Applications (INISTA)* (pp. 1–6). IEEE. DOI: 10.1109/INISTA.2015.7276759

Yala, N., Fergani, B., & Fleury, A. (2015). Feature extraction and incremental learning to improve activity recognition on streaming data. In *2015 IEEE International Conference on Evolving and Adaptive Intelligent Systems (EAIS)* (pp. 1–8). IEEE. DOI: 10.1109/EAIS.2015.7368804

Yin, R., & Yin, J. (2023). A two-stream hybrid CNN-transformer network for skeleton-based human interaction recognition. *arXiv preprint arXiv:2401.00409.*

Zhao, J., Han, R., Gan, Y., Wan, L., Feng, W., & Wang, S. (2020, October 12–16). Human identification and interaction detection in cross-view multi-person videos with wearable cameras. In *Proceedings of the 28th ACM International Conference on Multimedia* (pp. 2608–2616). Seattle, WA, USA. DOI: 10.1145/3394171.3413903

Chapter 12
Investigating Motivation for Skill Acquisition Among Indian Students Pursuing Professional Courses: A Predictive Analytics Framework With Artificial Neural Networks

Mohit Agrawal
https://orcid.org/0009-0009-4336-0384
Lloyd Business School, India

Fehmina Khalique
https://orcid.org/0000-0002-2519-3174
Lloyd Business School, India

Neetu Bali Kamra
Lloyd Business School, India

Aliza Ahsan
https://orcid.org/0009-0009-2864-4485
Jamia Millia Islamia, India

ABSTRACT

This study explores the factors influencing the motivation of Indian students in professional courses regarding skill acquisition and personal growth, using a pre-

DOI: 10.4018/979-8-3373-0735-0.ch012

dictive analytics framework with artificial neural networks (ANNs). It examines the relationship between student motivation and the significance of skill acquisition, focusing on career aspirations, societal pressures, personal interests, and educational goals. Through both descriptive and inferential statistical methods, such as correlation analysis and regression modeling, the study identifies key predictors of student satisfaction. The Multilayer Perceptron (MLP) neural network model, powered by TensorFlow, demonstrates its effectiveness in predicting motivation for skill acquisition and personal growth. The findings highlight the critical role of intrinsic motivation, self-confidence, career relevance, and institutional support in enhancing student satisfaction and success. The results have practical implications for educational practices and policies.

1. INTRODUCTION

In India, education is pivotal for individual and societal advancement. Professional courses like engineering, medicine, and management are highly popular due to their career prospects and opportunities for skill and personal growth. In today's competitive landscape, personal development extends beyond skill acquisition to include competencies like critical thinking and adaptability (Merma-Molina et.al, 2022). Despite extensive research on student motivation, there is a gap in understanding what drives skill acquisition and personal growth among Indian students in these fields.

Research is needed in India, where education plays a crucial role in both individual and societal progress. Professional courses such as engineering, medicine, and management are highly sought after due to their career prospects and opportunities for skill development and personal growth. In today's competitive environment, personal development now encompasses not just skill acquisition but also competencies such as critical thinking and adaptability. While there has been considerable research on student motivation, there remains a gap in understanding the factors that drive skill acquisition and personal growth among Indian students in these fields.

This study seeks to fill this gap by examining the motivations of students in professional courses. Through the use of predictive analytics and artificial neural networks (ANNs), it will analyse extensive datasets on student demographics and attitudes. The goal is to deepen our understanding of student motivation and provide insights that can inform strategies for fostering holistic development in Indian education. Existing research often neglects the social, cultural, and economic factors affecting Indian students in professional courses, highlighting the need for this study (Grishma, 2014). By using empirical methods and predictive analytics, the study will uncover motivations behind student behaviour and find patterns and correlations in the data. This can guide evidence-based interventions tailored to Indian students' needs (Deshmukh, 2017).

The research has two primary objectives:

1. To examine the relationship between student motivation and the significance of skill acquisition in professional education, with a focus on career aspirations, societal pressures, personal interests, and educational goals.
2. To utilize artificial neural networks (ANNs) to analyze student demographics and attitudes, identifying patterns and correlations that explain the dynamics of motivation, skill acquisition, and personal development among Indian students. This research aims to accomplish first, it seeks to investigate the relationship between student motivation and the significance of skill acquisition in professional education, taking into account various influencing factors such as career aspirations, societal expectations, personal interests, and educational goals. Second, it leverages artificial neural networks (ANNs) to analyze student demographics and attitudes, identifying patterns and correlations that provide insights into the interaction between motivation, skill development, and personal growth among Indian students. The impacts of this study could be far-reaching, particularly in enhancing educational practices and student outcomes in India.

Here are several potential ways the study could make a significant impact.

- Improved Understanding of Motivation: By uncovering the factors that drive student motivation in professional courses, the study could offer valuable insights into how students' career aspirations, societal pressures, and personal interests influence their learning. This understanding can help tailor educational strategies to better align with students' intrinsic motivations, fostering greater engagement and academic success.
- Holistic Development Strategies: The study's focus on skill acquisition, personal development, and critical competencies such as adaptability and critical thinking is essential for preparing students to thrive in an increasingly competitive and complex world. By highlighting the importance of these elements in student development, the study could guide educators and policymakers in creating more comprehensive learning environments that nurture both cognitive and emotional growth.
- Data-Driven Educational Interventions: The use of artificial neural networks (ANNs) to analyse large datasets allows for a deeper understanding of the patterns and correlations that influence student performance and well-being. This data-driven approach could lead to the development of targeted interventions and personalized learning experiences that address specific needs,

ensuring that students from diverse backgrounds receive the support they require to succeed.

- Promotion of Student Success and Well-Being: With a focus on factors like societal pressures and personal development, the study's findings could inform programs designed to enhance students' mental health, motivation, and overall well-being. Interventions based on these insights could help reduce dropout rates and improve academic persistence, ensuring that students not only succeed academically but also thrive in their personal lives.
- Societal Progress: By fostering a better-equipped and motivated student population, the study can contribute to the broader goal of societal progress. Well-rounded individuals who are both skilful and adaptable can make meaningful contributions to various sectors of society, thus driving economic and social development in India. The insights gained from this research could guide policies that support long-term growth in both education and the workforce.
- Policy and Curriculum Development: Findings from the study could influence educational policy and curriculum reforms by emphasizing the integration of motivation and personal development into professional education. Policymakers could use the results to design frameworks that incorporate motivational elements, enhance student engagement, and better prepare graduates for real-world challenges.

Overall, the study's findings could play a critical role in shaping the future of education in India, ensuring that students are not only equipped with technical skills but also empowered to grow personally and professionally in a rapidly evolving world.

2. LITERATURE REVIEW

The literature review explores various motivational theories that influence student motivation, along with studies on predictive modelling and analytics. It addresses the factors impacting motivation through both intrinsic and extrinsic motivational elements.

In the ongoing study on skill acquisition and personal development among Indian students in professional courses, motivation theories form the basics. Self-Determination Theory (SDT) posits that internal motivation arises from fulfilling needs for autonomy, competence, and relatedness (Legault, 2017; Ten Cate et. al, 2011; Moore et.al, 2020). According to SDT, students are more motivated to learn when they feel self-directed and supported by their community (Moore et.al, 2020). Expectancy-Value Theory (EVT) emphasizes perceived competence and task value in influencing behaviour (Eccles & Wigfield, 2020). EVT suggests students invest in skill acquisition when they believe they can succeed and see the skill's relevance to their goals. Social Cognitive Theory (SCT) highlights observational learning, self-efficacy, and outcome expectations (Bandura, 1986). SCT suggests students are motivated by seeing others' successes, believing in their abilities, and expecting positive results.

Integrating these theories provides a deeper understanding of what drives Indian students in professional courses to get skills. Personal growth, crucial in professional education, involves developing critical thinking, problem-solving, communication, adaptability, and self-awareness (Cook & Artino, 2016). This study examines how motivation for skill acquisition aligns with personal growth aspirations, influencing educational experiences and outcomes (Sharma & Rani, 2013).

Using predictive analytics and artificial neural networks (ANNs), the study analyses large datasets to find patterns and relationships between student demographics, attitudes, and personal growth indicators (Brahme, (2014). This approach informs strategies for holistic development, enhancing our understanding of personal growth in professional education. Predictive analytics is pivotal in educational research, analysing extensive datasets to uncover patterns and relationships not clear through traditional methods (Kurni & Mohammed, 2023). By employing ANNs, researchers can find key predictors of student motivation, skill acquisition, and personal growth, easing evidence-based decisions and interventions. Predictive models allow educational stakeholders to expect student needs, tailor interventions, and improve educational experiences. Predictive analytics also forecasts future trends, offering insights into the long-term impacts of educational policies. In Indian professional education, this can promote holistic development, improve retention rates, and ensure fair access to opportunities (Burke et.al, 2017). Several studies have explored the experiences of Indian students in professional courses, examined factors influencing course choice (Rajput & Chouhan (2021), highlighting parental influence, career aspirations, and societal expectations, challenges in engineering courses, such as curriculum overload and employability concerns (Madheswari & Mageswari, 2020), role of internships in enhancing employability skills in management courses (Dhar, 2012), factors affecting medical academic performance, focusing on study habits, learning environment, and socio-economic background (Siddiky & Haque, 2024).

These studies provide insights into the experiences and challenges of Indian students in professional courses, informing educators, policymakers, and stakeholders. The present study addresses a research gap by exploring predictive analytics' practical application in Indian professional education. By analysing large datasets with ANNs, it looks to uncover insights into student motivations, skill acquisition patterns, and personal growth, enhancing understanding and informing educational practices and policies in India.

2.1 Conceptualization of Predictive Analytics Framework

Developing a predictive analytics framework for this research on skill acquisition and personal growth among Indian students in professional courses requires careful consideration of several essential aspects. These components ensure that the model effectively analyses student data, provides accurate predictions, and generates meaningful insights to enhance educational strategies and student outcomes.

2.1.1 Choosing Predictive Analytics Techniques

Selecting the appropriate predictive analytics techniques is a critical first step. Artificial Neural Networks (ANNs) are particularly well-suited for this study due to their ability to process large datasets and identify complex relationships between multiple variables. ANNs excel at analysing student demographics, attitudes, and academic performance, making them a powerful tool for uncovering patterns that influence skill acquisition and personal growth. Their capacity to model nonlinear relationships ensures that subtle but important connections between various factors are not overlooked (Singu & Singu, 2021).

2.1.2 Data Collection Process

A well-structured data collection process is fundamental to the success of the predictive model. The gathered data must align closely with the research objectives to provide accurate and relevant insights. This involves collecting comprehensive demographic information, academic records, attitudinal survey responses, and self-reported motivations. Each of these data points contributes to a holistic understanding of the factors that drive student learning and development. Ensuring data accuracy and completeness is essential, as inconsistencies or gaps can impact the reliability of the model's predictions.

2.2.3 Model Development

Once the data is collected, the next step involves developing and training the ANN models. This process entails feeding the model with large datasets, allowing it to learn from historical patterns and relationships. Training the ANNs is an iterative process that requires continuous refinement to enhance prediction accuracy. This includes adjusting parameters, validating results, and fine-tuning the model based on performance evaluations (Fan et.al, 2022). The goal is to create a robust predictive system capable of accurately forecasting student motivations, skill acquisition tendencies, and personal growth trajectories. Proper model validation techniques, such as cross-validation and performance metrics analysis, ensure that the predictions are reliable and applicable across different student populations.

2.2.4 Interpreting Results

Extracting meaningful insights from the model's forecasts requires not only a strong grasp of data analysis techniques but also domain expertise in education and student development. The results must be contextualized within the broader framework of professional education to ensure their relevance and applicability. Understanding how various factors interact helps in identifying key drivers of student success and areas where interventions may be necessary (Shams et.al, 2021). Statistical and visualization techniques, such as heat maps, graphs, and correlation matrices, further aid in interpreting and presenting the results in a comprehensible manner.

2.2.5 Applying Insights

The final and most crucial step is translating the predictive insights into actionable strategies aimed at improving student outcomes. These insights can be leveraged to design personalized learning experiences that cater to individual student needs. By identifying at-risk students early, institutions can implement targeted interventions, such as mentorship programs, skill development workshops, or career counselling sessions, to enhance student motivation and engagement. Furthermore, the findings can inform policy decisions and curriculum enhancements, ensuring that educational programs align with industry demands and student aspirations (Batina et.al, 2019)

2.2 Role of Artificial Neural Networks in Predictive Modelling

Artificial Intelligence (AI) is rapidly transforming the world, revolutionizing industries such as entertainment, transportation, healthcare, and economics. Python has become a preferred language for developing and implementing AI solutions due to its flexibility and beginner-friendly nature (Jana & Pal, 2024). This paper explores the intriguing intersection of Python and AI, providing a comprehensive overview of the field along with practical resources and examples to support learning. It delves into the role of AI and the Python programming language, highlighting various AI applications where Python is utilized. Additionally, another study outlines the advantages and disadvantages of Python for AI development (Raschka et.al, 2020).

Given the wide range of programming languages available for AI, this paper also includes a comparison of selected AI-focused languages.

Artificial Neural Networks (ANNs) are crucial in predictive modeling for skill acquisition and personal growth among Indian students in professional courses (Okewuet.al, 2021). Inspired by biological neural networks, ANNs can process complex, nonlinear relationships in large datasets, unlike traditional statistical methods (Al-Sayid & Kirkil, 2023), especially in education (Pinheiro et.al, 2020).

Compared to linear regression, ANNs excel in capturing the complexities of real-world data, which are often multifaceted and dynamic in educational research. ANNs manage high dimensional datasets with multiple input variables, extracting meaningful features and uncovering hidden patterns effectively (Müller et.al, 2018).

Compared to other machine learning algorithms, such as decision trees or support vector machines, ANNs are particularly adept at modelling highly nonlinear relationships and capturing intricate interactions between variables (Kirkos et.al, 2008). This makes them suitable for predictive modelling, especially in educational research, where understanding subtle factors influencing student behaviours and outcomes is essential (Narkhede et.al, 2025).

Overall, the versatility, adaptability, and ability for capturing complex relationships make ANNs indispensable for predictive modelling in studying skill acquisition and personal growth among Indian students in professional courses. Using these strengths, researchers can gain deeper insights into student dynamics and inform interventions to improve educational experiences and foster holistic development (Qamar and Zardari, 2023). Neural networks, also referred to as artificial neural networks (ANNs) or artificially generated neural networks (SNNs), are a subset of machine learning that serve as the foundation for deep learning techniques. Their structure and functionality are inspired by the human brain, mimicking the way real neurons communicate with each other. ANNs are highly parallel systems consisting of numerous interconnected basic processors. This paper explores artificial neural networks, their fundamental types, and core concepts. It provides an overview of ANNs, outlining the basic structure of neurons and their computational models. Additionally, it discusses network architectures, learning methods, and some of the most widely used ANNs.

The use of AI in Predictive analytics involves utilizing data, statistical algorithms, and machine learning techniques to analyze historical data and forecast future events or outcomes is highly recognized. By applying advanced analytical methods, it identifies patterns, trends, and relationships within data to make informed predictions or forecasts. This approach is widely used across various industries, including business, finance, marketing, healthcare, and sports. The predictive analytics process typically consists of several key steps: data collection and preparation, data analysis, model development, model validation, and model deployment. Data is gathered from multiple sources, cleaned, and pre-processed to eliminate inconsistencies and errors. It is then analyzed to detect meaningful patterns and trends. Statistical algorithms and machine learning models are developed based on historical data, followed by validation processes to ensure accuracy and reliability. Once validated, these models are deployed in real-world applications to predict future outcomes.

Predictive analytics provides valuable insights, enabling organizations to make data-driven decisions, optimize operations, identify opportunities, and mitigate risks. Its applications range from predicting customer behavior and detecting fraud to optimizing marketing campaigns, forecasting product demand, predicting equipment failures, and even anticipating disease outbreaks. However, ethical considerations must be taken into account, including addressing biases, ensuring data privacy, and using predictive analytics as a tool to support, rather than replace, human decision-making. Predictive analytics is closely related to artificial intelligence (AI). AI involves developing computer systems that can perform tasks requiring human intelligence, such as natural language processing, pattern recognition, and decision-making based on data analysis.

This research aimed to demonstrate that the primary role of the philosophy of science is to develop a functional understanding of knowledge, viewing it as a tool for prediction. Prediction serves as the core function of science and is essential for the success of any scientific endeavor. Essentially, prediction is the ultimate outcome of description and interpretation. Furthermore, science is fundamentally focused on forecasting events that occur in the universe, with mature predictions validating scientific models. This study introduced the application of machine learning techniques to improve the accuracy of predictive processes. A pollution dataset, along with data on the harmful effects of polluted air, was utilized. Various models were built, trained, and tested to identify the optimal model capable of enhancing the accuracy and effectiveness of the prediction process.

2.3 Motivation and factors

Recent literature has explored various facets of student motivation, encompassing intrinsic and extrinsic factors, self-determination, and their impact on academic performance and personal growth.

2.3.1 Intrinsic and Extrinsic Motivation

As per latest studies cited on the impact of motivational factors among students in professional studies, one such latest study (Sheokand et.al, 2024) examines the approach and avoidance elements influencing students' motivation to learn in three different educational settings, highlighting the complex interplay between intrinsic and extrinsic motivational factors. This study aims to explore the factors of approach and avoidance that affect students' motivation to learn in three distinct learning environments: online learning, blended learning, and conventional face-to-face learning (Bunn & Wake, 2015). The study identified five motivating factors related to the approach to online learning and four motivating factors for the approach to traditional learning. Most of the motivational factors, including social interaction, campus life experience, physical well-being, and flexibility, were also observed in the blended learning environment. Another, recent study on motivational factors impacting the students in skill acquisition has been discussed (Chandran et.al, 2024) which discusses the typology of intrinsic, altruistic, and extrinsic motivation, this research provides insights into the motivational drivers of student-teachers, emphasizing the role of personal and professional aspirations in career choice. Based on a three-fold classification of motivation—intrinsic, altruistic, and extrinsic—participants were found to be primarily motivated by intrinsic and altruistic factors, with their motivation further shaped by four demographic variables: gender, social category, type of school attended, and discipline at the undergraduate level.

These findings are analysed within the broader structural context of teacher education, with implications for research, policy, and practice discussed. Another, important variable found to be determining academic performance and self-determination of students discussed in the paper (Akram and Li, 2024): This study investigates how teacher-student relationships influence students' intrinsic and extrinsic academic motivation, underscoring the importance of supportive interactions in fostering self-determined learning environments. The findings highlighted the importance of communication, personalized support, and fostering a sense of belonging in virtual education. Intrinsic motivation, in particular, had the most significant mediating effect on the relationship between teacher-student interactions and online learning engagement (Anggraeni et.al, 2024).

The practical implications of our study suggest that professional educators should prioritize building positive teacher-student relationships and incorporate motivational factors into the design of online courses. Study related to this has been the "Factors Influencing Students' Academic Self-Efficacy in Related Disciplines" (Hinduja et.al, 2024; Braun and Clark, 2006). This research explores how family, behaviour, values, and out-of-school experiences impact students' beliefs in their academic abilities, highlighting the role of self-efficacy in academic motivation. Another facet of motivation among students has been found to be Personal Growth and Critical Thinking (Kelly et.al, 2024; Bonk and Graham, 2012). Their study proposes that university students who possess a higher sense of belonging also experience greater achievement, motivation, and retention, highlighting the role of social integration in personal growth.

A similar study (Graefe, 2024; Beatson et.al, 2021) examines how classroom environments influence motivation among gifted students, providing insights into factors that support critical thinking and adaptability. These studies collectively offer a comprehensive understanding of the multifaceted nature of student motivation, encompassing intrinsic and extrinsic factors, the role of teacher-student relationships, the impact of technology, and the importance of social integration in fostering academic and personal growth. The current research has examined the role of motivation by analysing four key factors: skill development, personal growth, academic performance, and career aspirations, all of which impact student motivation. The first two parameters (skill development and personal growth) have been considered as intrinsic and the last two (academic performance and career aspirations) as extrinsic motivating factors.

3. METHODOLOGY

This study adopts a quantitative research approach to systematically collect and analyse data from Indian students enrolled in professional courses. The primary objective is to gain a deeper understanding of their motivations, skill acquisition, and personal development. By utilizing structured data collection methods, this research ensures an objective and comprehensive evaluation of various factors that influence students' academic and professional journeys. A key aspect of this study involves gathering demographic information, which includes details such as age, gender, socioeconomic background, and geographical location. These variables help in identifying patterns and trends that might influence students' educational and career choices. Understanding the demographic distribution of students provides valuable insights into the external factors that shape their aspirations and decision-making processes. In addition to demographics, academic performance plays a crucial role in this research. The study examines students' grades, coursework engagement, and overall academic achievements to assess their level of competency and dedication to professional education. By analysing academic performance, this study aims to identify correlations between students' success and their motivations, learning strategies, and external influences.

Furthermore, the research focuses on students' attitudes toward education, skill acquisition, and career development. Attitudes encompass a wide range of factors, including personal interests, societal expectations, peer influence, and career goals (Alshamrani et.al,2025). By evaluating these aspects, the study aims to determine how students perceive the importance of acquiring new skills and how their motivation shapes their academic and professional choices. Understanding these attitudes is essential in identifying the driving forces behind students' engagement in professional education. A significant component of this research is the application of data analysis techniques to interpret the collected information effectively. Statistical tools and machine learning models are employed to identify patterns, relationships, and trends within the dataset.

3.1 Data Collection

Data were collected using surveys and interviews. The survey collected comprehensive information on students' demographics (age, gender, and study field), academic performance, and attitudinal responses concerning their motivations, skill acquisition, and personal development. The interview process provided further qualitative insights, allowing participants to elaborate on their experiences and offer a deeper understanding of the factors influencing their academic journeys.

3.2 Data Analysis

Predictive analytics, specifically artificial neural networks (ANNs), were utilized to analyze the collected data. This method helps uncover patterns and correlations between various factors, such as motivation, skill acquisition, and student outcomes. By using ANNs, the study can detect complex, nonlinear relationships among multiple variables, providing a deeper understanding of student behavior and performance. The results were validated to ensure reliability, with careful interpretation to offer robust insights. The study gathered data through surveys and interviews from Indian students in professional courses. The surveys collected information on demographics, academic backgrounds, motivations, and beliefs about skill acquisition, providing quantitative insights into student experiences. Interviews allowed participants to share additional perspectives not covered in the surveys, giving a deeper qualitative understanding of their experiences and motivations.

The questionnaire used in the study focused on skill acquisition and personal growth among Indian students in professional courses. It included:

- Demographic questions (age, gender, and study field) to understand participant backgrounds.
- Likert scale items to evaluate feelings, attitudes, and educational experiences.
- Questions on academic performance and career aspirations to offer a comprehensive view of student experiences.
- A focus on quantitative data for predictive modeling through artificial neural networks.
- Structured scales to ensure consistency and reliability in responses across various constructs.

Figure 1 and Figure 2 exhibits the research methodology and the measures for the questionnaire.

Figure 1. Research Methodology

Aspect	Description
Methodology	Quantitative approach
Data Collection	Demographic information, academic records, and attitudinal surveys gathered from Indian students in professional courses
Quantitative Analysis	Utilizes predictive analytics techniques, particularly artificial neural networks, to uncover patterns and relationships within the data
Validation and Interpretation	Rigorous validation and interpretation process ensures robust findings
Focus of Exploration	Detailed examination of student motivations, skill acquisition, and personal growth, offering valuable insights into educational research
Research Design	Cross-sectional approach
Data Collection Method	Survey-based methodology
Sample	Indian students enrolled in professional courses across diverse institutions
Variables Investigated	Demographic information, academic records, motivation, skill acquisition, and personal growth
Experimental Design	Non-experimental; focuses on observational data
Analysis Method	Predictive analytics techniques, particularly artificial neural networks, used to identify patterns and associations among variables
Emphasis	Rigor and validity; measures in place to ensure reliability of findings and minimize bias
Overall Objective	To provide a comprehensive understanding of student motivations, skill acquisition patterns, and personal growth trajectories within Indian professional education settings
Outcome	Aims to generate meaningful insights that inform educational practices and policies, contributing to the enhancement of student outcomes and holistic development

Figure 2. Questionnaire Variables

Variable	Scale
Age	Continuous (years)
Gender	Categorical (Male, Female, Other)
Field of Study	Categorical (Engineering, Medicine, Management, etc.)
Motivation	Likert scale (1-5; strongly disagree to strongly agree)
Skill Development	Likert scale (1-5; strongly disagree to strongly agree)
Personal Growth	Likert scale (1-5; strongly disagree to strongly agree)
Academic Performance	Likert scale (1-5; poor to excellent)
Career Aspirations	Likert scale (1-5; low to high)

The study involved Indian students in engineering, medicine, and management across various institutions. Purposive sampling ensured representation from different disciplines and institutions. With five hundred participants, the sample captured diverse demographics, academic backgrounds, and specializations. This size allowed a thorough examination of factors affecting skill acquisition and personal growth among Indian students in professional education. The study on skill acquisition and personal growth among Indian students in professional courses examined various variables to capture the research topic's multidimensional aspects. These included:

- Demographic variables: Age, gender, ethnicity, socio-economic status, educational background.
- Academic variables: Course of study (e.g., engineering, medicine, management), academic performance (GPA, examination scores), years of study.
- Motivation variables: Intrinsic motivation (interest in the subject), extrinsic motivation (career aspirations), self-determination (autonomy, competence, relatedness).
- Skill acquisition measures: Self-reported skill development, perceived competence, participation in extracurricular activities or internships.
- Personal growth variables: Critical thinking, critical thinking skills, communication skills, adaptability, resilience.

Data was collected using structured questionnaires, validated scales, and qualitative interviews, ensuring comprehensive analysis. This approach provided a holistic understanding of factors influencing skill acquisition and personal growth among Indian students in professional education.

3.3 Research Design

A non-experimental, observational design was employed (Thompson & Panacek, 2007) meaning that no variables were manipulated, and the study focused on naturally occurring relationships. This design was chosen to capture a comprehensive snapshot of student experiences in professional education without intervention. The use of surveys, including demographic information, academic records, and attitudinal responses, allows for a broad view of student experiences, motivations, and skill development across various professional courses. As part of the data collection process, a comprehensive questionnaire was administered to 507 respondents from two institutions, enrolled in various courses. The questionnaire assessed students' motivation for skill acquisition and experiences of personal growth, with responses recorded on a Likert scale (Joshi et.al, 2015). Each row in the dataset stood for a respondent, and columns represented questionnaire items.

The dataset underwent Cronbach's alpha (Taber, 2018) analysis using Python for reliability. The "pandas" and "pinguin" libraries helped efficient computation of the Cronbach's alpha coefficient, which was **0.72**, showing high internal consistency and reinforcing the data's reliability as seen in Figure 3.

Figure 3. Cronbach's alpha Python Code

```
import pandas as pd
from scipy.stats import pearsonr
import numpy as np


df = pd.read_csv('cronf.csv')

# Calculate Cronbach's alpha
def cronbach_alpha(df):
    df_corr = df.corr()
    N = df.shape[1]
    mean_corr = df_corr.values[np.triu_indices(N, k=1)].mean()
    return (N * mean_corr) / (1 + (N - 1) * mean_corr)

# Selecting Likert scale variables
likert_variables = df.columns[3:]

# Calculate Cronbach's alpha for the Likert scale items
alpha = cronbach_alpha(df[likert_variables])
print(f"Cronbach's alpha: {alpha}")

Cronbach's alpha: 0.7244761697175927
```

The sample size of 507 respondents balanced statistical power and practical constraints, aligning with guidelines for adequate representation of Likert scale variables (Yurdugül, 2008). The diverse sample, including students from various courses and institutions, enhanced the findings' generalizability. Combining a well-designed questionnaire, rigorous statistical analysis using Python, and a justified sample size provided a robust foundation for investigating skill acquisition motivation and personal growth among Indian students in professional courses.

3.4 Data Analysis Techniques

For this study, data analysis employed a range of techniques to uncover patterns, relationships, and insights within the collected data. The analytical process was designed to systematically interpret the dataset, providing a comprehensive understanding of the factors influencing skill acquisition and personal growth among Indian students enrolled in professional courses. By utilizing a combination of statistical and advanced analytical methods, this study ensured accuracy, reliability, and depth in its findings.

The initial phase of data analysis involved descriptive statistics, which were used to summarize and organize the data effectively. Descriptive statistics provided an overview of participants' demographic characteristics, such as age, gender, socioeconomic background, and geographic location. Additionally, key variable distributions were analysed to present a clear picture of the dataset's overall structure. This step was essential in identifying general trends, variations, and possible anomalies in the data before proceeding to more complex analyses.

Following the descriptive analysis, inferential statistical techniques were applied to examine relationships between different variables. Correlation analysis was conducted to assess the strength and direction of associations between key factors such as student motivation, skill acquisition, and academic performance. By measuring how strongly variables were related, correlation analysis helped establish potential links that could explain trends in the data.

Regression modelling was also employed to further explore predictive relationships within the dataset (Lindley, 1990). This technique allowed for the identification of factors that had a significant impact on students' learning outcomes, motivation levels, and overall skill development. By analysing these predictive relationships, the study was able to determine the extent to which certain variables influenced student success and personal growth. Regression modelling provided a data-driven basis for understanding how different elements interacted within the educational environment.

To enhance the accuracy and depth of predictions, advanced techniques, such as artificial neural networks (ANNs), were incorporated into the analysis. ANNs were particularly suitable for this study due to their ability to handle nonlinear relationships and process large datasets effectively (Al-Sayid & Kirkil, 2023). These machine learning algorithms allowed for the modelling of intricate connections between various student-related factors, offering a more sophisticated and precise approach to prediction. By leveraging ANNs, this study improved the reliability of its findings and provided valuable insights into how different influences shape students' academic and professional journeys.

Additionally, data visualization techniques were utilized to present findings in a more accessible and interpretable format. Visual representations such as charts, graphs, and heatmaps were employed to illustrate key relationships and trends. These visualization methods helped simplify complex data patterns, making it easier for researchers, educators, and policymakers to understand the results. By translating statistical findings into graphical formats, this study enhanced the clarity and usability of the insights derived from the analysis.

By integrating descriptive and inferential statistics, machine learning techniques, and data visualization methods, this study ensured a well-rounded approach to data analysis. The combination of these techniques provided a holistic understanding of the factors affecting skill acquisition and personal growth among Indian students pursuing professional education. This comprehensive methodology not only contributed to a more profound interpretation of the data but also reinforced the study's potential impact on improving educational strategies and policies.

3.4.1 Artificial Neural Network Architecture and Functionality

Artificial Neural Networks (ANNs) are computational models inspired by human brain networks. They consist of interconnected neurons organized into layers. Each neuron processes input signals using an activation function and produces an output. ANNs learn complex data patterns by adjusting neuron connections through training algorithms.

For our study on skill acquisition motivation and personal growth among Indian students in professional courses, a Multilayer Perceptron (MLP) is ideal. MLPs have an input layer, one or more hidden layers, and an output layer, capable of learning nonlinear relationships. Figure 4 depicts the strengths and weaknesses of the model for ANN applied.

Figure 4. ANN: Strengths and Weaknesses

Strengths	Weaknesses
Ability to capture complex relationships	Prone to overfitting with large, noisy datasets
Flexibility in model architecture	Requires careful tuning of hyperparameters
Robustness to noisy data	Computationally intensive for large networks
Generalization to diverse datasets	Interpretability can be challenging

3.4.2 MLP Architecture Design using TensorFlow.

Multilayer Perceptron (MLP) architecture serves as a robust framework and provides a systematic design and implementation process eased by the TensorFlow library in Python. The steps undertaken have been exhibited in Fig 5 below.

Figure 5. MLP Architecture

Step	Description
1	Importing Libraries: Essential libraries including TensorFlow are imported, laying the groundwork for subsequent model construction.
2	Defining the MLP Architecture: The structure of the MLP is outlined, specifying input features, hidden layers, and activation functions for non-linearity.
3	Compiling the Model: Compilation involves configuring optimizer, loss function, and evaluation metric, pivotal for training and assessing model performance.
4	Displaying the Model Summary: A concise summary of the MLP architecture is presented, offering insights into its complexity and parameter distribution.
5	Training the Model: The model is trained on training data, enabling it to learn patterns and relationships present in the dataset through an iterative process.
6	Evaluating the Model: Post-training, the model's performance is evaluated using test data, quantifying its ability to generalize and make accurate predictions.
7	Making Predictions: Finally, the trained model is employed to make predictions on new data, validating its efficacy in real-world scenarios.

These steps help in creating a MLP model that is expected to predict skill acquisition motivation and personal growth scores among Indian students in professional courses. This iterative process, using TensorFlow's capabilities (Microsoft, n.d.), underscores the importance of robust deep learning frameworks in addressing complex research questions and generating actionable insights.

4. ANALYSIS AND RESULTS

This study explored skill acquisition motivation and personal growth among Indian students in professional courses. Initial statistical descriptions detailed variable distributions, followed by analyses of factors influencing motivation and growth. Correlation and regression analyses revealed connections, while Multilayer Perceptron neural networks predicted scores. The findings offer nuanced insights into these dynamics, informing interventions and support initiatives to foster skill development and personal growth among students.

4.1 Descriptive Statistics

The descriptive analytics offer a comprehensive overview of the dataset, which includes 472 samples from various fields of study with a balanced gender distribution. The average age of respondents is 21.93 years, showing a youthful demographic. Likert scale item analysis reveals high mean scores for motivation to get new skills (3.44), the importance of skill acquisition for career prospects (3.61), confidence in learning new skills (3.61), and the belief in the essential nature of personal growth for success (3.58). These high scores reflect strong positive attitudes towards skill acquisition and personal growth among the students. The figure 6, below as descriptive statistics applied using pandas.

Figure 6. Descriptive Statistics with Pandas

```
import pandas as pd

# Load the dataset into a Pandas DataFrame
df = pd.read_csv('data.csv')

# Create an empty DataFrame to store the results
detailed_stats = pd.DataFrame(columns=['Variable', 'Type', 'Count', 'Unique', 'Top', 'Frequency',
                                       'Mean/Median', 'Standard Deviation', 'Min', '25%', '50%', '75%', 'Max'])

# List to hold the results before converting to DataFrame
stats_list = []

# Iterate through each column in the DataFrame
for col in df.columns:
    dtype = df[col].dtype
    if dtype == 'object':  # Categorical variable
        count = df[col].count()
        unique = df[col].nunique()
        top = df[col].mode().iloc[0]
        freq = df[col].value_counts().iloc[0]
        stats = [col, dtype, count, unique, top, freq, '-', '-', '-', '-', '-', '-', '-']
    else:  # Numeric variable
        count = df[col].count()
        unique = df[col].nunique()
        top = '-'
        freq = '-'
        mean_median = df[col].mean() if count > 0 else '-'
        std = df[col].std() if count > 1 else '-'
        min_val = df[col].min()
        q25 = df[col].quantile(0.25)
        median = df[col].median()
        q75 = df[col].quantile(0.75)
        max_val = df[col].max()
        stats = [col, dtype, count, unique, top, freq, mean_median, std, min_val, q25, median, q75, max_val]

    # Add the statistics to the list
    stats_list.append(stats)

# Convert the list to a DataFrame
detailed_stats = pd.DataFrame(stats_list, columns=['Variable', 'Type', 'Count', 'Unique', 'Top', 'Frequency',
                                                   'Mean/Median', 'Standard Deviation', 'Min', '25%', '50%', '75%', 'Max'])
```

The low standard deviations across these items show consistent responses clustered around the mean, highlighting a consensus among respondents (Al-Saleh & Yousif, 2009). This consistency is crucial for the Multilayer Perceptron (MLP) model's success, as it implies a reliable dataset with minimal noise, enabling more correct training and prediction (Kordos & Rusiecki 2016). This robust dataset, marked by high engagement levels and consistent responses, enhances the MLP model's ability to effectively learn and predict factors influencing skill acquisition motivation and personal growth. Consequently, the insights derived from the MLP model will be more dependable and actionable, aiding in the development of targeted educational interventions. Figure 7 below elaborates the data profiling.

Figure 7. Data Profile

Variable	Type	Count	Unique	Top	Frequency	Mean/Median	Standard Deviation	Min	25%	50%	75%	Max
Age (In years)	int64	472	10	-	-	21.93220339	2.335832984	18	20	22	24	27
Gender	object	472	2	Male	247	-	-	-	-	-	-	-
Field of Study	object	472	3	Management	187	-	-	-	-	-	-	-
I was motivated to acquire new skills in my field of study	int64	472	4	-	-	3.438559322	1.158572059	2	2	3	5	5
Acquiring new skills is important for my future career prospects.	int64	472	4	-	-	3.612288136	1.005345299	2	3	4	4	5
I felt confident in my ability to learn new skills.	int64	472	4	-	-	3.608050847	1.001579863	2	3	4	4	5
I believe that personal growth is essential for success in my field of study	int64	472	4	-	-	3.578389831	0.950024669	2	3	4	4	5
I actively sought opportunities for personal development and growth.	int64	472	4	-	-	3.552966102	1.020673612	2	3	4	4	5
Personal growth involved more than just acquiring technical skills.	int64	472	4	-	-	3.56779661	0.985920532	2	3	4	4	5
How satisfied were you with your overall educational experience?	int64	472	4	-	-	3.588983051	0.98423099	2	3	4	4	5
Did you feel supported in your efforts to acquire new skills and grow personally at your educational institution?	int64	472	4	-	-	3.588983051	0.962417683	2	3	4	4	5
How likely are you to recommend your field of study to others?	int64	472	4	-	-	3.610169492	0.971211062	2	3	4	4	5

Figure 8. Data Visualization

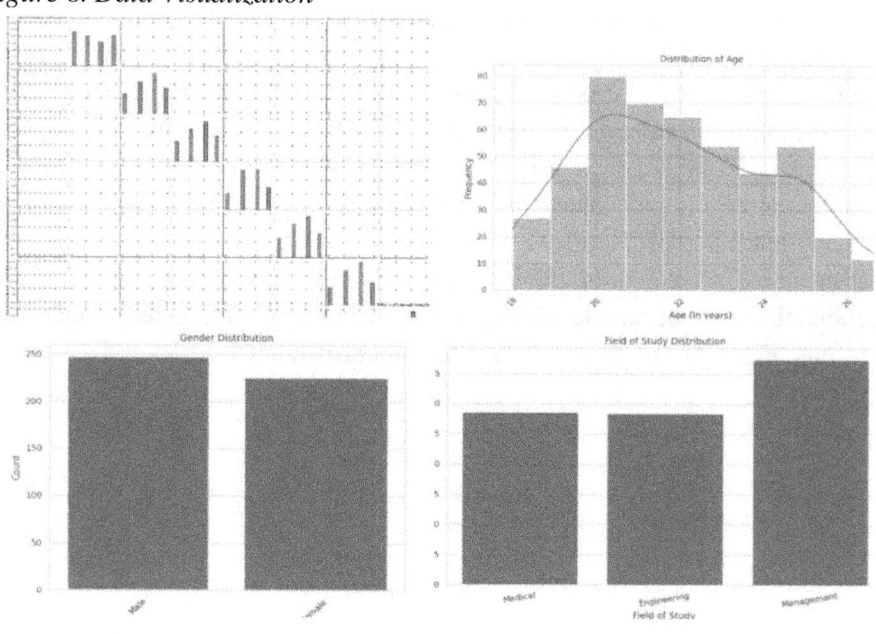

The correlation matrix was computed to analyse relationships between various variables, identifying the strongest connections (Lindley, 1990). This analysis provided valuable insights into the factors influencing skill acquisition, motivation, and personal growth among Indian students enrolled in professional courses. The key findings highlight several important aspects of student engagement and development.

One of the most significant findings was the strong association between students' motivation to acquire new skills and their recognition of these skills' importance for future career prospects. Students who understood the relevance of skill acquisition were more confident in learning new abilities and actively pursued opportunities for personal and professional growth. This indicates that career-oriented motivation plays a crucial role in encouraging students to develop their competencies.

Another important insight was the value placed on personal growth. Students who prioritized personal development actively sought opportunities to enhance their skills and knowledge, recognizing that growth extends beyond technical expertise. This suggests that fostering a mindset that values continuous learning can drive students to explore new areas of knowledge and expand their capabilities beyond their academic curriculum.

Additionally, overall student satisfaction was closely linked to the level of support they received in their skill acquisition efforts. Students who felt encouraged and supported by their institutions were more likely to express satisfaction with their learning experience. Moreover, satisfied students were more inclined to recommend their field of study to others, reflecting the positive impact of institutional support on motivation and engagement.

These findings emphasize the critical role of confidence, career relevance, and institutional support in shaping student motivation and satisfaction. When students recognize the long-term benefits of acquiring new skills and feel supported in their learning journey, they are more likely to stay engaged and proactive in their personal and professional development. Institutions that focus on fostering confidence, providing career-oriented training, and offering strong support systems can significantly enhance students' overall. The study highlights that motivation, personal growth, and institutional support are key drivers of skill acquisition and student satisfaction. By addressing these factors, educators and policymakers can create more effective learning environments that encourage students to pursue continuous development and career readiness.

Figure 9. Correlation Analysis

Variable	Highly Correlated With	Correlation Coefficient
I was motivated to acquire new skills in my field of study	Acquiring new skills is important for my future career prospects	0.6
	I felt confident in my ability to learn new skills	0.45
	Personal growth is essential for success in my field of study	0.28
	I actively sought opportunities for personal development and growth	0.42
Personal growth is essential for success in my field of study	I actively sought opportunities for personal development and growth	0.3
	Personal growth involved more than just acquiring technical skills	0.2
I actively sought opportunities for personal development and growth	How satisfied were you with your overall educational experience	0.32
	Did you feel supported in your efforts to acquire new skills and grow personally at your educational institution	0.2
How satisfied were you with your overall educational experience	Did you feel supported in your efforts to acquire new skills and grow personally at your educational institution	0.28
	How likely are you to recommend your field of study to others	0.27
How likely are you to recommend your field of study to others	I was motivated to acquire new skills in my field of study	0.31
	Acquiring new skills is important for my future career prospects	0.19

Regression analysis was performed to understand the impact of factors on students' motivation for skill acquisition and personal growth. Linear regression models helped find significant predictors (Lindley, 1990). The regression analysis aimed to figure out the impact of factors on students' overall satisfaction with their educational experience. The results reveal that motivation to get new skills has a significant positive impact on overall satisfaction **(coefficient = 0.4041, p < 0.0001).** This shows that students who are motivated to get new skills tend to be more satisfied with their educational experience. Conversely, the importance placed on getting new skills for future career prospects has a significant negative impact on satisfaction **(coefficient = -0.0843, p < 0.0001),** suggesting that students who see high career importance in getting new skills might experience lower satisfaction, due to increased stress or pressure. Other factors, such as confidence in learning new skills, belief in the essential nature of personal growth, and active pursuit of personal development, showed positive but non-significant impacts on overall satisfaction.

These findings have important implications for the current study and its outcomes. The significant positive impact of skill acquisition motivation on satisfaction underscores the need for educational institutions to foster intrinsic motivation among students. At the same time, the negative impact of career-related pressures suggests that institutions should address potential stressors associated with skill acquisition for future careers. By creating an environment that can enhance motivation and manage career-related pressures, institutions can improve overall educational satisfaction among students. However, the modest **R-squared value of 0.234** indicates that further analysis is needed to uncover additional factors influencing satisfaction. Future research should explore other potential predictors, such as peer support, faculty engagement, and extracurricular activities, to provide a more comprehensive understanding of the determinants of student satisfaction. These insights can guide the development of targeted programs and policies aimed at fostering motivation, reducing stress, and enhancing the overall student experience. Figure 10 below highlights the OLS regression with pandas.

Figure 10. OLS Regression with Pandas

```
import statsmodels.api as sm
import pandas as pd

# Load the dataset into a Pandas DataFrame
df = pd.read_csv('data.csv')
# Define the independent variables (X) and the dependent variable (y)
X = df[['I was motivated to acquire new skills in my field of study',
        'Acquiring new skills is important for my future career prospects.',
        'I felt confident in my ability to learn new skills.',
        'I believe that personal growth is essential for success in my field of study',
        'I actively sought opportunities for personal development and growth.',
        'Personal growth involved more than just acquiring technical skills.']]
y = df['How satisfied were you with your overall educational experience?']

# Add a constant to the independent variables
X = sm.add_constant(X)

# Create and fit the model
model = sm.OLS(y, X).fit()

# Print the summary of the regression model
print(model.summary())
```

Figure 11. Regression Analysis Results

```
                                          OLS Regression Results
===========================================================================================================
Dep. Variable:     How satisfied were you with your overall educational experience?   R-squared:                       0.234
Model:                                                                         OLS   Adj. R-squared:                  0.224
Method:                                                              Least Squares   F-statistic:                     23.65
Date:                                                             Wed, 05 Jun 2024   Prob (F-statistic):           1.97e-24
Time:                                                                     12:35:22   Log-Likelihood:                -598.88
No. Observations:                                                              472   AIC:                             1212.
Df Residuals:                                                                  465   BIC:                             1241.
Df Model:                                                                        6
Covariance Type:                                                         nonrobust
=====================================================================================================================================
                                                                                coef    std err          t      P>|t|      [0.025      0.975]
-------------------------------------------------------------------------------------------------------------------------------------
const                                                                         2.1683      0.258      8.415      0.000       1.662       2.675
I was motivated to acquire new skills in my field of study                    0.4041      0.055      7.385      0.000       0.297       0.512
Acquiring new skills is important for my future career prospects.           -0.0033      0.045     -0.073      0.942      -0.092       0.085
I felt confident in my ability to learn new skills.                           0.0439      0.045      0.970      0.332      -0.045       0.133
I believe that personal growth is essential for success in my field of study -0.0021      0.048     -0.043      0.966      -0.097       0.092
I actively sought opportunities for personal development and growth.          0.0076      0.046      0.165      0.869      -0.082       0.098
Personal growth involved more than just acquiring technical skills.          -0.0379      0.046     -0.824      0.410      -0.128       0.052
==============================================================================
Omnibus:                      239.235   Durbin-Watson:                   2.148
Prob(Omnibus):                  0.000   Jarque-Bera (JB):               28.111
Skew:                           0.127   Prob(JB):                     7.86e-07
Kurtosis:                       1.832   Cond. No.                         58.6
==============================================================================

Notes:
[1] Standard Errors assume that the covariance matrix of the errors is correctly specified.
```

4.2 Predictive Modeling with MLP

A Multilayer Perceptron (MLP) neural network was designed to predict student satisfaction and recommendations based on their responses to the Likert scale items. The architecture included an input layer, hidden layers, and an output layer.

Figure 12. MLP with TensorFlow

```python
import tensorflow as tf
from tensorflow.keras.models import Sequential
from tensorflow.keras.layers import Dense

# Prepare the data
X = df[['I was motivated to acquire new skills in my field of study',
        'Acquiring new skills is important for my future career prospects.',
        'I felt confident in my ability to learn new skills.',
        'I believe that personal growth is essential for success in my field of study',
        'I actively sought opportunities for personal development and growth.',
        'Personal growth involved more than just acquiring technical skills.']].values
y = df['How likely are you to recommend your field of study to others?'].values

# Define the MLP model
model = Sequential()
model.add(Dense(12, input_dim=X.shape[1], activation='relu'))
model.add(Dense(8, activation='relu'))
model.add(Dense(1, activation='linear'))

# Compile the model
model.compile(loss='mean_squared_error', optimizer='adam')

# Train the model
model.fit(X, y, epochs=50, batch_size=10, verbose=1)

# Evaluate the model
loss = model.evaluate(X, y)
print(f'Model Loss: {loss}')
```

Figure 12 above exhibits the MLP with tensor flow. Initially, the data is prepared by selecting relevant features from the dataset: motivation to acquire new skills, the importance of these skills for future career prospects, confidence in learning new skills, the belief in the essential nature of personal growth, the active pursuit of personal development opportunities, and understanding that personal growth involves more than just technical skills. The target variable is the likelihood of students recommending their field of study to others. These selected features and the target variable are then converted into NumPy arrays (X and y respectively) to be used in the neural network model.

The MLP model is defined using the Sequential class from Keras (Chollet & Chollet, 2021), with three layers: an input layer with 12 neurons and ReLU activation function, a hidden layer with 8 neurons and ReLU activation function, and an output layer with 1 neuron and a linear activation function. The model is compiled with the mean squared error (MSE) as the loss function and the Adam optimizer, which is known for its efficiency and adaptability in training deep learning models. The model is trained over 50 epochs with a batch size of ten, which means the dataset is divided into batches of ten samples and the weights are updated after each batch. Finally, the model's performance is evaluated on the same training data using the MSE loss function, providing a sign of how well the model has learned to predict the likelihood of students recommending their field of study. The MSE value is printed to give a quantitative measure of the model's accuracy as seen in figure 13.

Figure 13. MLP epoch Losses.

Epoch	Loss	Epoch	Loss
1	13.6553	26	0.755
2	3.253	27	0.758
3	1.2834	28	0.7519
4	1.0666	29	0.7592
5	0.9399	30	0.7526
6	0.8841	31	0.7618
7	0.8606	32	0.7603
8	0.8418	33	0.7468
9	0.8309	34	0.7487
10	0.8279	35	0.7479
11	0.8171	36	0.7442
12	0.8018	37	0.7446
13	0.7959	38	0.7462
14	0.7976	39	0.742
15	0.7872	40	0.731
16	0.7861	41	0.741
17	0.7858	42	0.7353
18	0.7853	43	0.7359
19	0.7835	44	0.7393
20	0.772	45	0.7314
21	0.7729	46	0.7424
22	0.7658	47	0.7258
23	0.7701	48	0.7311
24	0.7669	49	0.7227
25	0.7907	50	0.7316

The output highlights the training process of a Multilayer Perceptron (MLP) model designed to predict the likelihood of students recommending their field of study based on their motivation and experiences related to skill acquisition and personal growth. The training involved 50 epochs with a batch size of ten, utilizing the mean squared error (MSE) as the loss function and the Adam optimizer for model optimization.

The training process shows a significant reduction in the loss from the first epoch to the final epoch, showing that the model is learning and improving its predictions. Starting with a loss of 13.6553 in the first epoch, the model's loss consistently decreases, reaching 0.7316 by the 50th epoch. The final evaluation of the model on the training data shows an MSE of 0.7230, which suggests that the model has achieved a reasonable level of accuracy in predicting the target variable.

Retrieving Model Weights and Biases

Retrieving model weights and biases is crucial for understanding the influence of each input variable, ensuring model reliability, and enhancing transparency. This knowledge helps to find key predictors, guide model improvements, and develop targeted educational interventions and policies based on evidence, improving student outcomes (Rojas et.al, 2022). After training the model, we retrieved the weights and biases for each layer using the get weights () method as seen in figure 14.

Figure 14. Model Weights and Biases

```
[ ] import tensorflow as tf
    from tensorflow.keras.models import Sequential
    from tensorflow.keras.layers import Dense

    # Prepare the data
    X = df[['I was motivated to acquire new skills in my field of study',
            'Acquiring new skills is important for my future career prospects.',
            'I felt confident in my ability to learn new skills.',
            'I believe that personal growth is essential for success in my field of study',
            'I actively sought opportunities for personal development and growth.',
            'Personal growth involved more than just acquiring technical skills.']].values
    y = df['How likely are you to recommend your field of study to others?'].values

    # Define the MLP model
    model = Sequential()
    model.add(Dense(12, input_dim=X.shape[1], activation='relu'))
    model.add(Dense(8, activation='relu'))
    model.add(Dense(1, activation='linear'))

    # Compile the model
    model.compile(loss='mean_squared_error', optimizer='adam')

    # Train the model
    model.fit(X, y, epochs=50, batch_size=10, verbose=1)

    # Evaluate the model
    loss = model.evaluate(X, y)
    print(f'Model Loss: {loss}')

    # Retrieve weights and biases
    weights_layer_1, biases_layer_1 = model.layers[0].get_weights()
    weights_layer_2, biases_layer_2 = model.layers[1].get_weights()
    weights_output, biases_output = model.layers[2].get_weights()

    # Print model summary
    model.summary()

    # Print weights and biases
    print("Weights and biases of layer 1 (input layer):")
    print(weights_layer_1)
    print(biases_layer_1)
```

5. INTERPRETATION OF RESULTS

The reduction in the loss over the epochs shows that the MLP model is effectively learning from the data. The low final loss value of 0.7230 implies that the model can predict the likelihood of students recommending their field of study with a reasonable degree of accuracy. However, the reader can interpret the loss values to understand the model's performance better:

- Initial High Loss: The high loss at the start (13.6553) is usually expected as the model begins with random weights and learns from the data.
- Rapid Decrease in Loss: The loss decreases rapidly in the first few epochs, showing that the model quickly learns the first patterns in the data.
- Gradual Stabilization: The loss stabilizes and shows slower decreases in later epochs, suggesting that the model is fine-tuning its predictions and approaching a best solution.

5.1 Model Architecture

The Multilayer Perceptron (MLP) model built in this study consists of the following layers:

- Input Layer: twelve neurons with ReLU activation function. This layer receives the input features related to students' motivation and experiences.
- Hidden Layer: eight neurons with ReLU activation function. This layer processes the inputs through non-linear transformations to capture complex patterns in the data.
- Output Layer: one neuron with a linear activation function. This layer produces the final output, predicting the likelihood of students recommending their field of study.
- The model was trained over 50 epochs with a batch size of ten, using the mean squared error (MSE) as the loss function and the Adam optimizer for training.

Weights and biases for each layer were extracted and analysed. Below are the details: **5.1.1 Input Layer Weights and Biases:**

The input layer consists of twelve neurons, and the weights are a twelve-by-eight matrix representing connections to the hidden layer. The biases are a vector of length twelve. The weights show how each input feature influences the neurons in the hidden layer. Positive values show a direct relationship, while negative values show an inverse relationship.

5.1.2 Hidden Layer Weights and Biases:

The hidden layer has eight neurons, and the weights are an eight-by-one matrix representing connections to the output layer. The biases are a vector of length eight. The weights in this layer show how the activations from the hidden layer neurons affect the final output. Positive weights increase the predicted likelihood, while negative weights decrease it.

- **Output Layer Weights and Biases:**

The output layer has one neuron, and the weights are a vector of length eight, representing the influence of each hidden neuron on the output. The bias is a single value. The weights and biases at this layer figure out the final prediction of the model as seen in Figure 15.

Figure 15. Model Weights and Bias

Layer	Weights Shape	Biases Shape	Example Weights	Example Biases
Input Layer	(6, 12)	(12,)	[[-0.374, -0.207, ..., 0.496, -0.262], ...]	[0.037, 0.219, ..., -0.148]
Hidden Layer	(12, 8)	(8,)	[[-0.409, -0.537, ..., 0.249], ...]	[0.159, -0.082, ..., 0.190]
Output Layer	(8, 1)	(1,)	[[0.112], [-0.127], [0.297], ..., [0.388]]	[0.186]

6. IMPLICATIONS OF THE STUDY

The implications of the study have been the following:

6.1 Understanding the Role of the Multilayer Perceptron (MLP) Model in Skill Development:

The analysis of the Multilayer Perceptron (MLP) model offers valuable insights into the factors influencing skill acquisition, motivation, and personal growth among Indian students enrolled in professional courses. The MLP model, commonly used in artificial intelligence and data analysis, helps identify patterns and correlations in students' learning behaviors(Alwan &Rajendran et.al,2006). By applying this analytical model, we can better understand how various factors impact students' educational experiences and personal development. The findings provide guidance on improving educational strategies and institutional support to enhance student learning outcomes.

6.2 Motivation as a Driving Force in Skill Acquisition

One of the most critical factors identified in the study is the role of motivation in skill acquisition. There exists a strong positive correlation between students' motivation to acquire new skills and their overall satisfaction with their educational experience. This relationship highlights the importance of fostering intrinsic motivation among students, as it directly contributes to their engagement and academic success.

To enhance motivation, educational institutions should design engaging coursework that integrates real-world applications. Theoretical knowledge alone is insufficient; students benefit significantly from hands-on experiences that demonstrate the practical relevance of their learning. Project-based learning, case studies, internships, and industry collaborations can bridge the gap between academic theory and real-world practice, making learning more meaningful and stimulating.

Furthermore, recognizing and celebrating student achievements can reinforce motivation. Institutions should implement reward systems, such as certificates, scholarships, or public recognition, to acknowledge students' progress. Gamification, where students earn points or badges for skill mastery, can also be an effective strategy to sustain motivation. Providing constructive feedback and setting achievable yet challenging goals can further encourage students to persist in their learning journey.

6.3 Career Prospects, Stress, and Student Well-Being

While acquiring new skills is essential for career growth, the study reveals a significant negative impact when excessive importance is placed on skill acquisition solely for career prospects. Students who perceive skill acquisition as a mandatory requirement for securing a job often experience increased stress and lower overall satisfaction with their education. This finding suggests that a high-pressure learning environment, driven by external expectations, can lead to anxiety and burnout, ultimately hindering the learning process.

To address this issue, institutions must strike a balance between career readiness and stress management. Career counseling services should be readily available to help students navigate their professional aspirations without feeling overwhelmed. Personalized career guidance can help students set realistic expectations and create structured pathways toward their goals.

Additionally, integrating stress management workshops into the curriculum can equip students with coping mechanisms to handle academic and career-related pressures. Mindfulness training, time management strategies, and relaxation techniques can foster resilience and emotional well-being. By creating a supportive environment where skill acquisition is seen as a journey rather than a high-stakes requirement, institutions can promote both career development and mental health.

6.4 The Role of Confidence in Learning New Skills

The study indicates that confidence in learning new skills, while not statistically significant in correlation with overall satisfaction, still holds a positive coefficient. This suggests that confidence plays a contributory role in shaping students' educational experiences. When students believe in their ability to acquire new skills, they are more likely to take on challenges, persist through difficulties, and achieve higher levels of competence.

To build student confidence, institutions should adopt supportive teaching practices. Encouraging a growth mindset—where students view challenges as opportunities to learn rather than obstacles—can boost their self-efficacy. Providing self-paced learning resources allows students to progress at their comfort level, reducing the fear of failure. Digital platforms offering interactive tutorials, simulations, and practice exercises can support self-directed learning.

Mentorship programs can also enhance student confidence. Pairing students with experienced mentors, such as faculty members, industry professionals, or senior peers, can provide valuable guidance, encouragement, and constructive feedback. A strong support system reassures students that they are not alone in their learning journey and that they have access to resources and people who can assist them in overcoming difficulties.

6.5 Beyond Technical Skills: The Importance of Holistic Personal Growth

While technical skills are vital for professional success, the study highlights that students highly value personal growth beyond academic and technical competencies. In today's dynamic work environment, soft skills such as leadership, communication, teamwork, adaptability, and emotional intelligence are equally crucial for career advancement and personal fulfilment.

Educational institutions should incorporate holistic development programs into their curriculum. Leadership training programs can empower students to take initiative, make informed decisions, and develop problem-solving abilities. Communication skills workshops can enhance students' ability to articulate their ideas clearly and collaborate effectively in team settings.

6.6 Integrating Technology and Innovation in Skill Development

With advancements in technology, educational institutions must leverage innovative learning tools to enhance skill acquisition. Online learning platforms, virtual reality (VR) simulations, and artificial intelligence (AI)-driven tutoring systems can create immersive and interactive learning experiences. These technologies enable students to practice and refine their skills in a risk-free environment before applying them in real-world scenarios.

Blended learning, which combines traditional classroom instruction with digital resources, offers a flexible and personalized approach to education. Students can access recorded lectures, participate in discussion forums, and engage in collaborative online projects, fostering a more interactive and engaging learning process.

6.7 Bridging the Gap between Academia and Industry

To ensure that students are industry-ready, educational institutions should strengthen their partnerships with businesses and organizations. Industry collaborations can provide students with hands-on experiences through internships, apprenticeships, and live projects. Guest lectures and industry seminars can expose students to current trends, challenges, and expectations in their respective fields.

7. LIMITATIONS OF THE STUDY

Despite the insightful findings, this study has limitations that call for consideration. Firstly, the sample size of 507 respondents is small, which may limit the generalizability of the results to a broader population of Indian students in professional courses. Larger sample sizes in future research could provide more robust and generalizable insights.

The study has been conducted using questionnaire filled by respondents not under observation, which can be subject to response biases such as social desirability bias or recall bias. This could potentially affect the accuracy of the reported motivations and experiences.

Thirdly, while the Multilayer Perceptron (MLP) model captured significant relationships, the low R-squared value (0.234) indicates that there are other unmeasured factors influencing student satisfaction and motivation. Future studies should consider incorporating added variables such as peer relationships, faculty support, and institutional resources to provide a more comprehensive understanding.

Lastly, the design of the study prevents inference of causal relationships. Longitudinal studies are needed to better understand how motivations and experiences evolve over time and impact long-term educational outcomes.

8. RECOMMENDATIONS FOR FUTURE RESEARCH

Enhance the understanding of skill acquisition motivation and personal growth among students, increasing the sample size will improve the generalizability of the findings. Including a diverse range of institutions and student demographics will offer a more comprehensive view of the factors influencing student motivation and satisfaction.

Secondly, future studies should incorporate added variables such as peer relationships, faculty support, campus facilities, and extracurricular activities to capture a broader spectrum of influences on student outcomes. Utilizing mixed methods approaches, combining quantitative surveys with qualitative interviews, can offer deeper insights into the nuanced experiences of students.

Thirdly, addressing the potential biases in self-reported data by employing objective measures and triangulating data from multiple sources will improve the reliability of the findings.

Additionally, longitudinal research designs are recommended to track changes in student motivations and experiences over time, allowing for a better understanding of causal relationships and long-term impacts (Liu, Y. et.al, 2024).

Finally, exploring the impact of specific interventions, such as mentorship programs, stress management workshops, and holistic development initiatives, on student motivation and satisfaction will offer practical insights for educational institutions aiming to enhance student outcomes. By addressing these recommendations, future research can significantly contribute to the development of effective strategies for fostering skill acquisition and personal growth in educational settings.

9. CONCLUSION

This study investigated the factors influencing skill acquisition motivation and personal growth among Indian students in professional courses. The findings reveal that intrinsic motivation to get new skills significantly enhances overall educational satisfaction. Conversely, the pressure to get skills for future career prospects negatively affects satisfaction, highlighting the need for balanced stress management. Confidence and support systems, while not statistically significant, showed positive influences on student satisfaction.

The study contributes to knowledge by finding key predictors of student satisfaction and highlighting the complex interplay between motivation, career pressures, and personal growth. It underscores the importance of fostering intrinsic motivation and managing career-related stress to improve educational outcomes.

Practical applications of these findings include the development of strategies to enhance student motivation, such as engaging and relevant coursework, recognition of achievements, and supportive teaching practices. Policy implications suggest that educational institutions should provide holistic development programs and stress management resources to create a supportive learning environment.

Future research should expand on these findings by exploring added factors, employing longitudinal designs, and implementing mixed methods approaches to gain a deeper understanding. Overall, this study offers valuable insights for educational institutions aiming to foster skill acquisition and personal growth, enhancing student satisfaction and success.

REFERENCES

Akram, H., & Li, S. (2024). Understanding the role of teacher-student relationships in students' online learning engagement: Mediating role of academic motivation. *Perceptual and Motor Skills, 131*(4), 1415–1438. DOI: 10.1177/00315125241248709 PMID: 38647390

Al-Saleh, M. F., & Yousif, A. E. (2009). Properties of the standard deviation that are rarely mentioned in classrooms. *Austrian Journal of Statistics, 38*(3), 193–202.

Al-Sayid, F., & Kirkil, G. (2023). Exploring non-linear relationships between perceived interactivity or interface design and acceptance of collaborative web-based learning. *Education and Information Technologies, 28*(9), 11819–11866. DOI: 10.1007/s10639-023-11635-6 PMID: 37361814

AL-Sayid, F., & Kirkil, G.AL-Sayid. (2023). Students' web-based activities moderate the effect of human-computer-interaction factors on their E-Learning acceptance and success during COVID-19 pandemic. *International Journal of Human-Computer Interaction, 39*(14), 2852–2875. DOI: 10.1080/10447318.2022.2087013

Alamer, A., & Almulhim, F. (2024). Optimizing EFL learning: Exploring the role of learner background, intrinsic, and extrinsic motivation. *BMC Psychology, 12*(1), 34. PMID: 38238867

Alshamrani, K. M., Alkhayyat, A. A., Arif, R. N., Alahmadi, A. A., Aldahery, S. T., Alsharif, W. M., & Qurashi, A. A. (2025). Are Saudi Radiological Sciences Students Prepared for Emergencies? Exploring Knowledge, and Attitudes Towards Basic Life Support and Cardiopulmonary Resuscitation. *Open Access Emergency Medicine : OAEM, 17*, 91–103. DOI: 10.2147/OAEM.S507046 PMID: 39958799

Alwan, M., Rajendran, P. J., Kell, S., Mack, D., Dalal, S., Wolfe, M., & Felder, R. (2006). An artificial neural network–based fall detection. *Journal of Ambient Intelligence and Smart Environments, 2*(4), 311–322.

Bandura, A. (1986). Social foundations of thought and action. *Englewood Cliffs, NJ, 1986*(23-28), 2.

Batina, L., Bhasin, S., Jap, D., & Picek, S. (2019). {CSI}{NN}: Reverse engineering of neural network architectures through electromagnetic side channel. In *28th USENIX Security Symposium (USENIX Security 19)* (pp. 515-532).

Beatson, N., De Lange, P., O'Connell, B., Tharapos, M., & Smith, J. K. (2021). Factors impacting on accounting academics' motivation and capacity to adapt in challenging times. *Accounting Research Journal*, *34*(2), 184–195. DOI: 10.1108/ARJ-08-2020-0240

Bonk, C. J., & Graham, C. R. (2012). *The handbook of blended learning: Global perspectives, local designs*. Wiley+ ORM.

Brahme, A. (2014). *Comprehensive biomedical physics*. Newnes.

Braun, V., & Clarke, V. (2006). Using thematic analysis in psychology. *Qualitative Research in Psychology*, *3*(2), 77–101. DOI: 10.1191/1478088706qp063oa

Bunn, G., & Wake, D. (2015). Motivating factors of nontraditional post-baccalaureate students pursuing initial teacher licensure. *Teacher Educator*, *50*(1), 47–66. DOI: 10.1080/08878730.2014.975304

Burke, M., Parnell, A., Wesaw, A., & Kruger, K. (2017). Predictive analysis of student data: A focus on engagement and behavior. *NASPA report*.

Chandran, M., Padalkar, S., & Shimray, R. A. (2025). Motivation to Become a Teacher: Emerging Trends From a Study of Preservice Teacher Education. *Contemporary Education Dialogue*, *22*(1), 127–153. DOI: 10.1177/09731849241300796

Chollet, F., & Chollet, F. (2021). *Deep learning with Python*. Simon and Schuster.

Cook, D. A., & Artino, A. R.Jr. (2016). Motivation to learn: An overview of contemporary theories. *Medical Education*, *50*(10), 997–1014. DOI: 10.1111/medu.13074 PMID: 27628718

Deshmukh, D. (2017). Inclusion-evidence based strategies. *International Journal of Education and Management Studies*, *7*(3), 290–293.

Dhar, S. (2012). Employability of management students in India: Some concerns and considerations. *AIMA Journal for management research, 6*(4/4), 0974-497.

Eccles, J. S., & Wigfield, A. (2020). From expectancy-value theory to situated expectancy-value theory: A developmental, social cognitive, and sociocultural perspective on motivation. *Contemporary Educational Psychology*, *61*, 101859. DOI: 10.1016/j.cedpsych.2020.101859

Fan, C., Lei, Y., Sun, Y., Piscitelli, M. S., Chiosa, R., & Capozzoli, A. (2022). Data-centric or algorithm-centric: Exploiting the performance of transfer learning for improving building energy predictions in data-scarce context. *Energy*, *240*, 122775. DOI: 10.1016/j.energy.2021.122775

Graefe, A. K. (2024). Gifted high school students' perceptions of the impact of classroom power dynamics on motivation and empowerment. *Journal of Advanced Academics*, *35*(1), 6–55. DOI: 10.1177/1932202X231220414

Grishma, S., & Esi, A. (2014). The Impact of Socio-Cultural Factors on Professional Aspiration in India. Conference: Subsistence Markets Conference, Chicago https:// search. informit. org/doi/epdf/10.3316/ielapa. 721100117642410.

Hinduja, P., Fakir Mohammad, R., & Siddiqui, S. (2024). Factors influencing students' academic self-efficacy in related domains. *SAGE Open*, *14*(4), 21582440241289738. DOI: 10.1177/21582440241289738

Iqbal, S., Razalli, M. R., & Taib, C. A. B. (2023). Influence of intrinsic and extrinsic motivation on higher education performance: Mediating effect of quality culture. *Frontiers in Education*, *8*, 1099415. DOI: 10.3389/feduc.2023.1099415

Jana, S., & Pal, C. (2024). A study of stellar evolution based on structural equation modelling of stellar parameters. *International Journal of Data Analysis Techniques and Strategies*, *16*(2), 105–125. DOI: 10.1504/IJDATS.2024.137872

Joshi, A., Kale, S., Chandel, S., & Pal, D. K. (2015). Likert scale: Explored and explained. *British Journal of Applied Science and Technology*, *7*(4), 396–403. DOI: 10.9734/BJAST/2015/14975

Kelly, M. L., Nieuwoudt, J., Willis, R., & Lee, M. F. (2024). Belonging, enjoyment, motivation, and retention: University students' sense of belonging before and during the COVID-19 pandemic. *Journal of College Student Retention*, •••, 15210251241231242. DOI: 10.1177/15210251241231242

Khan, A., & Kim, N. (2020). Application of artificial neural networks for quantitative damage detection in fiber-reinforced composite structures. *Advances in Mechanical Engineering*, *12*(4), 1–12.

Kirkos, E., Spathis, C., & Manolopoulos, Y. (2008). Support vector machines, Decision Trees and Neural Networks for auditor selection. *Journal of computational Methods in Sciences and Engineering, 8*(3), 213-224.

Kordos, M., & Rusiecki, A. (2016). Reducing noise impact on MLP training: Techniques and algorithms to provide noise-robustness in MLP network training. *Soft Computing*, *20*(1), 49–65. DOI: 10.1007/s00500-015-1690-9

Kurni, M., & Mohammed, M. S. (2023). *A beginner's guide to introduce artificial intelligence in teaching and learning*. Springer Nature.

Legault, L. (2017). Self-Determination Theory. In V. Z.-H. Shackelford, Encyclopaedia of Personality and Individual Differences. DOI: 10.1007/978-3-319-28099-8_1162-1

Lindley, D. V. (1990). Regression and correlation analysis. In *Time series and statistics* (pp. 237–243). Palgrave Macmillan UK. DOI: 10.1007/978-1-349-20865-4_30

Liu, Y., Ma, S., & Chen, Y. (2024). The impacts of learning motivation, emotional engagement and psychological capital on academic performance in a blended learning university course. *Frontiers in Psychology, 15*, 1357936. DOI: 10.3389/fpsyg.2024.1357936 PMID: 38800675

Madheswari, S. P., & Mageswari, S. U. (2020). Changing paradigms of engineering education-An Indian perspective. *Procedia Computer Science, 172*, 215–224. DOI: 10.1016/j.procs.2020.05.034

Merma-Molina, G., Gavilán-Martín, D., Baena-Morales, S., & Urrea-Solano, M. (2022). Critical thinking and effective personality in the framework of education for sustainable development. *Education Sciences, 12*(1), 28. DOI: 10.3390/educsci12010028

Michael, E., & Moore, D. M. (2020). Connecting Theory to Practice: Using Self-Determination Theory To Better Understand Inclusion in STEM. *Journal of Microbiology & Biology Education*. PMID: 32431768

Microsoft. (n.d.). Introduction to natural language processing with TensorFlow. Retrieved from Learn.microsof.com: https://learn.microsoft.com/en-us/training/modules/intro-natural-language-processing-tensorflow/

Müller, O., Fay, M., & Vom Brocke, J. (2018). The effect of big data and analytics on firm performance: An econometric analysis considering industry characteristics. *Journal of Management Information Systems, 35*(2), 488–509. DOI: 10.1080/07421222.2018.1451955

Narkhede, G., Pasi, B., Dhamak, P., Mahalle, P., & Ambhore, N. (2025). In the pursuit of educational excellence: Investigating CSFs for implementing NEP 2020 to redefine the higher education ecosystem. *Journal of Applied Research in Higher Education*. Advance online publication. DOI: 10.1108/JARHE-09-2024-0454

Okewu, E., Adewole, P., Misra, S., Maskeliunas, R., & Damasevicius, R. (2021). Artificial neural networks for educational data mining in higher education: A systematic literature review. *Applied Artificial Intelligence, 35*(13), 983–1021. DOI: 10.1080/08839514.2021.1922847

Pinheiro, P. O., Almahairi, A., Benmalek, R., Golemo, F., & Courville, A. C. (2020). Unsupervised learning of dense visual representations. *Advances in Neural Information Processing Systems*, *33*, 4489–4500.

Qamar, R., & Zardari, B. A. (2023). A Study on Implementing Technology in Educational Institutions. *SBBU Journal of Social Sciences*, *1*(2), 127–137.

Rajput, G., & Chouhan, P. S. (2021). Exploring the factors affecting students' choice of higher education institutes in India: A factor analysis approach. *Journal of Business and Social Sciences Research*, *6*(1), 21–34. DOI: 10.3126/jbssr.v6i1.38126

Rojas, M. G., Olivera, A. C., & Vidal, P. J. (2022). Optimising Multilayer Perceptron weights and biases through a Cellular Genetic Algorithm for medical data classification. *Array (New York, N.Y.)*, *14*, 100173. DOI: 10.1016/j.array.2022.100173

Shams, S. R., Jahani, A., Kalantary, S., Moeinaddini, M., & Khorasani, N. (2021). The evaluation on artificial neural networks (ANN) and multiple linear regressions (MLR) models for predicting SO2 concentration. *Urban Climate*, *37*, 100837. DOI: 10.1016/j.uclim.2021.100837

Sharma, H. L., & Rani, R. (2013). Relationship of personal growth initiative with self-efficacy among university postgraduate students. *Journal of Education and Practice*, *4*(16), 125–135.

Sheokand, K., Garima, , Deswal, R., & Jyoti, . (2024). Learning in Transition: Exploring Factors Shaping Students' Motivation Across Diverse Learning Modalities. *International Journal of Educational Reform*, *0*(0), 10567879241302833. Advance online publication. DOI: 10.1177/10567879241302833

Siddiky, M. R., & Haque, I. E. (2024). Factors Affecting Students' Academic Performance Mediated by their Motivation for Learning. *Asian Journal of University Education*, *20*(1), 15–27. DOI: 10.24191/ajue.v20i1.25696

Singu, S., & Singu, S. (2021). Comparative analysis of artificial neural networks. *International Journal of Machine Learning for Sustainable Development*, *3*(4).

Taber, K. (2018). The Use of Cronbach's Alpha When Developing and Reporting Research Instruments in Science Education. *Research in Science Education*, *48*(6), 1273–1296. DOI: 10.1007/s11165-016-9602-2

Ten Cate, O. T. J., Kusurkar, R. A., & Williams, G. C. (2011). How self-determination theory can assist our understanding of the teaching and learning processes in medical education. AMEE guide No. 59. *Medical Teacher*, *33*(12), 961–973. DOI: 10.3109/0142159X.2011.595435 PMID: 22225433

Thompson, C. B., & Panacek, E. A. (2007). Research study designs: Non-experimental. *Air Medical Journal*, *26*(1), 18–22. DOI: 10.1016/j.amj.2006.10.003 PMID: 17210489

Yurdugül, H. (2008). Minimum sample size for Cronbach's coefficient alpha: A Monte-Carlo study. *Hacettepe Üniversitesi eğitim fakültesi dergisi, 35*(35), 1-9.

Chapter 13
Data Quality Management Technique in Big Data Analytics for Machine Learning and Deep Learning Applications in Gaming

Kunjesh Patadiya
https://orcid.org/0009-0001-7515-0965
Marwadi University, India

Jay Moteriya
Marwadi University, India

Shreyal Faldu
Marwadi University, India

Rituraj Jain
https://orcid.org/0000-0002-5532-1245
Marwadi Uinversity, India

Damodharan Palaniappan
https://orcid.org/0009-0003-0721-3068
Marwadi University, India

Kumar Parmar
https://orcid.org/0000-0002-2502-5680
Marwadi University, India

T. Premavathi
https://orcid.org/0009-0003-0172-2021
Marwadi University, India

ABSTRACT

This chapter focused on analyzing data quality management in enhancing the state-of-the-art ML and DL for gaming industry. The existence of gaming has led to the generation of large sets of data hence making data quality an important quality that is needed when analyzing the behavior of a player or the occurrence of cheats

DOI: 10.4018/979-8-3373-0735-0.ch013

in real time. This chapter discusses the problems of different types of data, such as player activity, session data, performance data, and communications during the game. Importance is given to data quality dimensions: accuracy, completeness, timeliness, and relevance and discusses issues such data cleaning, preprocessing, and use of automated validation techniques. It also covers, the applied ML/DL techniques often used as well as the anomaly detection, and the implicated tools such as Apache Spark, and Hadoop whereas discussing problems of volume, data consistency and privacy.

1. INTRODUCTION TO DATA QUALITY IN BIG DATA FOR GAMING INDUSTRY

1.1 Overview of Big Data in Gaming

In the current scenario, the gaming industry is involved at a huge level and has become a competitor of the movie and music industry. The exponential growth of the gaming industry has led to increased entertainment and business growth. The core of growth in gaming is the variety of games and player interaction with the game. The growth of any particular game depends on how the game is developed and how it has been monetized (Xiang et al., 2023). Any game can touch the peak of the market when a large number of players are playing games, and the company behind developing games will arrange tournaments and events at the national or international level. As a result of the huge growth in the gaming industry, it is expected that by 2025, the gaming industry will cross \$320 - \$340 billion at the global level.

Gaming industry versus other industries: When the gaming industry becomes very large and millions of players are connected to the game server, it is necessary to maintain and manage a very large amount of data for each player. On an annual basis 10000 to 15000 games developed, including mobile and PC games. If we analyze this figure, we will know that from 2000 to 2025, more than 1.1 million games have been developed, and by looking at the number of games, we can clearly say that all the data generated from this game probably cross 1000 tbs easily; to store this data in a traditional ecosystem is not suitable, for that we require a very powerful and very large data storage such as a distributed file system. DFS can be utilized to store and process an extremely large amount of data. A very popular framework, HDFS, is used to store and process the data of multiplayer games, MMORPG, Battle royale, RPG, and Open World games (Liu et al., 2021). Table 1 shows the different companies that have already used HDFS to store the game environment and data while playing parallel users.

Table 1. Companies using HDFS to store data.

Game Name	Developer	Big Data Tool	Use Case
League of Legends	Riot Games	HDFS	Player Behavior Analysis
Candy Crush Saga	King	Cloud Storage	In-Game Purchases Analysis
Call of Duty	Activision	Apache Spark	Cheat Detection
Clash of Clans	Supercell	Data Lakes	Player Retention Analysis

These are some companies that use Big Data tools for their business. HDFS gives them the ability to work on very large amounts of daily data, which can be further utilized for business ideas such as business growth and strategy making, or it can be utilized for analysis of players' behavior, mentality, like-dislike, choice, and much more. These data can be used to identify hidden patterns, predictions, and classifications using machine-learning and deep-learning algorithms. Using the ML/DL algorithm, we can utilize the data for future decisions. Here, one point is that if the quality of data generated by the data is poor, it cannot be used further. Therefore, the data quality should be maintained while applying the ML/DL algorithm(Aldoseri et al., 2023).

Key Source of Data:

i) In-Game Actions: This captures a player's move, choice, and interaction, such as combat style, gameplay strategy, skill, and game progression path. Session Metrics: Logs details, such as session length (how much time players played in one session), session frequency, and session pattern.
ii) Performance metrics: win-loss ratio, game achievements, score, and level completion.
iii) Interaction events: Data from in-game events such as encounters, races, battles, and items purchased.
iv) Environment metrics: With respect to the game world environment, some specific locations on the map and time spent on different game locations. NPC interaction etc.
v) In-game communication: Players are usually used in game communication facilities to talk to each other while playing; they use a microphone and a speaker to instruct each other.
vi) In-game Chat System: Player also uses text format to chat with teammates. This system can be used in the case of hardware failure for a mic or a speaker.

1.2 Significance of Data Quality in ML/DL Applications

The quality of data in ML and DL applications directly affects the performance of the model, its interpretation, and, ultimately, the business outcome. Data quality is crucial in the gaming industry. Because different games have data in different formats as well as there is verity of players which using different play style. This diversity in play styles and data formats can help us understand the various hidden patterns. However, for that, we should maintain data quality such that any minor details of the data are not missing. Data should be complete and consistent(McGowan et al. 2022).

Model accuracy and reliability in high-quality data: Quality is provided to ML and DL models according to the type of data on which the model is being trained. Hence, the better the condition of the data, the better the performance of the model in terms of prediction or its classification capability (Aldoseri et al., 2023). Noisy, Biased, and Incomplete Poor-quality data showed incorrect outcome tendencies through incorrect predictions and weak generalization. In turn, this has a significant impact on the efficiency of the model.

Improved Generalization of Models: Quality data directly determine the generalization of the model towards even new, unseen data. If the quality of the data is good, there is a higher probability for the model to perform well in the range of inputs (Li et al., 2024).

Reduces Issues related to Bias and Unfairness: Relevant data quality leads to a decrease in bias that may appear while using training data, in addition to providing much more accurate and less biased models. Except for lack of completeness, which results in biased models more so those used during developing unfair decisions, particularly those in sensitive applications in cases of player analysis as well as cheat detection so that quality data tends to decrease biasing; instead, it enhances the truthfulness of the models (Liu et al., 2024).

Decidability and interpretability: The results produced by models using high-quality data are more interpretable and explainable. This establishes the trust of the stakeholders in the model decision. Low-quality data are difficult to interpret or make predictions trustworthy because of noise or errors in the data that may hide the information derived from the model(Zhao et al., 2023).

Training and Development Productivity: Quality data saves much time from preparing, cleaning, and anomalous-handling the same and is an efficient opportunity for the development of more accurate models. Poor diluent quality consumes even more time and man-hours in the cleansing feature design and the repetition of those experiments to move it slowly through the pipeline of the operation and at higher operating expenses(Gehrmann et al., 2022).

2. THE ROLE OF DATA QUALITY IN GAMING ML/DL APPLICATIONS

2.1 Key ML/DL Use Cases for Gaming

ML/DL is used to improve players' experience, game design, and architecture. Further applications of ML/DL could include the generation of an auto player mode in open-world games.

Procedural Content Generation **(PCG)** is a technique that is mainly used to generate dynamic game content, such as terrains and levels. It can be performed using three deep learning algorithms, such as GANs. This technique also reduces the need for manual design and the architecture required for each individual level.

Examples of PCG are shown in figure 1.

Figure 1. Some examples of PCG

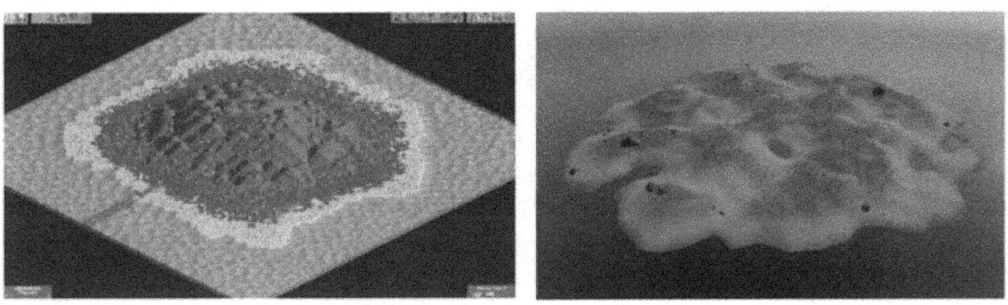

NPC Behavior: There is a different type of NPC in open-world games, which interacts with a player during a gameplay session, as shown in figure 2. In this context, the NPC reacts and responds to the player using a DL model. The machine learning algorithm may also be used for voice creation of an NPC; hence, an NPC could be used in real-world applications for better experience(Poalelungi et al., 2023).

Figure 2. Examples of NPC

Cheat Detection: Cheat and Fraud detection are also very common in the 2020 era. However, behavioral analysis can be performed for cheat detection using various techniques.

Figure 3. Example of cheat detection

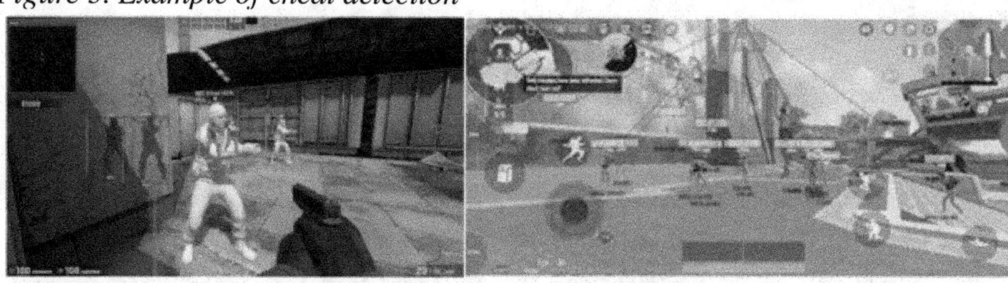

High graphics with animation: Nowadays, games are available with high-resolution graphics, which make use of GPU and CPU to render the graphics of a game. The DL model up-scales the game texture and graphics and enhances the player's experience.

Figure 4. Example of Deep learning algorithm improve resolution

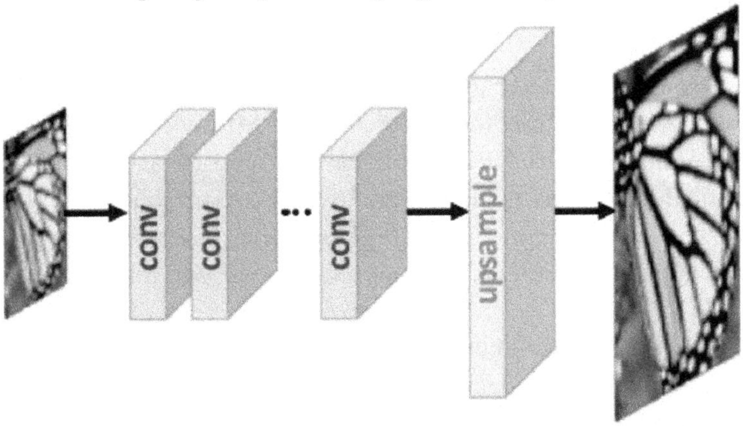

2.2 Data Quality Requirements for ML/DL Models in Gaming

In games, data quality is essential for the ML/DL model to perform well. This is because they use high-quality and reliable data to perform well. These are the key requirements for data quality in ML/DL in gaming, with actual examples of games utilizing the technology (Mystakidis et al., 2023):

i. Accuracy and Precision of Data Requirement: Data must indicate the correct behavior, interest, and interaction of players. Valid data guarantee that results that would be generated or expected from the models built on the basis of ML will be correct. For example, the League of Legends bases its matchmaking as well as game balance on accurate data about the actual behavioral activities of the players involved. This is because actual data about the performance or actual status of every single player are valid (Galekwa et al., 2024).
ii. Completeness Requirement: The data that should be used to train the ML models should be as holistic as possible, ensuring that all aspects of the interactions between players and events that occur in the game are captured. Incomplete data will lead to a model predicting something wrong or biased results in the favor of certain entities (Maffey et al., 2023).

Example: FIFA by EA Sports makes use of reams of player data, and with the help of that, it tries its best to make AI-driven attributes in the game almost close to real life in terms of player behavior and strategies of opposing teams. To achieve perfect player movements and decisions, complete datasets must be available to the model for all varieties of situations.

iii. Timelessness Requirement: The captured data must be processed in real time for real-time application. Therefore, the response of the ML model was real-time. For in-game recommendations, NPC interactions, and anti-cheat measures, time is the most critical factor. Example: Fortnite used ML to personalize real-time player experience, as well as recommending game modes. The time taken to base the recommendations on players' data makes the experience interactive(Dixit & Sarangi, 2023).
iv. Consistency: The demand would be for model forecasts to mean anything in a realistic setting with the participant; the data needs to have consistencies both from and to sources and both through and between versions.

Example: PUBG works on coherent data regarding players and game play, for instance, heatmaps showing hot spots as well as risky dropping areas.

v. Relevance Requirement: It use of data relevant only to the outcome. Using such irrelevant data causes dilution of the output quality of the models and slows down training. Example: Call of Duty uses data on players' behavior and detects whether someone is cheating by discovering patterns that show a variation from normal players' activities. Focusing only on relevant actions enables the system to maintain its efficiency and precision when flagging suspicious activities (Kanervisto et al., 2022).
vi. Data Volume and Variety Requirements for Complex Models: Complex models, including deep architectures for learning, require sufficient and diverse data to adequately generalize to scenarios. There may be player demographics or types of players, types of play, and styles, along with diverse game modes. Example: Red Dead Redemption 2 applies ML-driven systems to the interactions of nonplayer characters and dynamic world creation. The variety of different player actions and the reactions of NPCs allow this game to provide a unique experience and engage in its own way for each player (Romero-Mendez et al., 2023).
vii. Bias Reduction Requirement: There data bias that may result in biased or non-inclusive predictions of the model. Bias in data might cause biased results and even separate the parts of the player base.

Example: Sims 4 uses ML to develop diverse and inclusive characters. Bias-free data reflects diverse backgrounds of the players without developing stereotypes.

viii. Security and Privacy Requirement: The data of the players are safe and compliant with Privacy and Regulations, such as the GDPR. Information security is a very important feature, especially because such games usually gather personal information about one's personality and behavior.

2.3 Impact of Data Quality on Game Analytic:

Data quality plays an essential role in game analytics in several areas. Insights from poor data lead to futile and ineffective strategies, and ultimately yield irrelevant rewards or poorly timed promotions as a result of poor retention and poor engagement of the players. Bad monetization flips spending trends told by bad data into low value, optimized revenue in a poor store. As data are suboptimal for the prediction of player behavior, segmentation is inaccurate, and content recommendations are irrelevant. Poor data quality hinders game design and balances the lack of player interaction, patterns, and imbalances of gameplay. Low-quality data can produce false positives or negatives in cheat detection, where legitimate players will be angered by false positives, whereas false negatives will prevent the detection of real cheaters. On the last part, it is the last part that bad data quality also affects the server maintenance and can cause unexpected downtime and poor user experiences. Conversely, high-quality data provide accurate insight, effective strategies, and enhanced player experience in all these areas, which in turn helps the game to be successful and profitable. Here is how the poor quality of data impacts all aspects of game analytics in depth:

i. Analysis of player retention and engagement: The negative effect on poor data quality affects the ways in which player activities and preferences are recorded. Therefore, it sometimes causes bad insights about players' behaviors that further confuse one on how to engage the player either to be retained or churn. This again creates poor retention strategies, which may look like irrelevant rewards in games or even improper timing with respect to a particular promotion(Hazra and Anjaria, 2022).
ii. Monetization and Revenue Optimization: Poor data quality will end up poorly monetizing the data and misrepresenting spending trends in-game, leading to inefficiencies in stream optimization, and the wrong models or layout in in-game stores negatively affects both the player's experience and revenue. High-quality data: Proper data will yield accurate insights into the spending behavior of gamers, which allows optimization of the offers, price, and ad placement to maximize monetization(Burelli, 2022).

iii. Player Behavior Prediction and Segmentation: Poor quality data would mean an uncertain player segment and all inaccuracies related to the identification of different kinds of players. It ranges from irrelevant content recommendations to misguided targeting marketing, which signifies inappropriate alignment with player needs. Advantage of high-quality data: High-quality data facilitate proper player segmentation based on specific behavioral patterns. There is a good capacity to predict the behavior of players as well as group similar preferences, which can help enhance the personalization of gameplay, offers, and communications (Burelli, 2022).
iv. Game Design and Balancing: Poor quality data will deny the understanding of the interaction of players with game mechanics and point out imbalances in gameplay. This will result in the uneven advantages of certain characters or items and frustration. The advantages of good data to game developers are as follows: good data will give them much more realistic and accurate information on how players play games. It can then be used to determine if flaws exist in the design and balance fair gameplay. Such right information from mechanics, items, and characters informs them of appropriate adjustments to balance experience(Hazra & Anjaria, 2022).
v. Cheat Detection and Anti-Fraud Systems: Low quality of data causes false positives or negatives in cheat detection, which might frustrate the rightful players or simply fail to detect actual cheats. Thus, it not only diminishes the sense of the game, but also the belief of the player. An advantage of high-quality data: Quality data ensures that cheat detection algorithms are able to point out abnormal behavior in the game without flagging the honest player. Thus, good-quality data improve the integrity of the game as well as the experience of honest players.
vi. Game Server Predictive Maintenance Bad Quality of Data: Poor quality information about the performance in a server may lead to its downtimes, thus creating a lousy experience for the users. Advantages of Good Quality Data: Predictive models can predict the exact server performance technical faults to minimize downtime. This allows fixes in a timely manner and maintains the player. In addition, it does not cause frustration.

3. DATA QUALITY DIMENSIONS IN GAMING ANALYTICS

3.1 Defining Key Quality Dimensions

Table 2 lists the different quality factors/dimensions used in the games.

i. Accuracy: The more accurate the information about the characters' statistical data, scoring systems, physics calculations, etc., the more trustful and satisfied players will be. For instance, with the counting of ammo and damage taken, a character's health level and hitboxes should fit the model for a fair game.
ii. Completeness: Complete data ensure that all the assets required are available to generate an integrated game experience. In this scenario, the missing assets may be textures, sounds, or narrative details that would break the immersion of the game. For online gaming, complete player profile information helps match players with a similar level of skill, which will make matches closer and more enjoyable for players involved(Zhu & Ontañón, 2021).
iii. Consistency: The inconsistencies in the data presented in the gaming environment are most likely to cause confusion and reduce the stability of the experience. For instance, weapon stats or gameplay mechanisms should not change or vary depending on the level or game mode. If a weapon exhibits a specific range in one location but features a different type of range without any reason, it can prove frustrating for gamers(Toh, 2023).
iv. Validity: Data validity ensures that the data are valid according to specified formats and logical requirements. This may include validating input data: any accepted usernames, limits to game actions such as the use of teleportation, etc.. Validity checks could end cheating and glitching more often, thus promoting fairness and integrity.
v. Timeliness: In competitive online multiplayer games, players obtain real-time information for their knowledge of the position or actions of other players and in-game events; thus, timely data is of high demand. The update and syncing of such data on multiple players would be impeded, thus causing "lag" in gameplay if latency had resulted(Burelli, 2022).

Table 2. Quality Dimensions used in games

Quality Dimension	Definition	Impact on Model	Gaming Example
Accuracy	Data reflects true values	Improves model reliability	League of Legends Matchmaking
Completeness	All necessary data is present	Reduces bias	FIFA Player Attributes
Consistency	Uniform data standards	Enhances user experience	PUBG Heatmaps
Validity	Data follows valid formats	Reduces errors	Fortnite Real-time Recommendations

3.2 Challenges in Each Dimension

i. Accuracy Problems: Guaranteeing the accuracy of the amount and diversity of data in a game can be challenging. In telemetry, the data are incorrect. Player metrics are not precise, and in-game events are incorrectly tracked. All of these can wreak havoc using analytics. The more real-time the data, the more likely a problem can be created in terms of latency, packets dropped, and synchronization. Some Examples Problems: Misleading Player Metrics: Inaccurate record of the levels of skills or achievements by players may result in incorrect matchmaking and bad game balance. Error in Economic Balances: In virtual economies, incorrect pricing of items or currency exchange rates results in inflation or deflation, which affects player satisfaction (Lundy et al., 2024).
ii. Completeness Problems: Inadequate data will not permit full analysis. Missing data points may be caused by failure at the network level, failure at the server level, or even at the point of capture, leading to an incomplete player journey and overall gameplay trends. Interplay between complex platforms or regions may also lead to partial data collection, which continues to affect cross-platform or cross-region analysis. Example Problems: Partial Session Data: Retention analysis will partially lose the session data, and it would be impossible to derive a conclusion that makes a judgment about why users churned or returned Gaps in Telemetry Data: All the telemetry data of any application, such as movement log data or game decision logs, are missing. Thus, the inference about preference cannot be seen; hence, people never come to know what all is in practice (Burelli, 2022).
iii. Consistency Issues: It is difficult to be consistent in gaming, especially when there are different systems, game versions, or sources of data. Because the updates and patches would change the nature of the game, discrepancies may come from the shift in gameplay; if they support multi-platform, inconsistencies may arise because the recording or processing of data differs from the device. Example Problems Mixed Metrics Over Different Versions of the Game: Changes in weapon status or level difficulties due to updates or patches make it difficult to compare player performance over time before and after updates. Cross-Platform Variation: Differences in mechanics can create inconsistent player behavior data; thus, it is difficult to compare cross-platforms(Pfau & El-Nasr, 2023).
iv. Validity Challenges: These arise due to wrongly entered data, bad telemetry reading, or non-genuine inputs by the users that fail to strictly follow any pattern of expected inputs, such as oddball characters in the name and chat. Keeping the data valid in games that are based on dynamic interactions with the environment and other interacting players is sometimes quite challenging because some

interactions may create invalid data that do not strictly follow a desired format. Example Problems Player Movement out of Bounds: Player's drift into areas unsupported by the game; therefore, the location data generated might not be valid and could not be used in further analysis of popular locations. Character encodings for players' chats or usernames are not supported; this would lead to errors while processing or even extra steps in interpreting data, especially if there exists a global version with multilanguage support(Song et al., 2024).

v. Timeliness Problems: The demand for real-time or near-real-time data in gaming analytics poses many problems because any lag in the collection and processing will only give stale insights; this is particularly true for online and multiplayer games, whose nature demands timely information about the behavior and metrics of players. Such a system of effective matchmaking and leaderboard updates depend on this information. Latency in Player Action Data: In real-time games, some disparity would arise in the leaderboards or progressions of player skills owing to the delayed data on a player's actions, such as shooting or movement.

4.COMMON DATA QUALITY CHALLENGES IN GAMING DATA

4.1 Data Collection Challenges

The major challenge in gaming data collection is high-quality data collection. The first major problem is the integration/treatment of heterogeneous data sources, such as telemetry data, in-game transactions, player behavior logs, and external data from online databases, such as leaderboards and social media websites from the game's community. There is often a technical and logistical challenge of integration owing to the diversity of these sources in other formats. There are many factors that can disrupt data flows, and these factors can cause you to lose some data or even miss data. Because online multiplayer games involve real-time data, this is especially unhygienic. These games also have to deal with privacy concerns as they collect sensitive information such as the location, chat logs, or behavioral patterns. In specific regulated regions or for younger audiences, compliance with regulations such as the GDPR or CCPA may add a limitation when it comes to data collection. Another challenge is that data capture is limited to each device. It is a game across different platforms that can capture different data (consoles, PCs, mobile phones, and VR headsets). It is possible that mobile devices do not provide telemetry that is as rich as consoles or PCs. The amount of data that can be collected poses a hardware limitation that does not affect game performance. In addition, stereotyping data consistency across platforms becomes more complicated with different control schemes (touch, gamepad, and keyboard), which would skew analytics and result in a lack of gameplay insight accuracy across platforms.

Data source problems: Games rely on numerous data sources, including telemetry data, in-game transactions, player behavior logs, social interactions, and external sources, such as leaderboards and community forums. The integration of such heterogeneous sources is technically and logistically challenging, because they may use different formats and standards.

i. Network failures or server crashes: This may stop data flows, which might mean that some datasets would be missing or unavailable. This is worse in the case of an online game in which multiplayer interactions occur in real time. Continuous data flow is crucial in this case. Effects Disconnected Data Analysis: Since broken or incomplete data sources do not provide an appropriate understanding of the behavior of players, there could be misleading conclusions about the trends and preferences of players. Data inconsistency: Due to differences in metrics released by certain sources, such as the level of a player or perhaps the balances in currencies inside the game, this leads to an inconsistent experience for playing. The solution builds integration pipelines for strong data by combining information from more than one source in a single centralized database; therefore, the data are all in line. Redundant servers or data caching techniques are used to minimize the impact of data loss in the case of network or server disruption, especially in real-time gameplay data(Baima et al., 2024).
ii. Privacy concerns: Privacy concerns about users' problem games collect a significant amount of sensitive information. Examples include location, chat logs, and behavioral patterns. All of these pose privacy concerns. The regulations governing these include the GDPR and CCPA. Data collection will be limited, depending on privacy compliance regulations such as younger audiences or more strictly governed regions. There is a fine line between the value of the information and personal privacy. Effect: Reduced Data Granularity: Privacy regulations can limit the amount of detail that can be revealed for analysis. This challenges the ability to personalize experiences or identify subtle behavioral patterns. For instance, anonymized data could prevent the precise targeting of in-game offers or the motivation of players(Hu et al., 2023).
iii. Data capture limitations on different device Challenges: Gaming occurs on many devices such as consoles, PCs, mobile phones, and VR headsets. Each captured different data. Mobile devices may not capture telemetry data like a console or a PC; hence, the data quality could differ from one platform to another. Hardware limitations include less processing power or memory on some devices, meaning that the amount of data collected without affecting the game performance can be limited. Other control schemes, such as touch, gamepad,

and keyboard, can also make the type of player interaction different, which complicates cross-platform data consistency. Impact: The inconsistent quality of data across devices: Since not all devices capture sufficient data, skewed analytics can result in comparisons from behavior on one platform to another. Therefore, this reduces the accuracy of insights. For example, movement data will be less accurate on mobile devices, where touch controls offer different capabilities than game controllers. Detailed information gathering through the lower-end device may carry a performance trade-off in the form of an increase in lags or battery consumption, which has a tendency to impact the overall game experience. Solutions: Employ adaptive data-gathering methodologies that vary along a device's capability, record the most relevant data when optimizing performance on respective platforms, and implement cross-platform data mapping and normalization mechanisms to account for differences generated as a result of data acquisition from the various devices, thus homogenizing analytics across each and every platform used (Aldoseri et al., 2023).

4.2 Data Processing Challenges

i. Real-Time Data Processing Challenges: Low Latency Requirements: Any real-time game environment, especially multiplayer games, requires fast processing of data to almost zero latency. Data referring to the actions of players, along with updating the game state and matchmaking, should be processed almost in real time to avoid delaying the sequences of games. Data Overload: At times, a bottleneck point in the system might result in high data loads during peak gaming hours; this will result in inefficient gaming. Consistency and Synchronization: The Real-time data across different servers or regions is difficult to maintain because high-speed processing may often lose consistency. Effect Delayed Responses: Player responses are delayed in games that require prompt action such as first-person shooters. This irritates the user and provides unnecessary advantages. Old Matchmaking and Leaderboards: Leaderboards and matchmaking should be updated in real time. Processing delays can result in incorrect rankings or unbalanced matches. Solutions Apply the consumption of stream processing frameworks such as Apache Kafka and Apache Flink to process large amounts of data in real time, thus allowing low-latency processing. Make use of edge computing solutions to process data closer to the location of the player in a manner that reduces latency and allows faster synchronization of data among servers (Mehran et al., 2021).

ii. Feature Engineering for ML Model Problems High dimensionality and complexity: Data related to gaming include a large number of variables, their interactions, the action taken by the player session duration, and records of win and loss. Such variables are transformed into meaningful features that require deep knowledge of game mechanisms and the behavior of players for high-quality features. Real-time Feature Generation: Most ML game-related models, whether to use them in the match-making procedure or to forecast churn, require real-time generation of features. Such load pressure computations, especially on intricate features. Games continue to update on changes in items, new mechanics, and event-keeping that updates them, which can change their feature importance; hence, some become irrelevant constantly, so there should be reengineering too. Effects: Poor feature engineering means that ML models cannot forecast the behavior or preferences of players sufficiently well for any personalization or retention approach to be meaningful. Tighter Computation Costs: Real-time feature extraction, particularly complex ones, is computationally expensive and affects the cost of servers and scalability. Solutions Use tools such as feature stores (Feast) to automate feature engineering, which means that features are managed and served in real time at scale. Apply techniques for dimension reduction, including PCA, and feature selection techniques that aim to extract the most informative features without sacrificing the goodness of performance by reducing the processing time. Flexible feature application features consider basic patterns of player behavior as opposed to game-specific, which change over changes in games(Maffey et al., 2023).
iii. Cleaning and transforming game data problems data noise and anomalies: This may arise from bugs, cheaters, or unknown player behavior. It is critically important to determine its importance, but at the same time it is extremely challenging because of the very high volume and variability of the players. Data Standardization: On different devices, game versions, and even platforms, data can be represented in different formats. This can make the integration and analysis of gameplay data quite difficult. Normalization of such differences is required, but it is very difficult. Dealing with Missing or Incomplete Data: There may be gaps or breaks in the gameplay data caused by networking issues and server outages among other interferences. This is a very sensitive task because there is a very good possibility that attempts to deal with missing data will introduce bias or considerably downplay the importance of the obtained results (Larson et al., 2023). Dirty data may also push incorrect player insights and will have a direct impact on the balance of games, matchmaking, and revenue strategies. Resource-intensive: It takes too much time because big data is undergoing cleansing in gameplay, particularly in a more complex multiplayer game dealing with thousands of different types of data Solution Developing

effective, robust pipelines for cleaning and utilizing rules as well as ML-based anomaly detection to filter out noise/anomalies/invalid data within a system. Format your data uniformly such that the structures of your data become comparable with the schema-alignment technique to make them fit cross-platform and cross-version data. Missing values are filled using imputation methods, such as the interpolation of a time-series dataset. Alternatively, design strategies that minimize the impact of gaps, such as aggregate statistics, are less sensitive to gaps.

4.3 Data Integration and Aggregation Issues

Diverse types and formats of data: Data vary in form and structure. Some were structurally similar to database information or log information, whereas others were purely unstructured, such as tweets and comments for social media activities. This leads to a tremendous demand in that one has to try and normalize the data so that it can be correctly integrated(Chang & Mukherjee, 2023). This difficulty is caused by data schemes, data types, naming conventions, and so on. The collection of data from multiple formats has led not only to relatively complex ETL processes, as shown in figure 5, but also to more time and resources to prepare the data. Because the formats may carry errors, there is always a risk that data might be lost or interpreted incorrectly when it comes to the behavior and preferences of the players(Sundberg & Holmström, 2024).

Figure 5. ETL in online game

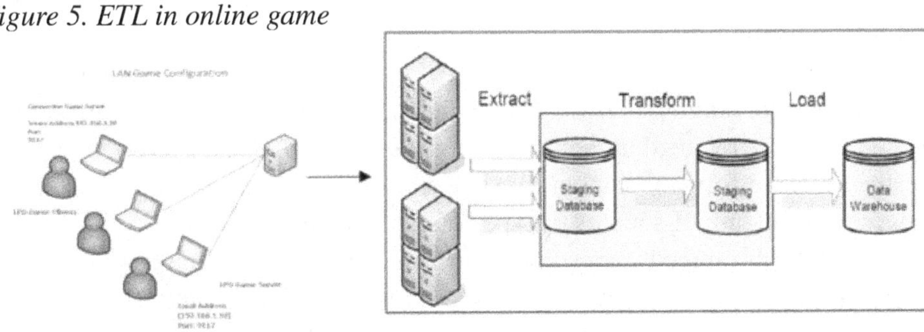

Volume and Velocity of Gameplay Data Problems: The volume and velocity of the gameplay data generated from gaming are high, particularly in real-time multiplayer scenarios that are difficult to process and integrate. This requires gigantic infrastructure to be handled by the streaming of data from several sources in real time while updating such data streams and collecting analytics. Too much data coming into a system will slow down the system and thus act as a bottleneck in integration, which will eventually lead to delays in the delivery of insights. Slow integration might lead to decisions not being made in real time, and thus, the effect of custom content or real-time engagement strategies might be watered down(Rydén & El Sawy, 2023).

Data Quality and Consistency Issues: Quality of data among sources is extremely diverse, making integration very complicated. While noisy or irrelevant content may be present on social media, gameplay data may simply be blanked in specific areas or wrong. Most importantly, consistency between sources of data collection and reporting is a challenge, especially when dealing with different teams or platforms involved in data generation(Musa & Zulkifli, 2022). Poor data quality results in unreliable insights. This could affect the design of the game, marketing strategies, and how efforts are made to engage the players. Inconsistencies in data and services may render one unable to trust the integrity of the data, making it difficult to make a decision based on a conclusive outcome.

Real-Time Data Integration Challenges: Most gaming scenarios require real-time or near real-time integration to respond quickly to the actions of players, social media trends, or gaming events. This requires superior data processing capabilities and infrastructure. Live sources, specifically social networks, do not integrate data too well because of the pace of social interactions. The processes of gameplay or marketing strategy may delay the integration of real-time data, which alters the impact on player engagement and satisfaction. Failure to respond in a timely manner to social media sentiment or trends may result in missing opportunities to engage with communities in a timely manner (Avalle et al., 2024).

Fluid and changing data sources Challenges: The gaming ecosystem is forever fluid and dynamic, meaning new updates and versions of games are constantly added coupled with a constantly changing population of players. Whenever new sources of data go online, such as a new social media platform, they challenge these new sources to be retained in their existing data systems. This calls for continuous investments and efforts to maintain flexible architectures that can respond easily to changes in the nature of sources or types of data(Zibani et al., 2021). The rigidity of data architecture breeds, overtime, and technical debt; it is impossible to take account of new sources of data, as well as to respond appropriately to changes in the gaming environment. This results in old or obsolete insights, where failing to integrate data sources would lead to old insights, as well as failure marketing and player engagement strategies.

5.TECHNIQUES FOR MANAGING DATA QUALITY IN BIG DATA ANALYTICS FOR GAMING

5.1 Data Cleaning and Preprocessing

Initial data cleaning and preprocessing are crucial steps in managing the data quality for gaming analytics.

Gameplay and Player Behavior Data Errors Types of Major Errors Data Ingression Errors: Spelling mistakes or inappropriate data in a database can be due to input errors when a session is collected or at the logging stage. Hardware and Technical Errors: There may be bugs in the game or a data capture tool, and thus, missing and corrupted data. For example, an incomplete session may not log all transactions in a system(Woodard et al., 2023). Logical Mistakes: These refer to inconsistencies in data on the behavior of players, where values may be unrealistic (for example, negative scores or impractical achievement).

Detection Techniques: Validation Rules: Determine rules to validate incoming data against how it should look, that ranges, and any logical constraints (such as, in this case, a score cannot be negative).

Scripted Checks: Create scripted checks to scan for common error patterns, such as missing values or out-of-range metrics, using libraries such as Pandas or Apache Spark.

Cross-Reference: Compare the data against other reliable sources, which include, but are not limited to, game logs and player profiles, for discrepancies.

Outliers in Gameplay Data Attributes of Outliers: Outliers can be caused by exceptional player behavior or errors while recording data. Envision a situation in which a player scores something ridiculously high; it may either be an exceptional skill or an anomaly in data recording.

Detection Strategies: Z-scores or IQR were used to determine outliers by identifying points that fell beyond the expected values.

Data Visualization Tools: Visual methods such as box plots and scatter plots were used to identify outliers in gameplay metrics such as scores, session lengths, and in-game purchases.

Machine Learning-Based Methods: Anomaly detection algorithms, such as Isolation Forest and DBSCAN, are used to find outliers from complex patterns based on player behavior(Greige et al., 2022).

Redundancy in game and player states types of redundancy: Redundancies can occur because of capturing multiple log entries for the same player activity owing to inadequate data capture or failure in the logging operation. Redundancy can also be caused by the wrong confluence of different sessions or by submissions of user-generated work.

Detection techniques: Unique identifiers: Unique identifiers, including player identification numbers and timestamps, are used to track and control redundancies effectively.

Deduplication Algorithms: Apply algorithmic deduplication by identifying and eliminating duplicated records using appropriate key fields, such as grouping gameplay logs for the same player ID and session timestamp.

Database Constraints: Utilize database constraints such as primary keys at the point of data insertion to prevent duplicate entries from entering the database. the game.

5.2 Data Validation Frameworks

Data Entry Validation Systems Input Validation Rules: Type Checking Data Entries: That entry has the specified expected data type upon inputting, say, numeric, string, or date.

Valid Range and Format: The number of entries can be restricted. For example, the scores may fall in the range of 0–100. In addition, formatting restrictions may be applied to some fields, such as timestamps or player ID. Improved User Interface Real-time Validations: Use form validation for the user interface wherein a person will get back immediately returns the errors that occur in data entry by the player or developer. This will help to prevent most mistakes at the source.

Dropdown and Auto-complete: Use fields whose values are pre-defined and relatively smaller, such as character name and game modes. All of these help prevent typing errors(Barchard & Pace, 2008).

Automated data validation framework ETL process: Develop robust ETL frameworks that can automatically fetch data from various sources and transform the same according to valid criteria to load in a database or analytics platform. Transformation steps during the ETL process include data transformation, removal of inconsistencies for cleaning, and duplicate data quality monitoring tools.

It continuously tracks the quality of data in the pipeline with tools such as Apache NiFi, Talend, or Alteryx, so that only accurate and complete data are processed. Alerts and Reporting: It throw up alerts for anomalies or validation failures that are likely to help and enable timely intervention before issues have an impact on analytics(M et al., 2020).

Checks and Rules of Consistency Cross-Source Validation: Verify which data from different sources, for example, play logs against player profiles and matchup. Such inconsistencies may render alerts to be noteworthy for further examination.

Historical Comparison: Compare new data against old data to detect sudden spikes or anomalies that could raise an error.

Data Integrity Constraints: Maintain integrity constraints such as foreign keys and unique constraints on the database against related datasets such as the player profile and gameplay records so that there may not be any mismatch in related datasets(Daimler & Wisnesky, 2020).

Feedback Mechanisms Player Feedback Mechanisms: Consider interfaces through which players may report any mismatches or errors they come across, such as wrong scores or achievements. This can be correlated with greater problems within the corpus.

Data quality dashboards: Real-time data quality dashboards are designed by making it easier for the relevant stakeholders to track accuracy, completeness, and consistency metrics(Gupta et al., 2021).

Continuous improvement framework iterative processes: Design iterative processes to review and update validation rules and practices at regular intervals based on feedback, new technologies, or changes in data sources.

Data Governance: Design a data governance framework to define roles, policies, and procedures that ensure the quality of the data being maintained and accountability as a pervasive phenomenon among the teams.

6. ADVANCED ML AND DL TECHNIQUES FOR QUALITY MANAGEMENT

6.1 Anomaly Detection

Understanding Video Game Anomalies, Anomalies can occur in different shapes or forms in video game data.

Unusual Player Behavior: Deviations from usual play actions, for example, a very high score, an extremely low score, very long session length, and so on, or the change of style in gameplay with a sudden speed. Changes in Gameplay Metrics: Upswing or downswing, for example, the user engagement, in-game purchases, or session counts that do not fit the historical trend.(Huang et al., 2019)Technical Artifacts: Existence of errors or outliers in the gameplay data as a result of bugs, glitches, or missing data collection.

ii. **Machine Learning Techniques for Outlier Detection:** There Many machine learning models can be used to detect outliers in gaming data.

Supervised learning model classification algorithms: Supervised algorithms such as Decision Trees, Random Forests, and SVMs are used to classify behaviors as normal or anomalous. Models require labelled datasets in which normal and anomalous behaviors are known(Goldstein, 2023).Consider the following: Train a classifier to decide whether a game session should be classified under "normal" or "anomalous" headers based on features like time taken, player score and in-game actions.

Unsupervised model clustering algorithms: Apply clustering algorithms such as K-Means, DBSCAN, or Hierarchical Clustering to group similar data points. Anomalies can be identified as points that do not belong to any cluster, or are in small clusters. Example: Cluster player sessions based on gameplay metrics and flag sessions that are significantly different from the rest are anomalies. **Statistical Approaches**: The Z-score method calculates Z-scores of the gameplay metrics such as scores and session length. The numbers are ranked over a specified limit; for example, Z>3.

Example Assignment: Score analysis of player; Mark the occurrences where Z is more than 3 Moving Averages and Control Charts Analyze game performance metrics in terms of variations over time and monitor data points that fall beyond the control limits as outlier.Example: Monitor session length using control charts and alert when these are beyond the expected limit.

iii. **Feature Engineering**: This supports Anomaly Detection To improve the performance of models for detecting anomalies. Feature engineering has become one of the most significant approaches, including session length, the number of actions executed during the session, and score accrued.
iv. **Implementation Considerations:** Data Quality: Ensuring the quality of input data because anomalies found in noisy or incomplete data may result in false positives. Real-Time Monitoring: Develop models that can operate in real time to detect anomalies as they occur, thereby providing immediate responses to problems. Feedback mechanisms: This includes feedback loops to improve anomaly detection models over time. For instance, cross-validation of flagged anomalies by human reviewers improves model accuracy.
v. **Tools and Frameworks:** Some tools and frameworks will help in the implementation of anomaly detection in a game, including the following ones.1. Scikit-learn: Several algorithms are available for the classification, clustering, and regression.2. TensorFlow/Keras: It is helpful to design and train neural network models for the construction and training of autoencoders, including anomaly detection purposes.3. PyOD: This is a library for Python to find anomalies in high-dimensional data using a wide array of algorithms and methods. Using both techniques together, supervised and unsupervised learning techniques could possibly come in handy for an added advantage in detection.

6.2 Explainable AI and Model Interpretability

Significance of Explainable AI in GamingPlayer trust and confidence in decision outcomes: In general, an AI-driven decision for matching and game balancing, among others, will find favor with players and all stakeholders if it is explained(Chang & Mukherjee, 2023).Enhanced performance by the model: Knowledge of how a model came up with a certain decision enlightens one on its vulnerability spots, bias points, or parts that require improvement.

Data Quality Insights: XAI methods will make it possible to find poor-quality data with an understanding of which input data influences the predictions that come from the model, allowing developers to fix mistakes and biases within the data.

i. XAI methods for explaining model decisions in games

Feature Importance Analysis Explanation: This will be one such technique identifies which of the input features has the strongest impact on the model's predictiveness.

Application in Gaming: Feature importance analysis would thus enable developers to know which aspects of player behavior or the gameplay metrics most influence the results of the model.

B. LIME Overview: LIME is used to explain individual predictions by approximating the model locally with an interpretable model such as a linear model around the prediction of interest. Using LIME in Games: Apply LIME to explain particular predictions made by the models. For instance, why was a player matched with a specific set of opponents, or why was a recommendation made for in-game purchases? This might reveal patterns in data quality, such as unexpected influences from outlier behaviors.

C. PDP Description: PDPs describe how a variable is related to the prediction of a given value of the other variables.

Application in Gaming: Build PDPs to observe how changes in game-play metrics (e.g., the player's score and session time) affect model predictions. This can be useful for detecting unexpected relationships that could arise from data problems, such as noise and bias.

ii. Using XAI in Data Quality Issues XAI methods can reveal various data quality issues in gaming datasets.

Outliers and Anomalies: Using feature importance and model predictions, developers can flag outlier behaviors with high impacts on outcomes. For example, if a few players with odd engagement patterns dominate matchmaking algorithms, this could suggest a problem in how the gameplay data are captured or represented.

Bias Detection: XAI can help identify bias in the training data. For instance, if retention is predicted to be lower for certain demographics and the model is consistent with its predictions, it may raise red flags about biases in the data that need to be fixed, such as the underrepresentation of certain types of players.

7.TOOLS AND FRAMEWORKS FOR DATA QUALITY IN BIG DATA ANALYTICS

A number of open-source and commercial tools are available to assist in data quality assurance.

Apache Spark: Apache Spark is a popular big-data processing framework that enables real-time analytics and distributed data processing. Key features Distributed Computing: Apache Spark can process large datasets in a cluster, which makes it ideal for the big scale of data in gaming.Data Processing: Through Data Frames and SQL capabilities, Spark allows cleaning, transforming, and validation of data. Real-time Analytics: Analysis of streaming data is one of the strengths that Spark Streaming exhibits, and this is very valuable when handling in-game event processing(Cheng et al., 2021).Integration of machine learning: Therefore, for all the machine learning model development and their validation, that will happen here, as the Spark MLlib is considered. Thus, it can perfectly support a player retention prediction application as well as conduct churn analysis and cheat-detecting applications. Spark is also used by game companies to obtain player data from multiple servers, clean and preprocess it, and feed it into ML models for real-time analytics as game recommendations or anomaly detection, indicative of cheating.

Apache Hadoop: Apache Hadoop is an open-source framework used to store and process huge data sets in a distributed way. Sometimes, it is a skeleton for most big-data architectures. Distributed File System (HDFS): It holds big data by spreading it over several servers, which makes it scalable. MapReduce: Process data in parallel, which is great for analyzing large datasets resulting from player interactions. Use with Other Tools: It used along with tools such as Spark, Hive, and Pig. These additional advantages help perform data-quality-related tasks. Game Development Usage Hadoop is primarily implemented in storing game logs about gameplay, player behavioral information, and purchase history, which will be a fundamental source for even more precise analysis and ensures that it is stored consistently and reliably (Burelli, 2022).

Apache NiFi: Apache NiFi is a tool for the automation of data flow. It facilitates the movement, transformation, and monitoring of data across the systems.

Key Features: Data Flow Management: This makes it easier to extract, transform, and load data between the systems. Real-Time Processing: Real-time data-streaming support is important for in-game data processing. Data Provenance: It follows and transforms the data flow. This would help in tracing and debugging while maintaining quality.

Integrations: This supports numerous databases, APIs, and other data storage solutions. Therefore, this helps integrate the data easily. NiFi utilizes transformation and validation for real-time ingestion events and user-interaction streams. These streams then provide timely information of good quality with data lakes or analytics platforms(Cheng et al., 2021).

Microsoft Azure Data Factory It is the enterprise level cloud-based Microsoft product, that supports to build and schedule ETL workflows with the help of integration services.Data Pipeline Automation: Supports automatic workflows that include data moving and transforming Scalability and Integration: Integrate well with other Azure services and external databases in order to process big amount of data.

Data Quality Monitoring: Monitor data quality with in-built monitoring and error handling abilities to ensure that data quality is maintained in pipelines.

Use Case in Gaming: Gaming companies may use ADF to pipeline the player and gameplay data to cloud storage and preprocess and transform it before handing it over to advanced analytics and ML workloads.

Google Cloud Dataflow: Google Cloud Dataflow is a fully managed service for real-time streaming and batch data processing.

Key Features: It supports real-time streaming analytics and batch processing. This approach is ideal for capturing in-game events. Integrate natively with BigQuery for analytics and Google Cloud ML Engine for machine learning, scale up and down automatically, based on volumes of changing data common to games.

Use Case in Gaming: Dataflow to clean real-time data from gameplay and player interactions as they happen, which could feed into personalizing in-game experiences or flagging anomalies, such as cheating(Romero-Mendez et al., 2023).

CONCLUSION

In conclusion, proper management and analysis of big data, particularly in the gaming industry, requires robust data quality practices. The different tools and frameworks outlined in this study provide a solid foundation for addressing common data quality challenges, such as data ingestion, data cleaning, and data validation. By leveraging these tools and techniques, game developers and data scientists can ensure that the data driving their machine learning models and analytics are of high quality, leading to more accurate insights and better decision-making. Maintaining high-quality data is crucial for gaming companies as it enables them to make informed decisions, enhance player experiences, and gain a competitive edge in the industry. Proactive data quality management, facilitated by the tools discussed, can help gaming organizations stay ahead of the curve, identify and address issues early, and continuously improve their data-driven processes and outcomes.

REFERENCES

Aldoseri, A., Al-Khalifa, K. N., & Hamouda, A. M. S. (2023). Re-Thinking Data Strategy and Integration for Artificial Intelligence: Concepts, Opportunities, and Challenges. In Applied Sciences (Vol. 13, Issue 12, p. 7082). Multidisciplinary Digital Publishing Institute. DOI: 10.3390/app13127082

Avalle, M., Marco, N. D., Etta, G., Sangiorgio, E., Alipour, S., Bonetti, A., Alvisi, L., Scala, A., Baronchelli, A., Cinelli, M., & Quattrociocchi, W. (2024). Persistent interaction patterns across social media platforms and over time. In Nature (Vol. 628, Issue 8008, p. 582). Nature Portfolio. DOI: 10.1038/s41586-024-07229-y

Baima, R. L., Chovet, L., Sedlmeir, J., Olivares-Méndez, M. A., & Fridgen, G. (2024). Designing Trustful Cooperation Ecosystems is Key to the New Space Exploration Era (Vol. 9, p. 87). DOI: 10.1145/3639476.3639760

Barchard, K. A., & Pace, L. A. (2008). Meeting the challenge of high quality data entry: a free double-entry system. In International Journal of Services and Standards (Vol. 4, Issue 4, p. 359). Inderscience Publishers. DOI: 10.1504/IJSS.2008.020053

Bosch, J., Olsson, H. H., & Wang, T. J. (2020, December). Towards automated detection of data pipeline faults. In 2020 27th Asia-Pacific Software Engineering Conference (APSEC) (pp. 346-355). IEEE.

Burelli, P. (2022). Predicting Customer Lifetime Value in Free-to-Play Games. In arXiv (Cornell University). Cornell University. https://doi.org/DOI: 10.48550/arXiv.2209

Chang, H. H., & Mukherjee, A. (2023). Machine Learning and Consumer Data. In arXiv (Cornell University). Cornell University. https://doi.org/DOI: 10.48550/arXiv.2306

Cheng, W., Tang, Y., & Yang, W. (2021). Multi-channel VideoStreaming Technology for Processing Based on Distributed Computing Platform. In Journal of Physics Conference Series (Vol. 1757, Issue 1, p. 12172). IOP Publishing. DOI: 10.1088/1742-6596/1757/1/012172

Daimler, E., & Wisnesky, R. (2020). Informal Data Transformation Considered Harmful. In arXiv (Cornell University). Cornell University. https://doi.org/DOI: 10.48550/arXiv.2001

Dixit, A., & Sarangi, S. R. (2023). Minimizing the Motion-to-Photon-delay (MPD) in Virtual Reality Systems. In arXiv (Cornell University). Cornell University. https://doi.org//arxiv.2301.10408DOI: 10.48550

Galekwa, R. M., Tshimula, J. M., Tajeuna, E. G., & Kyamakya, K. (2024). A Systematic Review of Machine Learning in Sports Betting: Techniques, Challenges, and Future Directions [Review of A Systematic Review of Machine Learning in Sports Betting: Techniques, Challenges, and Future Directions]. arXiv (Cornell University). Cornell University. https://doi.org//arxiv.2410.21484DOI: 10.48550

Gehrmann, S., Clark, E. A., & Sellam, T. (2022). Repairing the Cracked Foundation: A Survey of Obstacles in Evaluation Practices for Generated Text. In arXiv (Cornell University). Cornell University. https://doi.org/DOI: 10.48550/arXiv.2202

Goldstein, M. (2023). Special Issue on Unsupervised Anomaly Detection. In Applied Sciences (Vol. 13, Issue 10, p. 5916). Multidisciplinary Digital Publishing Institute. DOI: 10.3390/app13105916

Greige, L., Silva, F. de M., Trotter, M. V., Lawrence, C., Chin, P., & Varadarajan, D. (2022). Collusion Detection in Team-Based Multiplayer Games. In arXiv (Cornell University). Cornell University. https://doi.org//arxiv.2203.05121DOI: 10.48550

Gupta, N., Patel, H., Afzal, S., Panwar, N., Mittal, R. S., Guttula, S., Jain, A., Nagalapatti, L., Mehta, S., Hans, S., Lohia, P., Aggarwal, A., & Saha, D. (2021). Data Quality Toolkit: Automatic assessment of data quality and remediation for machine learning datasets. In arXiv (Cornell University). Cornell University. https://doi.org//arxiv.2108.05935DOI: 10.48550

Hazra, T., & Anjaria, K. (2022). Applications of game theory in deep learning: a survey. In Multimedia Tools and Applications (Vol. 81, Issue 6, p. 8963). Springer Science+Business Media. DOI: 10.1007/s11042-022-12153-2

Hu, Y., Wu, F., Li, Q., Long, Y., Garrido, G. M., Ge, C., Ding, B., Forsyth, D., Li, B., & Song, D. (2023). SoK: Privacy-Preserving Data Synthesis. In arXiv (Cornell University). Cornell University. https://doi.org/DOI: 10.48550/arXiv.2307

Huang, Y., Jasin, S., & Manchanda, P. (2019). "Level Up": Leveraging Skill and Engagement to Maximize Player Game-Play in Online Video Games. In Information Systems Research (Vol. 30, Issue 3, p. 927). Institute for Operations Research and the Management Sciences. DOI: 10.1287/isre.2019.0839

Kanervisto, A., Kinnunen, T., & Hautamäki, V. (2022). GAN-Aimbots: Using Machine Learning for Cheating in First Person Shooters. In IEEE Transactions on Games (Vol. 15, Issue 4, p. 566). Institute of Electrical and Electronics Engineers. DOI: 10.1109/TG.2022.3173450

Kang, M., & Tian, J. (2023). Machine Learning: Data Pre-processing. https://onlinelibrary.wiley.com/doi/10.1002/9781119515326.ch5

Larson, D. M., Bungula, W., Lee, A., Stockdill, A. K., McKean, C., Miller, F. W., Davis, K., Erickson, R. A., & Hlavacek, E. (2023). Reconstructing missing data by comparing interpolation techniques: Applications for long-term water quality data. In Limnology and Oceanography Methods (Vol. 21, Issue 7, p. 435). Wiley. DOI: 10.1002/lom3.10556

Li, K., Rubungo, A. N., Lei, X. L., Persaud, D., Choudhary, K., DeCost, B., Dieng, A. B., & Hattrick-Simpers, J. (2024). Probing out-of-distribution generalization in machine learning for materials. In arXiv (Cornell University). Cornell University. https://doi.org/DOI: 10.48550/arXiv.2406

Liu, G., Caragea, D., Ou, X., & Roy, S. (2024). The Impact of Train-Test Leakage on Machine Learning-based Android Malware Detection. In arXiv (Cornell University). Cornell University. https://doi.org//arxiv.2410.19364DOI: 10.48550

Liu, M., Xue, Z., He, X., & Chen, J. (2021). SCADS: A Scalable Approach Using Spark in Cloud for Host-based Intrusion Detection System with System Calls. In arXiv (Cornell University). Cornell University. https://doi.org/DOI: 10.48550/arXiv.2109

Lundy, T., Raman, N., Fu, H., & Leyton-Brown, K. (2024). Pay to (Not) Play: Monetizing Impatience in Mobile Games. In *Proceedings of the AAAI Conference on Artificial Intelligence* (Vol. 38, Issue 9, p. 9856). Association for the Advancement of Artificial Intelligence. DOI: 10.1609/aaai.v38i9.28846

Maffey, K. R., Dotterrer, K., Niemann, J., Cruickshank, I. J., Lewis, G. A., & Kästner, C. (2023). MLTEing Models: Negotiating, Evaluating, and Documenting Model and System Qualities. In arXiv (Cornell University). Cornell University. https://doi.org/DOI: 10.48550/arXiv.2303

McGowan, L. D., Peng, R. D., & Hicks, S. C. (2022). Design Principles for Data Analysis. In Journal of Computational and Graphical Statistics (Vol. 32, Issue 2, p. 754). Taylor & Francis. DOI: 10.1080/10618600.2022.2104290

Mehran, N., Kimovski, D., & Prodan, R. (2021). A Two-Sided Matching Model for Data Stream Processing in the Cloud – Fog Continuum. DOI: 10.1109/CCGrid51090.2021.00061

Musa, M. A., & Zulkifli, N. (2022). The US-Malaysia Maritime Security Cooperation and Implication Towards Malaysia's National Security. In Malaysian Journal of Social Sciences and Humanities (MJSSH) (Vol. 7, Issue 2). DOI: 10.47405/mjssh.v7i2.1306

Mystakidis, A., Ntozi, E., Afentoulis, K., Koukaras, P., Gkaidatzis, P. A., Ioannidis, D., Tjortjis, C., & Tzovaras, D. (2023). Energy generation forecasting: elevating performance with machine and deep learning. In Computing (Vol. 105, Issue 8, p. 1623). Springer Science+Business Media. DOI: 10.1007/s00607-023-01164-y

Pfau, J., & El-Nasr, M. S. (2023). On Video Game Balancing: Joining Player- and Data-Driven Analytics. In arXiv (Cornell University). Cornell University. https://doi.org//arxiv.2308.07576DOI: 10.48550

Poalelungi, D. G., Mu at, C. L., Fulga, A., Neagu, M., Neagu, A., Piraianu, A. I., & Fulga, I. (2023). Advancing Patient Care: How Artificial Intelligence Is Transforming Healthcare [Review of Advancing Patient Care: How Artificial Intelligence Is Transforming Healthcare]. Journal of Personalized Medicine, 13(8), 1214. Multidisciplinary Digital Publishing Institute. DOI: 10.3390/jpm13081214

Romero-Mendez, E. A., Santana-Mancilla, P. C., García-Ruiz, M. A., Montesinos-López, O. A., & Anido, L. (2023). The Use of Deep Learning to Improve Player Engagement in a Video Game through a Dynamic Difficulty Adjustment Based on Skills Classification. In Applied Sciences (Vol. 13, Issue 14, p. 8249). Multidisciplinary Digital Publishing Institute. DOI: 10.3390/app13148249

Rydén, P., & El Sawy, O. A. (2023). How Managers Perceive Real-Time Management: Thinking Fast & Flow. https://journals.sagepub.com/doi/10.1177/0008125618818840

Schoeffer, J., Jakubik, J., Voessing, M., Kuehl, N., & Satzger, G. (2023). On the Interdependence of Reliance Behavior and Accuracy in AI-Assisted Decision-Making. In arXiv (Cornell University). Cornell University. https://doi.org/DOI: 10.48550/arXiv.2304

Song, X., Zhang, J., Yan, P., Hahn, J., Krüger, U., Mohamed, H., & Wang, G. (2024). Integrating AI in College Education: Positive yet Mixed Experiences with ChatGPT. In arXiv (Cornell University). Cornell University. https://doi.org/DOI: 10.48550/arXiv.2407

Sundberg, L., & Holmström, J. (2024). Fusing domain knowledge with machine learning: A public sector perspective. In The Journal of Strategic Information Systems (Vol. 33, Issue 3, p. 101848). Elsevier BV. DOI: 10.1016/j.jsis.2024.101848

Toh, W. (2023). Gamers and Their Weapons: An Appraisal Perspective on Weapons Manipulation in Video Games. https://www.sciencedirect.com/science/article/pii/B9780128017388000051

Wolniak, R. (2023). *Functioning of real-time analytics in business*. Zeszyty Naukowe. Organizacja i Zarządzanie/Politechnika Śląska.

Woodard, M., Sarvestani, S. S., & Hurson, A. R. (2023). A Survey of Research on Data Corruption in Cyber-Physical Critical Infrastructure Systems. https://www.sciencedirect.com/science/article/pii/S0065245815000285

Xiang, C., Yan, Y., Hu, T., Lv, Y., & Zeng, Y. (2023). A review of the effect of the light environment of the VDT workspace on the "learning to learn" effect of video game training [Review of A review of the effect of the light environment of the VDT workspace on the "learning to learn" effect of video game training]. Frontiers in Neuroscience, 17. Frontiers Media. DOI: 10.3389/fnins.2023.1093602

Zhao, Z., Shi, Y., Wu, S., Yang, F., Song, W., & Liu, N. (2023). Interpretation of Time-Series Deep Models: A Survey. In arXiv (Cornell University). Cornell University. https://doi.org/DOI: 10.48550/arXiv.2305

Zhu, J., & Ontañón, S. (2021). Player-Centered AI for Automatic Game Personalization: Open Problems. In arXiv (Cornell University). Cornell University. https://doi.org/DOI: 10.48550/arXiv.2102

Zibani, P., Rajkoomar, M., & Naicker, N. (2021). A systematic review of faculty research repositories at higher education institutions [Review of A systematic review of faculty research repositories at higher education institutions]. Digital Library Perspectives, 38(2), 237. Emerald Publishing Limited. DOI: 10.1108/DLP-04-2021-0035

Compilation of References

Abdelouafi, H. (2019). *Teaching Sign Language to the Deaf Children in Adrar.*

Abdul, W., Alsulaiman, M., Amin, S. U., Faisal, M., Muhammad, G., Albogamy, F. R., Bencherif, M. A., & Ghaleb, H. (2021). Intelligent real-time Arabic sign language classification using attention-based inception and BiLSTM. *Computers & Electrical Engineering*, *95*, 107–395. DOI: 10.1016/j.compeleceng.2021.107395

Abidine, B. M., Fergani, L., Fergani, B., & Oussalah, M. (2018). The joint use of sequence features combination and modified weighted SVM for improving daily activity recognition. *Pattern Analysis & Applications*, *21*(1), 119–138. DOI: 10.1007/s10044-016-0570-y

Ads, O. S., Alfares, M. M., & Salem, M. A. M. (2021). Multi-limb Split Learning for Tumor Classification on Vertically Distributed Data. *International Conference on Intelligent Computing and Information Systems (ICICIS)*, 88-92. http://dx.doi.org/DOI: 10.1109/ICICIS52592.2021.9694163

Ahamed, F., Shahrestani, S., & Cheung, H. (2020). Internet of things and machine learning for healthy ageing: Identifying the early signs of dementia. *Sensors (Basel)*, *20*(21), 6031. DOI: 10.3390/s20216031 PMID: 33114070

Akram, H., & Li, S. (2024). Understanding the role of teacher-student relationships in students' online learning engagement: Mediating role of academic motivation. *Perceptual and Motor Skills*, *131*(4), 1415–1438. DOI: 10.1177/00315125241248709 PMID: 38647390

Al Moaiad, Y., Alobed, M., Alsakhnini, M., & Momani, A. M. (2024). Challenges in natural Arabic language processing. *Edelweiss Applied Science and Technology*, *8*(6), 4700–4705. DOI: 10.55214/25768484.v8i6.3018

Alamer, A., & Almulhim, F. (2024). Optimizing EFL learning: Exploring the role of learner background, intrinsic, and extrinsic motivation. *BMC Psychology*, *12*(1), 34. PMID: 38238867

Alawwad, R. A., Bchir, O., & Maher, M. (2021). Arabic sign language recognition using Faster R-CNN. *International Journal of Advanced Computer Science and Applications*, *12*(3), 3. DOI: 10.14569/IJACSA.2021.0120380

Al-Barham., …. (2023). RGB Arabic Alphabets SL dataset. url: https://paperswithcode .com/dataset/rgbarabic-alphabets-sign-language-dataset

Aldausari, N., Sowmya, A., Marcus, N., & Mohammadi, G. (2020). Video Generative Adversarial Networks [PDF]. *RE:view.*

Aldoseri, A., Al-Khalifa, K. N., & Hamouda, A. M. S. (2023). Re-Thinking Data Strategy and Integration for Artificial Intelligence: Concepts, Opportunities, and Challenges. In Applied Sciences (Vol. 13, Issue 12, p. 7082). Multidisciplinary Digital Publishing Institute. DOI: 10.3390/app13127082

Ali Almahri, H. G. (2022). Arabic Sign Language Recognition: A Deep Learning Approach. P*hD thesis. The British University in Dubai (BUiD).*

Aliyu, I., Feliciano, M. C., Van Engelenburg, S., Kim, D. O., & Lim, C. G. (2021). A Blockchain-Based Federated Forest for SDN-Enabled In-Vehicle Network Intrusion Detection System. *IEEE Access : Practical Innovations, Open Solutions*, *9*, 102593–102608. DOI: 10.1109/ACCESS.2021.3094365

Almansor, E. (2018). Translating Arabic as low resource language using distribution representation and neural machine translation models, Master thesis, *School of Biomedical Engineering, Faculty of Engineering and Information Technology, University of Technology Sydney*, 2018.

Alnahhas, A.. (2020). Enhancing the recognition of Arabic sign language by using deep learning and leap motion controller. *International Journal of Scientific and Technology Research*, *9*(4), 1865–1870.

Aloysius, N., Geetha, M. (2020). Understanding vision-based continuous sign language recognition". *Multimedia Tools and Applications: 79.31-32, 22177-22209.*

Al-qaness, M. A., Dahou, A., Abd Elaziz, M., & Helmi, A. M. (2024). Human activity recognition and fall detection using convolutional neural network and transformer-based architecture. *Biomedical Signal Processing and Control*, *95*, 106412. DOI: 10.1016/j.bspc.2024.106412

Al-Saleh, M. F., & Yousif, A. E. (2009). Properties of the standard deviation that are rarely mentioned in classrooms. *Austrian Journal of Statistics*, *38*(3), 193–202.

Al-Sayid, F., & Kirkil, G. (2023). Exploring non-linear relationships between perceived interactivity or interface design and acceptance of collaborative web-based learning. *Education and Information Technologies*, *28*(9), 11819–11866. DOI: 10.1007/s10639-023-11635-6 PMID: 37361814

AL-Sayid, F., & Kirkil, G.AL-Sayid. (2023). Students' web-based activities moderate the effect of human-computer-interaction factors on their E-Learning acceptance and success during COVID-19 pandemic. *International Journal of Human-Computer Interaction*, *39*(14), 2852–2875. DOI: 10.1080/10447318.2022.2087013

Alshamrani, K. M., Alkhayyat, A. A., Arif, R. N., Alahmadi, A. A., Aldahery, S. T., Alsharif, W. M., & Qurashi, A. A. (2025). Are Saudi Radiological Sciences Students Prepared for Emergencies? Exploring Knowledge, and Attitudes Towards Basic Life Support and Cardiopulmonary Resuscitation. *Open Access Emergency Medicine : OAEM*, *17*, 91–103. DOI: 10.2147/OAEM.S507046 PMID: 39958799

Alwan, M., Rajendran, P. J., Kell, S., Mack, D., Dalal, S., Wolfe, M., & Felder, R. (2006). An artificial neural network–based fall detection. *Journal of Ambient Intelligence and Smart Environments*, *2*(4), 311–322.

Aly, S., & Aly, W. (2020). DeepArSLR: A novel signer-independent deep learning framework for isolated arabic sign language gestures recognition. *IEEE Access : Practical Innovations, Open Solutions*, *8*, 83199–83212. DOI: 10.1109/ACCESS.2020.2990699

Amin, R., Rojas, E., Aqdus, A., Ramzan, S., Casillas-Perez, D., & Arco, J. M. (2021). A Survey on Machine Learning Techniques for Routing Optimization in SDN. *IEEE Access : Practical Innovations, Open Solutions*, *9*, 104582–104611. DOI: 10.1109/ACCESS.2021.3099092

Amodei, D., & Hernandez, D. (2018). AI and Compute. *OpenAI*. https://openai.com/blog/ai-and-compute/

Anderson, J. A. (1995). *An Introduction to Neural Networks*. The MIT Press., DOI: 10.7551/mitpress/3905.001.0001

Anguita, D., Ghio, A., Oneto, L., Parra, X., & Reyes-Ortiz, J. L. (2013). A public domain dataset for human activity recognition using smartphones. In *The European Symposium on Artificial Neural Networks*.

Angwin, J., Larson, J., Mattu, S., & Kirchner, L. (2016). Machine bias: There's software used across the country to predict future criminals. And it's biased against blacks. *ProPublica*. https://www.propublica.org/article/machine-bias-risk-assessments-in-criminal-sentencing

Ansari, M. A., & Singh, D. K. (2021). Human detection techniques for real-time surveillance: A comprehensive survey. *Multimedia Tools and Applications*, *80*(6), 8759–8808. DOI: 10.1007/s11042-020-10103-4

Ansari, M. A., & Singh, D. K. (2021). Monitoring social distancing through human detection for preventing/reducing COVID spread. *International Journal of Information Technology : an Official Journal of Bharati Vidyapeeth's Institute of Computer Applications and Management*, *13*(3), 1255–1264. DOI: 10.1007/s41870-021-00658-2 PMID: 33870073

Ansari, M. A., Singh, D. K., & Jayaswal, R. (2024). Using postural data and recurrent learning to monitor shoplifting activities in megastores. *Concurrency and Computation*, *36*(2), e7900. DOI: 10.1002/cpe.7900

Anwar, S. M., Majid, M., Qayyum, A., Awais, M., Alnowami, M., & Khan, M. K. (2018). Medical Image Analysis using Convolutional Neural Networks: A review. *Journal of Medical Systems*, *42*(11), 1–13. DOI: 10.1007/s10916-018-1088-1 PMID: 30298337

Arjovsky, M., & Bottou, L. (2017). Towards Principled Methods for Training Generative Adversarial Networks. arXiv preprint arXiv:1701.04862.

Arroyo, R., Yebes, J. J., Bergasa, L. M., Daza, I. G., & Almazán, J. (2015). Expert video-surveillance system for real-time detection of suspicious behaviors in shopping malls. *Expert Systems with Applications*, *42*(21), 7991–8005. DOI: 10.1016/j.eswa.2015.06.016

ArSL Alphabets. url: https://www.arabamerica.com/do-you-know-about-deafcommunities-and-arabic-sign-languages-in-the-arab-world/

Avalle, M., Marco, N. D., Etta, G., Sangiorgio, E., Alipour, S., Bonetti, A., Alvisi, L., Scala, A., Baronchelli, A., Cinelli, M., & Quattrociocchi, W. (2024). Persistent interaction patterns across social media platforms and over time. In Nature (Vol. 628, Issue 8008, p. 582). Nature Portfolio. DOI: 10.1038/s41586-024-07229-y

Azroumahli, C., El Younoussi, Y., Moussaoui, O., & Zahidi, Y. (2019). An Arabic Dialects Dictionary Using Word Embeddings. [IJRSDA]. *International Journal of Rough Sets and Data Analysis*, *6*(3), 18–31. DOI: 10.4018/IJRSDA.2019070102

Babaali, B. (2024). Arabic Machine Translation of Social Media Content (Doctoral dissertation). *University of Mascara.* http://dspace.univ-mascara.dz:8080/jspui/handle/123456789/1073

Babaali, B., & Salem, M. (2023). Survey of the Arabic Machine Translation Corpora. In Chikhi, S., Diaz-Descalzo, G., Amine, A., Chaoui, A., Saidouni, D. E., & Kholladi, M. K. (Eds.), *Modelling and Implementation of Complex Systems. MISC 2022. Lecture Notes in Networks and Systems* (Vol. 593). Springer., DOI: 10.1007/978-3-031-18516-8_15

Bahdanau, D., Cho, K., & Bengio, Y. (2014). Neural machine translation by jointly learning to align and translate. arXiv preprint arXiv:1409.0473.

Baima, R. L., Chovet, L., Sedlmeir, J., Olivares-Méndez, M. A., & Fridgen, G. (2024). Designing Trustful Cooperation Ecosystems is Key to the New Space Exploration Era (Vol. 9, p. 87). DOI: 10.1145/3639476.3639760

Bandura, A. (1986). Social foundations of thought and action. *Englewood Cliffs, NJ, 1986*(23-28), 2.

Banerjee, S., & Lavie, A. (2005). METEOR: An automatic metric for MT evaluation with high levels of correlation with human judgments. In Proceedings of the ACL workshop on intrinsic and extrinsic evaluation measures for machine translation and/or summarization (pp. 65-72).

Barchard, K. A., & Pace, L. A. (2008). Meeting the challenge of high quality data entry: a free double-entry system. In International Journal of Services and Standards (Vol. 4, Issue 4, p. 359). Inderscience Publishers. DOI: 10.1504/IJSS.2008.020053

Batina, L., Bhasin, S., Jap, D., & Picek, S. (2019). {CSI}{NN}: Reverse engineering of neural network architectures through electromagnetic side channel. In *28th USENIX Security Symposium (USENIX Security 19)* (pp. 515-532).

Beatson, N., De Lange, P., O'Connell, B., Tharapos, M., & Smith, J. K. (2021). Factors impacting on accounting academics' motivation and capacity to adapt in challenging times. *Accounting Research Journal*, *34*(2), 184–195. DOI: 10.1108/ARJ-08-2020-0240

Belmadoui, S. (2022). ArSL Arabic Sign Language Dataset. https://www.kaggle.com/datasets /sabribelmadoui/arabic-sign-language-unaugmented-dataset

Beloucif, R., Choukri, K., & Gotti, R. (2016). Automatic evaluation of machine translation for dialectal Arabic. *Proceedings of the Tenth International Conference on Language Resources and Evaluation (LREC 2016).*

Bencherif, M., Algabri, M., Mekhtiche, M. A., Faisal, M., Alsulaiman, M., Mathkour, H., Al-Hammadi, M., & Ghaleb, H. (2021). Arabic sign language recognition system using 2D hands and body skeleton data. *IEEE Access : Practical Innovations, Open Solutions*, *9*, 59612–59627. DOI: 10.1109/ACCESS.2021.3069714

Bender, E. M., & Friedman, B. (2018). Data statements for natural language processing: Toward mitigating system bias and enabling better science. *Transactions of the Association for Computational Linguistics*, *6*, 587–604. DOI: 10.1162/tacl_a_00041

Bengio, Y.. (2015). Learning deep architectures for AI. *Foundations and Trends in Machine Learning*, *2*(1), 1–127. DOI: 10.1561/2200000006

Benziane, S. (2024). Innovating Prosperity: Intelligent Approaches and Economic Paradigms for Sustainable Futures. In *Intelligent Methods and Alternative Economic Models for Sustainability,* pp. 194-241, IGI Global.

Bercovich, E., & Javitt, M. C. (2018). Medical Imaging: From Roentgen to the Digital Revolution, and Beyond. *Rambam Maimonides Medical Journal*, *9*(4), e0034. DOI: 10.5041/RMMJ.10355 PMID: 30309440

Bies, A., Song, Z., Maamouri, M., Grimes, S., Lee, H., Wright, J., Strassel, S., Habash, N., Eskander, R., & Rambow, O. (2014). Transliteration of Arabizi into Arabic Orthography: Developing a Parallel Annotated Arabizi-Arabic Script SMS/ Chat Corpus, In: *Proceedings of the EMNLP 2014 Workshop on Arabic Natural Langauge Processing (ANLP)*, pp 93–103, Doha, Qatar, October 25, 2014. DOI: 10.3115/v1/W14-3612

Binns, R. (2018). Transparent design decisions: Bias, fairness, and the ethical implications of AI. *Proceedings of the 2018 CHI Conference on Human Factors in Computing Systems*, 1-15.

Bishop, C. M. (2006). Pattern Recognition and Machine Learning. *Springer*. https://dl.acm.org/doi/10.5555/1162264

Boden, M. A. (2019). *AI: Its nature and future*. Oxford University Press.

Bommasani, R., Klyman, K., Longpre, S., Kapoor, S., Maslej, N., Xiong, B., ... & Liang, P. (2025). The 2023 Foundation Model Transparency Index. Transactions on Machine Learning Research.

Bonk, C. J., & Graham, C. R. (2012). *The handbook of blended learning: Global perspectives, local designs*. Wiley+ ORM.

Bosch, J., Olsson, H. H., & Wang, T. J. (2020, December). Towards automated detection of data pipeline faults. In 2020 27th Asia-Pacific Software Engineering Conference (APSEC) (pp. 346-355). IEEE.

Boukdir, A.. (2021). Isolated Video-Based Arabic Sign Language Recognition Using Convolutional and Recursive Neural Networks. *Arabian Journal for Science and Engineering*, •••, 1–13.

Bowman, S. R.. (2016). *Generating Sentences from a Continuous Space*. In arXiv:1511.06349. DOI: 10.18653/v1/K16-1002

Brahme, A. (2014). *Comprehensive biomedical physics*. Newnes.

Braun, V., & Clarke, V. (2006). Using thematic analysis in psychology. *Qualitative Research in Psychology*, *3*(2), 77–101. DOI: 10.1191/1478088706qp063oa

Brock, A., ... (2018). Large Scale GAN Training for High Fidelity Natural Image Synthesis. arXiv preprint arXiv:1809.11096.

Brown, T., Mann, B., Ryder, N., Subbiah, M., & Kaplan, J. (2020). Language models are few-shot learners. *Advances in Neural Information Processing Systems*, *33*, 1877–1901.

Brusilovsky, P., & Peylo, C. (2003). Adaptive and intelligent web-based educational systems. *International Journal of Artificial Intelligence in Education*, *13*(2–4), 159–172.

Brynjolfsson, E., & McAfee, A. (2014). *The second machine age: Work, progress, and prosperity in a time of brilliant technologies*. W.W. Norton & Company.

Bunn, G., & Wake, D. (2015). Motivating factors of nontraditional post-baccalaureate students pursuing initial teacher licensure. *Teacher Educator*, *50*(1), 47–66. DOI: 10.1080/08878730.2014.975304

Burelli, P. (2022). Predicting Customer Lifetime Value in Free-to-Play Games. In arXiv (Cornell University). Cornell University. https://doi.org/DOI: 10.48550/arXiv.2209

Burke, M., Parnell, A., Wesaw, A., & Kruger, K. (2017). Predictive analysis of student data: A focus on engagement and behavior. *NASPA report*.

Callison-Burch, C., Osborne, M., & Koehn, P. (2007). Re-evaluation of the evaluation of machine translation: Human vs. automatic evaluation. *Proceedings of the 45th annual meeting of the association for computational linguistics*, 688–695.

Calvo, R., & Wright, M. (2021). AI governance in a globalized world. *Journal of AI Research*, *80*, 115–136.

Camgo, N. C.. (2017). Subunets: End-to-end hand shape and continuous sign language recognition. *Proceedings of the IEEE international conference on computer vision*, 3056-3065.

Cao, Z.. (2017). Realtime multi-person 2d pose estimation using part affinity fields. *Proceedings of the IEEE conference on computer vision and pattern recognition,* 7291-7299. DOI: 10.1109/CVPR.2017.143

Cath, C., Wachter, S., & Mittelstadt, B. D. (2018). The ethics of algorithms: Mapping the debate. *Big Data & Society, 5*(2), 1–21. DOI: 10.1177/2053951718786327

Chandran, M., Padalkar, S., & Shimray, R. A. (2025). Motivation to Become a Teacher: Emerging Trends From a Study of Preservice Teacher Education. *Contemporary Education Dialogue, 22*(1), 127–153. DOI: 10.1177/09731849241300796

Chang, H. H., & Mukherjee, A. (2023). Machine Learning and Consumer Data. In arXiv (Cornell University). Cornell University. https://doi.org/DOI: 10.48550/arXiv.2306

Chavarriaga, R., Sagha, H., Calatroni, A., Digumarti, S. T., Tröster, G., Millán, J. R., & Roggen, D. (2013). The opportunity challenge: A benchmark database for on-body sensor-based activity recognition. *Pattern Recognition Letters, 34*(15), 2033–2042. DOI: 10.1016/j.patrec.2012.12.014

Chen, C., Jafari, R., & Kehtarnavaz, N. (2015). UTD-MHAD: A multimodal dataset for human action recognition utilizing a depth camera and a wearable inertial sensor. In *2015 IEEE International Conference on Image Processing (ICIP)* (pp. 168–172). DOI: 10.1109/ICIP.2015.7350781

Cheng, W., Tang, Y., & Yang, W. (2021). Multi-channel VideoStreaming Technology for Processing Based on Distributed Computing Platform. In Journal of Physics Conference Series (Vol. 1757, Issue 1, p. 12172). IOP Publishing. DOI: 10.1088/1742-6596/1757/1/012172

Chen, L., & Li, Z. (2023). Natural Language Processing with Transformer-based Neural Networks. *Journal of Natural Language Processing, 38*(3), 134–149.

Chen, W., & Liu, L. (2023). BERT and Transformers: Modern Neural Networks for NLP. *Computational Linguistics, 48*(7), 865–887.

Chesney, R., & Citron, D. K. (2019). Deepfakes: A looming challenge for privacy, democracy, and national security. *California Law Review, 107*(6), 1753–1819.

Ching, T., Himmelstein, D. S., Beaulieu-Jones, B. K., Kalinin, A. A., Do, B. T., Way, G. P., Ferrero, E., Agapow, P.-M., Zietz, M., Hoffman, M. M., Xie, W., Rosen, G. L., Lengerich, B. J., Israeli, J., Lanchantin, J., Woloszynek, S., Carpenter, A. E., Shrikumar, A., Xu, J., & Greene, C. S. (2018). Opportunities and Obstacles for Deep Learning in Biology and Medicine. *Journal of the Royal Society, Interface, 15*(141), 20170387. DOI: 10.1098/rsif.2017.0387 PMID: 29618526

Cho, K., ... (2014). *Learning phrase representations using RNN encoder-decoder for statistical machine translation*. In EMNLP, 2014. DOI: 10.3115/v1/D14-1179

Chollet, F. (2017). Deep learning with Python. Manning Publications. https://www.manning.com/books/deep-learning-with-python

Chollet, F., & Chollet, F. (2021). *Deep learning with Python*. Simon and Schuster.

Clark, A., & Sivasankaran, P. (2023). Creative artificial intelligence and its impact on creative industries. *Journal of Innovation & Creativity*, *12*(3), 35–49. DOI: 10.1016/j.jiic.2023.01.006

Clark, C., & Sivasankaran, R. (2023). Generative AI and its impact on creative industries. *Journal of Creative Technologies*, *9*(2), 20–33. DOI: 10.1080/123456789

Conneau, A., Khandelwal, K., Goyal, N., Chaudhary, V., Wenzek, T., Guzmán, F., Grave, E., Ott, M., Zettlemoyer, L., & Stoyanov, V. (2020). Unsupervised cross-lingual representation learning at scale. *Proceedings of the 58th Annual Meeting of the Association for Computational Linguistics*, 8440–8451. DOI: 10.18653/v1/2020.acl-main.747

Cook, D. A., & Artino, A. R.Jr. (2016). Motivation to learn: An overview of contemporary theories. *Medical Education*, *50*(10), 997–1014. DOI: 10.1111/medu.13074 PMID: 27628718

Cook, D. J. (2010). Learning setting-generalized activity models for smart spaces. *IEEE Intelligent Systems*, *2010*(99), 1. DOI: 10.1109/MIS.2010.95 PMID: 21461133

Cook, D. J., Crandall, A. S., Thomas, B. L., & Krishnan, N. C. (2012). CASAS: A smart home in a box. *Computer*, *46*(7), 62–69. DOI: 10.1109/MC.2012.328 PMID: 24415794

Cosmos, N. V. I. D. I. A. (n.d.). *What is NVIDIA Cosmos?*https://www.nvidia.com/en-in/ai/cosmos/

CS2R, Center of Smart Robotics Research, (2022). KSU-ArSL, Arabic Sign language. *IEEE Dataport, doi: https://dx.doi.org/*DOI: 10.21227/8axv-ma58

Daimler, E., & Wisnesky, R. (2020). Informal Data Transformation Considered Harmful. In arXiv (Cornell University). Cornell University. https://doi.org/DOI: 10.48550/arXiv.2001

Darwish, K., Magdy, W., & Yamani, M. (2014). Arabic dialect identification using n-grams and character-level svm. *Proceedings of the First Arabic Natural Language Processing Workshop*, 124–131.

Dash, A., Ye, J., & Wang, G. (2021). A review of Generative Adversarial Networks, GANs, and its applications in a wide variety of disciplines—from medical to remote sensing. *arXiv preprint arXiv:2110.01442*. arXiv

Dastin, J. (2021). The social impact of artificial intelligence and the rise of new media consumption patterns. *Journal of Science and Technology*, *7*(1), 52–65.

Deng, J., Dong, W., Socher, R., Li, L. J., Li, K., & Fei-Fei, L. (2009, June). Imagenet: A large-scale hierarchical image database. In 2009 IEEE conference on computer vision and pattern recognition (pp. 248-255). Ieee. DOI: 10.1109/CVPR.2009.5206848

Dense Layers. url: https://www.oreilly.com/library/view/tensorflowfordeep/9781491980446/ch04.html

Deshmukh, D. (2017). Inclusion-evidence based strategies. *International Journal of Education and Management Studies*, *7*(3), 290–293.

Dessí, D., Osborne, F., Recupero, D. R., Buscaldi, D., & Motta, E. (2022). SCICERO: A deep learning and NLP approach for generating scientific knowledge graphs in the computer science domain. *Knowledge-Based Systems*, *258*, 109945. DOI: 10.1016/j.knosys.2022.109945

Devlin, J., ... (2018). *BERT: Pre-training of deep bidirectional transformers for language understanding*. In NAACL, 2018.

Devlin, J., Chang, M. W., Lee, K., & Toutanova, K. (2018). Bert: Pre-training of deep bidirectional transformers for language understanding. arXiv preprint arXiv:1810.04805.

Devlin, J., Chang, M. W., Lee, K., & Toutanova, K. (2018). BERT: Pre-training of deep bidirectional transformers for language understanding. arXiv. https://arxiv.org/abs/1810.04805

DGV-5 Gloves. url: http://www.dg-tech.it/vhand3/products.html

Dhar, S. (2012). Employability of management students in India: Some concerns and considerations. *AIMA Journal for management research, 6*(4/4), 0974-497.

Doshi-Velez, F., & Kim, B. (2017). Towards a rigorous science of interpretable machine learning. *arXiv preprint arXiv:1702.08608*.

Duan, Y.. (2023). EduChat: Towards Multi-role Multi-turn Open-ended Conversation for Education. https://arxiv.org/abs/2308.02773

Dumoulin, V., ... (2017). *Adversarially learned inference*. In Advances in Neural Information Processing Systems, NeurIPS, 2017.

Eccles, J. S., & Wigfield, A. (2020). From expectancy-value theory to situated expectancy-value theory: A developmental, social cognitive, and sociocultural perspective on motivation. *Contemporary Educational Psychology*, *61*, 101859. DOI: 10.1016/j.cedpsych.2020.101859

Eisa, S., & Moreira, A. (2017). A behaviour monitoring system (BMS) for ambient assisted living. *Sensors (Basel)*, *17*(9), 1946. DOI: 10.3390/s17091946 PMID: 28837105

El Ghoul, O.. (2022). JUMLA-QSL-22: A dataset of Qatari sign language sentences. *IEEE Dataport, doi: https://dx.doi.org/*DOI: 10.21227/ckzp-3754

ElBadawy, M., ... (2014). A proposed hybrid sensor architecture for arabic sign language recognition. *Intelligent Systems: Proceedings of the 7th International Conference Intelligent Systems IS'2014, Warsaw, Poland, Tools, Architectures, Systems, Applications: Springer, 2, 721-730.*

ElBadawy, M., ... (2017). Arabic sign language recognition with 3d convolutional neural networks". IEEE *Eighth international conference on intelligent computing and information systems (ICICIS), 66-71.* Electromygrophy(EMG). url: https://www .myupchar.com/en/test/emg-electromyography

Elgammal, A., Liu, B., Elhoseiny, M., & Mazzone, M. (2017). CAN: Creative adversarial networks, generating "art" by learning about styles and deviating from style norms. *arXiv preprint arXiv:1706.07068.* https://arxiv.org/abs/1706.07068

Elhage, N., Pustokhina, I., & Leckie, C. (2021). AI creativity and its limitations: An exploration of artificial intelligence-generated content. *AI & Society*, *36*(4), 823–834. DOI: 10.1007/s00146-021-01174-1

Elkin-Koren, N., & Salzberger, E. (2020). Who owns AI-generated content? The legal and ethical implications of AI and copyright. *Journal of Technology and Policy*, *12*(3), 74–91.

ElNokrashy, M., & Kocmi, T. (2023, December). ebleu: Unexpectedly good machine translation evaluation using simple word embeddings. In *Proceedings of the Eighth Conference on Machine Translation* (pp. 744-748). https://doi.org/DOI: 10.18653/v1/2023.wmt-1.61

Elons, A. S. (2014). GPU implementation for arabic sign language real time recognition using multi-level multiplicative neural networks. *IEEE2014 9th International Conference on Computer Engineering & Systems (ICCES), 360-367.*

Energy, R. (2020). Energy-efficient AI models for sustainable futures. *Journal of Sustainable Computing*, *3*(4), 221–234.

Espinilla, M., Medina, J., & Nugent, C. (2018). UCAMI CUP: Analyzing the UJA human activity recognition dataset of activities of daily living. *Proceedings - MDPI, 1267.* Advance online publication. DOI: 10.3390/proceedings1267

Esteva, A., Kuprel, B., Novoa, R. A., Ko, J., Swetter, S. M., Blau, H. M., & Thrun, S. (2017). Dermatologist-level classification of skin cancer with deep neural networks. *Nature, 542*(7639), 115–118. DOI: 10.1038/nature21056 PMID: 28117445

Ezzeldin, M.. (2025). Survey on multimodal complex human activity recognition. *FCI-H Informatics Bulletin, 7*(1), 26–44.

Fan, C., Lei, Y., Sun, Y., Piscitelli, M. S., Chiosa, R., & Capozzoli, A. (2022). Data-centric or algorithm-centric: Exploiting the performance of transfer learning for improving building energy predictions in data-scarce context. *Energy, 240*, 122775. DOI: 10.1016/j.energy.2021.122775

Fidalgo-Blanco, Á., García-Peñalvo, F. J., Sein-Echaluce, M. L., & Conde-González, M. Á. (2014, November). Learning content management systems for the definition of adaptive learning environments. In *2014 International Symposium on Computers in Education (SIIE)* (pp. 105–110). IEEE. DOI: 10.1109/SIIE.2014.7017713

Floridi, L., Cowls, J., Beltrametti, M., Chatila, R., Chazerand, P., & Luetge, C. (2018). AI4People—An ethical framework for a good AI society. *Minds and Machines, 28*(4), 689–707. DOI: 10.1007/s11023-018-9482-5 PMID: 30930541

Frid-Adar, M., Diamant, I., Klang, E., Ben-Cohen, A., & Goldberger, J. (2018). GAN-based synthetic medical image augmentation for increased CNN performance in liver lesion classification. *Neurocomputing, 321*, 321–331. DOI: 10.1016/j.neucom.2018.09.013

Ganaie, M. A., Hu, M., Malik, A. K., Tanveer, M., & Suganthan, P. N. (2022). Ensemble deep learning: A review. *Engineering Applications of Artificial Intelligence, 115*, 105151. DOI: 10.1016/j.engappai.2022.105151

Ganesh, S., Gomathi, R., & Kannadhasan, S. (2025). Brain Tumor Segmentation and Detection in MRI using Convolutional Neural Networks and VGG16. *Cancer Biomarkers: Section. Disease Markers, 42*(3), 18758592241311184. Advance online publication. DOI: 10.1177/18758592241311184 PMID: 40183298

Gao, J., Liu, Q., & Huang, W. B. (2021, January). Learning path generator based on knowledge graph. In Proceedings of the 2021 12th International Conference on E-Education, E-Business, E-Management, and E-Learning (pp. 27–33). DOI: 10.1145/3450148.3450155

Gao, T., & Zhang, K. (2023). Deep Neural Networks for Social Media Analytics. *Journal of Data Science and Analytics*, *19*(1), 82–99.

Gatys, L. A., ... (2016). *Image style transfer using convolutional neural networks*. In CVPR, 2016. DOI: 10.1109/CVPR.2016.265

Gayathri, K., Elias, S., & Ravindran, B. (2015). Hierarchical activity recognition for dementia care using Markov logic network. *Personal and Ubiquitous Computing*, *19*(2), 271–285. DOI: 10.1007/s00779-014-0827-7

Gehrmann, S., Clark, E. A., & Sellam, T. (2022). Repairing the Cracked Foundation: A Survey of Obstacles in Evaluation Practices for Generated Text. In arXiv (Cornell University). Cornell University. https://doi.org/DOI: 10.48550/arXiv.2202

Ghazanfar, L.. (2020). An automatic Arabic sign language recognition system based on deep CNN: An assistive system for the deaf and hard of hearing. *International Journal of Computing and Digital Systems*, *9*(4), 715–724. DOI: 10.12785/ijcds/090418

Gogarty, B., & O'Mara, D. (2020). The liability of AI: A legal perspective. *Stanford Technology Law Review : STLR : An Online High-Technology Law Journal from Stanford Law School*, *23*(1), 34–57.

Goldstein, M. (2023). Special Issue on Unsupervised Anomaly Detection. In Applied Sciences (Vol. 13, Issue 10, p. 5916). Multidisciplinary Digital Publishing Institute. DOI: 10.3390/app13105916

Goodfellow, I. J., ... (2014). Generative Adversarial Networks. arXiv preprint arXiv:1406.2661.

Goodfellow, I. J., Pouget-Abadie, J., Mirza, M., Xu, B., Warde-Farley, D., Ozair, S., Courville, A., & Bengio, Y. (2014). Generative Adversarial Networks. *arXiv preprint arXiv:1406.2661*. arXiv

Goodfellow, I., ... (2014). *Generative Adversarial Nets*. In Advances in Neural Information Processing Systems, 27, 2672-2680.

Goodfellow, I., Bengio, Y., & Courville, A. (2016). *Deep learning*. MIT Press.

Goodfellow, I., Pouget-Abadie, J., Mirza, M., Xu, B., Warde-Farley, D., Ozair, S., & Bengio, Y. (2014). Generative adversarial nets. *Advances in Neural Information Processing Systems*, •••, 27.

Graefe, A. K. (2024). Gifted high school students' perceptions of the impact of classroom power dynamics on motivation and empowerment. *Journal of Advanced Academics*, *35*(1), 6–55. DOI: 10.1177/1932202X231220414

Grishchenko, L., ... (2020). Attention mesh: High-fidelity face mesh prediction in realtime. *arXiv preprint arXiv:2006.10962.*

Grishma, S., & Esi, A. (2014). The Impact of Socio-Cultural Factors on Professional Aspiration in India. Conference: Subsistence Markets Conference, Chicago https:// search. informit. org/doi/epdf/10.3316/ielapa. 721100117642410.

Guerberof, A. (2009). *Pupil: An automatic evaluation metric for translation quality assessment of web pages*. Dublin City University.

Gulrajani, I., ... (2017). Improved Training of Wasserstein GANs. arXiv preprint arXiv:1704.00028.

Guo, D., Zhou, W., Li, H., & Wang, M. (2018). Hierarchical LSTM for sign language translation. *Proceedings of the AAAI Conference on Artificial Intelligence*, *32*(1), 1. DOI: 10.1609/aaai.v32i1.12235

Guo, Z., & Zhang, L. (2023). Exploring Neural Networks for Traffic Prediction. *Transportation Research Part C, Emerging Technologies*, *98*, 215–229.

Guyon, I., & Elisseeff, A. (2003). An Introduction to Variable and feature selection. *Journal of Machine Learning Research*, *3*, 1157–1182. DOI: 10.1162/153244303322753616

Habash, N. (2010). Introduction to Arabic natural language processing. *Synthesis Lectures on Human Language Technologies*, *3*(1), 1–187. DOI: 10.1007/978-3-031-02139-8

Habash, N., Roth, R., Rambow, O., & Eskander, R. (2017). A multi-dialectal arabic treebank. *Proceedings of the Eleventh International Conference on Language Resources and Evaluation (LREC 2018).*

Hachiuma, R., Sato, F., & Sekii, T. (2023). Unified keypoint-based action recognition framework via structured keypoint pooling. In *2023 IEEE/CVF Conference on Computer Vision and Pattern Recognition (CVPR)* (pp. 22962–22971). Vancouver, BC, Canada. DOI: 10.1109/CVPR52729.2023.02199

Haque, M. A. (2022). A Brief analysis of "ChatGPT"–A revolutionary tool designed by OpenAI. EAI endorsed transactions on AI and robotics, 1, e15-e15. DOI: 10.4108/airo.v1i1.2983

Haroon, U., Ullah, A., Hussain, T., Ullah, W., Sajjad, M., Muhammad, K., Lee, M. Y., & Baik, S. W. (2022). A multi-stream sequence learning framework for human interaction recognition. *IEEE Transactions on Human-Machine Systems*, *52*(3), 435–444. DOI: 10.1109/THMS.2021.3138708

Harrat, S., Meftouh, K., & Smaïli, K. (2017). Machine translation for Arabic dialects (survey). *Information Processing & Management*, *56*(2), 262–273. DOI: 10.1016/j.ipm.2017.08.003

Hassan, N., Miah, A. S. M., & Shin, J. (2024). A Deep Bidirectional LSTM Model Enhanced by Transfer-Learning-Based Feature Extraction for Dynamic Human Activity Recognition. *Applied Sciences (Basel, Switzerland)*, *14*(2), 603. DOI: 10.3390/app14020603

Hayani, S.. (2019). Arab sign language recognition with convolutional neural networks. *IEEE International Conference of Computer Science and Renewable Energies (ICCSRE):* 1-4. DOI: 10.1109/ICCSRE.2019.8807586

Hazra, T., & Anjaria, K. (2022). Applications of game theory in deep learning: a survey. In Multimedia Tools and Applications (Vol. 81, Issue 6, p. 8963). Springer Science+Business Media. DOI: 10.1007/s11042-022-12153-2

He, K., Zhang, X., Ren, S., & Sun, J. (2016). Deep Residual Learning for Image Recognition. *IEEE Conference on Computer Vision and Pattern Recognition (CVPR)*, *6*, 770-778. https://doi.org/DOI: 10.48550/arXiv.1512.03385

He, K., Zhang, X., Ren, S., & Sun, J. (2016). Deep residual learning for image recognition. In *Proceedings of the IEEE conference on computer vision and pattern recognition* (pp. 770-778). DOI: 10.1109/CVPR.2016.90

Herrera, J. L., Galán-Jiménez, J., Foschini, L., Bellavista, P., Berrocal, J., & Murillo, J. M. (2022, August 1). QoS-Aware Fog Node Placement for Intensive IoT Applications in SDN-Fog Scenarios. *IEEE Internet of Things Journal*, *9*(15), 13725–13739. Advance online publication. DOI: 10.1109/JIOT.2022.3143948

Heusel, M., ... (2017). GANs Trained by a Two Time-Scale Update Rule Converge to a Local Nash Equilibrium. arXiv preprint arXiv:1706.08500.

He, Y., & Zhang, J. (2023). Improving GANs with Neural Architecture Search. *Machine Learning*, *29*(1), 1–22.

Hinduja, P., Fakir Mohammad, R., & Siddiqui, S. (2024). Factors influencing students' academic self-efficacy in related domains. *SAGE Open*, *14*(4), 21582440241289738. DOI: 10.1177/21582440241289738

Hinton, G. E. (2009). Deep belief networks. *Scholarpedia Journal*, *4*(5), 5947. DOI: 10.4249/scholarpedia.5947

Hisham, B., & Hamouda, A. (2017). Arabic Static and Dynamic Gestures Recognition Using Leap Motion. *Journal of Computational Science, 13*(8), 337–354. DOI: 10.3844/jcssp.2017.337.354

Hoffer, E., Hubara, I., & Soudry, D. (2017). *Train longer, generalize better: closing the generalization gap in large batch training of neural networks. Conference on Neural Information Processing Systems*, DOI: 10.48550/arXiv.1705.08741

Holzinger, A., Biemann, C., Pattichis, C. S., & Kell, D. B. (2017). What do we need to build explainable AI systems for the medical domain? arXiv, 1, https://doi.org/ DOI: 10.48550/arXiv.1712.09923

Huang, G., Liu, Z., van der Maaten, L., & Weinberger, K. Q. (2017). Densely Connected Convolutional Networks. *arXiv, 5*. https://arxiv.org/abs/1608.06993 DOI: 10.1109/CVPR.2017.243

Huang, Y., Jasin, S., & Manchanda, P. (2019). "Level Up": Leveraging Skill and Engagement to Maximize Player Game-Play in Online Video Games. In Information Systems Research (Vol. 30, Issue 3, p. 927). Institute for Operations Research and the Management Sciences. DOI: 10.1287/isre.2019.0839

Huang, Z., ... (2015). Bidirectional LSTM-CRF models for sequence tagging. *arXiv preprint arXiv:1508.0199.*

Hughes, R., & Lothian, T. (2022). The regulation of AI: Challenges and opportunities for copyright law. *Journal of Technology Law & Policy, 24*(1), 1–25. DOI: 10.1234/jtlp.2022.0123

Hu, H., Salcic, Z., Dobbie, G., Chen, Y., & Zhang, X. (2021, July). EAR: An enhanced adversarial regularization approach against membership inference attacks. In *2021 International Joint Conference on Neural Networks (IJCNN)* (pp. 1-8). IEEE.

Husain, F. (2022). Arabic Natural Language Processing, [Online]. Available: https://infoscilab.ku.edu.kw/arabic-natural-language-processing/

Hussain, S., Mubeen, I., Ullah, N., Shah, S. S. U. D., Khan, B. A., Zahoor, M., Ullah, R., Khan, F. A., & Sultan, M. A. (2022). Modern Diagnostic Imaging Technique Applications and Risk Factors in the Medical Field: A Review. *BioMed Research International, 1*(1), 1–19. DOI: 10.1155/2022/5164970 PMID: 35707373

Hu, Y., Wu, F., Li, Q., Long, Y., Garrido, G. M., Ge, C., Ding, B., Forsyth, D., Li, B., & Song, D. (2023). SoK: Privacy-Preserving Data Synthesis. In arXiv (Cornell University). Cornell University. https://doi.org/DOI: 10.48550/arXiv.2307

Hwang, Y. M., Park, S., Lee, H. O., Ko, S.-K., & Lee, B.-T. (2021). Deep learning for human activity recognition based on causality feature extraction. *IEEE Access : Practical Innovations, Open Solutions*, *9*, 112257–112275. DOI: 10.1109/ACCESS.2021.3103211

IBM. (2021). *What is strong AI?* Retrieved 5 Feb 2025 from https://www.ibm.com/think/topics/strong-ai

Ihianle, IK. et al. (2020). A deep learning approach for human activities recognition from multimodal sensing devices. *IEEE Access 8:179028–179038. . 2020. 30279 79*DOI: 10. 1109/ ACCESS

Iqbal, S., Razalli, M. R., & Taib, C. A. B. (2023). Influence of intrinsic and extrinsic motivation on higher education performance: Mediating effect of quality culture. *Frontiers in Education*, *8*, 1099415. DOI: 10.3389/feduc.2023.1099415

Jalal, A., Khalid, N., & Kim, K. (2020). Automatic recognition of human interaction via hybrid descriptors and maximum entropy Markov model using depth sensors. *Entropy (Basel, Switzerland)*, *22*(8), 817. DOI: 10.3390/e22080817 PMID: 33286588

Jana, S., & Pal, C. (2024). A study of stellar evolution based on structural equation modelling of stellar parameters. *International Journal of Data Analysis Techniques and Strategies*, *16*(2), 105–125. DOI: 10.1504/IJDATS.2024.137872

Jin, L., Tan, F., & Jiang, S. (2020). Generative Adversarial Network Technologies and Applications in Computer Vision. ncbi.nlm.nih.gov

Johnson, J. M., & Khoshgoftaar, T. M. (2019). Survey on Deep Learning with Class Imbalance. *Journal of Big Data*, *6*(1), 1–54. DOI: 10.1186/s40537-019-0192-5

Jonsdottir, A. H., & Stefansson, G. (2013). Enhanced learning with web-assisted education. arXiv. https://arxiv.org/abs/1310.4667

Joshi, A., Kale, S., Chandel, S., & Pal, D. K. (2015). Likert scale: Explored and explained. *British Journal of Applied Science and Technology*, *7*(4), 396–403. DOI: 10.9734/BJAST/2015/14975

Jung, K.-H., Park, H., & Hwang, W. (2017). Deep Learning for Medical Image Analysis: Applications to Computed Tomography and Magnetic Resonance Imaging. *Hanyang Medical Reviews*, *37*(2), 61–70. DOI: 10.7599/hmr.2017.37.2.61

Kaggle. (n.d.). Stack Sample – Stack Overflow Data. Kaggle. https://www.kaggle.com/datasets/stackoverflow/stacksample

Kahraman, H. T., Sagiroglu, S., & Colak, I. (2010, October). Development of adaptive and intelligent web-based educational systems. In 2010 4th International Conference on Application of Information and Communication Technologies (pp. 1–5). IEEE. DOI: 10.1109/ICAICT.2010.5612054

Kanervisto, A., Kinnunen, T., & Hautamäki, V. (2022). GAN-Aimbots: Using Machine Learning for Cheating in First Person Shooters. In IEEE Transactions on Games (Vol. 15, Issue 4, p. 566). Institute of Electrical and Electronics Engineers. DOI: 10.1109/TG.2022.3173450

Kang, M., & Tian, J. (2023). Machine Learning: Data Pre-processing. https://onlinelibrary.wiley.com/doi/10.1002/9781119515326.ch5

Karras, T., ... (2017). *Progressive growing of GANs for improved quality, stability, and variation.* In International Conference on Machine Learning, ICML, 2017.

Karras, T., ... (2019). A Style-Based Generator Architecture for Generative Adversarial Networks. arXiv preprint arXiv:1812.04948. DOI: 10.1109/CVPR.2019.00453

Katz, S., Downs, T. D., Cash, H. R., & Grotz, R. C. (1970). Progress in development of the index of ADL. *The Gerontologist, 10*(1_Part_1), 20–30. DOI: 10.1093/geront/10.1_Part_1.20 PMID: 5420677

Kelly, M. L., Nieuwoudt, J., Willis, R., & Lee, M. F. (2024). Belonging, enjoyment, motivation, and retention: University students' sense of belonging before and during the COVID-19 pandemic. *Journal of College Student Retention*, •••, 15210251241231242. DOI: 10.1177/15210251241231242

Kendall, A., Grimes, M., ... (2015). Posenet: A convolutional network for real-time 6-dof camera relocalization. Proceedings of the IEEE international conference on computer vision, 2938-2946. Kinect Microsoft Sensor. https://www.reallusion.com/iclone/help/iclone5/pro/08_animation/device_mocap/using_the_device_mocap_panel.html

Ker, J., Wang, L., Rao, J., & Lim, T. (2018). Deep Learning Applications in Medical Image Analysis. *IEEE Access : Practical Innovations, Open Solutions, 6*, 9375–9389. DOI: 10.1109/ACCESS.2017.2788044

Khan, A., & Kim, N. (2020). Application of artificial neural networks for quantitative damage detection in fiber-reinforced composite structures. *Advances in Mechanical Engineering, 12*(4), 1–12.

Khan, A., Rauf, Z., Sohail, A., Khan, A. R., Asif, H., Asif, A., & Farooq, U. (2023). A survey of the vision transformers and their CNN-transformer-based variants. *Artificial Intelligence Review, 56*(S3, Suppl. 3), 2917–2970. DOI: 10.1007/s10462-023-10595-0

Khiloun, I. E., Belmabrouk, K., & Dekhici, L., (2024). Literature Review on Supply Chains Optimization Using Multi-Agents Communication and Collaboration. *Intelligent Methods and Alternative Economic Models for Sustainability*, 74-94.

Kingma, D. P., & Welling, M. (2013). Auto-Encoding Variational Bayes. *International Conference on Learning Representations (ICLR).*

Kirkos, E., Spathis, C., & Manolopoulos, Y. (2008). Support vector machines, Decision Trees and Neural Networks for auditor selection. *Journal of computational Methods in Sciences and Engineering, 8*(3), 213-224.

Kitbutrawat, N., Portet, F., Yamaguchi, H., & Higashino, T. (2019). *Automatic localization of passive infrared binary sensors in home: From dense to scattered network. In 2019 IEEE Intl Conf on Dependable, Autonomic and Secure Computing, Intl Conf on Pervasive Intelligence and Computing, Intl Conf on Cloud and Big Data Computing, Intl Conf on Cyber Science and Technology Congress (DASC/PiCom/CBDCom/CyberSciTech).* IEEE., DOI: 10.1109/DASC/PiCom/CBDCom/CyberSciTech.2019.00149

Kitchenham, B. (2004). Procedures for performing systematic reviews. *Keele, UK, Keele University: 33.2004, 1-26.*

Klein, G., Kim, Y., Deng, Y., Senellart, J., & Rush, A. M. (2017). Opennmt: Open-source toolkit for neural machine translation, arXiv preprint, arXiv:1701.02810. DOI: 10.18653/v1/P17-4012

Koehn, P. (2010). *Statistical machine translation.* Cambridge university press.

Kolluri, J., Kotte, V. K., Phridviraj, M. S. B., & Razia, S. (2020, June). Reducing overfitting problem in machine learning using novel L1/4 regularization method. In 2020 4th international conference on trends in electronics and informatics (ICOEI) (48184) (pp. 934-938). IEEE.

Kordos, M., & Rusiecki, A. (2016). Reducing noise impact on MLP training: Techniques and algorithms to provide noise-robustness in MLP network training. *Soft Computing, 20*(1), 49–65. DOI: 10.1007/s00500-015-1690-9

Koshino, K., Werner, R. A., Pomper, M. G., Bundschuh, R. A., ... (2021). Narrative review of generative adversarial networks in medical and molecular imaging. ncbi.nlm.nih.gov

Krizhevsky, A., Sutskever, I., & Hinton, G. E. (2012). ImageNet Classification with Deep Convolutional Neural Networks. Advances in Neural Information Processing Systems, 25. https://proceedings.neurips.cc/paper_files/paper/2012/file/c399862d3b9d6b76c8436e924a68c45b-Paper.pdf

Krizhevsky, A., Sutskever, I., & Hinton, G. E. (2012). Imagenet classification with deep convolutional neural networks. *Advances in Neural Information Processing Systems, 25*. Advance online publication. DOI: 10.1145/3065386

Kukačka, J., Golkov, V., & Cremers, D. (2017, October). Regularization for Deep Learning. *Taxon.*

Kumar, R., & Gupta, A. (2023). Advanced Computing and Related Applications Leveraging Brain-inspired Spiking Neural Networks. *Journal of Advanced Computing, 40*(6), 1234–1250.

Kumar, R., & Patel, V. (2021). Generative AI in content creation: Enhancing productivity and creativity. *International Journal of Artificial Intelligence, 15*(2), 98–110.

Kumar, S., & Patel, R. (2021). The evolution of AI in content creation: Improving productivity in text generation. *International Journal of Artificial Intelligence, 16*(3), 45–58. DOI: 10.1016/j.ijai.2021.03.004

Kurni, M., & Mohammed, M. S. (2023). *A beginner's guide to introduce artificial intelligence in teaching and learning*. Springer Nature.

Kwapisz, J. R., Weiss, G. M., & Moore, S. A. (2011). Activity recognition using cell phone accelerometers. *SIGKDD Explorations, 12*(2), 74–82. DOI: 10.1145/1964897.1964918

Lalwani, P., & Ganeshan, R. (2025). HAR: A stacked ensemble learning approach based on smartphone sensors for activity detection. *Internet of Things : Engineering Cyber Physical Human Systems, 30*, 101487. DOI: 10.1016/j.iot.2024.101487

Larrazábal, A. J., Nieto, N., Peterson, V., Hitschfeld-Kahler, N., & González, E. (2020). Gender Imbalance in Medical Imaging Datasets Produces Biased Classifiers for Computer-aided Diagnosis. *Proceedings of the National Academy of Sciences of the United States of America, 117*(23), 12592–12594. DOI: 10.1073/pnas.1919012117 PMID: 32457147

Larson, D. M., Bungula, W., Lee, A., Stockdill, A. K., McKean, C., Miller, F. W., Davis, K., Erickson, R. A., & Hlavacek, E. (2023). Reconstructing missing data by comparing interpolation techniques: Applications for long-term water quality data. In Limnology and Oceanography Methods (Vol. 21, Issue 7, p. 435). Wiley. DOI: 10.1002/lom3.10556

LeCun, Y., Bengio, Y., & Hinton, G. (2015). Deep learning. nature, 521(7553), 436-444. DOI: 10.1038/nature14539

LeCun, Y., Bottou, L., Bengio, Y., & Haffner, P. (1998). Gradient-based learning applied to document recognition. *Proceedings of the IEEE, 86*(11), 2278–2324. DOI: 10.1109/5.726791

Ledig, C., ... (2017). *Photo-realistic single image super-resolution using a generative adversarial network.* In CVPR, 2017. DOI: 10.1109/CVPR.2017.19

Lee, D.-G., & Lee, S.-W. (2022). Human interaction recognition framework based on interacting body part attention. *Pattern Recognition, 128*, 108645. DOI: 10.1016/j.patcog.2022.108645

Lee, K.. (2019). *Adversarial Feature Matching for Text Generation.* In arXiv:1910.01888.

Lee, Y., & Wang, H. (2023). Multi-modal Neural Networks for Cross-Domain Learning. *Machine Learning, 58*(3), 431–446.

Legault, L. (2017). Self-Determination Theory. In V. Z.-H. Shackelford, Encyclopaedia of Personality and Individual Differences. DOI: 10.1007/978-3-319-28099-8_1162-1

Li, Y., & Luong, M.-T. (2015). *I2T: Improving the quality of machine translation with GANs.* In ACL, 2015.

Li, F., & Guo, Y. (2023). Neural Networks in Game AI: Achievements and Challenges. *Journal of Game Design and AI, 16*(3), 198–215.

Li, H., & Zhang, Y. (2023). Quantum Neural Networks: From Theory to Practice. *Quantum Computing Journal, 7*(1), 13–29.

Li, K., Rubungo, A. N., Lei, X. L., Persaud, D., Choudhary, K., DeCost, B., Dieng, A. B., & Hattrick-Simpers, J. (2024). Probing out-of-distribution generalization in machine learning for materials. In arXiv (Cornell University). Cornell University. https://doi.org/DOI: 10.48550/arXiv.2406

Lin, T. Y., Maire, M., Belongie, S., Hays, J., Perona, P., Ramanan, D., . . . Zitnick, C. L. (2014). Microsoft coco: Common objects in context. In Computer Vision–ECCV 2014: 13th European Conference, Zurich, Switzerland, September 6-12, 2014, Proceedings, Part V 13 (pp. 740-755). Springer International Publishing. DOI: 10.1007/978-3-319-10602-1_48

Lindley, D. V. (1990). Regression and correlation analysis. In *Time series and statistics* (pp. 237–243). Palgrave Macmillan UK. DOI: 10.1007/978-1-349-20865-4_30

Liouane, Z., Lemlouma, T., Roose, P., Weis, F., & Messaoud, H. (2020). An intelligent knowledge system for designing, modeling, and recognizing the behavior of elderly people in smart space. *Journal of Ambient Intelligence and Humanized Computing*, *11*(12), 6059–6075. Advance online publication. DOI: 10.1007/s12652-020-01876-5

Li, Q., Gravina, R., Li, Y., Alsamhi, S. H., Sun, F., & Fortino, G. (2020). Multi-user activity recognition: Challenges and opportunities. *Information Fusion*, *63*, 121–135. DOI: 10.1016/j.inffus.2020.06.004

Li, Q., & Liu, H. (2023). Adversarial Attacks on Neural Networks: A Comprehensive Review. *AI & Security*, *5*(2), 223–240.

Litjens, G., Kooi, T., Bejnordi, B. E., Setio, A. A. A., Ciompi, F., Ghafoorian, M., van der Laak, J. A. W. M., van Ginneken, B., & Sánchez, C. I. (2017). A Survey on Deep Learning in Medical Image Analysis. *Medical Image Analysis*, *42*, 60–88. DOI: 10.1016/j.media.2017.07.005 PMID: 28778026

Liu, B., & Wang, Z. (2023). Federated Learning with Neural Networks for Privacy-Preserving Applications. *Journal of Privacy and Security*, *41*(3), 301–318.

Liu, F., Wang, C., Tian, Z., Du, S., & Zeng, W. (2025). Advancing skeleton-based human behavior recognition: Multi-stream fusion spatiotemporal graph convolutional networks. *Complex & Intelligent Systems*, *11*(1), 94. DOI: 10.1007/s40747-024-01743-2

Liu, J., Zhang, L., & Lee, D. (2023). Graph Neural Networks for Decentralized Multi-Robot Path Planning. *Journal of Robotics*, *34*(2), 215–225.

Liu, M., Xue, Z., He, X., & Chen, J. (2021). SCADS: A Scalable Approach Using Spark in Cloud for Host-based Intrusion Detection System with System Calls. In arXiv (Cornell University). Cornell University. https://doi.org/DOI: 10.48550/arXiv.2109

Liu, X., Chen, S., & Ma, Y. (2021). AI and governance: Policy recommendations for artificial intelligence in China. *AI Open*, *2*(2), 107–120. DOI: 10.1016/j.aiopen.2021.03.003

Liu, Y., & Li, Q. (2023). Neural Networks for Fraud Detection in E-commerce. *Journal of E-commerce Technology*, *32*(5), 410–425.

Liu, Y., Ma, S., & Chen, Y. (2024). The impacts of learning motivation, emotional engagement and psychological capital on academic performance in a blended learning university course. *Frontiers in Psychology*, *15*, 1357936. DOI: 10.3389/fpsyg.2024.1357936 PMID: 38800675

Li, Y., & Wu, F. (2021). Multimodal AI: Integration of text, visual, and audio data for versatile applications. *Journal of AI Research*, *29*(2), 102–116. DOI: 10.1093/jair.2021.123

Li, Z.. (2019). *Boosting expressive power in GAN-based NLP models: Challenges and directions*. In *Proceedings of the International Conference on NLP*, 2019.

Li, Z., Yang, X., Wang, C., Ma, K., & Jiang, C. (2021). Crowd-learning: A behavior-based verification method in software-defined vehicular networks with MEC framework. *IEEE Internet of Things Journal*, *9*(2), 1622–1639.

Li, Z., Zhao, Y., Li, Y., Rahman, S., Wang, F., Xin, X., & Zhang, J. (2021, July 1). Fault Localization based on Knowledge Graph in Software-Defined Optical Networks. *Journal of Lightwave Technology*, *39*(13), 4236–4246. DOI: 10.1109/JLT.2021.3071868

Lo, C. K., Larkin, S., & Knowles, R. (2023, December). Metric score landscape challenge (MSLC23): Understanding metrics' performance on a wider landscape of translation quality. In Proceedings of the Eighth Conference on Machine Translation (pp. 776-799).

Lu, C.-H., & Chiang, Y.-T. (2014). Interaction-feature enhanced multiuser model learning for a home environment using ambient sensors. *International Journal of Intelligent Systems*, *29*(11), 1015–1046. DOI: 10.1002/int.21674

Luckin, R., & Holmes, W. (2016). Intelligence unleashed: An argument for AI in education.

Lugaresi, C., ... (2019). Mediapipe: A framework for building perception pipelines. inarXiv preprint arXiv:1906.08172.

Lundberg, S. M., & Lee, S.-I. (2017). A Unified Approach to Interpreting Model Predictions. Advances in Neural Information Processing Systems, 30, 4765-4774. https://proceedings.neurips.cc/paper_files/paper/2017/file/8a20a8621978632d76c43dfd28b67767-Paper.pdf

Lundervold, A. S., & Lundervold, A. (2019). An Overview of Deep Learning in Medical Imaging Focusing on MRI. *Zeitschrift für Medizinische Physik*, *29*(2), 102–127. DOI: 10.1016/j.zemedi.2018.11.002 PMID: 30553609

Lundy, T., Raman, N., Fu, H., & Leyton-Brown, K. (2024). Pay to (Not) Play: Monetizing Impatience in Mobile Games. In *Proceedings of the AAAI Conference on Artificial Intelligence* (Vol. 38, Issue 9, p. 9856). Association for the Advancement of Artificial Intelligence. DOI: 10.1609/aaai.v38i9.28846

Madheswari, S. P., & Mageswari, S. U. (2020). Changing paradigms of engineering education-An Indian perspective. *Procedia Computer Science*, *172*, 215–224. DOI: 10.1016/j.procs.2020.05.034

Maffey, K. R., Dotterrer, K., Niemann, J., Cruickshank, I. J., Lewis, G. A., & Kästner, C. (2023). MLTEing Models: Negotiating, Evaluating, and Documenting Model and System Qualities. In arXiv (Cornell University). Cornell University. https://doi.org/ DOI: 10.48550/arXiv.2303

Manning, C. (2020). AI Definitions. *Stanford University Human-Centered Artificial Intelligence*. https://hai.stanford.edu/sites/default/files/2020-09/AI-Definitions-HAI.pdf

Marsden, P. (2019). Artificial Intelligence defined: Useful List of Popular Definitions from Business and Science. *Digital Wellbeing*. https://digitalwellbeing.org/artificial-intelligence-defined-useful-list-of-popular-definitions-from-business-and-science/

Mateos, P., & Bellogín, A. (2025). A systematic literature review of recent advances on context-aware recommender systems. *Artificial Intelligence Review*, *58*(20). https://link.springer.com/article/10.1007/s10462-024-10939-4

McCormick, K. (2022). AI-generated art: Ethical and legal implications. *Ethics and Information Technology*, *24*(3), 301–313.

McCormick, M. (2022). Ethical implications of generative AI in creative industries. *Creativity and Technology*, *5*(1), 77–89.

McCulloch, W. S. (1943). A logical calculus of ideas immanent in nervous activity Bulletin of Mathematical Biophysics 5: 115-133. *The Bulletin of Mathematical Biophysics*, *5*, 115–133. DOI: 10.1007/BF02478259

McGowan, L. D., Peng, R. D., & Hicks, S. C. (2022). Design Principles for Data Analysis. In Journal of Computational and Graphical Statistics (Vol. 32, Issue 2, p. 754). Taylor & Francis. DOI: 10.1080/10618600.2022.2104290

Mediapipe, 2023. MediaPipe Holistic. *Github. url:*https://github.com/google/mediapipe/blob/master/docs/solutions/holistic.md

Medscience, O. (2024). Revolutionising medical imaging with AI and Big Data analytics. URL: https://openmedscience. com/revolutionising-medical-imaging-with-ai-and-big-data-analytics/#:~: text= AI% 20can% 20help% 20researchers% 20develop, and% 20develop% 20personalised% 20treatment% 20plans.

Mehrabi, N., Morstatter, F., Saxena, N., Lerman, K., & Galstyan, A. (2021). A Survey on Bias and Fairness in Machine Learning. *ACM Computing Surveys*, *54*(6), 1–35. DOI: 10.1145/3457607

Mehran, N., Kimovski, D., & Prodan, R. (2021). A Two-Sided Matching Model for Data Stream Processing in the Cloud – Fog Continuum. DOI: 10.1109/CCGrid51090.2021.00061

Men, Q., Ho, E. S., Shum, H. P., & Leung, H. (2021). A two-stream recurrent network for skeleton-based human interaction recognition. In *2020 25th International Conference on Pattern Recognition (ICPR)* (pp. 2771–2778). Milan, Italy. DOI: 10.1109/ICPR48806.2021.9412538

Meritt, R. (2025). *NVIDIA. What Are Foundation Models?*https://blogs.nvidia.com/blog/what-are-foundation-models/

Merma-Molina, G., Gavilán-Martín, D., Baena-Morales, S., & Urrea-Solano, M. (2022). Critical thinking and effective personality in the framework of education for sustainable development. *Education Sciences*, *12*(1), 28. DOI: 10.3390/educsci12010028

Miao, X., & Xu, L. (2023). Deep Learning for Autonomous Vehicles: A Review. *Autonomous Systems Review*, *47*(3), 230–246.

Michael, E., & Moore, D. M. (2020). Connecting Theory to Practice: Using Self-Determination Theory To Better Understand Inclusion in STEM. *Journal of Microbiology & Biology Education*. PMID: 32431768

Microsoft. (n.d.). Introduction to natural language processing with TensorFlow. Retrieved from Learn.microsof.com: https://learn.microsoft.com/en-us/training/modules/intro-natural-language-processing-tensorflow/

Miller, T., & Schneider, J. (2022). Personalization with generative AI: Applications and challenges. *Journal of Artificial Intelligence Applications*, *3*(2), 112–125. DOI: 10.1002/jai.2022

Miller, T., & Schneider, L. (2022). Customized content generation using AI: Personalization and its potential. *AI & Marketing Review*, *11*(4), 122–136. DOI: 10.1234/aimr.2022.1019

Minsky, M., & Papert, S. (1969). An introduction to computational geometry. Cambridge tiass. *HIT*, *479*(480), 104. DOI: 10.1007/978-1-4612-1098-6

Mirza, M., & Osindero, S. (2014). *Conditional Generative Adversarial Nets*. In arXiv:1411.1784.

Miyato, T., ... (2018). Spectral Normalization for Generative Adversarial Networks. arXiv preprint arXiv:1802.05957.

Moghe, N., Fazla, A., Amrhein, C., Kocmi, T., Steedman, M., Birch, A., Sennrich, R., & Guillou, L. (2025). Machine translation meta evaluation through translation accuracy challenge sets. *Computational Linguistics, 51*(1), 73–137. DOI: 10.1162/coli_a_00537

Mohamed Aktham, A., ... (2018). A review on systems-based sensory gloves for sign language recognition state of the art between 2007 and 2017. *In Sensors: 18.7, 2208.*

Montalvo, J., Torrijos, J., Cortes, D., Chundury, R., & St. Peter, M. (2021, August). Journey toward software-defined passive optical networks with multi-PON technology: An industry view [Invited]. *Journal of Optical Communications and Networking, 13*(8), D22–D31. DOI: 10.1364/JOCN.423034

Moryossef, A.. (2021). Evaluating the immediate applicability of pose estimation for sign language recognition. *Proceedings of the IEEE/CVF Conference on Computer Vision and Pattern Recognition,* 3434-3440. DOI: 10.1109/CVPRW53098.2021.00382

Morze, N., Varchenko-Trotsenko, L., Terletska, T., & Smyrnova-Trybulska, E. (2021, March). Implementation of adaptive learning at higher education institutions by means of Moodle LMS. [IOP Publishing.]. *Journal of Physics: Conference Series, 1840*(1), 012062. DOI: 10.1088/1742-6596/1840/1/012062

Müller, O., Fay, M., & Vom Brocke, J. (2018). The effect of big data and analytics on firm performance: An econometric analysis considering industry characteristics. *Journal of Management Information Systems, 35*(2), 488–509. DOI: 10.1080/07421222.2018.1451955

Murphy, K. P. (2012). *Machine learning: A probabilistic perspective.* MIT Press.

Musa, M. A., & Zulkifli, N. (2022). The US-Malaysia Maritime Security Cooperation and Implication Towards Malaysia's National Security. In Malaysian Journal of Social Sciences and Humanities (MJSSH) (Vol. 7, Issue 2). DOI: 10.47405/mjssh.v7i2.1306

Mystakidis, A., Ntozi, E., Afentoulis, K., Koukaras, P., Gkaidatzis, P. A., Ioannidis, D., Tjortjis, C., & Tzovaras, D. (2023). Energy generation forecasting: elevating performance with machine and deep learning. In Computing (Vol. 105, Issue 8, p. 1623). Springer Science+Business Media. DOI: 10.1007/s00607-023-01164-y

Nam, S., Kim, H., & Min, S.-G. (2021). Simplified Stream Reservation Protocol Over Software-Defined Networks for In-Vehicle Time-Sensitive Networking. *IEEE Access : Practical Innovations, Open Solutions*, *9*, 84700–84711. DOI: 10.1109/ACCESS.2021.3088288

Narayanan, A., Huey, J., & Kang, L. (2018). Data privacy in the age of AI. *Journal of Privacy & Technology*, *8*(4), 193–204.

Narkhede, G., Pasi, B., Dhamak, P., Mahalle, P., & Ambhore, N. (2025). In the pursuit of educational excellence: Investigating CSFs for implementing NEP 2020 to redefine the higher education ecosystem. *Journal of Applied Research in Higher Education*. Advance online publication. DOI: 10.1108/JARHE-09-2024-0454

Nguyen, P., & Wang, Y. (2023). Generative AI and accessibility in text-based content creation. *Journal of Inclusive Technology*, *7*(2), 79–91. DOI: 10.1016/j.jit.2023.05.007

Njah, Y., & Cheriet, M. (2021). Parallel Route Optimization and Service Assurance in Energy-Efficient Software-Defined Industrial IoT Networks. *IEEE Access : Practical Innovations, Open Solutions*, *9*, 24682–24696. DOI: 10.1109/ACCESS.2021.3056931

Nusrat, I., & Jang, S.-B. (2018). A Comparison of Regularization Techniques in Deep Neural Networks. *Symmetry*, *2018*(10), 648. www.mdpi.com/journal/symmetry. DOI: 10.3390/sym10110648

Nyanteh, A. O., Li, M., Abbod, M. F., & Al-Raweshidy, H. (2021). CloudSimHypervisor: Modeling and Simulating Network Slicing in Software-Defined Cloud Networks. *IEEE Access : Practical Innovations, Open Solutions*, *9*, 72484–72498. DOI: 10.1109/ACCESS.2021.3079501

O'Neil, C. (2016). *Weapons of math destruction: How big data increases inequality and threatens democracy*. Crown Publishing Group.

Obando Ceron, J., Bellemare, M., & Castro, P. S. (2023). Small batch deep reinforcement learning. *Advances in Neural Information Processing Systems*, *36*, 26003–26024.

Obermeyer, Z., Powers, B., Vogeli, C., & Mullainathan, S. (2019). Dissecting racial bias in an algorithm used to manage the health of populations. *Science*, *366*(6464), 447–453. DOI: 10.1126/science.aax2342 PMID: 31649194

Odena, A., ... (2017). *Conditional image generation with PixelCNN decoders*. In Advances in Neural Information Processing Systems, NeurIPS, 2017.

Okewu, E., Adewole, P., Misra, S., Maskeliunas, R., & Damasevicius, R. (2021). Artificial neural networks for educational data mining in higher education: A systematic literature review. *Applied Artificial Intelligence*, *35*(13), 983–1021. DOI: 10.1080/08839514.2021.1922847

Okwuibe, J., Haavisto, J., Kovacevic, I., Harjula, E., Ahmad, I., Islam, J., & Ylianttila, M. (2021). SDN-Enabled Resource Orchestration for Industrial IoT in Collaborative Edge-Cloud Networks. *IEEE Access : Practical Innovations, Open Solutions*, *9*, 115839–115854. DOI: 10.1109/ACCESS.2021.3105944

Open, A. I. (2023). GPT-4 Technical Report. https://arxiv.org/abs/2303.08774

Ordónez, F. J., De Toledo, P., & Sanchis, A. (2013). Activity recognition using hybrid generative/discriminative models on home environments using binary sensors. *Sensors (Basel)*, *13*(5), 5460–5477. DOI: 10.3390/s130505460 PMID: 23615583

Oren, O., Gersh, B. J., & Bhatt, D. L. (2020). Artificial Intelligence in Medical Imaging: Switching from Radiographic Pathological Data to Clinically Meaningful Endpoints. *The Lancet. Digital Health*, *2*(9), e486–e488. DOI: 10.1016/S2589-7500(20)30160-6 PMID: 33328116

Orozco-Santos, F., Sempere-Payá, V., Silvestre-Blanes, J., & Albero-Albero, T. (2021). Multicast Scheduling in SDN WISE to Support Mobile Nodes in Industrial Wireless Sensor Networks. *IEEE Access : Practical Innovations, Open Solutions*, *9*, 141651–141666. DOI: 10.1109/ACCESS.2021.3120917

Ouzzani, M., Hammady, H., Fedorowicz, Z., & Elmagarmid, A. (2016). Rayyan-a web and mobile app for systematic reviews. *Systematic Reviews*, *5*(1), 1–10. DOI: 10.1186/s13643-016-0384-4 PMID: 27919275

Paciorek, A. M., von Schacky, C. E., Foreman, S. C., Gassert, F. G., Gassert, F. T., Kirschke, J. S., Laugwitz, K. L., Geith, T., Hadamitzky, M., & Nadjiri, J. (2024). Automated Assessment of Cardiac Pathologies on Cardiac MRI using T1-mapping and Late Gadolinium Phase Sensitive Inversion Recovery Sequences with Deep Learning. *BMC Medical Imaging*, *24*(43), 43. Advance online publication. DOI: 10.1186/s12880-024-01217-4 PMID: 38350900

Papernot, N., ... (2016). *The limitations of deep learning in adversarial settings*. In Proceedings of the IEEE European Symposium on Security and Privacy, EuroS&P, 2016, 372–387. DOI: 10.1109/EuroSP.2016.36

Papineni, K., Roukos, S., Ward, T., & Zhu, W. J. (2002). BLEU: a method for automatic evaluation of machine translation. In *Proceedings of the 40th annual meeting on association for computational linguistics* (pp. 311-318).

Patel, P., & Gupta, A. (2023). Transfer Learning for Neural Networks in Healthcare. *Journal of Healthcare Engineering*, *39*(5), 57–72.

Patel, R., & Gupta, P. (2023). Neural Networks in Predictive Maintenance Systems. *Journal of Industrial Engineering*, *58*(3), 228–242.

Pathak, D., ... (2016). *Context encoders: Feature learning by inpainting*. In CVPR, 2016. DOI: 10.1109/CVPR.2016.278

Pinheiro, P. O., Almahairi, A., Benmalek, R., Golemo, F., & Courville, A. C. (2020). Unsupervised learning of dense visual representations. *Advances in Neural Information Processing Systems*, *33*, 4489–4500.

Poalelungi, D. G., Mu at, C. L., Fulga, A., Neagu, M., Neagu, A., Piraianu, A. I., & Fulga, I. (2023). Advancing Patient Care: How Artificial Intelligence Is Transforming Healthcare [Review of Advancing Patient Care: How Artificial Intelligence Is Transforming Healthcare]. Journal of Personalized Medicine, 13(8), 1214. Multidisciplinary Digital Publishing Institute. DOI: 10.3390/jpm13081214

Puchała, S., Kasprzak, W., & Piwowarski, P. (2023). Human interaction classification in sliding video windows using skeleton data tracking and feature extraction. *Sensors (Basel)*, *23*(14), 6279. DOI: 10.3390/s23146279 PMID: 37514573

Qamar, R., & Zardari, B. A. (2023). A Study on Implementing Technology in Educational Institutions. *SBBU Journal of Social Sciences*, *1*(2), 127–137.

Quantology, N., ... (2022). YOGA POSE CORRECTION USING POSENET. 20. 1758-1763. : https://www.researchgate.net/figure/Posenet-Dataof-Yoga-Pose-A-Pose-object-contains-17-key-points-for-identifying-17-key_fig3_362280366DOI: 10.14704/nq.2022.20.7.NQ33220.url

Radford, A., ... (2015). Unsupervised Representation Learning with Deep Convolutional Generative Adversarial Networks. arXiv preprint arXiv:1511.06434.

Radford, A., ... (2016). *Unsupervised learning with generative adversarial networks*. In ICLR, 2016.

Radford, A.. (2016). *Unsupervised representation learning with deep convolutional generative adversarial networks*. arXiv:1511.06434.

Radford, A., Ramesh, A., Muthukumar, S., & Sutskever, I. (2021). Learning transferable visual models from natural language supervision. *Proceedings of the International Conference on Machine Learning (ICML)*, 139, 8748-8763. https://arxiv.org/abs/2103.00020

Rajendran, S., Rajagopal, S. K., Thanarajan, T., Shankar, K., Kumar, S., Alsubaie, N. M., Ishak, M. K., & Mostafa, S. M. (2023). Automated Segmentation of Brain Tumor MRI Images using Deep Learning. *IEEE Access : Practical Innovations, Open Solutions*, *11*, 64758–64768. DOI: 10.1109/ACCESS.2023.3288017

Raj, N. S., & Renumol, V. G. (2022). A systematic literature review on adaptive content recommenders in personalized learning environments from 2015 to 2020. *Journal of Computers in Education*, *9*(1), 113–148. DOI: 10.1007/s40692-021-00199-4

Rajpurkar, P., Irvin, J., Ball, R. L., Zhu, K., Yang, B., Mehta, H., Duan, T., Ding, D., Bagul, A., Langlotz, C. P., Patel, B. N., Yeom, K. W., Shpanskaya, K., Blankenberg, F. G., Seekins, J., Amrhein, T. J., Mong, D. A., Halabi, S. S., Zucker, E. J., & Lungren, M. P. (2018). Deep Learning for Chest Radiograph Diagnosis: A Retrospective Comparison of the CheXNeXt Algorithm to Practicing Radiologists. *PLoS Medicine*, *15*(11), e1002686. DOI: 10.1371/journal.pmed.1002686 PMID: 30457988

Rajput, G., & Chouhan, P. S. (2021). Exploring the factors affecting students' choice of higher education institutes in India: A factor analysis approach. *Journal of Business and Social Sciences Research*, *6*(1), 21–34. DOI: 10.3126/jbssr.v6i1.38126

Ramanujam, E., & Perumal, T. (2023). MLMO-HSM: Multi-label multi-output hybrid sequential model for multi-resident smart home activity recognition. *Journal of Ambient Intelligence and Humanized Computing*, *14*(3), 2313–2325. DOI: 10.1007/s12652-022-04487-4

Rapidops. (10.11.2024). 26 Generative AI Tools: Disrupting every prominent sector. https://www.rapidops.com/blog/generative-ai-tools/

Razzak, M. I., Naz, S., & Zaib, A. (2018). Deep Learning for Medical Image Processing: Overview, Challenges, and the Future. *Classification in BioApps*, *26*, 323–350. DOI: 10.1007/978-3-319-65981-7_12

Redhouane, L., Sarah, B., & Abdelkader, B. (2014, June). Dorsal hand vein pattern feature extraction with wavelet transforms. In *The 2014 international symposium on networks, computers and communications* (pp. 1–5). IEEE.

Rei, R., Stewart, C., Farinha, A. C., & Lavie, A. (2020). COMET: A neural framework for MT evaluation. arXiv preprint arXiv:2009.09025. DOI: 10.18653/v1/2020.emnlp-main.213

Reiss, A., & Stricker, D. (2012). Introducing a new benchmarked dataset for activity monitoring. In *2012 16th International Symposium on Wearable Computers* (pp. 108–109). DOI: 10.1109/ISWC.2012.13

Renotte, N. (2023). Github Repository. url: https://github.com/nicknochnack/ActionDetectionforSignLanguage

Rezaeezade, A., & Batina, L. (2024). Regularizers to the rescue: Fighting overfitting in deep learning-based side-channel analysis. *Journal of Cryptographic Engineering*, *14*(4), 609–629. DOI: 10.1007/s13389-024-00361-5

Ritonga, M. et al. (2021). Machine Learning Approach for Gesture Based Arabic Sign Language Recognition for Impaired People.

Rojas, M. G., Olivera, A. C., & Vidal, P. J. (2022). Optimising Multilayer Perceptron weights and biases through a Cellular Genetic Algorithm for medical data classification. *Array (New York, N.Y.)*, *14*, 100173. DOI: 10.1016/j.array.2022.100173

Romero-Mendez, E. A., Santana-Mancilla, P. C., García-Ruiz, M. A., Montesinos-López, O. A., & Anido, L. (2023). The Use of Deep Learning to Improve Player Engagement in a Video Game through a Dynamic Difficulty Adjustment Based on Skills Classification. In Applied Sciences (Vol. 13, Issue 14, p. 8249). Multidisciplinary Digital Publishing Institute. DOI: 10.3390/app13148249

Ronneberger, O., Fischer, P., & Brox, T. (2015). U-Net: Convolutional networks for biomedical image segmentation. *arXiv, 1*. https://doi.org//arXiv.1505.04597DOI: 10.1007/978-3-319-24574-4_28

Rosenblatt, F. (1958). The perceptron: A probabilistic model for information storage and organization in the brain. *Psychological Review*, *65*(6), 386–408. DOI: 10.1037/h0042519 PMID: 13602029

Rumelhart, D. E., Hinton, G. E., & Williams, R. J. (1986). Learning representations by back-propagating errors. nature, 323(6088), 533-536. DOI: 10.1038/323533a0

Rydén, P., & El Sawy, O. A. (2023). How Managers Perceive Real-Time Management: Thinking Fast & Flow. https://journals.sagepub.com/doi/10.1177/00081256188 18840

Sajeeda, A., & Hossain, B. M. (2022). Exploring generative adversarial networks and adversarial training. *International Journal of Cognitive Computing in Engineering*, *3*, 78–89.

Salehi, A. W., Khan, S., Gupta, G., Alabduallah, B. I., Almjally, A., Alsolai, H., Siddiqui, T., & Mellit, A. (2023). A Study of CNN and Transfer Learning in Medical Imaging: Advantages, Challenges, Future Scope. *Sustainability (Basel), 15*(7), 1–28. DOI: 10.3390/su15075930

Salehin, I., & Kang, D. K. (2023). A Review on Dropout Regularization Approaches for Deep Neural Networks within the Scholarly Domain. *Electronics (Basel), 2023*(12), 3106. DOI: 10.3390/electronics12143106

Salimans, T., ... (2016). Improved Techniques for Training GANs. arXiv preprint arXiv:1606.03498.

Salimans, T., ... (2016). *Improved techniques for training GANs.* In Advances in Neural Information Processing Systems, NeurIPS, 2016.

Samaan, G. et al. (2022). MediaPipe's Landmarks with RNN for Dynamic Sign Language Recognition. *Electronics: 11.19, 3228.*

Samek, W., Wiegand, T., & Müller, K. R. (2017). Explainable Artificial Intelligence: Understanding, Visualizing, and Interpreting Deep Learning Models. *arXiv, 1*, 1-8 https://arxiv.org/abs/1708.08296

Sangodoyin, A. O., Akinsolu, M. O., Pillai, P., & Grout, V. (2021). Detection and Classification of DDoS Flooding Attacks on Software-Defined Networks: A Case Study for the Application of Machine Learning. *IEEE Access : Practical Innovations, Open Solutions*, *9*, 122495–122508. DOI: 10.1109/ACCESS.2021.3109490

Schmidt, R. M. (2019). Recurrent neural networks (rnns): A gentle introduction and overview. https://doi.org//arXiv.1912.05911DOI: 10.48550

Schoeffer, J., Jakubik, J., Voessing, M., Kuehl, N., & Satzger, G. (2023). On the Interdependence of Reliance Behavior and Accuracy in AI-Assisted Decision-Making. In arXiv (Cornell University). Cornell University. https://doi.org/DOI: 10.48550/arXiv.2304

Sellam, T., Das, D., & Parikh, A. P. (2020). BLEURT: Learning robust metrics for text generation. arXiv preprint arXiv:2004.04696. DOI: 10.18653/v1/2020.acl-main.704

Setio, A. A. A., Ciompi, F., Litjens, G., Gerke, P., Jacobs, C., Van Riel, S. J., Wille, M. M. W., Naqibullah, M., Sanchez, C. I., & Van Ginneken, B. (2016). Pulmonary nodule detection in CT images: False positive reduction using multi-view convolutional networks. *IEEE Transactions on Medical Imaging*, *35*(5), 1160–1169. DOI: 10.1109/TMI.2016.2536809 PMID: 26955024

Shafiqul, I. M., Jannat, M. K. A., Kim, J.-W., Lee, S.-W., & Yang, S.-H. (2022). HHI-AttentionNet: An enhanced human-human interaction recognition method based on a lightweight deep learning model with attention network from CSI. *Sensors (Basel)*, *22*(16), 6018. DOI: 10.3390/s22166018 PMID: 36015776

Shahriar, S., & Hayawi, K. (2022, March). NFTGAN: Non-fungible token art generation using generative adversarial networks. In *Proceedings of the 2022 7th International Conference on Machine Learning Technologies* (pp. 255-259).

Shams, S. R., Jahani, A., Kalantary, S., Moeinaddini, M., & Khorasani, N. (2021). The evaluation on artificial neural networks (ANN) and multiple linear regressions (MLR) models for predicting SO2 concentration. *Urban Climate*, *37*, 100837. DOI: 10.1016/j.uclim.2021.100837

Sharma, H. L., & Rani, R. (2013). Relationship of personal growth initiative with self-efficacy among university postgraduate students. *Journal of Education and Practice*, *4*(16), 125–135.

Sharma, P., Kumar, M., Sharma, H. K., & Biju, S. M. (2024). Generative adversarial networks (GANs): Introduction, Taxonomy, Variants, Limitations, and Applications. *Multimedia Tools and Applications*, *83*(41), 88811–88858. DOI: 10.1007/s11042-024-18767-y

Sharma, S., Gupta, R., & Kumar, A. (2023). Continuous Sign Language Recognition Transfer Learning. *Journal of Ambient Intelligence and Humanized Computing*, *14*, 1531–1542. DOI: 10.1007/s12652-021-03418-z

Shboul, Z. A., Shboul, M. Z., & Al-Husain, M. (2020). A review on deep learning algorithms in medical image analysis. *Journal of Healthcare Engineering*, •••, 1–12. DOI: 10.1155/2020/6619801

Shen, T., ... (2017). *Mapping representations for GAN-based NLP models*. In NeurIPS, 2017.

Shen, D., Wu, G., & Suk, H.-I. (2017). Deep Learning in Medical Image Analysis. *Annual Review of Biomedical Engineering*, *19*(1), 221–248. DOI: 10.1146/annurev-bioeng-071516-044442 PMID: 28301734

Sheokand, K., Garima, , Deswal, R., & Jyoti, . (2024). Learning in Transition: Exploring Factors Shaping Students' Motivation Across Diverse Learning Modalities. *International Journal of Educational Reform*, *0*(0), 10567879241302833. Advance online publication. DOI: 10.1177/10567879241302833

Siddiky, M. R., & Haque, I. E. (2024). Factors Affecting Students' Academic Performance Mediated by their Motivation for Learning. *Asian Journal of University Education, 20*(1), 15–27. DOI: 10.24191/ajue.v20i1.25696

Sidig., ... (2021). KArSL: Arabic Sign Language Database. in KArSL Dataset. url: https://paperswithcode.com/dataset/karsl

Singh, D. K., Ansari, M. A., & Pallawi, S. (2022). Computer vision-based visual activity classification through deep learning approaches. In *2022 IEEE Region 10 Symposium (TENSYMP)*. IEEE. DOI: 10.1109/TENSYMP54529.2022.9864443

Singh, M., & Kumar, R. (2023). Neural Networks in Drug Discovery: A Survey. *Journal of Computational Biology, 31*(5), 423–438.

Singu, S., & Singu, S. (2021). Comparative analysis of artificial neural networks. *International Journal of Machine Learning for Sustainable Development, 3*(4).

Snover, M., Dorr, B., Schwartz, R., Micciullo, L., & Makhoul, J. (2006). A study of translation edit rate with targeted human annotation. In Proceedings of the 7th conference of the association for machine translation in the Americas: technical papers (pp. 223-231).

Sønderby, C. K., ... (2016). Amortised MAP Inference for Image Super-resolution. arXiv preprint arXiv:1610.04490.

Song, X., Zhang, J., Yan, P., Hahn, J., Krüger, U., Mohamed, H., & Wang, G. (2024). Integrating AI in College Education: Positive yet Mixed Experiences with ChatGPT. In arXiv (Cornell University). Cornell University. https://doi.org/DOI: 10.48550/arXiv.2407

Srivastava, N., Hinton, G., Krizhevsky, A., Sutskever, I., & Salakhutdinov, R. (2014). Dropout: A Simple Way to Prevent Neural Networks from Overfitting. *Journal of Machine Learning Research, 15*(1), 1929–1958.

Statista Market Insights on Technology. (n.a.) *Artificial Intelligence: Worldwide*. https://www.statista.com/outlook/tmo/artificial-intelligence/worldwide

Staudemeyer, R. C., ... Rothstein, E. M. (2019). Understanding LSTM–a tutorial into long short-term memory recurrent neural networks. inarXiv *preprint arXiv:1909.09586.*

Stergiou, A., & Poppe, R. (2019). Analyzing human–human interactions: A survey. *Computer Vision and Image Understanding, 188*, 102799. DOI: 10.1016/j.cviu.2019.102799

Strubell, E., Ganesh, A., & McCallum, A. (2019). Energy and policy considerations for deep learning in NLP. *Proceedings of the 57th Annual Meeting of the Association for Computational Linguistics*, 3645-3650. DOI: 10.18653/v1/P19-1355

Suliman, W.. (2021). Arabic Sign Language Recognition Using Deep Learning. *4th International Symposium on Advanced Electrical and Communication Technologies (ISAECT),* Alkhobar, Saudi Arabia, 1-4, DOI: 10.1109/ISAECT53699.2021.9668405

Sundberg, L., & Holmström, J. (2024). Fusing domain knowledge with machine learning: A public sector perspective. In The Journal of Strategic Information Systems (Vol. 33, Issue 3, p. 101848). Elsevier BV. DOI: 10.1016/j.jsis.2024.101848

Sutskever, I., Vinyals, O., & Le, Q. V. (2014). Sequence to sequence learning with neural networks. In Advances in neural information processing systems (pp. 3104-3112).

Szegedy, C., Liu, W., Jia, Y., Sermanet, P., Reed, S., Anguelov, D., & Rabinovich, A. (2015). Going deeper with convolutions. In *Proceedings of the IEEE conference on computer vision and pattern recognition* (pp. 1-9). DOI: 10.1109/CVPR.2015.7298594

Sztyler, M., Stuckenschmidt, H., Van Laerhoven, J., Amft, B., & Tröster, G. (2017). On-body localization of wearable devices: An investigation of position-aware activity recognition. *Pervasive and Mobile Computing*, *38*, 281–295. DOI: 10.1016/j.pmcj.2017.01.008

Taber, K. (2018). The Use of Cronbach's Alpha When Developing and Reporting Research Instruments in Science Education. *Research in Science Education*, *48*(6), 1273–1296. DOI: 10.1007/s11165-016-9602-2

Tadesse, A., Bent, O., Weldemariam, K., Istiak, M. A., Hasan, T., & Cavallaro, A. (2022). BON: An extended public domain dataset for human activity recognition. *arXiv preprint arXiv:2209.05077.*

Tam, A. Y., Zha, L.-W., So, B. P.-H., Lai, D. K.-H., Mao, Y.-J., Lim, H.-J., Wong, D. W.-C., & Cheung, J. C.-W. (2022). Depth-Camera-Based Under-Blanket Sleep Posture Classification Using Anatomical Landmark-Guided Deep Learning Model. *International Journal of Environmental Research and Public Health*, *19*(20), 2022. DOI: 10.3390/ijerph192013491 PMID: 36294072

Tang, X. (2020). The Role of Artificial Intelligence in Medical Imaging Research. *BJR|Open, 2*(1), 1-5. https://doi.org/DOI: 10.1259/bjro.20190031

Tan, T.-H., Badarch, L., Zeng, W.-X., Gochoo, M., Alnajjar, F. S., & Hsieh, J.-W. (2021). Binary sensors-based privacy-preserved activity recognition of elderly living alone using an RNN. *Sensors (Basel), 21*(16), 5371. DOI: 10.3390/s21165371 PMID: 34450809

Tapia, E. M., Intille, S. S., & Larson, K. (2004). Activity recognition in the home using simple and ubiquitous sensors. In *International Conference on Pervasive Computing* (pp. 158–175). Springer. DOI: 10.1007/978-3-540-24646-6_10

Tayyab, M., Alateyah, S. A., Alnusayri, M., Alatiyyah, M., AlHammadi, D. A., Jalal, A., & Liu, H. (2025). A Hybrid Approach for Sports Activity Recognition Using Key Body Descriptors and Hybrid Deep Learning Classifier. *Sensors (Basel), 25*(2), 441. DOI: 10.3390/s25020441 PMID: 39860811

Tehrani, M. S. (2020). What's the difference between all the different head scans (X-Ray, CT, MRI, MRA, PET scan)? And what do they show in the head? *San Diego Brain Injury Foundation*, https://sdbif.org/whats-the-difference-between-all-the-different-head-scans/

Ten Cate, O. T. J., Kusurkar, R. A., & Williams, G. C. (2011). How self-determination theory can assist our understanding of the teaching and learning processes in medical education. AMEE guide No. 59. *Medical Teacher, 33*(12), 961–973. DOI: 10.3109/0142159X.2011.595435 PMID: 22225433

Thompson, C. B., & Panacek, E. A. (2007). Research study designs: Non-experimental. *Air Medical Journal, 26*(1), 18–22. DOI: 10.1016/j.amj.2006.10.003 PMID: 17210489

Thukral, M., Haresamudram, H., & Ploetz, T. (2025). Cross-Domain HAR: Few-Shot Transfer Learning for Human Activity Recognition. *ACM Transactions on Intelligent Systems and Technology, 16*(1), 1–35. DOI: 10.1145/3704921

Toh, W. (2023). Gamers and Their Weapons: An Appraisal Perspective on Weapons Manipulation in Video Games. https://www.sciencedirect.com/science/article/pii/B9780128017388000051

Topol, E. J. (2019). High-performance medicine: The Convergence of Human and Artificial Intelligence. *Nature Medicine, 25*(1), 44–56. DOI: 10.1038/s41591-018-0300-7 PMID: 30617339

Tulyakov, S., ... (2017). *Mocogan: Generating motion sequences with generative adversarial networks*. In CVPR, 2017.

Turing, A. (1950). Computing machinery and intelligence. *Mind, 59*(236), 433–460. DOI: 10.1093/mind/LIX.236.433

Tu, X., He, Z., Huang, Y., Zhang, Z.-H., Yang, M., & Zhao, J. (2024). An overview of large AI models and their applications. *Vis. Intell.*, *2*(1), 34. DOI: 10.1007/s44267-024-00065-8

Van Kasteren, T. L., Englebienne, G., & Kröse, B. J. (2011). Human activity recognition from wireless sensor network data: Benchmark and software. In *Activity Recognition in Pervasive Intelligent Environments* (pp. 165–186). Springer., DOI: 10.2991/978-94-91216-05-3_8

Vaswani, A., Shazeer, N., Parmar, N., Uszkoreit, J., Jones, L., Gomez, A. N., & Polosukhin, I. (2017). Attention is all you need. In Advances in Neural Information Processing Systems, 30.

Vaswani, A. (2017). Attention is all you need. *Advances in Neural Information Processing Systems*. arXiv1706.03762

Vavoulas, G., Chatzaki, C., Malliotakis, T., Pediaditis, M., & Tsiknakis, M. (2016). The MobiAct dataset: Recognition of activities of daily living using smartphones. In *Proceedings of the International Conference on Information and Communication Technologies for Ageing Well and E-Health* (pp. 143–151). DOI: 10.5220/0005792401430151

Vilar, D., Xu, J., & Ney, H. (2010). Error analysis of statistical machine translation output. *Proceedings of the Workshop on Statistical Machine Translation*, 107–116.

Voigt, P., & Von dem Bussche, A. (2017). The EU General Data Protection Regulation (GDPR): A Practical Guide. *Springer International Publishing*, *10*. Advance online publication. DOI: 10.1007/978-3-319-57959-7

Wang, Z., ... (2018). *Perceptual loss for real-time style transfer and super-resolution.* In ECCV, 2018.

Wang, J., Chen, Y., Hao, S., Peng, X., & Hu, L. (2019). Deep learning for sensor-based activity recognition: A survey. *IEEE Transactions on Cognitive and Developmental Systems*, *11*(3), 313–325. DOI: 10.1109/TCDS.2018.2869999

Wang, J., & Li, Y. (2023). AutoML and Neural Networks: Revolutionizing Automated Model Design. *Journal of Artificial Intelligence Research*, *60*(4), 907–922.

Wang, Q., & Zhao, W. (2023). Recurrent Neural Networks for Time Series Forecasting. *Journal of Time Series Analysis*, *48*(4), 568–583.

Wang, R., Bashyam, V., Yang, Z., Yu, F., Tassopoulou, V., Chintapalli, S. S., & Davatzikos, C. (2023). Applications of generative adversarial networks in neuroimaging and clinical neuroscience. *NeuroImage*, *269*, 119898.

Wang, S., Yang, D. M., Rong, R., Zhan, X., Xiao, G., & Xiao, G. (2018). Pathology Image Analysis using Segmentation Deep Learning Algorithms. *American Journal of Pathology, 189*(9), 1686–1698. DOI: 10.1016/j.ajpath.2019.05.007 PMID: 31199919

Wang, X., & Li, P. (2023). Artificial Neural Networks in Human-Computer Interaction. *Journal of Human-Computer Interaction, 41*(2), 167–180.

Wang, X., Liu, J., Moore, S. J., Nugent, C. D., & Xu, Y. (2023). A behavioural hierarchical analysis framework in a smart home: Integrating HMM and probabilistic model checking. *Information Fusion, 95*, 275–292. DOI: 10.1016/j.inffus.2023.02.025

Wang, Z., Ying, K., Meng, J., & Ning, J. (2023, November 20–23). Human-to-human interaction detection. In *International Conference on Neural Information Processing* (pp. 120–132). Changsha, China.

Wikizer. (01.04.2025). *Timeline of artificial intelligence*. Wikizero. https://wikizero.com/en/Timeline_of_artificial_intelligence

Wolniak, R. (2023). *Functioning of real-time analytics in business*. Zeszyty Naukowe. Organizacja i Zarządzanie/Politechnika Śląska.

Woodard, M., Sarvestani, S. S., & Hurson, A. R. (2023). A Survey of Research on Data Corruption in Cyber-Physical Critical Infrastructure Systems. https://www.sciencedirect.com/science/article/pii/S0065245815000285

Xiang, C., Yan, Y., Hu, T., Lv, Y., & Zeng, Y. (2023). A review of the effect of the light environment of the VDT workspace on the "learning to learn" effect of video game training [Review of A review of the effect of the light environment of the VDT workspace on the "learning to learn" effect of video game training]. Frontiers in Neuroscience, 17. Frontiers Media. DOI: 10.3389/fnins.2023.1093602

Xu, L.. (2018). Data augmentation using generative adversarial networks for improving deep learning in healthcare applications. *Journal of Healthcare Engineering*, •••, 2018.

Xu, Z., Wang, G., & Guo, X. (2022). Online activity recognition combining dynamic segmentation and emergent modeling. *Sensors (Basel), 22*(6), 2250. DOI: 10.3390/s22062250 PMID: 35336420

Xu, Z., Zhang, H., Wang, Y., Chang, X. Y., & Liang, Y. (2010). L1/2 regularization. *Science China. Information Sciences, 53*(6), 1159–1169. DOI: 10.1007/s11432-010-0090-0

Yala, N., Fergani, B., & Fleury, A. (2015). Feature extraction and incremental learning to improve activity recognition on streaming data. In *2015 IEEE International Conference on Evolving and Adaptive Intelligent Systems (EAIS)* (pp. 1–8). IEEE. DOI: 10.1109/EAIS.2015.7368804

Yala, N., Fergani, B., & Fleury, A. (2015). Feature extraction for human activity recognition on streaming data. In *2015 International Symposium on Innovations in Intelligent Systems and Applications (INISTA)* (pp. 1–6). IEEE. DOI: 10.1109/INISTA.2015.7276759

Yamashita, R., Nishio, M., Do, R. K. G., & Togashi, K. (2018). Convolutional Neural Networks: An Overview and Application in Radiology. *Insights Into Imaging*, *9*(4), 611–629. DOI: 10.1007/s13244-018-0639-9 PMID: 29934920

Yang, H., & Lee, S. (2024). Neural Networks Made of Light: Photon Power Drives the Next AI Revolution. *Science Daily*, *23*(1), 48–53.

Yin, R., & Yin, J. (2023). A two-stream hybrid CNN-transformer network for skeleton-based human interaction recognition. *arXiv preprint arXiv:2401.00409.*

Yosinski, J., ... (2014). *How transferable are features in deep neural networks?* In NeurIPS, 2014.

Yousuf, F. H., Alwarfalli, A. B., ... (2021). Arabic Sign Language Recognition System by Using Surface Intelligent EMG Signal. *The 7th International Conference on Engineering & MIS 2021, 1-6.*

Yu, L., ... (2017). *SeqGAN: Sequence Generative Adversarial Nets with Policy Gradient.* In AAAI, 2017. DOI: 10.1609/aaai.v31i1.10804

Yurdugül, H. (2008). Minimum sample size for Cronbach's coefficient alpha: A Monte-Carlo study. *Hacettepe Üniversitesi eğitim fakültesi dergisi, 35*(35), 1-9.

Zaidan, O., & Callison-Burch, C. (2011). Task-oriented intrinsic evaluation of machine translation using semantic role labeling. *Proceedings of the 49th Annual Meeting of the Association for Computational Linguistics: Human Language Technologies*, 181–189.

Zawacki-Richter, O., Marín, V. I., Bond, M., & Gouverneur, F. (2019). Systematic review of research on artificial intelligence applications in higher education – Where are the educators? *International Journal of Educational Technology in Higher Education, 16*(1), 1–27. DOI: 10.1186/s41239-019-0171-0

Zellers, R., Holtzman, A., & Clark, C. (2019). Defending against deepfakes: A comparative analysis of AI detection models. *AI Research Review*, *15*(3), 206–220.

Zellers, R., Holtzman, A., Yu, L., & Lu, Y. (2019). Defending against neural fake news. *Advances in Neural Information Processing Systems, 32*, 9081–9093.

Zhang, T., Kishore, V., Wu, F., Weinberger, K. Q., & Artetxe, M. (2019). BERTScore: Evaluating text generation with BERT. arXiv preprint arXiv:1904.09675.

Zhang, Y., ... (2017). *Adversarial feature matching for text generation*. In ICML, 2017.

Zhang, Y., ... (2019). *Catalonia Generative Network: A new approach to generative modeling*. In Neural Networks, 2019.

Zhang, F., & Wang, M. (2023). Deep Neural Networks for Financial Forecasting. *Journal of Finance and Technology, 45*(2), 213–229.

Zhang, L.. (2019). *Learning to generate ambiguous sentences using GANs*. In arXiv:1904.11991.

Zhang, L., & Wu, J. (2023). Neural Networks for Anomaly Detection in Industrial IoT Systems. *Journal of Industrial IoT Research, 9*(6), 1023–1037.

Zhang, Q., & Li, T. (2023). Neural Networks-based Video Analytics for Smart Cities. *Smart City Technologies, 22*(1), 56–68.

Zhang, S., & Wang, Q. (2021). Graph Neural Network for Traffic Forecasting: A Survey. *International Journal of Geographical Information Science, 35*(7), 1476–1491.

Zhang, X.. (2018). Improving GANs for NLP tasks: A survey of recent developments and future directions. *Journal of Machine Learning Research, 19*(1), 52–58.

Zhang, X.. (2018). *Leveraging GANs for transfer learning: A new frontier in synthetic data generation*. arXiv:1811.11247.

Zhang, X., & Lee, T. (2023). A Review of Validation and Verification of Neural Network-based Policies for Sequential Decision Making. *Journal of Machine Learning Research, 55*(2), 1050–1073.

Zhang, X., & Yang, Z. (2023). Neural Network-based Approaches for Image Segmentation in Medical Imaging. *Medical Image Analysis, 74*, 112–125.

Zhang, Y., & Luo, C. (2023). Reinforcement Learning with Neural Networks in Robotics. *Robotics and Automation Letters, 8*(2), 3501–3512.

Zhao, J., ... (2016). Energy-based Generative Adversarial Network. arXiv preprint arXiv:1609.03126.

Zhao, J., Han, R., Gan, Y., Wan, L., Feng, W., & Wang, S. (2020, October 12–16). Human identification and interaction detection in cross-view multi-person videos with wearable cameras. In *Proceedings of the 28th ACM International Conference on Multimedia* (pp. 2608–2616). Seattle, WA, USA. DOI: 10.1145/3394171.3413903

Zhao, S., & Zhang, L. (2023). Neural Networks for Environmental Monitoring and Climate Change Modeling. *Environmental Informatics*, *40*(8), 2103–2120.

Zhao, Z., & Chen, S. (2023). Neural Networks in Cybersecurity: A Survey. *Journal of Cybersecurity Research*, *15*(4), 101–120.

Zhao, Z., Shi, Y., Wu, S., Yang, F., Song, W., & Liu, N. (2023). Interpretation of Time-Series Deep Models: A Survey. In arXiv (Cornell University). Cornell University. https://doi.org/DOI: 10.48550/arXiv.2305

Zhavoronkov, A., Ivanenkov, Y. A., Aliper, A., Veselov, M. S., Aladinskiy, V. A., Aladinskaya, A. V., Terentiev, V. A., Polykovskiy, D. A., Kuznetsov, M. D., Asadulaev, A., Volkov, Y., Zholus, A., Shayakhmetov, R. R., Zhebrak, A., Minaeva, L. I., Zagribelnyy, B. A., Lee, L. H., Soll, R., Madge, D., & Aspuru-Guzik, A. (2019). Deep learning enables rapid identification of potent DDR1 kinase inhibitors. *Nature Biotechnology*, *37*(9), 1038–1040. DOI: 10.1038/s41587-019-0224-x PMID: 31477924

Zhou, Y.. (2020). Generative AI in drug discovery. *Trends in Pharmacological Sciences*, *41*(11), 827–832.

Zhu, J., & Ontañón, S. (2021). Player-Centered AI for Automatic Game Personalization: Open Problems. In arXiv (Cornell University). Cornell University. https://doi.org/DOI: 10.48550/arXiv.2102

Zibani, P., Rajkoomar, M., & Naicker, N. (2021). A systematic review of faculty research repositories at higher education institutions [Review of A systematic review of faculty research repositories at higher education institutions]. Digital Library Perspectives, 38(2), 237. Emerald Publishing Limited. DOI: 10.1108/DLP-04-2021-0035

About The Contributors

Sarah Benziane is a distinguished researcher and university lecturer in computer science and distributed systems, currently based at the Computer Science Department of the University of Science and Technology in Oran, Algeria. With a strong academic foundation, she holds an engineering degree in Parallel and Distributed Systems, a Magister in Electronics specializing in Vision and Pattern Recognition, and a Ph.D. in Artificial Intelligence and Pattern Recognition. Her research has produced a wealth of publications primarily focused on biometrics, hand vein recognition, and the application of convolutional neural networks (CNNs) in image processing. In addition to her research contributions, Sarah Benziane has supervised numerous undergraduate and master's projects on topics ranging from biometric systems and irrigation optimization to intelligent asset management. She has also been actively involved in organizing national and international conferences, such as doctoral workshops and conferences on embedded and distributed systems, and has served on scientific committees for conferences focused on artificial intelligence and the Internet of Things (IoT). Sarah Benziane is the author of several academic books, including one on reactive navigation for mobile robots and another on computer networks. Her recent work includes innovative research on AI applications for weather prediction and anti-theft systems for agriculture.

Fatiha Guerroudji Meddah is an Associate Professor at the University of Science and Technology Mohamed Boudiaf of Oran (USTOMB), Algeria. She holds both a Magister and a Ph.D. in Computer Science from the same institution. Her research focuses on Artificial Intelligence, Data Science, Geographic Information Science, interactive cartography, and geovisualization. Dr. Guerroudji is actively involved in interdisciplinary research projects at both national and international levels. She has served as principal investigator and project leader in several initiatives dealing with the integration of AI, data science, and geospatial technologies to address complex challenges in environmental monitoring, spatial data analysis, and smart decision-making systems. Her work aims to develop intelligent, user-centered tools that enhance geospatial data interpretation and communication. She has authored and co-authored numerous scientific papers published in peer-reviewed international journals and conference proceedings. In addition to her research, Dr. Guerroudji contributes to the academic and scientific communities as a reviewer and program committee member for various national and international conferences and journals in the fields of computer science, geoinformatics, and data driven technologies. She also supervises Master's and Ph.D. students, and is deeply committed to advancing education and innovation in intelligent systems, spatial data science, and interdisciplinary research.

***

Mohit Agrawal, Associate Professor of IT and Analytics at Lloyd Business School, Mohit Agrawal brings over 20 years of experience spanning industry and academia. With 15 years of teaching at prestigious institutions in Delhi-NCR, he specializes in Business Analytics, Advanced Excel, Power BI, Tableau, and CRM. His extensive industry background includes leadership roles in credit analysis at Bajaj Allianz, ICICI Bank, and Magma Fincorp. As an academic collaborator with institutions like BML Munjal University, Galgotias University,, IILM, Accurate Institute and AIMA he has conducted numerous training sessions, emphasizing practical applications of analytics tools. An advocate for knowledge dissemination, Mr. Agrawal contributes his expertise as an author, blending his industry insights and teaching acumen to provide readers with actionable perspectives on analytics and management.

Neetu Kamra is a distinguished academic and industry expert, serving as the Head of Analytics and AI at Lloyd Business School. She holds a doctorate and brings extensive experience in data science and AI. ERP and IBM-certified, she has a strong technical foundation, complemented by her corporate tenure at TCS. With a passion for research, she has published over 25 articles in reputed journals. Dr. Kamra plays a pivotal role in bridging academia and industry, ensuring students gain practical insights alongside theoretical knowledge. Her expertise in AI, analytics, and enterprise solutions makes her a leader in the field.

Linda Benachenhou, PhD student in Artificial Intelligence, specializing in Learning Analytics and Education. My research focuses on analyzing learning data to optimize educational processes and enhance the learner experience. My goal is to develop innovative AI-based approaches to foster more personalized and effective education.

Efan received the S.Kom. degree from Bina Darma University, Palembang, Indonesia, in 2007 and the M.Kom. degree from the University of Putera Indonesia YPTK, Padang, Indonesia, in 2013. In June 2023, He received the Dr. degree from Universitas Negeri Padang, Indonesia and become the best graduate on TVET Program. He is currently a Lecturer of the Department of Informatics Engineering, Sekolah Tinggi Teknologi Pagaralam (now reformed to Institut Teknologi Pagar Alam), Indonesia. His research interests include TVET, Information System, Artificial Intelligence, and Database.

Semra Erpolat Taşabat is a faculty member at the Department of Statistics, Faculty of Arts and Sciences, Mimar Sinan Fine Arts University. Additionally, she serves as a part-time lecturer at various universities and provides consultancy services to BORUSAN CAT. Her academic interests include artificial intelligence, decision theory, applied statistics, data science, and operations research. The author is recognized for her extensive research in these fields and has published numerous articles and scientific papers in international peer-reviewed journals.

Shreyal Faldu, My Research interest is in Machine learning, Big data analysis, Cloud Computing, Game Development and Deep learning.

Rituraj Jain is currently working in the Department of Information Technology, Marwadi University, Rajkot, GUjarat, India. He has published many papers in International Journals and Conferences. He has published 4 books. He is an Oracle Database SQL Certified Expert. He is also associated with professional bodies like the Indian Society of Technical Education (ISTE), Computer Science Teachers Association (CSTA), Academy & Industry Research Collaboration Center (AIRCC), International Association of Computer Science and Information Technology (IACSIT), International Association of Engineers (IAENG). His research interests include Cloud Computing, Machine Learning, Deep Learning, Fuzzy Logic, IoT, Genetic Algorithms, Big Data and Software Engineering.

Fehmina Khalique is a PhD from Sharda University, Noida, India and MBA specializing in Human Resource Management. She is currently associated as a Professor with Lloyd Business School, Noida, India, whereby she plays a role of Head-research Cell. She is editor-in-chief for a bi-annual International Journal, Lloyd Business Review and published 4 issues successfully. She is associated with academics for the past 17 years in the area of Human Resource Management, Business Ethics and Organisational Behaviour. She has 4 years of industry experience and enjoys being a corporate trainer, counsellor and consultant. Her research interest lies International Management, Human Resource Management, Business Analytics, Sustainable Development and she has to her credit several high-quality research papers. She is also involved in copywriting, editing and reviewing of research articles for high quality Journals. She has authored 2 books, 15 Research Papers, 10 Book chapters and 5 patents till now. In her free time, she likes to do some social work and deliver free career counseling sessions for students on honing their inter-personal and corporate-communication skills.

Ravi Teja Kothuru, With 7+ years of diverse experience spanning various domains, I am adept in developing software products as well as crafting advanced AI models, seamlessly integrating development and AI research, particularly focusing on NLP, LLMs, Transformers, Computer Vision (CV) and Generative AI to foster innovation within the AI landscape.

Lila Meddeber received the engineering degree in Computer Science and the magister's degree, both from the University of Science and Technology of Oran (USTO), Algeria. She obtained a Ph.D. in Vision and Pattern Recognition in 2014. She is currently Associate Professor at USTO, in the Electronics Department and Director of the Intelligent Systems Research Laboratory. Her teaching activities mainly concern object-oriented programming (C++, Python, Java, PHP, ...), information theory, image processing and pattern recognition. Her research interests include pattern recognition, artificial intelligence, deep learning, medical image analysis, remote sensing and geographic information systems.

Damodharan Palaniappan works as an Associate Professor & Head in the Department of Information Technology, Marwadi University, Rajkot, Gujarat. He completed his Ph.D. at Anna University, Chennai, M.E. in Computer Science and Engineering at C.I.E.T, Coimbatore and B.E. in Computer Science and Engineering at CSI College of Engineering, Ketty, Nilgiri. He has 19 years' experience of teaching and research. Currently, he guides 6 Ph.D. research scholars. He has authored 8 book chapters, and he has published research papers in reputed journals. His interested areas of research are Data Mining, Image Processing, Software, Machine Learning and Deep Learning.

Pallavi Pandey is currently associated with IILM university GURUGRAM as associate professor. She has done PhD from Indira Gandhi Delhi Technical University foe women, Delhi and MTech in CSE from Jamia Hamdard Delhi. She has published various books, book chapters, conference papers and journal papers.

Kumar Parmar, I am an Assistant Professor with a strong foundation in Computer Science and Engineering, currently pursuing my PhD at Marwadi University. With a Master's in Computer Engineering and extensive teaching experience across various institutions, I am dedicated to fostering a dynamic and innovative learning environment. My expertise spans Operating Systems, Linux Administration, Cybersecurity, IoT, and Software Engineering, Machine Learning, Deep learning. In addition to teaching, I have contributed to research with multiple publications and patents, and I am actively involved in guiding projects, mentoring students, and coordinating academic clubs. My professional journey is driven by a passion for continuous learning and collaboration

Affaan Shaikh is the Founder & CEO of Neuratia Labs. As an AI engineer, researcher and neuroscientist, he develops cutting-edge solutions at the intersection of artificial intelligence, neuroscience, and medical technology. His research spans neurodegenerative disease diagnosis, brain-computer interfaces (BCIs), and AI in aerospace. With over 10 peer-reviewed papers in journals like IEEE and Springer, Affaan is an active contributor to the tech community. He has mentored 20+ aspiring researchers and writers and is passionate about innovation, leadership, and public engagement.

Singaravelan Shanmugasundaram is a professor in the Computer Science and Engineering Department at PSR Engineering College, Sevaplatti, India.

Tarik Zouagui received the engineering degree in electronics and the Magister degree (Signal and Image Processing) both from the University of Science and Technology of Oran (USTO), Algeria. He received also a PhD in Image and Systems from INSA de Lyon, France in 2004. He is currently Full Professor at USTO, at the electronics department. His teaching activities mainly concern signal and image processing, and medical imaging. His research interests are in the area of image processing with particular focus on image segmentation, medical image analysis with variational methods, registration and remote sensing.

Index

N

O

P

Q

R

S

T

V

www.ingramcontent.com/pod-product-compliance
Lightning Source LLC
LaVergne TN
LVHW080615300926
849162LV00005B/1161
* 9 7 9 8 3 3 7 3 0 7 3 5 0 *